THE WRITINGS OF RABASH

ESSAYS

Volume Two

LAITMAN
KABBALAH
PUBLISHERS

Rav Baruch Shalom Halevi Ashlag

The Writings of RABASH
Volume Two—Essays

Copyright © 2016 by Michael Laitman
All rights reserved
Published by Laitman Kabbalah Publishers

Contact Information
E-mail: info@kabbalah.info
Web site: www.kabbalah.info
Toll free in USA and Canada: 1-866-LAITMAN

1057 Steeles Avenue West, Suite 532, Toronto,
ON, M2R 3X1, Canada
Tel. 1-416-274-7287

2009 85th Street #51, Brooklyn, New York, 11214, USA
Tel. 1-800-540-3234

Printed in Canada

No part of this book may be used or reproduced
in any manner without written permission of the publisher,
except in the case of brief quotations embodied
in critical articles or reviews.

ISBN: 978-1-77228-016-6
Library of Congress Control Number: 2016938484

Translation: Rinah Shalom, Chaim Ratz
Editors: Mary Pennock, Mary Miesem, Mordakhay Kholdarov
Transcription: Brenda Jones, Linda Narbonne, Jazmin Delgado,
David Prosser, Mary Miesem, Katia Wilson, Karen Larkins
Layout: Chaim Ratz
Cover: Baruch Khovov
Administrative Editor: Simona Gamarnik
Executive Editor: Chaim Ratz
Printing and Post Production: Uri Laitman

FIRST EDITION: SEPTEMBER 2016
First printing

Table of Contents

Tav-Shin-Mem-Dalet (1984)

The Purpose of Society (1) 9
The Purpose of Society (2) 12
Concerning Love of Friends 14
Love of Friends 16
They Helped Every One His Friend 18
What Does the Rule, "Love Thy Friend as Thyself," Give Us? 19
Love of Friends 21
According to What Is Explained
Concerning "Love Thy Friend as Thyself" 25
Which Keeping of Torah and Mitzvot Purifies the Heart? 30
One Should Always Sell the Beams of His House 33
What Is the Degree One Should Achieve
in Order Not to Have to Reincarnate? 38
Ancestral Merit 42
Concerning the Importance of Society 45
Sometimes Spirituality Is Called "a Soul" 48
One Should Always Sell Everything He Has
and Marry a Wise Disciple's Daughter 53
Can Something Negative Come Down from Above 58
Concerning Bestowal 65
Concerning the Importance of Friends 78
The Agenda of the Assembly 82
And It Shall Come to Pass
When You Come to the Land that the Lord Your God Gives You 85
You Stand Today, All of You 93

Tav-Shin-Mem-Hey (1984 - 1985)

Make for Yourself a Rav and Buy Yourself a Friend (1) 102
The Meaning of Branch and Root 111
The Meaning of Truth and Faith 117
These Are the Generations of Noah 124
Go Forth From Your Land 131
And the Lord Appeared to Him at the Oaks of Mamre 136
The Life of Sarah 140

Make for Yourself a Rav and Buy Yourself a Friend (2)	145
And the Children Struggled within Her	151
Jacob Went Out	157
Concerning the Debate between Jacob and Laban	164
Jacob Dwelled in the Land Where His Father Had Lived	170
Mighty Rock of My Salvation	179
I Am the First and I Am the Last	185
And Hezekiah Turned His Face to the Wall	190
But the More They Afflicted Them	196
Know Today and Reply to Your Heart	202
Concerning the Slanderers	207
Come unto Pharaoh – 1	213
He who Hardens His Heart	220
We Should Always Discern between Torah and Work	224
The Whole of the Torah Is One Holy Name	229
On My Bed at Night	236
Three Times in the Work	243
In Every Thing We Must Discern between Light and Kli	249
Show Me Your Glory	254
Repentance	258
The Spies	273
The Lord Is Near to All Who Call upon Him	281
Three Prayers – 1	286
One Does Not Regard Oneself as Wicked	293
Concerning the Reward of the Receivers	299
The Felons of Israel	303
And I Pleaded with the Lord	308
When a Person Knows What Is Fear of the Creator	314
And There Was Evening and There Was Morning	321
Who Testifies to a Person?	327
A Righteous Who Is Happy, a Righteous Who Is Suffering	339
Hear Our Voice	351

Tav-Shin-Mem-Vav (1985 - 1986)

Moses Went	360
Lend Ear, O Heaven	367
Man Is Rewarded with Righteousness and Peace through the Torah	380
Concerning Hesed	387
Concerning Respecting the Father	395
Confidence	401
The Importance of a Prayer of Many	420
Concerning Help that Comes from Above	430

Concerning the Hanukkah Candle..441
Concerning Prayer 449
A Real Prayer Is over a Real Deficiency..............................455
What Is the Main Deficiency for which One Should Pray?..................460
Come unto Pharaoh – 2 467
What Is the Need to Borrow Kelim from the Egyptians?.......................483
A Prayer of Many 493
The Lord Has Chosen Jacob for Himself..499
The Agenda of the Assembly..504
Who Causes the Prayer...511
Concerning Joy 517
Should One Sin and Be Guilty 532
Concerning Above Reason 539
If a Woman Inseminates..553
Concerning Fear and Joy 562
The Difference between Charity and Gift 570
The Measure of Practicing Mitzvot..584
A Near Way and a Far Way..594
The Creator and Israel Went into Exile..608
A Congregation Is No Less than Ten 620
Lishma and Lo Lishma 629
The Klipa that Precedes the Fruit..648
Concerning Yenika and Ibur...663
The Reason for Straightening the Legs
and Covering the Head During the Prayer 683
What Are Commandments that a Person Tramples with His Feet 694
Judges and Officers..704
The Fifteenth of Av 714
What Is Preparation for Selichot..722

Tav-Shin-Mem-Dalet

(1984)

The Purpose of Society (1)

Article No. 1, Part 1, Tav-Shin-Mem-Dalet, 1984

We have gathered here to establish a society for all who wish to follow the path and method of Baal HaSulam, the way by which to climb the degrees of man and not remain as a beast, as our sages said (*Yevamot*, 61a) about the verse, "And you My sheep, the sheep of My pasture, are men." And Rashbi said, "You are called 'men,' and idol worshipers are not called 'men.'"

To understand man's merit, we shall now bring a verse from our sages (*Berachot*, 6b) about the verse, "The end of the matter, all having been heard: fear God, and keep His commandments; for this is the whole man" (Ecclesiastes, 12:13). And the Gemarah asks, "What is 'for this is the whole man'"?

Rabbi Elazar said, "The Creator said, 'The whole world was created only for that.' This means that the whole world was created for the fear of God."

Yet, we need to understand what the fear of God is, being the reason for which the world was created. From all the words of our sages, we learn that the reason for creation was to benefit His creations. This means that the Creator wished to delight the creatures so they would feel happy in the world. And here our sages said about the verse, "For this is the whole man," that the reason for creation was the fear of God.

But according to what is explained in the essay, *Matan Torah* ["The Giving of the Torah"], the reason why the creatures are not receiving delight and pleasure, even though it was the reason for creation, is the disparity of form between the Creator and the creatures. The Creator is the giver and the creatures are the receivers. But there is a rule that the branches are similar to the root from which the branches were born.

And since there is no reception in our root, since the Creator is in no way deficient and needs nothing to satisfy His want, man feels unpleasantness when he needs to be a receiver. This is why every person is ashamed to eat the bread of shame.

To correct that, the world had to be created. *Olam* [world] means *He'elem* [concealment], so that delight and pleasure must be concealed. Why is it so? The answer is, for fear. In other words, it is so that man would fear using his vessels of reception, called "self-love." This means that one should prevent oneself from receiving pleasures because one craves them, and should have the strength to prevail over the craving, the object of one's desire.

Instead, one should receive pleasures that bring contentment to the Creator. This means that the creature will want to bestow upon the Creator and will have fear of the Creator, of receiving for oneself, since reception of pleasure—when one receives for one's own benefit—removes him from cleaving to the Creator.

Therefore, when a person performs one of the *Mitzvot* [commandments] of the Creator, one should aim that this *Mitzva* will bring him pure thoughts that he will bestow upon the Creator by keeping God's *Mitzvot*. It is as our sages said, "Rabbi Hanania Ben Akashia says, 'The Creator wanted to cleanse Israel; hence, He gave them plentiful Torah and *Mitzvot*.'"

And this is why we gather here—to establish a society where each of us follows the spirit of bestowing upon the Creator. And to achieve bestowal upon the Creator, we must begin with bestowal upon man, which is called "love of others."

And love of others can only be through revoking of one's self. Thus, on the one hand, each person should feel lowly, and on the other hand, be proud that the Creator has given us the chance to be in a society where each of us has but a single goal: for The *Shechina* [Divinity] to be among us.

And although we have not yet achieved this goal, we have the desire to achieve it. And this, too, should be appreciated by us, for even though we are at the beginning of the way, we do hope to achieve the exalted goal.

The Purpose of Society (2)

Article No. 1, Part 2, Tav-Shin-Mem-Dalet, 1984

Since man is created with a *Kli* called "self-love," where one does not see that an act will yield self-benefit, one has no motivation to make even the slightest motion. And without annulling self-love, it is impossible to achieve *Dvekut* [adhesion)] with the Creator, meaning equivalence of form.

And since it is against our nature, we need a society that will form a great force so we can work together on annulling the will to receive, called "evil," as it hinders the achievement of the goal for which man was created.

For this reason, society must consist of individuals who unanimously agree that they must achieve it. Then, all the individuals become one great force that can fight against itself, since everyone is integrated in everyone else. Thus, each person is founded on a great desire to achieve the goal.

To be integrated in one another, each person should annul himself before the others. This is done by each seeing the friends' merits and not their faults. But one who thinks that he is a little higher than his friends can no longer unite with them.

Also, it is important to remain serious during the assembly so as not to lose the intention, as it is for this aim that they have gathered. And to walk humbly, which is a great thing, one should be accustomed to appear as though one is not serious. But in truth, a fire burns in their hearts.

Yet, to small people, during the assembly one should be wary of following words and deeds that do not yield the goal of the gathering—that thus they should achieve *Dvekut* with the Creator. And concerning *Dvekut*, see the essay, "*Matan Torah.*"

But when one is not with one's friends, it is best to show nothing of the intent in one's heart and appear to be like everyone else. This is the meaning of "walk humbly with the Lord your God." While there are higher interpretations of that, the simple explanation is also a great thing.

Hence, it is good that there will be equality among the friends who unite, so one can be annulled before the other. And there should be careful watch in the society, disallowing frivolity, since frivolity ruins everything. But as we have said above, this should be an internal matter.

But when there is someone who is not from this society, no seriousness should be shown, but to equalize with the person who has just come in. In other words, avoid speaking of serious matters, but only of things that suit the one who has just entered, who is called "an uninvited guest."

Concerning Love of Friends

Article No. 2, Tav-Shin-Mem-Dalet, 1984

1) The need for love of friends.

2) What is the reason I chose specifically these friends, and why have the friends chosen me?

3) Should each of the friends disclose his love for the society, or is it enough to feel love in one's heart and practice love of friends in concealment, and thus not need to openly show what is in his heart?

It is known that being humble is a great thing. But we can also say the opposite—that one must disclose the love in his heart towards the friends, since by revealing it he evokes his friends' hearts toward the friends so they, too, would feel that each of them is practicing love of friends. The benefit from that is that in this manner, one gains strength to practice love of friends more forcefully, since every person's force of love is integrated in each other's.

It turns out that where a person has one measure of strength to practice love of friends, if the group consists of ten members, then he is integrated with ten forces of the need, who understand that it is necessary to engage in love of friends. However, if each of them does not show the society that he is practicing love of friends, then one lacks the force of the group.

This is so because it is very hard to judge one's friend favorably. Each one thinks that he is righteous and that only he engages in love of friends. In that state, one has very little strength to practice love of others. Thus, this work, specifically, should be public and not concealed.

But one must always remind oneself of the purpose of the society. Otherwise, the body tends to blur the goal, since the body always cares for its own benefit. We must remember that the society was established solely on the basis of achieving love of others, and that this would be the springboard for the love of God.

This is achieved specifically by saying that one needs a society to be able to give to one's friend without any reward. In other words, he does not need a society so the society would give him assistance and gifts, which would make the body's vessels of reception content. Such a society is built on self-love and prompts only the development of his vessels of reception, as now he sees an opportunity to gain more possessions by his friend assisting him to obtain corporeal possessions.

Instead, we must remember that the society was established on the basis of love of others, so each member would receive from the group the love of others and hatred of himself. And seeing that his friend is straining to annul his self and to love others would cause everyone to be integrated in their friends' intentions.

Thus, if the society is made of ten members, for example, each will have ten forces practicing self-annulment, hatred of self, and love of others. Otherwise, one remains with but a single force of love of others, since he does not see that the friends are practicing it, since the friends are practicing love of others in concealment. Moreover, the friends make him lose his strength of desire to walk the path of loving others. In that state, he learns from their actions and falls into the dominion of self-love.

4) Should everyone know his friend's needs, specifically for each friend, so he would know how he can satisfy them, or is it enough to practice love of friends in general?

Love of Friends

Article No. 3, Tav-Shin-Mem-Dalet, 1984

"And a certain man found him, and behold, he was wandering in the field. And the man asked him, saying, 'What are you seeking?' And he said, 'I seek my brothers. Tell me, I pray you, where they are feeding the flock?'" (Genesis, 37).

A man "wandering in the field" refers to a place from which the crop of the field to sustain the world should spring. And the works of the field are plowing, sowing, and reaping. It is said about that: "They that sow in tears shall reap in joy," and this is called "a field which the Lord has blessed."

Baal HaTurim explained that a person wandering in the field refers to one who strays from the path of reason, who does not know the real way, which leads to the place he should reach, as in "an ass wandering in the field." And he comes to a state where he thinks that he will never achieve the goal he should achieve.

"And the man asked him, saying, 'What are you seeking?'" meaning, "How can I help you?" "And he said: 'I seek my brethren.'" By being together with my brothers, that is, by being in a group where there is love of friends, I will be able to mount the trail that leads to the house of God.

This trail is called "a path of bestowal," and this way is against our nature. To be able to achieve it, there is no other way but love of friends, by which everyone can help his friend.

"And the man said: 'They are departed hence.'" And Rashi interpreted that they had departed themselves from the brotherhood, meaning they do not want to bond with you. This, in the end, caused Israel's exile in Egypt. And to be redeemed from Egypt, we must take it upon ourselves to enter a group that wants to be in love of friends, and by that we will be rewarded with exodus from Egypt and the reception of the Torah.

They Helped Every One His Friend

Article No. 4, Tav-Shin-Mem-Dalet, 1984

We must understand how one can help his friend. Is this matter specifically when there are rich and poor, wise and fools, weak and strong? But when all are rich, smart, or strong, etc., how can one help another?

We see that there is one thing that is common to all—the mood. It is said, "A concern in one's heart, let him speak of it with others." This is because with regard to feeling high-spirited, neither wealth nor erudition can be of assistance.

Rather, it is one person who can help another by seeing that one's friend is low. It is written, "One does not deliver oneself from imprisonment." Rather, it is one's friend who can lift his spirit.

This means that one's friend raises him from his state into a state of liveliness. Then, one begins to reacquire strength and confidence of life and wealth, and he begins as though his goal is now near him.

It turns out that each and every one must be attentive and think how he can help his friend raise his spirit, because in the matter of spirits, anyone can find a needy place in one's friend that he can fill.

What Does the Rule, "Love Thy Friend as Thyself," Give Us?

Article No. 5, Tav-Shin-Mem-Dalet, 1984

What does the *Klal* ["rule," as well as "collective"], "Love thy friend as thyself" give us? Through this rule, we can come to love the Creator. If this is so, what does keeping the 612 *Mitzvot* [commandments] give us?

First, we need to know what a rule is. It is known that a collective [*Klal*] consists of many individuals. Without individuals, there cannot be a collective. For example, when we refer to an audience as "a sacred audience," we are referring to a number of individuals who have gathered and formed a unit. Afterwards, a head is appointed to the audience, etc., and this is called a *Minian* [ten/quorum] or a "congregation." At least ten people must be present, and then it is possible to say *Kedusha* (a specific part of a Jewish prayer) at the service.

The Zohar says about it: "Wherever there are ten, the *Shechina* [Divinity] dwells." This means that in a place where there are ten men, there is a place for the dwelling of the *Shechina*.

It therefore follows that the rule, "Love thy friend as thyself," is built on 612 *Mitzvot*. In other words, if we keep the 612 *Mitzvot*, we will be able to achieve the rule, "Love thy friend as thyself." It turns out that the particular elements allow us to achieve the collective, and when we have the collective, we will be able to achieve the love of the Creator, as it is written, "My soul yearns for the Lord."

However, one cannot keep all 612 *Mitzvot* alone. Take, for example, the redemption of the first-born. If one's first-born is a girl, he cannot keep the *Mitzva* of redemption of the first-born. Also, women are exempted from observing time-dependent *Mitzvot*, such as *Tzitzit* and *Tefillin*. But because "all of Israel are responsible for one another," through everyone, they are all kept. It is as though everyone keeps all the *Mitzvot* together. Hence, through the 612 *Mitzvot*, we can achieve the rule, "Love thy friend as thyself."

Love of Friends

Article No. 6, Tav-Shin-Mem-Dalet, 1984

"Love thy friends as thyself." Rabbi Akiva says, "It is a great rule (in Hebrew: also collective) in the Torah." It means that if one keeps this rule, all the details are included in it, meaning it is taken for granted that we will come to the particulars effortlessly, without having to work for it.

However, we see that the Torah tells us, "What does the Lord seeketh of thee? To fear Me." Thus, the primary requirement from a person is only fear. If one keeps the commandment of fear, all the Torah and *Mitzvot* are contained in that, even the commandment, "Love thy friend as thyself."

Yet, according to the words of Rabbi Akiva, it is the opposite, meaning fear is contained in the rule of "Love thy friend." Moreover, according to our sages (*Berachot* p. 6), the meaning is not as Rabbi Akiva says. They referred to the verse, "The end of the matter, all having been heard: fear God, and keep His commandments; for this is the whole man." The Gemarah asks, "What does it mean, 'this is the whole man?' Rabbi Elazar said, 'The Lord said the whole world was not created but for this.'" However, according to the words of Rabbi Akiva, it seems that everything is contained in the rule, "Love thy friend."

Nevertheless, we find in the words of our sages (*Makot* 24) that they said faith is the most important. They said that Habakkuk came and declared that there is only one: "the righteous shall live by his faith."

The Maharsha interprets, "The thing that is most conclusive for any person from Israel, at any time, is faith." In other words, the essence of the rule is faith. Accordingly, it turns out that both fear and "Love thy friend" are contained in the rule of faith.

If we are to understand the above, we must examine closely the following:

1. What is faith?

2. What is fear?

3. What is "Love thy friend as thyself"?

The most important thing is to always remember the purpose of creation, which is known to be "to do good to His creations." Thus, if He wants to give them delight and pleasure, why are these three above matters—faith, fear and "Love thy friend"? It means that they need only qualify their vessels to be able to receive the delight and pleasure that the Creator wishes to give to the creatures.

Now, we must understand for what these three above-mentioned things qualify us. Faith, confidence included, gives us a preliminary belief in the goal, which is to do good to His creations. We must also believe with certainty that we can promise ourselves that we, too, can reach that goal. In other words, the purpose of creation is not necessarily for a select group. Rather, the purpose of creation belongs to all creations without exception. It is not necessarily the strong and skillful, or the brave people who can overcome. Rather, it belongs to all the creatures.

(Examine the "Introduction to The Study of the Ten Sefirot," item 21, where it quotes *Midrash Rabba*, Portion, "This is the Blessing": "The Creator said unto Israel: 'Regard, the whole wisdom and the whole of Torah are easy: Anyone who fears Me and does the words of Torah, the entire wisdom and the whole of the Torah are in his heart.'")

Thus, we must also use faith to have confidence that we can reach the goal and not despair mid-way and flee the campaign.

Rather, we should believe that the Creator can help even a low and ignoble person like myself. It means that the Creator will bring me near Him and I will be able to attain adhesion with Him.

Yet, to acquire faith, fear must come first, as it is related in the "Introduction of The Book of Zohar": "Fear is a commandment that contains all the commandments in the Torah, since it is the gate to faith in Him. According to the awakening of one's fear (in His guidance), so one believes in His guidance."

It ends there: "The fear is lest he will lessen the giving of contentment to his Maker." This means that the fear that one should have with regard to the Creator is that perhaps he will not be able to give contentment to the Creator, and not that fear will concern one's own benefit. It follows that the gate to faith is fear; it is impossible to reach faith by any other way.

To acquire fear, the fear that one might not be able to give contentment to his Maker, he must first desire and yearn to bestow. Afterwards, he can say that there is room for the fear that he might not be able to sustain the fear. However, one is usually afraid that perhaps his self-love will not be complete, and he does not concern himself with not being able to bestow upon the Creator.

By which substance can one be brought to acquire a new quality that he must bestow, and that reception for self is faulty? This is against nature! Though at times, one receives a thought and desire that he must abandon self-love, which comes to us by hearing of it from friends and books, it is a very small force, which does not always shine for us so we can constantly appreciate it and say that this is the rule for all the *Mitzvot* in the Torah.

Thus, there is but one counsel: Several individuals must come together with the desire to abandon self-love, but without the sufficient force and appreciation for bestowal to become independent, without help from the outside. Now, if these individuals annul before one another, since each of them has at least potential love of the Creator, though they cannot actually keep it, then by each joining the society and annulling oneself before it, they become one body.

For example, if there are ten people in that body, it has ten times more power than a single person does. However, there is a condition: When they gather, each of them should think that he has now come for the purpose of annulling self-love. It means that he will not consider how to satisfy his will to receive now, but will think as much as possible only of the love of others. This is the only way to acquire the desire and the need to acquire a new quality, called "the will to bestow."

And from love of friends one can reach love of the Creator, meaning wanting to give contentment to the Creator. It turns out that only in this does one obtain a need and understanding that bestowing is important and necessary, and this comes to him through love of friends. Then we can talk about fear, meaning that one is afraid that he will not be able to bestow contentment to the Creator, and this is called "fear."

Hence, the primary basis upon which the building of sanctity can be erected is the rule of "Love thy friend." By that, one can acquire the need to bestow contentment upon the Creator. After that, there can be fear, meaning fear of perhaps not being able to give contentment to the Creator. When actually past that gate of fear, he can come to faith, because faith is the vessel for instilling the Shechina [Divinity], as it is explained in several places.

We thus find that there are three rules before us: The first rule is that of Rabbi Akiva, being "Love thy friend as thyself." Prior to that, there is nothing that provides a person with the fuel enabling him to modify his situation even a bit, as this is the only way to exit from self-love toward love of man, and the feeling that self-love is a bad thing.

Now we come to the second rule, which is the fear. Without fear, there is no room for faith, as Baal HaSulam says.

Finally, we come to the third rule, which is faith. After all the above-mentioned three rules have been acquired, one comes to sense the purpose of creation, which is to do good to His creations.

According to What Is Explained Concerning "Love Thy Friend as Thyself"

Article No. 7, Tav-Shin-Mem-Dalet, 1984

According to what is explained concerning "Love thy friend as thyself," all the details of the 612 *Mitzvot* [commandments] are contained in this rule. It is as our sages say, "The rest is its commentary; go study." This means that by keeping the 612 *Mitzvot* we will be rewarded with the rule, "Love thy friend," and following that, the love of God.

Thus, what does love of friends give us? It is written that by gathering a few friends together, since they each have but a small force of love of others—meaning they can carry out the love of others only potentially—when they implement it, they remember that they have decided to relinquish self-love in favor of love of others. But in fact, one sees that he cannot relinquish any pleasure of the will to receive in favor of another, not even a bit.

However, by assembling a few people who agree that they have to achieve the love of others, when they annul themselves before one another, they are all intermingled. Thus, in each person there accumulates a great force, according to the size of the association. And then each can execute the love of others in actual fact.

So what do the details of the 612 *Mitzvot* give us, which we said are in order to keep the rule, since the rule is kept by love of friends? And we see that in reality, there is love of friends among the secular, too. They, too, gather in various circles in order to have love of friends. What, then, is the difference between religious and secular?

The verse says (Psalms 1), "...nor sat in the seat of the scornful." We must understand the prohibition of the "seat of the scornful." If he slanders or speaks idle words, then the prohibition is not because of a "seat of scornful." So what does the "seat of the scornful" give us?

Actually, the meaning is that when a few people come together for the purpose of love of friends, with the intention that each and every one will help his friend improve his corporeal state, each anticipates that by having more meetings they will profit from society and improve their corporeal state.

However, after all the meetings, everyone calculates and sees how much they have received from the association for the self-love, what the will to receive has gained by that, since they invested time and effort to benefit society. So what have they gained by it? One could probably succeed more if engaged in self-benefit, at least the part of his own efforts. But, "I entered the association because I thought that through it, I would be able to gain more than I could gain alone. But now I see that I have gained nothing."

Then one regrets it and says, "I would be better off using my own little strength instead of giving my time to society. However, now that I have given my time to society, in order to gain more properties through help from the society, I finally realize that not only did I not gain anything from society, I even lost what I could have gained alone."

According to What Is Explained Concerning "Love Thy Friend as Thyself"

When someone wishes to say that love of friends should be engaged in for the purpose of bestowal, that everyone should work to benefit others, everyone laughs and mocks him. It seems to them like a kind of joke, and this is a seat of seculars. It is said about it, "but sin is a reproach to any people, and every grace that they do, they do for themselves." Such a society detaches one from holiness and casts him into the world of mockery. This is the prohibition of the seat of the scornful.

Our sages said about such societies, "Disperse the wicked; better for them and better for the world." In other words, it is better that they do not exist. However, it is the opposite with the righteous: "Assemble the righteous; better for them and better for the world."

What is the meaning of "righteous"? It is those who want to keep the rule, "Love thy friend as thyself." Their sole intention is to exit self-love and assume a different nature of love of others. And although it is a *Mitzva* [commandment] that should be kept, and that one can force oneself to keep, love is still something that is given to the heart, and the heart disagrees with it by nature. What, then, can one do to make love of others touch the heart?

This is why we were given the 612 *Mitzvot*: they have the power to induce a sensation in the heart. However, since it is against nature, that sensation is too small to have the ability to keep love of friends *de facto*, even though one has a need for it. Hence, now he must seek advice on how to actually implement it.

The advice for one to be able to increase his strength in the rule, "Love thy friend," is by love of friends. If everyone is nullified before his friend and mingles with him, they become one mass where all the little parts that want the love of others unite in a collective force that consists of many parts. And when one has great strength, he can execute the love of others.

And then he can achieve the love of God. But the condition is that each will annul before the other. However, when he is separated from his friend, he cannot receive the share he should receive from his friend.

Thus, everyone should say that he is nothing compared to his friend. It is like writing numbers: If you first write "1" and then "0," it is ten times more. And when you write "00" it is a hundred times more. In other words, if his friend is number one, and the zero follows it, it is considered that one receives from his friend ten (10) times more. And if he says that he is double zero compared to his friend, he receives from his friend a hundred (100) times more.

However, if it is to the contrary, and he says that his friend is zero and he is one, then he is ten times less than his friend 0.1. And if he can say that he is one and he has two friends who are both zeros compared to him, then he is considered a hundred times less than them, meaning he is 0.01. Thus, his degree lessens according to the number of zeros he has from his friends.

Yet, even once he acquires that strength and can keep the love of others in actual fact, and feels his own gratification as bad for him, still, do not believe in yourself. There must be fear of falling into self-love in the middle of the work. In other words, should one be given a greater pleasure than he is used to receiving, although he can already work in order to bestow with small pleasures and is willing to relinquish them, he lives in fear of great pleasures.

This is called "fear," and this is the gate to receive the Light of faith, called "The inspiration of the *Shechina* [Divinity]," as it is written in The *Sulam* Commentary, "By the measure of fear is the measure of faith."

Hence, we must remember that the matter of "Love thy friend as thyself" should be kept because it is a *Mitzva*, since the Creator commanded to engage in love of friends. And Rabbi Akiva only interprets this *Mitzva* that the Creator commanded. He intended to make this *Mitzva* into a rule by which to be able to keep all the *Mitzvot* because of the commandment of the Creator, and not because of self-gratification.

In other words, it is not that the *Mitzvot* should expand our will to receive, meaning that by keeping the *Mitzvot* we would be generously rewarded. Quite the contrary; by keeping the *Mitzvot* we will reach the reward of being able to annul our self-love and achieve the love of others, and subsequently the love of God.

Now we can understand what our sages said about the verse, *VeSamtem* [Place them]. It comes from the word, *Sam* ["potion," as well as "placing"]. "If granted, it is a potion of life; if not granted, it is a potion of death."

Not granted means that one engages in Torah and *Mitzvot* to multiply self-love, so the body would acquire possessions in return for its work. If granted, one's self-love is nullified and he aims to receive a reward that is the strength for love of others. By this he will reach the love of the Creator—that his only wish will be to give contentment to the Creator.

Which Keeping of Torah and Mitzvot Purifies the Heart?

Article No. 8, Tav-Shin-Mem-Dalet, 1984

Question: Does keeping Torah and *Mitzvot* in order to receive reward purify the heart, too? Our sages said, "I have created the evil inclination; I have created the spice of Torah." This means that it does purify the heart. But is it so when one aims specifically at not receiving a reward, or does it also purify the heart if one works in order to receive a reward?

Answer: In the "Introduction to the Book of Zohar" (Item 44), it is written, "When one begins to engage in Torah and *Mitzvot*, even without any intention, meaning without love and fear, as is appropriate when serving the King, even in *Lo Lishma* [not for Her sake], the point in one's heart begins to grow and show its activity. This is so because *Mitzvot* do not require intention, and even actions without intention can purify one's will to receive, but in its first degree, called 'still.' And to the extent that one purifies the still part of the will to receive, one gradually builds the 613 organs of the point in the heart, which is the still of *Nefesh de Kedusha* [holiness]." Thus, we see that observing Torah and *Mitzvot*, even *Lo Lishma* purifies the heart.

Which Keeping of Torah and Mitzvot Purifies the Heart?

Question: Is the path of observing Torah and *Mitzvot* in order not to be rewarded meant only for a chosen few? Or can anyone walk this path of observing everything in order not to be rewarded, by which they will be rewarded with *Dvekut* [adhesion] with the Creator?

Answer: Although the will to receive for oneself alone emerged at the thought of creation, being given a correction that the souls will correct it to being in order to bestow, meaning by observing Torah and *Mitzvot*, we will turn our will to receive to be in order to bestow. This is given to everyone, without exception, for everyone was given this remedy, not necessarily a chosen few.

But since this is a matter of choice, some advance more quickly and others more slowly. But as it is written in the "Introduction to the Books of Zohar" (Items 13, 14), in the end, everyone will achieve their complete perfection, as it is written, "The outcast shall not be outcast from Him."

Still, when beginning to learn to observe Torah and *Mitzvot*, one begins in *Lo Lishma*. This is because man is created with a will to receive; hence, he does not understand anything that does not yield him self-benefit and he will never want to begin to observe Torah and *Mitzvot*.

It is as the Rambam wrote (*Hilchot Teshuva*, Chapter 10), "Sages said, 'one should always engage in Torah, even *Lo Lishma*, because from *Lo Lishma*, one comes to *Lishma*.' Hence, when teaching children and women and the populace, they are only taught to work out of fear and to receive reward. And when they gain knowledge and acquire wisdom, that secret is revealed to them bit by bit. They are accustomed to it calmly until they attain Him and serve Him with love." Thus, we see from the Rambam's words that everyone should achieve *Lishma*, but the difference is in the timing.

Question: If a person sees and feels that he is treading a path that leads to *Lishma*, should he try to influence others so they will tread the right path, too?

Answer: This is a general question. It is like a religious person examining a secular person. If he knows that he can reform him, then he is must reform him, due to the *Mitzva*, "Thou shalt surely rebuke your friend." Similarly, in this case it can be said that you should tell your friend about the better way that one can go, provided your intention is only the *Mitzva*. But there are many times when a person rebukes another only for the purpose of domination, and not in order to "rebuke your friend."

And we learn from the above that everyone's desire that others will tread the path of truth has created disputes between orthodox and secular, between the Lithuanian faction and *Hassidim*, and among the *Hassidim* themselves. This is because everyone thinks that he is in the right, and everyone is trying to persuade the other to tread the right path.

One Should Always Sell the Beams of His House

Article No. 9, Tav-Shin-Mem-Dalet, 1984

"Rabbi Yehuda said, 'Rav said, 'One should always sell the beams of his house and put shoes on his feet''" (*Shabbat*, 129). We should understand the precision about the beams of one's house and the great importance of shoes, to the point that it is worth selling the beams of his house for it, meaning to have the ability to put shoes on his feet.

We should interpret it in the work. The *Korot* [beams] of his house comes from the word Mikreh [incident/event], meaning everything that a person experiences in his home. We perceive man by two discernments—by knowledge, meaning with the intellect, and by emotion, meaning what we feel in our hearts—whether we are happy or unhappy.

These incidents that we experience evoke questions in our everyday lives. This applies between a person and his Creator, and between a person and his friend.

Between a person and the Creator means that he has complaints that the Creator is not satisfying all his needs. In other words, the

Creator should fulfill what the person thinks he needs because the rule is that the conduct of the Good is to do good. And sometimes he complains as though he feels the opposite—that his situation is always worse than that of others, who are at a higher degree than he is.

It follows that he is in a state called "spies," who slander Providence because he doesn't feel that delight and pleasure in his life and it is hard for him to say, "Only goodness and grace will follow me all the days of my life." Thus, at that time he is in a state of "spies."

Our sages said about that (*Berachot* [Blessings], 54), "One must bless for the bad as he blesses for the good," since the basis of Judaism is built on faith above reason. This means not relying on what the intellect compels one to think, say, and do, but on faith in a benevolent, higher Providence. And precisely by justifying Providence, one is later rewarded with feeling delight and pleasure.

Baal HaSulam gave an allegory about a person who had complaints and demands of the Creator that He wasn't granting all his wishes. It is like a person who is walking on the street with a little child, and the child is crying bitterly. All the people on the street are looking at the father and thinking, "How cruel is this man who can hear his son crying without paying any attention? The child's cries make even people on the street feel sorry for the child, but this man, who is his father, doesn't. And there is a rule, 'As a father has compassion on his children.'"

The child's cries made people go to his father and ask, "Where is your mercy?" Then his father replied, "What can I do if my son, whom I keep like the apple of my eye, demands of me to give him a pin so he can scratch his eye because he has an itch in his eyes? Can I be called "cruel" for not granting his wish, or is it for mercy that I will not give it to him so he will not poke his eye and remain blind forever?"

Therefore, we must believe that everything that the Creator gives us is for our own good, although we must pray, just in case, that the Creator will lift these troubles from us. However, we must know that the prayer and the granting of the prayer are two separate issues. In other words, if we do what we must, then the Creator will do what is good for us, as with the above allegory. It is said about that, "And the Lord will do that which seems good to Him."

The same principle applies to a person and his friend, meaning that he should sell the beams of his house and put shoes on his feet. In other words, a person should sell the beams of his house, meaning all the incidents that his house experienced in regards to love of friends.

One may have questions and complaints about his friend, since he is working devotedly in love of friends, yet he sees no response on the part of the friends that would help him in any way. They are all behaving not according to his understanding of how love of friends should be, meaning that each one will speak to his friend in a respectable manner, as it is among distinguished individuals.

Also, regarding actions, he sees no action on the part of the friends that he can look at in relation to love of friends. Instead, everything is normal, as it is among ordinary people who still did not have an interest in coming together and deciding to build a society where there is love of friends, where each cares for the well-being of the other.

Thus, now he sees that there is no one to look at who engages in love of friends. And since he feels that he is the only one who is walking on the right path, and he is looking at everyone with contempt and scorn, this is called "spies." That is, he is spying on his friends to see if they are behaving properly toward him in regards to "Love thy friend." And since he constantly hears that the friends are preaching all day long that love of others is the most important, he wants to see if what they say is what they do.

And then he sees that it is all lip service. He finds that even in speaking there is no love of others, and this is the smallest thing in love of others. In other words, if he asks someone a question, he answers him offhandedly, indifferently, not in the way one answers a friend. Rather, it is all cold, as though he wants to get rid of him.

And don't ask me, "If you're thinking about love of others, why are you criticizing if your friend loves you, as though love of friends is established on the basis of self-love, and this is why I want to see what my self-love gained from this engagement?" These are not my thoughts. Rather, I truly want love of others.

This is why I was interested in establishing this society, so I would see that each and every one is engaging in love of others, so that through it, the little bit of force that I have in love of others would increase and I would have the strength to engage in love of others more powerfully than I could by myself. But now I see that I have gained nothing because I see that not even one is doing good. Thus, it would be better if I weren't with them and hadn't learned from their actions.

To that, there is the reply that if a society is established with certain people, and when they gathered, there must have been someone who wished to establish specifically this "bunch." Thus, he sorted out these people to see that they were suitable for each other. In other words, each of them had a spark of love of others, but the spark could not ignite the light of love to shine in each, so they agreed that by uniting, the sparks would become a big flame.

Hence, now, too, when he is spying on them, he should overcome and say, "As all of them were of one mind that they must walk on the path of love of others when the society was established, so it is now." And when everyone judges his friends favorably, all the sparks will ignite once more and again there will be one big flame.

It is as Baal HaSulam once said when he asked about the covenant that two friends make, as we find in the Torah (Gen 21:27), "And Abraham took sheep and oxen, and gave them unto Abimelech; and they two made a covenant." He asked, "If the two of them love each other, of course they do good to each other. And naturally, when there is no love between them because the love has waned for some reason, they do not do good to one another. So how does making a covenant between them help?"

He answered that the covenant that they do is not for now, since now when the love is felt between them, there is no need to make a covenant. Rather, the making of the covenant is done purposely for the future. In other words, it is possible that after some time, they will not feel the love as they do now, but they will still keep their relations as before. This is what the making of the covenant is for.

We can also see that although now they do not feel the love as it was when the society was established, everyone must still overcome his view and go above reason. By that, everything will be corrected and each will judge his friend favorably.

Now we can understand the words of our sages, who said, "One should always sell the beams of his house and put shoes on his feet." *Min'alim* [shoes] comes from the word *Ne'ilat Delet* [locking a door], meaning closing. Once a person has spied on his friend—and *Rigel* [spied] comes from the word *Raglaim* [feet/legs]—he should "Sell the beams of his house," meaning all that has happened to his house in the connection between him and his friend, meaning the spies that he has, who slander the friends.

Then, "Sell everything" means remove all the incidents that the spies have brought to him and put shoes on his feet, instead. The meaning is that he should lock away the spies as though they no longer exist in the land, and he will shut away all the questions and demands that he has about them. And then everything will come to its place in peace.

What Is the Degree One Should Achieve in Order Not to Have to Reincarnate?

Article 10, Tav-Shin-Mem-Dalet, 1984

Question: What is the degree one should achieve in order not to have to reincarnate?

It is written in *Gate of Reincarnations* (p 10b), "All of the children of Israel must reincarnate until they are completed with all the NRNHY. However, most people do not have all five parts called NRNHY, but only *Nefesh*, which is from *Assiya*." This means that each one should correct only his part and the root of his soul, and nothing more. By that, he completes what he must correct.

The thing is that we have to know that all of the souls extend from the soul of *Adam Harishon*, for after he sinned in the sin of the Tree of Knowledge, his soul divided into 600,000 souls. This means that the one light that *Adam Harishon* had, which the Holy *Zohar*

What Is the Degree One Should Achieve in Order Not to Have to Reincarnate?

called *Zihara Ila'a* [upper brightness], which he had in the Garden of Eden at once, spreads into numerous pieces.

It is written in the book *Panim Masbirot* [*Welcoming Face*] (p 56), "Once good and bad have been mingled (meaning after the sin), a big structure was made for the *Klipot* [shells] as they have the strength to grip to holiness. To keep from them, the light of the seven days of creation was divided into very small pieces from which the *Klipot* cannot suckle due to their smallness.

"For example, a king wanted to send a large number of gold coins to his son overseas, but all of his countrymen were thieves and swindlers, and he did not have one loyal messenger. What did he do? He divided, he broke all the coins into pennies, and sent them through many messengers, so that the joy of stealing would not be worth blemishing the glory of the kingship."

In this way, through an order of times in many souls, it is possible, through the illumination of the days, to scrutinize all the holy sparks that were robbed by the *Klipot* due to the sin of the tree of knowledge.

The meaning of many souls is division into inner lights, and many days means division into outer lights. And each penny accumulates into the amount of great light with which *Adam Harishon* sinned, and then will be the end of correction.

It follows that each one is born with only a tiny part of the soul of *Adam Harishon*. When he corrects his part, he no longer needs to reincarnate. Therefore, one can correct only that which belongs to his part. It is written about it in the book, *Tree of Life*, by the Ari, "There is not a day that is like another, or a moment that is like another; there is not a person who is like another, and the *Helbona* [resin] will correct what the *Levona* [incense] will not correct. Rather, each one must correct that which belongs to his part."

However, we must know that each person who is born has the work of choice, for one is not born righteous, as our sages said (*Nidah*, 16b), and these are their words: "Rabbi Hanina Ben Papa said, 'That angel appointed over pregnancy is called *Laila* [night].

He takes a drop, places it before the Creator, and says to Him, 'Lord of the world, what shall become of this drop? A mighty one or a weakling, a wise or a fool, wealthy or poor?' But wicked or righteous he did not say.'"

This means that one is not born righteous, as he did not say, "righteous or poor." Rather, this is given to man's choice. According to each one's labor in Torah and *Mitzvot* [commandments], so he is rewarded with cleansing his heart and correcting that which he must according to the root of his soul, and then he is completed.

The First Degree in Which a Man Is Born

It is written in *The Zohar* (*Mishpatim*, 4:11 in the *Sulam*): "Come and see. When a person is born, he is given a soul from the side of the beast, the side of purity, the side of those who are called holy *Ofanim*, meaning from the world of *Assiya*. If he merits more, he is given *Ruach* from the side of holy animals, meaning from the side of *Yetzira*. If he merits more, he is given *Neshama* from the side of the throne, meaning from the world of *Beria*. If he merits more, he is given *Nefesh* in the way of *Atzilut*. If he merits more, he is given *Ruach de Atzilut* from the side of the middle pillar, and he is called a "son of the Creator," as it is written, "You are the sons of the Lord your God." If he merits more, he is given *Neshama*, which is *Bina*, of which it was said, the whole *Neshama* (soul) will praise the Lord, and the name *HaVaYaH* is completed in them.

Thus, the completion of the soul is when he has *NRN* from *BYA* and *NRN* from *Atzilut*. This is the completion that *Adam Harishon* had before the sin. Only after the sin he descended from his degree and his soul divided into 600,000 souls.

Because of it, a person's spirituality is called *Neshama* [soul], even when he has only *Nefesh de Nefesh*, since there is a rule: whenever we speak of some discernment, we speak of the uppermost discernment. And because the uppermost discernment of a person is the degree of *Neshama*, in general, we always refer to man's spirituality by the name, *Neshama*.

However, although each person is born in the smallest degree, they said (see Gate of Reincarnations, p 11b), "Every person can be as Moses, if he wishes to cleanse his works, since he can take another, higher spirit, from the height of *Yetzira*, and also a *Neshama* from the height of *Beria*." By that you will also understand the famous matter in the words of our sages, that the spirits of the righteous, or their souls, come and become impregnated in a person, in what is called impregnation to assist him in the work of the Creator.

It is also presented in the *Sulam* (*Introduction of the Book of Zohar*, p 93), and these are its words: "That thing of the donkey driver is the assistance to the souls of the righteous, which is sent to them from Above in order to raise them from degree to degree. Were it not for this assistance that the Creator sends to the righteous, they would not be able to exit their degree and rise higher. Therefore, the Creator sends each and every righteous a high soul from Above—to each according to his merit and degree—which assists him on his way. And this is called, 'the impregnation of the soul of the righteous,' and it is called, 'the revealing of the souls of the righteous.'"

It follows that when we say that there is no generation in which there is none such as Abraham, Isaac, and Jacob, it does not mean that they were born this way and they have no choice. Rather, these are people who exert in walking on the path of truth, and make the effort they have to make. These people always receive help from Above through the impregnation of the soul of the righteous. That is, they receive the strength to rise up the upper degrees.

It follows that everything that is given from Above is as assistance, but not without any work and choice.

And the persistence of the world is through these righteous who extend abundance from Above, and by that there is persistence to the world.

Ancestral Merit

Article No. 11, Tav-Shin-Mem-Dalet, 1984

A dispute is introduced regarding ancestral merit (*Shabbat*, p 55): "Shmuel said, 'Ancestral merit has ended.' Rabbi Yohanan said, 'Ancestral merit pardons.'" In the *Midrash* (*Midrash Rabah, Vayikra*, 37), "Rav Aha said, 'Ancestral merit exists forever and is forever mentioned.'" And there, in the *Tosfot*, it is said, "Rabeinu Tam says that ancestral merit has ended, but ancestral covenant has not ended." To Rabbi Yohanan it seems that there is no dispute between Shmuel and Rabbi Yohanan: Shmuel said that it ended for the wicked but not for the righteous, and Rabbi Yohanan is referring to the righteous.

According to the above, we can interpret what is being asked about the choice: "If there is ancestral merit, then there is no choice here, since ancestral merit causes a person to be righteous. And according to the words of the *Tosfot*, in the name of the ARI, who says that ancestral merit is only for the righteous, it follows that initially one has choice, so as to be righteous, and subsequently one can enjoy the ancestral merit.

From the essay *Matan Torah* ["The Giving of the Torah"] (item 19), it appears that thanks to ancestral merit we have the power to make the choice, and were it not for ancestral merit we would not be able to make the choice. In reality, we see that even though we have ancestral merit, we still do not see that everyone has the strength to make the choice. Rather, everyone finds it difficult. However, the ancestral merit assists us in making the choice.

This means that choosing applies where there are two equal things, and I must decide. But when one side is more difficult than the other, it cannot be said that I must decide, since I naturally lean toward the stronger side. Therefore, thanks to ancestral merit they are two equal forces and we can decide. This is called that we were given the strength to make the choice.

To understand these matters we should look at what is written in the essay, "The Giving of the Torah" (item 19): "Therefore, the Creator did not find a nation or a tongue qualified to receive the Torah, except for the children of Abraham, Isaac, and Jacob, whose ancestral merit reflected upon them, as our sages said, 'The Patriarchs observed the whole Torah even before it was given.' This means that because of the exaltedness of their souls, they had the ability to attain all the ways of the Creator with respect to the spirituality of the Torah, which stems from their *Dvekut* [adhesion] with Him, without first needing the ladder of the practical part of the Torah, which they had no possibility of observing at all (as written in item 16). Undoubtedly, both the physical purity and the mental exaltedness of our holy fathers greatly influenced their sons and their sons' sons."

It therefore follows that thanks to ancestral merit we can make the choice. Otherwise, it would be impossible.

However, we need great mercy even once we have ancestral merit, so we can make the choice, meaning abandon self-love and take upon ourselves love of others, and that all our aspirations will be only to bestow contentment upon the Creator. And even with all the powers of Torah and *Mitzvot* [commandments], that we will be able to defeat the evil in us and turn it into good.

However, we should understand why he says "Ancestral merit has ended." The question is, "What existed prior to the end of ancestral merit?" And if so, there was no need for choice then, since he had ancestral merit. However, we should say that a person's request that He will help him come close to Him—to the true service of the Creator—is the prayer itself. His request that He will help him with ancestral merit is itself considered a "choice." The choice is that he is doing what he can, and this is already regarded as a choice.

Concerning the Importance of Society

Article No. 12, Tav-Shin-Mem-Dalet, 1984

It is known that one is always among people who have no connection to the work on the path of truth, but to the contrary, always resist those who walk on the path of truth. And since people's thoughts mingle, the views of those who oppose the path of truth permeate those with some desire to walk on the path of truth.

Hence, there is no other solution but to establish a separate society for themselves, to be their framework, meaning a separate community that does not mingle with other people whose views differ from that society. And they should constantly evoke in themselves the issue of the purpose of society, so they will not follow the majority, because following the majority is our nature.

If the society isolates itself from the rest of the people, if they have no connection with other people in regards to spiritual matters, and their contact with them is only on corporeal matters, they will not mingle with their views, since they have no connection in matters of religion.

But when a person is among religious people and begins to converse and argue with them, he immediately mingles with their views. Their views subconsciously penetrate his mind to such an extent that he will not be able to discern that these are not his own views, but what he received from the people he connected with.

Therefore, in matters of work on the path of truth, one should isolate oneself from other people. This is because the path of truth requires constant strengthening, since it is against the view of the world. The view of the world is knowing and receiving, whereas the view of Torah is faith and bestowal. If one strays from that, he immediately forgets all the work of the path of truth and falls into a world of self-love. Only from a society in the form of "They helped every man his friend" does each person in the society receive the strength to fight against the view of the world.

Also, we find the following in the words of *The Zohar* (Pinhas, p 31, Item 91, and in the *Sulam*): "When a person dwells in a city inhabited by evil people, and he cannot keep the *Mitzvot* of the Torah, and does not succeed in the Torah, he relocates and uproots himself from there and plants himself in a place inhabited by good people, with Torah and with *Mitzvot*. This is because the Torah is called 'tree,' as it is written, 'She is a tree of life to them that lay hold upon her.' And man is a tree, as it is written, 'For is the tree of the field man.' And the *Mitzvot* in the Torah are likened unto fruits. And what does it say? 'Only the trees of which thou knows that they are not trees for food, them thou may destroy and cut down,' destroy from this world and cut down from the next world."

For this reason, one must uproot himself from the place where there are wicked, for he will not be able to succeed there in Torah and *Mitzvot*, and plant himself elsewhere, among righteous, and he will succeed in Torah and *Mitzvot*.

And man, whom *The Zohar* compares to the tree of the field, suffers, like the tree of the field, from bad neighbors. In other words, we must always cut down the bad weeds around us that affect us, and we must also keep away from bad environments and from

Concerning the Importance of Society

people who do not favor the path of truth. We need a careful watch so as to not be drawn to follow them.

This is called "isolation," when one has thoughts of the "single authority," called "bestowal," and not "public authority," which is self-love. This is called "two authorities"—the Creator's authority and one's own authority.

Now we can understand what our sages said (*Sanhedrin*, p 38), "Rav Yehuda said, 'Rav said, '*Adam Harishon* was heretic,' as it is written, 'And the Lord God called unto the man, and said unto him: 'Where art thou?'' Where has thine heart gone?'"

In Rashi's interpretation, "heretic" refers to a tendency towards idol worship. And in the commentary, *Etz Yosef* (Joseph's Tree), it is written, "When it writes, 'Where, where has thine heart gone?' it is heresy, as it is written, 'that ye go not about after your own heart,' this is heresy, when his heart leans towards the other side."

But all this is very perplexing: How can it be said that *Adam Harishon* was inclined towards idolatry? Or according to the *Etz Yosef* commentary, that he was in the form of "that ye go not about after your own heart," is it heresy? According to what we learn about the work of God, that it is solely about the aim to bestow, if a person works in order to receive, this work is foreign to us, for we need to work only to bestow, and he took everything in order to receive.

This is the meaning of what he said, that he failed in "go not about after your own heart." In other words, he could not take the eating from the Tree of Knowledge in order to bestow, but received the eating from the Tree of Knowledge in order to receive. This is called "heart," meaning the heart wishes only to receive for self-gratification. And this was the sin of the Tree of Knowledge.

To understand this matter, see the introduction to the book *Panim Masbirot*. And from this we can understand the benefits of the society—it can introduce a different atmosphere—one of working only in order to bestow.

Sometimes Spirituality Is Called "a Soul"

Article No. 13, Tav-Shin-Mem-Dalet, 1984

We must understand why spirituality is sometimes called "a soul" [Heb: *Neshama*], as it is written, "Body and soul," and sometimes spirituality is called "soul" [Heb: *Nefesh*], as in, "And you shall love the Lord your God with all your heart and with all your soul."

Usually, when speaking of spirituality, we speak of its highest discernment, which is *Neshama*, so that one will know that a high degree has been made ready for him, which is *Neshama*, to evoke in his heart the desire to achieve it and to think what is the reason that he has not achieved it yet. Then he will come to know that all we need in order to attain spirituality is equivalence of form.

The body is born with a nature of self-love, which is disparity of form from the Creator, whom we attain as only giving. Thus, one should cleanse one's body and come to equivalence of form so he, too, will want to do things that are only to bestow. By that, he will be able to reach this high degree called *Neshama*. This is why we always speak in terms of body and *Neshama* [soul].

But when referring to the order of the work, following the degree of the body comes the degree of *Nefesh*. This is why the writing says, "And you shall love the Lord your God with all your heart and with all your soul [Heb: *Nefesh*]," for this is the next degree after the body.

This is why it says, "With all your heart," and subsequently, "With all your soul." In other words, one must be willing to give everything he has to the Creator. But afterwards, if he obtains a higher degree, meaning *Ruach* [spirit], and then *Neshama*, he should still be willing to give everything to the Creator. But the text begins with the first degree that comes after the body.

All that a man has, he must give to the Creator. This means that he does not do anything for his own benefit. Rather, everything is for the sake of the Creator. This is considered that all his deeds are only to bestow, while he is completely inconsequential. Rather, everything is for the sake of the Creator.

Now you can understand what is written in *The Zohar* (*Teruma* [Contribution], p 219, Item 479 in the *Sulam* Commentary), "'With all your soul.' He asks, 'It should have said, 'In your soul,' what is 'With all your soul?' Why does it say, 'With'?' He replies that it comes to include *Nefesh, Ruach, Neshama*. This is 'With all your soul,' where 'all' means what this *Nefesh* grips."

From this, we see that *The Zohar* interprets the "all" that the Torah adds to us as coming to tell us that *Nefesh* and *Ruach* are included in the *Neshama*. However, it deliberately begins with *Nefesh*, since after the body comes the *Nefesh*. But when we speak of spirituality in general, we refer to spirituality as *Neshama*, as it is written, "And he blew into his nostrils the *Neshama* ["soul" or "breath"] of life."

To obtain the degree of *NRN* [*Nefesh-Ruach-Neshama*], we must go by a path of bestowal and try to come out of self-love. This is called "the path of truth," meaning that by so doing, we will achieve the quality of truth that exists in His Providence, who behaves toward us with the quality of benevolence.

This is called "The Creator's seal is truth." This means that the objective of the work of the Creator, meaning His work in creating the worlds—which is to do good to His creations—is that man must reach the Creator's quality of truth. Man will know that he has reached his completeness after he has attained the guidance of the Creator as benevolent, whether he has abundance. But also, he should see that others have abundance, too, meaning see that everyone has complete abundance.

This is presented in "Introduction to the Study of the Ten Sefirot" (Item 150), "The fourth discernment of love, which is unconditional love, is eternal. This is so because after he has judged the whole world favorably, the love is eternal and absolute. There cannot be covering and hiding in the world because there, it is a place of complete disclosure of the face, as it is written, 'Your Teacher will no longer hide Himself, but your eyes will see your Teacher,' since he already knows all of the Creator's dealings with all the people in the form of true Providence that appears from His name, 'The Good Who Does Good to the good and to the bad.'"

It therefore follows that if one reaches complete perfection, he attains his true state. However, there are preliminary degrees before that, as it is written in "Introduction to the Study of the Ten Sefirot," that the first discernment is repentance from fear. It is written about it (Item 63), "The first degree of attainment of the disclosure of the face, meaning attainment and sensation of the Providence of reward and punishment in a way that He who knows all mysteries will testify that he will not turn back to folly, is called 'repentance from fear.' At that time, his sins become mistakes for him, and he is called 'incomplete righteous' or 'medium.'"

However, according to the above, there is another sign that one is walking on the path of truth—the state of negation. In other words, even though he sees that now he is in a worse state, that is, before he began to walk on the path of truth he felt closer to *Kedusha* [holiness], whereas now that he's begun to walk on this path he feels more remote. But according to the known rule,

"Holiness is increased, not decreased," there rises the question, "Why now that he is walking on the path of truth does he feel that he is regressing instead of progressing, as it should be if he is walking on the path of truth? At the very least, he should not decline from his previous state."

The answer is that there must be absence before there is presence. This means that first there must be a *Kli* [vessel], which is called "a lack," and then there will be room to fill the lack. Therefore, first, one must go forward and bring himself closer to the truth each time. In other words, each time he goes forward, he sees his situation: that he is immersed in self-love. And each time he should see more clearly that self-love is bad because self-love is what hinders us from reaching the delight and pleasure that the Creator has prepared for us, as this is what separates us from the Creator.

Accordingly, we can understand that what a person thinks—that he is regressing now that he has begun on the path of truth—he must know that this is not so. Rather, he is advancing toward the truth. Previously, when his work was not based on bestowal and faith, he was far from seeing the truth. But now he must come to feel the evil within him, as it is written, "There shall be no strange god within you."

Our sages said, "Who is the strange God in a man's body? It is the evil inclination." In other words, within a person, the will to receive is his very evil.

And then when he has achieved the recognition of evil, he can say that he is going to correct it. It turns out that prior to attaining his evil to an extent where he couldn't tolerate it any longer, there was nothing to correct. Thus, he has indeed gone a long way forward in the truth, to see his real situation.

And when a person sees the evil in himself to an extent that he cannot tolerate it, he begins to seek advice for how to come out of it. But the only advice for a man of Israel is to turn to the Creator, so He will open his eyes and his heart and fill it with sublime abundance, as our sages said, "He who comes to be purified is aided."

Then, when he receives help from the Creator, all the lacks will be filled with the light of the Creator, and he begins to rise on the degrees of holiness because the need has already been prepared within him by coming to see his true state. Hence, now there is room to receive his completeness.

And then a person begins to see how each day, according to his work, he rises ever upwards. However, we must always awaken what the heart forgets, what is needed for the correction of the heart—Love of friends—whose purpose is to achieve love of others.

This is not a pleasant thing for the heart, which is called "self-love." Hence, when there is a gathering of friends, we must remember to bring up the question, meaning everyone should ask himself how much we have advanced in love of others, and how much we have done to promote us in that matter.

One Should Always Sell Everything He Has and Marry a Wise Disciple's Daughter

Article No. 14, Tav-Shin-Mem-Dalet, 1984

"One should always sell everything he has and marry a wise disciple's daughter" (*Psachim*, 49). This means that he should sell all the possessions that he has acquired through his labor. That is, he should give everything and relinquish everything, and in turn take the daughter of a wise disciple.

This means that if he does not take a wise disciple's daughter, all the labor that he has given in Torah and *Mitzvot* [commandments] his whole life is incomplete. Only if he marries a wise disciple's daughter will he be rewarded with his completeness. This is why our sages said that he should sell everything he has, meaning that it is worthwhile to sell everything for a wise disciple's daughter. Therefore, we should understand the meaning of "a wise disciple's daughter."

Baal HaSulam said that a wise disciple is one who is a disciple of a wise, meaning he learns from the wise, and then he is considered a disciple. A wise is the Creator, whose quality is only to bestow. One who learns from Him the quality of bestowal is called a "wise disciple" because he is learning from Him the quality of bestowal.

By that we will understand what our sages said, "One should always sell everything he has and marry a wise disciple's daughter." That is, he should give all the labor he has given in Torah and work, and in return receive a possession of bestowal.

This means that he will establish in his heart a new nature, instead of the one that he naturally has—a desire of self-love. Now he will receive a second nature: the desire to bestow. That is, his every thought, word, and action will be only in order to bestow upon the Creator, for this is the whole man. This means that one should achieve only this degree, for all we need to attain are the *Kelim* [vessels]. But the abundance, which is the filling of the *Kelim*, comes from the Creator, since more than the calf wants to suckle, the cow wants to nurse. Therefore, all we are missing is the power of bestowal.

By that we can interpret what is written in *The Zohar* (Pinhas, p 78, item 218), "If Israel are rewarded, He would come down like a lion of fire to eat the offerings. If they were not rewarded, He would come down there like a dog of fire." It is known that lion implies *Hesed* [mercy], which is the right of the *Merkava* [chariot], "If they are rewarded," where being rewarded means pure, meaning bestowal. Then we are shown an eye for an eye—that from above, too, comes the discernment of lion, meaning that the quality of *Hesed* expanded to the lower ones, and then the abundance was plentiful for the lower ones.

"If they are not rewarded," meaning that they did not engage in bestowal, but only in self-love, then from above the discernment of dog would be extended. A dog implies, as it is written in *The Zohar* about the verse, "The leach has two daughters that howl as dogs, give us the wealth of this world and give us the wealth of the next world." In other words, two daughters that bark like dogs: "Give us the wealth of this world and give us the wealth of the next world," which is only about reception and not about bestowal. Therefore, from above, too, we are shown that we cannot bestow abundance downward, and this is called an "eye for an eye."

It turns out that our work is only to be rewarded with *Kelim* [vessels] that are suitable for reception of the abundance, which are vessels of bestowal. Therefore, a person should focus all of his efforts on one thing only, called "vessels of bestowal." This should be the only reward that he wants to attain from Torah and *Mitzvot* [commandments]. By that he will achieve *Dvekut* [adhesion] with the Creator, which is man's purpose: to achieve *Dvekut* with the Creator.

We also see in the words of *The Zohar* that it was said about the verse, "The mercy of the nations is a sin," "All the good that they do, they do for themselves." This means their aim with all the mercy, meaning the acts of bestowal that they do, is not to bestow. Rather their intention is for themselves, meaning to receive reward for it. Otherwise, they cannot perform acts of bestowal.

But the people of Israel are capable of performing acts of bestowal. We should understand why the people of Israel can perform acts of bestowal, and we should also understand, according to what we hear from people who became religious, who say that before they became religious they were more capable of performing acts in order to bestow, but afterwards, meaning once they have become religious, it has become more difficult for them to perform acts of bestowal.

To understand the above we should remember the known that a person is called a "created being" only in that there is a will to receive in him, for this is called "created existence from absence." It therefore turns out that by nature he is incapable of performing any act of bestowal unless he receives some reward in return.

The reward does not have to be that he receives something for the effort. Rather, it can be some pacifying that he receives. That is, if some compassion awakened in him toward another, and his conscience does not let him rest, to the point that he must help another, this, too, is regarded as reward. But simply doing something for another, for the other to enjoy, then he tells himself, "What will I get out of it?"

But the people of Israel, through the power of Torah and *Mitzvot*, are capable of obtaining a second nature. That is, instead of the nature they were born with—a desire only to receive—they will receive a second nature, where now they work only in order to bestow. He obtains this through the Torah and *Mitzvot*, which instilled in him sparks of bestowal that bring him a sensation of wanting to resemble his root. But without the Torah and *Mitzvot*, a person cannot come out of his own nature, which is the desire to receive only for himself, and he cannot perform any act of bestowal without reward.

By this we will understand what they asked about those who become religious and say that before they became religious they had more strength to perform acts of bestowal. But later, when they have become religious, they feel that it is more difficult for them to perform acts of bestowal.

We should reply to that, as is explained in "The Introduction to the Book of Zohar" (items 29-30), where he writes that at the time of his birth his will to receive is only for corporeality. Therefore, although he has obtained the excessive will to receive prior to being thirteen, it is still not the end of the growth of the will to receive. The main growth of the will to receive is depicted only in spirituality, since, for example, prior to being thirteen his desire to receive wants to devour all the wealth and honor in this corporeal world, which is revealed to all, which is to him a transient world that is accessible to everyone, and is perceived by everyone only as a fleeting shadow.

But when he obtains the excessive, spiritual will to receive, he wants to devour for his own pleasure all the delight and wealth of the next, eternal world, which is to him an everlasting possession for all eternity. Thus, the will to receive is completed only with the desire to receive spirituality.

It turns out that before they have become religious they had a corporeal will to receive, which is not yet so great. This is why they had more strength to perform acts of bestowal. But once they have become religious and their will to receive has grown with the will to receive for spirituality, it has become more difficult because now the will to receive has more strength than when they had only a corporeal will to receive. Therefore, before they have become religious, they had some strength to perform acts of bestowal. But once they have become religious, obtaining the spiritual will to receive, it is now more difficult for them to engage in matters of bestowal.

For this reason, it cannot be said that now they have become worse, or to say that the religious are worse because it is more difficult for them to perform acts of bestowal. Rather, the will to receive has grown bigger, so it is more difficult to overcome it. For example, before he obtained the spiritual will to receive, his evil was thirty percent. Afterwards, once he has obtained the spiritual will to receive, his evil acquired another seventy percent. Therefore, now he needs greater powers to be able to overcome it.

However, we should not say that now his strength has diminished. On the contrary, now he must find the remedy to defeat the evil power he has obtained. And the remedy for this is keeping Torah and *Mitzvot* with the intention for the light in it to reform him.

It therefore follows that he has advanced and has obtained more evil in order to correct it. But every beginning is difficult, and therefore now he thinks that he has become worse. However, he should know that each time he is given more bad to correct until he is rewarded with correcting everything.

[For the continuation of the clarification of the article, see next article]

Can Something Negative Come Down from Above

Article No. 15, Tav-Shin-Mem-Dalet, 1984

An explanation on what was said in article no. 14 about the words in *The Zohar*, Pinhas (item 78) "If Israel were rewarded, it would come down like a lion of fire to eat the offerings. If they were not rewarded it would come down there like a dog of fire." It was asked about it, "How can something negative come down from above?" We understand that what comes from above is to do good. When something not positive comes, what correction comes out of it, of which we can say that it came from above like a dog of fire? After all this is not positive.

We should understand this with an allegory. A person who had a sick son went to the doctor, who gave him a medicine. However, this didn't help his son. Friends advised him that since there is a great professor here, although he charges a lot of money it is worthwhile seeing him because he is a great expert. When they came to him, he examined the sick child and said that his son was dangerously ill, and named the child's illness.

The man paid him the price they agreed on in advance, and when he returned to his home he told his friends, "You advised me to go see this great expert and that it's worthwhile to pay him a lot of money. But in the end, what did the great expert do? He said that my son has a worse illness than the doctor who is not an expert told me. Was it worthwhile for me to pay so much money, so he would tell me that my son has such a terrible illness? After all, why do I go to a doctor? To heal the patient, not to say that my son has a terrible disease."

The friends told him that according to the great expert's diagnosis of his precise illness, now we know how to cure him. Curing the illness does not require a great doctor because we already know which medicine to prescribe to every illness. The important thing is to know what is the real illness. It turns out that the large sum you pay a great expert compared to a doctor who is not an expert is to determine precisely what is the illness.

It turns out that determining the flaw, which is considered negative, is nonetheless positive. That is, knowing the illness is actually a correction because now he knows what to correct. It turns out that knowing the illness is part of the healing of the illness, since it is impossible to heal the illness if he is not known the cause of the illness. Therefore, when a dog of fire comes down, the image of the dog indicates that the lower ones are under the rule of self-love, which *The Zohar* calls *Hav! Hav!* [bark, but also "give"] like a dog, it is considered positive, for now we know what to correct, that all you need is to correct the vessels of reception.

It turns out that the image of the dog of fire that comes down from above comes for the purpose of correction, not for the purpose of corruption. Therefore, this, too, is regarded as positive and not negative. Everything that comes from above, though it seems like a flaw to the lower one, when the lower ones examine, they see that it is all for their sake, so they will know what they must correct in themselves.

An explanation to article no. 14 (1984) concerning the corporeal will to receive, which is only half a degree of the will to receive.

When he receives the spiritual will to receive, he is complemented with the complete will to receive. It therefore follows that when he has a corporeal will to receive, he is not as bad, so why does he need to receive the spiritual will to receive, to be worse? Therefore, I would say that it is better to stay in the corporeal will to receive. Why should I exert to obtain the spiritual will to receive and become worse? And why should one enter a place of danger that he may not be able to correct? Therefore, it is certainly better to stay with the corporeal will to receive meaning that all of his passions will be only for corporeal things and not desire spirituality at all.

It is written in the "Introduction to the Book of Zohar" (item 29): "The first division is to obtain the excessive will to receive without restraints, in its full, corrupted measure from under the hands of the four impure worlds ABYA. If we do not have that corrupted will to receive, we will not be able to correct it, for one cannot correct that which is not in him."

Thus, we have no choice but to do things that will bring us the attainment of the spiritual will to receive. But that, too, is not easy. A person may obtain the spiritual will to receive because it depends on the measure of faith. That is, a person must first believe that there is spirituality, and it is more important than any corporeal pleasure, to the extent that it is worth relinquishing corporeal pleasures in order to obtain spiritual pleasures. Hence, this is a lot of work, and not everyone can obtain it.

And yet, this is still regarded as bad, meaning that he has obtained a corrupt will to receive. This is the meaning of from *Lo Lishma* [not for Her sake] one comes to *Lishma* [for Her sake]. That is, first one must achieve the degree of *Lo Lishma*, and then it is possible to correct it to *Lishma*, for it is impossible to intend where there is no action. Once there is an act, it is possible to try to make the act follow the right path called "for the Creator."

According to the above, it turns out that we have four general discernments in man's work, which he needs in order to achieve the completeness for which he was created. 1) Receive in order to

Can Something Negative Come Down from Above

receive, 2) bestow in order to receive, 3) bestow in order to bestow, 4) receive in order to bestow.

The first discernment, receiving in order to receive, is the first degree, and the creatures were born with this discernment. That is, they understand nothing more than self-love. They have no interest in doing anything good to anyone, and are totally immersed—according to the nature with which they were born—in the will to receive only for themselves. The whole world is in this state, and there is no difference from one to another.

The second discernment is bestowing in order to receive. This is a degree that transcends the majority of the people, who are used to doing things only in order to receive, while that person performs an act of bestowal. However, he must explain why he wants to be different from the rest of the world, meaning to do things contrary to the nature with which he was born. At that time he tells his body: "Know, that by performing an act of bestowal, you will receive more pleasure." He lets his body understand that it is worthwhile to believe that it will pay off. If the body believes it, it lets him work to the extent that it believes that it will pay off to cancel acts of self-reception and perform acts of bestowal. This is called *Lo Lishma*, of which our sages said, "From *Lo Lishma* we come to *Lishma*."

This is a springboard for moving from state to state—from a state of *Lo Lishma* to a state of *Lishma*, since with respect to the act they are the same. That is, you cannot discern and say that there is something to add to an act *Lishma*. Therefore, because in terms of the act they are the same, there is no work here as far as action. Rather, their entire work is in the intention. This means that they need only to think if the act they are performing is truly because of the commandment of the Creator, for the Creator commanded us to do *Mitzvot* [commandments] and we want to keep his *Mitzvot* because it is a great reward for us to serve Him, and He has also let us know how we can serve Him.

At that time comes the work of scrutiny if this is really so—that his sole intention in Torah and *Mitzvot* is to bestow or he has other considerations, meaning considerations of self-love, and this is why he observes Torah and *Mitzvot*.

When he sees that he is still far from performing all his actions for the Creator, he needs a true scrutiny. There are many people who do not have that scrutiny of the truth, who think that they are really working for the Creator. Although they are not one hundred percent *Lishma*, they usually feel that this is *Lishma*, though there is still more to add concerning *Lishma*. However, the truth is that they do not have the true perception, either because of their nature or because they did not have a good teacher to show them how not to deceive themselves.

Therefore, they cannot achieve *Lishma* because *Lishma* is called "truth," and *Lo Lishma* is called "falsehood." However, there should be a medium between truth and falsehood, so as to be a springboard from falsehood to the truth. The medium between truth and falsehood is a lie in truth. In other words, there is a lie but it is not really a lie because he is thinking of a lie that is true. That is, he is going by the path of falsehood, but thinks it is the truth. It turns out that it is not really a lie. However, if he knows that he is going in falsehood then he is walking on the path of truth because he knows that it is actually a lie. At that time he has a springboard, for only then he can really come into the actual truth, meaning from truth of falsehood into truth of truth.

As long as one does not know that he is going by the path of falsehood, why should he change his way and go by another way, if he does not have the understanding that he is in falsehood? Only if he comes to know that he really is in falsehood he will be able to change his way and go by the path of truth.

It therefore turns out that if a person already has the path of truth he is going on the path of *Lishma*, though he is still half way through. For example, a person who wants to go to Jerusalem gets in a car and drives according to sign that says, "Jerusalem." However, even when has travelled eighty or ninety percent of the way to Jerusalem, he is still not in Jerusalem. Only when he actually comes to Jerusalem can you say that he is in Jerusalem.

It is likewise in spirituality. If we say that Jerusalem is called "truth," meaning *Lishma*, then before a person enters *Lishma*, which is the truth, we have to say that he is still in falsehood, meaning in *Lo Lishma*, which is called "falsehood." Even when he has gone almost all the way and he is standing by the gate, called "truth," which is *Lishma*, he is still outside. It turns out that a person cannot know if he has achieved *Lishma* before he is rewarded with entering *Lishma*.

But when can one know if he has already entered the degree of *Lishma*? What is the sign by which to know that now he is in the degree of truth?

We find the answer to this in the "Introduction to Talmud Eser Sefirot" (item 56): "By this you will understand what our sages said, 'How is repentance? Until He who knows all mysteries will testify that he will not turn back to folly.'" This seems perplexing, for who can go up to Heaven and hear the Creator's testimony? Also, before whom should the Creator testify? Is it not enough that the Creator Himself knows that the person has repented wholeheartedly and will not sin again? From what is explained, the matter is very simple. Indeed, one is not completely certain that he will not sin again before he has been rewarded with the above clarified guidance of reward and punishment, meaning the revelation of the face. That revelation of the face on the part of the Creator is called "testimony." This is why he was given a clear sign, meaning "until He who knows all mysteries will testify to him."

It turns out that when a person has achieved bestowal he is rewarded with the revelation of the face of the Creator. This is called He who knows all mysteries testifies about him that he has achieved *Lishma*. This is called the "third discernment," bestowing in order to bestow, regarded as having achieved *Lishma*, which means that he has achieved the degree of truth. This came to him through the springboard which is to come from *Lo Lishma* to *Lishma*, but certainly with all the conditions that we have to abide by so as not to remain in *Lo Lishma*.

And after he has completed the degree of bestowing in order to bestow comes the fourth discernment, which is receiving in order to bestow. This is the degree of wholeness. This means that he has achieved a degree where he says, "I want to receive the light and pleasure because I know that I want to keep the purpose of creation, for the Creator created creation because He desires to do good to His creations." Therefore, he wants to receive the delight and pleasure from the Creator, as this is His will.

For the reason of self-love, he has no desire or craving for this, since he has already achieved the degree of equivalence of form called "bestowing in order to bestow." Therefore, now he wants to obey the Creator's will, which is His desire to do good to His creations.

We should know that there is the matter of the purpose of creation and the matter of correction of creation. The purpose of creation is to do good to His creations, meaning that the creatures will receive delight and pleasure. It turns out that the more they receive pleasure, the more the Creator enjoys. Therefore, one who is on a degree of completeness wants to always receive much delight and pleasure. As was explained, this is the purpose of creation—to do good to his creations.

But one who has achieved the degree of bestowing in order to bestow, which is *Dvekut* [adhesion] and equivalence of form, it is still only the correction of creation. This means that creation must come to a state where they received delight and pleasure, and after receiving all the pleasures they will still remain in bestowal. This is called "receiving in order to bestow."

Concerning Bestowal

Article No. 16, Tav-Shin-Mem-Dalet, 1984

Explaining the matter of bestowal. When a person serves someone whom the world regards as important, the important person doesn't need to reward him for his service. Rather, the very service of an important person is regarded by him as though he has rewarded him. This means that if one knows that he is an important person, he already enjoys the service and doesn't need further reward for his service. Instead, the service itself is his pleasure.

But if he is serving an ordinary person, he takes no pleasure in the service and must be rewarded for the service. This means that if he does that same service for an important person, he needs no reward.

If, for example, an important person comes by plane, carrying a small suitcase, many people are waiting for his arrival, and the important person gives his suitcase to someone to take it to the car that will take him home. For this service he wants to give him, say, one hundred dollars. He will certainly refuse to receive from him because the pleasure he derives from his service is more than the hundred dollars he is giving him.

But if he were an ordinary person, he wouldn't serve him even for money. Instead, he would tell him, "There are porters here; they will carry your suitcase to the car. As for me, it is beneath me to serve you. But since it is the porters' job, they will be happy to serve you if you pay them."

It follows that in his same action, there is a difference and significant distinction not in the act, *but for whom* he does it—if he is doing it for an important person. It depends only on the importance of that individual in that person's eyes, meaning what he feels about that person's greatness. It doesn't matter if he understands that he is an important person or if others around him say that he is an important person; this already gives him the strength to serve him without needing any reward.

According to the above, we should understand the true intention of the one who is serving the important person. Is his intention to enjoy serving him, since he considers it a great privilege? Or is it because he takes great pleasure in serving him? From which source does the pleasure of serving the important person come to him? He doesn't know. However, he is seeing something natural—that there is great pleasure involved here—so he wants to serve him.

In other words, is his aim that this is an important person, which is why he wants that person to enjoy? Or does he want to serve him because it gives him joy? Meaning, if he could have the same pleasure that he takes in serving him through some other means, would he relinquish this service, since he only wants to serve him because he feels that here he could find a good feeling, and this is why he serves him?

The question is whether the service is because he wants the important person to feel good, the pleasure that he derives from serving him is only a result, but his aim is not for himself but only for the important person to feel good. Or, is he in fact not considering the important person, but all his calculations are about how much pleasure he can derive from it?

And if we asked, "Does it matter with which intention he is working?" The answer is that we should know what vessels of bestowal mean.

There are three discernments that we find in an act of bestowal:

1) He engages in bestowal upon others—whether with his body or with his money—in order to be rewarded for it. In other words, the service itself is not enough to give him pleasure. Instead, he wants to be given something else in return for it. For example, he wants to be given honor in return for his work in bestowal. For that, he has the strength to work. But if he weren't confident that he would receive honor in return for it, he wouldn't do what he does for others.

2) He engages in bestowal upon others and does not wish to be given any reward for his work, meaning another thing, something else. Rather, he settles for performing acts of bestowal. It is in his nature to enjoy doing good to others and this is his whole pleasure. Certainly, this is a greater degree than the first, since from here we see that he does things with the aim to do good to others. We should call it, "Bestowing in order to bestow."

However, if we look a little deeper and scrutinize his real intention in giving to others, does he do all those deeds because he wishes to enjoy—meaning for self-love, since by his nature, he enjoys acts of bestowal—or is his aim that he enjoys others having good things?

In other words, is he enjoying others having a good mood and this is why he tries to do good to others, so they would be in high spirits and enjoy their lives? And if by chance he sees that there is another person, and that person would succeed more than he in doing what he wishes to do for his town's people, would he relinquish his pleasure in performing acts of bestowal and try to have the other person do it?

Indeed, if that person—who engages in acts of bestowal without wanting any reward for his work—couldn't make the concession of having the other person do those things for his town's people, although he knows the other person is more competent, we still cannot call this "bestowing in order to bestow," since at the end of the day, self-love is his determining factor.

3) He is working in order to not receive any reward. And even if he sees that there is another person who is more competent, he relinquishes his pleasure in giving to others and cares only for the well-being of the other. This is called "bestowing in order to bestow."

Thus, there is broad scrutiny that must be made here about his real intention: whether he wants high spirits for himself and this is why he serves him, or is he aiming to give high spirits to the important person.

To understand the above distinction, we can understand the matter by a person picturing for himself that he is a very important person, and this is why he wishes to please him, so he would be in high spirits, and this is why he wants to serve him. But during the service that he does for him, he himself is in high spirits and feels elated. Now he feels that all the pleasures he would feel in his life are nothing compared to what he is feeling now, since he is serving the most important person in the world, and he has no words to describe the contentment he derives from wanting to make that important person be in high spirits.

Now he can scrutinize himself, meaning what is his aim in wanting to give contentment to the important person—is he caring for his own good, meaning that he wants to delight him because it would give him high spirits—or is he aiming only for the important person to enjoy, so the important person will have high spirits, and he has a great desire to serve him only because of the greatness of that person?

Thus, although during the service he feels the great pleasure that is derived during the service, still, if he knows that there is someone who would give more contentment to the important person if he were to serve him, he concedes his own pleasure, which he can feel during the service. Instead, he wishes wholeheartedly for the other to do this service because it would bring him more contentment than if he were to serve him.

It therefore follows that if he agrees to concede his service—even though he experiences great delight from his service, and yet, to benefit the important person and make him more content, he relinquishes it because he is not thinking of himself but only of the benefit of the important person—this is considered that he has no intention of self-benefit. Instead, it is all in order to bestow and he has no consideration of himself. At that time, he has the complete scrutiny, for he cannot deceive himself, and this is called, "complete bestowal."

However, we should know that one cannot achieve this on his own. Rather, it is said about that (*Kidushin*, 30), "Man's inclination overcomes him each day and seeks to kill him, as it is said, 'The wicked watches the righteous, and seeks to slay him.' And if the Creator did not help him, he would not overcome it, as it is said, 'The Lord will not leave him in his hand.'"

This means that first, one must see if he has the strength to come to be able to act with the aim to bestow contentment upon the Creator. Then, when he has already come to realize that he cannot achieve it by himself, that person focuses his Torah and *Mitzvot* on a single point, which is that "the light in it reforms him," that this will be the only reward that he wants from the Torah and *Mitzvot*. In other words, the reward for his labor will be for the Creator to give him this strength called "the power of bestowal."

There is a rule that one who makes an effort, meaning cancels his rest, it is because he wants something, since he knows that without labor he will not be given, so he must toil. For this reason, a person who exerts to keep Torah and *Mitzvot* must certainly be missing something, and this is why he exerts in Torah and *Mitzvot*, to obtain what he wishes through it.

Accordingly, one must pay attention and contemplate what he wants—what is the reward that he wants for his work—before he begins his work in serving the Creator. Or, put simply, what is the reason that compels him to engage in Torah and *Mitzvot*? Then, when he determines what he needs, for which he must toil, a person begins to think very hard until it is difficult for him to know what he really wants.

This is why many people cannot determine the real goal when they begin to contemplate the purpose of their work. Instead, they say, "Why should we tire ourselves with scrutinizing?" Instead, they work without any purpose and say, "We are working for the next world."

And what is the next world? "Why should we think about that? We only believe that it's good and settle for that. When we receive the reward of the next world, then we'll know what it is. Why should we get into scrutinies?"

Only a few say that there is the matter of *Dvekut* [adhesion] with the Creator, and that to achieve *Dvekut* they must achieve equivalence of form, meaning "As He is merciful, you, too, are merciful." And then he begins to try to achieve equivalence of form—that all his actions will be in bestowal—for only then the restriction and concealment that exist in the world are removed from him and he begins to feel the *Kedusha* [holiness].

But when he begins to reach the degree of bestowal in his work, he sees that he is very far from it, that he has no desire for a thought, word, or deed that he would have the ability to aim in order to bestow. And then he doesn't know what to do to obtain the power of bestowal. And each time he adds effort, he sees that this whole matter is far from him. In the end, he realizes that it is not humanly possible that he will ever reach it.

At that time, he realizes that only the Creator can help him, and only then does he understand that he must engage in Torah and *Mitzvot* in order to receive reward. And the reward for his labor will be for the Creator to give him the power of bestowal. This is the reward he hopes for, since he wants to achieve *Dvekut* with the Creator, which is equivalence of form, meaning bestowal.

And this is the only reward he hopes for—that through his toil in Torah and *Mitzvot* he will be given what he cannot obtain by himself, and instead, he needs another to give him. It is like labor in corporeality: since one cannot obtain money by himself, he works, and in return, he is paid money. Likewise, in spirituality, what he cannot obtain by himself, he needs someone to give it to him, so this is what we call "reward."

Therefore, when a person wishes to achieve the quality of bestowal because he wants to achieve *Dvekut* with the Creator, and he cannot obtain this quality, but needs the Creator to give it to him, that which he wants to be given is called "reward." And since there is a rule that if one wants reward he must make an effort and work, he keeps Torah and *Mitzvot* to be given this reward, which is called "the power of bestowal," meaning to exit self-love and receive a desire to have the strength to engage only in love of others.

This is the meaning of, "One should always engage in Torah and *Mitzvot* in *Lo Lishma* [not for Her sake], for from *Lo Lishma* one comes to *Lishma* [for Her sake] because the light in it reforms him." Thus, through the labor in Torah and *Mitzvot* to achieve *Lishma*, he will achieve the degree of *Lishma* by laboring first. This is why he is rewarded with the light in it, which reforms him, and it is considered that he was given the power of bestowal from above.

However, we should ask, "Why does he first need to exert himself and afterwards be given the light of Torah? Why is he not given the light of Torah immediately, so it will reform him instantly? Also, why exert and toil for nothing and waste time for nothing? Wouldn't it be better if he were given the light right at the beginning of his work, meaning that he would immediately receive the light and would immediately begin his work in *Lishma*?"

The thing is that there is no light without a *Kli* [vessel], and a *Kli* means a desire. In other words, when a person has a need and craves to satisfy that need, this is called "a *Kli*." Only then, when he has a *Kli*—meaning a desire for some fulfillment—can it be said that he is given the filling and he is content with the filling that he was given, since this is what he craved. Reward is considered a fulfillment, when the craving receives. Moreover, the measure of the importance of the fulfillment depends on the measure of the craving. And by the measure of his suffering, to that extent one enjoys the fulfillment.

For this reason, it is impossible to give a person a light that will reform him when he has no desire for it whatsoever. This is because reforming him means he will lose the power of self-love and receive the power of love of others.

If a person has no desire to exit self-love, and he is told, "Do some work and in return you will have no desire for self-love," he does not regard it as a reward. On the contrary, he thinks that for the work he did for the owner, he should have rewarded him in return for his labor. But in return, he is giving him something very bad, and so much so that he would lose all the self-love in an instant. Who would agree to that?

For this reason, first one must study in *Lo Lishma*, so that through it, the body will assist him, since a person is willing to give up a small pleasure to receive a great pleasure. But by nature, one is incapable of imagining pleasure unless it is based on self-love. Therefore, he is told that he will be rewarded for engaging in Torah and *Mitzvot*. This is not a lie, for he will certainly be rewarded. In other words, he is told that for his effort in Torah and *Mitzvot*, he will be rewarded, and this is the truth, since he will indeed be rewarded, but the reward will change.

For example, a father tells his child, "If you are a good boy, I will buy you a toy car, a plastic car." Afterwards, the father goes abroad and returns several years later. The son has already grown, and he comes to his father and tells him, "Dad, before you went abroad, you promised me a plastic toy car." So his father goes and buys him a real car, one that can travel great distances.

The son is already clever and understands that now is not the time for a plastic car, but for a real car. Is this considered a deception by his father? Of course not! Instead, now the boy sees that when he was a child, he could only understand a trifle reward.

Here, too, he begins with a trifling reward, called *Lo Lishma*, meaning he is waiting to be rewarded with something that is worthless compared to the real reward that he will receive—being rewarded with *Lishma*, which is the *Kli* in which one can receive the delight and pleasure that the Creator wishes to impart. Those are the real pleasures.

It follows that by telling him to work in *Lo Lishma*, meaning to receive a reward, this is true, meaning that when he aims in order to bestow, he will be rewarded, too. The only falsehood is in the actual reward. While a person is in *Lo Lishma*, he thinks that he will be given a different reward, that the *Kli* that receives it is called "self-love."

But afterwards, when a person grows, he begins to understand that the *Kelim* [vessels] that actually receive the reward are the *Kelim* of bestowal, that it is precisely through those *Kelim* that the real delight and pleasure is received. At that time, he feels that he is the happiest man on earth. But the reward that he wished to receive while he was in *Lo Lishma* could only be a reward suitable for a little boy.

Thus, when teaching to receive reward and pleasure for one's work in *Lo Lishma*, it is not considered a lie, since he did not lose anything by his reward being exchanged for a greater reward. We should only explain that the *Lo Lishma*, meaning this reward, is not the real name, as he thinks. Instead, the reward has a different name than what he thought. However, a reward remains a reward, and the reward is not changed; only the name of the reward changes—from a false and imaginary reward to a true reward.

From all the above, it follows that the main thing that a person needs in return for his toil in Torah and *Mitzvot* is for the Creator to give him the vessels of bestowal, which one cannot obtain by himself because they are contrary to nature. However, this is a gift from above—that his reward will be always to wait for the time when he can bring contentment to the Creator. And since this is the reward that he awaits, this is called "his reward."

To understand the above, we should look in "General Preface to the Tree of Life" (Item 3), where it is written, "The root of the darkness is the *Masach* in the *Kli* of *Malchut*, and the root of the reward is rooted in the Reflected Light that comes out through a *Zivug de Hakaa*."

There he offers the root to what we see in this world—that everything that we see in this world is a branch that extends from the roots, from the upper worlds. He says there, "The root of the labor that a person feels in this world extends from the root of the *Masach* in the *Kli* of *Malchut*."

This means that the *Kli* that the creatures have is called "a desire to receive pleasure," which the Creator created because of His desire to delight His creatures. Hence, He created in the creatures a desire to receive pleasure. In the upper *Sefirot*, this is called *Malchut*.

Afterwards, we learn that there was a *Tzimtzum* [restriction]. This means that one doesn't want to be a receiver because he wants equivalence of form with the Creator; hence, a rule was made in the *Kedusha* [holiness] that nothing is received unless there is an aim to bestow.

This is the meaning of the correction of the *Masach* [screen]. Since we are speaking of upper lights, not wanting to receive light is called "a *Masach*." It is like a person who places a curtain or a veil when the sun shines too brightly and he doesn't want to receive the sunlight, so that the sun will not shine into the house.

Hence, when speaking of upper lights, although *Malchut* had a great desire and craving to receive the light of pleasure, she still relinquished the pleasure, not receiving it because she wanted equivalence of form. This is called "labor," meaning doing something against her will—preventing herself from receiving the pleasure.

In the corporeal world, too, when a person must give up some pleasure, it is considered an effort. For example, if a person enjoys rest, and for some reason must give up his rest and do something, this is called "labor."

He also shows us how, when the corporeal branch receives a reward, where it is rooted in the upper worlds. He shows us that the root of the reward extends from the Reflected Light—the desire to bestow that comes out of the *Zivug de Hakaa* that occurred between the upper light and the *Masach* and *Aviut* [thickness] (see *The Study of the Ten Sefirot*, Part 4, Item 8). He writes, "The clothing Reflected Light comes out as a result of two forces."

In spirituality, a *Zivug de Hakaa* means that if two things are opposite to one another, it is regarded as *Hakaa* [striking/beating]. This means that on the one hand, one truly wants that thing because he sees that it will give him immense pleasure, but on the other hand, he overcomes and does not receive it because he wants equivalence of form.

Indeed, there are two desires here: 1) One's desire to receive pleasure, and 2) his desire for equivalence of form. And of those two, a new thing is born, called "clothing Reflected Light." With this force, he can later obtain the upper abundance because this Reflected Light is the appropriate *Kli* for reception of the bounty.

In other words, with this *Kli*, he has two things: 1) He receives the pleasure that is found in the upper abundance, which comes from the thought of creation, to do good to His creations. 2) At the same time, he finds himself in equivalence of form, which is the second discernment that he has upon reception of the abundance.

From all the above, we see that the whole reward is only the Reflected Light, which is the power of bestowal that the lower one receives from the upper one, which he calls "Reflected Light," meaning what the lower one gives to the upper one. This means that the abundance that initially came from the Creator is called "Direct Light," as it is written, "God created man straight." It is as we learn, that the thought of creation was to do good to His creations, meaning for the lower ones to receive abundance, and this is called "straight."

But the receivers of the abundance wish for equivalence of form, hence we have a correction called "Reflected Light." This means that the receiver of the abundance does not receive it because he wishes to enjoy, but because he wishes to give to the upper one. In other words, as the upper wishes for the receiver to enjoy, the receiver of the abundance aims to return pleasure to the giver, meaning for the upper one to enjoy the fulfillment of His thought. It therefore follows that the reward is primarily the Reflected Light, meaning the power of bestowal that the lower one receives from the upper one.

But we should still understand why we say that the *Kli*, which is called "power of bestowal," is the whole reward. After all, "reward" implies something that is received. We say, "I work for the pay," or we say that the purpose of creation is to do good to His creations, meaning that they will receive reward. And here we are saying that the reward is called "the power of giving." And what do we understand? That the reward should be for a person to be imparted with attaining Godliness and the secrets of Torah, and so on. But why is he saying that the reward is in obtaining the power of giving, meaning the power of bestowal? Moreover, he is telling us that this extends from the upper root, called "Reflected Light."

There is a known rule that the cow wants to nurse more than the calf wants to suckle. It therefore follows that the Creator wishes to give to the creatures more than the creatures wish to receive. So who is inhibiting? We must remember the *Tzimtzum* occurred so that the creatures would have equivalence of form. This is a correction to prevent the bread of shame, which extends from our root because the Creator is about bestowal and not reception, for He has no needs and there is no such thing as reception in Him. Thus, according to the rule that exists in our nature—that each branch wishes to resemble its root—when the lower one must carry out an action that is not present in the root, he feels unpleasantness.

It follows that one does not need to do anything to receive abundance, which is light and pleasure, since the Creator wants to give to the creature more than the creature wants to receive. However, the creature has no *Kli* in which to enjoy the pleasures that he will be given, due to the shame. It follows that the only reward we need is the *Kli*, which is called "the power of bestowal." Thus, all we need are *Kelim* [plural of *Kli*], and not lights, and this is why the reward is primarily the power of bestowal.

However, to obtain that *Kli*, called "the desire to bestow," we need a desire, meaning to feel that we need this *Kli*. This is why we must first engage in Torah and *Mitzvot* in *Lo Lishma*, and this is our labor—to see that everything we do is for self-benefit, without any intention to bestow.

And then we see that we need the power of bestowal, and we want a reward for our work—that the Creator will give us this reward—the desire to bestow. And when we have that power, we will be able to receive the delight and pleasure that is already available and for which we don't need to work at all because the Creator gives it. But for a person to rise from degree to degree, he must acquire the power of bestowal each time, and then nothing else is missing.

Concerning the Importance of Friends

Article No. 17, Part 1, Tav-Shin-Mem-Dalet, 1984

Concerning the importance of the friends in the society and how to appreciate them, meaning with which kind of importance everyone should regard his friend. Common sense dictates that if one regards one's friend as being at a lower degree than one's own, he will want to teach him how to behave more virtuously than the qualities he has. Hence, he cannot be his friend; he can take the friend as a student, but not as a friend.

And if one sees one's friend as being at a higher degree than his own, and sees that he can acquire good qualities from him, then he can be his Rav, but not his friend.

This means that precisely when one sees one's friend as being at an equal degree to one's own, one can accept the other as a friend and bond with him. This is so because "a friend" means that both parties are in the same state. This is what common sense dictates. In other words, they have the same views and thus decide to bond. Then, both of them act towards the goal that they both wish to achieve.

It is like two like-minded friends who are doing business together to achieve a profit. In that situation, they feel that they have equal powers. But should one of them feel that he is more competent than the other, he will not want to accept him as an equal partner. Instead, they would create a proportional partnership according to the strength and qualities that one has above the other. In that state, the partnership is a thirty-three or twenty-five percent partnership, and it cannot be said that they are equal in the business.

But with love of friends, when friends bond to create unity among them, it explicitly means that they are equal. This is called "unity." For example, if they do business together and say that the profits will not be distributed equally, is this called "unity"? Clearly, a business of love of friends should be when all the profits and possessions that the love of friends yields will be equally controlled by them. They should not hide or conceal from one another, but everything will be with love, friendship, truthfulness, and peace.

But in the essay, "A Speech for the Completion of *The Zohar*," it is written, "The measure of the greatness comes under two conditions: 1) to always listen and receive the appreciation of society, to the extent of their greatness; 2) the environment should be great, as it is written, 'In the multitude of people is the king's glory.'"

To accept the first condition, each student must feel that he is the smallest among all the friends, and then he will be able to receive the appreciation of the greatness from everyone. This is so because the greater one cannot receive from the smaller one, much less be impressed by his words. Only the lower one is impressed by the appreciation of the greater one.

And for the second condition, each student must extol each friend's merit as though he were the greatest in the generation. Then the environment will affect him as a great environment should, since quality is more important than quantity.

It follows that in the matter of love of friends, they help each other, meaning it is enough for everyone to regard his friend as being of the same degree as his own. But because everyone should learn from his friends, there is the issue of Rav and disciple. For this reason, he should consider the friend as greater than himself.

But how can one consider one's friend greater than himself when he can see that his own merits are greater than his friend's, that he is more talented and has better natural qualities? There are two ways to understand this:

1. He is going with faith above reason: once he has chosen him as a friend, he appreciates him above reason.
2. This is more natural—within reason. If he has decided to accept the other as a friend, and works on himself to love him, then it is natural with love to see only good things. And even though there are bad things in one's friend, he cannot see them, as it is written, "love covers all transgressions."

We can see that a person may see faults in his neighbor's children, but not in his own. And when someone mentions some faults in his children, he immediately resists his friend and begins to declare his children's merits.

And the question is, which is the truth? After all, there are merits to his children, and hence he is upset when others speak of his children. The thing is this, as I had heard it from my father: Indeed, each person has advantages and disadvantages. And both the neighbor and the father are saying the truth. But the neighbor does not treat the other's children like a father to his children, since he does not have the same love for the children as the father does.

Hence, when he considers the other's children, he sees only the children's faults, since this gives him more pleasure. This is because he can show that he is more virtuous than the other because his own children are better. For this reason, he sees only the other's faults. What he is seeing is true, but he sees only things he enjoys.

But the father, too, sees only the truth, except that he regards only the good things that his children have. He does not see his children's faults, since it gives him no pleasure. Hence, he is saying the truth about what he sees in his children. And because he regards only the things that can please him, he sees only the virtues.

It turns out that if one has love of friends, the rule in love is that you want to see the friends' merits and not their faults. Hence, if one sees some fault in one's friend, it is not a sign that his friend is at fault, but that the seer is at fault, meaning that because his love of friends is flawed, he sees faults in his friend.

Therefore, now he should not see to his friend's correction. Rather, he himself needs correction. It follows from all the above that he should not care for the correction of his friend's faults, which he sees in his friend, but he himself needs to correct the flaw he has created in the love of friends. And when he corrects himself, he will see only his friend's merits and not his faults.

The Agenda of the Assembly

Article No. 17, Part 2, Tav-Shin-Mem-Dalet, 1984

In the beginning of the assembly, there should be an agenda. Everyone should speak of the importance of the society as much as he can, describing the profits that society will give him and the important things he hopes society will bring him, which he cannot obtain by himself, and how he appreciates the society accordingly.

It is as our sages wrote (*Berachot* 32), "Rabbi Shamlai said, 'One should always praise the Creator, and then pray.' Where did we get that? From Moses, as it is written, 'And I besought the Lord at that time.' It is also written, 'O Lord God, Thou hast begun,' and it is written, 'Let me go over, I pray Thee, and see the good land.'"

And the reason we need to begin with praising the Creator is that it is natural that there are two conditions when one asks for something of another:

1. That he has what I ask of him, such as wealth, power, and repute as being wealthy and affluent.
2. That he will have a kind heart, meaning a desire to do good to others.

From such a person you can ask for a favor. This is why they said, "One should always praise the Creator, and then pray." This means that after one believes in the greatness of the Creator, that He has all sorts of pleasures to give to the creatures and He wishes to do good, then it is pertinent to say that he is praying to the Creator, who will certainly help him since He wishes to bestow. And then the Creator can give him what he wishes. Then, also, the prayer can be confident that the Creator will grant it.

Similarly, with love of friends, at the very beginning of the assembly, when gathering, we should praise the friends, the importance of each of the friends. To the extent that we assume the greatness of the society, one can appreciate the society.

"And then pray" means that everyone should examine himself and see how much effort he is giving to the society. Then, when he sees that he is powerless to do anything for society, there is room for prayer to the Creator to help him and give him strength and desire to engage in love of others.

And afterwards, everyone should behave the same as in the last three of the "Eighteen Prayer." In other words, after having pleaded before the Creator, *The Zohar* says that in the last three of the "Eighteen Prayer," one should think as though the Creator has already granted his request and he has departed.

In love of friends we should behave the same: After examining ourselves and following the known advice of praying, we should think as though our prayer has been answered and rejoice with our friends, as though all the friends are one body. And as the body wishes for all its organs to enjoy, we, too, want all our friends to enjoy themselves now.

Hence, after all the calculations comes the time of joy and love of friends. At that time, everyone should feel happy, as though one had just sealed a very good deal that will earn him lots of money. And it is customary that at such a time he gives drinks to the friends.

Similarly, here everyone needs his friends to drink and eat cakes, etc. Because now he is happy, he wishes his friends to feel good, too. Hence, the dispersion of the assembly should be in a state of joy and elation.

This follows the way of "a time of Torah" and "a time of prayer." "A time of Torah" means wholeness, when there are no deficiencies. This is called "right," as it is written, "at His right hand was a fiery law."

But "a time of prayer" is called "left," since a place of deficiency is a place that needs correction. This is called "the correction of the *Kelim* (vessels)." But in the state of Torah, called "right," there is no room for correction, and this is why Torah is called a "gift."

It is customary to give presents to a person you love. And it is also customary not to love one who is deficient. Hence, at a "time of Torah," there is no room for thoughts of correction. Thus, when leaving the assembly, it should be as in the last three of the "Eighteen Prayer." And for this reason, everyone will feel wholeness.

And It Shall Come to Pass When You Come to the Land that the Lord Your God Gives You

Article No. 18, Tav-Shin-Mem-Dalet, 1984

Interpreters ask about the verse, "And it shall come to pass that when you come to the land that the Lord your God gives you as inheritance, and you will inherit and dwell in it." They asked what is the precision, "that the Lord your God gives you"? After all the people of Israel concurred it by war. They explained that one should know in one's heart that not by his own might and strength does he come to inherit the land. Rather, it is the gift of the Creator, as they said, "that the Lord your God gives you as inheritance and not my strength and the might of my hand."

To understand the above in the work, we need to know that *Eretz* [land] means *Ratzon* [desire], meaning that the desire in man's heart is called land. The nations of the world live in that land, which is called man's heart, and the people of Israel live in it. However we should know that they cannot live in it together. The people of Israel and the nations of the world cannot rule together. Either there is governance of the nations of the world there, or the governance of Israel.

To understand the real reason why both of them cannot be in one place, it is known that the creation of the world was because of His desire to do good to His creations. For this reason He has created the will to receive delight and pleasure. That is, He created in the creatures a lack to always crave pleasures, for we see that the creature feels the pleasure according to his desire.

This is the *Kli* [vessel] that was created by the Creator, and it is the first discernment we discern in the creatures. If the creatures do not have that desire, they are still not regarded as created beings. It turns out that you cannot speak of any discernment if there is no will to receive there. And this is the whole of creation of which we speak, which is the *Kli* for the reception of the pleasure.

But because of the shame, which our sages call "bread of shame," there was a restriction not to receive in order to receive unless one can aim to bestow, regarded as equivalence of form. That is, if one can receive the pleasures with the intention to bestow contentment upon the Creator, then one receives. Otherwise, he does not want to receive. This is called Israel, meaning *Yashar-El* [straight to the Creator], meaning everything he thinks of is only that everything will get to the Creator, and he is not taken into account because he is not thinking of himself at all. Rather all his thoughts are only for the Creator.

This is called the "land of Israel," meaning that he has a desire directly to the Creator. That is, he has no desires of self-love, but of love of others, and for himself—that he will enjoy life—he has no desire at all. All he wants is to have the means to bestow upon the Creator, and all the nourishments he gives to his body are only to have the strength to work in order to bestow.

This is similar to a person who has a horse and he gives it food and water. That is, everything he gives to the horse is not because he loves it, but because he has to work with it. Therefore, all his thoughts of pleasing the horse are not because of love, but simply because he wants to use the horse for his own benefit, and he is not thinking at all about the horse's favor. This is called the "land of Israel," meaning that all his thoughts are only *Eretz* [land], *Ratzon* [desire] that everything will be straight to the Creator.

This is not so with the land of the nations. This is a land, a desire of self-love, which is called the "peoples of the land." This means that all their desires are only the desires of the people, whose intention is not the Creator's will, but the people's will, meaning the creature's will who are called "nations," while the Creator is the one who created the nation. Also (*Ki Tavo*), "and all the nations of the earth shall see that the name of the Lord is called upon you and they shall fear you." It is also written (*Hayei Sarah*) "Abraham arose and bowed before the people of the land, the sons of Heth". This means that they do not know or feel anything but the people, which is self-love, and only this is regarded as creatures.

But the people of Israel are not so. They want to annul themselves and their being, which is the will to receive that was created existence from absence. This is why we say and the *Kiddush* [sanctification] of a good day "who has chosen us from every nation."

Those two governances cannot be together. Either the will to bestow governs or the will to receive governs. Both cannot exist together because each one contradicts the other and two opposites cannot be in the same subject.

From this comes the war of the inclination, that one should fight with oneself to subdue the heart, which is where these desires clothe, expel the domination of the will to receive, and give full governance to the desire to bestow upon the Creator. When one begins to work the holy work, which is to aim all of his work for the Creator, the wars between those two desires begin. Then, through great labor, a person is rewarded with overcoming and he wins the war. At that time the ruling of the will to bestow upon the Creator enters his heart and a person can say, "My might and the strength of my hand has gotten me these riches," and only through his work, he inherited the heart, which is now called the "land of Israel" because his desire is straight to the Creator.

In this regard, the verse comes and tells us, "When you come to the land that the Lord your God gives you." That is, you did not concur it by your own strength, but rather "the Lord your God gives you," meaning that once a person has made the sufficient efforts to concur the heart through the wars he has fought with the nations of the world and has defeated them, he has inherited the heart, which is now called the "land of Israel," and not the "land of the nations." Still, he should believe that he did not concur the land but "the Lord your God gives you," and "not my strength and the might of my hand has gotten me these riches."

By that we should understand what is difficult about it, that the Creator promised Abraham, as it is written (*Lech Lecha*), "and he said to him I am the Lord who took you out from Ur of the Chaldeans to give you this land to inherit it."

Therefore, why did he first give the land to the nations of the world and then the people of Israel came and had to fight them and drive them out of their land, and the whole world complains, "Why did you concur a land that was never yours, and only by concurring through war you say that this is your land?" Everyone understands that it would certainly be better if He did not give this land to the nations of the world, for then there would be no shortage of places for the nations of the world to dwell. After all, afterwards new countries were made, and the Creator could have made it that they would not dwell in this place.

But this was not what happened. Rather, first the seven nations sat here, as well as the rest of the kings, and the people of Israel had to fight with them and drive them out, and all the nations of the world are yelling at the people of Israel, "You are robbers! You have conquered the lands of seven nations!" Why do I need this trouble? RASHI introduces our sage's interpretation (*Beresheet*, Chapter 1): "What is the reason that it begins with *Beresheet* [in the beginning]?

Because of the might of His deeds, He told His people to give them an inheritance of nations, for if the idol worshipers would to say to Israel, 'You are robbers, you have stolen the lands of seven nations,' they tell them, 'The whole earth belongs to the Creator. He has created it and He has given it to whom He pleases. Upon His will He gave it to them, and upon His will He took it from them and gave to us.'"

This is perplexing. Why do I need this order that occurred, meaning that before He gave it to us, He first gave it to the nations of the world, and only once they settled, He told us go, "Drive them out of this land for I have promised it to Abraham"?

By way of root and branch we can interpret this whole matter. It is known that *Eretz* [land] is called *Malchut*, which is the roots of the creatures, which is called "receiving in order to receive." This is the root, meaning the first receiver, called the world of *Ein Sof* [infinity]. Afterwards corrections were made not to receive because of self-reception, but because the lower one wants to bestow upon the Creator. That is, he wants the will to receive for himself to be annulled, meaning not to use it, and all of his work will be only to bestow contentment upon the Creator.

According to the above it turns out that in the order of creation of the corporeal world, too, there should be the same order as in spirituality. That is, first this land is given to the nations of the world, and then, by overcoming and wars, the nations of the world are driven out of this land, and the people of Israel concur it and inherit the place of the nations of the worlds.

This is so because the root of the nations of the world is the middle point on which there was the restriction. That is, since the first discernment that emerged in the world had to be a receiver in order to receive, for otherwise you cannot say that he is restricting himself not to receive, since overcoming relates to a place where there is a desire and craving to receive, and he overcomes his craving and wants equivalence of form.

Therefore, the nations of the world had to first receive this land, like the root, where the will to receive emerged first, which is the essence of creation, and then it can be said that we need to make corrections there. Therefore, once the nations of the world received this land, the people of Israel came and corrected the land to be entirely for the Creator. This is called the "land of Israel," as it is written (*Ekev*) "A land that the Lord your God always demands; the eyes of the Lord your God are on it from the beginning of the year to the end of the year."

We should understand about what is written that the land of Israel is called "a land that the eyes of the Lord your God are on it from the beginning of the year to the end of the year." It means that the guidance of the Creator is on it, meaning specifically on the land of Israel. But the guidance of the Creator is all over the world, as the poet says "the eyes of the Lord roam everywhere." Thus, how can we say that His guidance is only in the land of Israel?

We should interpret what is the land of Israel. It means that the land has already come out of the authority of the nations of the world and has already entered the authority of Israel. This is what the verse is trying to tell us, and to hint to us so as to know whether they are in the land of Israel or still in the land of the nations.

The sign for this is as it is written, "a land that the Lord your God always demands." The verse tells us what is the land of Israel. It says that we need to know that the Creator always demands it. And what is His demand? The verse says onward, "The eyes of the Lord your God are on it from the beginning of the year to the end of the year," for the guidance of the Creator is called "the eyes of the Lord." Therefore, if a person sees His guidance from the beginning of time, which is called "the beginning of the year," to the end of the year, which means that he sees the unending guidance of the Creator, this is called the "land of Israel."

But the land of the nations means that only the Creator knows that He is watching over the whole world, but the nations of the world do not see it. This is why He has given us a sign, so as to know if we are in the land of Israel, or is the land where we are dwelling still the land of the nations of the world.

It turns out from all of the above that first, the nations of the world should enter this land, which implies the will to receive, which is the place where it is born first, and then they wage war with the will to receive and subdue it into the authority of holiness, meaning that everything he does will be according to the Creator's demand.

By what the interpreters explained about the words, "And it shall come to pass that when you come to the land that the Lord your God gives you," it means that one should not say after all the wars with the inclination, that he had to always overcome it, every single day, he should not think that he has achieved what he has achieved by his own strength. Rather, the Creator let him win this war.

This is the meaning of "that He gives you." We need to make two discernments in the "He gives you": 1) *Mitzva* (commandment), which is faith. This is called the "hand *Tefillin*." Concerning the hand *Tefillin*, our sages said "and let it be for you as a token, and not for others as a token." Because of it, the hand *Tefillin* should be covered, which means that faith is called "be humble with the Lord your God," which is above reason.

2) Torah, which is the head *Tefillin*. Concerning the head *Tefillin*, our sages said about the verse (*Ki Tavo*): "And all the nations of the earth shall see that the name of the Lord is called upon you, and they shall fear you." These are the head *Tefillin*, meaning that it is written there, "and all the nations of the earth shall see," for the head *Tefillin* should be revealed to all. This is discerned as "Torah," and the Torah is called so precisely that it is revealed.

But the hand *Tefillin* should be covered, which means above reason. Therefore, we cannot say words to another because everything that one can say to another is only through reason, and with something that is above reason, there are no words. This is why it is said, "for you as a token, and not for others." It therefore follows that this giving—that the Creator has given the land to the people of Israel—is in order to produce fruits out of it.

As we explained above, when we speak of work, land means the "heart," and the Creator gave two discernments in the heart: 1) faith,

2) Torah. Through both of them, a person achieves completeness. And although both come through me, we should still know that both come from the Creator, and one should not say, "My strength and the might of my hand has done these riches."

By this we will understand what the interpreters asked, "Why is it written concerning the first born, 'and You shall answer and You shall say out loud,' but in reading a confession of the tithing, it is written, 'and You said,' and it is not written, 'and You answered,' as it is written in the first born?" Therefore, the confession of the tithing is said in a soft voice.

Tithing is regarded a *Mitzva* [commandment], which is the kingdom of heaven, and in that there is the matter of being humble, which is the *Tefillin* of the hand, of which our sages said "for you as a token, and not for others as a token." Therefore, with a tithing, which implies a *Mitzva*, it is written only, "and You said," which is with a soft voice that is not heard outside because this is regarded as being humble.

But firstborn implies to the head *Tefillin*, which is the Torah, of which it is written, "and all the nations of the earth shall see that the name of the Lord is called upon you and they will fear you." This is why it is written about the firstborn, "and You shall answer and You shall say." That is, it should be with a loud voice which is the Torah, which should be revealed to all, meaning that doing good to His creations should be revealed to the entire world.

You Stand Today, All of You

Article No. 19, Tav-Shin-Mem-Dalet, 1984

The interpreters ask about the words, "You stand today, all of you ...your heads, your tribes, your elders and your officers, every man of Israel." It begins with the plural form, "You" [plural form in Hebrew], and ends in singular form, "Every man of Israel." The author of the book, *Light and Sun*, explains that by using plural form and singular form, it points to the matter of love of friends. Although among you are "heads, tribes," etc., still no one sees greater merit in himself than in any man of Israel. Instead, everyone is equal in that no one complains about the other. For this reason, from above, too, they are treated accordingly, and this is why great abundance is imparted below.

It is our way to study everything within one subject. It turns out that a person should take upon himself the burden of the kingdom of heaven as an ox to the burden and as a donkey to the load, which are mind and heart. In other words, all of one's work should be in order to bestow.

Accordingly, if one works in order to bestow and does not wish for any reward in return—except to serve in the holy work without hoping to be given any addition to what he has—he has no wish even for additional work. In other words, receiving some knowledge that he is walking on the right path is certainly a just demand, and yet he relinquishes even that because he wishes to go with his eyes shut and believe in the Creator. And what he can, he does and he is content with his lot.

And he even feels that there are people who have some understanding of the work of the Creator, while he sees that he is completely empty. In other words, many times he feels a good taste in the work, and at times he feels that he is in a state of "Your heads." In other words, at times he thinks that now he has reached a degree where it is impossible that he will ever decline to a state of lowliness, a state where if he wishes to engage in the work of God, he has to make great efforts to force his body. At that time, what he does is by compulsion because he has no desire for the work, and the body only wishes to rest and does not care for anything.

Instead, at that time he feels that he has already come to know for sure that there is nothing else in the world except to work in order to bestow, and then he certainly finds good taste in the work. And when he regards his previous states, he cannot understand, now that he is in a state of ascent. Hence, by all calculations, he decides that now it is impossible that he will ever suffer a decline.

But sometimes, after a day, an hour, or a few minutes, he descends to such a state of lowliness that he cannot immediately feel that he has fallen from his uplifted state to the "depth of the great abyss." Rather, at times, after an hour or two he suddenly sees that he has fallen from the highest level, meaning from his previous certainty that he was the strongest man, and he is like any man of Israel, meaning like an ordinary person. Then he begins to seek advice in his heart, "What should I do now?" "How can I pick myself up to the state of *Gadlut* [greatness/adulthood] that I had before?"

At that time, one should walk on the path of truth—to say, "My current state, being in utter lowliness, means that I was deliberately thrown out from above to know if I truly wish to do the holy work in order to bestow, or if I wish to be God's servant because I find it more rewarding than other things."

Then, if one can say, "Now I want to work in order to bestow and I do not want to do the holy work to receive some gratification in the work. Instead, I will settle for doing the work of holiness like any man of Israel—praying or taking a lesson on the daily portion. And I don't have time to think with which intent I study or pray, but I will simply observe the actions without any special intent." At that time, he will reenter the holy work because now he wishes to be God's servant without any preconditions.

This is the meaning of what is written, "You stand today, all of you," meaning everything you went through, all the states you have experienced—whether states of *Gadlut* or states of less than *Gadlut*, which were considered intermediate or so. You take all those details and you do not compare one degree to another because you do not care for any reward, but only for doing the Creator's will. He has commanded us to observe *Mitzvot* [commandments] and to study Torah, and this is what we do, like any common man of Israel. In other words, the state he is in right now is as important to him as when he thought he was in a state of *Gadlut*. At that time, "The Lord your God makes with you this day."

This means that then the Creator makes a covenant with him. In other words, precisely when one accepts His work without any conditions and agrees to do the holy work without any reward, which is called "unconditional surrender," this is the time when the Creator makes a covenant with him.

Baal HaSulam explained the matter of making a covenant: When two people see that they love each other, they make a covenant between them that their love will always endure. And he asked, "If they love each other and understand that this love will never leave them, why this covenant? Why do they make this covenant, meaning for what purpose?" In other words, what do they gain by this making of a covenant? Is it only a ritual or is it for some benefit?

He said that the matter of making a covenant is that now they understand that it is in their interest for each to love the other because of reasons they can now see—that each one feels the other and cares only for his well-being—so they make a covenant. And as now neither has any complaints against his friend, or they would not make the covenant, they tell each other, "It is worthwhile for us to make a covenant once and for all." In other words, if there is ever a state where one will have complaints against the other, they will both remember the covenant that they made when love was revealed between them.

Similarly, even though they currently do not feel the love as they did then, they still evoke the old love and do not look at the state they are currently in. Instead, they go back to doing things for each other. This is the benefit of the covenant. Thus, even when the love that was between them has lost its fancy, because they made the covenant, they have the strength to reawaken the shining love that they had before. In this way, they usher each other back into the future.

It follows that making the covenant is for the future. It is like a contract that they sign that they will not be able to regret when they see that the ties of love are not as they were, that this love gave them great pleasure while they were doing good to each other, but now that love has been corrupted, they are powerless and none can do anything for the other.

But if they do wish to do something for their friends, they must consider the making of the covenant that they had before, and out of that they should rebuild the love. It is like a person who signs a contract with his friend, and the contract connects them so they cannot part from one another.

It follows that, "You stand today, all of you." In other words, he thinks of details, "Your heads, your tribes, your elders and your officers, every man of Israel." This means that of all the high degrees that he had, it is now considered for him that he is in a state of "Every man of Israel," and he assumes that state, as when he was in a state that he considered good. He says, "Now I do my part, and I agree that the Creator will give me what He wants, and I have no criticism." At that time, he is rewarded with making a covenant. In other words, the connection remains forever because the Creator made a covenant with him for all eternity.

According to the above, we should interpret the verse, "The secret things belong to the Lord our God, but the things that are revealed belong to us and to our sons forever, that we may do all the words of this law." We should understand what this verse comes to tell us. We cannot say that it comes to tell us that we do not know what is hidden and only the Creator knows. We cannot say that because without the verse, we do not know what is hidden from us. Thus, what does the verse come to tell us?

It is known that there is a thing that is hidden and a thing that is revealed. It means that the active part of what we do is when we can see whether or not we are doing it. And if the body does not wish to perform the *Mitzva* [commandment], there is a tactic—one can force oneself, meaning that he is compelled to do the *Mitzva* against his will. It turns out that coercion is relevant with revealed things.

The hidden thing is the intention in the *Mitzva*. This, one cannot see, meaning what the other one intends while doing. It is the same with the person himself, the one who acts. He, too, cannot know, unless he lies to himself while doing. He thinks that he has no other goal and that he is completely dedicated to the Creator. But with the action, called "the revealed part," it is irrelevant to speak of a person lying to himself, that he thinks that he is wearing *Tefillin* [phylacteries] when in truth, it is not *Tefillin*. Similarly, a woman cannot lie to herself saying that she lights the Sabbath candles when in fact she isn't.

But with intention, it can be said that one lies to oneself. He thinks that he is working *Lishma* [for Her sake] when in fact he is entirely in *Lo Lishma* [not for Her sake]. Also, there cannot be coercion because one cannot coerce one's thought into thinking what he wants to. Regarding things that belong to emotion or knowledge, a person is powerless. He cannot force his mind to understand differently than it does or feel differently than how he feels.

Now we can understand the above matter—that all that is left for us is the practical part. This is called "The things that are revealed belong to us and to our sons forever, that we may do all the words of this law." We are commanded to perform the action, meaning it is the deed that we are commanded to do, even coercively.

But as for the intention, called "the hidden part," in that, no man has any view or governance. Thus, what should we do to keep the hidden part, as well? Here all that one can do is test, meaning examine himself to see if he is truly doing everything in order to bestow, or whether the body resists the aim to bestow. He feels that he is removed from it to the extent that there is nothing he can do alone, since whatever he plans to do, all the tactics to be able to aim in order to bestow do not help him.

It is about that that the verse comes to tell us that this matter of *Lishma*, called "the hidden part," belongs to the Lord our God. In other words, only the Creator can help him, while there is absolutely no possibility that he himself would realize it. It is not in the hands of man because it is above nature. This is why the verse says, "The secret things belong to the Lord our God," meaning that it belongs to Him, that the Creator should provide this force called "to bestow."

This is why our sages said (*Kidushin* 30), "Man's inclination overpowers him every day and seeks to put him to death, as it is said, 'The wicked watches the righteous, and seeks to slay him.' And if the Creator did not help him, he would not overcome it, as it is said, 'The Lord will not leave him in his hand.'"

The matter of seeking to slay him means that it wishes for man to do everything in order to receive, which is regarded as being separated from the Life of Lives. Naturally, one remains a beast. This is why our sages said, "The wicked are called 'dead' while they are alive." It turns out that it is called "death" when his intention is to receive. This is considered separation. To be rewarded with

Dvekut [adhesion], meaning to be granted the strength to bestow—to have such a thing—only the Creator can give it to him; it is not in man's power to obtain.

This is why our sages said, "Man's inclination overpowers him every day and seeks to slay him, and if the Creator did not help him, he would not overcome it, as it is said, 'The Lord will not leave him in his hand.'" From what we explained, we can understand the verse, "The secret things belong to the Lord our God, but the things that are revealed belong to us and to our sons."

Thus, only the act is for us to do, but the hidden part is for the Creator to do.

However, there is still something for us to do about the hidden, so the Creator will give us the hidden part. This follows the rule that everything requires an awakening from below. There is a rule that there is no light without a *Kli* [vessel], meaning there is no fulfillment without a deficiency. You cannot insert anything unless there is a vacancy, and then you put in whatever you want. But if there is no cavity, no empty place, how can we insert anything?

Therefore, first we should see that we do not have the vessel of bestowal, called "desire to bestow," and that this is our light. As we explained in previous articles, our primary reward is to obtain the desire to bestow, called "Reflected Light," as it is said, "The whole reward that we hope for is the Reflected Light" (General Preface to the Tree of Life).

Therefore, if the desire to bestow is called "the light," then this deficiency, when one sees that he does not have the power to bestow, is called "a *Kli*." He feels that this is what he is missing, meaning he sees what he is losing by not having this power called "the power of bestowal." Hence, his deficiency is built in him according to his sensation. This is called "a *Kli*" and "a vacancy," for here—where he lacks the power of bestowal—there is room for this filling to enter. This is called "the arrival of the light into the *Kli*."

However, we should know that receiving this *Kli* requires a lot of work. We have *Kelim* [plural of *Kli*], called "deficiencies," which we wish to fill. They are called "*Kelim* of self-love," meaning that we wish to receive fulfillment. These are very important *Kelim* because they come from the side of the Creator, who created them existence from absence because He wishes to do good to His creations, meaning that He wishes to give fulfillment. Yet, how is it possible to give fulfillment if there is no vacancy in which to place the filling? For this reason, He created these *Kelim* existence from absence to place the delight and pleasure in them. It turns out that this is the essence of the *Kli* that the Creator created.

However, because this *Kli* is called a "desire to receive," it wished to have equivalence of form, called "*Dvekut* [adhesion] with the Creator." This is why this *Kli* was disqualified from being a *Kli* for reception of the upper abundance. Now there is a need for a new *Kli* for reception, which dresses in the former *Kli*, where only by both—by clothing the will to bestow within the will to receive—will this *Kli* befit reception.

The previous *Kli*, called "desire to receive," came from the Emanator. The lower one has no part in the work of the desire to receive, although everything comes from the Emanator. Similarly, the second *Kli*, called "desire to bestow," comes only from the Emanator, as well, and the lower one cannot add, just as in the first *Kli*, called "desire to receive."

However, the difference is that the vessel of bestowal must first have a demand from the lower one, who seeks of the Creator to be given the new *Kli*. This, the first *Kli* did not have because it came to him without any awakening on the part of the lower one.

Tav-Shin-Mem-Hey

(1984 - 1985)

Make for Yourself a Rav and Buy Yourself a Friend (1)

Article No. 1, Tav-Shin-Mem-Hey, 1984-85

In the *Mishnah* (*Avot*, 1), Yehoshua Ben Perachia says, "Make for yourself a rav [great/teacher], buy yourself a friend, and judge every person favorably." We see that there are three things here: 1) Make for yourself a rav; 2) buy yourself a friend; 3) judge every person favorably.

This means that besides making for himself a rav, there is something more that he must do in relation to the collective. In other words, engaging in love of friends is not enough. Additionally, he should be considerate toward every person and judge them favorably.

We must understand the difference in wording between "make," "buy," and "favorably." Making is a practical thing. This means that there is no mind involved here, only action. In other words, even if one does not agree with the thing he wishes to do, but on the contrary, the mind makes him see that it is not a worthwhile deed, this is called doing, meaning sheer force, with no brains, since it is against his reason.

Accordingly, we should interpret in relation to the work, that the fact that one needs to assume the kingdom of heaven is called "an act." It is like putting the yoke on an ox so it would plow the ground. Although the ox does not wish to take this work on itself, we force it nonetheless.

Similarly, with the kingdom of heaven we should also force and enslave ourselves because it is the Creator's commandment, without any rhyme or reason. This is so because man must accept the kingdom of heaven not because the body feels that some benefit will come to it as a result, but in order to give contentment to the Creator.

But how can the body agree to it? This is the reason why the work must be above reason. It is called, "Make for yourself a rav," since there should be the kingdom of heaven because "He is great and ruling."

It is written in *The Zohar* ("Introduction of The Book of Zohar"), "'Fear is the most important, for man to fear the Upper One because He is great and ruling, the essence and the root of all the worlds, and all are of no consequence compared to Him.' Thus, one should fear the Creator because He is great and rules over everything. He is great because He is the root from which all the worlds expand, and His greatness is seen by His actions. And He rules over everything because all the worlds that He created, both upper and lower, are regarded as nothing compared to Him for they add nothing to His essence."

Therefore, the order of the work is for one to begin with "Make for yourself a rav," and take upon himself the burden of the kingdom of heaven above logic and above reason. This is called "doing," meaning action only, despite the body's disapproval. Afterwards, "Buy yourself a friend." Buying is just as when a person wishes to buy something; he must let go of something that he has already acquired. He gives what he's had for some time and in return purchases a new object.

It is similar with the work of God. For one to achieve *Dvekut* [adhesion] with the Creator, which is equivalence of form, as in, "As

He is merciful, so you are merciful," he must concede many things that he has in order to buy bonding with the Creator. This is the meaning of "Buy yourself a friend."

Before a person makes for himself a rav, meaning the kingdom of heaven, how can he buy himself a friend, meaning bond with the rav? After all, he has no rav yet. Only after he has made for himself a rav is there a point in demanding that the body make concessions to buy the bonding, that he wishes to give contentment to the Creator.

Moreover, we should understand that he has the strength to observe "buy yourself a friend" to the same extent as the greatness of the rav. This is so because he is willing to make concessions so as to bond with the rav to the very same extent that he feels the importance of the rav, since then he understands that obtaining *Dvekut* with the Creator is worth any effort.

It turns out that if one sees that he cannot overcome the body because he thinks that he is not strong enough and was born with a weak nature, it is not so. The reason is that he is not feeling the greatness of the rav. In other words, he still does not have the importance of the kingdom of heaven, so he has no strength to overcome for something that is not very important. But for an important thing, anyone can concede important things that he loves and receive what he needs.

For example, if a person is very tired and goes to sleep at around 11 pm, if he is awakened at three in the morning, of course he will say that he has no energy to get up to study because he's very tired. And if he feels a little weak or has a slight temperature, the body will certainly have no power to rise at the time he is accustomed to rising.

But if a person is very tired, feeling sick, and goes to sleep at midnight, but is awakened at one in the morning and told, "There is a fire in the yard; it's about to come into your room, quick, get up and you'll save your life in return for the effort you are making," then he will not make any excuses about being tired, mindless, or sick. Rather, even if he is very sick, he will make every effort to save his life. Evidently, because he will obtain an important thing, the body has the energy to do what it can to get what he wants.

Therefore, while working on "Make for yourself a rav," a person believes that it is, "For they are our lives and the length of our days." To the extent that he feels that this is his life, the body has enough strength to overcome all the obstacles, as written in the allegory. For this reason, in all of man's works, in studying or in praying, he should focus all his work on obtaining the greatness and importance of the rav. Much work and many prayers should be made on that alone.

In the words of *The Zohar*, this is called "Raising the *Shechina* [Divinity] from the dust," which means raising the kingdom of heaven, which is lowered to the dust. In other words, one does not place an important thing on the ground, while something that is unimportant is tossed to the ground. And since the kingdom of heaven, called *Shechina*, is "Lowered to the very bottom," it is said in the books that before every spiritual action one must pray to "raise the *Shechina* from the dust." This means that we should pray that we will regard the kingdom of heaven as important and that it will be worthwhile exerting for it and raising it to its importance.

Now we can understand what we say in the *Rosh Hashanah* [New Year's Eve] prayer, "Give glory to Your people." This seems quite perplexing. How is it permitted to pray for honor? Our sages said, "Be very, very humble," so how can we pray for the Creator to give us glory?

We should interpret that we pray that the Creator will give the glory of God to Your people, since we have no glory of God, but "The city of God is lowered to the very bottom," called "*Shechina* in the dust." Also, we do not have the real importance in the matter of "Make for yourself a rav." Hence, on *Rosh Hashanah*, the time when we take upon ourselves the kingdom of heaven, we ask of the Creator to give the glory of God to Your people, for the people of

Israel to feel the glory of the Creator. And then we will be able to keep the Torah and *Mitzvot* [commandments] in full.

Hence, we should say, "Give the glory of God to Your people," meaning that He will give the glory of God to the people of Israel. This does not mean that He will give the glory of Israel to the people of Israel, but that the Creator will give the glory of God to the people of Israel, for this is all we need to feel the importance and greatness of *Dvekut* with the Creator. If we have this importance, each person will be able to make efforts and there will be no one in the world saying he has no strength to save his life, so he wishes to remain a beast, if he feels that life is a very important thing because he can enjoy life.

But if a person does not feel that life has meaning, many people choose to die. This is so because no person can experience suffering in his life because it is against the purpose of creation, since the purpose of creation was to do good to His creations, meaning that they would enjoy life. Hence, when one sees that he cannot be happy now, or at least later, he commits suicide because he does not have the goal of life.

It follows that all we lack is, "Make for yourself a rav," to sense the greatness of the Creator. Then, everyone will be able to achieve the goal, which is to adhere to Him.

And we should also interpret the words of Rabbi Yehoshua Ben Perachia—who says three things: 1) Make for yourself a rav. 2) Buy yourself a friend. 3) Judge every person favorably—in regards to love of friends.

It would make sense to think that friendship relates to two people with equal skills and qualities, since then they find it easy to communicate, and they unite as one. And then, "They helped everyone his friend," like two people who make a partnership and each invests equal energy, resources, and work. Then the profits, too, are divided equally among them.

However, if one is superior to the other, meaning he invests more money or more expertise or more energy than the other, the division of profits is unequal, too. This is called "one-third partnership" or a "one-quarter partnership." Thus, it is not considered a real partnership because one is of higher status than the other.

It turns out that real friendship—when each makes the necessary payment to buy his friend—is precisely when both are of equal status, and then both pay equally. It is like a corporeal business, where both of them give everything equally, or there cannot be a real partnership. Hence, "Buy yourself a friend," since there can be bonding—when each buys his friend—only when they are equal.

But on the other hand, it is impossible to learn from one another if one does not see that his friend is greater than he. But if the other one is greater, he cannot be his friend, but his rav [teacher/great], while he is considered a student. At that time, he can learn knowledge or virtues from him.

This is why it is said, "Make for yourself a rav and buy yourself a friend"; both have to exist. In other words, each should regard the other as a friend, and then there is room for buying. This means that each must pay with concessions to the other, like a father concedes his rest, works for his son, spends money for his son, and all is because of the love.

However, there it is natural love. The Creator gave natural love for raising children so there would be persistence to the world. If, for instance, the father would raise the children because it is a *Mitzva* [commandment], his children would have food, clothing, and other things that are necessary for children to the extent that a person is committed to keep all the *Mitzvot* [plural of *Mitzva*]. At times he would keep the *Mitzvot*, and at times he would only do the very minimum, and his children could starve to death.

This is why the Creator gave parents natural love for their children, so there would be persistence to the world. This is not so with love of friends. Here everyone must make great efforts by himself to create the love of friends in his heart.

It is the same with "And buy yourself a friend." Once he understands, at least intellectually, that he needs help and he cannot do the holy work, to the extent that he understands it in his mind, he begins to buy, to make concessions for his friend's sake.

This is so because he understands that the work is primarily in bestowing upon the Creator. However, it is against his nature because man is born with a desire to receive only for his own benefit. Hence, we were given the *cure* by which to go from self-love to love of others, and by that he can arrive at the love of the Creator.

Therefore, he can find a friend at his level. But afterwards, making the friend a rav, meaning for him to feel that his friend is at a higher degree is something that one cannot see, that his friend is like a rav and he is like a student. But if he does not regard his friend as a rav, how will he learn from him? This is called "Make," meaning a mindless action. In other words, he must accept, above reason, that his friend is greater and this is called "Make," meaning *acting above reason*.

In the essay, "A Speech for the Completion of *The Zohar*," it is written, "To receive the first condition, each student must feel the smallest among all the friends. In that state, one can receive the appreciation of the greatness of the great one." Thus, he is explicitly stating that everyone should see himself as the smallest among the students.

And yet, how can one see oneself as the smallest of the students? Here, only above reason is pertinent. This is called "Make for yourself a rav," meaning that each of them is considered a rav compared to him, and he is regarded as merely a student.

This is a great exertion, since there is a rule that the other's deficiencies are always visible while his own faults are always hidden. And yet, he must regard the other as being virtuous, and that it is worthwhile for him to accept what he says or does, to learn from the other's actions.

But the body does not agree to it because whenever one must learn from another, meaning if he has high regard for the other, the other commits him to labor, and the body revokes the views and actions of the other. Because the body wants to rest, it is better for it and more convenient to rule out his friend's views and actions so he will not have to make an effort.

This is why it is called, "Make for yourself a rav." It means that for the friend to be your rav, you have to make it. In other words, it is not by reason, since the reason asserts otherwise, and sometimes even shows him the opposite, that he can be the rav and the other his student. This is why it is called "Make," meaning doing and not reasoning.

3) "And judge every person favorably."

After we said, "Buy yourself a friend," there remains the question, "What about the rest of the people?" For example, if a person chooses a few friends from his congregation and leaves the others and does not bond with them, the question is, "How should he treat them?" After all, they are not his friends, and why didn't he choose them? We should probably say that he did not find virtues in them to make it worth his while to bond with them, meaning he does not appreciate them.

Thus, how should he treat the rest of the people in his congregation? And the same applies for the rest of the people who are not from among the people of the congregation. How should he treat them? Rabbi Yehoshua Ben Perachia says about it, "Judge every person favorably," meaning one should judge everyone favorably.

This means that the fact that he does not find qualities in them is not their fault. Rather, it is not in his power to be able to see the merits of the general public. For this reason, he sees according to the qualities of his own soul. This is true according to his attainment, but not according to the truth. In other words, there is such a thing as truth in itself, regardless of the one who attains.

There is truth that each attains according to his attainment, meaning that truth changes according to the ones who attain. Meaning, it is subject to change according to the changing states in the one who attains.

But the actual truth did not change in its essence. This is why each person can attain the same thing differently. Therefore, in the eyes of the public, it could be that the public is just fine, but he sees differently, according to his own quality.

This is why he says, "And judge every person favorably," meaning he should judge all the others besides his friends favorably—that they are all worthy in and of themselves and he has no complaints whatsoever concerning their conduct. But for himself, he cannot learn anything from them because he has no equivalence with them.

The Meaning of Branch and Root

Article No. 2, Tav-Shin-Mem-Hey, 1984-85

The meaning of root and branch. The land of Israel is a branch from the *Sefira Malchut*. *Malchut* is called the *Kli* [vessel] that was emanated by the Emanator to become a *Kli* for the reception of the abundance that the Emanator wanted to bestow upon His creations. That *Kli* is called *Malchut*.

The order was that first was the vessel of reception in order to receive, and then there was a correction that it is forbidden to receive in that *Kli*, unless we can aim in order to bestow, and then the abundance is drawn into that *Kli*. That correction was made so that when the abundance comes to the creatures, there will not be any deficiency in them, called "bread of shame."

Instead, they will be able to receive the abundance unboundedly because there will be no shame in them upon the reception of the abundance. Rather, they will aim all the delight and pleasure they receive only to the benefit of the Creator. Then they will continually extend abundance because they will not be able to say they have given the Creator enough and they do not need to bestow upon Him anymore. Therefore, they will always have a reason to extend abundance.

This is not so if they receive the abundance for themselves, meaning because of self-love. At that time they must be limited because of the shame. They will have to say that the delight and pleasure that He has given us is enough. Because of it there was the correction called restriction so as not to receive light into the *Kli* of *Malchut* unless we can receive in order to bestow.

From the root of *Malchut* extends downward into the corporeal branch the *Eretz* [land] which is a branch of *Malchut* of above. That land is called the Holy Land. For this reason, here in the Holy Land there are special corrections, meaning *Mitzvot* [commandments] that are dependent upon the earth, such as donations and tithing. This is not so in the rest of the lands.

And also there is a special root to Jordan, a special root to Syria, a special root to Babylon, and a special root to the rest of the lands (See Talmud Eser *Sefirot*, Part 16, p 1930). For this reason, with respect to the branch and root, the place of the Temple is precisely the Holy Land, which is the land of Israel. This is so after it was sanctified.

But before the people of Israel came into this land, it was a place of seven nations, which correspond to the seven holy *Sefirot*. They were the opposite of holiness, extending from *Malchut*, where there is no correction of the *Masach* [screen] which is the intention to bestow. For this reason, first the nations of the world came there, for so was the order in spirituality: 1) the coming of the will to receive came, 2) the correction of making it in order to bestow. For this reason for the Holy Land: 1) The nations of the world had to come first, for they belong to *Malchut* before it was corrected with a *Masach* so that everything will be in order to bestow. 2) Afterwards, Israel will come and conquer them.

It turns out that the Holy Land extends from *Malchut* and the will to receive in a person also extends from *Malchut*. For this reason there were 1) the nations of the world in the land first, 2) then the people of Israel came.

It is likewise in man's heart: 1) First comes the evil inclination; 2) and then comes the good inclination. Everything extends from the upper roots.

However, there's a difference between man's heart, which extends from *Malchut*, and the land of Israel, which extends from *Malchut*, since we should discern between internality and externality. In the externality, there should be the place of the branch that corresponds to the root. But in internality, it is not necessarily the place of the branch that corresponds to it.

In the land of Israel, which aims to a person's heart, which extends from the root of *Malchut*, a person does need to be specifically in the land of Israel to be awarded with the kingdom of heaven, called the "land of Israel." Internally, a person can be rewarded with the instilling of the *Shechina* [divinity] and with the greatest attainments overseas as well, just like all of our great sages who were overseas.

Also, people who live in the land of Israel can be the worst criminals. The land of Israel, called the "Holy Land," does not obligate them in any way to keep Torah and *Mitzvot*, since what concerns the internality, the externality does not obligate them at all, as internality is the work in the heart and it is completely unrelated to the externality.

However, at the same time there is the matter of externality. That is, there is a rule that it is forbidden to say *Kaddish* unless ten men are present. And we do not check if these ten men are with complete fear, but rather when ten simple men come together they can say *Kaddish*, and "Bless," and read in the Torah, etc. However, if there are nine righteous sages, they are forbidden to say *Kaddish*, and "Bless" because the revealed law is according to the externality and not according to the quality of the internality.

65) Hence, we could ask, "Why, then, is it forbidden to disagree with the first in the revealed Torah?" It is because, as far as the practical part of the *Mitzvot* [commandments] is concerned, it is to the contrary: the first were more complete in them than the last. This is because the act extends from the holy *Kelim* [vessels] of the

Sefirot (called 'externality' because *Kelim* are called 'externality' with respect to the lights, and the lights are called 'internality'). And the secrets of the Torah and the *Taamim* [flavors] of the *Mitzva* [commandment] extend from the Lights in the *Sefirot*. You already know that there is an inverse relation between Lights and vessels."

It turns out that with respect to the revealed, meaning the practical part, belongs to the externality. Therefore, with respect to the practical part, there are things that can be done only in the land of Israel, such as the prohibition on building the Temple abroad.

But in the internality, which concerns man's heart, it does have to be specifically in the land of Israel, although the branch of *Malchut* is specifically the land of Israel. Yet, there are unifications that if one wants to make a unification on the outside, as well, they have to make that unification specifically in the external land.

It is as we find, that there is a unification of ASHAN, which is an acronym for *Olam, Shanah, Nefesh* [world, year, soul respectively], meaning that that unification should be specifically according to these three conditions which are: *Olam* [world]—specifically the place of the Holy of Holies; *Shanah*—with respect to time, it should be specifically on *Yom Kippur* [Day of Atonement], which is regarded as *Shanah* [year]; *Nefesh* [soul]—with respect to *Nefesh*, it should be specifically through the high priest.

Therefore, with respect to internality, when we speak of man's heart, where he begins to serve the Creator, meaning the work of exiting self-love, which is called the "land of the peoples," and instill the people of Israel instead of them, meaning that his intention will be only to love the Creator, then there is the matter of day and night.

"Day" means that he has high spirts without any need for corrections, such as when the sun shines and a person does not need to make any correction to make the sun shine. However, one needs to be careful not to put interferences so that the sun will not be able to shine where it should shine, such as not entering a house with no windows, for this interrupts the shining of the sun.

Conversely, "night" is the time when a person should make corrections so it will illuminate for him. For example, in corporeality, night is the time when it is dark in the house. Through corrections, meaning by placing a candle or a lamp there, there is light. Without corrections, even if one does not pose any interferences, still, without effort, which is called corrections, nothing will shine for him. Instead, wherever he looks it is as though he is looking through black glasses: everything is dark.

This is a time when one should reflect on one's current state, how remote he is from spirituality and immersed in self-love, and that he has no chance of exiting his situation by himself. At that time he must see his real situation—how by nature a person cannot do anything. Rather, as our sages said, "Were it not for the Creator's help, he would not have overcome it."

However, we should know that the Creator created the night, and He certainly created it for a purpose, which is to do good to His creations. Therefore, each one is asking: Why did He create darkness which is night? After all, according to the purpose of creation, He should have created only day and not night. The verse says, "And there was evening and there was morning, one day." That is, specifically through both, which are night and day, comes one day.

However, the night was created deliberately as not illuminating without corrections, in order to perform the corrections that the night reveals to a person. This is so because the *Kelim* are founded over the sensation of darkness. These are needed in order for them to have a need for the Creator to help them. Otherwise, there is no need for the Creator's salvation. That is, at that time there is no need for the Torah, which is regarded as "the light in it reforms him."

For this come corrections called "Torah and *Mitzvot*." Torah is what is revealed to us in the part that is called revealed, which is rules and stories of the fathers, etc. All of this is called Torah. This part is called the revealed Torah, and the Torah teaches us to perform *Mitzvot*, and how to do them. It also tells us the stories of the fathers.

However, we should know that there is a hidden part in the Torah, meaning that that Torah is hidden from us. We should know that the whole Torah is the names of the Creator, meaning the revelation of Godliness, called the "secrets of Torah," which a person begins to attain specifically after he has been rewarded with Torah *Lishma* [for Her sake].

In the words of Rabbi Meir (*Avot*, Chapter 6), "Rabbi Meir says, 'Anyone who engages in Torah *Lishma* is rewarded with many things, the secrets of Torah are revealed to him, and he becomes like an ever-flowing fountain.'" It turns out that the revealed part in the Torah is to bring us, by its merit, into *Lishma*, meaning to have the ability to aim every thought, word, and action to be in order to bestow.

Afterwards, once he has been rewarded with *Lishma*, begins the engagement in the hidden Torah and the flavors of the *Mitzvot*. By doing them, he extends upper abundance downward. And we have already spoken about the 613 *Mitzvot* being called "613 counsels," as well as "613 deposits."

It is written in the "Introduction of the Book of Zohar," "*The Zohar* calls the *Mitzvot* in the Torah by the name "deposits." However, they are also called "613 counsels." The difference between them is that in everything there is anterior and posterior. The preparation for something is called the "posterior" and attainment of that thing is called the "anterior." With that respect of the anterior of the *Mitzvot*, which are then called "deposits," Rabbi Shimon explains the fourteen above-mentioned deposits.

We see from above that the hidden part is called "anterior," and one is rewarded with the anterior after one is rewarded with attaining *Lishma*.

The Meaning of Truth and Faith

Article No. 3, Tav-Shin-Mem-Hey, 1984-85

Truth and faith are two contradicting things. We see that in our prayer, which was established by the members of the Great Assembly, we also have two things that contradict one another. On the one hand, they have arranged for us the procession of the prayer, and prayer should be said specifically when a person is deficient. Moreover, our sages said, "A prayer should be from the bottom of the heart," meaning that the prayer that we pray to the Creator should be from the bottom of the heart, meaning that we will feel the deficiency throughout the heart.

This means that within the heart there should be no place that is whole, but rather only deficiencies. And the greater the deficiency, the more the prayer is accepted compared to other prayers. It is written in *The Zohar* about the verse, "A prayer for the poor when he is weak and pours out his words before the Lord" (Balak, items 187-88): "But there are three that are called a 'prayer': a prayer for Moses, man of God—there is none like this prayer in another man. A prayer for David—there is none like it in another king. A prayer for the poor. Of the three prayers, which is the most important? It is a prayer for the poor. This prayer comes before the prayer of Moses, before the prayer of David, and before all other prayers in the world. What is the reason? The poor is brokenhearted. It is written, 'The Lord is near to the brokenhearted.' And the poor always quarrels with the Creator, and the Creator listens and hears his words." Thus far its words.

It turns out, according to the words of the holy *Zohar*, that the prayer is precisely when a person is broken, when he has nothing with which to revive his soul. Then it is called a "prayer from the bottom of the heart." This prayer is more important than all the prayers in the world because he has no merit with which to say, "I am not like my friends because I have some merit that my friends do not have." It turns out that he is full of deficiencies, and then there is room for an honest prayer from the bottom of the heart. That is, the bigger the deficiency, the more important is the prayer.

And corresponding to the prayer that they have arranged for us in the order of the prayers, they have arranged for us an order of praise and gratitude. This contradicts the prayer in litany that exists in the order of the prayers, since normally, when one does something good to another, he is grateful for it. But the measure of the gratitude is always according to the measure of the benefit that he does for him. This is how he expresses the gratitude to the receiver of the benefit.

For example, if one person helps another for half his sustenance, meaning that if he has obtained through him provision that suffices to provide only half his household needs, the gratitude he gives him is incomplete. But if he has tried to find someone full provision, and even with luxuries, meaning that he has no deficiency that he did not fulfill, he certainly thanks and praises such a person with his heart and soul.

It therefore turns out that when a person thanks and praises the Creator, and wants to praise and thank the Creator from the bottom of his heart, he should see that the Creator has given him all of his wishes and he is not lacking anything. Otherwise, his gratitude cannot be complete.

Therefore, a person should try to see that he is not lacking anything, but the Creator complimented all of his deficiencies, and he is left with no deficiencies. Only then can he give thanks to the Creator, and this is the meaning of the songs and praises which they have arranged for us in the prayer.

For this reason, they, meaning the prayer and litany, and songs and praises, are opposites, since if he has no completeness during the prayer and litany, and he is full of deficiencies, his prayer is complete. But with songs and praises it is the opposite: if he has no place of deficiency that is not completely filled, specifically then he can give true thanks.

We should understand why they have arranged for us those two opposites, for what purpose, and what this order gives to us. Also, we should understand how it is possible to maintain those two opposites, since they contradict one another.

The holy Ari says (*Talmud Esser Sefirot*, p 788, item 83), "There should be two doors in a woman, so as to close them and hold the fetus inside, so it does not come out until it is completely fashioned. There should also be in her a force that fashions the shape of the fetus."

It explains there the reason: "As in corporeality, if there is a malfunction in the mother's abdomen, the mother aborts the fetus. That is, if the fetus comes out of the mother's abdomen before the shape of the fetus has been sufficiently fashioned in the degree of *Ibur* [impregnation], that birth is not regarded as birth because the *Ibur* cannot exist in the world. Rather, it is called "abortion," meaning that it was not born, but fell out of the mother's abdomen and cannot live."

Likewise, in spirituality, there are two discernments in the *Ibur*:

1. The shape of the *Ibur*, which is the degree of *Katnut* [smallness/infancy], which is its real shape. However, since it only has *Katnut*, it is regarded as a deficiency, and wherever there is a deficiency in holiness, there is a grip to the *Klipot* [shells/peels]. At that time the *Klipot* can cause abortion—that the spiritual fetus will fall out before

its stage of *Ibur* has been completed. For this reason, there should be a detaining element, which is that it is given wholeness, meaning *Gadlut* [adulthood/greatness].

2. However, we should understand how the newborn can be given *Gadlut* while it is still unfit to receive even *Katnut* sufficiently, since it still does not have the *Kelim* [vessels] in which to receive them in order to bestow. To that there is an answer there: Our sages said, "An embryo in its mother's abdomen eats what its mother eats." He also said, "A fetus is its mother's thigh." This means that since a fetus is its mother's thigh, the *Ibur* does not merit its own name. For this reason, the fetus eats what its mother eats. That is, the fetus receives everything that it receives in the mother's *Kelim*. For this reason, although the fetus has no *Kelim* that are fit to receive *Gadlut*, but in the *Kelim* of the upper one, which is its mother, it can receive because it is completely annulled before the mother and has no authority of its own. This is called *Ibur*, when it is completely annulled before the Upper One.

Then, when it receives *Gadlut*, it is in wholeness. This is why there is no grip to the *Klipot* there, and this is why it is called the "detaining force." This keeps the fetus from falling in spirituality, like an abortion in a corporeal fetus, from where the mother must watch over her fetus so there will not be any malfunction there. It is likewise in spirituality.

It turns out from all of the above that we should discern two states in man's work:

1. One's true state, meaning one's *Katnut*, when everything he does and thinks is *Katnut*. The sensation of *Katnut* begins when it wants to walk on the path of truth, which is to work in order to bestow. At that time he begins to see his *Katnut*, how remote he is from matters of bestowal, and he cannot do anything in order to bestow. This is called "truth," meaning his true state.

Then, because it is *Katnut*, there can be a grip to the *Sitra Achra*, and he can come to despair. It turns out that his entering the work is regarded as *Ibur*, and he can come into abortion, meaning to fall from his degree, similar to the corporeal fetus that falls out from the mother's abdomen and cannot stay alive. Likewise, in spirituality, he falls from his degree and needs a new *Ibur*. That is, he needs to start his work anew as though he never served the Creator.

For this reason, there should be a detaining force so that the fetus will not fall out. This means that at that time he should be in wholeness, meaning to feel that he is not lacking anything in the work, but that now he is close to the Creator in complete *Dvekut* [adhesion], and no one can tell him, "But you see that you have no progress in the work of the Creator. Therefore, you're exerting in vain, and you are unfit to serve in holiness. Therefore, you need to be like everyone else. Why are you making such a noise that you want to be at a higher degree than everyone else, although you derive no satisfaction from the work of the general public? This is what gave you the push so as to be able to have thoughts and desires that you must come out of the work of ordinary people, and go further ahead toward the truth. It is true that this is the truth, but you see that although you want to walk on the path of truth, you are unfit for it, either because you lack talent or because you lack the strength to overcome, as you are unable to overcome the nature of self-love with which you were born. Therefore, drop this work. Don't dwell in lowliness like the rest of the people, and do not raise your heart above your brother, to be haughty. Rather, it is better for you to retire from this path."

For this reason, in order not to fall into such thoughts, he needs the detaining force. That is, he must believe above reason that the grip he has on the path of truth is great and very important, and he cannot even appreciate the importance of touching the path of truth for this is the entire *Kli* in which the Light of the Creator will be. However, this is in the *Kelim* of the upper one. That is, the Creator knows when a person should feel his *Dvekut* with the Creator.

In his own *Kelim* he feels the opposite—that now he is worse than when he walked on the path of the general public, where he felt that each day he was adding good deeds and Torah and *Mitzvot*. But now, since he has started walking on the path of the individual, to always keep the intention how much he can work in order to bestow and how much he can relinquish self-love, at that time he usually sees how much he is nearing the truth. At that time, he always sees more of the truth, that he is unable to exit self-love.

Still, in the *Kelim* of the upper one, meaning above reason, he can raise himself and say, "I don't care how I am bestowing upon the Creator. I want the Creator to bring me closer to Him, and the Creator certainly knows when the time will come when I feel that the Creator has brought me closer to Him. In the meantime, I believe that the Creator knows what is best for me, and this is why He makes me feel the feelings that I am feeling. But what is the reason that the Creator wants to guide me on this path, meaning that I must believe in the path of faith that He is behaving with me benevolently? And if I believe it, He has given me a sign: the amount of joy I have, the amount of gratitude that I can give to Him for this, and how much I can thank and praise His name. Surely, we must say that it is to our benefit, that specifically through faith we can achieve the goal, which is called "receiving in order to bestow." Otherwise, the Creator could certainly lead us by the path of knowledge and not by the path of faith.

By that you will understand what we asked, "Why we need two things that deny one another?" That is, on the one hand, we should walk by the path of truth, meaning to feel our situation, that we feel that we are moving farther from self-love and toward love of others, and how much we would like the world to be in, "May His blessed name grow and be sanctified."

And when we see that spirituality is still not important, we feel ourselves in great deficiency, and also to see how much we regret it, and how it pains us that we are removed from Him. This is called "truth," meaning the state we feel in our *Kelim* according to our sensation.

Also, we were given the path of faith, which is above reason, namely not to take our sensations and reason into account, but say, as it is written, "They have eyes and see not. They have ears and hear not." Rather, we should believe that the Creator is certainly

The Meaning of Truth and Faith

the Messiah, and He knows what is good for me and what is not good for me. Therefore, He wants me to feel my state as I do, and for myself, I do not care how I feel myself because I want to work in order to bestow.

Therefore, the main thing is that I need to work for the Creator. And although I feel that there is no wholeness in my work, still, in the *Kelim* of the upper one, meaning from the perspective of the upper one, I am utterly complete, as it is written, "The cast out will not be cast out from Him." Hence, I am satisfied with my work—that I have the privilege of serving the King even at the lowest degree. That, too, I regard as a great privilege that the Creator has allowed me come closer to Him at least to some degree.

This gives us two things: 1) With respect to the truth, he sees his true state—that he has room for prayer, and then he has room for deficiency. At that time he can pray that the Creator will complement his deficiency, and then he can rise by the degrees of holiness. 2) The path of faith, which is wholeness—that from here he can praise and thank the Creator, and then he can be in joy.

These Are the Generations of Noah

Article No. 4, Tav-Shin-Mem-Hey, 1984-85

"These are the generations of Noah. Noah was a righteous man. He was complete in his generations. Noah walked with God."

RASHI interprets, to teach you that the generations of the righteous are primarily good deeds. RASHI explains why he says, "These are the generations of Noah." It should have said the names of his sons, meaning Shem, Ham, and Japheth. And why does it say, "These are the generations of Noah. Noah was a righteous man?" He explains that it is because the generations of the righteous are primarily good deeds.

"In his generations," since some of our sages praise him—that if he were in a generation of righteous, he would have been more righteous. Others condemn him—if he were in the generation of Abraham, he would be regarded as nothing.

"Noah walked with God." RASHI interprets, with Abraham he says, "Before whom I walked." Noah needed assistance to support him, but Abraham was strong and walked with his righteousness by himself.

To explain all the above in the work, we should know that father and son, fathers and generations [offspring], mean cause and consequence. Normally, when a person does something, he is certain that this act will engender something. For example, a person who goes to work in some factory wants to beget a salary through his actions, so he can provide for himself. It turns out that the father is the labor and the generation is the provision. Likewise, when a person learns some wisdom he wants to be appreciated as wise by that, meaning that everything a person does is only to see generations from his actions.

Therefore, when a person engages in Torah and *Mitzvot* [commandments], he certainly wants some generations to be born out of his actions.

According to what is written in the holy *Zohar* ("Introduction of The Book of Zohar," item 189) and in the *Sulam*, and these are its words (in the *Sulam*, item 190), "Fear is interpreted in three ways, two of which do not have the proper root, and one is the root of fear. There is person who fears the Creator so his sons will live and not die, or fears a monetary punishment. For this reason, he always fears Him. It turns out that his fear of the Creator is not the root, since his own benefit is the root, and the fear is its consequence [generation]. And there is a person who fears the Creator because he fears the punishment of that world, and the punishment of hell. Those two fears—fear of punishment in this world and fear of punishment in the next world—are not the essence of the fear and its root." (In item 191) "Fear, which is the essence, is that one should fear one's Master because He is great and ruling, the essence and root of all the worlds, and everything is regarded as nothing compared to Him."

It follows from the above that from the work in which a person labors, which is called the "father," he wants to see generations from his work, which is called the "fruit of his work."

There are three types of generations we should see here. 1) Reward in this world, meaning that his sons will live and he will succeed in provision, etc. 2) Reward in the next world. 3) Because He is great and ruling. This means that all the generations he aspires for are to be able to bestow contentment upon the Creator.

It follows from the above that there is the matter of generations which are called "good deeds," and good means bestowing upon the Creator, as it is written (Psalms 45), "My heart overflows with a good thing. I say, 'My work is for the King.'" This means that he wants all of his actions to be for the Creator, and this is called "good deeds." For his own benefit he wants no reward, and all the reward he hopes for is to be able to do things that bring contentment to the Creator without any reward for his own labor. This means that his reward is that he will be given that gift of being able to do things only for the sake of the Creator, without any mixture of intention to benefit himself. This is the reward for which he engages in Torah and *Mitzvot*. For such good deeds he hopes to attain this by his labor. It was said about this (*Kidushin* 30): "I have created the evil inclination; I have created for it the Torah as a spice."

Accordingly, what are the generations of the righteous? Only good deeds, meaning the result that stems from the reason, and the reason is the labor in Torah and *Mitzvot*. For the rest of the people, the results of the reason are reward in this world or reward in the next world. But to the righteous, their result from the reason is that their father, who begets generations, is only good deeds. This is the only reward they hope for—to be able to bring contentment to the Creator.

This is the meaning of what RASHI interprets, "That the generations of the righteous is primarily good deeds." This is regarded as all their actions being only to bestow contentment upon the Creator. However, we should understand what RASHI interprets about the essence of the generations of the righteous, and what they consider secondary, which they do not regard as the essence.

It is known that there are actions and there is understanding and knowing. That is, that which is within reason is called understanding and knowing, meaning that the body, too, agrees that we should engage in Torah and *Mitzvot*, since once a person has achieved the degree of *Lishma* [for Her sake], he is rewarded with the light of life, which is found in Torah and *Mitzvot*. It is as it is written (Psalms 19), "More desirable than gold, then much fine gold, and sweeter than honey and the honeycomb." This is called "understanding," where the body, too, understands that it is worthwhile to be a servant of the Creator.

Rabbi Meir says (*Avot*, Chapter 6), "Anyone who engages in Torah *Lishma* is rewarded with many things. Moreover, the whole world is worthwhile for him, and the secrets of Torah are revealed to him."

To the righteous, all these things attained by engaging in *Lishma* are not regarded as the essence. That is, this is not their intention in the work in Torah and *Mitzvot*. Rather, what is most important for them is good deeds, meaning to bestow contentment upon the Creator. It is in that regard that they expected to achieve a degree of deeds above reason. Their intention was not to have generations of understanding and knowing, but rather, their intention was only the actions. This is the meaning of what RASHI explained, "To teach you that the generations of the righteous are primarily good deeds."

According to the above, we can interpret what RASHI explains about, "in his generations." "Some of our sages praise him: Moreover, if he were in a generation of righteous, he would have been more righteous. Others condemn him: If he were in Abraham's generation, he would be regarded as nothing."

In his generations means his two generations, because two is plural. But concerning the work, each and every state is called a "generation." This is the meaning of, "One generation shall praise your work to another." It means that whether a person is in a generation of wicked, meaning if a person has thoughts and desires of the wicked, at which time a person has great exertion to be able to overcome the arguments of the wicked, which peck his mind and thought with the questions of who and what. At that time, he cannot overcome them unless with the power of faith above reason. This is regarded as subduing the arguments of the wicked not with answers within reason, but rather only with the power of faith above reason can he defeat them.

This is called an "act," meaning without intellect, and this is called, "If he has performed one *Mitzva* [commandment] he is happy, for he has sentenced himself and the entire world to a scale of merit," for only with an act can we defeat the argument of the wicked, and not with intellect and reason.

Accordingly, we should say that Noah's generation refers to a generation of wicked. He should be praised because then he has the primary hard work. But he should be condemned because in the end, he is in a generation of wicked, meaning he has foreign thoughts, and it is unbecoming of a servant of the Creator to have such wickedness in his mind and heart.

We should also say, that in the generation of Abraham, meaning in a generation where there are righteous, namely when he has good thoughts, of righteous, it is when there only one desire is in his mind and heart—to bring contentment to the Creator—and thoughts and desires of the wicked never crossed his mind or heart. Such a person is in a generation of righteous.

Others praise, for if Noah had been in the state of righteous, meaning if he had equalized the powers of overcoming that he had in the generation of the wicked, what would he have felt then compared to the feeling he has now, which is the pleasantness and sweetness of the Torah? Certainly, the time of Noah's generation, which was called a "generation of wicked," that time was regarded as nothing, for then he still did not feel the delight and pleasure that he feels in a generation of righteous.

But with respect to the work, the time when he was in a generation of wicked was a place for work. It turns out that Noah's generation is more important because he has what to do, for the generations of the righteous are primarily good deeds.

"Noah walked with God." RASHI interprets that with Abraham he says, "Before whom I walked." Noah needed assistance to support him, but Abraham was strong and walked by his righteousness. This means that there are two types of forces in a person, which are called "vessels of reception" and "vessels of bestowal." Vessels of bestowal relate to the Creator, as the Creator is the giver, and vessels of reception relate to the creature, who is the receiver.

The vessels of reception. which relate to the receiver, come before the vessels of bestowal. In the words of Kabbalah, the vessels of bestowal are called *Keter*, *Hochma*, and *GAR de Bina*, and below them are the vessels of reception, which are *ZAT de Bina*, *Zeir Anpin*, and *Malchut*.

Accordingly, the vessels of bestowal are called, "God walked with Noah," meaning that in a place of vessels of bestowal, it was possible to walk in holiness, meaning vessels of bestowal that relate to the Creator, which are vessels of bestowal. This is called, "Noah needed assistance to support him," since the upper one gives the vessels of bestowal, which is regarded as Noah needing assistance to support him.

This means that the upper one awakens him to work, called "awakening from above," as it is written in *The Study of the Ten Sefirot* (part 9, p 735, item 6, and in *Ohr Pnimi*): "However, in the beginning, in the first time, the *MAN* that were not by *ZON* in *AVI* went up, and then the *ZON* were made of those *MAN*. After *ZON* were established, they raised *MAN* a second time. Once he has the vessels of bestowal, which he acquired through awakening from above, which is called, 'Noah needed assistance to support him,' which comes from the upper one, and this was the degree of Noah."

But Abraham did not need assistance to support him. RASHI makes that precision from the words, "Before whom I walked." It means, that he walked with vessels of reception, which stand before the vessels of bestowal. The vessels of bestowal—which are *Keter*, *Hochma*, and *GAR de Bina*—stand above, and below them stand the vessels of reception, which are *ZAT de Bina* and *ZON*.

Since Abraham walked with vessels that are before him, before the vessels of bestowal, which relate to the Creator, and we relate the vessels of reception to the receivers, this is why using the vessels of reception is called "awakening from below," which is attributed to the lower one.

This is the meaning of Abraham not needing assistance to support him because he walked with vessels of reception. With those *Kelim* [vessels] he was serving the Creator. But the words, "God walked with Noah," mean the *Kelim* that are attributed to God, which are vessels of bestowal, which are vessels of the Creator, and those *Kelim* the Creator gives.

Go Forth From Your Land

Article No. 5, Tav-Shin-Mem-Hey, 1984-85

"Go forth from your land, and from your homeland, and from your father's house to the land that I will show you."

This is perplexing, for it is not according to the order of reality. This is so because first one comes out of one's father's house, then from one's homeland, and then from one's land. This is what the interpreters ask.

In the work, we should interpret that "your land" comes from the word *Ratzon* [desire] as our sages said about, "Let the earth put forth grass," it was delighted to do its Maker's will. Accordingly, "Go forth from your land" means from your desire, which is the desire with which one is created, called "desire to receive delight and pleasure," which is regarded as self-love. This is why he was told to go out of self-love.

"From your homeland" means that father and offspring are cause and consequence, reason and result. This is so because the result comes from the drop in the father's brain. By that, the result later emerges, as we explained in previous articles. In other words, the labor, when a person is going to work, is in order to receive reward. It turns out that the labor gives him reward. Were it not for the reward, he would not have made any effort. It therefore follows that a person keeps Torah and *Mitzvot* [commandments] in order to beget a son, which is called the reward.

Considering the reward, we've already said that there are two kinds of reward: 1. reward in this world; 2. reward in the next world.

It is written in *The Zohar* ("Introduction of the Book of Zohar," item 190), "And those two, says the Holy *Zohar* are not the essence." It is explained there in the *Sulam* [Ladder (commentary on *The Zohar*)], that it is because they were built on a foundation of self-love, called "desire to receive in order to receive."

It therefore follows that if a person exerts in Torah and *Mitzvot* in order to receive reward for his will to receive, then both the father, meaning the labor, and the offspring, which was born out of that labor, and which is called "reward," were all on the basis of self-love. This means that the drop in the father's brain, called "labor," from the beginning of his work his thought was only of self-love. Naturally the offspring that was born, meaning the reward he expects to receive, is also a reward of self-love.

He was told "Go forth from your land," meaning from your will to receive, "and from your homeland," meaning the offspring that were born. "From your father's land" means the reward that was born out of your father's house, which is the labor that begets a reward of self-love. From all these he should depart.

"To the land that I will show you." That land means desire to bestow. On that land, meaning on the desire to bestow, on that land, that is, on the desire to bestow, he will be rewarded with the Creator revealing to him.

"That I will show you" means that the Creator will reveal Himself to him. Conversely, on the will to receive there were restriction and concealment, and it became dark there and separated from the life of lives, which causes darkness.

Therefore, I cannot be revealed to you on your desire, but only on the desire to bestow, called "equivalence of form." At that time, the restriction and concealment are removed and the Creator is revealed to him.

"And I will make you a great nation." In Midrash Raba (Chapter 39) "Rabbi Levi said, 'When Abraham our father was walking in Aram Naharaim and saw them reckless and eating and drinking, he said, 'I wish that I will not have a portion in this land.' When he came to *Sulam Tzor*, and saw them weeding at the time of weeding, and hoeing at the time of hoeing, he said, 'I wish that I might have a portion in this land.' The Creator told him, 'To your descendants I have given this land.'"

To understand his words in the work, we should interpret that *Eretz* [land] means *Ratzon* [desire]. *Be-Aram* [in Aram] has the letters of Avram. When Abraham walked from Naharaim—Naharaim comes from the word *Nahor* [illuminated]—then he saw that there are people who desire only the lights. This is called "eating and drinking," when the aim is for the reward. This is why he said "that I will not have a portion in this land," meaning I will not have a portion in this desire, when the intention is only on the reward, and the work is not appreciated, only the reward is appreciated. This is why he said, "I will not have a portion in this desire."

"When he came to *Sulam Tzor*," *Tzor* comes from the word *Tzar* [narrow], meaning that they felt *Tzarut* [narrowness] in the work. He saw that they were in the *Sulam* [ladder], which is as a ladder set on the earth with its top reaching to heaven. "He saw them weeding at the time of weeding, and hoeing at the time of hoeing," meaning that all their thoughts were about man's work, and they were focusing their intentions on the correctness of their work. That is, the *Kelim* [vessels] where the abundance should come should be proper. And they did not pay attention to the fruits, which is the reward. Instead, they were looking at the order of the work, and this is the meaning of what he said, that they were weeding at the time of weeding, and hoeing at the time of hoeing.

Then he said, "I wish I will have a part in this land," in this desire, which is aiming for the work to be proper. And the reward, which is the fruits, is not their business. It was said about this, "The concealed things are to the Lord our God." In other words, the reward is the Creator's business, and we need not look at the reward, but in any situation we are in, we are satisfied that we have been privileged with having any contact with the work. This, to him, is a great privilege. And only the revealed things are to us, which is the actions.

By this we should interpret, "and I will make you a great nation." *Gadlut* [adulthood/greatness] is precisely the action. Among those who work, greatness is only work above reason. Only there they feel its importance, but they do not take into account the lights that they receive through their work, since the lights have to do with "the concealed things are to the Lord our God." This is the work of the Creator—who does what He wants.

They did not ask of Him to give them because this was not their purpose. They have only one purpose: to bring contentment to the Creator without any reward, for all the reward is in that they have the privilege of serving the King. They do not care what service they do for the King, whether an important role or an unimportant role, since all they think of is how they can delight the King.

This means that, for example, not many people want to take upon themselves unimportant roles. They immediately jump on them because here they can delight the King, since not many people want it.

The lesson is that not many people want to go in the direction of work above reason, as everyone thinks it is regarded as a lowly work and regard such work as exile. Therefore, those who want to look at that—at their ability to delight the King—want specifically that role. This work of theirs is called, "Raising the *Shechina* [Divinity] from the dust." This work is also called "*Shechina* in Exile," and this is the only work they want. But work in order to receive lights and abundance from above is something many people want.

By that, we should interpret what our sages said (*Shabbat* 127), "Rav Yehuda said, 'Rav said, 'Welcoming guests is greater than welcoming the face of the *Shechina*, as it is written, 'And he said, 'My lord, if you have found favor with me, please do not pass.'" RASHI interprets, please do not pass, and he left Him alone and went to greet the guests.'" We can say that he learned this matter from what the Creator had told him, "And I will make you a great nation," meaning that the main thing is the act and not the lights. That is, the essence of their work is love of others, and he has no consideration of himself.

Therefore, although welcoming the *Shechina* certainly delights the body more than work on love of others, here, after the Creator had told him, "And I will make you a great nation," it means that you will have the greatness primarily in actions. Therefore, here he had a place where he could show himself, meaning that he would be certain that he does not want to look at the profits, as it is a great profit to be rewarded with welcoming the *Shechina*. Still, he chose the act, meaning he did not intend for any reward for his work, but the main thing was the work.

Here he found the place of scrutiny—for this is certainly a great thing to relinquish the reward and receive the reward of work. Normally, it is to the contrary: one labors in order to receive reward. But he did the opposite—giving the reward in order to receive labor. He learned this from what the Creator had told him, "I will make you a great nation," as was said, that the greatness is primarily the action.

And the Lord Appeared to Him at the Oaks of Mamre

Article No. 6, Tav-Shin-Mem-Hey, 1984-85

"And the Lord appeared to him at the oaks of Mamre." RASHI interprets, "He gave him an advice about the circumcision. Therefore, He appeared to him partially." It is written in *The Zohar* (VaYera, item 17), "'And the Lord appeared to him at the oaks of Mamre.' He asks, 'Why in the oaks of Mamre and not elsewhere?' And he replies, "It is because Mamre gave him an advice about his circumcision.' When the Creator said to Abraham to circumcise himself, Abraham consulted with his friends. Aner told him, 'You are already more than 90 years old; you will afflict yourself.'

"Mamre told him, 'Remember the day when the Chaldeans threw you in the furnace and the hunger that the world experienced, as it is written, 'There was famine in the land and Abraham went down to Egypt.' And those kings that your men chased, and you struck them. The Creator saved you from all of them, and no one could harm you. Arise, and do as your Lord commands.' The Creator said to Mamre, 'Mamre, you advised him about the circumcision, therefore I will appear to him only in your place.'"

There is a question, "How can it be said that if the Creator told him to circumcise himself, he consulted the friends whether or not to listen to the Creator? Can such a thing be said?"

We should interpret this in the work. When the Creator told him to circumcise himself, he consulted with his friends, meaning with his body, since the body is the one that has to perform the act. Therefore, he asked his body if it agreed, or did it think that he should not obey the Creator's commandment. This is so because man's friends are in the body, meaning they are the desires which are together, connected to the body, and he must ask them because they are the ones who have to keep the commandment that he received from the Creator. Then, when he knew their opinions, he could know what to do.

We have to know that there are three souls in the body, as it is written in *The Zohar*, VaYera (item 315), "Rabbi Yehuda said, 'There are three forms of guidance in man: the guidance of intellect and wisdom is the power of the holy soul. The guidance of lust, which lusts for every wicked passion. This is the power of lust. And a guidance that guides people and strengthens the body is called the 'soul of the body.' These three forms of guidance are called Abraham's friends. That is, he contains them. Abraham went to ask their opinion; he wanted to know the view of each and every one of his friends.'"

Aner told him: "You are more than 90 years old; you will afflict yourself." In *Gematria*, Aner is 320, implying 320 sparks that are present there, including *Malchut* which is called the "stony heart," which is the will to receive in order to receive, meaning self-love. This is why he told him: "You are already more than 90 years old; you will afflict yourself." The stony heart, which is the lusting soul, told him, "You have to always try to receive the Light and pleasure, and not afflict yourself." Therefore, he told him that he should not obey the Creator's commandment.

Mamre told him, "Remember the day when the Chaldeans threw you into the furnace." In other words, he told him, "You see that the Creator is behaving with you above reason, because it stands to reason that one who is cast into the furnace is burned, but your saving is above what seems reasonable. Therefore, you, too, cling on to His qualities, and you, too, go above reason. That is, even though it seems reasonable that Aner is right, you should go above reason."

Eshkol is the soul of the body and sustains the body. It comes from the word, Eshkol [I will consider], meaning that he needs to consider with whom to unite—with a lusting soul, which is Aner, or with Mamre, who is the soul of intellect and wisdom. This is the power of the holy soul, as was written in the words of *The Zohar*.

Mamre comes from the words, "because he *Himrah* [disobeyed] Aner." He told him to go above reason. This is the meaning of "And the Lord appeared to him at the oaks of Mamre," for precisely where one goes above reason, where there is no intellect, precisely there the Creator appears, and one is rewarded with the *Daat* [knowledge] of holiness. This is why it is called Mamre [disobeying], which is regarded as above reason, named "the soul of the intellect and wisdom," because precisely where one goes above reason the intellect and wisdom appear.

It therefore turns out that the meaning of what *The Zohar* says, that Abraham went to consult his friends, refers to Abraham's own body. The body needs to keep the commandment, therefore he asked the body for its opinion in order to know what he must do. That is, if he should coerce it or agree to what the Creator had told him. When it says that he consulted with his friends, it refers to the three souls that exist in his body, which are his friends who are always with him.

It is written in *Midrash Raba* (end of the portion *Lech Lecha*, and in the beginning of the portion *VaYera*): "Abraham said, 'Before I was circumcised, passersby would come to me. Now that I am circumcised, they do not come to me.' The Creator told him, 'Before you were circumcised, uncircumcised people came to you. Now, I and my entourage appear to you.'"

We should understand this, as he did not receive an answer to his question. He asked, "Why are passersby not coming now?" What was the answer? No answer is written as to why they are not coming. Instead, he received a different kind of answer—that previously they were uncircumcised and now the Creator comes to him. This does not correspond to the question.

We should interpret this in the work. He said that before he was circumcised the order of his work was that passersby would always come to him, meaning that he had thoughts of people who come and then, people who go. This means that before he was circumcised he had room for work, for he had thoughts of transgression. Afterwards, he had room for those who come, meaning for repentance, and then, he knew that he was truly working.

But now he does not have room for passersby, yet he longed for work. So the Creator told him, "You should not regret this, for in the end, your work is on the work of people who are circumcised. That is, your work was not yet in pure bestowal because you were still not rewarded with removing the foreskin, which is called the will to receive."

Now, however, you do not need to regret the work you had then, as in the end, it was the work of people, which is good work, but still outside, for they were uncircumcised. But now that you are circumcised there is equivalence of form, so I and my entourage may come, which was not so before.

The Life of Sarah

Article No. 7, Tav-Shin-Mem-Hey, 1984-85

It is written in *The Zohar*, in the portion, *Hayei Sarah* [The Life of Sarah] (item 17), "Another interpretation: 'A king is a woman who fears the Lord, as you say, 'A woman who fears the Lord, she shall be praised,' meaning the *Shechina* [Divinity]. '...to a cultivated field' is foreign fire, meaning the *Sitra Achra*, as you say, 'to protect you from a foreign woman,' for there is a field and there is a field. There is a field that all the blessings and sanctities are in it, as you say, 'as the scent of a field which the Lord has blessed,' meaning the *Shechina*. There is a field that every ruin, impurity, destruction, killing, and war is in it, meaning the *Sitra Achra*," thus far its words.

According to our way, the meaning is that we have two ways—either to follow the path of those who come to the Creator, whose way is the path of bestowal, or a path that leads to people, which is reception, since the creatures are called "creatures" only with respect to reception and self-love, which comes to us from the core of creation.

There was a *Tzimtzum* [restriction] and concealment on that aspect, for in this place it is not evident that the whole earth is full of His glory, as it is possible to attain that the whole earth is full of His glory only when one exits the place of reception. But prior to exiting reception, one can only believe that this is so.

To be able to feel this, we are given the advice to exit the place of reception, which the place of darkness and death. That is, the light of life cannot appear although it is present, but it is covered from man, and one who comes to that place becomes separated from the source of life.

Hence, that place is called "darkness and death," and every kind of calamity is present there. This is called the *Sitra Achra* [other side], meaning it is the opposite of *Kedusha* [holiness/sanctity]. A place of *Kedusha*, called a "place of bestowal," is a place of equivalence of form. This is why in that place appear all the delight and pleasure, as it is a place of blessing and holiness. This is called "a woman who fears the Lord." Our work is only to come to fear the Lord, called "assuming the burden of the kingdom of heaven."

By this we will understand what our sages said about the verse, "as black as a raven" (*Iruvin*, 22): "In whom do you find them? Raba said, 'In one who pretends to be as cruel as a raven to his sons and to his household.' And some say, 'In whom you exclude the orders of Torah.'" RASHI interprets that a raven is cruel to its young, as it is written, "to the young ravens which cry."

The word *Orev* [raven] comes from the word *Arev* [pleasant], as it is written, "for your voice is *Arev* [pleasant]." It is the opposite of the dove, as our sages said about the verse, "The dove came to him ... and behold, in her beak was a freshly picked olive leaf" (*Iruvin* 18). "Rabbi Yirmiah Ben Elazar said, 'Why is it is written, 'and behold, in her beak was a freshly picked olive leaf'?' The dove said to the Creator, 'Lord of the world, let my food be as bitter as an olive but be given by You, and let them not be as sweet as honey but be given by flesh and blood.'"

It is known that when a person works in order to receive, when his direction is only self-love, that work is called "sweet work." This is why the dove said, "let my food be as bitter as an olive but be given by the Creator." This refers to his sustenance, on which one sustains oneself, the sustenance on which one lives. If his work is intended for the Creator, even though it is bitter because the body does not agree with his nourishment, it will be dependent on the measure of his ability to aim to bestow, since it is against the nature in which the body was born.

The body was born with a desire to receive. It craves only that which can sustain self-love. This is regarded as provision that comes from "flesh and blood." The body enjoys this provision and finds it sweet. It is regarded as *Orev* [raven] because only provision of flesh and blood is *Arev* [pleasant] to it. But it runs from provision that is given from above—meaning from being able to work for the Creator—since it feels bitterness in acts of bestowal.

It therefore follows that the raven is called "work of self-love." Since there was a restriction on the will to receive, which is concealment and the upper light does not appear there, the work of the raven is black. This is the meaning of "as black as a raven." That is, where is the Torah found? In whom can the light of Torah shine? Only in one who has come to realize that a raven, meaning work in reception, causes only blackness, that he can receive only darkness and not light. Our sages said about this that the Torah is found only "in one who pretends to be as cruel as a raven to his sons and to his household."

It is known that father and son are cause and consequence. Therefore, we should interpret the above words to mean that one who has realized that by serving flesh and blood, which is work in self-love, though it is sweet work, it is a raven. However, by this he knows the outcome, meaning what will come out of such work—only darkness, called "blackness." At that time he knows that he has become cruel to his sons, meaning he has no mercy on the results that will come out of this.

It follows that if he knows he has become cruel by walking on the degree of raven, he changes his way and begins to walk on the path of the dove, agreeing to work for the Creator even though these nourishments are as bitter as olives. But the results, meaning the sons, will enjoy his work, since because it is in order to bestow, abundance will flow into that place. This is the opposite from the raven, who becomes cruel to his sons.

The Life of Sarah

We can interpret that this is why Israel are compared to a dove. This is the assembly of Israel, which is regarded as *Yashar-El* [straight to the Creator]. This means that everything that the people of Israel do is with the intention *Yashar-El*. Conversely, the nations of the world are regarded as a foreign God, not wanting to dedicate their work to the Creator.

By this we can interpret the verse, "He gives to the beast its bread, and to the young ravens which cry." We should understand the reason for the proximity of "beast" to "raven." It is as our sages said about the verse, "Man and beast" (*Hulin*, 5): "Rav Yehuda said, 'Rav said, 'these people are cunning and pretend to be as a beast.''" Baal HaSulam interpreted that it is faith above reason, whose basis is vessels of bestowal.

The young of the raven—when one looks and sees one's results, meaning what will come out of self-love—begin to call out to the Creator to give them vessels of bestowal and faith above reason, once they have realized what results self-love, called "raven," will bring them. We can say that this is called "The Lord is near to all who call upon Him, to all who call upon Him in truth."

Baal HaSulam interpreted what is written in the songs of Shabbat, "Extend Your mercy to one who knows You, O jealous and vengeful God." This means that since one has acknowledged that if he does not walk on the path of bestowal he will immediately suffer revenge, he is guaranteed to keep himself from failing and entering the road that leads to self-love, since he knows he will lose his life, meaning that he will fall into a place of darkness and the shadow of death. At that time he says, "Extend Your mercy to those who know You," who is a "jealous and vengeful God."

This is why they ask of the Creator to give them the mercy, for they know that otherwise they are doomed. Only through the mercy that the Creator will give them they will receive vessels of bestowal. This is regarded as a "dove." But the raven, meaning the sweetness that they demand as a condition in their work, which is called "raven," makes them cruel, meaning killing all their sons. That is, by measuring his work according to the sweetness that he feels in his work, when his only consideration is how his will to receive guides him, he loses all his future.

This is the meaning of "He gives to the beast its bread." When does he give them bread, which is called "faith"? When the young of the raven cry. That is, they understand that the results, called "sons," which are born to the raven, are destined to die, for it is separation from the life of lives. Then, when they call upon the Creator to help them, they call upon the Creator in truth. This is the meaning of what is written, "The Lord is near to all who call upon Him, to all who call upon Him in truth."

Make for Yourself a Rav and Buy Yourself a Friend (2)

Article No. 8, Tav-Shin-Mem-Hey, 1984-85

Considering what we discussed in article no. 1 (1984-5), we should elaborate a little:

We should discern between a) man and the Creator, b) a man and his friend, and c) a man and the rest of the people, who are not his friends, although there is a saying, "All of Israel are friends."

At one time, we find that the words, "make for yourself a rav [teacher/important person] and buy yourself a friend," are the path of correction, and another time, it is in the words, "And judge every person favorably" (*Avot*, Chapter 1). We should understand the difference between "make" and "buy," and the meaning of judging favorably.

We should interpret "make" as coming to exclude from reason. This is because when reason cannot understand if something is worth doing or not, how can it determine what is good for me? Or vice versa, if reason considers them as equal, who will determine for a person what he should do? Thus, the act can decide.

We should know that there are two ways before us: to work in order to bestow or to work in order to receive. There are parts in man's body that tell him, "You will succeed in life if you work in order to bestow, and this is the way you will enjoy life." This is the argument of the good inclination, as our sages said, "If you do so, you will be happy for this world and happy for the next world."

And the argument of the evil inclination is the opposite: It is better to work in order to receive. In that state, only the force called "action that is above reason" determines, not the intellect or emotion. This is why doing is called "above reason" and "above reasoning," and this is the force called "faith that is against the intellect."

"Buy" is within reason. Normally, people want to see what they want to buy, so the merchant shows them the goods and they negotiate whether or not it is worth the price that the merchant is asking. If they do not think it is worth it, they don't buy. Thus, "buy" is within reason.

Now we will explain the matter of "rav" and the matter of "friend." A friend is sometimes called "society," when people come together and wish to bond. This can happen through equivalence of form, by everyone caring in love of others. By that, they unite and become one.

Therefore, when a society is established to become a single group, we see that people who consider creating such a society usually seek people who are alike in views and attributes, whom they can see as more or less equal. Otherwise, they will not accept them into the group that they want to establish. And after that begins the work of love of friends.

But if they had no equivalence with the goals of the society from the beginning, before they even entered the society, it cannot be expected that anything will come out of that bonding. Only if there was apparent equality among them before they entered the society can it be said that they can begin to exert in the work of love of others.

Between Man and the Creator

Between man and the Creator, the order begins with "Make for yourself a rav," and afterwards, "Buy yourself a friend." In other words, first one must believe above reason that the Creator is great, as written in *The Zohar* (p 185, Item 191 in the *Sulam* Commentary), "Fear, which is the rudiment, means that man should fear his Master because He is great and ruling."

To the extent that one believes in the greatness of the Creator, who is called "Great," he has the strength to give to the "buy," meaning to buy through conceding self-love in order to achieve equivalence of form, called *Dvekut* [adhesion] with the Creator. And this is called a *Haver* [friend]: one who is in *Hibur* [bonding/connection] with the Creator.

When buying corporeal things, we must relinquish money, honor, or simply make an effort to obtain it. Similarly, when a person wishes to buy bonding with the Creator, he must relinquish self-love, because otherwise he cannot achieve equivalence of form.

When one sees that he is unfit to make concessions to buy the equivalence of form, it is not because he was born with a weak character and hence cannot overcome his self-love. Rather, the fault is in "Make for yourself a rav," meaning that he is not working on the faith, since he will be able to make concessions according to the importance of his faith in the greatness of the Creator.

Moreover, one should know that if he wishes to measure his degree of faith, he can see it in the degree of concessions he can make in self-love. Then, he'll know his degree in the work of faith above reason. This applies between man and the Creator.

Between a Man and His Friend

Between a man and his friend, we should begin with "Buy yourself a friend," and then "Make for yourself a rav." This is so because when a person looks for a friend, he should first examine him to see if he is really worth bonding with. After all, we see that a special prayer has been set up concerning a friend, which we say after the blessings in the prayer, "May it please ... Keep us away from an evil person and from a bad friend."

This means that before one takes a friend for himself, he must examine him in every possible way. At that time, he *must* use his reason. This is why it was not said, "Make yourself a friend," since "making" implies above reason. Therefore, concerning a man and his friend, he should go with his reason and examine as much as he can if his friend is okay, as we pray each day, "Keep us away from an evil person and from a bad friend."

And when he sees that it is worthwhile for him to bond with him, he must pay in order to bond with him, meaning make concessions in self-love, and in return receive the power of love of others. And then he can expect to be rewarded with love for the Creator, too.

After he has bonded with a group of people who wish to achieve the degree of love of the Creator, and he wishes to take from them the strength to work in order to bestow and be moved by their words about the necessity for obtaining the love of the Creator, he must regard each friend in the group as greater than himself.

It was written in the book, *Matan Torah* (The Giving of the Torah, p 143), that one is not impressed by the society or takes their appreciation of something unless he regards the society as greater than himself. This is the reason why each one must feel that he is the smallest of them all, since one who is great cannot receive from one who is smaller than himself, much less be impressed by his words. Rather, it is only the smaller one who is impressed through appreciating the greater one.

It follows that in the second stage, when everyone must learn from the others, there is the matter of "make for yourself a rav." This is because to be able to say that his friend is greater than himself, he must use "making," which is doing without reason, since only above reason can he say that his friend is at a higher degree than himself. Therefore, between a man and his friend, the order is to begin with keeping, "Buy yourself a friend," and then, "Make for yourself a rav."

Between a Man and Every Person

The *Mishnah* tells us, "Make for yourself a rav, buy for yourself a friend, and judge every person favorably" (*Avot*, Chapter 1).

We have explained that between a man and his friend the order is that first you go and buy yourself a friend—and we explained that buying is within reason—and then you must engage in "Make for yourself a rav." And between man and the Creator, the order is to first "Make for yourself a rav," and then "Buy yourself a friend."

We should understand the meaning of saying that concerning every person, "Judge favorably." Is this buying or making? According to the above, we should interpret the meaning of "And judge every person favorably" as "making," not "buying."

For example, assume there are many people in the congregation, and a small group among them decides that they want to unite in a society that engages in love of friends. And let us say, for instance, that there are 100 men in the congregation, and ten of them decide to unite. We should examine why those ten specific individuals decided to unite, and exclude others in the congregation. Is it because they find that those people are more virtuous than the rest of the people in the congregation, or because they are worse than the others and that they must take some action to ascend on the ladder of Torah and fear?

According to the above-mentioned, we can interpret that the reason those people agreed to unite into a single group that engages in love of friends is that each of them feels that they have one desire that can unite all their views, so as to receive the strength of love of others. There is a famous maxim by our sages, "As their faces differ, their views differ." Thus, those who agreed among them to unite into a group understood that there isn't such a great distance between them in the sense that they recognize the necessity to work in love of others. Therefore, each of them will be able to make concessions in favor of the others, and they can unite around that. But the rest of the people have no understanding of the necessity of work on love of others; hence, they cannot bond with them.

It therefore follows that when engaging in unity of love of friends, everyone examines the other, his reason and his attributes, to see if he qualifies or is worthy of joining the society that those people decided to allow inside. It is as we pray, "Keep us away from an evil person and from a bad friend," within reason.

It turns out that he prides himself over the rest of the people in the congregation. How is this permitted? After all, it is against an explicit rule that says, "Rabbi Levitas, man of Yavne, would say, 'Be very, very humble'" (*Avot*, Chapter 4).

Rabbi Yehoshua Ben Perachia says about that, "'Judge every person favorably' (*Avot*, Chapter 1) means that with regards to the rest of the people, he should go above reason, which is called "making," that is, acting and not reasoning. This is so because his reason shows him that they are not as suitable as the people to whom he associated himself, and this is what everyone says to himself. Thus, everyone prides himself over the others. The advice for that is what he says, "And judge every person favorably."

This means that with regard to the rest of the people at the congregation, he should judge them favorably and say that they truly are more important people than himself, and that it is his own fault that he cannot appreciate the greatness and importance of the public, called by our sages, "Every person." Hence, within reason, he doesn't see their greatness, and we said that between a man and his friend there should be "buying." However, he must use the "making," which is above reason. And this is called, "Judge every person favorably."

And the Children Struggled within Her

Article No. 9, Tav-Shin-Mem-Hey, 1984-85

"And the children struggled within her." According to RASHI's interpretation, "Our sages explained it as running, when she would pass by the doors of Torah of Shem and Ever, Jacob was running and wiggling to come out. When she passed by doors of idol-worship, Esau was wriggling to come out."

Baal HaSulam said that this is the order of the work. The beginning of the work is called *Ibur* [impregnation], when a person begins to work on the path of truth. When he passes by the doors of Torah, the Jacob in a person awakens and wishes to walk on the path of Torah. When he walks by the doors of idol-worship, the Esau in a person awakens to come out.

We should interpret his words. Man consists of vessels of reception by nature, called "self-love," which is the evil inclination, and also consists of a point in the heart, which is his good inclination. When he begins to work in bestowal, it is regarded as *Ibur*, form the word, *Avra* [passed]. This is why he experiences ascents and descents and is unstable. He is influenced by the environment and is unable to overcome.

For this reason, when one moves to an environment where people engage in work that is alien to us, meaning self-love, the self-love in a person awakens and comes out from concealment to disclosure, and takes control over the body. At that time one is unable to do anything except that which concerns his receiver.

When he passes through an environment where people engage in work of bestowal, the Jacob in him awakens and comes out from concealment to disclosure. At that time works of bestowal govern the body. That is, at that time, when he looks back and sees how before he has reached the state he is in he was so immersed in self-love, he cannot understand how can one be so low and derive satisfaction from such base things that are inappropriate for an adult to build his house among lowly and despicable desires and thoughts. He is insulted by these desires and thoughts where his house once was.

But later, when he passes by the doors of idol-worship, meaning when he comes to an environment that engages in self-love, the Esau in him reawakens and wriggles to come out. This continues in the worker repeatedly, day after day. One who works harder may go through these changing states each and every hour.

"And she said, 'If it is so, then why me?' And she went to inquire of the Lord." RASHI interprets "And she went to inquire" to mean Shem's seminary, to inquire the Lord so as to tell her what shall become of her. And what was the reply? The verse says, "The Lord said to her, 'Two nations are in your womb, and two peoples will be separated from your abdomen, and one people shall be stronger than the other, and the older shall serve the younger.'" RASHI interprets "one people shall be stronger than the other" to mean that they will not be of equal greatness; when one rise, the other falls. He also says, "She is laid waste; *Tzor* is filled only by the ruin of Jerusalem."

To understand the Creator's answer to her, as it is written, "The Lord said to her," we need to explain that it was said that these two forces must exist, as it is known that the creature is the vessel of reception, called Esau. But afterwards comes the second force, called Jacob, which is the desire to bestow. Each wants to rule alone, and this is the struggle between Esau and Jacob.

This is why RASHI interpreted, "When one rises the other falls; *Tzor* was filled only by the ruin of Jerusalem." That is, she was told that we must clearly know—either the will to receive governs, or the will to bestow governs. They cannot both exist together. Therefore, we must decide once and for all that it is not worthwhile to dwell in abominable and lowly thoughts and desires.

Then, when one sees that one cannot overcome one's will to receive, it is regarded as seeing that he is nothing, worthless, except that then he sees that even though he has already realized that the will to receive is the harm-doer, he still cannot overcome it. This is why specifically then he sees that he needs heaven's mercy, that without His help it is impossible to come out of the governance of the will to receive.

This is the meaning of what our sages said (*Kidushin* 30), "Man's inclination overcomes him every day. Were it not for the Creator's help, he would not overcome it." This pertains specifically to one who has begun the work and has done everything he could. At that time he does not need to believe that only the Creator can help him because now he sees that there is no tactic or ploy that he has not tried, and nothing helped him. Only the Creator helped him.

Only then can he understand that only the Creator helps. Thus, what is the difference between him and another? As He helped him, he can also help others. For this reason, there is no reason to be proud over others, since it is not his strength. But those who have not begun the holy work, which is only to bestow and not to receive, they do not see that only the Creator helped them. Instead, they say, "My strength and the power of my hand has done this riches." Naturally, they have something with which to boast over others who are not working as they do.

At that time it follows that the difference between good and bad is not so great, since his good is also built on a basis of self-love.

And although he engages in Torah and *Mitzvot* [commandments], the struggle between Jacob and Esau is still not apparent then, and naturally, he does not need help from above to save him from the will to receive, have mercy on him, and give him the *Kli* [vessel] of the desire to bestow, since he sees that by nature he cannot work in order to bestow.

This is so because he does not think that one needs to work in Torah and *Mitzvot* in order to be awarded *Dvekut* [adhesion] with the Creator, and the matter of bestowal does not interest him at all. Therefore, it cannot be said that when one rises, the other falls.

However, when one wishes to walk on the path of bestowal, this is when the matter of "struggling" begins. Afterwards, one should do what one can, and then he comes to a state where he sees the truth—that he cannot help himself. Afterwards he sees that he has no choice, and he needs heaven's mercy. Then the words of our sages, "He who comes to purify is aided," come true.

We should understand what, "And the older shall serve the younger," comes to tell us. We should interpret that it is not enough that he has been rewarded with the good inclination being the ruler, and the evil inclination being powerless to resist it, which is regarded as being able to serve the Creator only with the good inclination. Rather, one needs to achieve the degree of wholeness, as our sages said, "'And you shall love the Lord your God with all your heart,' with both your inclinations," where the evil inclination is also used to serve the Creator. This can be interpreted only in a manner that first we need to know what is the evil inclination.

We must know that the essence of the evil in us is the will to receive, from which all the bad things come to us, namely bad thoughts and desires. The will to bestow brings us all the good things, which are our good thoughts and desires. Therefore, when the good inclination governs a person, namely the desire to bestow, upper abundance pours upon us from above, meaning that by this, abundance of *Hassadim* [mercies] comes from above.

However, we must know that this is only the correction of creation. That is, to have equivalence of form, we must aim everything for the Creator, so we will have equivalence of form, called *Dvekut* [adhesion] with the Creator. However, the purpose of creation is to do good to His creations, meaning for the lower ones to receive delight and pleasure from the Creator, and not to bestow upon Him contentment, as though the Creator needs the lower ones to give Him something.

Therefore, when the creatures wish to receive something from the Creator, they must use their vessels of reception, which is the evil inclination. Otherwise, who will receive the pleasure? The receiver of the pleasure is only the craving for that thing. The craving for pleasures is called "will to receive." It follows that at that time one must use the evil inclination, but with a correction placed on it, called "in order to bestow." It follows that then he serves the Creator with the evil inclination, too.

The evil inclination is called "older" because it was born first. Likewise, when a person is born the evil inclination comes first, and the good inclination comes after thirteen years. Therefore, when a person works with the will to receive in order to bestow, it is considered that he loves the Creator with all his heart, meaning with both his inclinations. This is the meaning of the verse, "and the older shall serve the younger," meaning that the will to receive, called "older," will serve the younger, meaning serve the desire to bestow upon the Creator.

It follows that the desire to bestow will be the ruler. Sometimes the desire to bestow uses vessels of bestowal, called "vessels of Jacob," and then it is regarded as serving the Creator with the good inclination. Sometimes it uses the vessels of reception, and then it is regarded as serving the Creator also with the evil inclination. All this was said to her in Shem's seminary, as it is written, "The Lord said to her."

By this we will understand what Ben Zoma said (*Avot deRabbi Natan,*, Chapter 23), "Who is the hero of heroes? He who turns his enemy into his friend." In *Masechet Avot* (Chapte 4), "Ben Zoma says, 'Who is a hero? He who conquers his inclination.'"

We should understand the difference between referring to a "hero" when he says, "Who is a hero? He who conquers his inclination," and the interpretation he gives to "hero of heroes," when he says "He who turns his enemy into his friend."

According to the above we should interpret the words of Ben Zoma, that a hero means "and one people shall be stronger than the other," as RASHI interpreted, "When one rises, the other falls." This is called a "hero," who has surrendered the evil in him, and only the good inclination governs, meaning that he is serving the Creator only with the good inclination.

A "hero of heroes" is regarded as "and the older shall serve the younger." This means that the "older," meaning the evil in him, "will serve the younger," namely serve the desire to bestow. At that time he will be serving the Creator also with the evil inclination, and then he keeps the verse, "With all your heart," meaning with both your inclinations.

Jacob Went Out

Article No. 10, Tav-Shin-Mem-Hey, 1984-85

"Jacob went out." According to RASHI's interpretation, "It should have written only 'Jacob went to Haran.' Why does it mention his exit? It says that the exit of a righteous from a place leaves an impression. When the righteous is in town, he is its splendor, he is its brilliance, he is its majesty. When he exits it, its splendor exits, its brilliance exits, and its majesty exits." Thus far his words.

We should understand the above in the work. What is a righteous, and what is the impression that a righteous makes upon his exit?

We should interpret that the Creator is called "righteous," as it is written, "The Lord is the righteous, and I and my people are the wicked." This means that when a person is close to the Creator, meaning feels that the Creator is close to him, he feels how the Creator does him good. At that time he feels good taste in Torah and in prayer, and in all his engagements, he feels that the Creator is close to him. Whatever he does, he does it with joy and elation.

Afterwards he comes into a descent, feeling tastelessness in the study of Torah and good deeds. However, he is left with the impression that he had during the ascent, when he felt good taste in Torah and *Mitzvot* [commandments], and was in a state of joy. That remaining impression make him long to return to the previous state.

That is, after some time he awakens through the impression left in him, so as to seek advice how to return to the state he had, which was called a "state of ascent," while now he feels his lowliness—how remote he is from anything spiritual.

This brings up the question, "Why did he get this descent? Who is gaining by this?" Or, perhaps it came to him as a punishment, for now he must correct himself for his sin. However, he does not know what was the sin for which he has descended from the state of ascent he was in. Thus, he does not know what to correct. It follows that on the one hand he does not see any deficiency in himself that could have caused him a descent, so he is compelled to say that it came from the Creator. This begs the question, "What did He gain from lowering him from his degree?"

By this we can interpret what our sages said, "The exit of the righteous from the place leaves an impression." During the ascent it is regarded as the Creator being present in the place, meaning in the body. At that time He causes him the sensation of excitement from Torah and *Mitzvot*. But he could not give that importance—that the Creator is in him, as it is written, "I am the Lord, who dwells within them, in the midst of their impurity—to appreciate it, to know who is in him and pay the due respect. Thus, they could never help him receive a higher degree, since he was satisfied with the work.

Therefore, he was lowered from heaven so as to know once more how to appreciate it, since from above they raised him and brought him closer, but he did not value it. If you should ask, "Why must one value his state of ascent?" It is as I heard from Baal HaSulam, that there is no distinction of degrees in the light. Rather the matter of *Gadlut* [adulthood/greatness] and *Katnut* [infancy/smallness] depends on the attainment of the *Kelim* [vessels]. According to the vessels' attainment of the light, so is the measure of the light. This is why he said that if a person receives something from above, and has the sense to value it, to that extent the illumination grows for him and he does not need a greater light at all. Rather, by himself, by appreciating (the illumination), it grows and illuminates for him each time on a higher degree.

It follows that the whole sin for which he fell from his degree was that he did not value his condition and was content. It therefore follows that he would have had to stay in this degree forever. Therefore, the descent he had received was for his own good, so as to give him the ability to ascend in the degrees of holiness.

Therefore, "The exit of a righteous from a place leaves an impression. When the righteous is in town, he is its splendor, he is its brilliance, he is its majesty," means that all the importance was in it, but he did not know how to appreciate its value. Hence, "its splendor departs, its brilliance departs, and its majesty departs."

It follows that "The exit of a righteous from a place leaves an impression." He should know that when the righteous was in town, he did not pay attention to appreciating it: its splendor, its brilliance, and its majesty." Instead, he turned, meaning that he did not have the importance of all the above-mentioned degrees of importance.

This is called "leaves an impression," meaning that it had to be imprinted in him that the exit of the righteous from the place was because of the turning, meaning that in fact, all the degrees were there, but he did not notice it because he should have known that there are no changes in the light, but everything depends on the *Kelim* [vessels]. It follows that we can say that this departure was not due to a sin, but so as to allow him to rise in the degrees of holiness.

We should also interpret regarding the above-mentioned verse, that the exit of a righteous from the place leaves an impression refers to a person, for when the righteous is in town, it means that a person can justify Providence. Then, when he overcomes the state he is in and says, "There is no doubt that the Creator, who is good and does good, is behaving benevolently with me. However, He wants me to feel as I do." It follows that he is justifying Providence. At that time he immediately sees the importance of the work of bestowal and above reason. This is called, "When the righteous is in town, he is its splendor, he is its brilliance, he is its majesty," for then he (sees) all the virtues.

"When he departs from there" means that he has departed from justifying Providence and wants to see everything within reason. At that time he feels no taste in the work in order to bestow. And then, "its splendor departs, its brilliance departs, and its majesty departs," and he falls once more into self-love. In other words, at that time he knows nothing but work that is built on a basis of within reason.

This is regarded as the "exit of the righteous from the place leaves an impression." It means that only then, through the exit of the righteous, when he thinks, "Now that I feel good taste in the work, I no longer need to work above reason," it causes him the exit of the righteous from the place. This creates in him an impression, so he will know how to keep himself from exiting the work of above reason from here on. As I heard from Baal HaSulam, when a person says, "Now that he has support and no longer stands between heaven and earth," he must fall from his degree because then he flaws the discernment of above reason.

It therefore follows that precisely the departure of the degree he had leaves an impression on him so he will know how to be careful next time and will not blemish the faith above reason, but always justify Providence.

"And behold, a ladder was set on the earth with its top reaching to heaven; and behold, the angels of God were ascending and descending on it." The interpreters ask, "It should have said, 'descending,' and then 'ascending.'" To understand this in the work we need to explain that the ladder implies a person: A person stands below, on the earth, but the man's head reaches the heaven. That is, when a person begins to advance upward, he reaches the heaven, and he should not complain that the ladder is set on the earth.

However, first we need to understand what "on the earth," means. We see that the earth is the lowest thing. And yet, we also see that all the stately buildings and wholesome fruits come specifically from the earth.

It is known that *Eretz* [earth] implies the will to receive, which is the foundation, since all of creation and all the bad that exists in the world extend from this desire, as it is known that all the wars, murders, and so forth are rooted in the will to receive. This is called "a ladder set on the earth," for when a person first comes to the world, he is placed on the *Eretz* [earth], from the word *Ertzeh* [I will want], meaning I want to receive. This is regarded as lowliness, that there is nothing lower than that. However, "its top reaching to heaven." That is, precisely through the ladder being set on the earth, I will want, for *Ertzeh* ["earth," "I will want"] has two meanings: 1) from the word, *Ertzeh*, meaning "I want," 2) from the word *Eretz* [land], which is regarded as lowliness.

It is known that the essence of creation is only the desire to receive, that in the beginning of creation only the will to receive emerged. Afterwards there were corrections, called "equivalence of form," which means that the lower one, called "earth," achieves equivalence with heaven, which is called the "giver." We can interpret this as man, although he is in worldliness, can still correct, by his head—called "the end of the ladder"—reaching to heaven, namely being in equivalence of form with the heaven, which is regarded as receiving in order to bestow.

As in the beginning of creation, the receiver emerged first, and then was corrected in order to bestow, so is the ladder, which is akin to a person standing on the earth. The beginning is on the earth, and then he reaches heaven. This means that we should not be impressed when we see that man is full of worldliness and has no sparks of bestowal, and he cannot believe that it is realistic that his body will ever agree to work only in order to bestow. Instead, he should believe that it is the way and the order of the work that the Creator wants it specifically in this way—that a ladder will be placed on the earth with its top reaching to heaven.

By this we will understand what is written, "The angels of God were ascending and descending on it." The interprets ask, "Angels are in the sky, so it should have been written there 'descending' and then 'ascending.'" We should interpret that this refers to man, who is the emissary of the Creator, since an angel is called a "messenger." These men, who are walking on the path of the Creator, are called

"God's angels." First they ascend, by the ladder being set on the earth, and reach the top of the ladder, regarded as "its head reaching to heaven." Afterwards they descend, meaning that all the ascents and descents are because there are two ends to the ladder: 1) "set on the earth," meaning the place of lowliness, 2) but "its top reaching to heaven."

This means that to the extent that he appreciates "its top reaching to heaven," he can feel the lowliness of being "set on the earth," and regret being in worldliness. But if he has no real clue about "its top reaching to heaven," he has nothing to impress him about being in a state of descent.

It follows that to the extent that he ascends and "its top reaching to heaven," he can appreciate the measure of lowliness of the descent. This is why it is first written "ascending", and then "descending," since one can feel that he is in a state of descent only to the extent that he feels the importance of reaching to heaven.

This is the meaning of "ascending" and then "descending," since the ladder that one should climb in order to carry out his vocation—for he was sent to this world by the Creator—begins from the degree of "a ladder set on the earth with its top reaching the heaven," meaning from the beginning of lowliness, which is the will to receive, which is his nature. "Its head" means that at the end of the ladder he should reach the heaven, which is only to bestow. This is called "heaven," as earth is called "receiving," and heaven is called "giving."

We should also interpret ascending and descending as a person having to know that when he feels that he is in descent, such as when he engages in commerce or works at a factory, or simply walks on the street, and he suddenly wakes up from his sleep and finds himself in a state of descent, at that time he should know that knowing that he is in a descent has come to him from the ascent. This is called "ascending" first, and then "descending," for if there were no ascent in degree, owing to the awakening from above, he would not come to feel this. However, he is being called upon from above.

It follows according to the above that our entire work is as "a ladder set on the earth with its top reaching the heaven." That is, man's ladder has two discernments, and with those two discernments he ascends on the ladder of the living.

1) From his perspective, the "ladder set on the earth," which is the will to receive, is set on the earth, which is lowliness. Earth means receiving, *Nukva* [female], who receives from the heaven, where heaven is called "male," giver. "Its head reaching to heaven" means that bestowal, called "heaven," is to him the head, meaning important. To the extent that he regards bestowal as the head, he regards the earth, which is the will to receive, as "earth," meaning lowliness.

2) He regards the *Eretz*, meaning *Ertzeh* [I will want], as the head, and heaven is regarded as lowliness.

Also, "angels of God" means that one who makes the calculation that he has come to this world on a mission from the Creator to correct corrections is called "angels of God ascending and descending" on it. That is, they see the ladder of the living set on the earth, meaning that the will to receive is regarded as lowliness.

"Its top reaching to heaven" means that to him bestowal means heaven. That is, they are awaiting bestowal because the essence of their work is to bestow contentment upon the Creator, and this is what they regard as "head." When they receive a desire with which they can bestow, they consider it elation, and this is what they wait for. Conversely, when they are placed under the rule of the earth, they feel lowliness, and are looking only to bestow upon the Creator.

Concerning the Debate between Jacob and Laban

Article No. 11, Tav-Shin-Mem-Hey, 1984-85

We see that the debate between Jacob and Laban was different from the debate between Jacob and Esau. With Jacob and Laban, it is written, (Genesis, 31): "And Laban replied and said to Jacob: 'The daughters are my daughters, and the sons are my sons, and the flocks are my flocks, and all that you see is mine.'" With Jacob and Esau, it is written (Genesis, 33), "And Esau said, 'I have plenty, my brother; let what you have be yours.'"

We should understand why Laban claimed that everything was his and Esau said to the contrary, "Let what you have be yours."

Baal HaSulam explained it in this way: It is known that there is the grip of the *Klipot* [shells/peels], and there is the suckling of the *Klipot*. He said that a grip means that the *Klipa* [singular of *Klipot*] grips him and does not let him do anything in *Kedusha* [holiness].

For example, when a person needs to rise before dawn and go to the synagogue to engage in Torah, the *Klipa* comes and tells him, "Why are you tormenting yourself? You're tired; it's cold outside," and other such arguments of the inclination that it is not worthwhile to get up and engage in work. He replies to it, "As you say, but it is worthwhile to engage in this world in order to be rewarded with the next world." Then the evil inclination replies to him: "You think that you will have the next world in return for your labor in this world. This is possible if a person engages in Torah and *Mitzvot* [commandments] for the Creator. But I know that you are doing everything not for the Creator. Therefore, whom are you serving? Only me." With this allegory we can understand his words. This is the meaning of the grip of the *Klipa*, which does not let him engage in Torah and *Mitzvot*.

This was Laban's argument: "The daughters are my daughters ... and all that you see is mine." That is, you are working for me and not for the Creator, so you cannot hope to have the next world. Hence, why trouble yourself for nothing? With this force she grips a person and he cannot exit her influence and do anything against her will. This was Laban's argument, because he thought that with this argument he would have the strength to grip him and he would be unable to engage in Torah and *Mitzvot*.

But once he overcame Laban's argument and said, "Not true, I do engage for the Creator, but I must believe that you were sent to me with all the just arguments only to veer me off from *Kedusha*. But I want simply to serve the Creator, and you have no grip on my Torah and *Mitzvot*. This is why I overcome you and go and engage in Torah and *Mitzvot*, and you have no foothold in me at all."

At that time the *Klipa* approaches in a different way. She tells him, "Look, is there anyone else like you, who can overcome the evil inclination? Look at the lowliness of the rest of the people; they have no power to overcome, while you, thank God, are the strongest among men. It is certainly not good for you to join them." At that time all his engagement falls into the *Klipa* because she admits him into pride.

At that time, one should overcome and tell the *Klipa*: "Not true, I am no better than other people. Everything I did in Torah and

Mitzvot was not for the Creator; it was all for you, so now I am in a state that is as our sages said, 'He who learns Torah *Lo Lishma* [not for Her sake] would be better off if his placenta had been turned inside out on him.' So now I am worse than the rest of the people.'" This was Jacob's argument when he said to Esau, "'Take my gift,' and I want to begin to engage in Torah and *Mitzvot* anew, and until now it is as though I never did anything for the Creator."

But what does it say? "And Esau said, 'I have plenty, my brother; let what you have be yours.'" He did not want to receive from him until after several efforts and great exertion. Then, "And he took from him," as it is written, "He pleaded with him and he took."

It follows that here, meaning after the fact, the matter was overturned. Laban's argument, who said, "All that you see is mine," means that everything belongs to the *Klipa*. Here Jacob claims that he has sent everything to him as a gift. That is, he is saying that it is a possession of the *Klipa*. But what Jacob claimed with Laban was that the act comes first. Jacob argued that everything belongs to the *Kedusha*, and not to the *Klipa*. Now Esau is claiming it, as it is written, "let what you have be yours."

Concerning the verse, "The camp that is left will escape," RASHI interpreted that he had prepared himself for three things: for a gift, for a prayer, and for war. That is, two things belong to Esau, gift and war, and one thing belongs to the Creator, a prayer.

In the work we should interpret that all three things refer to the Creator. It is as Baal HaSulam said about the verse, "Behold, there is a place with Me, and you shall stand on the rock" (Exodus, 33), that Moses said to the Creator, "Show me Your glory." To that came the reply, "And the Lord said, 'Behold, there is a place with Me.'" He interprets *ETY* [with Me] to be an acronym for *Emuna* [faith], *Tefillah* [prayer], *Yegia* [labor].

He said that to be rewarded with the glory of the Creator one must believe in the Creator, then pray to the Creator to bring him closer to Him. Afterwards one must labor to subdue his inclination and want to annul himself for the sake of the Creator. After these three actions he is rewarded with the glory of the Creator. This is the reply that the Creator gave to Moses concerning what Moses said to the Creator, "Show me Your glory."

In the same way we should interpret what RASHI interpreted, that he prepared himself for a gift, for a prayer, and for war. "For war" means the war of the inclination; a prayer means that the Creator will bring him closer, so as to achieve his completeness—the degree he should achieve. A gift means faith, for one who believes in someone, this is regarded as giving, as it is written about Abraham, "And he believed in the Lord and He regarded it to him as righteousness" (Genesis, 15). RASHI interpreted that the Creator regarded it for Abram as a merit and righteousness for the faith that he had had in Him.

It therefore follows that all three things—gift, prayer, and war—are with the intention that with these three things he will defeat Esau. Also, all of these three things are between man and the Creator. We should not say that only prayer is between man and the Creator, but gift and war refer to Esau. Rather, he attributes everything to the Creator.

But the main thing we should know is what is the discernment of Esau we must correct. It is known that opposite *Kedusha* there is *Klipa*. In general, it is called "the *Klipa* of Esau." However, there are many degrees in the *Klipa*, and each discernment has its own name. *Kedusha*, too, has many discernments, and each discernment has its own name.

In general, *Kedusha* is called *Sefirot* and *Partzufim* [plural of *Partzuf*], and worlds. And in general, *Kedusha* means "in order to bestow," while *Tuma'a* [impurity] means "in order to receive," which is self-love.

When a person observes Torah and *Mitzvot* in order to receive this world or the next world in return, these two discernments are considered *Lo Lishma*. Only one who observes Torah and *Mitzvot* because "He is Great and ruling," meaning because of the greatness and importance of the Creator, this is called *Lishma* (see *The Book* of *Zohar*, item 190). This is called "in order to bestow and not to receive any reward for his work," and it is called "pure work."

Work in order to bestow can only be to the extent that one values the receiver of one's work. At that time one has the motivation. But if one cannot increase the importance of the one he serves, he has no energy to work. This is so because we see that in nature, the little one annuls itself before the great one as a candle before a torch. However, all the great work is to extol the receiver of the work, meaning to recognize His importance. If he has nothing with which to revere Him within reason, then our work is as Baal HaSulam said when he interpreted the verse, "Here is a place with Me," that the *Aleph* of *ETY* [with Me] implies faith above reason.

It follows that the essence of man's work is to work above reason, to appreciate the Creator. In general, all the creatures feel the *Kedusha* as *Shechina* [Divinity] in the dust. This is why it is said in all the books that every person should aim, prior to engaging in Torah and *Mitzvot*, to raise the *Shechina* from the dust. There is no point working on the little one annulling itself before the great one, for this is natural for the little one to annul before a great one. Rather, man's work is only to exert to recognize the greatness and importance of the Creator.

In fact, a person understands that he needs to work for everything he feels he needs, except for the greatness and importance of the Creator. Here, we do not understand that this is all we need.

We can interpret this with regard to the verse, "The righteous has perished and no one notices." The Creator is called "righteous," as it is written, "The Lord is the righteous." He has lost His importance and no one notices that we need to work in order to acquire His importance.

When a person feels somewhat elated, he understands that it is only worthwhile to work for spirituality. We should say that the reason is that he feels the importance of spirituality to the extent that it is worthwhile to exert for spirituality and not for corporeality because at that time corporeality loses its value for him, and spirituality is valued.

Therefore, at that time he decides that only spirituality is worth working for, and not corporeality. It turns out that all the ascents and descents do not refer to man, but to the *Kedusha*. That is, sometimes the value of *Kedusha* is high, meaning it has become more important to him, and sometimes the value of *Kedusha* is down and so unappreciated that it is not worthwhile to even think about it.

Concerning the little one annulling before the great one, we found that it is said (*Yalkut Hadash*, Chapter 1) that after the Creator promoted Abraham's reputation, since everyone saw Abraham's greatness, Pharaoh gave Sarah a girl who was his daughter, to be a servant in Abraham's house. Although a servant is a very inferior degree, since at that time servants and maids had no rights of humans at all. They were as beasts. Still, he gave away his daughter to be Sarah's maid and appeased her by saying, "My daughter, it is better for you to be a servant in Blessed Abraham's house than to be a queen in my house."

The difference between a person doing the holy work for a reward or because he wants to serve the king because of His importance and greatness is that if one is working in corporeality to obtain a corporeal reward, we see that if a person has a way to be rewarded without working so many hours, if such a thing is possible he promptly chooses this way, since man loves rest and relinquishes the pleasure of rest in order to be paid.

Therefore, if he can find a way not to have to labor, he regards this as happiness. But one who works because of the greatness of the King, and his pleasure is his great privilege of serving the king, it cannot be said that he will not work and still be paid, since his reward is the service of the king. This is a clear sign by which one sees the true purpose of his work—whether it is for a reward or because of the greatness of the Creator.

Jacob Dwelled in the Land Where His Father Had Lived

Article No. 12, Tav-Shin-Mem-Hey, 1984-85

"Jacob dwelled in the land where his father had lived, in the land of Canaan." It is written in *The Zohar* (*Vayeshev*, item 11): "Rabbi Hiya started and said, 'Many are the afflictions of the righteous, but the Lord delivers him out of them all.' But the righteous who fears his master, how much affliction he suffers in this world so as not to believe or partake with the evil inclination? And the Creator saves him from them all. This is the meaning of what is written, 'Many are the afflictions of the righteous, but the Lord delivers him out of them all.' It does not say 'many to the righteous,' but 'Many are the afflictions of the righteous.' This indicates that that one who suffers many afflictions is righteous because the Creator desires him, since the afflictions he suffers remove him from the evil inclination, and therefore the Creator desires that person and saves him from them all."

We should understand these words:

1. This implies that one who suffers many afflictions is righteous, and one who does not suffer many afflictions is not righteous.

2. Why must he suffer many afflictions if he does not want the evil inclination to partake with him?

3. Do the words, "And for this reason the Creator desires that person and saves him from all of them," mean that the Creator does not save other people, God forbid? Can this be?

4. Even more perplexing, on the one hand it says that the troubles he suffers remove him from the evil inclination. On the other hand it says that the Creator saves him from all of them, meaning saves him from many afflictions. Thus, he will bring himself close to the evil inclination once again, since the reason that removed him from the evil inclination has been cancelled.

We should interpret his words. Here is a verse that concerns this (*Kidushin* 30b): "Rabbi Shimon Ben Levi said, 'Man's inclination overpowers him each day and seeks to put him to death, as it was said, 'The wicked watches for the righteous and seeks to put him to death.' Were it not for the Creator's help, he would not have overcome it, as it was said, 'God will not leave him in his hand.'"

In *Masechet Sukkah* (p 52), there is another similar verse: "The evil inclination has seven names. Solomon called it "enemy," as it is said (Proverbs, 25), "If your enemy is hungry feed him bread; if he is thirsty give him water to drink, for you are burning coals on his head and the Lord will pay you." Do not pronounce it as *Yashlim* [pay], but as *Yashlimenu* [complement] you.

According to RASHI, "If your inclination is hungry and craves transgression, feed it bread and trouble it with the war of Torah, as it is written (Proverbs, 9): 'Go, eat of my bread.' 'Give him the water of Torah to drink,' as it is written about it (Isaiah, 25), "All who are thirsty, go to the water.' 'Will complement you' means that your inclination will be completely with you, love you, and will not incite you to sin and be lost from the world."

To understand all the above we must know that the essence of the evil inclination—which is called the "essence of creation," which the Creator created existence from absence—is the will to receive. It is known (see in the introductions) that this is something new that did not exist before He has created it. Man's work is only to work the opposite of his nature, meaning that he will want only to bestow. But since it is against his nature—since by nature he needs to see only to the needs of self-love—he has no desire to work for others.

Although we see that sometimes people do work for others, this is possible only if they see that they will be rewarded for their work, namely that the will to receive will be satisfied by it. That is, the reward should satisfy the self-love; otherwise one cannot exit the vessels of reception by nature.

However, being able to perform acts in order to bestow and not receive any reward is unnatural. And although we see that there are people who kill themselves for their country and do not want anything in return, it is because their country is very important to them, and that importance is also natural, as our sages said, "The favor of the place is with its dwellers."

However, there is certainly a difference in the measure of favor, for not everyone favors the same. This is why there are many who volunteer to the army because of the importance of their homeland, but think that this is not so dangerous that their lives are at stake, "because I see that many people return unharmed from the war."

And if there is sometimes a danger of certain death, they are not willing to go to certain death, except for a chosen few for whom the homeland is important. But here, too, the power of reward is involved, because he thinks that after his death everyone will know that he was dedicated to the public and that he was above everyone else because he cared for the public's well-being.

But in the work of the Creator, when a person is walking on the path of truth, he must work in humbleness so that the external ones will have no grip. That is, in serving the Creator he will not have the grip of working for the outer ones, meaning that people outside of him will know about his work, so he is working devotedly so that people outside will say that he was above the common folk. This assists him in his ability to work without return, so that people outside will say that he was working only for the Creator. The Creator gave this power to the creatures because "from *Lo Lishma* [not for Her sake] he will come to *Lishma* [for Her sake]," and he will not have any assistance from outside. He can achieve that if he first has *Lo Lishma*, but he should not remain in *Lo Lishma*, God forbid.

This is the meaning of what our sages said (*Sukkah*, 45), "Anyone who joins working for the Creator with something else is uprooted from the world, as it is said, 'Only for the Lord.'" The meaning of "only for the Lord" is that there will be no mingling of self-love at all, but only for the Creator. This is the meaning of the word, "only."

Still, there is a fundamental issue to understand here. We should discern if a person is devoted in order to acquire something. Even if he receives the reward for the public, this is certainly a great thing because if the reward he is receiving is not for self-love but for love of others, because he loves the others and puts himself to death for them, to benefit the public, but there is no doubt that if he could achieve the same thing not by giving up his life, he would have chosen that other way. This is so because to him the key is to receive a reward for the public, and not the work. The contentment he can bring his homeland is what makes him work, therefore he does not regard the means by which to obtain that thing for the homeland. If he sees that specifically by giving up his life for the country (he can bring contentment to the country), he is willing to do this, too.

Conversely, with love of the Creator, we say that a person should work only for the Creator, meaning without any reward. This means that he is ready for complete devotion without any reward, without any return being born out of his devotion. Rather, this is the core—his purpose, that he wants to annul his self before the Creator, meaning (cancel) his will to receive, which is the existence of the Creator. This is what he wants to annul before the Creator. It follows that this is his goal, meaning his goal is to give his soul to the Creator.

This is not so in corporeality with respect to love of others. Although this is a great degree, and not all the people can work for the general public, still, devotion is only a means and not a goal, and he would be happier if he could save the public without giving up his life.

Let us ask all those who volunteer to go to war for their country. If someone could advise them how to save their country without losing their lives, they would certainly be happy. But when there is no choice, they are willing to go, for the public, so that the public will receive the reward, while they are giving up everything. Although this is a great force, it has nothing to do with devotion to the Creator, where devotion is the goal, and what comes out as a result is not their purpose, as this was not their intention. Therefore, devotion in spirituality is worthless to corporeal people, since for them devotion is a means and not the goal, while in spirituality it is the opposite: devotion is the goal.

By this we will understand the meaning of receiving in order to bestow. Man's purpose is only to bestow upon the Creator, for this is the meaning of equivalence of form, "As He is merciful, so you are merciful." When he achieves the degree of devotion to the Creator because he wants to annul himself in order to delight the Creator, he sees that the purpose of the Creator, as it was in the thought of creation, is to do good to His creations. At that time he wants to receive the delight and pleasure that was in the purpose of creation—to delight His creatures.

This is called "receiving in order to bestow." Otherwise, he might want to receive the delight and pleasure and this is why he gives everything, so he can receive. This is regarded as "bestowing in order to receive." But if his purpose is to bestow, and he has no desire to receive for his own benefit at all, but only for the Creator, then he can become a receiver in order to bestow.

Concerning devotion, I heard from Baal HaSulam that one should depict devotion as we find with Rabbi Akiva (*Berachot* 61b): He said to his disciples, "My whole life I have regretted the verse, 'With all your soul, even if He takes your soul.' I said, 'When will I be able to keep it?' And now that this has come to me, will I not keep it?"

Certainly with such a desire to bestow, when a person says that he wants to receive delight and pleasure because this is the purpose of creation, he certainly means (only) to receive in order to bestow upon the Creator.

By this we will understand the four above questions:

Question no. 1) It seems from the words of *The Zohar* that only one who suffers many afflictions is righteous, but one who does not suffer afflictions cannot be righteous. Can this be? The thing is that afflictions refer to the evil inclination. That is, specifically one who feels that the evil inclination is causing him many afflictions by not letting him approach the Creator is called "righteous." But if a person does not feel that it is removing him from the Creator and does not feel that by this it is causing him afflictions, is not considered righteous because he has not achieved recognition of evil, meaning that it hurts him.

Question no. 2) Why must he suffer many afflictions if he wants the evil inclination not to take part in him? This means that there is no other choice but to suffer afflictions. According to the above-said, this is very simple: Afflictions refer to the evil inclination. If he does not feel that the evil inclination is causing him many afflictions, he does regard it as evil inclination that he does not want to have a part in him. Rather, he regards it as a good inclination, which brings him only good, so why should it not have a part in him? But if he sees the afflictions that the evil inclination causes him then he does not partake with it.

Question no. 3) *The Zohar* says that the Creator desires a person who suffers many afflictions. This means that the Creator does not desire one who does not suffer afflictions. Can this be? The answer is that if a person feels that the evil inclination is causing him many afflictions, and the person cries out to the Creator to help him, the Creator desires that person. But when a person does not feel that the evil inclination is afflicting him, the Creator does not want him because he has no *Kli* [vessel], meaning desire that the Creator will save him.

Question no. 4) If the Creator saves him from afflictions, he will reconnect with the evil inclination.

Answer: Salvation that comes from the Creator is a different matter than salvation that occurs in corporeality. The evil that takes place at the time of the *Achoraim* [posterior], which is the time of concealment of the face, when he sees that he is under concealment, for it is known that the little one is annulled before the great one, and certainly here, in serving the Creator, a person must annul before the Creator as a candle before a torch. Yet, he sees that his body does not annul, and it is hard for him to subdue it and take upon himself faith above reason. At that time he sees that the body is afflicting him by not wanting to assume the burden of the kingdom of heaven, by which he is removed from all the spirituality.

It follows that one must believe that the Creator has created the world with benevolence, and the evil in his body removes him from all the good. That is, when he comes to learn Torah, he finds it utterly tasteless. And also, when he comes to perform some *Mitzva* [good deed/correction], he finds it utterly tasteless because the evil inclination in his body has the power not to let him believe in the Creator above reason by taking out every flavor. Whenever he begins to approach something spiritual, he feels that everything is dry without any moisture of life.

When the person began his work, he was told—and he believed what he was told—that the Torah is a Torah of life, as it is written, "For they are your life and the length of your days," and as it is written (Psalms 19), "More desirable than gold, than much fine gold, and sweeter than honey and the honeycomb."

But when one consider this and sees that the evil inclination is to blame for everything, and strongly feels the bad that it is causing him, then he feels on himself what is written (Psalms 34) "Many are the afflictions of the righteous." That is, that verse was said about him.

At that time he looks at what the verse says afterwards, "but the Lord delivers him out of them all." At that time he begins to cry out to the Creator to help him because he has already done everything that he could think of doing, but nothing helped, and he thinks that "Everything that you find within your power to do, that do," was said about him. At that time comes the time of salvation—the salvation of the Creator delivering him from the evil inclination— to the extent that from this day forth the evil inclination will surrender before him and will not be able to incite him into any transgression.

It is written in the "Introduction to the Study of the Ten Sefirot" (item 54): "When the Creator sees that one has completed one's measure of exertion and finished everything he had to do in strengthening his choice in faith in the Creator, the Creator helps him. Then, one attains open Providence, meaning the revelation of the face. Then, he is rewarded with complete repentance, meaning he cleaves to the Creator once more with all his heart, soul, and might, as though naturally drawn by the attainment of the open Providence."

It is also written there (item 56): "What is repentance like? When He who knows the mysteries will testify that he will not turn back to folly." The words, 'What is repentance like?' mean "When can one be certain that he has been rewarded with complete repentance?" For this he was given a clear sign: "When He who knows the mysteries will testify that he will not turn back to folly." This means that he has been rewarded with disclosure of the face, and then His salvation itself testifies that he will not turn back to folly.

This answers the fourth question, that if the Creator saves him from the evil inclination He will not afflict him. The holy *Zohar* says that the afflictions that the righteous suffers are in order not to partake with it. It follows that if the Creator saves him and he sees that He will not afflict him, then he will reconnect with the evil inclination, since the only reason that the evil inclination is afflicting him is in order not to partake with it. But since the reason has been cancelled, the situation returns as before.

However, according to what we explained, the salvation of the Creator is the revelation of the face, until the Creator testifies that he will not sin. The afflictions that the righteous suffers are for him to be able to ask of the Creator, as is said above, "If there is no *Achoraim* [posterior/back], there is no disclosure of the *Panim* [face/anterior]." It follows that when there is disclosure of the face of the Creator, everything is as it should be.

Mighty Rock of My Salvation

Article No. 13, Tav-Shin-Mem-Hey, 1984-85

In the Hanukah song we say, "Mighty rock of my salvation, to praise You is a delight; Restore my House of Prayer, and there we will bring a thanksgiving offering." The song begins with words of praise, "To praise You is a delight," and then begins with words of prayer, "Restore my House of Prayer."

Afterwards, it returns to words of thanksgiving and praise, "And there we will bring a thanksgiving offering."

Thus, there are three things here, similar to the order of the prayer:

1. The first three of the Eighteen [a sequence of prayers] are praise and thanksgiving.

2. The middle three are pleas.

3. The last three are praise and thanksgiving once more.

Thus, we begin with the present, as it says, "To praise You is a delight," meaning we thank and praise You for the good we have received from You. It is as our sages said, "One should always praise the Creator and then pray" (*Berachot* [Blessings], 32).

The reason is that one who believes that the Creator is merciful and gracious, and that He desires to do good to the creations, has room for prayer. This is why we must first establish the praise of the Creator, meaning a person himself should establish praise of the Creator. This does not mean that the Creator should see that the person is praising Him, since the Creator doesn't need people. Rather, the person himself should see the praise of the Creator, and then he can ask Him to help him, since His conduct is to do good to His creations.

Thus, after he said, "To praise You is a delight" comes the prayer, and we say, "Restore my House of Prayer."

What is "My House of Prayer"? It means, as it is written, "Even them will I bring to My holy mountain, and make them joyful in My house of prayer." "My holy mountain." *Har* [mountain] comes from the word *Hirhurim* [thoughts/contemplations], meaning that He will bring them thoughts of *Kedusha* [holiness]—that all their thoughts will be only of *Kedusha*.

"And make them joyful in My house of prayer" is man's heart, so there will be a place for the presence of the *Shechina* [Divinity] there. The *Shechina* is called "prayer," as it is known that *Malchut* is called "prayer," as it is written, "But I am all prayer."

After "Restore my House of Prayer" comes "And there we will bring a thanksgiving offering." It follows that first there is praise, then there is prayer, and then praise once more, like the order of the prayer, which concludes with praise and thanksgiving.

But what can one do if he wants to begin with praise but his heart is closed, and he feels that he is full of faults and cannot open his mouth and sing and praise? The advice is to go above reason and say that everything is "covered *Hassadim* [mercies]." In other words, he should say that everything is *Hesed* [grace/mercy], but it is covered from him because he is not yet qualified to see the delight and pleasure that the Creator has prepared for His creations.

And after he establishes the praise of the Creator—meaning that he believes above reason that everything is good and gracious—he should pray that the Creator will mend his heart to become "My House of Prayer," meaning that the mercies of the Creator will appear there. This is called "revealed *Hassadim*."

And then, "There we will bring a thanksgiving offering," meaning that he will give thanks for having been privileged with offering the vessels of reception. This is called, "There we will bring a thanksgiving offering" for having been rewarded with sacrificing his will to receive. In return for it came the will to bestow, which is called "the place of the Temple."

But the important thing is for a person to first have a desire to sacrifice the will to receive. And since the will to receive is the very essence of the Creator, the creature loves it and it is very difficult for him to understand that it must be annulled or else it is impossible to be rewarded with anything spiritual.

In corporeality, we see that a person has a desire and deficiency that concerns him, which comes from inside his body, and there is a desire that one acquires from the outside, not from himself. In other words, if there were no people outside who begot this desire in him, he would never feel that he needed it, but people on the outside begat this desire in him.

For example, a person alone will still want to eat, drink, sleep, and so on, even when there are no other people around him. However, if there are people around him, there is the matter of shame, where others compel him. Then he must eat and drink what people around him compel him to.

This is apparent primarily in clothing. At home, a person wears what is comfortable for him. But when he is among people, he must dress according to the way others see it. He has no choice, since shame compels him to follow their fancies.

It is the same in spirituality. A person has a desire within him, which comes from himself. In other words, even when he is alone and there are no people around him to affect him, or from whom to absorb some desire, he receives an awakening and craves to be a servant of the Creator. But his own desire is probably not big enough for him not to need to enhance it so he can work with it to obtain the spiritual goal. Therefore, there is a way—just like in corporeality—to enhance that desire through people on the outside who will compel him to follow their views and their spirit.

This is done by bonding with people whom he sees that also have a need for spirituality. And the desire that those people on the outside have begets a desire in him, and thus he receives a great desire for spirituality. In other words, in addition to the desire that he has from within, he receives a desire for spirituality that they beget in him, and then he acquires a great desire with which he can reach the goal.

Hence, the issue of love of friends is where each person in the group, besides having a desire of his own, acquires desire from the friends. This is a great asset that can be obtained only through love of friends. However, one should take great care not to be among friends who have no desire to examine themselves, the basis of their work—whether it is to bestow or to receive—and to see if they are doing things in order to reach the path of truth, which is the way of nothing but bestowal.

Only in such a group is it possible to instill the friends with a desire to bestow, meaning that each will absorb a lack from the friends, which he himself lacks the power to bestow, and wherever he walks, he is eagerly searching for a place where perhaps someone will be able to give him the power to bestow.

Hence, when he comes into a group where everyone is thirsty for the power to bestow, everyone receives this strength from everyone else. This is considered receiving strength from the outside in addition to the small power that he has within him.

However, opposite that, there is a force from the outside from which it is forbidden to receive any assistance, even though this force, which he can receive from the outside, will give him fuel for the work. One should be very careful not to receive it. And one needs take great care because the body tends to receive strength for the work specifically from people on the outside. It comes to a person when he hears that it is said about him, for instance, that he is a virtuous person, or a wise disciple, or a man with fear of heaven, or when it is said about him that he is a man who seeks the truth. When a person hears these things, that his work is appreciated, these words give him strength for the work because he is receiving honor for his work.

And then he doesn't need faith above reason and the power of bestowal, meaning that the Creator will help him and this will be his motivation. Instead, he receives fuel from the externals. In other words, the external ones compel him to engage in Torah and *Mitzvot* [commandments].

This is the issue with being humble—one of its reasons is so that there will be no nursing to the external ones. This is why one must walk humbly, as it is written, "And to walk humbly with the Lord your God."

The external ones are people who are outside of him. They nurse on his work by afterwards—meaning after he hears that he is respected—he learns to work for the outer ones and not for the Creator. This is so because he no longer needs the Creator to bring him closer to His work, since now he is the operator because people on the outside give him the fuel to study and work for them. In other words, they are the ones who are compelling him to work, and it is not the Creator who compels him to work for Him. Rather, others are compelling him to work for them—so they will respect him, etc.

It follows that this is similar to working for a foreign god. That is, they order him to work for the reward of respect and the like, which they will give him in return for engaging in Torah and *Mitzvot*. This means that if they do not know of his work, and he did not see that there is someone who sees and engages in the Torah, there is no one to obligate him to work. This is called "the grip of the external ones," and this is why a person must work in a concealed manner.

However, working in a concealed manner is not enough. Although it is true that now only the Creator compels him to do the holy work, there must be one more thing: a person must work not in order to receive reward. This is a completely different matter because it is against our nature. We are created with a nature called "will to receive." But now we must work only in the work of bestowal and receive nothing for ourselves.

For that, we must seek out a society where each one believes that we must work to bestow. Since this is a small force within a person, he must look for people who are seeking such powers, too. Then, united, each of them can receive strength from the others, and this is all that one needs. And the Creator will send him help from above that we may be able to walk on the path of bestowal.

I Am the First and I Am the Last

Article No. 14, Tav-Shin-Mem-Hey, 1984-85

The verse says, "I am the first and I am the last, and there is no God besides Me." It is known that the order of the work on the way to achieve the goal of *Dvekut* [adhesion] with the Creator is to work in order to bestow. However, according to what man has received, the order of the work with regard to education is actually *Lo Lishma* [not for Her sake], as Maimonides said (*Hilchot Teshuva*, Chapter 10), "The sages said, 'One should always engage in Torah, even in *Lo Lishma*, since from *Lo Lishma* he comes to *Lishma* [for Her sake].' Therefore, when teaching little ones, women, and uneducated people, they are taught to work only out of fear and to be rewarded. Until they gain knowledge and acquire much wisdom, they are taught this secret bit by bit, and they are accustomed to this matter peacefully until they attain Him, know Him, and serve Him with love."

Therefore, when a person wants to walk on the way to the goal of *Dvekut* with the Creator, which means to aim that everything will be in order to bestow, he must first have a deficiency, meaning dissatisfaction with the work in *Lo Lishma*.

At that time he begins to search for another order in the work, since the engagement in Torah and *Mitzvot* [commandments] he was used to was on the basis of the will to receive, called *Lo Lishma*. But now that he needs to replace his entire basis on which he built his entire life's order, it depends on the extent to which he sees that the state of *Lo Lishma* is the wrong way, does not let him rest, and he will not be at peace until he comes out of that state into a state of *Lishma*.

However, who is making him feel, while he is in the state of *Lo Lishma*, that this is still not the right way and he is still far from *Dvekut* with the Creator? When he looks at the rest of the people, they go by this path, so why does he need to be different? Another difficulty is that when he looks at the rest of the people he sees people who are more talented and more capable in the work than him. But they settle for the order of the work they had received when they were little, when the instructors taught them to work only in *Lo Lishma*, as in the above words of Maimonides. And then he sees about himself that although "a sorrow shared is a sorrow halved," he cannot accept the state of *Lo Lishma*. At that time comes the question: "If I am really less talented and less capable in the work, where did I get this restlessness in the state of *Lo Lishma*?"

To this comes the answer: "I am the first." That is, the Creator has given him this deficiency so he will not be able to continue on this path. One should not think that he has obtained this by his own wisdom. Rather, the Creator says, "I am the first," meaning "I have given you the first push, so you will begin to walk on the path of truth. By giving you a deficiency of feeling that with the respect to the truth, you are deficient."

Then begins the work that he begins to wait for a state where he repels self-love, and all his works are only in order to bestow. At that time he must dedicate to it all the thoughts and resources at his disposal, as in "Everything that you find within your power to do, that do."

Afterwards, when he is rewarded with *Dvekut* with the Creator, he thinks that it is through his labor in Torah and *Mitzvot*, and by overcoming his self-love. He thinks that he has been rewarded with it only through his work, that he was very persistent, and only he had the strength to make the most of his opportunities, which gave him this riches and he was rewarded what he was rewarded.

The verse says about that: "And I am the last. That is, as I was the first, giving you the deficiency, I am also the last, meaning I have given you the filling of the deficiency." The deficiency is called the *Kli* [vessel], and the filling is called "the light." Since there is no light without a *Kli*, the *Kli* is made first, and then the abundance is poured into the *Kli*. This is why the Creator first gives the *Kli*, which is called "I am the first," and then He gave the abundance, called "I am the last."

By this will understand the difference between work that a person does in corporeal work, in some factory, and a worker doing spiritual work. Ordinarily, a worker who is not working does not receive reward. However, he is also not punished if he is not working.

Conversely, in spiritual work, one who is not working, who is not keeping Torah and *Mitzvot*, is punished, as our sages said (*Avot*, Chapter 5), "The world was created with ten utterances. What does that teach us? It could have been created with one utterance. However, to avenge the wicked, who are destroying the world, it was created with ten utterances, and to give a good reward to the righteous, who are sustaining the world, it was created in ten utterances."

This has already been explained in previous articles, but the gist of the matter is that "to avenge the wicked" means that there will be the suffering that the wicked suffer in their lives. This means that when he looks at his own wicked, meaning at his own will to receive, if he sees that everything he does for the will to receive does not satisfy him in this life, and to the extent that he sees and feels the unpleasantness of this life, by these he receives a *Kli* and deficiency for spirituality. This is so because the unpleasantness that one feels in one's life pushes him to search for a place where he can derive life.

It therefore follows that the punishment that he suffers for taking the wrong path is not regarded as vengeance for not walking on the path of the Creator, regarded as having to work for the Creator. On the contrary, it is assistance—he is being pushed toward happiness and bounty.

It therefore follows that the punishment he sees that the wicked are suffering, he needs to feel the suffering that the wicked suffer. This is the meaning of what is written (Psalms, 94), "Happy is the man whom You chasten, Lord." This means that the suffering he feels when he is marching the wrong path is regarded as the Creator giving him a *Kli*, which is "I am the first."

However, He does not let anyone feel suffering when walking on the path of *Lo Lishma*. Rather, only "He whom the Lord loves He admonishes." This is regarded as feeling the taste of the wicked, who are immersed in self-love, and this pushes him from the path of falsehood to the path of truth.

It follows that when a worker is not working in corporeality, he is not paid, but he is not punished for not wanting to work. But this is not so in spirituality: If he is idle in the work, he is punished, as our sages said, "to avenge the wicked," where it is not regarded as being punished, but as being elevated to walk on the right path. It is not considered a punishment, but as a correction.

This means that there are two manners of correction: 1) the path of Torah, 2) the path of suffering. However, this is not regarded as a punishment, but as a correction, and the correction comes to him by suffering.

Afterwards, when he has a *Kli*, called "vessel of bestowal," where he previously had only a desire for self-reception, now he receives a desire, meaning he expects the Creator to give him the *Kli* called "desire to bestow." When he has the *Kli* of the desire to bestow, he is rewarded with the bounty and happiness that were in the thought of creation, which is called "to do good to His creations." This is the meaning of "I am the last," referring to the filling, that what he lacked before, now He fills all his deficiencies.

However, this is so only with respect to private Providence. That is, for himself, a person should say that everything depends on him, for only according to his overcoming in the work he will be able to be rewarded with the goal for which he was created. This is regarded as a person having to believe in reward in punishment. At that same time, once he has done his work, he must say that everything is under private Providence, as was said in the interpretation to "I am the first and I am the last."

Regarding this matter, that one should reach the goal, he should know that the most important thing is to come to aim all his thoughts and actions to be *Lishma*, as it is written, "Everything that is called by My name, I have created, made, and fashioned for My glory." We should understand what is written about "Everything that is called by My name, I have created." Did the Creator Himself not create for His glory what is not called "by My name"? We should also understand the meaning of "called by My name."

We should interpret "called by My name," that he relates to Him, as it is written, "Israel, Your people," or "His people, Israel," meaning that he relates to the Creator. At that time he must be in equivalence of form with the Creator, as it is written, "As He is merciful, so you are merciful," meaning that his intention is only to bestow upon the Creator, that all his actions are only for His glory, and he has no concern for his own benefit.

By that we should interpret, "Everything that is called by My name." That is, who relates to Me? These are people who say that the whole of creation is only for His glory, and not for one's own benefit. Then one can relate oneself to Me, and is regarded in the collective called "His people, Israel," or "Israel." At that time one can feel what is written, "Who chooses His people, Israel, with love."

It follows that one should acquire a deficiency—to feel that he needs the Creator's help to come to "all his actions are for the Creator." Then begins the order of the work *Lishma*, and then he is rewarded with things, as in the words of Rabbi Meir.

And Hezekiah Turned His Face to the Wall

Article No. 15, Tav-Shin-Mem-Hey, 1984-85

It is written in *The Zohar* (*Vayechi*, item 386): "Rabbi Yehuda started and said, 'And Hezekiah turned his face to the wall and prayed to the Lord.'" These are his words there in the *Sulam* [Ladder commentary]: "One should pray only next to a wall and nothing should part between him and the wall, as it is written, 'And Hezekiah turned his face to the wall.'"

We should understand what is the "wall" next to which we should pray. Also, what is the "partition" where he says that nothing should part. *The Zohar* interprets there and in the *Sulam* (item 392): "A wall is the Lord of all the land, and it is the *Shechina* [Divinity]."

Accordingly, we should interpret what he says, that we must pray next to a wall, meaning close to the *Shechina*. However, it is still not known what is the measure of proximity to the wall. He interprets that nothing should part between him and the wall. This is why we should interpret the issue of parting, such as with the *Tevillah* [ritual bathing], with *Netillat Yadaim* [ritual washing of the hands], and with the four species, where the palm branch, myrtle, and willow are tied with a palm branch leaf because it is of the same kind.

It follows that parting between him and that wall is—as the *Shechina* bestows upon the lower ones, so man should remove the force of reception—that his desire will be only to bestow upon the Creator. At that time it is called nearing and proximity to the wall.

However, first we must know, and it is our duty to try to understand as much as we can with our little minds what we need to pray for, meaning which deficiency we should regard and say that this is the main thing we need, and that if we can satisfy that deficiency we will not need anything else.

It is known that the essence of the prayer is for the *Shechina* being in exile. However, this requires explanation, too. It is written in many places that the main thing we need to pray for is to raise the *Shechina* from the dust. There are many interpretations to it, and the little we can understand is the kingdom of heaven. This is what one takes upon himself—that he has nothing in the world that is his purpose, except to serve the king not in order to receive reward. By that he will be rewarded with *Dvekut* with the Creator, and will be able to delight the king, as in "As He is merciful, so you are merciful." At that time he will be fit to keep the thought of creation to do good to His creations.

However, the discernment called "bestowing contentment upon the Creator" does not have a place in the creatures for they are born with a desire to receive. For this reason, the are utterly incapable of comprehending the concept of bestowal. This is similar to an object lying in the dust and no one notices that it should be picked up. This is called "*Shechina* in the dust." It is as it is written (The *Selichot* [forgiveness] of the thirteen qualities): "I will remember God and long for Him when I see every city built on its foundations, and the city of God lowered to the very bottom."

A "city" means as it is written (Ecclesiastes, 9), "a small city with few men in it." Eben Ezra interprets as follows, "The ancient interpreters said that it is an allegory: "A small city" is man's body, and "few men in it" means those with power to beget, the servants of the soul.

Therefore, here, too, we should interpret the "city of God" to mean that when the body wants God to dwell in it, in this body, all the organs resist it. The work of bestowal, meaning to work for the Creator, is work in utter lowliness, and there is a taste of dust in this work. It is written in the curse of the serpent (Genesis, 3), "You are more cursed than all beast, and more than every animal of the field; you will walk on your belly, and you will eat dust all the days of your life." This means that everything he will eat will taste like dust.

It is likewise here: when a person begins to work for the Creator and does not see that self-love will draw any benefit from it, this work is degraded, and everything he does in it tastes like dust. This is called "The city of God is lowered to the very bottom." That is, if there is a partition between him and the *Shechina*, meaning if his work is built on a basis of self-love, he thinks that he is at the height of perfection.

But when he wishes to remove the partition between him and the wall, and wants to work on the basis of bestowal, he feels that he is at the very bottom, since he does not see that in this work he will have anything to receive for his will to receive. At that time all the organs resist this work.

Now we will understand for what we need to pray. The prayer should be primarily for the *Shechina* being in the dust. This means that work to bestow upon the Creator is despicable and contemptible, and we ask of the Creator to open our eyes and remove the darkness that is floating before our eyes.

We ask about this, as it is written (Psalms 113), "He raises the poor from the dust, and lifts the destitute from the trash." It is known that the holy *Shechina* is called poor and meager, as it is written in *The Zohar*, "and it is placed in the dust." "He lifts the poor from the trash" refers to those who want to cling to her but feel that they are lowly, and they do not see how they can emerge from this mud. At that time they ask of the Creator to lift them.

Where the body agrees with the work, where it is on the basis of the will to receive, since they have no clue about bestowal, their work is with pride, meaning they take pride in being servants of the Creator while others are in utter lowliness, and they always see others' faults.

But those who walk on the path of truth, who want to achieve bestowal, are lowly because they see that "Were it not for the Creator's help, he would not have overcome it." Thus, they find no special merit in themselves over others. These people are called "lowly" because they want to connect to bestowal, which is lowliness, and this is another reason why they are called "lowly."

At that time they can say what is written, "The Lord is high, great, and terrible. He lowers the proud to the ground, and raises the lowly to the heavens," for at that time they say that what was lowly before is now high and sublime, great and terrible. This is because now they feel that what was previously work in self-love, which is pride, when they felt proud about this work, has now become lowliness, since they are ashamed to work for self-love.

But who gave them the strength to feel this? It was the Creator who gave them. This is why at that time a person says, "Lowers the proud to the ground," while the work of bestowal, which was previously lowly, now the work of bestowal has become to him of the highest merit. And who did this for him? Only the Creator. At that time a person says, "And raises the lowly to the heaven."

Shechina in exile means that one should feel that she is in exile. That is, since a person is called a "small world," for he consists of seventy nations, and the Israel in him is in exile, meaning the people of Israel (in him) is enslaved to the nations of the world in him and cannot do anything for their own good, but only for the nations of the world, and the people of Israel are called *Yashar-El* [straight to the Creator], wanting to bestow upon the Creator, while they want to work in order to receive, which is called the "nations of the world."

Accordingly, we should interpret "Israel that have exiled" to mean that if Israel are in exile and cannot do anything *Yashar-El*, the *Shechina* is with them. She, too, is in exile, as though she cannot rule over them because they seemingly rule over her. This is the meaning of what King David said (Psalms, 115), "Not to us, O Lord, not to us, but to Your name give glory, for Your mercy, for Your truth. Why should the nations say, 'Where is their God?' and our God is in the heavens; He does whatever He pleases."

According to the above, we should interpret that we ask of the Creator to help us come out of exile. This is the meaning of saying, "Not to us," meaning to our will to receive. That is, we want our thoughts and desires and deeds not to be for our will to receive, which is regarded as the importance being only for the nations of the world.

Rather, "To Your name give glory," so that the *Shechina* will not be in exile and regarded as dust, but that the glory of heaven will be revealed, which is called "May His great name grow and be sanctified." This is the meaning of "Why should the nations say," meaning the nations of the world in a person, which are called "nations." What do they say? "Where is their God?" meaning they oppose the faith of Israel, for their work is in mind and heart, and all of their (the nations) work is within reason.

But "our God is in the heavens," meaning specifically above reason, called "heaven," which is above our intellect. And why did (the Creator) make our work be above reason? We do not say that He could not do otherwise. Rather, "He does whatever He pleases," and He understood that work above reason is a better way to achieve the goal, to be able to receive the delight and pleasure, yet remain in order to bestow and not for self-gratification.

We should interpret "for Your mercy, for Your truth," that we pray to the Creator, "Give glory to Your name." "Your mercy" means that the quality of mercy will be poured upon us so we will have the strength to walk in the quality of mercy, called "vessels of bestowal," and by that we will have equivalence of form.

Subsequently, we will be able to receive the delight and pleasure, which is called the "quality of truth," as interpreted in *The Study of the Ten Sefirot* (Part 13 p 1,419, and in *Ohr Pnimi* there): "This is why the disclosure of His guidance is called 'truth,' since it is truly His will. We discover this truth in His guidance, which is to do good to His creations, and this is why that correction in ZA is called 'truth.'" This is the meaning of "Your truth."

But the More They Afflicted Them

Article No. 16, Tav-Shin-Mem-Hey, 1984-85

It is written, "But the more they afflicted them, the more they multiplied and the more they spread out, so that they were in dread of the sons of Israel" (Exodus 1:12). The meaning of the words, "But the more they afflicted them" is that they will multiply and spread to that same extent that they are afflicted. It seems as though it is a condition—that there cannot be multiplication and spreading in the work before there is a basis of affliction first.

But to understand the above written, we must know our tenet, meaning know what is our essence. As it is explained in the introductions, it is only our will to receive. And certainly, when the will to receive fulfills its wish, that fulfillment is not considered work, since work means that for which one is rewarded.

In other words, work is actions that man would avoid, and he does them only because he has no choice, since he wishes to receive some reward. The reward is considered the thing that he craves, and his only desire and wish is for that thing. True craving means that this thing touches his heart so deeply that he says, "I'd rather die than to live if I cannot obtain it." It follows that if he has no affliction or pain for not having what he craves, it is not considered a craving. And his craving is measured by the extent of his suffering.

It therefore follows that if one wishes to receive some satisfaction, there must first be a lack. This is so because there is no light without a *Kli* [vessel], and no one can fill it with anything if there is no deficiency. For example, one cannot eat without appetite or enjoy rest without fatigue.

Hence, one is not suffering because the Egyptians in his body are afflicting him unless he does not want to obey them and wishes to go by a way that displeases them. The root of reception in man is called "self-love," and this is regarded as "Egypt." There are many nations, which are generally called "the seventy nations," that are the opposite of *Kedusha* [holiness], which are the seven *Sefirot*, where each *Sefira* [singular of *Sefirot*] consists of ten, hence the number seventy nations. And also, each nation has its own unique desire.

The *Klipa* [shell] of Egypt is a general *Klipa*. It is where the sparks of *Kedusha* fell, which the people of Israel—who were in Egypt—had to correct. Thus, first there must be pain and affliction for not being able to exit their governance, as it is written, "And the children of Israel sighed because of the labor, and they cried, and their cry came up unto God because of the labor. And God heard their groaning."

We should be precise about the words "because of the labor" being written twice. We should explain that all the sighs were from the labor, meaning that they could not work for the Creator. Indeed, their suffering was from not being able to make the work that they were doing be for the Creator, due to the *Klipa* of Egypt. This is why it is written, "Because of the labor" twice.

1) All the sighs were not because they were lacking anything. They lacked only one thing, meaning they did not wish for any luxuries or payment. Their only lack, for which they felt pain and suffering, was that of not being able to do anything for the Creator. In other words, they wished that they would have a desire to give contentment to the Creator and not to themselves, but they

couldn't, and this afflicted them. This is called "wanting to have some grip in spirituality."

2) The second "Because of the labor" comes to teach that, "And their cry came up unto God," that God heard their groaning, was because their only request was work. This comes to imply to the other "because of the labor." It turns out that the whole exile that they felt was only because they were under the rule of the *Klipa* of Egypt and they could not do anything to make it only in order to bestow.

It is written in *The Zohar* (Exodus, Item 381 in the *Sulam* Commentary), "Rabbi Yehuda said, 'Come and see that this is so, as Rabbi Yehoshua of Sakhnin said, 'As long as their minister was given dominion over Israel, the cry of Israel was not heard. When their minister fell, it writes, 'The king of Egypt died,' and promptly, 'And the children of Israel sighed because of the labor, and they cried, and their cry came up unto God because of the labor.' But until then they were not answered in their cry.'"

For this reason, we can say that if it is not time to dethrone Egypt's minister, there is no room for choice or for them to repent and to be able to be redeemed from exile. He says (Exodus, Item 380 in the *Sulam* Commentary), "'In those many days.' 'Many' refers to Israel's stay in Egypt, that is, that the end has come. And since their exile has been completed, what does it say? 'The king of Egypt died.' What does that mean? It means that the minister of Egypt was lowered from his status and fell from his pride. This is why the writing says about him, 'The king of Egypt died,' since decline is regarded for him as dying. As when the king of Egypt—who was their minister—fell, the Creator remembered Israel and heard their groaning."

The Zohar asks this question about the verse, "In your distress, when all these things come upon you" (Deuteronomy 4). It means that before everything takes place, it is impossible to achieve perfection. It turns out that you give an excuse, a pretext that all the things that one should go through can be experienced through suffering, and this is measured by neither time nor quantity of affliction, but by the measure of feeling (see in *The Zohar*).

We can understand it through an allegory. If a person should make one kilogram worth of labor, which is a thousand grams of suffering, the reward comes for that as well. As our sages said, "The reward matches the pain." This means that the labor that one should exert before he receives the reward is because there is no light without a *Kli*, since there is no fulfillment without a deficiency. And the labor that one gives is the qualification for reception of the need, so that afterwards he will be able to receive the filling in it.

Let us say that that person can give the thousand grams of deficiency intermittently, which are discernments in quantity and quality. A person can exert for ten minutes a day, meaning regret his remoteness from the Creator, or he can regret his remoteness from the Creator ten minutes a week, or ten minutes a month.

It is similar with the *quality* of his suffering when he remembers that he is remote from the Creator. Although it pains him, it is not so terrible and there are things that pain him more, things that he craves. It turns out that in quality, too, one should contemplate. Thus, a person has a choice, although he must experience the whole process of labor and affliction through the end, until he comes to a state of, "And you will return to the Lord your God and listen to His voice."

Thus, man has a choice to shorten the time of the process of affliction due to the prolonging of time, which, as we said, is called "quantity," and to add in quality, which is the sensation of suffering at being remote from the Creator.

But we should know that there is a big difference between quantity and quality in the manner of the work. When considering quantity of time, a person can arrange his schedule, meaning the amount of time he allocates to himself, even by coercion. This means that even though the body does not wish to sit for the whole time of the lesson that he decided on, he must sit for several minutes or hours and regret being remote from the Creator. If he has a strong desire and he is not of weak character, he can sit and keep the schedule he arranged for himself, since this is an act, and with actions a person can do things by coercion.

But with quality, this is very difficult because one cannot force oneself to feel differently than he does. If he comes to examine his feelings of pain and suffering at being remote from the Creator, he sometimes comes to a state where he does not care. At that time, he does not know what to do because he cannot change how he feels, and then he is perplexed.

This causes the prolonging of the exile because it is hard for us to give the necessary quantity, much less the quality. And when he begins to scrutinize the quality of the deficiency, he sees that he feels no pain, that he is seemingly unconscious, unfeeling. And although remoteness from the Creator means not having life, it doesn't pain him that he has no life. Then he has no other choice but to pray to the Creator to give him some life, so he will feel that he is dangerously ill and needs to cure the soul.

And sometimes one comes to a state where he is in such a decline that he doesn't even have the strength to pray for it. Rather, he is in a state of complete indifference. This is called "being in a state of still," meaning he is completely motionless.

In that state, only his society can help him. In other words, if he comes among friends and does not criticize them in any way, testing if they, too, have the same obstructions and thoughts but have overcome them, or they just take no interest in introspection and this is why they can engage in Torah and *Mitzvot*, how can he be like them?

At that time, he cannot receive any assistance from society because he has no *Dvekut* [adhesion] with them at all, as they are too small to be his friends. Thus, naturally, he is not affected by them whatsoever.

But if he comes among his friends not with his head high, thinking that he is wise and the friends are fools—but rather tosses his pride away and follows the rule, "Poverty follows the poor," not only is he in a state of decline and feels no need for spirituality, he also receives thoughts of pride, meaning that he is wiser than all his society.

Now let us return to the first question, regarding what *The Zohar* says, "And since their exile has been completed," what does it say, "The king of Egypt died," since he regards dethroning as death. And since the king of Egypt—who is their minister—fell, the Creator remembered Israel and heard their prayer. It turns out that there is a pretext that no prayer will help before it is due time. Thus, there is nothing that can be done, because the Creator will not hear their prayer.

With the above words we can understand the matters as they are. This is the same issue that our sages described about the verse, "I the Lord will hasten it in its time." If they are rewarded, "I will hasten it." If they are not rewarded, "In its time." In other words, when the time comes, an awakening from the Creator will come, and through it Israel will repent. It turns out that the choice is in regards to time, as he says in the "Introduction to The Book of Zohar" (Item 16).

It follows from all the above that one should not consider the time of redemption—that it is written that before that, their prayer was not accepted—because this relates to the time of quantity and quality of suffering, that there is a certain time at which suffering will be completed. However, we can shorten the time. The whole quantity and quality by which the suffering will appear can be shortened in a way that all the suffering will come in a short time, but all the suffering will have appeared there.

Know Today and Reply to Your Heart

Article No. 17, Tav-Shin-Mem-Hey, 1984-85

It is written in *The Zohar, Vaera* (item 89): "Rabbi Elazar started and said, 'Know today and reply to your heart that the Lord, He is God.' He asks, 'It should have said, 'Know this day that the Lord, He is God,' and in the end, 'And reply to your heart,' since knowing that the Lord is God qualifies him to respond so to the heart.' He answers, 'But Moses said, 'If you want to insist on it and know 'that the Lord is God,' then 'reply to your heart.' Thus, we cannot know 'that the Lord, he is God," except by replying to the heart.' This is why the text first brings 'reply to your heart,' to know by this that 'the Lord he is God.'"

We should interpret this in the work. The order of the work is not what seems logical, as is the view of the nations of the world—first "we will hear," and then "we will do." Rather, first "we will do," and then "we will hear," as Israel said, "We will do and we will hear." Our sages said (*Shabbat*, 88), "When Israel preceded doing to hearing, a voice came out and told them, 'Who told my sons this secret, which the ministering angels used?'" It follows that by saying, "We will do and we will hear," they became similar to the ministering angels and not to people.

We should understand the reason for this: An angel is called a "messenger." There are two types of angels:

1) Those who do not mind what the sender tells them to do and take no interest in the act itself. Similarly, one who gives a package to give to another is not interested in the content of the package or the connection between the sender of the object and the messenger. But if he wants to carry out the sender's instructions he does it willingly. Certainly, the messenger receives some reward for this action, and this is called "serving the rav [great one/teacher] in order to receive reward."

2) Sometimes, if the sender is an important person, his reward is the privilege of serving the rav, and he does not need any other reward, called a "prize." It follows that the messenger has no interest or need to know the connection between the sender, who is sending the objet to the receiver of the object. Also, he has no need to know what is the object, meaning what is in that package that he has received from the sender to bring to this or that person.

This is the meaning of "we will do," like a messenger who is not interested at all, since we want to serve the king, to give him pleasure, and our pleasure is in having the possibility to serve him. This is the meaning of being an angel, meaning a messenger.

"We will hear" means that he already listens and understand the matter through and through. That is, at that time he is not regarded as an angel, a messenger. Rather, at that time he becomes the receiver of the gift from the messenger. And then it is not regarded as messenger and sender, but as receiver and giver, since he knows what is in that package because the giver wants him to receive the package and see the importance of the gift he is giving him.

According to the above we can interpret that the meaning of "reply to your heart" as "we will do," which is faith above reason. Afterwards we can be rewarded with "the Lord, He is God," which is "we will do."

An act means potential action, when he has nothing to reply to the body's question. He sees that what the body is asking is a correct question, to which he has no answer. At that time there is no room for deliberation because it is asking correct questions. At that time there is only one answer: "above reason." That is, although the body objects to all the things he wants to do for the Creator, he should say, "a *Mitzva* [good deed] induces a *Mitzva*."

And since he has one *Mitzva*, which he always keeps, the *Mitzva* of circumcision, a *Mitzva* that the body cannot resist, if he can be happy with one thing, even that he is keeping the Creator's commandment, if he is thinking about keeping this *Mitzva*, of which the body has no opinion, by that he can reawaken his work and toil diligently once again, as he did prior to the descent.

However, we must know that each ascent is a new thing. That is, when a person ascends, he does not return to the previous state. Rather, it is always a new discernment, as the ARI says, "One day is not like another; and one moment is not like another; and one cannot correct that which one's friend will correct."

By that we can interpret what our sages said (*Minchot* 43), "When David entered the bath-house and saw himself standing naked, he said, 'Woe unto me for I am standing naked, without *Mitzvot* [good deeds/corrections].' When he remembered the *Mitzva* of circumcision in his flesh, his mind was eased. When he came out he said a psalm about it, as it was said, 'To the chief musician on the eighth,' concerning the circumcision, which was given on the eighth."

We should interpret that a bath-house is when a person comes to purify himself. A state of purity is called "bath-house." At that time, when he looks at himself, at how much Torah and *Mitzvot* he has, and of which he can say he did for the Creator, he sees himself as naked. This concerns the past. Afterwards he looks at the present and sees that now, too, he does not want to do anything in order to bestow. This is the meaning of the words, "Woe unto me for I am standing naked, without *Mitzvot*."

"When he remembered the *Mitzva* of circumcision in his flesh, his mind was eased," since due in the commandment of circumcision he had no foreign thoughts because the view of the infant did not participate during the circumcision. Now, on the basis of the circumcision, he begins to build the order of his work, meaning that it will be above reason, too.

"When he came out he said a psalm about it." That is, once he was out of his state, meaning during the ascent, regarded as coming out of the bath-house, when he has been purified, "He said a psalm about it," since he built the whole structure henceforth on that basis of above reason, since the first *Mitzva* he had was above his reason.

This is why we should interpret that he "saw himself standing naked" means that he had no desire to do *Mitzvot*. Thus, he had no connection to *Kedusha* [holiness], since the body resisted anything of *Kedusha*. But "he remembered the *Mitzva* of circumcision in his flesh," to which the body cannot resist. Even those who circumcised themselves, although they had choice while they were circumcising themselves, at the time they were in ascent, or they would not circumcise themselves. Afterwards, during the descent, they no longer had choice concerning the circumcision.

But women, who do not need to circumcise their bodies, with what can they overcome? It is possible because of *Arvut* [mutual guarantee], that "Israel are responsible for one another." That *Mitzva* was literally carved in his flesh, meaning in his body, and not in a practical *Mitzva*, which is from the externality of his body. "His mind was eased," meaning that in such a state of descent he is still connected to the commandments of the Creator.

This can give him room to build his structure of *Kedusha* and say to his body, "You cannot bring me to despair, since you see that you are detached from the whole issue of Torah and *Mitzvot*, and you have no desire, so why are you still dreaming that it is possible that the Creator will bring you closer than others? You see that you are worse than others, so where do you get this insolence that He should bring you closer, to walk on the path of truth, which is to bestow and not receive anything, when you see that your body doesn't even agree to engage in Torah and *Mitzvot Lo Lishma* [not for Her sake]?"

To this comes the answer that the Creator deliberately left a *Mitzva* in your body, so you will be able to see that there is still something that connects you to the Creator, meaning the *Mitzva* of circumcision, which you cannot cancel. This is the meaning of saying, "The outcast shall not be outcast from Him." Rather, everyone will approach the Creator. This is why his mind was appeased by this, for he began to build all of his reason on the circumcision in his flesh. This is the circumcision that was given on the eighth, since *Bina* is called "eighth," which is covered *Hassadim*, meaning above reason.

Concerning the Slanderers

Article No. 18, Tav-Shin-Mem-Hey, 1984-85

It is written in *The Zohar* (*Bo*, item 1): "Rabbi Yehuda started and said, 'Happy are the people who know the cheer.' See how people must follow the path of the Creator and keep the *Mitzvot* [commandments] of the Torah so that through it they will be rewarded with the next world and be saved from all the slanderers above and below. This is so because as there are slanderers in the world below, there are slanderers above who stand ready to slander people."

We should understand what are the slanderers below. This is understandable with regard to the above, that if we want to give something to a person, slanderers come and complain about that person saying he should not be given what he is about to be given. But below? This begs the question, "Before whom are they complaining about the person?"

We should interpret that the slanderers come to the person himself. If a person wants to go by the path that ascends toward bestowal upon the Creator, slanderers come and tell him: "The way of bestowal is not for you; this way is suitable only for a chosen few, with special qualities and talents, brave hearts, strong, and who are able to overcome. But not you, for you don't have the qualities of those above the common folk. Therefore, it is better for you to dwell among your own people, meaning follow the path of the general public and not aspire to be exceptional."

In that regard, Rabbi Yehuda comes and tells us the verse, "Happy are the people who know the cheer." RASHI interpreted that they know how to appease their maker. How do they appease Him? By Him pouring abundance upon them. Rabbi Yehuda interprets about that that they must go by the path of the Creator and observe the *Mitzvot* [commandments] of the Torah." We should understand what are the "ways of the Creator." The verse comes and tells us about that, "For My thoughts are not your thoughts, nor are My ways your ways."

That is, only above reason can one walk by the path of the Creator. But within reason, the body itself is his slanderer and accuser, making him understand that the path of bestowing upon the Creator is not for him.

By this you will understand the verse (*Exodus*, 23): "You shall not take a bribe, for a bribe blinds the clear-sighted and distorts the words of the righteous." We therefore see that when one comes to scrutinize the order of his work and sees the conditions required of him, he decides that he cannot take upon himself this path, which is the work of bestowal, for two reasons:

1) He is not one hundred percent certain about the reward for the work, since he does not see anyone who has received the reward for which he labored. That is, when he comes to criticize people who he sees that they did toil and tolerated the conditions of the work, he sees that they really did make great efforts. However, he does not find that they have already received the reward for their work. If he asks himself why they did not receive reward, he comes up with a great excuse: One who keeps all the conditions of the work certainly receives reward. However, they made great efforts, but not the one hundred percent required of them. This is why they are in a state where they believe He is ejecting them (from the work, for they believe that they are right and the work of bestowal is not for them).

2) At that time a second question comes up: "Who knows if he will be more capable then they are, and he will be able to give the full one hundred percent required to be brought to *Dvekut* [adhesion] with the Creator?"

After those two reasons he decides that he is one hundred percent right in not wanting to take upon himself this path, which is built on faith above reason and on the basis of bestowal. He is so certain that he is right that he is sure that no one can criticize his unwillingness to take this path.

Accordingly, there is a question: "Those people who did commence on this path, who have taken upon themselves to walk on the path of bestowal, how did they overcome those questions?" Certainly, when one is told, "Go work, but not in order to receive reward," immediately asks all these questions, since these questions give one no rest. Thus, by which force could they emerge from the state of questions, which are called "evil waters"?

The only way is to go above reason and say, "What I see—that I am right and I must take the path that everyone takes—is not the truth, as I see it. Only one whose eyes are open can see the truth, but one whose eyes are not open cannot see the truth. When a person asks these questions he is biased toward his will to receive, since he is considering only the benefit he can derive for himself. Therefore, he can no longer see the truth. The verse comes and tells us about that: "You shall not take a bribe, for a bribe blinds the clear-sighted."

Therefore, it cannot be said that he is right according to his view because he is bribed by the will to receive, so he no longer has open eyes to see the truth. Instead, he should say, "Although I heard all your correct questions, now I am unable to answer you. But once I have been rewarded with the desire to bestow I will have open eyes. Then, if you come to me with all your questions, I will certainly give you the right answers.

"But now I have no choice but to go above reason because all the reason that I see comes from the side of biasness. And although

I think that all my calculations are correct, it should be said about them what the verse tells us, 'distorts the words of the righteous,' that I am unable to see who is right, meaning say that everything that must be done in order to bestow was not said about me, and 'I dwell among my own people,' like everyone else who settles for keeping Torah and *Mitzvot* saying, 'I do what I must do.'

"Concerning intentions, this pertains to one who feels he needs it. I, for one, do not feel that I need to be smarter than everyone and I am content with less." It was said about this, "distorts the words of the righteous," but I go above reason.

This is the meaning of the great importance of "cleanness," which is presented in all the books, that one must be clean before every *Mitzva* [commandment] one is about to do. And regarding cleanness, Baal HaSulam said that one should be careful that everything will be on the side of truth, and that no falsehood will be involved there. He also said that as there is a difference between people concerning keeping clean—there are people who make sure there is no dirt on their clothes, and there are people who are not so meticulous and the dirt is plainly visible, so they remove it. That is, it depends on the measure of loathing that one has for the dirt.

It is likewise in spirituality: No person is like another, and it depends on the extent to which one loathes falsehood. To the extent that he cannot tolerate falsehood, he comes closer to the path of truth.

He also said that we must know that this dirt in matters of the soul is the true harm-doer. Since the soul is eternal, one should be very careful with falsehood and keep one's truth clean from any manner of falsehood.

By this we will understand what our sages said (*Shabbat* 114), "Rabbi Hiya Bar Aba said, 'Rabbi Yohanan said, 'Every wise disciple who is found with a blemish on his clothes must die, as it was said, 'All who hate Me, love death.' Do not call it 'hate Me,' but 'cause to hate Me.' RASHI interprets that 'cause to hate Me' means that they make themselves loathsome in the eyes of people, and the people say, 'Woe unto the disciples of Torah for they are loathsome and dishonorable.' It turns out that they make the Torah loathsome.'"

Superficially, this is difficult to understand. If he has a blemish on his clothes, does he deserve to die? He brings evidence from the verse, "All who hate Me, love death." Here, too, we should understand: If he hates Me, is this a sign that he loves death?

According to what we explained above, that cleanness pertains to the need to be clean, so there will be no mixture of falsehood there when he wants to walk on the path of truth. Truth is called *Lishma* [for Her sake], as Maimonides says (*Hilchot Teshuva*, Chapter 10), "One who works out of love, engages in Torah and *Mitzvot*, and follows the paths of wisdom not because of anything in the world, or because of fear of harm, and not in order to inherit goodness. Rather, he does the truth because it is the truth, and the good will finally come because of it."

Therefore, it means that concerning finding a blemish in his clothes—which are regarded as clothes within which one receives goodness and life—they must be cleansed from any mixture of self-love, and be only for the Creator. According to this we will interpret "All who hate Me love death." We asked, "Why does the verse say, 'All who hate Me,' meaning the reason he hates Me is that he loves death?

According to the above, this is simple: The meaning of death is clarified, since precisely one who is adhered to the life of lives has life. But one who is separated from Him is separated from life.

This is why it was said, "All who hate Me," meaning who do not love the Creator, to work only for the Creator, but mix there a little bit of self-love, and self-love is death because it causes separation from the life of lives. For this reason, one who loves death, meaning self-love, becomes hateful of the Creator because of it.

RASHI interprets "cause to hate Me" to mean that they make themselves loathsome in the eyes of people. People say, "Woe unto the disciples of Torah, for they are loathsome and dishonorable." It follows that they cause to hate the Torah.

This is difficult to understand. If there is a stain on his clothes, is he already loathsome in the eyes of people? And also, does the Torah cause people to hate the Torah so much that for this he deserves a punishment of death, as our sages said, "Every wise disciple who is found with a blemish on his clothes must die"?

In the work, we should interpret that "making themselves loathsome in the eyes of people" means one's own organs, desires, and thoughts. Man's body is called "a world in and of itself." The organs of the body say, "Woe unto them who study Torah, for they are loathsome." But it is written, "For they are our lives and the length of our days," and they are "More desirable than gold, then much fine gold, and sweeter than honey and the honeycomb," but we don't see this with our disciples of Torah.

The reason why we do not see all those precious things in disciples of Torah is that there is a blemish on their clothes, meaning that there is self-love mingled in our disciples of Torah during the work. It follows that this blemish causes the good and the life in the Torah not to be able to clothe in these clothes, since they are not clean where everything is for the Creator. At that time the "people in our body" fall into despair. It follows they are causing them to hate the Torah.

That is, where the disciples of Torah should have revealed the preciousness of Torah, as it is written, "For it is your wisdom and understanding before the eyes of the nations," here they see the opposite. And who caused all this? It is all because they were not careful with cleanness, which is called a "blemish."

By this we will understand why he must die if there is a blemish on his clothes. It tells us that that blemish that he makes in his clothes separates him from the life of lives. This is why this is considered that he is compelling himself to come to a state of death. And it is all because he was not careful with cleanness, but falsehood, called *Lo Lishma* [not for Her sake] was mixed into his work. Rather, everything must be for the Creator.

Come unto Pharaoh — 1

Article No. 19, Tav-Shin-Mem-Hey, 1984-85

"Come unto Pharaoh." This is perplexing. Should it not have said, "Go unto Pharaoh"? *The Zohar* explains (*Bo*, item 36), "But He allowed Moses into rooms within rooms, to one high sea monster. ...When the Creator saw that Moses was afraid ... the Creator said, 'Behold, I am against you, Pharaoh King of Egypt, the great monster that lies in the midst of his rivers.' The Creator had to wage war against him, and no other, as you say, 'I the Lord,' and they explained, 'I, and no emissary.'" It follows that "Come" means both of us together.

To interpret this in the work of the Creator, we first have to know what is our demand for engaging in Torah and *Mitzvot* [commandments]. That is, what are we asking in return for it. The reward should be clear—to understand that it is worthwhile for us to relinquish bodily pleasures if we understand that this is what interferes with our achieving the goal, which is our reward—to achieve the sublime goal through our engagement in Torah and *Mitzvot*, meaning that the goal is a reward for relinquishing corporeal pleasures.

Therefore, we should know that the main reward we want for keeping Torah and *Mitzvot* is *Dvekut* [adhesion] with the Creator, which is equivalence of form, as in "and to cleave unto Him." It is as our sages said (*Baba Batra*, 16), "The Creator has created the evil inclination, He has created for it the Torah as a spice." This is the *Kli* [vessel] in which we can receive the purpose of creation, called "doing good to His creations," which is called "the revelation of His Godliness to His creatures in this world," as it is written in the essay, *Matan Torah* ["The Giving of the Torah"].

It is known that the heart of the work is in making the *Kli*. But the filling, which is the abundance poured into the *Kli*, comes from the upper one, which is His desire to benefit His creations. Certainly, from His perspective, nothing prevents Him from giving to us, and all the deficiencies we feel are because we haven't the *Kelim* [vessels] to receive the abundance, since our *Kelim* come from the shattering. This is so because due to the breaking of the vessels that occurred in the world of *Nekudim*, the *Klipot* [shells/peels] emerged, which receive in order to receive, for in spirituality, breaking is similar to breaking a vessel in corporeality. With a physical vessel, if it is broken and you pour into it some liquid, the liquid pours out. Likewise, in spirituality, if a thought of will to receive for oneself enters the *Kli*, the abundance pours out to the external ones, meaning outside of *Kedusha* [holiness].

Kedusha means "for the Creator." Anything outside of "for the Creator" is called *Sitra Achra* [other side], namely the other side of *Kedusha*. This is why we say that *Kedusha* means to bestow, and *Tuma'a* [impurity] means to receive.

For this reason, we, who were born after the breaking, desire only to receive. Therefore we cannot be given abundance, for it will all certainly go to the side of the *Sitra Achra*.

This is the only reason why we are far from receiving the delight and pleasure that the Creator has prepared for us, for everything that He may give us will not stay with us, but will be lost, as our sages said, "Who is a fool? He who loses what he is given." This means that the root of the reason we lose is that we are fools.

But why must a fool lose it and a wise keep what he is given? We should interpret that a fool is one who remains with his nature, which is self-love, and does not work on tactics to be able to exit the will to receive. Although there are many ways and tactics to exit one's nature, he remains as naked as on the day he was born, without another clothing, a clothing known as "the will to bestow," for with a clothing of bestowal he can dress the delight and pleasure he should receive.

However, sometimes a person begins the work of bestowal and explains to the body that this is the whole purpose of the work—to receive vessels of bestowal. However, after all his arguments with the body, the body tells him, "You cannot change the nature that the Creator has created. And since creation is regarded as 'existence from absence,' it is only in the form of desire to receive, so how dare you say that you can change the nature that the Creator has created?"

It was said about this, "Come unto Pharaoh," meaning we will go together. I will go with you so that I will change the nature, and all I want is that you will ask Me to help you change your nature from a desire to receive into a desire to bestow, as our sages said (*Sukkah*, 52), "Man's inclination overpowers him every day, and were it not for the Creator's help, he would not have overcome it."

However, we should understand why the Creator needs him to ask of Him. This is understandable with flesh and blood, who want the honor of being asked, so as to know that he has helped him. But how can such a thing be said about the Creator? However, the rule, "there is no light without a *Kli*," means that it is impossible to give to someone a filling if he has no desire. As long as there is no desire for something, if you give him, he will have no taste for it. Therefore, he will not be able to appreciate it and will not keep it from being stolen.

That is, there are people who do understand the importance of the matter and will take it from him. This is why a person should ask for the Creator's help, so that if he is given some illumination from above he will know how to keep it from the external ones stealing it from him, for they do know the value of any illumination of *Kedusha*.

For this reason, when a person asks of the Creator to help him—and a true request begins precisely when one sees that a person is unable to help himself—then he knows for certain that there is no other choice but to ask the Creator to help him. Otherwise, he will remain separated from *Kedusha* and will have no way out of the state of self-love. Therefore, when the Creator helps him, he already knows it is a valuable asset that must be guarded carefully so the external ones do not take it.

Likewise, the ARI says (*The Study of the Ten Sefirot*, Part 7, p 495), "This is the meaning of the pursuit of the evil inclination and *Sitra Achra* to make the righteous sin and to cling to *Kedusha*. It is because they have no vitality other than through them. When the good and *Kedusha* increase, their lives proliferate. Hence, from now on do not wonder why the evil inclination chases man so as to make him sin."

Thus, to keep from losing what he is given, one must first make great efforts, for something that comes to a person through labor causes him to keep the thing and not lose it. But during the exertion, when a person sees that the work is still far from finished, he sometimes escapes the campaign and falls into despair. At that time he needs great strengthening, to believe that the Creator will help him, and the fact that help has not arrived is because he has not given the required quantity and quality of labor for preparing the deficiency in order to receive the filing, as it is said ("Introduction to the Study of the Ten Sefirot," item 18), "And if one practices Torah and fails to remove the evil inclination from himself, it is either that he has been negligent in giving the necessary labor and exertion in the practice of Torah, as it is written, 'I have not labored but found, do not believe,' or perhaps one did put in the necessary amount of labor, but has been negligent in the quality."

Therefore, we should pay attention to "Come unto Pharaoh" and believe through the worst possible states, and not escape the campaign, but rather always trust that the Creator can help a person and give him, whether one needs a little help or a lot of help.

In truth, one who understands that he needs the Creator to give him a lot of help, because he is worse than the rest of the people, is more suitable for his prayer to be answered, as it is written, "The Lord is near to the brokenhearted, and saves the crushed in spirit."

Therefore, one should not say that he is unfit for the Creator to bring him closer, but that the reason is that he is idle in his work. Instead, one should always overcome and not let thoughts of despair enter his mind, as our sages said (*Berachot*, 10), "Even if a sharp sword is placed on his neck he should not deny himself of mercy," as it was said (Job, 13), "Though He slay me, I will hope for Him."

We should interpret the "sharp sword placed on his neck" to mean that even though one's evil, called "self-love," is placed on his neck and wants to separate him from *Kedusha* by showing him that it is impossible to exit this authority, he should say that the picture he sees is the truth.

However, "He should not deny himself of mercy," for at that time he must believe that the Creator can give him the mercy, meaning the quality of bestowal. That is, by himself, it is true that one cannot exit the authority of self-reception. But from the perspective of the Creator, when the Creator helps him, of course He can bring him out. This is the meaning of what is written, "I am the Lord your God, who took you out from the land of Egypt to be your God."

This is what we say in the *Shema* reading—which is assuming of the burden of the kingdom of heaven—that we must know that the Creator is the one who brings one out of the authority of reception, called "separation," and admits one into *Kedusha*. At that time, "to be your God" is kept true, for then one is regarded as "people of Israel," and not as "people of the earth."

Our sages said about it (*Pesachim*, 118): "Rabbi Yehoshua Ben Levi said, 'When the Creator said to *Adam HaRishon*, 'Thorns and thistles it shall grow for you,' his eyes teared. He said to Him, 'Master of the world, will I and my donkey eat from the same trough?' Because He had told him, 'By the sweat of your brow you will eat bread,' his mind was promptly eased.'"

However, we should understand *Adam HaRishon's* argument, who inquired about the Creator's action, why he deserved to eat from the same trough as the donkey. This is a just complaint. The evidence of this is that the Creator advised him to eat bread. Were this not a just complaint, the Creator would not have accepted his argument. This argument, saying, "Will I and my donkey eat from the same trough," is difficult to understand. What is his advantage? After all, our sages said (*Sanhedrin*, 38), "Our sages said, 'The man was born on the eve of Shabbat [Sabbath] so that should he become arrogant, he will be told, 'the mosquito came before you in the work of creation.'"

Accordingly, if a mosquito came before him, then what is the complaint about eating from the same trough as the donkey? However, we should interpret that after the sin he fell into self-love. It follows that he has become similar to a donkey, who understands nothing but self-love. This is the meaning of "His eyes teared and he said, 'Will I and my donkey eat from the same trough," meaning from the same discernment of self-love?

This is why he was given the advice, "By the sweat of your brow you will eat bread." Bread is regarded as man's food. That is, through labor in "By the sweat of your brow you will eat bread," which is man's food, he emerges from being "the people of the earth," and is then called "the people of Israel," which is *Yashar-El* [straight to the Creator].

But Egypt—which was the people of Israel in exile, for Egypt is called "a nation that is akin to a donkey"—means that the aim is only for self-love. For this reason, at that time the salvation to

Israel was that the Creator took them out of Egypt. This is the meaning of needing to intend upon the acceptance of the burden of the kingdom of heaven, "I am the Lord your God, who took you out from the land of Egypt, to be your God," for precisely by the force of God can we come out of Egypt and be rewarded with "to be your God."

He who Hardens His Heart

Article No. 20, Tav-Shin-Mem-Hey, 1984-85

It is written in *The Zohar* (item 186): "Rabbi Yitzhak said, 'We did not find anyone who hardened his heart before the Creator as Pharaoh.' Rabbi Yosi, said, 'But Sihon and Og also hardened their hearts.' He replied, 'This is not so. They hardened their hearts against Israel, but they did not harden their hearts against the Creator, as Pharaoh hardened his heart against Him, for he saw His might and did not repent.'"

We should understand the difference between not hardening their hearts before the Creator, or hardening their hearts against Israel. After all, all the hatred that the nations feel toward Israel is only because they are the Creator's people, as our sages said (*Shabbat*, 89), "What is Mt. Sinai? It is that *Sinaa* [hatred] came down to the idol-worshippers."

To return to the topic, meaning concerning the hatred of Israel: Pharaoh hated the people of Israel and wanted to enslave them. Moses came as a messenger of the Creator but he wouldn't listen and said, "Who is the Lord that I should obey His voice?" Sihon and Og also hated Israel, but what is the difference with respect to Israel? The reason why they hate Israel. Did Sihon and Og harden their hearts because the people of Israel was unimportant, and this is why they hated them? Or did they harden their hearts against the Creator, that the Creator was unimportant in their eyes, and this is why they hated Israel? In that case, what is the difference with respect to Israel?

We should interpret the above words of *The Zohar* in the work. We need to know that there are two obstructers standing opposite a person and not letting him cross the barrier and achieve love of the Creator, since man is born with a desire to receive for himself and cannot do anything without a profit. That is, one can relinquish self-reception in order to bestow something upon someone if this gives him emotional satisfaction. In that case he can relinquish self-reception.

For example, a person can work for an important person. If, say, the ADMOR of Lubavitch comes to the airport with a suitcase, gives it to one of his followers, and gives him 100 dollars for his work. Certainly, the follower will not want to receive the pay from the rabbi and will give it back to him. If they rabbi should ask him, "Why don't you want to receive it? Did I pay you too little for the work? If I had given an ordinary porter 10 dollars he would have been happy; why don't you want to take it?" The follower would reply, "My privilege of serving the rabbi is worth to me more than any fortune in the world that the rabbi might give me."

We therefore see that for an important person, a person can work without any reward. For this reason, when one comes to engage in Torah and *Mitzvot* [commandments] in order to bestow, a person can relinquish self-love for the sake of the Creator. At that time, what does the obstructer to the work of the Creator do so that one will not be able to walk on the path of the Creator? He does one thing: He does not let a person depict the greatness and importance of the Creator. It follows that all the strength that the *Sitra Achra* [other side] has is against the Creator. He tells him, "I know you are very powerful, meaning you can overcome your lusts, unlike weak-minded and soft-hearted people. You are the strongest of the strong. However, the reason why you are not walking on the path of truth is that the goal is not so important to you, to make you annul yourself for it. With this force it obstructs him from achieving the goal.

This is what *The Zohar* says in the name of Rabbi Yitzhak: "We did not find anyone who hardened his heart before the Creator as Pharaoh." That is, he did not appreciate the Creator and said, "Who is the Lord that I should obey His voice?" This is the first obstructer.

The second obstructer is that when one sees that he has overcome his arguments, goes above reason, and does not regard what it tells him, then he comes with a complaint against Israel. That is, one who wants to walk on the path of the Creator is called *Yashar-El* [straight to the Creator], which is directly to the Creator. This means that he wants all the actions that he does to rise straight to the Creator, and does not want to have any other intention.

For this reason, what does the other obstructer do? He degrades the Israel in him and tells him, "The Israel in you is very weak, both in skill and in strength to overcome. You have a weak character, and this way you want to go—where all the works are only for the Creator—can be demanded from an Israel who has all the required qualities, namely good education, skills, and the courage to fight the evil in him. He can walk on this path, but not you."

Thus, by what does he obstruct him? He no longer speaks to him about the importance of the goal, as with Pharaoh's argument, who disputed the importance of the goal. Rather, he tells him that the goal is very important, but "You are not important enough to be able to walk on such a lofty path, so walk on the path of the general public, and you do not need to be exceptional. Only this way is suitable for you."

Likewise, we find in *The Zohar* (*Shlach*, item 63) concerning the spies: "'And they returned from touring the land.' 'They returned' means that they returned to the bad side, returned from the path of truth, saying, 'What will we get out of it? To this day we have not seen good in the world. We have toiled in Torah and the house is empty. Who will be awarded that world? Who will come and be in it? It would have been better had we not toiled so. We labored and learned in order to know the part of that world, as you advised us. 'It is also flowing with milk and honey,' that upper world is good, as we know in the Torah, but who can be rewarded with it?

'However, the people ... are strong,' meaning the people that has been rewarded with that world is strong, not considering the rest of the world at all—to engage in it, to have great wealth—who can do so and be rewarded with it? 'However, the people ... are strong.' 'The rich man answers roughly, 'and we also saw the descendants of the giant there,' meaning you need a body as strong and as mighty as a lion, since the Torah weakens man's strength."

It follows that the argument of the spies, according to the interpretation of *The Zohar*, is that Israel is unimportant, as we explained that it is similar to the argument of the second obstructer, meaning that all the hardening is against Israel.

By that we can interpret the difference between Pharaoh's argument, who hardened his heart against the Creator, and the argument of Sihon and Og, who hardened their hearts against Israel. Pharaoh said, "Who is the Lord that I should obey His voice," meaning that all his strength was to lessen the importance of the Creator, as it was said, that he is the first obstructer. Sihon and Og, however, hardened their hearts against Israel, meaning to lessen the importance of Israel, which corresponds to the second obstructer.

To this, meaning to all those arguments, there is no other tactic but to walk on the path of faith above reason, disregard their arguments, and trust in the Creator that He can help everyone and there is no force that can resist the power of the Creator, so we should trust in the Creator to help.

We find such as this in *The Zohar* (*Beshalach*, item 187): "Rabbi Yehuda said, 'Rabbi Yitzhak said, 'Pharaoh was wiser than all his sorcerers. ...In their entire side he did not see that Israel would have redemption... And Pharaoh did not think that there is another tie of faith that governs all the forces of the *Sitra Achra*. This is why he hardened his heart.'"" It follows from the words of *The Zohar* that Pharaoh means within reason, that it seems irrational that they would be able to exit their authority, unless through faith above reason, for this power cancels all the powers in the world.

We Should Always Discern between Torah and Work

Article No. 21, Tav-Shin-Mem-Hey, 1984-85

We should always discern between Torah and work. "Torah" stands in and of itself. At that time we cannot speak of a person, but it is as though man is not there at all. Instead, we speak of the Torah in and of itself, which is regarded as the names of the Creator, and we note its importance, namely of whom we speak.

That is, we must always remember that we are speaking of the King, how He has placed order and guidance, how His holy names bestow upon the souls, and they will receive them and be able to exist as they reveal them, as it is written, "Who will climb up the mountain of the Lord, and who will rise in His holy place?"

When one pays attention and feels of whom he speaks, that he is speaking of the Creator, but we haven't the understanding so as to have some connection so we will understand that we are speaking of the Creator, and we must only believe that the whole Torah is the names of the Creator. However, He is dressed either in rules and conducts that one must keep the *Mitzvot* between man and God or between man and man, or in stories and tales, or they are clothed in the language of Kabbalah and the holy names. At that time we must remember that the internality clothed inside those dresses is only Godliness. This is called "the whole Torah is the names of the Creator."

Therefore, when we learn Torah we should learn with manners. That is, we must remember of whom we are speaking, and in this way we can draw the light of the Torah and feel that "They are our lives and the length of our days." Naturally, when learning with the above intention, one can be happy because he is attached to the life of lives, which is called "For they are our lives and the length of our days." This is so because one begins to feel the discernment of "to do good to His creations," which was the reason for the creation of the worlds.

We must elicit this good from the Torah, and this is regarded as saying only the praise of Torah, and not thinking at all of man. Therefore, when learning Torah, a person is in wholeness, according to the rule, "Where one thinks, there he is." One should receive vitality from this time to the rest of the day, for this is called "A separate time for Torah, and a separate time for prayer," since they contradict one another.

Work time is something altogether different. Work relates specifically to man, while Torah relates specifically to the Creator, which is called "the Lord's Torah." However, work relates specifically to man because man must work, as it is written, "For man is born for labor."

Since man is the creation, and creation is deficiency, which his existence from absence, and that existence, called "desire to receive," must be satisfied, since this is the purpose of creation. And since there was a *Tzimtzum* [restriction] on that desire for the purpose of equivalence of form, it is necessary to correct and remove the *Tzimtzum* on that desire so it can achieve the goal called "His desire to do good."

To remove the *Tzimtzum*, we were given the remedy of Torah and *Mitzvot* [commandments]. This is called, "I have created the evil inclination; I have created the Torah as a spice." And here, in the matter of work, we should discern that one is advancing toward the goal of removing the *Tzimtzum*, meaning if there are already sparks of bestowal, meaning that he has already received something from the remedy of the Torah and *Mitzvot* in the form of cleansing the thought and the desire, and is in a state of self-criticism in matters of work.

But one should not criticize oneself at all in the Torah. Rather, he should learn Torah as is. All we have to do is seek advice on how to appreciate the Torah, but the Torah itself is a reality called "the names of the Creator." It follows that when we learn some laws or morals from the Torah, or even just stories, or the manner of the work, all this is still not regarded as Torah. We only learn this from the Torah, but the Torah itself has no relation to the creature, only to the Creator, since it is the names of the Creator.

That is, the Torah is called "the revelation of Godliness," and this is called the "internality of the Torah." What is revealed outside, the laws and morals, and manners of work, and stories, these are all called "dresses on the Torah." This is why they are called the "externality of the Torah." But the names of the Creator are called the "internality of the Torah."

According to the above we should ask, "If the Torah in and of itself relates to the Creator, which is Godliness, then it is similar only to interpretation. What can one deduce from learning Torah if he does not understand anything in relation to himself?" Our sages said about this: "Great is the learning that leads to action," for man certainly needs only actions, as it is written, "Which God has created to do."

Therefore, "The learning is not the most important, but the action." To this comes the reply: "Great is the learning that leads to action" (*Kidushin*, p 40, and *Baba Kama* 207). In other words, the light of Torah, which is the internality, shines for a person so he will have the strength to do good deeds. This is done by the power of Torah, which gives him the strength to be able to do it, as it is written, "Which God has created to do."

This is the meaning of what our sages said, "A separate time for Torah, and a separate time for prayer," for they contradict one another. This is so because while learning Torah, one must think only about the importance of Torah, and not at all about himself. But during the prayer one must first of all have his deficiencies revealed, so he can ask that they will be fulfilled, since there is no deficiency if it is not looked for.

Only in corporeality are the deficiencies revealed, since the deficiencies come from the will to receive, and the will to receive is revealed. This is not so in spirituality, where the whole structure of *Kedusha* [holiness] is built on the basis of desire to bestow, and because we attribute the desire to bestow to the creature.

It was explained that *Malchut*, called the "will to receive," desires equivalence of form, called "to bestow." Therefore, when this matter extends to the creatures, who come after the breaking of the vessels that occurred, and also after the sin of the tree of knowledge, then that deficiency, where one feels that he is lacking the *Kli* [vessel], called "desire to bestow," is no longer present.

Instead, one must exert until he feels the lack of the desire to bestow. To the extent that he feels that deficiency he can pray to the Creator to help him, to give him that *Kli*, that all his concerns will be only that he lacks this force called "desire to bestow. To the extent that he is far from that *Kli* he should regret and ask for the Creator's mercy, that He will deliver him and give him that desire.

Moreover, we can say that one should ask the Creator to give him that deficiency, meaning to feel that he is devoid of the desire to bestow, and that this is all that is stopping him from achieving spirituality, since that deficiency does not come by itself.

It therefore follows that the Creator should give man both the *Kli* and the light. By this we can interpret the verse, "You have fashioned me from behind and from before." "From behind" means the *Kli*;

"from before" means the anterior, which is the filling. It turns out that the light, as well as the *Kli* all come from Him.

This is the meaning of what our sages said (*Kidushin*, 30), "Our sages said, '*Vesamtem* [and you shall put] means *Sam Tam* [complete potion]; the Torah is as a potion of life.'" This is what the Creator said to Israel: "My sons, I have created the evil inclination; I have created for it the Torah as a spice. If you engage in Torah, you will not be given to its hand." The thing is that the light in the Torah, which is the internality of the Torah, reforms him. However, we must intend to receive the light of Torah during the study, as is explained in the "Introduction to the Study of the Ten Sefirot," item 17.

The Whole of the Torah Is One Holy Name

Article No. 22, Tav-Shin-Mem-Hey, 1984-85

It is written in *The Zohar* (*Shmini*, item 1): "Rabbi Yitzhak started, 'The whole Torah is one holy name of the Creator, and the world was created in the Torah,' which was His tool of craftsmanship for creating the world." It is written there in item two: "Man was created in the Torah, as it is written, 'And God said, 'Let us make man...' It is written in plural form. He said to her, 'You and I will establish him in the world.' Rabbi Hiya said, 'The written Torah, which is ZA, and the oral Torah, which is *Malchut*, established man.'"

We see three things here: 1) the whole Torah is one holy name; 2) the world was created with the Torah; 3) man was created with the Torah.

Our sages said about *Beresheet* [in the beginning] that it is because the Torah is called *Resheet* [beginning], and because Israel were called *Resheet*, for the creation of the worlds was in order to do good to His creations, meaning for the souls, so the souls would receive the delight and pleasure. It follows that from the perspective of the Creator it is to bestow, and all that the creatures need is to receive.

We already learned that to have equivalence of form the creatures must obtain the *Kli* [vessel] called "desire to bestow."

But since we do not have the desire to bestow by nature, we need something to give us that force called "desire to bestow." That force, which the lower one receives, so as to be able to bestow, is through the Torah, since "the light in it reforms him." It follows that as *Resheet* is Israel, we also need the Torah so we can receive the delight and pleasure. Therefore, the Torah is also called *Resheet* because one does not work without the other.

We know the words of *The Zohar* that "the Torah and Israel and the Creator are one." Accordingly, by Israel's exertion in Torah they are rewarded with the Creator, meaning with the "names of the Creator."

It follows that we should discern two things in the Torah: 1) the light of Torah, which comes in order to reform him. This is the correction of the *Kelim* [vessels]. 2) Obtaining the light of Torah, which is the "holy names," called the "revelation of His Godliness to His creatures in this world" (see in the essay *Matan Torah* ["The Giving of Torah"]).

It therefore follows that when we study Torah we should discern the two above matters: 1) to extend light so it will create for us vessels of bestowal. It is impossible to obtain these *Kelim* [vessels] without the light of Torah. Therefore, what does he expect? To be rewarded for studying Torah. His only desire is to obtain that *Kli*, called "vessel of bestowal." This is precisely once he has begun the work of bestowal and has made great efforts to be able to do things only with the intention to bestow.

Only then can he come to know that the will to receive that was installed in him by nature cannot be cancelled. At that time he begins to understand that he needs "heaven's mercy," and only the Creator can help him be rewarded with vessels of bestowal, and this help comes from the light of Torah.

For this reason, during the study we must always pay attention to the purpose of the study of Torah, meaning what we should demand from the study of Torah. At that time we are told that first we must ask for *Kelim*, meaning to have vessels of bestowal, called "equivalence of form," by which the restriction and concealment that were placed on the creatures are removed. To the extent that this is so he begins to feel the holiness and begins to have a taste for the work of the Creator. At that time he can be happy because *Kedusha* [holiness] yields joy, for the light of doing good to His creations shines there.

But if he has not yet decided that he should always walk on the path of bestowal, as our sages said, "all your works will be for the Creator," this is regarded as "preparation of the *Kelim*" to be fit for reception of the upper abundance. He wants to be rewarded with vessels of bestowal through the study, as our sages said, "The light in it reforms him."

And once he has been rewarded with vessels of bestowal, he comes to a degree called "attainment of the Torah," which is the "names of the Creator," as *The Zohar* calls it: "The Torah, the Creator, and Israel are one."

By this we will understand what is written there in *The Zohar*, item 2: "Man was created in the Torah." We should understand the connection between the Torah and man that we can say that man was created from the Torah.

First, we must bring the words of our sages (*Yevamot*, 61): "Rabbi Shimon Ben Yochai would say, 'The graves of idol-worshippers are not defiled in the tent, as it was said, 'And you, you are My flock, the flock of My pasture; you are man; you are called 'man,' and the idol-worshippers are not called 'man.''"

We need to know what the discernment of "man" is, meaning what is the degree of "man" that idol-worshippers cannot be called "man." Our sages said about the verse (*Berachot* 212b): "'In the end of the matter, all having been heard, fear God,' what is 'for this is the whole man'? Rabbi Elazar said, 'The Creator said, 'The whole world was created only for this.''"

It follows that man is someone in whom there is fear of heaven. Since man was created with the evil inclination, which removes him from fear of heaven, what is the advice that we can say that by this he will be awarded fear of heaven? To this comes the answer that through Torah he will be able to defeat the evil inclination, as our sages said, "I have created the evil inclination; I have created the Torah as a spice, for the light in it reforms him." Accordingly, we can interpret that "Man was created by the Torah," since the reason why the discernment of "man" can emerge is specifically through the Torah. This is the meaning of "Man was created in the Torah."

In this way we can interpret what he wrote there in the holy *Zohar*, "The world was created in the Torah." This, too, is difficult to understand. What is the connection between the Torah, which is a spiritual thing, and the Torah being called the "names of the Creator"? How does the corporeal world extend from it? According to the above, we can resolve that "the world was created" refers to the whole world, meaning a world in which there are souls, for the purpose of creation was to do good to His creations, to the souls, for the creatures to receive delight and pleasure. Since the creation of the world refers to the will to receive, in order to have equivalence of form between branch and root, there was the *Tzimtzum* [restriction], meaning concealment, so the upper light, which is delight and pleasure, will not be revealed.

Thus, how can the world exist, so they can receive and not die, as it occurred in the breaking of the vessels, which broke and died because they could not aim to bestow? Through the Torah, whose light reforms, they will receive vessels of bestowal, and with these *Kelim* they will be able to receive abundance and pleasure and exist because they will be able to receive in order to bestow.

This is the meaning of "The world was created with the Torah." The creation of the world, which was in order to "do good to His creations," was immediately with the intention to bestow, and this was done by the Torah. It follows from all the above that we must always consider the goal, which is to "do good to His creations." If the evil inclination comes to a person and asks him all of Pharaoh's questions, he should not reply with lame excuses, but say, "Now, with your questions, I can begin with the work of bestowal."

This means that we should not say about the questions of the evil inclination that it came to us in order to lower us from our degree. On the contrary, now it is giving us a place to work, by which we will ascend on the degrees of wholeness. That is, any overcoming in the world is called "walking in the work of the Creator," since each penny joins into a great amount." That is, all the times we overcome accumulate to a certain measure required to become a *Kli* for the reception of the abundance.

Overcoming means taking a part of a vessel of reception and adding it to the vessels of bestowal. It is like the *Masach* [screen], which we must put on the *Aviut* [thickness/will to receive]. It follows that if one has no will to receive, one has nothing on which to place a *Masach*. For this reason, when the evil inclination brings us foreign thoughts, this is the time to take these thoughts and raise them above reason.

This is something one can do with everything one's soul desires. He should not say that now he has received rejection from the work. Rather, he should say that he was given thoughts and desires from above so as to have room to admit them into *Kedusha* [holiness]. It therefore follows that it is to the contrary: because he is brought closer from above, he was sent work.

It was said about this: "The ways of the Lord are straight; righteous walk in it and transgressors fail in it." That is, if he is rewarded, he receives an ascent by it. If he is not (rewarded), he receives by it a descent in spirituality. The order of descents is gradual, each according to his order. Normally, a person forgets, meaning he forgets that there is the matter of work at all, that he must yearn for *Dvekut* [adhesion] with the Creator. Instead, all the energy he had goes into corporeal things, meaning that at that time he finds more flavor in corporeal things.

That is, while he was connected to the work of the Creator, he was slightly removed from corporeal things. This means that he did not appreciate (corporeal things) as something to consider. But when he begins to veer off from the work, every corporeal thing, which he regarded as unimportant, becomes so important to him that the smallest thing becomes a great disturbance to him, and blocks him in the middle of the way, and he cannot move forward.

Sometimes, during the descent he has received, he remembers that there is such a thing as spiritual work. When he remembers it he is saddened, and this sadness makes him want only to sleep. That is, he wants to remove himself from the situation he is in, and he thinks that through sleep he will forget about his situations. Sometimes he gives up altogether, meaning he says, "I don't see any progress in me. On the contrary, as much as I exert—and I should have made some progress, according to the efforts I have made in order to obtain something in spirituality—I see that I keep going backwards. It must be that this work, meaning work of bestowing, is not for me because I am unfit for it."

Usually, people say, "I have a weak character so I haven't the strength to overcome my desires." Sometimes they become smarter and say, "I don't see anyone who was awarded anything in spirituality." So after all his arguments with his body, the body makes him see that he is one hundred percent right, which brings him into a state where he wants to escape the campaign, reenter the corporeal world like everyone else, and not be smarter than everyone, but go with the flow. And most of all, he is certain it cannot be any different from what he has decided.

What does the Creator do? Once (one) has forgotten everything, he suddenly receives some awakening from the Creator and a longing for spirituality begins to seep into his heart again. He begins to work persistently once more, and the force of confidence works within him, as though he is certain to be rewarded with nearing the Creator. He forgets all the promises he has made with a clear mind and precise calculation to the point that he regretted the beginning, meaning that his heart regretted ever getting into this mess called the "work of bestowal." He was one hundred percent certain that his calculation was one hundred percent right, but the awakening from above he has received now makes him forget it all.

The reason is that so is the order of the real work: from above they want to show him that man is nothing, with all of his intellect, unless he asks the Creator to help him. If this happens, meaning that he knows for certain that it is impossible that he will be able to come out of the state he is in, under the rule of self-love, called "exile in Egypt," which applies both in mind and in heart.

However, if a person only says and does not feel one hundred percent that he cannot do anything, then the real nearing does not come from above. Rather, what happened before repeats itself, namely that thoughts and desires from the body come to him once more, and he begins the old arguments once more, and falls into those states again, and decides once more to escape the campaign, and makes the above decisions once again. Later, an awakening from above comes to him once more, which is called a "call," when he is being called upon, and there is a desire to bring him closer to the Creator once again. But then, if he does not exert in the opportunity he is given, the same order as before repeats itself.

This is similar to what we find in *The Zohar* (*Tazria*, item 6): "'Her price is far above pearls.' It should have said 'worth,' that it is harder to buy her than pearls. Why does it say 'price'? He replies that she sells and turns over to other nations all those who do not fully cling to her and are not whole with her, as you say, 'And the children of Israel abandoned the Lord, and He sold them to the hand of Sisera.' And then they are all far from those high and holy pearls, which are the secrets and the internality of the Torah, for they will have no share in them. This is why it is written, 'For her price is far above pearls.'"

Therefore, we must not be frightened at the body sometimes showing us dark colors. Rather, we must always be strengthened above reason and not heed the body's advice, which tells us about separation from *Kedusha*. Rather, we must overcome with true prayer and we are certain to be saved and come out from the slavery of the rule of Egypt and be rewarded with redemption.

On My Bed at Night

Article No. 23, Tav-Shin-Mem-Hey, 1984-85

The *Zohar* (*Tazria*, item 1) asks about the verse, "On my bed": "Rabbi Elazar started, 'On my bed at night I sought him whom my soul loves.' He asks, 'It says, 'On my bed.' It should have said, 'In my bed.'' What is 'On my bed'? He answers, 'The assembly of Israel spoke before the Creator and asked Him about the exile, since she is seated among the rest of the nations with her children and lies in the dust. And because she is lying in another land, an impure one, she said, 'I ask on my bed, for I am lying in exile,' and exile is called 'nights.' Hence, 'I sought him whom my soul loves,' to deliver me from it.'"

It is known that the assembly of Israel is *Malchut*, who contains all the souls. It is also known that every man is considered a small world, as it is written in the holy *Zohar*, that man consists of the seventy nations of the world. This corresponds to the seven *Sefirot*, where each *Sefira* [singular of *Sefirot*] consists of ten, thus they are seventy discernments. They are the opposite of *Kedusha* [holiness], for there are seven *Sefirot* of *Kedusha* and the seventy nations of which man consists. This means that each nation has a special lust that pertains to it. Man consists of all seventy lusts that exist in general in the seventy nations.

Within man there is also Israel, which is his self. However, it is called a "point in the heart," meaning a point of darkness. This means that the Israel in her does not illuminate and she is regarded as *Achoraim* [posterior]. The reason is that she is in exile under the rule of the seventy nations in a person.

They have the strength to rule over the Israel in her by questions that they ask Israel when he wants to do something for the Creator, which is called *Yashar-El* [straight to the Creator]. At that time they make one understand that it is not worthwhile to work (but) only for self-love. But concerning in order to bestow, they ask "What," "What is this work for you," which we learned is the question of the wicked. And if one wants to overcome his argument, then Pharaoh's question comes, who said, "Who is the Lord that I should obey His voice?"

If these questions do not work on a person the first time, they repeat themselves all day, as it is written (Psalms, 42:11), "With the murder of my bones my adversaries revile me while they say to me all day long, 'Where is your God?'" and one cannot come out of their rule. They degrade the Israel in man to the dust, as it is written (Psalms 44), "For our soul has bowed down to the dust; Our belly clings to the ground." We should interpret that our soul's bowing down to the dust causes our belly to be attached to the ground.

The "belly" is one's vessels of reception. This is the meaning of the point in the heart being in the dust, which causes our *Kelim* [vessels] to have *Dvekut* [adhesion] only with worldliness, which is self-love.

But if the kingdom of heaven were honored, then we would certainly be honored if we had the chance to serve the Creator with anything. We would regard even the smallest service as a fortune. For such an honor, it would be worthwhile to relinquish all the pleasures that come to us through self-love. This is the meaning of what we say in the supplementary prayer of *Shalosh Regalim* [Three Pilgrimages], "Our Father, our King, show the glory of Your kingship upon us soon." That is, we ask of the Creator that since the kingdom of heaven is degraded and in a state of *Shechina* [Divinity] in the dust, we want the Creator to show us the importance and glory of the kingdom of heaven, and then it will be our great honor to be awarded by it with exiting self-love and to be granted with love of the Creator.

This is the meaning of what *The Zohar* interprets, "Hence, 'I sought him whom my soul loves,' to deliver me from it." It is known that man consists of three souls: 1) a soul of *Kedusha*; 2) a soul of *Klipat* [*Klipa* of] *Noga*; 3) a soul of the three impure *Klipot* [plural of *Klipa*]. The soul of *Kedusha* illuminates only as a point. Therefore, the soul of *Klipat Noga* should connect to the soul of *Kedusha*, as we explained in previous articles in the name of Baal HaSulam. But since the main operator is the soul of *Klipat Noga*—since the soul of the three impure *Klipot* cannot be corrected, and the soul of *Kedusha* does not need to be corrected because it is holy—then all the work is with the soul of *Klipat Noga*.

When (one) performs *Mitzvot* [good deeds/corrections], *Klipat Noga* joins the *Kedusha*. When he commits transgressions, the soul of *Klipat Noga* joins the soul of the three impure *Klipot*. However, the soul of *Kedusha* is in *Achoraim* [posterior], meaning it does not illuminate, and is in lowliness. This is why we do not want to exert to do good deeds so that *Klipat Noga* will join the *Kedusha*.

Therefore, "On my bed at night I sought him whom my soul loves," to bring him out of her, for the soul of *Kedusha* belongs to the assembly of Israel but is in another, impure land, asking from the one whom my soul loves to get me out of the impure land. That is, since the soul of *Kedusha* is in lowliness, the soul of *Noga* does things that the three impure *Klipot* want. It follows that at that time, when the soul of *Kedusha* must suffer the rule of the impure *Klipot* that govern at that time, the soul of *Kedusha* asks to be delivered from this exile, called "nights."

It is written there in *The Zohar* (item 9 in the *Sulam* [commentary]): "Rabbi Aha says, 'We learned that the Creator sentences whether a drop is male or female, and you say, 'A woman who inseminates first, delivers a male.' Thus, the Creator's sentence is redundant.'

Rabbi Yosi said, 'Indeed, the Creator decides between a drop of male and a drop of female. And because He has discerned it, He sentences whether it is to be a male or a female.'"

This explanation is unclear. Because "He has discerned it, He sentences whether it is to be a male." Why does He need to sentence? It will obviously be either male or female? He interprets there in the *Sulam*: "There are three partners in a man: the Creator, his father, and his mother. His father gives the white in him; his mother—the red in him; and the Creator gives the soul. If the drop is a male, the Creator gives the soul of a male. If it is a female, the Creator gives the soul of a female. It turns out that when the woman inseminates first, the drop has not become a male yet, if the Creator had not sent within her a soul of a male. This discernment that the Creator discerns in a drop—that it is fit for a soul of a male or a female—is considered 'the sentencing of the Creator.' Had He not discerned it and did not send a soul of a male, the drop would not have become a male. Thus, the two statements do not contradict one another."

To understand all the above in the work we should interpret that all three partners are in one person. "His father and mother" are the causes of the birth of a son. His "father" is the male, called "man," and "wholeness" because male is regarded as wholeness. His father gives the white because "white" is called "wholeness," where there is no dirt. His mother is called *Nekeva* [female] and "woman," and she is called a "deficiency," since *Nekev* [hole] means deficiency [lack] and is called "redness." It is as we say that when there is red light, you cannot cross, which is called a "barrier," when you cannot go forward. The Creator gives the soul, since man can do anything, but the spirit of life belongs to the Creator.

The order of the work is that man should divide the workday into day and night. "Day" means wholeness, and "night" means deficiency. In order for a son to be born and have a long life, that son needs to be born by his father and mother, since his father gives the whiteness, meaning the wholeness, regarded as "a male man," and his mother gives him the lack, called a "female woman." The wholeness and deficiency should be because a person needs to receive nourishment for sustenance, and then he can work. Likewise, here in the work of the Creator, a person must receive spiritual nourishment, and then he can see what needs to be corrected. Otherwise, without nourishment, he does not have the strength for work, and we receive nourishment only from wholeness.

Therefore, we can elicit wholeness while engaging in Torah and *Mitzvot* [commandments], for then we do not examine how much we are exerting in keeping Torah and *Mitzvot*, to do them perfectly and flawlessly, meaning examining ourselves to see if we are fine or not. Rather, at that time we examine the Torah and *Mitzvot* themselves, meaning whose Torah and *Mitzvot* we are keeping. We must think about the giver of the Torah, as we bless, "Blessed are you the Lord, Giver of the Torah." With the *Mitzvot* we say, "Who has sanctified us with His *Mitzvot*," meaning to know that we are keeping the *Mitzvot* of the Creator.

Therefore, we need to consider the importance of the giver, and derive from this vitality and joy from meriting observing what He has commanded us, to some extent. At that time we should say that although the work is still not "actual observing," in order to bestow in every way, we should still believe that there are people to whom it did not occur in mind or will to keep Torah and *Mitzvot* even in the slightest bit. But to us the Creator has given a desire and will to keep a little, meaning with little understanding, but after all we are doing something, while people do not even have that something. When we pay attention to this, we receive vitality and nourishment.

This is called "his father gives the white," as we said that wholeness is called "whiteness," where there is no dirt. There is a twofold gain here: 1) In this way he receives elation from being adhered to the Whole, meaning to the Creator, and we must believe that what He gives is wholeness. Wholeness makes a man whole, making him feel whole, too. Naturally, he derives nourishment from this, so he can live and persist and then have strength to do the holy work. 2) According to the importance he acquires during the work of wholeness, he will later have room to feel the deficiency with regard to his work, which is not truly pure. That is, at that time he can depict to himself how much he is losing by his negligence in the work, for he can compare between the importance of the Creator and his own lowliness, and this will give him energy to work.

However, one should also correct oneself, or he will remain in the dark and will not see the true light that shines on the *Kelim* [vessels] that are suitable for it, called "vessels of bestowal." The correction of the *Kelim* is called *Nukva*, deficiency, when he works on correcting his deficiencies. This is regarded as "His mother gives the red." That is, at that time he sees the red light, which are the barriers on his way, which prevent him from reaching the goal.

Then comes the time of prayer, since the man sees the measures of the work that he has in matters of "mind and heart," and how he has not progressed in the work of bestowal. He also sees how his body is weak, that he does not have great powers to be able to overcome his nature. For this reason, he sees that if the Creator does not help him, he is lost, as it is written (Psalms 127), "If the Lord does not build the house, they who build it labor in it in vain."

From those two, meaning from wholeness and deficiency, which are the "father and mother," it turns out that the Creator is the one who helps him, giving him a soul, which is the spirit of life. And then the newborn is born. This is why our sages said, "There are three partners in man." The newborn that was born is regarded as a sustainable descendant, meaning that he has a long life. Otherwise, if it does not have the soul that the Creator gives it, that newborn is called "aborted," meaning it is unsustainable and "falls from its degree." We should know that the Creator wants to give, as explained in several places that "the upper light does not stop illuminating," but we need *Kelim* that are fit to receive.

Therefore, there are two discernments we need to make in what depends on man's preparation, since there are two forces in man: 1) forces of reception, 2) forces of bestowal. We need to correct these two forces so they work in order to bestow. The force of bestowal in a person is called "man," and the force of reception in a person is called "woman," "female." Inseminating means that a person makes an effort in order to obtain something. For example, when a person needs wheat, he sows wheat. This means that his work will yield wheat. If he needs potatoes he will sow potatoes. That is, one exerts according to the kind that one wants, and this is what he gets.

It is similar in the work of the Creator. If one wants to correct the vessels of bestowal, called "male," "man," which is called "If the man inseminates first," meaning that his initial thought is to correct the vessels of bestowal, then she "delivers a female," as it is known that there is an inverse relation between *Kelim* and lights, since "female light" is called *Katnut* [smallness/infancy].

"If the woman inseminates first," meaning that he wants to correct the vessels of reception so they work in order to bestow, then "she delivers a son," meaning male light, which is the light of *Gadlut* [adulthood/greatness]. "And the Creator gives the soul." The Creator distinguishes about the drop, meaning about man's work, of which type was his "sowing," meaning preparation. That is, if he wants his vessels of reception to work in order to bestow then the Creator gives him a soul of a male, called "*Neshama* [soul] of *Gadlut*." If he is regarded as a "man," meaning wants only his vessels of bestowal to work in order to bestow, he receives from the Creator the light of *Katnut*, called "female."

Three Times in the Work

Article No. 24, Tav-Shin-Mem-Hey, 1984-85

A person should discern three times in his work: 1) past, 2) present, 3) future.

"Past" is when he begins with the work of the Creator. At that time he must look at the past, meaning the reason why he now wants to take upon himself the burden of the kingdom of heaven. That is, he must scrutinize the reason—if this reason is sufficient for him to begin with the work of the Creator to the point of "And you shall reflect on Him day and night," when he has nothing to think of but the Torah because he has come to a resolution that nothing is worth contemplating but the Torah.

This must be because he feels he is in big trouble, and he has nothing in the world worth living for, and he finds nothing but *Dvekut* [adhesion] with the Creator. But to be rewarded with *Dvekut* with the Creator, one must exit self-love. And to exit self-love he believes in the words of our sages: "I have created the evil inclination; I have created the Torah as a spice."

This is the reason that compels him to contemplate the Torah day and night, for otherwise he cannot exit self-love. It follows that the reason for the Torah is *Dvekut* with the Creator. And the reason that obligates him to be rewarded with *Dvekut* with the Creator must always be renewed, since there are many who are against this reason. Each time the body comes with new questions and wants to question that reason. At one time it tells him this is difficult; another time it tells him this is not for him, and brings him sparks of despair; and sometimes it brings foreign thoughts into his mind and heart.

Therefore, we must look at the past, meaning we must always examine at the reason that gave him the initial awakening for it. That is, perhaps there were other reasons that have made him begin the work of the Creator, meaning that his initial reason was not in order to achieve *Dvekut* with the Creator, but perhaps it was another reason. Afterwards, because "from *Lo Lishma* [not for Her sake] we come to *Lishma* [for Her sake]," the second reason was in order to achieve *Dvekut* with the Creator.

It could also be to the contrary, that the first reason was to achieve *Dvekut* with the Creator, and then, for various reasons, he acquired other reasons that obligated him to take upon himself the burden of Torah and *Mitzvot* [commandments]. It follows from all the above that we must always examine the reason that compels us to walk in the work of the Creator. This is regarded as having to learn from the past, referring to the reasons that surround all the ways of his work. That is, the reason is regarded as the goal: according to the greatness and importance of the goal, to that extent a person can exert.

However, there is a difference in what is regarded as "importance." With regard to importance, it depends on what a person regards as important. Usually, people appreciate things that yield self-gratification, meaning only what concerns self-love. But if the goal is to bestow, it is unnatural that one should regard this as important.

For this reason, if the reason is not a real reason, he cannot go all the way, meaning achieve *Dvekut*. This is so because when he sees that he will not have self-gratification, he promptly escapes the campaign because the reason for which he took upon himself to keep Torah and *Mitzvot* was not so as to bestow, but for his own benefit.

For this reason, when he does not feel self-gratification during the work, he is compelled to be negligent in the work, since he sees that he does not feel that this will be a reward for him because the whole basis of his work was in *Lo Lishma*. However, from *Lo Lishma* we come to *Lishma*, so the order is that he is shown what *Lishma* feels like, meaning not for his own benefit but for the benefit of the Creator, and then he promptly escapes the campaign.

Hence, one must always scrutinize one's goal, meaning his reason. He must always remember that the goal is to bestow upon the Creator. Then, when he is shown the feeling of bestowal, he does not become confused but knowns that it is difficult because it is against his nature.

Only now, once he sees that it is difficult to work in order to bestow, there is room for prayer from the bottom of the heart because he sees that he cannot do anything except pray to the Creator to give him that strength. For this reason we must always study the past, meaning to have a real reason that compels us to engage in the work of holiness.

"Present" is a discernment that a person feels during the work. A person should do the work of holiness on several aspects. It is as our sages said (*Avot*, Chapter 1, Discourse 2), "He would say, 'The world stands on three things—on the Torah, on work, and on good deeds.'"

"World" means "man," for every person is a small world in and of itself, as it is written in the holy *Zohar*. In order for man to exist, meaning for man to exist in the world, and feel and attain the Creator as benevolent, he needs the three above-mentioned things, since man was created with the evil inclination, which is the desire to receive only for himself.

There was a *Tzimtzum* [restriction] on that will to receive, meaning concealment of the upper abundance, so the delight and pleasure are not felt before a person achieves equivalence of form, when all his actions are only in order to bestow. For this reason, we need the Torah, as our sages said (*Kidushin*, 30b), "I have created the evil inclination; I have created for it the Torah as a spice."

Work is required because work is prayer. A prayer is work in the heart. That is, since the root of man's heart is the will to receive, and he needs the opposite, meaning that it will work only to bestow and not receive, it follows that he has a lot of work in inverting it.

And since this is against nature, he must pray to the Creator to help him come out of his nature and enter what is discerned as above nature. This is called a "miracle," and only the Creator can perform miracles. That is, for man to be able to exit self-love is a miraculous act.

RASHI interprets "good deeds" to mean "lending his money to the poor. This is greater than charity because he is not ashamed. Moreover, good deeds applies to rich and poor, to the living and to the dead, to one's body and to one's money." But charity is as was said, "Good deeds is greater than charity," and as was said, "And the mercy of the Lord is from everlasting to everlasting on those who fear Him," "For I said, 'A world of mercy shall be built,' to teach you that the world exists for mercy."

Because mercy is the exit from self-love to love of the Creator, as Rabbi Akiva said, "Love your neighbor as yourself, this is the great rule of Torah," in the "present," we should see that the three above discernments operate in him in the present. At that time he should also include the past in the present, meaning the goal for which he is making all the efforts.

"Future": He needs to see the future, what can be attained until he achieves his wholeness, since it is known that *Ohr Pnimi* [Inner Light] means what illuminates in the present, and *Ohr Makif* [Surrounding Light] is what he should receive in the future.

Usually, when a person makes a deal and invests a lot of money, it is certainly in order to make a lot of money. Accordingly, we understand that if he bought a lot of goods it was in order to make a lot of money by selling the goods right away. That is, the merchant bought goods in the fair. When he brought the goods, and his town's people saw he brought a lot of goods, they all thought that he would soon rent many shops in order to sell the goods right away. But then they saw that he put all the goods in warehouses and did not want to sell the goods. Yet, everyone saw that although he did not sell the goods, he was as happy as if he had made a fortune. The people close to the merchant could not understand him. They asked, "Why the happy face? After all, you did not sell a thing, and you did not make any money, so why are you so happy?"

He told them: "I bought a lot of goods cheaply because their prices dropped, and all the merchant were reluctant to buy them. I bought them because I know by calculation that two years from now they will be in great demand for they will be rare. At that time this will make me rich. So when I consider my future, I am happy, though at the moment, I have not made any profit."

Therefore, we see that if the future shines in the present, although he still has nothing in the present, it is of no consequence. Rather, he can be happy about the future as about the present. However, this is so precisely if the future shines in the present. In the language of Kabbalah, it is considered that he enjoys the *Ohr Makif*, meaning that he enjoys the light that will come in the future.

That is, if he sees that there is a valid way to achieve the goal, although he has not achieved wholeness, if the confidence of the goal illuminates for him he can enjoy in the present as though the *Ohr Makif* shines for him now in the *Kelim*.

Baal HaSulam said similarly about the words of our sages, "Righteous say psalms about the future," meaning that the righteous can say psalms about what is destined to come to them later. That is, they believe that in the end they will be rewarded with wholeness, and based on that they say psalms, even though they have no yet attained wholeness.

This matter is brought in *The Zohar* (*Vayelech*, item 47): "Rabbi Elazar said, 'Israel are destined to say psalms from below upward and from above downward, and tie the knot of faith, as it is written,

'Then Israel shall sing this singing.' It does not say, 'sang,' but 'Shall sing,' meaning in the future.'" It follows that man should receive illumination from *Ohr Makif*, which is from the future, after the present, and needs to draw it into the present.

This is why all three times—past, present, and future—are included in the present. However, the counsel of the evil inclination is always to the contrary, meaning to divide the three times so they do not illuminate together. Therefore, we must always go against the evil inclination and say, "What it says is certainly not in our favor, as it is not its role to assist us in the work."

For example, it is written in article no. 11 (*Tav-Shin-Mem-Hey*) that when the evil inclination says to a person, "Why are you exerting so long is prayer and Torah? After all, your aim is not for the Creator. I can understand why other people exert in Torah and prayer, since their intention is for the Creator, but this is not so with you." At that time we should reply to it: "On the contrary, I do work for the Creator, and I do not want to listen to you," since it wishes to obstruct him in the work, meaning cause not to engage in Torah and *Mitzvot*.

Afterwards it comes and argues, "You are righteous, and your intention is only for the Creator. You are not like other people." At that time one should say to it: "On the contrary, all my work is not for the Creator, and I know that everything you say is not for my benefit," since it wishes to fail him with the transgression of pride, which is the worst thing of all, as our sages said, "Anyone who is proud, the Creator says, 'He and I cannot dwell in the same abode.'" Therefore, one cannot determine which way to go—on the path of lowliness or on the path of greatness. It is all done on a case by case basis.

In Every Thing We Must Discern between Light and Kli

Article No. 25, Tav-Shin-Mem-Hey, 1984-85

In every thing we must discern between light and *Kli* [vessel], meaning between the Giver, who is the Creator, and the receiver, who is the creature.

And since there is no light without a *Kli*, meaning if there is no one to attain it, then who can speak of it? Therefore, we can only speak of light that is clothed in a *Kli*, meaning the abundance that the Giver gives to the body, namely the measure of impression of the body from the abundance that pours down to it. We must believe that everything a person receives into his body comes from Him, both corporeality and spirituality, since it is known that there is no other force in the world that will bestow upon him.

Therefore, when a person begins to come into the work of the Creator, we must thank and praise the Creator, for this is the beginning of man's entrance into the work. The order of the work begins as our sages said, "One should always establish the praise of the Creator and subsequently pray. From where do we know this? From Moses, as it is written, 'And I pleaded with the Lord at that time,' and as it is written, 'God, You have begun,' and 'afterwards is written, 'Let me go over, I pray Thee, and see the good land'"" (*Berachot* 32a).

Therefore, when he begins to thank the Creator, he first needs to thank the Creator for creating the world, as we say during the prayer, "Blessed are You who said, 'Let there be the world.'" And then begins the work, meaning the extent to which he can thank the Creator for creating the world. In other words, the extent of the gratitude is as the extent of the pleasure.

Here begins the scrutiny of true and false, and here lies the difference between the work of the individual and the work of the public, meaning between one whose Torah is his craft or not. The meaning is as Baal HaSulam explained: His Torah is his craft means that through the Torah he wants to be rewarded with faith. Or, according to people who belong to the general public, it means that they study Torah in order to be rewarded with the next world, meaning in order to receive, and not to people who belong to the individual, namely engage in order to bestow.

When a person begins to praise the Creator, there is a scrutiny of true and false. That is, usually, when one needs to thank another person for helping him, the measure of gratitude is according to the measure of feeling that he has helped him. Therefore, when a person begins to thank the Creator for what He has given him, the body begins to think of the benefits He has done to him, and to the extent that he is impressed with the benefit that He has done to him, so is the measure of the gratitude.

Therefore, when a person says, "Blessed is He who said, 'Let there be the world,'" it also depends on the extent to which he is enjoying the world. At that time the body begins to show him that he lacks corporeality and lacks spirituality, and does not let him establish the praises of the Creator. At that time there is a lot of work because then he needs to go above reason and believe that the Creator is doing only good to him, and there is also a scrutiny of true and false.

Since the general name of the Creator is Good Who Does Good, there is a lot of work to believe above reason that the Creator is good and does good. It therefore follows that when a person begins to establish the praise of the Creator, he has what to pray for so he can go above reason. Beforehand, there was not such a great lack of faith in the Creator above reason, but now he feels his lack of faith, and needs to learn Torah so that the light in it will reform him.

It turns out that his desire to establish the praise of the Creator causes him a deficiency. When he has a deficiency, called a *Kli*, to the extent of his impression from being far from wholeness he has room for work and a need for prayer and Torah.

However, there is another deficiency: Sometimes a person sees his lowliness, gives up, and escapes the campaign. At that time, all the pleasures he receives are only if he forgets about his situation, meaning that he is not thinking about spirituality or he can sleep, meaning feel great pleasure in sleep. This is so not because at that time he derives from sleep some special pleasure, but that when he sleeps he does not remember about the work. This is his pleasure, since whenever he remembers about the work, the body immediately brings him despair and lowliness.

Therefore, a person must always be careful not to fall into despair, namely that a state of suffering has come to him because he sees that he cannot continue the work. This is why Baal HaSulam said that one should be careful to criticize himself, except when he allocates for this a special time, and not whenever the body tells him to introspect. Rather, he should tell the body: "I have a special time for criticizing if I am going according to the line that I was given or have veered off from the correct line. Now I am engaging in Torah and prayer, and I am certain that the Creator will help me as He has helped all the servants of the Creator who wished to go by the right path and achieve the goal for which they were created."

In my previous article, and in article no. 11 [*Tav-Shin-Mem-Hey*], I have written that we must say the opposite of what the body tells us. And by this will understand the question of *The Zohar* and its answer (*Behukotai*, item 18): "'And do them.' He asks, 'What is, 'And do them'?' Since he already said 'walk' and 'keep,' why the 'do,' as well? He answers that one who performs the *Mitzvot* of the Torah and follows His ways, it is as though he has made Him above. The Creator said, 'It is as if he has made Me,' and established Him. Hence, 'And do them' as a law and ordinance," thus far its words.

This answer seems very perplexing. How can it be said that by keeping Torah and *Mitzvot* we make Him above? After all, "The whole earth is full of His glory," even before the creatures observed Torah and *Mitzvot*. Thus, what does it mean "As though you have made Me"?

As said above, we do not speak of a light without a *Kli*, for in regard to whom is it discerned that there is light? When there is a *Kli*, the *Kli* obtains the light. Therefore, when we say that the purpose of creation is to do good to His creations it pertains only to the creatures when they receive the delight and pleasure. This is regarded as having a *Kli*, and the *Kli* attains Him in a way that they receive from the Creator only delight and pleasure. But when the creatures do not receive from Him delight and pleasure, the question arises, "With regard to whom the name of the Creator, The Good Who Does Good, appears?"

For this reason, in order for the name of the Creator, the general name of all the names—The Good Who Does Good—to be revealed, and in order for the creatures to receive the delight and pleasure from the Creator, for His benefit to be complete, meaning that there will be no shame in the gift, hence there was the *Tzimtzum* and concealment, where we cannot attain and feel the good before we qualify ourselves with vessels of bestowal, which is equivalence of form. It turns out that then the name, Good Who Does Good is not revealed, which causes the creatures not to feel the Creator, and this is why there are wicked in the world who do not believe in the Creator.

In order for His name to be revealed in the world before everyone, all the *Kelim* need is equivalence of form. And in order to have the ability to acquire vessels of bestowal, which are *Kelim* [vessels] of equivalence of form, we can obtain this only by keeping Torah and *Mitzvot*. That is, while observing Torah and *Mitzvot* we must aim that it will be in order to raise the glory of Israel through observing the Torah and *Mitzvot*.

Israel means the letters *Yashar-El* [straight to the Creator], where the actions are directly toward the Creator and not for one's own benefit. This is called "equivalence of form." In the words of the holy *Zohar*, this is called "raising the *Shechina* [Divinity] from the dust," since spirituality is not honored in our eyes so we can tell our bodies that it is a great privilege to be able to serve the Creator, and then the body surrenders and annuls before the *Kedusha* [holiness]. This is the meaning of what the holy *Zohar* says, that through "walk in My statutes and keep My commandments," by that "And do them," meaning as though you make Me above. In other words, by this you make the name of the Creator be revealed as Good Who Does Good, meaning that everyone will feel the good because you will be rewarded with equivalence of form.

Show Me Your Glory

Article No. 26, Tav-Shin-Mem-Hey, 1984-85

"And he said, 'Show my Your glory ... Then I will take My hand away and you shall see My back, but My face shall not be seen'" (Exodus, 33). We should understand what the question about Moses implies to us, and the Creator's answer with regard to our work.

When a person begins with the work of the Creator, he longs to see the glory of the Creator. That is, when the Creator shines for him, when he has a taste for Torah and *Mitzvot* [commandments], and longs for spirituality, he can engage in the holy work. At that time he knows that he is walking on the path of the Creator and feels that he is above the ordinary people, that the whole public is worldly, and only he knows and understands what spirituality is.

It is known that our sages said (*Avot*, Chapter 4, item 4), "Rabbi Levitas, Man of Yavne says, 'Be very, very humble.'" Therefore, he has a lot of work finding some deficiency in himself so he can say that he is humble. But since it is a *Mitzva* [commandment/good deed] to do what our sages said, he takes it above reason and says, "Of course I am still incomplete."

Also, there is a time of *Achoraim* [posterior], when the craving for Torah and *Mitzvot* does not shine for him and he does not feel a lack in that he does not crave *Dvekut* [adhesion] with the Creator. In a state of *Achoraim*, a person can see himself, meaning his real situation, if he still sees that he is higher than the rest of the people. At that time he needs to work on lowliness, to take upon himself the *Mitzva* of humility above reason, while he is looking at other people, who are in a state of spiritual decline, while he is in an ascent. It turns out that only in a state of *Achoraim* he can see the truth, but during the *Panim* [anterior] he might deceive himself.

However, there are many discernments in the degree of *Achoraim*, too. If a person has already entered the work of truth, meaning on the way that one has to work in order to bestow, only then does one begin to feel real states of *Achoraim*. At that time one occasionally receives an image of *Achoraim*, when he sees his fall, although he had a state of *Panim* before the fall to the state he is in. But now that he sees that he has no desire for Torah and *Mitzvot*, or for prayer and so forth, he feels that now he is as an empty *Kli*, that he derives no "moisture" from the work of the Creator. In addition, he sees himself as though he has never worked the holy work and does not even know what the work of the Creator is.

Sometimes he comes into darkness where if he begins to say to himself that he must begin the work and it is pointless to remain without any purpose in life, it seems to him that he is saying to himself something new, that he has never heard about spiritual matters. At that time he is surprised at himself, that he can feel such a feeling—that he is in a state of a beginner who has never engaged in work—while there is still some recollection in his memory from when he thought that he was always among the advanced ones in the work, and suddenly he has forgotten everything and he remembers it as if he is dreaming.

It follows that he is seeing his real state only at a time of *Achoraim*. This is the meaning of "you shall see My back, but My face shall not be seen." At that time he has room for work, meaning to ask of the Creator to bring him to Him and show him the illumination of His face. At that time he comes to repentance: "Until He who knows the mysteries will testify that he will not turn back to folly."

It is written in the introduction to *The Study of the Ten Sefirot* (items 53-54): "We must know that the whole matter of work in keeping Torah and *Mitzvot* by way of choice applies primarily to the two aforementioned discernments of concealed Providence. And Ben Ha Ha says about that time: 'The reward is according to the pain.' Since His Guidance is not revealed, it is impossible to see Him but only in concealment of the face, meaning from behind. However, when the Creator sees that one has completed one's measure of exertion and finished everything he had to do in strengthening his choice in faith in the Creator, the Creator helps him. Then, one attains open Providence, meaning the revelation of the face."

According to the above, the beginning of the work on the path of truth is in *Achoraim*. This is so in order for a person to prepare for himself *Kelim* [vessels] where the light of the Creator can be. Also, *Kelim* are desires. This means that before a person passes the state of *Achoraim*, he does not know that he needs the Creator to help him, but thinks that he can achieve his wholeness by himself and he does not need any special help from the Creator.

Rather, he knows and believes, as is customary in Israel, that although a person sees that it makes sense that man is the operator, he still believes that the Creator helps him obtain his wish. But in the work of bestowal, a person sees that the mind is telling him that he cannot achieve the degree of bestowal, but he rather sits and waits for the Creator to help him. It follows that only this is regarded as needing the Creator. This is called a *Kli* and "desire."

The path of truth is called *Lishma* [for Her sake], meaning that he does everything in order to bestow contentment upon the Creator. At that time the resistance of the body comes to him when it argues that it understands that all his work is to satisfy the vessels of the body, which is self-love. At that time one begins to see that he cannot go against the body, and then he needs the Creator's help. This is considered that he already has a *Kli*, meaning a desire and need for the Creator to fulfill him, and then what our sages said, "He who comes to purify is aided" (*Zohar*, Noah, item 63) happens in him. These are its words: "If a person comes to purify, he is aided with a holy soul. He is purified and sanctified, and he is called 'holy.'" We therefore see that before he has a *Kli*, he cannot be given light. But once it has been established in his heart that he needs the Creator's help, he receives help, as was said, that precisely when he comes to purify but sees that he is unable, he receives from above a holy soul, which is light that pertains to him, to help him be able to go forward and defeat his vessels of reception so he can use them in order to bestow upon the Creator.

Now we can interpret what is written, "Peace, peace, to the far and to the near." "Peace" indicates a complete division, since division is as our sages said, "One should always anger the evil inclination on the good inclination." RASHI interpreted that he should wage war on it. A person thinks that only when he feels close to the Creator he is whole, when it seems to him that he has already been awarded *Panim* [anterior]. But when he feels removed from the Creator, he thinks that he is not walking on the path of wholeness.

This is when we say, "Peace, peace," meaning the peace that the Creator says, as it is written (Psalms 85), "I will hear what the Lord says, for He will speak peace unto His nation, and unto His pious ones, and let them not turn back to folly." Regarding this verse, we must believe that the Creator says "peace" even when he (a person) feels that he is far from the Creator. This is so because who has made him see that now he is farther than at another time? Normally, a person begins to feel that he is far when he increases Torah and *Mitzvot* and wishes to walk more on the path of truth. At that time he sees that he is farther.

It follows that according to the rule, "A *Mitzva* induces a *Mitzva*," he should have felt closer. However, the Creator brings him closer by showing him the truth, so he will pay attention to the Creator's help. That is, He shows him that a person cannot win the war without the help of the Creator. It follows that at the time of remoteness (when one feels removed), which is regarded as *Achoraim*, this is the time of nearing the Creator.

Repentance

Article No. 27, Tav-Shin-Mem-Hey, 1984-85

It is written in *The Zohar* (*Nasso*, item 28): "This commandment is the commandment of *Teshuva* [repentance], and this is *Bina*. What is *Bina*? She is the letters *Ben Yod-Hey* [Son of *Yod-Hey*]. That son is *Vav*, which is attached to her and receives from her *Mochin* of *Yod-Hey*. Anyone who repents, it is as though he has returned the letter *Hey*, which is *Malchut*, to the letter *Vav*, which is *Ben Yod-Hey*, by which *HaVaYaH* is completed."

In *The Zohar* (*Nasso*, item 29), "The letter *Hey* is certainly a confession of words. This is the meaning of "Take words with you and return to the Lord. Say to Him, '...that we may present the fruit of our lips.'" Certainly, when one sins, he causes the *Hey* to depart from the *Vav*. This is why the Temple was ruined and Israel were removed from there and were exiled among the nations. For this reason, anyone who repents causes the return of the *Hey* to the letter *Vav*.

In *The Zohar* (*Nasso*, item 31), "This answer is called 'life.' This answer, which is *Malchut*, and *Hey de HaVaYaH*, is called 'life,' as it is written, 'for from it flow the offspring of life,' which are the souls of Israel, who are the offspring of *Malchut*, called 'life.' She is the *Hevel* [mouth fume] that comes in and out of one's mouth effortlessly. This is also the meaning of the *Hey* of *Hibaraam* [they were created], since the letter *Hey* is pronounced by the mouth more easily than all the other letters. It was said about her, 'for man lives by that which proceeds out of the mouth of the Lord,' for *Malchut* is called 'that which proceeds out of the mouth of the Lord.' Also, she is on a man's head, as in, 'On my head is the Lord present.' It was said about her, 'And the image of the Lord does he behold,' since *Malchut* is called 'the image of the Lord,' and also, 'Only in the image does a man walk.'"

In *The Zohar* (*Nasso*, item 32), "And because she is on a man's head, he must not walk four *Amot* [approx. four feet] bare-headed, for if she is removed from the man's head, life promptly leaves him."

Also in *The Zohar* (*Nasso*, item 34), "It was certainly about this shape of the *Hey* that they asserted, 'I have a good gift in my treasury, whose name is 'Shabbat' [Sabbath]. Shabbat is *Malchut*, when she ascends to *Bina*. When this *Malchut*, who is Shabbat, is over Israel, they have neither labor nor enslavement, and in it, the laboring and toiling soul stops and rests."

We need to understand all those names which the holy *Zohar* gives to *Malchut*.

1. What does it mean that *Malchut* is called *Hey*, and that she is *Hevel* without labor and toil? After all, there is a rule, "I found but did not labor, do not believe."

2. What does it mean that *Malchut* is called "life"? In several places, the holy *Zohar* calls *Malchut* "the quality of judgment," from whom extends death.

3. What does it imply that *Malchut* is called "the Lord's mouth"?

4. What does it mean that she is on a man's head?

5. Why does he say that *Malchut* is called the "image of the Lord," as it is written, "The image of the Lord does he behold"?

6. What does it mean that *Malchut* is called "*Tzelem*" [image], as it is written, "Only in the image does a man walk"?

To explain the above said, we first need to understand the purpose of creation, meaning the connection that the creatures should have with the Creator. All of our labor surrounds this axle, as well as the punishments we suffer if we do not come to correct it. This is also all the reward we receive when the creatures connect with the Creator.

It is known that the purpose of creation is to do good to His creations. However, in order to prevent the bread of shame, which is the matter of equivalence of form—as disparity of form in spirituality is called "moving farther," and equivalence of form is called "moving closer"—therefore, although His desire to do good to His creations is unbounded, still, the matter of equivalence of form was made, meaning not to receive delight and pleasure unless it is in order to bestow contentment upon the Creator.

From this extends to us the matter of labor, meaning that we must make a *Masach* [screen] so we can receive the delight and pleasure in order to bestow. This is the root of the labor that we have, as it is written in "General Preface to the Book, *Panim Meirot Umasbirot*" (item 3): "Know that the *Masach* in the *Kli* [vessel] of *Malchut* is the root of the darkness because of the detaining force that exists in the *Masach*, to stop the upper light from spreading to *Behina Dalet*. This is also the root of the labor in order to receive reward, since labor is an involuntary act, for the worker feels comfortable only when resting. But because the landlord is paying his salary, he annuls his will before the will of the landlord."

Thus, all we need to do is work. This is the only thing incumbent upon us, as it is written, "Which God has created to do." "Created" is what we attribute to the Creator, which is the desire to do good to His creations. From "created," extends to us the matter of separation and disparity of form. However, by "to do," meaning through the work we do in order to achieve the degree of in order to bestow, we move closer to the Creator once again through equivalence of form.

This is the meaning of the partnership between the creatures and the Creator, as it is written in *The Zohar* ("Introduction of the Book of Zohar," item 67): "'And to say to Zion, "You are My people."' Do not pronounce 'You are My people [*Ami*],' but 'You are with Me [*Imi*],' which means partnering with Me." That is, the Creator gave the will to receive, which is the deficiency He has created, which is called "darkness," as it is written, "And creates darkness." This comes from His desire to do good. The creatures must give the *Masach*, by which we have equivalence of form, for only then we have *Kelim* [vessels] that are suitable to receive the abundance that comes from His doing good to His creations. It follows that "has created" comes from above, and "to do" comes from the lower ones.

We find two matters in the labor: 1) The work and the reward are two matters. The work is not in the place of the reward, meaning that the time of work and the time of reward are separate. 2) The work and the reward are in the same place and the same time.

Labor means that one has to make a movement, and movement also happens in three ways: 1) labor of the body, 2) labor of the mind, 3) inner labor, which is the hardest. This is done when he must work with the mind, while doing things that contradict the mind and the intellect. That is, he must annul his mind. This means that the mind mandates that he will do this or that, but he makes a movement and cancels his mind—what he understands to be one hundred percent true according to his mind. And yet, he annuls it. This is true labor.

Let us return to the matter of labor. For example, a person makes a movement in order to receive a reward for the movement. Otherwise, he would remain at rest, since by the nature of creation, man longs for rest. The reason for this is explained in *The Study of the Ten Sefirot* (Part 1, *Histaklut Pnimit* [Inner Reflection], item 19): "This is because our root is motionless and restful; there is no motion in Him at all."

Therefore, we see that to the extent of the size, importance, and necessity that he has for the reward, to that extent he can exert. However, if he were to find a tactic to receive the reward without exertion, he would promptly waive the effort because to him the effort is but a means to obtain the reward. Thus, if he can get the reward through some other means, meaning not through work, then he will think, "Why should I work for nothing?" for he does not receive any reward for his work, since he can get what he will be given for the work without the work. It follows that he is not paid, and as we said, it is impossible to work without pay. Therefore, he waives the work.

This is regarded as the work and the reward being in two places and two times, since the work is, for example, that he is in a factory, and the pay is the paycheck he receives at the office. "In two times" means a separate time for work and a separate time for reception of the reward, since the work is every hour and every moment, and the reward is received only at the end of the day, when he finishes the work, as it is written (Deuteronomy, 24:14), "You shall not oppress the hired ... You shall give him his wages each day before the sun sets."

But sometimes the work and the pay are in the same place and the same time. This is so where the work itself is the reward, and he does not expect to be given any other reward for his work. That is, every move the body makes. As was said above, the body cannot make a move at all without reward.

But here, when his work is the reward, he receives the reward right where he works. And also, he receives the reward while he is working. That is, he does not need to wait for another time to be given the reward, such as for the end of the day, but rather each and every movement is rewarded right there and then.

For example: If a great ADMOR [high ranking rabbi] comes to Israel. If, for instance, the ADMOR of Lubavitch comes, and all his followers go to greet him. And he has a small package in his hand, which he gives to one of the followers to take it to the taxi. Afterwards the ADMOR takes out a $100 note and gives it to him in return for carrying the package to the taxi. His follower will no doubt refuse to receive the money. And should the ADMOR ask him, "Why won't you take the money? Is this too little? To an ordinary porter, who is not a follower and does not know what is an ADMOR, and does not know that I am in important person, if I were to give him a $10 note, he would have thanked me. To you I give ten times more than to an ordinary porter, and you won't take it?"

What should we say about this? His follower did not want to receive from him the money for carrying precisely because he knows the greatness and importance of the ADMOR, and the ADMOR has chosen him to serve him. This is a great reward, which is worth a lot. If any of the followers could buy from him the service that the ADMOR had let him do, the follower would certainly tell him: "All the money in the world is worthless compared to this service, which the ADMOR has given me, and has chosen me over everyone else."

Here we see that the labor and the reward are in the same place and the same time, since during the work, meaning while he is carrying the load—and he should be rewarded, since it is impossible to work without reward—he does not receive reward elsewhere, meaning that the work is the package he is carrying, and his reward is elsewhere, namely the money, or on another time, meaning that he is rewarded when he has finished the job.

Rather, here the work and the pay are in the same place. The work is carrying the package, and the reward is also carrying the ADMOR's package. He does not need to be given anything else that can be regarded as reward. Rather, the work of carrying the ADMOR's package is itself his reward.

This is also regarded as "in the same time," meaning that while he is working, at the same time he is rewarded, and it cannot be said here that he receives the reward after he has finished his work. Rather, he is receiving his pay at that very moment. The time of work and the time of pay are inseparable here because his entire reward is the service he is giving to the ADMOR. He enjoys this service more than any fortune in the world.

It follows that there is something new here—that it cannot happen that there can be such a thing as receiving reward each and every moment of one's work. Rather, the reward always comes after the work, as it is written, "to do them today and to receive the reward for them tomorrow." But here it is different, meaning that the work and the reward come as one.

It therefore follows that the work is not regarded as labor for which to receive reward. Only when the work and the reward are in two places and two times is work regarded as labor. That is, when the work is only a means to receive reward. Therefore, if he could toss the means and receive the purpose right away, why would he need the means? For this reason, since the whole purpose is the reward, his attention is only on the reward, and he is always searching how to work less and gain more.

But if the work and the reward are simultaneous, this work is not regarded as labor, of which we can say that he wants to get rid of the work, since the work and the pay are in the same place and the same time, since he enjoys serving an important person.

Accordingly, the labor in Torah and *Mitzvot* [commandments] is only when he is carrying the burden of Torah and *Mitzvot* like the porter carrying the ADMOR's package without knowing the ADMOR's importance. At that time he is always bargaining and wants more reward than the ADMOR is paying him for his labor, as we said in the allegory about the ADMOR of Lubavitch. That is, the follower who takes the package that the ADMOR has given him, since the follower recognizes the importance and greatness of the ADMOR, he wants no reward from the ADMOR. Rather, the size of the reward is measured by his recognition of the greatness and importance of the ADMOR; this is how he receives additional reward.

Although by nature we derive great pleasure when serving an important person, there is a difference in the importance. If a person is serving the most important person in town, while it pleases him, this is nothing like knowing that he is serving the most important person in the country. And his pleasure would be even greater if he knew that he was serving the most important person in the world. Then his joy would grow unboundedly.

It follows that we labor in Torah and *Mitzvot* because we lack the importance and greatness of the Creator. In the words of the holy *Zohar*, it is called that all our thoughts should be only to "raise the *Shechina* [Divinity] from the dust." That is, to us spirituality is completely in concealment of the face, and we do not feel the importance of our work. That is, we do not feel the importance of the one for whom we work, and whom we are serving. Therefore, when we overcome in the work, that work is by coercion. This is called "labor," since the reward is not in the place of the work.

In other words, by working in coercion, he expects to receive reward after some time and in a different place. Since the reward is far from the time of the work, he has time to think that now he is working and later he will receive reward. Therefore, there is a time when there is work there, and this is called "labor."

This is not so when he feels the importance of the work, meaning when he feels whom he is serving. At that time the reward is in the place of the work. Such work is not regarded as labor because the work and the reward are in the same time and in the same place, and this is not labor.

We can discern this when here, if the work and the reward are in the same place, the work itself is the reward. Therefore, he will not want to relinquish the work because naturally, you don't waive the goal, you only waive the means. Therefore, when the reward and the work are in the same place and the same time, a person cannot relinquish the work. If he relinquishes the work, he relinquishes the reward, since they are in the same place.

But if a person works like a porter, as in the above allegory, since there, there is labor because the work and the reward are in two different places, then the person wants to relinquish the labor, which is only a means for the reward, and he wants the reward. For example, a person who works to obtain the next world is willing to relinquish the work, meaning if he is given the next world without labor, since he needs only the goal and not the means.

We can discern the same regarding a gift. If an important person gives someone a gift, the recipient distinguishes two things about the gift: 1) that he loves him, or he would not have given him the gift, 2) the gift itself.

Here, too, we should make the same discernments, meaning what is the goal and what is the means. We should also determine the importance of the giver—if the giver is an important person then the love is the goal and the gift is only a means, where by the gift the love appears here. It follows that here, too, he is willing to relinquish the gift, but not the love. But if the giver is an ordinary person then the gift is the goal and love is the means, and he can relinquish the love as long as he gives him gifts. It follows that whether he gives or receives, there is always the same calculation of the importance of the person.

Thus far we talked about the reward and the work. However, there is another matter, namely punishment. That is, if he does not keep the Torah and *Mitzvot*, he is punished for it. But here, too, we should discern if the punishment is where he broke the laws or in another place and another time.

Let us take, for example, reward and punishment in regard to the rules of the state. One who breaks the laws of the state is punished. His punishment is not in the same place and the same time. A person who stole another man's possessions and was caught receives a punishment, say incarceration or a fine. However, this is all not in the same place or in the same time. But if it is not known that he is the thief, he will never be punished.

The same thing applies to transgressors of the rules of Torah. And yet, there is a big difference between breaching the law of Torah and breaching the laws of the state. In the revealed part, meaning the work in Torah and *Mitzvot*, every person can see what the other is doing. Here the transgression and the punishment are also not in the same place and the same time. If a person has committed a transgression and there are witnesses who saw it, he is punished for his transgression. For example, if he ate pork and people saw it, afterwards the court sentences that for this transgression he deserves to be flogged. It follows that the transgression and the punishment are in two places and two times, such as when breaking the laws of the state.

However, in man's work, approaching the internality of the Torah, which is called the "hidden part," there the matter is concealed and no one can see man's inner work, since no one knows what is in one's heart. If, for example, a man comes and says, "I want to make a big donation for a seminary where people learn Torah. However, I want there to be a big stone nameplate in the seminary where it will be inscribed that I gave the big donation, and to advertise in the papers that I gave such a big donation, so that wherever I go I will be respected."

We can say that he is a great philanthropist, but we cannot say that his intention is specifically to support learners of Torah, but that pursuit of honor, called "self-love," is also mixed in the support of the learners of Torah. However, his real intention is hidden from us because perhaps all he wants is really only to support the learners of Torah. And in order to prevent the recipients of his money from respecting him he pretends to want respect, that he wants to pay to charity because he wants to exchange the desire for money with a desire for honor. Naturally, he will not be respected.

Between man and man we can discern between the revealed part and the concealed part. But between man and God there is certainly a big difference. Our sages said, "One should always engage in Torah and *Mitzvot*, even if *Lo Lishma* [not for Her sake], since from *Lo Lishma* he comes to *Lishma* [for Her sake]" (*Pesachim*, 50b). Thus, in the act of *Mitzvot* and in the study of Torah there is a big difference between the revealed part, meaning the act, and the concealed part, meaning the intention, since no person can look at the intention, for the act that one does between man and God does not have a person in the middle who can criticize his intention. Normally, each one is busy with himself and does not have time to think of his friend's calculations. It follows that only he thinks of the intention.

That is, when he engages in *Lo Lishma*, meaning expects reward, the work and the reward are not in the same place and in the same time. But here, when we are speaking of punishments, the transgression and the punishment are not in the same place and in the same time, since he receives the punishment after he commits the transgression, and afterwards he suffers the punishment—a punishment in this world or a punishment in the next world. This applies only to the part of *Lo Lishma*.

However, in those who work on the intention—to be able to aim their actions only to bestow—the reward and the punishment are in the same place and the same time, since his inability to aim the act of bestowing contentment upon the Creator is his punishment, and he does not need to be given any other punishments, for nothing torments him more than seeing that he is still far from the Creator.

The evidence is that he does not have the love of the Creator, that he wants to respect Him. All this is because he is in a state of *Achoraim* [posterior] and concealment from the Creator. This is what pains him, and this is his punishment. But here is his reward—if he has love for the Creator and wants to bestow contentment upon him. However, all this concerns specifically those who want come to work only for the Creator, and not in *Lo Lishma*. It can be said about them that the punishment and the reward are in the same place and in the same time.

But normally, punishment is when they are in two different places. This is so because generally, observing Torah and *Mitzvot* is in the revealed part, meaning only in the act. It is called "revealed because in terms of the act, it is revealed to everyone what one does and what one says. In the revealed part, we explained above that there the reward and punishment are in two different places.

With all the above we shall come to clarify the words of the holy *Zohar*, where we asked six questions. It is known that *Malchut* is called "the last *Hey* in the name *HaVaYaH*," called *Behina Dalet de Ohr Yashar* [fourth discernment in the Direct Light]. Her quality is to receive in order to receive. All the corrections we need to do through Torah and *Mitzvot* are to correct her, so the reception in her will be in order to bestow, which is called *Dvekut* [adhesion] with the Creator. But if her intention is not to bestow she becomes removed from the Creator.

Also, it is known that everything we learn about the upper worlds pertains to the souls, as our sages said (*Vayikra*, 36:4), "Rabbi Birkiya said, 'The heaven and earth were created only by Israel's merit, as it is written, 'In the beginning God created,' and there is no beginning but Israel, as it was said (Jeremiah, 2), 'Israel was holy to the Lord, the first of His harvest.'"

Therefore, everything we learn in upper worlds is only so the souls will receive the upper abundance, as it is known that the purpose of creation is to do good to His creations. In order to correct the disparity of form that governs *Malchut* herself, who is called "receiving in order to receive," since disparity of form causes separation in spirituality, and this *Kli*, called *Malchut*, is the *Kli* of all the souls from which man was created. He must correct it so that all the vessels of reception will work in order to bestow.

See what is written in the introduction to *The Book of Zohar* (items 10-11): "And in order to mend that separation, which lies on the *Kli* of the souls, He has created all the worlds and separated them into two systems, as in the verse: 'God has made them one opposite the other.' These are the four pure worlds *ABYA*, and opposite them the four impure worlds *ABYA*. And He ... removed the will to receive for themselves from them, and placed it in the system of the impure worlds *ABYA*. ...And the worlds cascaded onto the reality of this corporeal world, to a place where there is a body and a soul, and a time of corruption and a time of correction. For the body, which is the will to receive for itself, extends from its root in the Thought of Creation, and passes through the system of the impure worlds, as it is written, 'a man is born a wild ass's colt.' He remains under the authority of that system for the first thirteen years, which is the time of corruption. By engaging in *Mitzvot* from thirteen years of age onward, when he engages in order to bestow contentment upon his Maker, he begins to purify the will to receive for himself imprinted in him, and slowly turns it to be in order to bestow. By this he extends a holy soul from its root in the Thought of Creation. It passes through the system of the pure worlds and dresses in the body. ...And so he accumulates degrees of holiness from the Thought of Creation in

Ein Sof [Infinity], until they aid him in turning the will to receive for himself in him to be entirely in the form of reception in order to bestow contentment upon his Maker."

According to what he presents there in the introduction to *The Book of Zohar*, we see that everything we say about the upper worlds concerns only the souls. Therefore, when we say that *Malchut* moved farther from the name *HaVaYaH*, it pertains to the souls, which need to correct her so she will connect with the name *HaVaYaH*, because with respect to the souls, she drew farther.

However, when a person takes upon himself the burden of the kingdom of heaven above reason, and he is in bestowal, it causes man's root, which is *Malchut*, to also be in bestowal, which is equivalence of form. At that time it is considered that *Malchut*, which was remote from the giver, in disparity of form, now that man engages in bestowal, called "equivalence of form," it is regarded as *Malchut* moving herself closer to the name *HaVaYaH*, meaning to the giver. This is the meaning of "Retuning the *Hey* to the *Vav*," where *Yod-Hey-Vav* are called "the upper nine," who are the giver, and the letter *Vav* is regarded as giving to *Malchut*, since now *Malchut* is regarded as giving, like the *Vav*. This is why the holy *Zohar* calls *Malchut* by the name *Hey*. This is the answer to the first question we asked.

On the one hand, at her root, *Malchut* is the root of the created beings. She is named *Malchut* due to her root of receiving in order to receive. From this aspect extends death, since reception causes separation from the life of lives. For this reason, death extends from here. This is also why *Malchut* is called the "tree of death" (*Zohar*, *Behaalotcha*, item 96), as it is written, "Rabbi Yehuda said, 'Rabbi Hiya said, 'The text testifies that anyone who gives charity to the poor awakens the tree of life, which is ZA, to add life to the tree of death, which is *Malchut*. Then there is life and joy above, in *Malchut*.'"

We therefore see that on the one hand, *Malchut* is called the "tree of death," from the perspective of her root, but when the souls engage in bestowal, she is in equivalence of form, and then the *Tzimtzum* [restriction] and concealment that were on her are removed. Specifically from here, meaning from *Malchut*, life extends to the world, and in that respect *Malchut* is called "life."

By this we explained the second question, why *Malchut* is called "life," since *Malchut* is called the "tree of death." The answer is that after she is corrected, as in "Work below awakens work above," it means that the works of the lower ones awaken the upper roots, by which they cause the unification of the Creator and His *Shechina*, and from that unification life comes to the world.

The third question is what does it mean that *Malchut* is the mouth of the Creator? We see that in corporeality, the mouth reveals what is on one's mind. *HaVaYaH* is called "the quality of mercy." This means that the Creator imparts delight and pleasure upon the creatures. When *Malchut* is called "life," which is when the lower ones engage in bestowal, the upper life comes from *Malchut*. The purpose of creation is called "light of *Hochma*," which is *Ohr Haya*. When *Malchut* reveals it, she is called "the mouth of the Lord," revealing the thought of creation, which is to do good to His creations.

By this we come to interpret what we asked in the fourth question: what does it mean that because she is on a man's head, a man must not walk four *Amot* [approx. four feet] bare-headed. It is known that *Malchut* is called "faith," and faith is always above reason. Man's mind is referred to as man's "head." Accordingly, the kingdom [*Malchut*] of heaven that one must take upon oneself should be above reason and above mind. This is why it is considered that *Malchut* is on a man's head.

This is why it is forbidden to walk four *Amot* bare-headed, since if she departs from a man's head, life promptly departs from him. Bare-headed means that *Malchut*, which is regarded as faith, is not on his mind and reason. It is as we said, that faith is regarded as above his head, meaning above reason. And because he has no faith, the light of life, which comes from *Malchut*, certainly departs from him, since *Malchut* is called "life" only by correcting the vessels of bestowal. But in vessels of reception, *Malchut* is called the "tree of death." This is why life departs from him.

The fifth question, why *Malchut* is called "the image of the Lord," is because "image" means as we say, "I want to have a general picture of the matter." Therefore, when wanting to know the general picture of spirituality, we are told, "And the image of the Lord does he behold." That is, seeing the general picture of spirituality depends on the extent to which he has been rewarded with faith in the Creator. Faith is expressed in mind and heart, and according to the faith with which one has been awarded, so he receives the image of it. Therefore, since *Malchut* is called "faith," *Malchut* is called "the image of the Lord," meaning that according to his faith, so is the image of spirituality that he receives.

Also, in the above manner we can answer the sixth question: why is *Malchut* called *Tzelem* [image], as it is written, "Only in the image does a man walk"? *Tzelem* also means faith, since "sun" is called reason [knowledge] and *Tzel* [shadow] is something that hides the sun. This is the faith, which is called "clothing." If a person has that clothing, the upper light dresses in him, as it is written in *The Zohar* (*Vayechi*, item 201), "If the *Tzelem* [image] departs, the *Mochin* depart, and the *Mochin* dresses according to the *Tzelem*."

The Spies

Article No. 28, Tav-Shin-Mem-Hey, 1984-85

The holy *Zohar* interprets the matter of the spies that Moses sent to tour the land (*Slach*, items 56-58) concerning the spiritual land: "Why is it written that the Creator tells them, 'Go up there into the Negev,' delve in the Torah, and by that you will know that world. 'See what the land is like,' meaning from that you will see the world to which I bring you. 'And the people dwelling in it' are the righteous in the Garden of Eden.

"'The strong is the faint,' meaning that in it you will see if they were rewarded with all that because they overcame their inclination by strength and broke it, or by weakness, without effort. Or, if they were strengthened in the Torah, to engage in it day and night, or left it off and were still rewarded with all that. 'Whether they are few or many' means if many engage in My work and strengthen themselves in the Torah, and are rewarded with all this or not.

"'And what is the land like, is it fat or lean.' You will know what the land is like in the Torah, meaning what is that world, if the upper abundance is plentiful for its dwellers or if anything is missing there.

"'And they went up into the Negev and came to Hebron.' Going up in the Negev means that people are ascending in it, in the Torah. 'In the Negev" means with an idle heart, as one who tries in vain, dryly, thinking that there is no reward in it. He sees that the wealth of this world is lost for it, and thinks that all is lost. 'In the Negev' means that the water has dried out. 'And came to Hebron' means that he comes to connect with the Torah. Hebron was built in seven years, which are the seventy faces of the Torah.

"'And they came to the stream of Eshkol' are words of legend and interpretation, which come from the side of faith. 'And cut down a branch from there,' meaning learned chapter headings from there, headlines. Those who are faithful are happy with the words, and the words are blessed within them. They look at their being of one root and one kernel and there is no separation in them. Those who are not faithful and do not learn Torah *Lishma* [for Her sake] separate faith, which is *Malchut*, from ZA, since they do not believe that they are of one kernel and one root. This is the meaning of 'and they carried it on a pole between two,' meaning that they separated between the written Torah and the oral Torah.

"'With the pomegranates and with the figs,' meaning they put these words completely with the *Sitra Achra* [other side], to the side of idol-worship and the side of separation. *Rimonim* [Pomegranates] comes from the word, *Minim* [idol-worshipers], and *Te'enim* [figs] comes from the words, 'And the Lord is not by his side,' meaning when they do not believe in Providence and say that everything is incidental, and separate the Creator from the world.

"'And they returned from touring the land' means that they returned to the bad side, returned from the path of truth, saying, 'What did we get out of it? To this day we have not seen good in the world; we have labored in the Torah and the house is empty. We have dwelt among the lowest in the nation. Who will be rewarded with that world? Who will come into it? We'd be better off not laboring so much.'

"'They told him, and said,' we labored and learned in order to know a part of that world, as you advised us. 'And it is also flowing with milk and honey,' that upper world is good, as we know from the Torah, but who can merit it? 'However, the people

The Spies

... are strong,' the people that has been rewarded with that world is strong, dismissing the entire world as something to engage in and have great wealth. Who can do so and be rewarded with it? Of course the people who dwell in that land are strong. One who wishes to be rewarded with it must be strong in wealth, as the writing says, 'The rich man answers roughly.'

"'And the cities are big and fortified,' meaning houses filled abundantly; nothing is missing in them. And yet, 'we also saw there the descendants of the giant,' meaning it requires a body as strong and as mighty as a lion, since the Torah exhausts man's strength, who can be rewarded with it?

"'Also, Amalek is living in the land of the Negev.' If one should say that even with all this he will be rewarded with overcoming, 'Amalek is living in the land of the Negev,' meaning the evil inclination, the slandering accuser of a person is always in the body.

"With these words, 'they discouraged the hearts of the children of Israel,' since they gave it a bad name. 'These faithful ones, what did they say? 'If the Lord is pleased with us, He will ... give it to us.'" That is, when one tries with the desire of the heart toward the Creator, he will be rewarded with it because all He wants from him is the heart.

"'But do not rebel against the Lord.' We must not rebel against the Torah because the Torah does not need wealth or vessels of silver and gold. 'And you, do not fear the people of the land,' for if a broken body were to engage in Torah, there will be healing for all, and all of man's slanderers will become his helpers." Thus far its words.

According to how the holy *Zohar* interprets the matter of the spies in relation to man's entrance to the holy work, it is generally called "taking upon oneself the burden of the kingdom of heaven." By this, one is rewarded with the reception of the Torah, as it was at the foot of Mt. Sinai, when they said, "We will do and we will hear." It is just as each and every one who wants to be rewarded with the Torah must go through a period called "we will do," and then he can be rewarded with "we will hear."

There are many degrees in "we will do," which generally divide in two ways:

1) The revealed part is regarded as keeping the Torah and *Mitzvot* [commandments] in practice, learning day and night and being meticulous with all the details of the *Mitzvot*, until there is nothing more he can add as far as actions are concerned. His intention is that he does everything for the Creator, to keep the King's commandment, and in return he will receive reward in this world and in the next world. In this respect he is considered righteous.

2) The hidden part refers to the hidden part in the Torah, which is the intention. What a person intends while practicing is hidden from people. But mostly, it is hidden from the person himself because this work must be above reason. Thus, the reason cannot criticize his work—if he is on the way that ascends toward *Dvekut* [adhesion] with the Creator, meaning if he is on the path called "in order to bestow," called "not in order to receive reward." Therefore, it is hidden because he is working without reward, so the reward is hidden from him.

This means that a person who works for a reward knows that he is working well because he is receiving a reward. But one who works in order to bestow contentment upon his Maker, so the Creator will enjoy, cannot see if the Creator is enjoying his work. Rather, he must believe that the Creator is pleased. It follows that the reward, too, is called "in order to bestow," and it, too, is above reason.

There are other reasons, called "the hidden part." This work does not belong to the general public, but to individuals, as Maimonides says (at the end of *Hilchot Teshuva*), "Sages said, 'One should always engage in Torah, even if *Lo Lishma* [not for Her sake], since from *Lo Lishma* he comes to *Lishma* [for Her sake]. Therefore, when teaching children, women, and uneducated people, they are to be taught to work out of fear and in order to receive reward. Until they gain knowledge and acquire much wisdom, they are to be taught this secret bit-by-bit, and are to be accustomed to it pleasantly until they attain Him and know Him, and serve Him out of love."

The Spies

The matter of spies begins primarily in a person who wants to walk on the path of *Dvekut*, which is to bestow. At that time the spies come with their just arguments according to their views. Through reasoning, they make one understand that they are right.

It is known that the holy *Zohar* says, "Every man is a small world," consisting of seventy nations, as well as of Israel. This means that since there are seven qualities, which are seven *Sefirot*, and opposite them there are seven qualities in the *Sitra Achra*. Each one consists of ten, thus they are seventy. Also, each nation has its own passion and wants to ordain its passion over everyone. And the people of Israel in a person also has its own passion, which is to adhere to the Creator.

There is a rule that one cannot fight oneself. Rather, this requires a special power for a person to be able to go against his views. But he does have the power and strength to fight against another if he understands that his view is true, and he will never want to yield before the view of the other.

Accordingly, if the seventy nations are within the person, how can he fight himself? That is, once a certain nation prevails over the seventy nations with its passion, and then a person is governed by that passion. Then, when a person thinks about himself, he sees that this is his passion. He does not say that someone from the seventy nations wants to govern him, but thinks that this is he, himself, and it is very hard to fight against himself.

Therefore, a person should depict to himself that he has seventy nations in his body, as well as the people of Israel. He must determine for himself to which people he belongs. That is, there is a rule: every person loves his homeland and fights for his homeland. Therefore, he must determine if he belongs to the people of Israel or to a nation from the seventy nations. If he determines that he belongs to the people of Israel, then he can fight the seventy nations when he sees that they are coming to fight.

At that time he sees that the seventy nations want to obliterate the people of Israel, as it is written in the Passover *Haggadah* [story], "She stood for our fathers and for us, for not only one arose against us to obliterate us. Rather, each and every generation, there are those who arise against us to obliterate us, and the Creator saves us from their hands." If he knows that he belongs to the people of Israel, he has the strength to fight against the seventy nations, since there is strength in nature to fight for one's homeland, for he knows that he is an "Israelite," and they want to obliterate him. It follows that it is as though there are two bodies fighting one another, and then he has the strength to fight.

Thus, here, when we speak of the work of the Creator, the "people of Israel" is called that which is *Yashar-El* [straight to the Creator]. He wants to adhere to the Creator, wants *Malchut*, meaning to take upon himself the burden of the kingdom of heaven. *Malchut* is called *El* [God], as it is written in the holy *Zohar* (Korah, item 14): "This is why it is written, 'A God who has indignation every day,' meaning *Malchut*, while the seventy nations in him resist it and fight with the Israel in him. With all kinds of tactics, they wish to annul and obliterate the Israel in a man's body."

Here, in the work with the intention—when he wants to go specifically in a manner of bestowal—the argument of the spies begins, which the holy *Zohar* interprets their arguments according to the verses written in the Torah, which dispute and fight the Israel in him, and want to eradicate them from the face of the earth.

That is, he must not think that he will achieve what he thought he would achieve with all kinds of arguments, for they are fighting him, since the basis of the seventy nations is the will to receive, and Israel is precisely annulling before Him without any reward at all. Therefore, precisely when a person wants to go against their views begins the argument of the spies, who make him understand rationally that he has no chance of achieving the goal that he plans to achieve.

However, sometimes the spies make a person understand something that is harsher than anything the spies claim. They say to a person, "Know that the Creator cannot help an ignoble person such as you." This is the harshest of all because usually, whenever a person is in trouble he can pray. But when they come to a person saying "You are wasting your efforts because the Creator cannot help," they deny him the prayer, since what can he do then? To whom can he turn for help?

It is written in the holy *Zohar* (item 82): "Rabbi Yosi says, 'They took it upon themselves to slander everything. What is 'everything'? It is the earth and the Creator.' Rabbi Yitzhak said, 'With the earth, it's true. With the Creator, how do we know?' He told him: 'It is implied in the words, 'However, the people ... are strong.' That is, who can defeat them? 'The people are strong' is accurate, meaning that even the Creator cannot defeat them, and they slandered the Creator.'"

A person cannot argue with the words of the spies with his reason, or wait until he has what to reply to them, and in the meantime be under their governance. Rather, he must know that he will never be able to answer their doubts with the external mind. But specifically when he is rewarded with the inner mind, he will have the words to explain to them. In the meantime he must go above his mind, meaning say that although the intellect is very important, the importance of faith is still higher than the intellect. Therefore, he must not go according to the intellect, but according to the path of faith, to believe what our sages told us, that a man must take upon himself the burden of the kingdom of heaven as faith above reason. At that time there is no place for the argument of the spies because they speak only within the reason of the external mind.

This is the meaning of Israel saying at the time of the preparation for the reception of the Torah, "We will do," and then "We will hear." "Doing" means without the external intellect. Rather, he calculates according to the Commander, for the Commander probably knows what is good for him and what is not, meaning what is good for a person and what is not. But one big question remains, "Why did the Creator give us an external intellect, which we use in every single thing, while here in the work of the Creator we must go against this intellect, and not with the intellect with which we were born?"

This comes because the Creator wanted to be asked for help. The help He gives is the light of Torah, and if they could go without the help of the Creator they would have no need for the light of Torah, as our sages said, "I have created the evil inclination; I have created the Torah as a spice." Therefore, in order for him to need to extend the light of Torah, we were given this work in concealment on the intention, so that man will need an inner mind.

From the perspective of the outer intellect, the Creator made it so as not to give any help for the work. On the contrary, it is obstructing him to work in order to bestow. This is the meaning of what is written in the holy *Zohar* (Noah, item 63): "If a person comes to purify, he is aided with a holy soul. He is purified and sanctified, and he is called 'holy.'"

By that one comes to need to be rewarded with the NRNHY that pertains to the root of his soul. Hence, there was a correction of concealment, which is the *Daat*, meaning that a person's outer mind will be against working in order to bestow. This is called "within reason of the outer mind," which makes all of man's calculations that it is not worthwhile for him to work in order to bestow.

When he overcomes and does not escape the campaign, and prays to the Creator to help him go above reason, meaning not to be under the rule of the will to receive, then, when the Creator helps him he receives an inner mind called "inner reason." At that time, through this reason, the body agrees to work in order to bestow upon the Creator, as it is written, "When a man's ways are pleasing to the Lord, He makes even his enemies be at peace with him," referring to the evil inclination.

It follows that while he is within reason, meaning that the intellect tells him it is worthwhile to do this work, he can exert in the work. Therefore, when he has an outer intellect, the reason compels him, meaning the intention to receive. This is called "within reason." When he is rewarded with the inner mind, meaning the inner reason, the mind obligates him that it is worthwhile to work in order to bestow contentment upon the Creator.

The Lord Is Near to All Who Call upon Him

Article No. 29, Tav-Shin-Mem-Hey, 1984-85

It is written in *The Zohar, Hukat* (item 78): "From this we learn that anyone who wishes to evoke things above—in an act or in a word—if that act or that word is not done properly, nothing is evoked. All the people in the world go to the synagogue to evoke a matter above, but few are the ones who know how to evoke. The Creator is near to all those who know how to call upon Him and to evoke a matter properly. But if they do not know how to call upon Him, He is not close, as it is written, 'The Lord is near to all those who call upon Him, to all who call upon Him in truth.' What is 'in truth'? 'In truth' means that they know how to properly evoke a true matter. So it is in everything."

This means that one who does not know how to call upon Him should not go to the synagogue because if he does not know how to call upon Him, it means that his prayer is not accepted. Thus, there is an excuse here, so he explained that it is not enough to not go to the synagogue because he does not know how to call upon Him. Therefore, one should know what to do in order to know how to call upon Him and be close to the Creator.

The *Zohar* comes and explains to us about that what we should know, and then we should exert to come to know it. It says that knowing is only truth, that one who calls upon Him in truth is close to the Creator. Accordingly, if knowing means that he called upon Him in truth, what is new here when he says that with the Creator it means that there must be special knowledge in order to call upon the Creator? The meaning of the verse that says, "The Lord is near to all who call upon Him," is that it is without exceptions, meaning that He is close to everyone, without exceptions. Afterwards the verse ends with a condition, which appears to be a major stipulation. What is the condition? He should call upon Him in truth! This is the principal condition required of man.

Regarding this principal condition required of man, which is called "truth," usually, when someone calls another person, if the other person knows that he is calling him falsely, he is bound to ignore his calling him because he knows that he is calling him falsely, so he pretends not to hear him, since he is calling him falsely.

Thus, what is the principal condition required of man? Certainly, when it comes to the Creator there must be special requirements that do not apply to people, but this condition, that we must call upon Him in truth, is the smallest requirement that can be. Indeed, there is a special intention here in the stipulation of truth, and this intention is called "in truth."

To understand the meaning of truth we should precede with the words of our sages: "Anyone who is proud, the Creator says, 'He and I cannot dwell in the same abode.'" We should ask, "Why should the Creator care if he is proud?" If a person walks into a hen house and sees that one rooster is showing vanity over another, is the person impressed by that? Baal HaSulam said that the Creator loves the truth and cannot tolerate falsehood, as it is written, "He who speaks lies will not be established before My eyes."

Indeed, the Creator created man with a desire to receive, which is the self-love that there is in him. This is the source of all the evil lusts that exist in the world, namely thefts, murders, and wars, they all stem from man's will to receive. It follows that the Creator created man in utter lowliness, and he takes pride, meaning says that he is not like others. It follows that he is lying, and truth does not tolerate lies.

According to the above, if a person comes to the synagogue to ask the Creator to hear his prayer because he deserves to be heard by the Creator—to be given because he deserves, to be given by the Creator more than He gives to others, even when this concerns spirituality—then he is far from the Creator, since falsehood is far from the truth. This is why it is considered that he does not know how to call upon Him, since he is calling the Creator with a lie, and this is called "far" and not "near," according to the spiritual law that "nearness means equivalence of form, and remoteness means disparity of form."

Since there is no greater disparity of form than between truth and falsehood, it is regarded that he does not know how to call upon Him. The Creator is not close to him because when he is asking during the prayer, he is in falsehood for he feels that he is more virtuous than others because he sees all his faults in others. For this reason, he wants the Creator to help him.

But in truth, it is as our sages said (*Kidushin*, p 70), "Anyone who flaws is flawed and does not speak in praise of the world. And Shmuel said, 'faults in his own fault.'" Because there are people who always look at others. If the other is learning as he understands or prays as he understands, then the other is fine. If he is not fine then he has found a flaw in the other.

This is similar to what Baal HaSulam said, that among the jealous there is a custom where if someone is more meticulous than him [in observing commandments], he is called "frumer" [derogatory term: overly pious], meaning too extreme. There is no point mentioning this person and it's a waste to even think about him. But if he is less devout than him he says that the other person is far too lenient and should be persecuted to the point of banning, so he does not defile others.

That person, who comes to pray to the Creator to bring him closer because he is virtuous, is remote from the Creator, meaning in disparity of form from the Creator, since the Creator's quality is truth, and that man's quality is all falsehood. Therefore, it is regarded as the Creator being far from him, and therefore does not hear him.

We should ask, "If 'the whole earth is full of His glory,' what does it mean that the Creator is far from him?" It is as one who is standing far from another, and does not hear his voice. Therefore, in spirituality, it is known that the measure of remoteness and nearness depends on the equivalence or disparity of form.

But if a person comes to pray to the Creator and says to Him, "You must help me more than others, since others do not need Your help that much because they are more qualified than I, and are not as immersed in self-love as I am, and have better self-discipline than I, and I see that I need Your help more than the rest of the people, since I feel my lowliness, that I am farther from You than everyone and I have come to feel as it is written, "We have no redeeming and delivering King but You."

It follows that his argument is true, and such arguments the Creator tolerates because they are true. It was said about this, "I am the Lord, who dwells with them in the midst of their impurity." That is, although they are immersed in self-love, which is the source of impurity, since he is making a true argument, the Creator is close to him because truth with truth means equivalence of form, and equivalence of form is called "near."

By this we will understand the question of the holy *Zohar*, which implies that one who does not know how to call upon Him has no reason to go to the synagogue because the Creator will not hear his voice because he is far from the Creator if he does not know how to call upon Him. And another perplexity is that this contradicts the verse, "The Lord is high and the low will see" (Psalms 138). And what is the meaning of "low"? It is one who knows nothing, not even know how to call upon Him; he, too, will see.

With the above we will thoroughly understand that he does not need to know anything, but only his true spiritual state—that he does not know any wisdom and any moral word that will help him, and he is in the worst possible state that can be in the world. And if the Creator does not help him, he is lost. This is the only thing he needs to know—that he does not know anything and that he is the lowest of everyone. If he does not feel it, but thinks that there are worse people, then he is already in falsehood and already in remoteness from the Creator.

By this we will understand the second question we asked, "What can he do in order to know how to call upon Him and be closer to Him? What should he learn in order to know? In that state, he is told that he does not need to learn anything special but simply try to walk on the path of truth, and then he will have what to pray for, meaning for necessity and not for luxuries, as it is written (Psalms, 33), "Behold, the eye of the Lord is on those who fear Him, on those who hope for His mercy, to deliver their souls from death and to keep them alive in famine," or simply, the he needs spiritual life.

By this we will interpret the verse, "The Lord is near to all who call upon Him," without exception. And the condition he states, "to all who call upon Him in truth," is not regarded as a special condition. But among children, if one calls another, and he knows that he is lying, he will not mind him. But here, with the Creator, we should know to what the matter of truth pertains. It is difficult for one to know for himself what a state of truth is and what a state of falsehood is, since one cannot see the truth. Hence, he needs a guide to guide him and tell him what he lacks, and what he has, and even redundancies that interfere with his reaching the truth.

This is the meaning of "Seek the Lord while He is present; call upon Him while He is near." Certainly, we find him when He is near. But where is the place called "near"? It is as was said above, "to all who call upon Him in truth." If a person calls upon Him from his real state, one finds Him.

Three Prayers — 1

Article No. 30, Tav-Shin-Mem-Hey, 1984-85

It is written in *The Zohar*, Balak (item 187): "Three are the ones called 'prayer': a prayer for Moses, a prayer for David, a prayer for the poor. Of those three, which is the most important? A prayer for the poor. This prayer precedes the prayer of Moses and precedes the prayer of David. What is the reason? It is because a poor is brokenhearted, and it is written, 'The Lord is near to the brokenhearted.' The poor always quarrels with the Creator, and the Creator listens and hears his words, 'a prayer for the poor when he is weak [also: wraps].' It should have said, 'when he is wrapped'; what is 'when he wraps'? It means that he creates a delay, delaying all the prayers in the world, which do not enter until his prayer enters. The Creator alone is unified with these grievances, as it is written, 'and pours out his words before the Lord.' All the hosts of heaven ask one another, 'What does the Creator do? In what is He exerting?' They are told, 'He is becoming passionately unified with His *Kelim* [vessels],' meaning with the brokenhearted. This prayer causes delay and postponement to all the prayers in the world."

Concerning these three prayers, we should understand the difference between the prayers of Moses, David, and the poor. What is the importance of the poor, in that he has grievances against the Creator, and for which he delays all the prayers? We should also understand what it means that it delays all the prayers in the world? Is the Creator unable to answer all the prayers at once? Does He need to take up time, as though they need to stand in line one-by-one?

We will interpret this in the work, for all these prayers apply to one person. These are three consecutive states in the order of the work. We find that there are three deficiencies that one should ask the Creator to satisfy for him: 1) Torah, which is called "Moses," 2) the kingdom of heaven, 3) a poor, who is brokenhearted, pertaining to his *Kelim*.

We should understand why he says, "The Lord is near to the brokenhearted," which is called "close." We learn that "close" means equivalence of form. But how can we speak of equivalence of form with the Creator if he is brokenhearted? We should also understand what we learn, "The Lord is near to all who call upon Him in truth." That is, what is "close"? "Truth" is called "close," and brokenhearted is not called "close." We should also understand the grievance that the poor has against the Creator, as though the Creator is saying that the poor is right, for we see that because of the grievances He listens to him more than to others, as said in the above words of the holy *Zohar*.

But it is written in *The Zohar* ("Introduction of The Book of Zohar," item 174): "Rabbi Shimon started, 'One who rejoices in holidays and does not give his share to the Creator.'" In *The Zohar* (item 175), he explains what is the share of the Creator: "The share of the Creator is to delight the poor as much as he can, for on holidays the Creator comes to see His broken *Kelim*."

He interprets in the *Sulam* [Ladder commentary on *The Zohar*] why the Creator's share is for the poor, pertaining to the breaking of the vessels that preceded the creation of the world. In his words: "By the breaking of the *Kelim* of *Kedusha* [holiness] and their fall into the separated *BYA*, sparks of *Kedusha* fell into the *Klipot* [shells/peels]. From them, all sorts of pleasures and fancies come into the domain of the *Klipot*, for the sparks transfer them into man's reception and for his pleasure. By that, they cause all kinds of transgressions, such as theft, robbery, and murder."

Accordingly, we should interpret what it means that a poor's complaint is with a grievance. He says, "Why is it my fault that He has created me from broken vessels, because of which I have within me all the evil lusts and evil thoughts? All this came to me only because I extend from the breaking of the vessels, which was the first place where they wanted to extend the upper abundance into the vessels of reception with the intention to receive in order to receive, and not at all with the intention to bestow. Because of it, self-love has been installed in me, and for this reason I am far from anything spiritual and have no part in *Kedusha*, which is founded only on vessels that have the intention to bestow. It follows that all my suffering at having no access to *Kedusha* and seeing that I am far from You due to the disparity of form that I have as a result of self-love, which is the whole enemy that is in my heart, He is the one who causes all of my bad states. It all came because You created me this way!"

For this reason, he comes with complaints and says, "I cannot change the nature with which You created me, but I want that just as You have created me with self-love, now You will give me a second nature, as You have given me the first, meaning a desire to bestow, for I cannot fight against the nature that You have imprinted in me. Moreover, I have evidence that it is Your fault that I haven't the strength to overcome. Our sages said (*Kidushin* 30), 'Rabbi Shimon Ben Levi said, 'Man's inclination overpowers him each day and seeks to put him to death, as it was said, 'The wicked watches for the righteous and seeks to put him to death.' Were it not for the Creator's help, he would not have overcome it, as it was said, 'God will not leave him in his hand.'"

It follows that the grievances of the poor are justified. That is, he hasn't the strength to overcome it if the Creator does not help him, as our sages said. Therefore, he comes with a complaint to the Creator that only He can help, and none other, as it is implied from the words of our sages that the Creator did so deliberately, so there would be a need for prayer, since "The Creator awaits the prayer of the righteous," meaning those who pray that they want to be righteous. The reason for this was explained in the previous essays of Baal HaSulam.

It therefore follows that his grievances with the Creator for creating him in such lowliness is justified, meaning that the Creator Himself made it so that he cannot expect anything to help him but the Creator. This is why the prayer of the poor is called "brokenhearted," meaning it comes from the breaking of the vessels. It follows that the argument of the brokenhearted is a true argument, and truth is called "close" because it is in equivalence of form with the Creator. This is why this prayer is answered first, since here begins the order of the work.

By this we will understand what we asked, that here he says that "close" means brokenhearted, and there we learned that "near" is true, as it is written, "The Lord is near to all who call upon Him in truth." The answer is that the argument of the brokenhearted is a true argument. It follows that the two are the same, meaning that we must know that when we come to pray to the Creator we must speak to him words of truth.

This is what we explained in the previous article [29, *Tav-Shin-Mem-Hey*], that when he comes to pray to the Creator he needs to ask the Creator to help him: "Since I am truly in the worst state in the world, for although there might be lower people than I, both in Torah and in work, they do not feel the truth as I see my situation. Therefore, they still do not have the deficiency that I have, and therefore do not need Your help so much. But I do see my true state—that I am completely disconnected from spirituality after all the work that I have done both in time and in effort. And yet, now I see that 'the former days were better than these,' and as much as I may try to go forward, I feel that I am going backwards." This is called "a true argument," and to this it is possible to attribute equivalence of form with the Creator in that he is making a true argument.

By this we will understand the question, "Why does the prayer of the poor delay all the prayers? Is the Creator unable to answer all the prayers at once?" We need to learn all three prayers in one body. This means that it is impossible to answer everything a person asks, except by order of the degree that a person can receive. That is, if he receives this, it will be to his best. But if he receives some satisfaction that he wants it will be to his detriment, and his wish will certainly not be granted because the Creator wants to benefit him and not harm him.

Therefore, the lower one must receive from above according to what the lower one really needs. This is why he must pray for his poverty, that he has grievances that He created him with a will to receive, which he feels is causing all the evil in him and causing all his troubles. Afterwards he can ask to be given the kingdom of heaven, for he has already been given vessels of bestowal and can already receive faith, called the "kingdom of heaven."

That is, one cannot attain the burden of the kingdom of heaven, called "faith," before he has vessels of bestowal, as he says in the *Sulam* ("Introduction of the Book of Zohar," p 138): "It is a law that the creature cannot receive apparent harm from Him, for it is a flaw in His glory that the creature should perceive Him as doing harm, for it is inappropriate for the perfect Operator. Hence, when one feels bad, to that extent there is denial of His guidance upon him and the Operator is hidden from him."

Therefore, first one should receive strength from above to have a second nature, which is the desire to bestow. Subsequently, he can ask for another degree, which is David, meaning the kingdom of heaven. It follows that the prayer of the poor delays all the other prayers, meaning that before the poor receives his wish, one cannot acquire higher degrees. This is why it is written, "A prayer for the poor when he is weak [also "wraps"]."

Then comes the second prayer, which is the prayer for David, being the kingdom of heaven, when he asks to have faith, to feel the Operator who operates with His guidance over the entire world.

This is so because now he can already perceive the Creator as doing good, as written in the *Sulam*, since he already has vessels of bestowal. Thus, he can already see how He is doing good.

It follows that it is impossible to obtain faith, which is the kingdom of heaven, before one has acquired the correction of the qualities—to always be ready to bestow and not receive in order to receive. Otherwise from above he is not permitted to obtain faith. This is regarded as the prayer of the poor delaying all the prayers. That is, before a person reveals his deficiency—that he is immersed in self-love, and wants to emerge from it—it is pointless to ask for other things.

Afterwards comes the time for the prayer for Moses, which is regarded as the Torah. This is so because it is impossible to be rewarded with the Torah before he obtains faith, for "It is forbidden to teach idol-worshippers the Torah," as it was said, "This is the law [Torah] that Moses set before the children of Israel." And it is written in *The Zohar*: "It is forbidden to teach idol-worshippers the Torah," and "One who circumcised himself but does not keep the commandments of the Torah is as though he was not circumcised, as it is written (Jethro), 'If you make an altar of stone for Me, you shall not build it of cut stones, for if you wield your sword on it, you will profane it.' Although you wielded your sword on it, meaning he circumcised himself, he profanes it, which means that he profaned the circumcision."

This means that even one who is circumcised and has Jewish parents is still not regarded as "Israel" with respect to the Torah, meaning that it is permitted to learn with him Torah, if he is not keeping the commandments of the Torah. This is what is implied from the above words of *The Zohar*.

It is written in *The Zohar* (Pinhas, item 68): "'And wine makes man's heart glad.' This is the wine of Torah, for wine is the same number as *Sod* [secret]. As the wine must be concealed and sealed so it is not poured into idol-worship, so is the Torah: it must be concealed and sealed, and all her secrets are poured out only to those who fear Him."

Thus, the prayer for Moses, which is the Torah, is a degree that comes after the kingdom of heaven, called fear. This is the meaning of the Torah being given specifically to those who fear Him. This is also the meaning of what our sages said, "The hand *Tefillin* precedes the head *Tefillin*," since it is written, "You shall bind them as a sign on your hand and they shall be as frontals between your eyes."

The holy *Zohar* interprets that the hand *Tefillin* is *Malchut*, and the head *Tefillin* is ZA. The hand *Tefillin* should be covered because it is written, "And it shall be as a sign to you on your hand," and they explained "To you as a sign, and not to others as a sign." Baal HaSulam said that *Malchut* is called "faith." For this reason, it must be concealed, which means that because *Malchut* is faith above reason, it is called "concealment." Therefore, once he acquires faith, which is called "kingdom of heaven," he can be rewarded with the Torah, called ZA, which implies the head *Tefillin*, where there is already disclosure of Torah. This is why our sages said about the verse, "And all the peoples of the earth will see that you are called by the name of the Lord, and they will be afraid of you," that these are the head *Tefillin*, where there is seeing.

One Does Not Regard Oneself as Wicked

Article No. 31, Tav-Shin-Mem-Hey, 1984-85

Concerning "One does not regard oneself as wicked," it is written in *The Zohar* (Balak, item 193): "King David regarded himself in four ways. He regarded himself with the poor, regarded himself with the *Hassidim* [pious/devout followers]. Regarded himself with the *Hassidim*, as it is written, 'Preserve my soul, for I am pious,' for one must not regard oneself as wicked. And should you say, 'If so then he will never confess his sins,' it is not so. Rather, when he confesses his sins, then he will be a *Hassid*, for he has come to receive repentance and takes himself out of the evil side, in whose filth he was thus far. But now he has clung to the upper right, which is *Hesed* that is stretched out to welcome him. And because he has clung to *Hesed*, he is called *Hassid* [pious/devout follower]. Do not say that the Creator does not accept him until he details all his sins since the day he came to the world, or even those that were hidden from him. This is not so. Rather, he only needs to detail the sins that he remembers. If he sets his mind on them to regret during the confession, all the other sins follow them," thus far its words.

We should understand the following:

1) How can one say about himself that he is a *Hassid*? This is already a degree of importance, so how does he praise himself by himself?

2) He says that one should not regard oneself as wicked. On the other hand, he says that one should detail one's sins, but says that he does not need to detail all his sins since the day he came to the world, but should detail only the sins that he remembers. Thus, when he details the sins he has committed, he is already wicked. So why does he say that one must not regard oneself as wicked? Is there a difference between saying he did bad deeds and not saying about himself that he is wicked? If he says that he did bad deeds then he is saying about himself that he is wicked anyhow. It is as we find in the words of our sages (*Sanhedrin* 9b): "Rav Yosef said, 'A person came to force him; he and another conjoined to kill him. By his will, he is wicked. The Torah said, 'Do not make a wicked a witness.' Raba said, 'A person is close to himself, and one does not regard oneself as wicked.'"

Thus, this means that if he says that he has sinned, he cannot be trusted because he is wicked. But here, when he confesses his sins, we must say that by this saying alone he is called "wicked," since you are saying, "One does not regard oneself as wicked." Thus, the question remains, how can he detail his sins during confession?

We should know why they said, that "One does not regard oneself as wicked." It is so because "a person is close to himself." By this we should say that since "Love covers all transgressions," we cannot see any faults in the ones we love, since a fault is something bad, and one cannot harm oneself, for he is partial due to self-love. For this reason, "One does not regard oneself as wicked" and is not trustworthy to testify anything bad about himself, like a relative, who is disqualified.

We should know that when one comes to ask of the Creator to repent, and asks for the Creator's help so he can repent, the question arises, "If he wants to repent, who is stopping him?" He can choose to repent, so why does he need to ask the Creator to help him repent? In the Eighteen Prayer we pray, "Bring us back, our Father, to Your law, and bring us close, our King, to Your work, and return us in complete repentance before You." This means that without His help, one cannot repent. We should understand why this is so, that one cannot repent by himself.

In previous articles we explained that because the Creator created in us a nature of desire to receive, and that desire initially emerged in order to receive, only afterwards, we learn, there was a correction not to receive in order to receive, but in order to bestow. This is called the "correction of the *Tzimtzum* [restriction]." This means that before the lower one is fit for the aim to bestow, that place will be vacant from light. What extends from this correction down to the creatures is that before one emerges from self-love, one cannot feel the light of the Creator. For this reason, first we must exit self-love, or the *Tzimtzum* is on us.

However, a person cannot exit the nature that the Creator created because the Creator created that nature. Therefore, there is no other way but to ask of the Creator to give him a second nature, which is the desire to bestow. Thus, the choice we attribute to man is only in the prayer, to ask the Creator to help him and give him that second nature. For this reason, when one wants to repent, he must ask the Creator to help him exit from self-love to love of others. This is why we ask of the Creator and say and pray, "Bring us back, our Father."

But when does one truly ask the Creator to bring him back with repentance? This can be only when he feels that he must repent. Before he comes to the decision that he is wicked, there is no place for prayer to be reformed. After all, he is not so wicked so as to need the Creator's mercy. The meaning of the prayers that should be granted is precisely that the person needs mercy, as we say in the Eighteen Prayer, "For You hear the prayer of every mouth (so it is implied, but when?) of Your people, Israel."

Accordingly, when does the Creator hear the prayer of every mouth? If a person feels that he needs mercy. This pertains specifically to when he feels he is in great distress and no one can help him. Then it can be said that he comes to the Creator to ask for mercy. But previously, when he came to the Creator to ask for luxuries, meaning when the state he was in was not so bad, that there were people whose state he saw as worse than his, then his prayer to the Creator was not because he needed heaven's mercy, but because he wanted to be in a better state, superior to others. This is regarded as asking the Creator to give him a life of luxuries, meaning that he wanted to be happier than others.

Therefore, when one wants the Creator to grant his prayer, he first needs to see that he needs to be given life more than others, meaning that he sees that everyone is living in the world, but he has no life because he feels himself as wicked and sees that he is more immersed in self-love than others. At that time he sees that he needs heaven's mercy not because he wants to live a life of luxury, but because he has no life of *Kedusha* [holiness].

It follows that at that time he is really asking for mercy, something to revive his soul. He cries out to the Creator: "Since 'You give bread to the hungry; the Lord sets the prisoners free.'" That is, he sees that he simply needs faith, called "bread," and he sees that he is sitting in jail, called "self-love," and cannot come out of there, for only the Creator can help him. This is regarded as praying a real prayer.

We should know that prayer pertains to a deficiency. A deficiency does not mean not having. Rather, a deficiency is a need. Therefore, a great deficiency means he has a great need for the thing that he is asking. If he does not have a great need it means that he does not have a great deficiency, and so his prayer is not so great, because he is not as needy of the thing he asks. This is why the request is also not as big.

It follows from all the above that one cannot see a bad thing in himself. Accordingly, we should ask, "If a person knows that he is sick, and being sick is certainly bad, he goes to the doctor to cure his illness. If the doctor tells him that he sees nothing wrong with his body, he will not trust him. He will go to an expert, who will tell him that he has found something wrong with his body, and he needs to undergo surgery. That person will certainly be happy that he has found what was bad in him, and he pays him a large sum for having found his illness and for knowing how to cure his body so he can live and enjoy life.

We see that if we find the bad, it is a good thing, as with the illness. At that time it cannot be said that a person does not see bad in himself, since at that time he wants to correct the bad, so the bad is regarded as a good thing. It follows that at that time a person can find bad in himself.

Accordingly, we can understand the words of *The Zohar* when we asked how on the one hand he says "He does not regard himself as wicked," and then says that he must detail his sins? After all, when he details the sins he had committed he sees himself as wicked by saying that he did this and that transgression. We can answer this differently: When he comes to ask of the Creator, He brings him closer because he is immersed in evil, meaning in self-love. If he wants his prayer to be granted, he knows that he must pray to the Creator from the bottom of the heart, meaning that he needs more mercy than the rest of the people because he feels himself as worse than them.

At that time he must see for himself the bad that he has more than the rest of the people. Otherwise it is regarded as telling a lie that he is worse than them, and it is written, "The Lord is near to all who call upon Him in truth." Therefore, if he finds evil in himself, then he can see about himself that he has a great need that the Creator will help him, it is regarded for him as a good thing. Therefore, when he details his sins, it is not regarded as "regarding oneself as wicked." On the contrary, now he can make an honest prayer for the Creator to bring him closer to Him.

It follows that by finding bad in himself he becomes very needy of the Creator, and a need is called "deficiency." Also, the prayer he prays must be from the bottom of the heart, since "from the bottom" means that the prayer he is praying on his deficiency is not superficial. Rather, that deficiency touches the point in his heart, meaning that all the organs feel his deficiency, and only then it is called a "prayer."

By this we will understand the question we asked, "How he says about himself that he is a *Hassid*, since a *Hassid* is already a degree, for not everyone is called *Hassid*, so how could he say about himself that he is *Hassid*? According to what I heard from Baal HaSulam, he said, "'He will give wisdom to the wise.' But it should have said, 'He will give wisdom to the fools.'" He said about this: "A 'wise' is named after the future. That is, one who wishes to be wise is already regarded as wise."

Therefore, when he said "I am pious [*Hassid*]," it means that he wants to be pious, which is called "love of others." First he said a prayer for the poor, meaning that he was in self-love, and "I want to be a *Hassid*." This is why the holy *Zohar* ends there: "At that time he is a *Hassid*, for he has come to receive repentance, and he takes himself out of the evil side, in whose filth he was thus far. But now he has clung to the upper right that is *Hesed* that is stretched out to welcome him. And because he has clung to *Hesed*, he is called *Hassid* [pious/devout follower]. That is, now he has come to cling to *Hesed*, so he is called *Hassid*, after the future.

By this we will also understand what the holy *Zohar* says, "Do not say that the Creator does not accept him until he details all his sins since the day he came to the world." This is not so. "If he sets his mind on regretting them during the confession, all the other sins follow them." We should say that if he prays for the public and for the root, from which all the sins come, namely the will to receive, naturally all the sins follow them, meaning follow self-love.

Concerning the Reward of the Receivers

Article No. 32, Tav-Shin-Mem-Hey, 1984-85

It is known that man cannot work without reward. This means that if one were not given reward, he would not make a move. This stems from the root of the creatures, which is utterly motionless, as it is written in *The Study of the Ten Sefirot* (Part 1, item 19): "We love rest and vehemently hate movement, to the point that we do not make even a single move if not to find rest. This is because our Root is motionless and restful; there is no movement in Him whatsoever. For this reason, it is also against our nature and hated by us."

Accordingly, we must know what is the reward for which it is worth our while to work. To explain this we must look into what we know—that there is the purpose of creation and the correction of creation.

That purpose of creation is from the perspective of the Creator. That is, we say that the Creator created creation because of His desire to do good to His creations. This brings up the famous questions, "Why are the creatures not receiving delight and pleasure, for who can go against Him and say that he does not want delight and pleasure if He has installed in the creatures a nature where each one wants to receive?"

We learn that only the will to receive is called "creation," and "creation" means something new, which is called "existence from absence." Therefore, He has created this nature in the creatures, which means that everyone wants to receive and He wants to give. So who is delaying?

The answer to this is presented in the words of the ARI (in the beginning of the book, *Tree of Life*): "To bring to light the perfection of His deeds, He has restricted Himself." He explains there, in "Inner Reflection," that it means that since there is a difference between giver and receiver, it causes disparity of form, meaning unpleasantness to the receivers. To correct this there was a correction that the abundance shines only to a place where there is an aim to bestow, for this is called "equivalence of form," and "*Dvekut* [adhesion] with the Creator."

Then, when he receives the delight and pleasure, he does not feel unpleasantness, and the abundance can come to the receiver because the receiver will not feel any deficiency upon the reception of the abundance. That is, he will not feel deficient because he is a receiver, since his aim is to bestow contentment upon the Creator, and not because he wants to receive pleasure for himself.

It therefore follows that if we introspect into what we must do in order to receive the delight and pleasure, it is only to obtain the *Kelim* [vessels], which is a second nature, called "vessels of bestowal." This is called the "correction of creation." Therefore, we should know what reward we should demand of the Creator to give us in return for our labor in Torah and *Mitzvot* [commandments]: it is that He will give us vessels of bestowal.

It is written in the introduction to the book, *Panim Masbirot* [Welcoming Face], the root of the reward is the *Masach* [screen] and the *Ohr Hozer* [Reflected Light]. Therefore, we need not demand pleasure and abundance in return for work, but vessels of bestowal, for this is all we need in order to receive the delight and pleasure.

Before one obtains the vessels of bestowal, he suffers in his life, for he hasn't the suitable *Kelim* to receive delight and pleasure.

We see that we should make three discernments in our actions in the order of our work: 1) forbidden things, 2) permitted things, 3) *Mitzvot*. With forbidden things it is impossible to speak of intentions for the Creator, that I can do something forbidden even *Lishma* [for Her sake]. We cannot even speak of doing them. Our sages call this a "*Mitzva* [commandment] that comes by transgression." Only with the permitted things can it be said that we should aim for the Creator, or that he cannot aim, and then he has no *Mitzva*. However, when he can aim to bestow, this act is regarded as a *Mitzva*.

With acts of *Mitzva*, such as eating a *Matza* [Passover bread], eating in a *Sukkah* [Sukkot hut], etc., even when one does not aim to bestow with them, it is still regarded as a *Mitzva*, since *Lo Lishma* [not for Her sake] is also a *Mitzva*. But when he does aim with it in order to bestow, that *Mitzva* causes him to be rewarded with the light in the *Mitzva*.

When he can no longer aim, but does the *Mitzva Lo Lishma*, our sages said, "One should always engage in Torah and *Mitzvot Lo Lishma*, and from *Lo Lishma* he will come to *Lishma*." It follows that even when he does not aim, he is observing the *Mitzvot* of the Creator. But when he does permitted things, it is called "optional," and this cannot be added to the count of *Mitzvot*.

However, when he commits forbidden things the transgression is written in his account. At that time he regresses from the path of Torah, becoming farther from the Creator. When he observes *Mitzvot Lo Lishma* he also becomes close to the Creator, but this is a slow path, meaning that by that he is nearing the Creator by a long route until he can cling to the Creator.

But when he performs the *Mitzvot Lishma*, by this he becomes more adhered to the Creator each and every time, until he is rewarded with the flavors of Torah and *Mitzvot*.

We can also discern from this if he enjoys the *Mitzva* or not. That is, when he eats a tiny piece of *Matza*, he cannot observe the *Mitzva* if he is not enjoying, for one who eats a tiny piece of *Matza*, below the threshold of pleasure, does not do his due. Rather, he must enjoy, or else he cannot bless.

Also, the delight of Shabbat [Sabbath] is a *Mitzva*. If he does not enjoy eating a Shabbat meal, he also did not do his due. Therefore, the rule is that on the Eve of Shabbat, close to the afternoon prayer, one should not eat until it is dark, so he will enjoy the meal. Our sages said about it (*Pesachim*, p 99): "'One should not eat on the eve of Shabbat and good day from the afternoon prayer onward, so he will come into Shabbat hungry,' the words of Rabbi Yehuda."

Still, even if he cannot aim in order to bestow, he is still observing the *Mitzva* of eating a *Matza* etc. Also, in permitted things, even if he cannot aim in order to bestow, it is still regarded as not being more materialized by eating permitted things when they are necessary, meaning that without them a person cannot live. It is permitted to receive these things in any case, meaning even when he cannot aim to bestow with them.

But with permitted things that are not necessary, when one uses them he becomes more materialized even if he commits no transgression by eating them. On the one hand we can say that necessities stand one degree below *Mitzvot* when they are done *Lo Lishma*.

It therefore follows that we should discern from below upward: 1) forbidden things, 2) permitted things with which he cannot aim to bestow, 3) permitted, but necessary things, 4) *Mitzvot* with which he does not aim in order to bestow, 5) permitted things with which he aims in order to bestow. (However, a *Mitzva* without the aim and permitted things in order to bestow require scrutiny, which of them is more important because there is room for mistakes here. This is why I do not want to scrutinize it), 6) *Mitzvot* with which he aims in order to bestow.

It follows that the reward is only to obtain vessels of bestowal. When one attains these vessels he has everything.

The Felons of Israel

Article No. 33, Tav-Shin-Mem-Hey, 1984-85

"Rish Lakish said, 'The felons of Israel, the light of Hell does not govern them, much less from the altar of gold, etc. The felons of Israel are full of *Mitzvot* [commandments/good deeds] like a pomegranate, as it is written, 'Your Temple is like a slice of a pomegranate.' Do not pronounce it *Rakatech* [your Temple], but *Reikanin* [empty] in you are full of *Mitzvot* like a pomegranate, all the more so" (end of *Hagigah* [*Masechet*]).

Concerning the felons of Israel, we should understand with respect to whom they are called the "felons of Israel": 1) Is it with respect to the Torah, 2) or with respect to the whole of Israel that they are regarded as the felons of Israel, 3) or with respect to the individual himself? That is, he sees and feels about himself that he is the felons of Israel. Superficially, it is difficult to see how one can be full of *Mitzvot* like a pomegranate, yet be regarded as the felons of Israel.

If we interpret this with respect to the person himself, we can say and interpret, "Although they are full of *Mitzvot* like a pomegranate," he sees that he is still the felons of Israel. We should interpret *Rimon* [pomegranate] from the word *Rama'ut* [deceit]. That is, he sees that he is deceiving himself, meaning that although he is full of *Mitzvot*, namely sees that he has nothing more to add in quantity, and according to his efforts, he should certainly have been Israel by now, meaning

Yashar-El [straight to the Creator], where everything is for the Creator. Yet, after his self-scrutiny, he sees that he is deceiving himself, that the main reason he engages in Torah and *Mitzvot* is self-love, and not in order to bestow contentment upon his Maker, which is called *Yashar-El*, meaning that all his work goes straight to the Creator.

Since he saw that all his work was only in order to receive, he saw that he was a felon with regard to Israel. That is, he does not want his work to be for above, called "in order to bestow upon the Creator." Rather, all his work is on the basis of keeping everything below, which is regarded as a receiver because the receiver is regarded as being of inferior importance, and the giver is of superior importance.

This extends from the root. Since the Creator is the giver, He is regarded as "above." The creature, who receives from the Creator, is regarded as being of inferior importance. Hence, if his work is in order to receive, he is regarded as wanting his work in Torah and *Mitzvot* to remain below, meaning in reception.

This is called "transgressing in the aspect of Israel," for instead of serving the Creator, where he wants to work to bestow upon the Creator, he does the opposite—wanting the Creator to serve man. And since they said that nothing is given for free, but the reward is given according to the labor, as is done in the physical world, this is how he wants to labor. He works for the Creator on condition that the Creator will pay for his labor. Otherwise he will have no strength to make any move without reward.

However, how can one come to see the truth, that he is deceiving himself concerning the quality of the goal, and cannot do the holy work in truth? Our sages said in that regard that one cannot see the truth before one has light. That is, one sees that he is doing many *Mitzvot*, meaning that he is full of deeds and sees no place where he can do more deeds that will help him become "Israel," meaning only to bestow, without any need for self-love. He does not see that he will ever achieve this by himself unless he has help from above, and it is impossible that man will be able to do this.

It follows that the *Mitzvot* he has done caused him to see the truth, that thus far he was fooling himself thinking that a person can obtain the force that changes to the intention to bestow by himself. Now he has come to realize that this is not the case.

Now we can interpret, "even the empty ones among you are full of *Mitzvot* like a pomegranate." It means that even though they are full of *Mitzvot*, they feel that they are empty because they see that they are like a pomegranate, from the words, "I called to my lovers; they deceived me" (Lamentations, 1), meaning deceit, whose work in Torah and *Mitzvot* was only for their own benefit and not to benefit the Creator.

But who caused him to know this? It is precisely that he is full of *Mitzvot*. This caused him to see that he should not fool himself into thinking that he can become "Israel." Instead, now he sees that he is the "felons of Israel."

It turns out that it is impossible to obtain real knowledge of one's degree in spirituality, unless he is full of *Mitzvot*. At that time he sees his state, that until now he was in deceit, and now he is in the degree of the "felons of Israel." But without *Mitzvot* is regarded as being without light, and then one cannot see the truth, that he needs the Creator to help him become "Israel."

However, we should know that saying that if he is full of *Mitzvot* then he sees that he is as a pomegranate comes with a stipulation: It is said specifically when he is a person who is seeking the truth. At that time it is said that one who seeks the truth still cannot see the truth before he is full of *Mitzvot*, but not before.

Hence, this requires two things: 1) On the one hand he needs to engage in Torah and *Mitzvot* as much as he can, without any criticism whether it is on the path of truth or not. Only after the fact can he criticize, but not while engaging in Torah and *Mitzvot*, for at that time he needs to feel himself in wholeness, as our sages said, "One should always engage in Torah and *Mitzvot Lo Lishma* [not for Her sake], because from *Lo Lishma* we come to *Lishma* [for Her sake]." Thus, for now it is unimportant how he is engaging because in any manner of engagement he is keeping the words of our sages. 2) After the fact he must criticize himself to see if his actions were for the Creator, or if something else was involved in it. From the two of them he can come to being "as a pomegranate," according to what we explained above.

By this we will understand the words of our sages (*Avoda Zara*, p 17): "Our sages said, 'When Rabbi Eilezer Ben Parta and Rabbi Hanina Ben Tardion were caught, ... 'Woe unto me for I was caught for one thing and I am not saved. You engaged in Torah and good deeds, and I engaged only in the Torah.' It is as Rav Huna said, 'Anyone who engages only in Torah is as one who has no God, as it was said, 'and many days for Israel without a true God, without a teaching priest, and without Torah.' What is 'without a true God'? Rav Huna said, 'Anyone who engages only in Torah, it is as though he has no God.'"

We should understand why if he does not engage in good deeds he is as one who has no God. Another perplexity: why specifically the *Mitzva* [commandment] of good deeds? After all, there are other *Mitzvot* that need to be observed, so why specifically good deeds is akin to being without a true God? It is as though by good deeds it is possible to tell if the Torah he is learning is without a true God.

According to what we learn, all our work is in order to achieve equivalence of form, regarded as "as He is merciful, so you are merciful." For this reason, during the study of Torah one must not criticize his Torah, meaning whose Torah he is learning, and then he can learn even *Lo Lishma*, which is also a *Mitzva*, as our sages said, "One should always engage in Torah and *Mitzvot*, even *Lo Lishma* [not for Her sake], since from *Lo Lishma* he will come to *Lishma* [for Her sake]."

This is so when he tests himself, his situation with regard to equivalence of form, how remote he has become from self-love, and how close he has become to love of others, which is the meaning of "cleaving to His qualities." This is why he makes the precision that the main thing to know is to test himself through the quality of *Hesed* [mercy], how much he engages in it, exerting for it, and contemplating various tactics and tricks to achieve equivalence of form, or he will not reach the path of truth.

It follows that at that time he does not have a "true God," for "true" means as is explained (*The Study of the Ten Sefirot*, Part 13), "The seventh correction of the thirteen corrections of *Dikna* is called 'and truth.'" He interprets there in "Inner Reflection": "At that time appears the quality of the Creator, who has created the world with the intention to do good to His creations, since at that time appears the *Ohr Hochma* [Light of Wisdom], which is the light of the purpose of creation, when everyone feels the delight and pleasure. At that time everyone says with clear cognizance that this, meaning the goal, is true."

It follows that if he does not engage in good deeds, which is the power that can bring to love of others, by which he will acquire vessels of bestowal, as the upper abundance is drawn only into these vessels, and if he has no vessels of bestowal he cannot acquire the delight and pleasure that the Creator created in order to delight His creatures. It follows that in that state a person is regarded as being "without a true God." That is the reality of His guidance, which is to do good to His creations, is God forbid untrue. This is called "without a true God."

This can be obtained precisely by engaging in good deeds. However, without Torah, it is impossible to know one's state, meaning where he is, since without light it is impossible to see anything. Rather, to see that he is a felon of Israel he needs to be full of *Mitzvot*, meaning both *Mitzvot* of learning Torah and the rest of the *Mitzvot*. The test is that after some time of engaging in Torah and *Mitzvot* he needs to examine, but not during his work.

And I Pleaded with the Lord

Article No. 34, Tav-Shin-Mem-Hey, 1984-85

"And I pleaded with the Lord." RASHI interpreted that in all the places, *Hanun* [gracious] from the root, *Hanan*, the same root as for *Etchanan* [pleaded] means *Matnat Hinam* [free gift]. Although the righteous can refer to their good deeds, they are only asking the Creator for a free gift.

It is written in *Midrash Rabbah*: "'And I pleaded with the Lord.' Out of all of them, Moses prayed only with a language of pleading. Rabbi Yohanan said, 'You learn from this that one has nothing with one's Maker, for Moses, the greatest of the prophets, came only with words of pleading.' Rabbi Levi said, 'Why did Moses come only with words of pleading?' The allegory says, 'Take care that the place of your words will not be caught.' How so? The Creator said so to Moses: 'I will be gracious to whom I will be gracious.' He said to him: 'With one who has in My hand I will be merciful; I work with him with the quality of mercy. And one who has not in My hand I will pardon; I work with him with a free gift.'"

We should understand the above said: 1) How can it be said, "I will be merciful" in relation to someone who has in My hand? The words, "One who has in My hand" come from the words of our sages, "Count for Me in your hand," meaning that he should be paid a debt. Thus, what does it mean that the Creator said that one to whom the Creator is indebted, the Creator tells him, "I will be merciful." He should have said, "I will pay," as it is written, "Who has preceded Me and I will pay him?" Therefore, how can it be said that paying a debt has to do with being merciful? 2) We should understand how it is possible to have two such conflicting views, where one view is that he deserves a debt from the Creator, as he says, "One who has in My hand," and the other is that he has nothing in his hand. In what way are their arguments so remote from one another? What is the point from which they come to such opposite views?

To understand the above we should discern two kinds in those who engage in Torah and *Mitzvot* [commandments]. Although there is no difference between them in the actions, meaning that in terms of actions it cannot be recognized, but there is a huge difference in the intention between the two above kinds.

The purpose that the first kind wants to achieve through their engagement in Torah and *Mitzvot* is to receive reward for the labor, since there is a rule in our nature that it is impossible to work without reward. Thus, what compels them to keep Torah and *Mitzvot* is the fear of not getting the fulfillment for the deficiencies that they are feeling. They are deficient of this and that and have a strong desire and great craving to satisfy it.

Therefore, they do everything they can in order to obtain what they want. For this reason, this fear compels them to engage in Torah and *Mitzvot*. This is regarded as not observing the fear because of the commandment of the Creator, but because of self-benefit, as presented in the *Sulam* [commentary] ("Introduction of the Book of Zohar," item 191): "It follows that his own benefit is the root, and fear is a branch derived of his own benefit."

It turns out that this kind engages in Torah and *Mitzvot* so the creator will pay them. Thus, the Creator is indebted to them, since they made great efforts in the engagement in order to yield fruit.

For this reason they come to the Creator with a demand: "Pay us for our labor." By this we can interpret the words of the above homily [Midrash], when Rabbi Levi said that the Creator said, "With one who has in My hand," meaning who deserves to be paid a debt, namely that from the beginning, his intention was for the Creator to pay for his labor in Torah and *Mitzvot*.

It turns out that he comes with a complaint, as it is said by our sages, "Count for Me in your hand." By this we can explain the words of the above homily. However, we should still clarify why the Creator said about this argument, "I will be merciful." What mercy is there here if he deserves to be paid a debt? How can it be said here, "I work with him with the quality of mercy"?

The second kind is those who have a completely different intention, since they want to serve the Creator in order to bestow contentment upon the Maker without any reward. According to the rule that man was created with a desire to receive for himself, how can he work without any reward? As I said in the previous articles, there are those who work in order to later receive a reward, and there are those who work because they regard the work itself as reward and payment, and they have no greater reward than to be allowed to work.

This is similar to serving an important person. It stems from nature that there is no greater reward than to serve an important person. This means that he can give everything he has in order to have the privilege of serving the King. It follows that the work itself is the reward, and he expects no other pay. Rather, he expects to have the privilege of always serving the King, ceaselessly, and this is his whole life, the whole purpose of his life, and it is imprinted in nature.

However, we should understand why the Creator created such a nature, where if the lower one knows the importance of the upper one he wants to serve Him without any reward. Baal HaSulam said about this that since the Creator created the worlds in order to delight His creatures, He created in the creatures desire and craving to receive delight and pleasure. Otherwise, without a desire to enjoy, the creature cannot receive delight and pleasure, since there is no fulfillment without a lack.

However, along with it came the matter of the bread of shame—that there is no *Dvekut* [adhesion] here due to the disparity of form that has been born. For this reason, there was the correction of *Tzimtzum* [restriction], meaning not to receive, unless it is because he wants to bring contentment to the Creator. This is why he receives from Him, and otherwise he waives the pleasure.

However, this brings up the question: If he was born with a will to receive and this is his nature, from where can he receive a desire to bestow? This is against nature! This is why He has created a second nature—that the smaller one annuls before the greater one and derives delight and pleasure from serving the greater one. Then, when he has a desire to bestow upon the greater one, he thinks, "What can I give to the Creator so the Creator will enjoy?" since he wants to impart Him with pleasure so He will enjoy. At that time he sees that all he can give to the upper one, which you could say that the upper one lacks, is only one thing: that the lower one derives delight and pleasure. This gives pleasure to the Creator because this was the purpose of creation, which is to do good to His creations.

It therefore follows that all that man lacks in order to have the desire to bestow is the greatness of the Creator, for as soon as he obtains the greatness of the Creator he immediately wants to bestow upon Him due to the nature that the lower one, who is smaller, is annulled before the greater one.

This is why we were given the matter of wailing over the exile of the *Shechina* [Divinity]. This means that the whole matter of spirituality is degraded, which is called "*Shechina* in the dust," when her importance is as that of dust, which is stepped on and is meaningless. This is the meaning of what is presented, that with each *Mitzva* [commandment] we must intend to raise the *Shechina* from the dust. That is, with every action one should intend that by this the glory of the *Shechina* will grow. It is as we say (In the Eighteen in the Supplementary Prayer of *Rosh Hashanah* [beginning of the year]), "Our Father, our King, reveal the glory of Your kingdom upon us," namely that the kingdom of heaven will not be to us as dust, but rather glorified.

It follows that what this kind of people demands of the Creator is that He will reveal to them the glory of His kingship, and have nothing with the Creator since they do not require any reward from the Creator. Rather, all they want is to serve the King and please Him. They ask that the Creator will show them the glory of the kingdom of heaven.

Thus, they have nothing in the hands of the Creator that they can say that they gave something to the Creator for which they are demanding that He will satisfy their need, since anything they can do in order to bestow is only because the Creator has revealed to them with some importance, when they feel a little bit of the sublimity of the Creator. It follows that those people who have nothing of theirs in the hands of the Creator, whatever He gives them is only because "I will pardon," "I work with him with a free gift."

But those who work in order to receive reward say that they have something in the hands of the Creator. That is, they give Him work and ask of the Creator to pay the reward for their work in return. And since the Creator does not deny the reward of any being, He pays them according to their work.

However, we must understand the words, "I will have mercy," "I work with him with the quality of mercy [*Rachamim*]," since the Creator is saying that He feels mercy toward those who are walking on this path. And yet, the Creator does not deny the reward of any being, therefore He pays them according to their demand.

By this we will understand what we asked, "How can there be such a big difference between the two above views. The thing is that from the perspective of the Creator, we learn that the purpose of creation is to do good to His creations, but the creatures themselves turn it into two discernments, since those who cannot understand the importance of the greatness of the Creator have no way to begin the work, except in order to receive reward, as our sages said, "One should always engage in Torah and *Mitzvot*, even if *Lo Lishma* (*Pesachim* 50)." They feel that they are giving something to the Creator.

But those who want to work in order to bestow see that they cannot give anything to the Creator. This is regarded as not having anything. It follows that what they want is for the Creator to show them a little of His greatness. They ask this for the purpose of pardoning, and then the Creator tells them, "I will pardon," "I work with him with a free gift."

When a Person Knows What Is Fear of the Creator

Article No. 35, Tav-Shin-Mem-Hey, 1984-85

In the portion, *Vaetchanan* (item 68), the holy *Zohar* writes, "Afterwards in particular, meaning that when a person knows what fear of the Creator is, when he attains the quality of *Malchut* herself, which is fear out of love, the essence and the basis of love of the Creator, this fear makes him keep all the *Mitzvot* [commandments] of the Torah, so a person is a loyal servant of the Creator, as it should be."

We should understand what it means when he says, "when he attains the quality of *Malchut* herself, which is fear out of love." It means that since he has been rewarded with *Malchut* herself, she is regarded as love, and that love causes him fear. But why does love cause him fear? And also, we should understand what is fear once he has been rewarded with love?

We should interpret this according to what I heard that Baal HaSulam interpreted about the verse, "And there was a quarrel between the herdsmen of Abram's cattle and the herdsmen of Lot's cattle" (Genesis, 13:7). Abraham is called "father of faith," whose work was based entirely on faith above reason without any support, meaning something to support the entire building that he was going to build in his life. He went wholeheartedly, and precisely through faith above reason he could approach the Creator, when he saw only this as life's purpose.

To be rewarded with *Dvekut* [adhesion] with the Creator within reason, he saw that his mind mandated otherwise, for wherever he turned he saw contradictions in Providence, in how the Creator behaves with the creatures. Then he understood that the Creator wants him to serve Him precisely above reason. He understood that if the way of within reason was better suited for bringing man to *Dvekut* with the Creator, the Creator would certainly behave differently, "for who will tell You what to do?"

Rather, he believed that he has no other way but to go above reason, and that the Creator did so deliberately because precisely this way is to man's benefit. Therefore, he decided that he wanted to serve the Creator specifically above reason. This means that if he can attain His guidance within reason, he will oppose it because he regarded his work above reason, that this was more certain that his aim would be only to bestow contentment upon the Creator. But what could he do if he saw that His guidance dressed in him within reason, and he no longer had the option of going above reason because everything was revealed to him?

Baal HaSulam explained that when he saw some disclosure of light and abundance appearing to him he did not say about it that now he was happy that he will no longer have to go above reason because this is work to which the body does not agree, for the body enjoys more if it has some support on which to rely. That is, on which basis is his entire effort built? All the buildings that man builds are founded on the intellect, meaning that the intellect compels him that he must do so. For this reason, where the intellect cannot say that everything he does is fine, it is certainly difficult for him to walk in this way.

Therefore, where he has a chance to attain something within reason, he promptly throws his foundation of above reason and begins to work on a new basis, built on the intellect. Then he has support on which his labor can rely and he no longer needs the help of the Creator. Because it is difficult to go above reason, he always needs the help of the Creator, to have the strength to go above reason.

But now that the mind is telling him, "Now that you have the support of the mind and reason, you can advance alone, without the help of the Creator, and attain what there is to attain." Then his advice, when he said, "Now I see that the real way is to go specifically above reason because precisely by going above reason, a way that pleases the Creator, I was now rewarded with nearing the Creator." The evidence of this is that now he feels a taste for the work of the Creator both in Torah and in prayer.

It follows that he does not take being rewarded with nearing the Creator and feeling the love of the Creator as a basis for the work, meaning support for the work of the Creator, since the intellect necessitates that it is worthwhile to keep Torah and *Mitzvot* and he no longer needs to go with faith above reason. Rather, he is careful not to flaw the faith, meaning to accept the way of within reason and throw away the faith.

Faith is called *Malchut*. Therefore, it is considered that he has degraded and blemished the faith, for now it is evident that to begin with, he had no choice and therefore took to faith, but otherwise he would not have taken it. And as soon as he sees that he can get rid of it he promptly degrades it and throws it, and takes knowing in its stead. It was said about this, "I will honor those who honor Me, and those who despise Me will be disgraced." It is also written, "The ways of the Lord are straight; the righteous walk in it, and the wicked fail in it."

Accordingly, we can understand what we asked, since he has already been rewarded with *Malchut*, it is regarded as fear out of love. We asked, "If he already has love, how can we still speak of fear, and how can we speak of fear when he has already been rewarded with love?"

When a Person Knows What Is Fear of the Creator

According to the interpretation of Baal HaSulam, who explained concerning the herdsmen of Abraham's cattle, we can easily understand this. He said that the herdsmen of Abraham's cattle means that Abraham was pasturing the faith. *Mikneh* [cattle] comes from the word *Kinyan* [possessions], meaning that all the possessions he has been rewarded with were pasturing his faith. That is, he said, "Now I see that the path of faith is the real path because I was rewarded with nearing the Creator. For this reason, I take upon myself to henceforth go only by the way of faith above reason."

This was not so with the herdsmen of Lot's cattle. He took the possessions he acquired into the discernment of Lot. The holy *Zohar* calls Lot by the name of "land of the curse," meaning that it is not a place of blessing, called a "field that the Lord has blessed." Rather, it is a place of curse, which is within reason, meaning that he does what the mind mandates. However, when he began to walk on the path of the Creator, he also began with faith above reason, but he always waited for a time when he could be rid of this work of above reason.

The body always demands some basis on which to base his exertion in Torah and *Mitzvot*, since when the work is built on the intellect, and the intellect lets him understand that the work is worthwhile, the body makes great efforts, and very persistently, because the intellect compels it.

For example, a person went to bed at midnight, he is very tired, with fever, and is forbidden to get out of bed because he is shivering. But a fire breaks out in nearby rooms and he is told to quickly get out of bed because soon he won't be able to get out of the house and he might burn. At that time, the intellect mandates without any doubt, if he regards his situation, that it is inconvenient for him to get out of bed for several reasons, then he might burn. Surely, he jumps out of bed without any arguments because the basis on which he has to exert, the intellect, mandates its profitability. Therefore he is certain to make every effort.

It follows that where the intellect binds the effort, one does not regard the effort, but only the profit, meaning what one can obtain through the effort. However, when working above reason one is always under the body's pressure, which is asking, "What makes you certain that you're on the right path? Is the effort you are making in order to achieve the goal really worthwhile? Is this even doable? Can you achieve the goal you're seeking?"

Therefore, he is always going through ups and downs, where once the intellect prevails and once above reason prevails. He always thinks, "When will I be able to establish my work within reason and have a sound basis, since I will be able to build everything on the intellect? Surely, at that time I will not have any descents in the work of the Creator, as is with everything that is built on common sense." However, he does not know what he hopes to attain will not give him a blessing, but a curse, since within reason is the place of the grip of the *Sitra Achra* [other side], and the Creator has chosen that those who want to achieve *Dvekut* with the Creator, specifically above reason, is the real way to approach the Creator.

This is the degree of Lot, the cursed land, a land where there is a curse and not a blessing. This is called the "herdsmen of Lot's cattle," who was always searching possessions for within reason, called Lot, meaning a curse. This is the meaning of the verse, "And there was a quarrel between the herdsmen of Abram's cattle and the herdsmen of Lot's cattle." That is, the quarrel was that each one said that he was right.

Those who were in the state of herdsmen of Lot's cattle were saying, "If we can build our basis on the intellect, called 'within reason,' we will not have ups and downs because we will always be in a state of ascent." This is so because where the intellect binds doing the actions there is no one to interrupt them. Therefore, when we have no choice we must go above reason. But when we can choose to go within reason, it is to the contrary: we must say that there is contentment above in that from this day forth we will have no descents in the work. Therefore, our way is certainly better.

But the herdsmen of Abram's cattle are people whose basis was precisely on faith above reason. They said, "If the Creator wanted us to work on the basis of the intellect, He would not be concealed from us to begin with. Rather, this must be the best way. Therefore, we need not look for opportunities to be rid of faith above reason. Rather, if we receive some intellect and nearing to the Creator we will not take it as a basis for casting away faith, but to say, 'Now I see that this is the real way because by this I was rewarded with nearing.'" Therefore, he should brace himself and accept that henceforth he will not search for any opportunities to be rid of the faith, but on the contrary, grow stronger with faith above reason.

By this we will understand the words of the holy *Zohar*, that once he was rewarded with *Malchut* herself, which is love, being fear out of love, we asked, "How can you speak of fear if there is already love there?" And also, "What is fear?"

According to the above said, it turns out that once he was rewarded with love, there is nothing greater that mandates the work because it is a basis within reason, for now the intellect mandates the work for him. This is so because naturally, we want to serve the one we love. Therefore, there is no more room for faith because at that time how can we speak of faith above reason then?

Therefore, he is afraid that he might blemish the faith because now the body will enjoy the work more since he has a basis of within reason. And if he blemishes faith, then it becomes revealed that the faith above reason that he had had was out of necessity to begin with, not out of respect, but that he constantly longed for a time when he could be rid of it and work with knowledge instead of faith.

Then, because he has blemished faith, he promptly falls from his degree and soon parts from the Creator, since knowing is receiving. It is known that we understand receiving, which is self-love, in two ways: 1) with the mind, 2) with the heart.

It turns out that when he has been rewarded with love, the love itself causes him fear. He is afraid that he will not be drawn to knowledge. Therefore, at that time he needs great care that he will not fall into the will to receive. At that time we understand that love itself causes the fear. Now we already know what fear is, which love causes, meaning that he is afraid that through this love he will fall into self-love.

With this we can understand the great rule that Baal HaSulam said, that although it makes sense that sin induces punishment, in internality, it is a very different meaning, which is a little difficult to grasp. He said that we must know that the sin is the punishment, and the punishment is already the correction!

We should ask about this: If the sin is the punishment, what is the sin? Through the above said we can interpret that the sin was actually during the ascent, that precisely when he was rewarded with love, he had a desire to take love as the basis, and cast away the faith, as is the view of the herdsmen of Lot's cattle.

At that time he suffered a descent and fell once more into self-love, from which every kind of sin is derived. It follows that he failed precisely during the ascent, when he thought that by taking love as a basis and support on which to exert, and thought that by this he would not have any more descents, since where the intellect mandates is a healthy path and he will never fall, this was the actual sin. This is called "All who add subtract." It follows that his fall into self-love is the punishment for flawing the faith, and the punishment he has received is a correction so he will rise once more on the degree of the straight path.

And There Was Evening and There Was Morning

Article No. 36, Tav-Shin-Mem-Hey, 1984-85

The *Zohar* says about the verse, "And there was evening and there was morning" (Genesis 3, p 96, and Item 151 in the *Sulam* Commentary), "'And there was evening,' which the text writes, means that it extends from the side of darkness, meaning *Malchut*. 'And there was morning' means that it extends from the side of the light, which is ZA.

"This is why it writes about them, 'One day,' indicating that the evening and morning are as one body, and both make the day. Rabbi Yehuda said, 'What is the reason?' He asks, 'Since 'And there was evening and there was morning' points to the unification of ZON, that the light of day comes out of both of them, then after the text announces it on the first day, why does it says about each day, 'And there was evening and there was morning'?

"And he replies, 'It is to know that there is no day without a night and no night without a day, and they will never part from one another. This is why the text repeats and informs us each and every day, to indicate that it is impossible that there will ever be the light of day without the darkness of night. Likewise, there will never be the darkness of night that does not bring a day after it, since they will never part from one another.'" Thus far its words.

We should understand the above-written in the work, as to what light means and what darkness means, and why it is impossible to have a day unless it is from the both of them together, meaning that light and darkness produce a single day, that is, it takes both to build a single day. This means that the day begins when the darkness begins because this is when the sequence of the making of a new day begins.

We should also understand how the word "day" can be applied to darkness, since when the darkness has begun, we can already begin to count the day.

It is known that after the restrictions and the departure of the light that occurred in the upper worlds—after the second restriction and the breaking—the system of *Klipot* [shells] emerged, until the place of *BYA* divided into two discernments. From its middle and above it was the *BYA* of *Kedusha* [holiness], and from its middle and below it became the permanent section of the *Klipot*, as explained in TES (Part 16, p 1938, Item 88).

Consequently, in this world, "A man is born the foal of a wild donkey" and he has no desire for spirituality. Thus, from where does the sensation of need for spirituality come to a person, to the point of saying that he feels darkness, which he calls "night," by feeling that he is remote from the Creator? We must know that at the same time he begins to feel that he is far from the Creator, he is already beginning to believe in the existence of the Creator to some extent, or else how can he say that he is remote from something that doesn't exist? Instead, he must say that he has some illumination from afar that shines for him to the extent that he feels that he is remote from the Creator.

It therefore follows that as soon as the darkness begins, meaning the sense of the existence of darkness, the light immediately begins to shine to some extent. And the measure of illumination of the light is recognized only through negation. That means that one feels a lack, that he does not have the light of the Creator shining for him in an affirmative manner. However, the light shines for him in the form of lack, meaning that now he begins to feel that he is missing the light of the Creator, which is called "day."

But those for whom the light of day does not shine don't know if there is such a reality where a person must feel the absence of the light of the Creator, which is called "day." Let us speak of a single person, meaning within the same body. Sometimes one feels that he is in darkness, meaning that he is remote from the Creator and craves to draw near to the Creator. He feels suffering at being remote from the Creator.

The question is, "Who causes him to worry about spirituality?" And sometimes he feels darkness and suffering when he sees that another is successful in corporeality in possessions and with people, while he lacks both sustenance and respect. He sees about himself that in truth, he is more gifted than the other, both in terms of talent and in terms of ancestry, and he deserves more respect. But in fact, he is many degrees lower than the other one, and this pains him terribly.

At that time, he has no connection to spirituality, and he doesn't even remember that he ever was connected, and that he himself considered all the friends with whom he was studying at the seminary, that when he saw them suffering for their concerns to achieve wholeness in life, they seemed to him like children who cannot make a purposeful calculation, and all that their eyes see is what they want. At one time they see that the most important thing in life is money, and at another time they see that the most important thing in life is to have a respectable position among people, etc. And now he is within those very things that he mocked, and he feels that his life is tasteless unless he determines the whole of the hope and peace in life at the same level that they determine, that this is called "life's purpose."

And what is the truth? It is that now the Creator has taken pity on him and illuminated the discernment of day for him, and this day begins with negation. In other words, when the day begins to shine in his heart in the form of darkness, it is called "the beginning of the rise of day," and then *Kelim* begin to form in him, in which the light will be able to shine in an affirmative manner. This is the light of the Creator, when one begins to feel the love of the Creator and begins to feel the flavor of Torah and the taste of *Mitzvot*.

From this we can understand the above words of *The Zohar*, that a day comes out specifically of the both of them, as it writes, "This is why it writes about them, 'One day,' indicating that the evening and morning are as one body, and both make the day." Also, when Rabbi Yehuda said that this is why the text alerts every day anew—to indicate that it is impossible that there will ever be light without the darkness of the night that comes first. And also, there will not be the darkness of the night that does not bring the light of day after it, so they will never part from one another.

It is as mentioned above, 1) following the rule that there is no light without a *Kli*, and 2) it also requires light, which is called "day," to make a *Kli*.

But we should understand why, if one has already been granted a little bit of day in the negative form and feels that his whole life is only if he is rewarded with *Dvekut* with the Creator, and he begins to torment over being remote from the Creator, who, then, causes him to fall from his state of ascent? In other words, his whole life should be only in spiritual life, and this is all his hope, and he suddenly falls into a state of lowliness, a state where he would always laugh at people whose hope in life was to obtain the fulfillment of beastly lusts. But now he himself is among them, nourished by the same nourishments that they feed on.

Moreover, we should wonder how he has forgotten that he was once in a state of ascent. Now he is in a state of such amnesia that it doesn't even occur to him that he would consider the people that he is now among, meaning that his only ambitions are at such a low level and he is not ashamed of himself that he dared go into such an atmosphere that he always ran from. In other words, this air that they breathe so willingly, he would always say that it suffocates *Kedusha* [holiness], and now he is among them and feels that there is no fault in them.

The answer is as the writing says (Psalms 1), "Happy is the man that has not walked in the counsel of the wicked." We must understand what the counsel of the wicked is. It is known that the question of one who is wicked that is brought in the *Hagadah* (Passover narrative) is "What mean you by this service?" Baal HaSulam explained that it means that when a person begins to work in order to bestow, the wicked one's question comes and asks, "What will you get out of not working for yourself?"

And when a person receives such a question, he begins to contemplate that perhaps he is right. And then he falls into his net. Accordingly, we should interpret, "Happy is the man that has not walked in the counsel of the wicked" that when the wicked come to him and advise him that it is not worthwhile to work if he does not see some benefit and gain from it to himself, he does not listen to them. Instead, he strengthens himself in the work and says, "Now I see that I am going on the path of truth, and they wish to confuse me." It follows that when that man overcomes, he is happy.

Afterwards, the writings say, "Nor stood in the way of sinners." We should interpret "Way of sinners." He says, "Nor stood." A sin is as we explained in the previous essay (35, 1984-85), that the sin is if a person breaks "You shall not add." In other words, the real way is that we have to go above reason, called faith. And the opposite of that is knowing—the body understands that he has no other choice except to believe above reason.

Hence, when he feels some taste in the work and takes it as support, and says that now he does not need faith, since he already has some basis, he immediately falls from his degree. And when one is careful about it and does not stand for even a minute to look and see if it is possible to change his basis, it is considered that he is happy because he did not stand in the way of sinners, to look at their way.

And afterwards, the writing says, "Nor sat in the seat of the scornful," referring to those people who spend their days idly, who do not take their lives seriously and consider every moment precious. We should know to what "The seat of the scornful" refers. Those who cherish every moment and sit and think of others—if other people are all right and how much others should correct their actions, and have no pity for themselves, worrying about their own lives, this causes them all the descents. The RADAK interprets scornful as being of a shrewd mind in an evil way, finding faults in people and disclosing secrets to each other. This matter is for lazy people, idlers. This is why he said, "Nor sat in the seat of the scornful," and this is the reason for the descents.

Who Testifies to a Person?

Article No. 37, Tav-Shin-Mem-Hey, 1984-85

It is written in *The Zohar, Shoftim* [judges] (and in the *Sulam* Commentary p 8, Item 11), "It is a *Mitzva* [commandment/good deed] to testify in court so that his friend will not lose money because he is not testifying. This is why the authors of the *Mishnah* said, 'Who testifies to a person? The walls of his house.'

"What is the meaning of 'The walls of his house'? These are the walls of his heart, as it is written, 'Then Hezekiah turned his face to the wall.' The authors of the *Mishnah* asserted that it teaches that Hezekiah prayed from the walls of his heart. Moreover, his household testifies to him. His household are his 248 organs, since the body is called 'house.'

"This is what the authors of the *Mishnah* asserted: 'A wicked one, his iniquities are engraved in his bones. Likewise, a righteous one, his merits are engraved in his bones.' This is the reason why David said, 'All my bones shall say.' But why are the iniquities engraved in the bones more than in the flesh, tendons, and skin? This is because the bones are white, and a black writing is visible only from within white. It is like the Torah, which is white from within, meaning the parchment, and black from without, meaning the ink. Black and white are darkness and light. And moreover, the body is destined to rise on its bones, hence the sins and merits are engraved in its bones. If he is rewarded, the body will rise on its bones. If he is not rewarded, it will not rise and will not have revival of the dead." Thus far its words.

We should understand why *The Zohar* interprets that a person should testify before a court so that his friend will not lose money. This is interpreted in the work of the Creator. Thus, we should understand what it is that one is demanding, and from whom he is demanding it. And to make it reliable, a person must testify.

In the work of the Creator, a person demands of the Creator to give him what he wants of the Creator. Thus, to show that his argument is true, doesn't the Creator know whether or not a person is telling the truth? However, if the man testifies, then he knows that his argument is true. Moreover, how can one be trusted to testify for himself? And we should also understand why the testimony must be from the walls of his heart, since he brings evidence to the meaning of "walls of his house" from Hezekiah in the words, "Then Hezekiah turned his face to the wall," which we interpreted to mean "the walls of his heart."

Thus, a person's testimony should also be from the walls of his heart. However, it is known that a testimony must be from his mouth, as our sages said, "From their mouths, not from their writings," and here he says that it should be from the walls of his heart and not from the mouth.

We should also understand why it says, "This is what the authors of the *Mishnah* asserted: 'A wicked one, his iniquities are engraved in his bones. And likewise, a righteous one, his merits are engraved in his bones.'"

But are sins and merits engraved in corporeal bones? How is a spiritual matter, which is sins and *Mitzvot*, engraved in bones? And it is even more difficult to understand his answer, "This is because the bones are white, and a black writing is visible only from within white."

Also, we should understand why he says, "And moreover, the body is destined to rise on its bones." Why particularly, "On its bones," which means that whether or not he is revived depends on his bones?

To understand the above in the work, we must remember the known rule that "There is no light without a *Kli* [vessel]," meaning that it is impossible to receive any fulfillment if there is no hole or deficiency there, where the filling can enter. For example, a person cannot eat a meal if he is not hungry. Moreover, the amount of pleasure that person can derive from the meal is measured by the amount of desire he has for the meal.

It follows that where one does not feel any lack, he will not experience any pleasure, which he will be able to receive, since there is no room to receive any filling. Thus, when we speak of the order of the work, when a person begins to enter the work, meaning when he wishes to do the work of holiness with the aim to bestow contentment upon his Maker, according to the above-mentioned rule, he must have a need for it—to feel that he needs to bestow upon the Creator. And we can say that he has a *Kli* to the extent of his need to give to the Creator. And the filling for that *Kli* is while he gives to the Creator, meaning when he wishes to bring Him contentment. This means that the body already agrees to bestow upon the Creator.

And since man is born with a nature for reception and not for bestowal, if one wishes to engage in bestowal the body will certainly resist it. And if a person wants to engage in bestowal, meaning that he has a desire to obtain such a *Kli*, and a *Kli* means a desire and deficiency, then the body immediately comes and asks, "Why do you want to change the nature you were created in? What is the deficiency that you feel you are lacking? Are you one hundred percent sure that you understand that you need to work in order to bestow? Look at how the majority do the work of holiness; they are not meticulous about what they do. In other words, in their engagement in Torah or *Mitzvot*, they see primarily that the act will be proper, with all its precisions and details, but not the intent. They say, 'We certainly do what we can.' They pay no mind to the intent because they say that the work *Lishma* [for Her name] belongs to a chosen few, and not to everyone."

It follows that the body, which comes and asks its questions, is probably asking to the point. And since it is not given a sufficient answer, it doesn't allow a person to think thoughts of desire to bestow, since it is right, there is no light without a *Kli*. In other words, "If you don't feel the need to engage in bestowal, why are you making a fuss?" So first it tells him, "Give me this need, the desire to bestow, and then we'll talk." But according to the above-said, the need for the desire must be present, meaning that he should suffer at not being able to bestow. Thus, since he has no *Kli*, he certainly cannot be granted the light, meaning the filling.

Therefore, a person should try to have a great deficiency because he is unable to bestow upon the Creator. And it is known that a deficiency is determined by the sensation of suffering that he feels because of the deficiency. Otherwise, although he does not have what he is asking, it is still not considered a deficiency because a real lack is measured by the pain that he feels at not having. Otherwise, it is nothing but empty words.

Now we can understand what our sages said (*Taanit*, 2a), "'To love the Lord your God and to serve Him with all your heart.' What is the work of the heart? It is a prayer. We should understand why they extended the prayer beyond the literal meaning. Usually, when one wants another person to give him something, he asks him to, verbally, as it is written, 'For You hear the prayer of every mouth.' So why did they say that a prayer is called 'the work of the heart'?"

We said above that a prayer is called "a deficiency," and he wants his deficiency to be filled. And yet, no deficiency is sensed in a person's mouth; rather, all of man's sensations are sensed in the heart. This is why if a person doesn't feel a lack in his heart, what he utters in his mouth does not count at all, so we could say that he truly needs what he is asking for with his mouth. This is so because the filling he is asking for should enter a place of deficiency, which is the heart. This is why our sages said that a prayer should be from the bottom of the heart, meaning that the whole heart will sense the lack for which he is asking.

It is known that light and *Kli* are called "deficiency" and "filling" (or "fulfillment"). We ascribe the light, which is the filling, to the Creator, and the *Kli*, which is the lack, to the creatures. Thus, a person should prepare the *Kli* so the Creator will pour the abundance there, or there will be no room for the abundance. For this reason, when a person asks the Creator to help him so he can aim his actions to bestow, the body comes and asks him, "Why are you praying this prayer? What are you missing without it?"

For this reason, we must study and scrutinize the books that discus the necessity of the work of bestowal until we understand and feel that if we don't have this *Kli*, we will not be able to enter the *Kedusha*. We should not look at the majority, who say that the most important thing is the act and here is where all the energy should go, and that the acts of *Mitzvot* and establishing of the Torah that we do are enough for us.

Instead, he must perform every act of Torah and *Mitzvot* in order to bring himself into the aim to bestow. Afterwards, when he has a complete understanding of how much he needs to engage in order to bestow, and he feels pain and suffering at not having this force, then it is considered that he already has something for which to pray—for work in the heart—since the heart feels what it needs.

For such a prayer comes the answer to the prayer. This means that he is given this strength from above so he will be able to aim in order to bestow, for then he already has the light and *Kli*. However, what can one do if, after all the efforts he has made, he still does not feel the lack of not being able to bestow as pain and suffering? The solution is to ask the Creator to give him the *Kli* called, "A lack from not feeling," and that he is unconscious, without any pain from being unable to bestow.

It follows that if he can regret and ache over not having the deficiency, for not feeling how remote he is from *Kedusha* [holiness], that he is utterly mundane and doesn't understand that the life he is living—wanting to satisfy the corporeal needs—is no more important than that of any other animal that he sees, and that if he paid attention to see how similar he is to them with all their aspirations, and that the only difference is man's cunningness and his ability to exploit others while animals are not clever enough to exploit others.

Sometimes, even though he sees that he is studying Torah and keeping the *Mitzvot*, he cannot remember—while keeping the *Mitzvot* or while studying Torah—that he should obtain connection with the Creator by engaging in Torah and *Mitzvot*. It is as though they are separate things for him—the Torah and *Mitzvot* are one thing, and the Creator is another.

And if he regrets not having any sensation of deficiency, that he is like an animal, this is called "work in the heart," as well. It is called, "a prayer." This means that for this deficiency, he already has a place in which to receive fulfillment from the Creator, to give him the sense of deficiency, which is the *Kli* that the Creator fills with a filling.

Now we can understand the question, "why is a prayer in the heart and not in the mouth?" It is because a prayer is called, "a deficiency," and it cannot be said that he has a deficiency in the mouth. Rather, the deficiency is a sensation in the heart.

Now we should explain why we asked about his saying that the merits and the sins are engraved on the bones, and he can revive from the bones or not. *The Zohar* compares the bones, which are white, to the Torah, which is black over white, where the black is darkness and the white is light.

We should explain the meaning of bones being white. This is why both the merits and the sins are written on them, since concerning the work of the Creator, it should be interpreted that a person who engages in Torah and *Mitzvot* is called "a bone." The primary part of Torah and *Mitzvot* is considered white, since something in which there are no deficiencies is called "white." And since there is nothing to add to the actions that a person does, for it is said about it, "You shall neither add nor subtract," his engagement in

Who Testifies to a Person?

the Torah is called "bones." They are white because the merits and sins of a person are engraved in them.

However, if a person criticizes his actions—the reason why he is building his foundation (the reason that compels him to engage in Torah and *Mitzvot*, his aim while doing the deeds)—and tries to see if he is truly doing those deeds for the Creator, to bestow contentment upon his Maker, then he can see the truth: he is inside the nature he was born in, called "receiving in order to receive," and he doesn't want to engage in Torah and *Mitzvot* without any reward.

And the real reason why one cannot exit his nature is that he doesn't see the need for it, so he would have to change the nature that was imprinted in him, which is called "self-love," and assume the love of others in order to achieve the love of the Creator. This is so because a person feels that he is deficient of the love of his surroundings, meaning that the family will love him, and his town's people, etc. But what will he gain from loving the Creator? Also, what will he gain if he loves his friends? After all, he is always considering the profits related to self-love. Thus, how can he exit this love?

And if he asks himself why he is keeping Torah and *Mitzvot* in actions, and is even meticulous about all its precisions and details, then he answers himself that he received faith through education. In education, you begin to guide a person to engage in Torah and *Mitzvot* in *Lo Lishma* [not for Her name], as Maimonides says (end of *Hilchot Teshuva* [*Laws of Repentance*]). It follows that he has taken it upon himself to believe in the Creator, that he will serve in the holy work, and in return will be rewarded in this world and in the next world.

This is why a person is told that the real work is to believe in the Creator who gave us Torah and *Mitzvot* to keep, and by that, we will achieve equivalence of form, called "*Dvekut* [adhesion] with the Creator." This means that one should exit self-love and assume love of others. And to the extent that he exits self-love, he can be rewarded with complete faith. Otherwise he is separated, as written in the *Sulam* Commentary ("Introduction of The Book of Zohar," p 138), "It is a law that the creature cannot receive apparent harm from Him, for it is a flaw in His glory that the creature should perceive Him as doing harm, for it is inappropriate for the perfect Operator. Hence, when one feels bad, to the extent that there is denial of His guidance upon him and the Operator is hidden from him, this is the biggest punishment in the world."

If a person introspects, he recognizes the truth that the Torah and *Mitzvot* should be for the Creator. He feels how remote he is from the truth, and the scrutiny brings him into pain and suffering at constantly marching on the wrong road from being called a "servant of the Creator." Rather, all his work is for his own sake, which is called, "working for himself," which is the way of all the animals, but is inappropriate for the speaking.

It follows that through those sufferings, he receives a *Kli*, meaning a deficiency. And since he sees that he is incapable of exiting self-love by himself, for he doesn't have the strength to go against nature, the solution is to ask the Creator to help him, as our sages said, "He who comes to be purified is aided." It follows that then he has room for filling the deficiency, since there is no light without a *Kli*.

This brings up the question that we asked earlier: "What can one do if, even though he understands that it is worthwhile to work in order to bestow, he still doesn't have the pain and suffering at not being able aim in order to bestow? In that case, he should know that this does not mean that he doesn't have complete faith in the Creator, only that he cannot aim in order to bestow. He should know that he is lacking whole faith, since when he has whole faith in the Creator, there is a natural law that the small annuls itself before the big. Thus, if he truly had whole faith in the greatness of the Creator, he would be annulled before the Creator naturally, and he would wish to serve Him without any reward.

It follows that there is no deficiency here, for he cannot prevail over nature. Rather, there is lack of whole faith here, although he has faith. The evidence of that is that he is keeping Torah and *Mitzvot*. However, it is not whole faith, as it should be.

In other words, the entire wholeness is that they believe in His greatness, and if one wishes to know if he has whole faith, he can see how much he is willing to work in order to bestow and how much the body is annulled before the Creator. Thus, a person's inability to work in order to bestow is the deficiency, but there is a greater deficiency here—that he lacks whole faith—and this is the main one.

But what can one do if, even though he sees that he lacks whole faith, that deficiency still does not beget in him pain and suffering at his being deficient? The real reason is that he is looking at the majority, and sees that they are important people, of influence and status, and it is not apparent that they lack whole faith. When speaking to them, they say that this is only for a chosen few, which is their well-known view. This is the great partition, which becomes a barrier for a person, arresting his progress on the right path.

This is the reason why we need an *environment*, meaning a group of people who are all of the view that they must achieve whole faith. This is the only thing that can save a person from the views of the collective. At that time, *everyone strengthens everyone else* to crave to achieve whole faith, that he can bestow contentment upon the Creator, and that this will be his only aspiration.

However, this does not conclude the solution for achieving a deficiency for whole faith. Rather, one must exert in actions more than one is accustomed in both quantity and quality. And the body will certainly resist that and ask, "How is today different from other days?" And he will reply, "I am picturing myself as a servant of the Creator, how I would serve the Creator if I had whole faith. This is why I want to serve Him at the same pace *as though* I were already rewarded with whole faith." This creates in him a deficiency and pain at not having whole faith, since the resistance of the body causes him to have a need for whole faith. But this is certainly said specifically where he goes against the body, in coercion, when he works with the body not according to his will.

It follows that those two actions, his working more than he is accustomed to, and the resistance of the body, cause him to need whole faith. Only then is a *Kli* formed in him so that afterwards the light will clothe within it, since now he has room for prayer in his heart, meaning a place of deficiency. And then the Creator, who hears a prayer, gives him the light of faith by which he can serve the King not in order to be rewarded.

Now we can understand what we asked about the meaning of the merits and sins being engraved in corporeal bones. "Bones" refer to the heart of the matter ("bone of the matter" is an idiom in Hebrew), referring to the Torah and *Mitzvot* that he is keeping. We were given it to keep it in action, and there is nothing to add to it, as it is written, "You shall neither add nor subtract."

And on these actions, the sins and merits are engraved, meaning that if he wishes to walk on the path of truth and criticize his actions—whether they are with the intent to bestow or not—and he is a man who loves the truth and is not interested in what others do, but wants to know if he is engaging in Torah and *Mitzvot Lishma* [for Her name] or is it all for himself, then he sees that he is immersed in self-love and cannot come out of it by himself.

Then he cries for the Creator to help him out of self-love and be rewarded with the love of others and the love of the Creator, and "The Lord is near to all who call upon Him, to all who call upon Him in truth." This is why he is rewarded with *Dvekut* [adhesion] with the Creator.

It follows that then, the merits are engraved in his bones, meaning that the Torah and *Mitzvot* that he kept are called "white," since in terms of the actions, everything is white, positive, and there is nothing to add to them. But afterwards, he scrutinized and saw that the aim was not in order, and that there was darkness on them because he was separated and didn't have *Dvekut*, called "equivalence of form," that he will do everything with the aim to bestow. Instead, he is ruled by self-love.

Thus, he has darkness placed over the white, which are the white bones, as written in the words of *The Zohar*. This means that he sees that there is darkness on the Torah and *Mitzvot* that he performed, that he is separated from the light, since the light wants to bestow, while he does everything in order to receive and cannot do anything except what concerns self-love.

It follows that his bones, meaning the practical Torah and *Mitzvot*, are white, which means that there is no deficiency in the act that requires any additions. But through the criticism that he puts on this white, he sees that there is darkness there. And if he pays attention to mending it because it causes him pain and suffering that he is in the dark, and he prays for the Creator to help him and deliver him from self-love, by that, he is later rewarded with adhering to the Creator.

This is called, "A righteous one—his merits are engraved in his bones," meaning that his criticism of his white bones caused him to be rewarded with revival of the dead, since "the wicked in their lives are called 'dead,'" for they are separated from the Life of Lives. Thus, when they are rewarded with clinging to the Creator, it is considered that they have been rewarded with the revival of the dead.

But, "A wicked one, his iniquities are engraved in his bones," since a wicked one is one who is still immersed in self-love, and a righteous one is called "good," and "good" is called "bestowal," as it is written, "My heart overflows with a good thing; I say, 'My work is for the King.'" In other words, what is a good thing? It is when one can say, "My work is for the King," meaning that all his actions are for the Creator and not for his own sake.

This is why, "He who has a good eye will be blessed." For this reason, those people who have practical Torah and *Mitzvot*, which is considered the core, that the Torah and *Mitzvot* were given by the Creator to keep them, this is called "whites," since the actions have no deficiencies, as it is written, "You shall neither add nor subtract." This is why his bones are white.

"His iniquities are engraved in his bones," which are white, because he did not criticize his actions, whether or not they are in order to bestow. Instead, he trusted the majority and how they keep Torah and *Mitzvot*. And they say that working for the Creator is work that belongs to a chosen few, and not everyone must take this path of being concerned with his work being with the aim to bestow.

This is called "the view of landlords." But "the view of Torah" is different. It is known that "the view of landlords is opposite from the view of Torah," since the view of landlords is that by a person engaging in Torah and *Mitzvot*, his possessions grow and expand, since he becomes an owner of a bigger house. In other words, everything he does goes into self-love.

But the view of Torah is as our sages said about the verse, "When a man dies in a tent." They said, "The Torah exists only in one who puts himself to death over it." This means that he puts his self to death, meaning it is the self-love that he puts to death. Thus, he has no possessions, as there is no landlord to whom we can relate possessions, since his only aim is to bestow, not to receive. Thus, he annuls his self.

It follows that "A wicked one, his iniquities are engraved in his bones" means that he did not walk in the path of Torah, since the Torah is called "black over white." *The Zohar* says that this is why his merits are engraved in his bones, "Since the bones are white, and a black writing is visible only from within white." Like the Torah, meaning if there is white, which means that he keeps Torah and *Mitzvot*, it can be said that he is like the Torah, that he has black over the white. Then, he is trying to achieve *Dvekut* or remains with the white bones and doesn't write anything on them.

This is why he is called "wicked," for his iniquities are engraved in his bones. But those who have no white in them, who have no practical Torah and *Mitzvot*, do not belong to the discernment of "wicked." Rather, they belong to the discernment of animals, meaning they are only beasts.

A Righteous Who Is Happy, a Righteous Who Is Suffering

Article No. 38, Tav-Shin-Mem-Hey, 1984-85

The holy *Zohar* interprets the matter of "a righteous who is happy, a righteous who is unhappy (*Ki Tetze*, item 13): "One who is righteous and unhappy, it means that he is from the tree of knowledge of good and evil, since evil is with him. There is not a righteous who will not sin in this evil because it is with him. A wicked who is happy is one whose evil inclination has overcome his good inclination, and it was said about it, 'He is happy,' for the good is under the authority of the evil. And because the evil governs the good, he is wicked, for the one who prevails takes the name. If the good overcomes the bad, he is called "a righteous who is unhappy," for the evil is under his authority. If the evil prevails over the good, he is called a "wicked who is happy," thus far its words.

To understand the matter of good and evil in general, we need to know that since the root of the creatures extends from the *Sefira* of *Malchut*, and *Malchut* at her root is called "receiving in order to receive," this is the root of all the evil that is in the creatures. This is so because that desire separates us from the root, for we learn that the thought of creation is to do good to His creations, and created a deficiency existence from absence, called "desire to receive delight and pleasure."

But since in spirituality *Dvekut* [adhesion] and separation pertain to equivalence of form, and since the Creator is the giver and the creatures are the receivers, there is disparity of form between them, and that disparity of form separates us from the Creator. Thus, we cannot receive the delight and pleasure that He wants to give us, and which was the purpose of creation. For this reason, to receive the good, we need to qualify the *Kelim* [vessels] to work in order to bestow, and then we will receive the good.

It follows that our evil, for which we have no delight and pleasure, is nothing less and nothing more than the self-love within us. This is what interferes with our receiving the delight and pleasure, and this is what causes us death, as it separates us from the life of lives. This is why we are called "dead," as our sages said, "The wicked, in their lives, are called 'dead.'"

When we consider our evil, the way it speaks with us and wants to control us, with what force it comes to us to listen to its arguments, we should make four discernments here: 1) We can resemble and attribute to repentance from love (although repentance from love is a great matter, here we are speaking only with respect to the attribution). 2) To approximately resemble repentance from fear. 3) He cannot overcome and repent, but still remains broken and shattered because he cannot repent. 4) He is not impressed by his inability to overcome the evil and repent.

We will explain them one at a time. It is known that when one wants to go on the path of doing everything for the Creator, where in everything he does he thinks what benefit the Creator will derive from this, and does not think of his own benefit, then the body comes to him with arguments. It begins to slander this path, called "the path of bestowal and not for one's self-benefit," and argues the arguments of Pharaoh and the argument of the wicked, which are regarded as "mind and heart," namely "who and what."

When a person begins to listen to their arguments, he begins to wonder because he has never heard such strong arguments coming from his body as the ones he hears now. When he began the work he thought that each time he would advance further toward the goal, meaning that each time he would see that it is worthwhile to work for the Creator.

But suddenly he sees that where he should have had a greater desire to serve the Creator, he hears rejection from the body, which tells him now, "Why don't you want to go the way the whole world goes, where you should be meticulous with the nitty gritty actions, and concerning the intention you should say, 'May it be as though I intended.'" "But now," says the body, "I see that you are paying attention specifically to the intentions, meaning that you can aim that everything will be for the Creator and not for yourself. Can it be that you will be different? Don't you want to be like everyone else, who say that this is the safest way? And the evidence of this is to look at everyone else, how they behave."

At that time begins the work of overcoming. That is, he needs to overcome their arguments and not surrender to their demands. He must certainly give them clear answers to what they are making him see, that his desire to intend that all his works will be only to bestow and not for his own benefit is against reason, since reason mandates that since man was created with a will to receive delight and pleasure, and there is a natural demand to satisfy it—or else, why does he need life if not to enjoy it, to satisfy the body's demands—and so it lets him understand that this makes perfect sense, and there is no excuse to answer its arguments.

The clear reply should be that we believe in the words of the sages, who taught us that we must go above mind and reason. That is, true faith is specifically above reason, and what the mind understands is not all true, since with respect to the Creator, we learn that "My thoughts are not your thoughts, nor My ways your ways."

Here begin discernments in the order of the work:

The first degree is when he tells his body, "All your arguments you're telling me make sense, and I agree with you. However, you should know that since the real path, as I received it from faith in the sages, is above reason, but I did not have a chance to show that the way is really so, that I am going above reason. But now that you are coming to me with your arguments that we must go within reason, and slander the way of bestowal and faith, I am happy that you are coming to me with your slander because now I can show my thoughts, that the basis on which I built the work of the Creator is on the path of truth. That is, now I can say that I am going above reason. But before you came to me I did not have a chance to show my way.

"Therefore, I like your arguments because you did me a big favor by slandering before me. That is the slander I heard from you that caused me to repent, since now I must overcome with faith above reason. It turns out that the one who causes me to take upon me the burden of the kingdom of heaven in bestowal and above reason is specifically your slandering. Had you not come to me with complaints, I would not have needed to take upon myself the commandment of faith. But now I must repent." Thus, he is not upset with the slander he had heard.

We can compare this to how we relate to repentance from love (although in truth, repentance from love and repentance from fear are two great degrees), as our sages said, "Repentance from love—sins become to him as merits." We can also interpret here that sins became to him as merits.

We should understand how sins become merits. Sins means that a person is angry that sins came to him. Merits are when a person enjoys from having acquired merits. So how can it be said that sins have become merits? What is the sin here that the body comes with its complaints about faith, which he took upon himself above reason? Also, how can there be a greater sin than one who slanders holy faith?

However, if he repents from love, meaning now that he repents and takes upon himself faith above reason with a clear mind, he decides to go specifically by the path of faith, since now he has two ways before him and he decides. Thus, he has room for choice. But before it came to him with slander, although he took upon himself faith above reason, it was not so evident that he has two ways before him. But now he is making a real choice, determining that he must go specifically with faith above reason.

It therefore follows that he is happy with the slander he has heard, and likes the slander that they spoke about faith, although it is sins. And since they caused him to have room for choice, so it becomes revealed to him that he really wants to walk on the path of faith above reason, it turns out that these sins are as important to him as merits, for without them he would not have room for choice.

It turns out that with the repentance he is making now, he is happy with the work that has come to him now, and this is regarded as repentance from love. That is, he loves the act of repentance he has now performed. At that time, his causes, which are the sins, are regarded by him as merits, meaning that he loves them as merits, for one does not go without the other. He has approximately the relation that light and *Kli* [vessel] have. That is, the deficiency that the sins caused him is called a *Kli*, and the repentance, that he has made the choice, is similar to the relation of the light. This is the first degree in the order of the work.

The second degree is that although he overcomes the slander that the body speaks about the path of truth, which is bestowal and faith, and he repents, meaning answers the body, "All I hear from you is only what you say, that the mind dictates, but I go according to what I heard, that the basis of the work of the Creator is faith above reason. That is, I do not go according to the dictates of the mind, but above the mind." Therefore, this is real repentance.

However, he says he would be happier if he did not hear their slander because he was in danger of perhaps not being able to make the choice. It follows that this repentance is regarded as fear. That is, he fears the work of overcoming, for it is hard work, since when a person is tested it is very difficult to choose the good.

It follows that this repentance is related to repentance from fear, when sins become to him as mistakes. Because he has repented the sins, they become as mistakes, but not as merits, since merits mean that he is similar to merits. Thus, as a person longs for merits, he is happy with his work, with being given a chance to make choice. But when he fears slander, he himself is saying that this is not merits, but rather similar to mistakes.

It follows that although he has elevated the evil into *Kedusha* [holiness], meaning corrected the evil by repenting, that degree is lower than repentance from love, since he himself did not turn them into merits. Therefore, this is regarded as the second degree in the work.

The third degree we should discern in the work is that when the body comes to him with its known arguments, when it slanders the mind and heart, and he surrenders to them and cannot overcome them, he must descend from his degree. That is, where he previously thought that he was regarded as being among the servants of the Creator, now he sees that he is far from it, since before the body came to him with its known arguments, he thought that he was already fine, meaning that he had no desires for self-love and he is completely in order to bestow.

But now he sees that he cannot overcome its complaints. Although now he is not actually being tested—for now all the arguments are only in potential—he still sees that he surrenders to its arguments and cannot take upon himself faith above reason and say, "I want to walk only in a path of bestowal."

Now a man sits and wonders at himself, how the situation has been overturned. It seems to him as though it is a repeating cycle, and he who always looked at his lowliness, has fallen in there himself and cannot come out of that place though he remembers how he always loathed those people and regarded them as small and

A Righteous Who Is Happy, a Righteous Who Is Suffering

childish, and always stayed away from them. Now he is there and cannot come out of there by himself.

Now he sees similarly to the story that is told about Rabbi Yonatan, who had an argument with a priest. The priest said that he could change nature, and Rabbi Yonatan said that it is impossible to change the nature that the Creator created. Only the Creator Himself can change it, but man himself cannot.

What did the priest do? He took a few cats and taught them to be waiters. He dressed them in waiters' clothes, went to the king, and told him about his issue with Rabbi Yonatan. The priest prepared a meal and invited the king and the ministers. Before the meal, the priest reiterated the matter of being able to change into a second nature, and Rabbi Yonatan said that only the Creator can change it but not man.

Subsequently, the priest commanded and said, "Let us eat first, and then we will conclude our debate." Promptly, the waiters, meaning the cats, walked in, dressed just like real waiters, and set the table. They brought the dishes to each and every one, and the priest and the king and ministers were in awe at the wondrous acts of the waiters. Now everyone saw that there is no point in arguing after the meal, and everyone were surprised at Rabbi Yonatan sitting so calmly, unimpressed with the act that proved unequivocally that man can change nature.

What did Rabbi Yonatan do then? It is said that once they finished the meal and the waiters stood and waited to serve the guests, Rabbi Yonatan took out a box of tobacco. When everyone thought he was going to smell tobacco, he opened the box and out came several mice. When the waiters saw the mice coming out of the box and running away, they promptly left the guests and chased the mice, as is in their nature. Then everyone saw that Rabbi Yonatan was right.

The same thing applies to us. When the body comes and begins its slandering, showing tangibly the taste of self-love, he promptly leaves the Torah, the work, and the Creator, and runs to obtain self-love, where the body shows him the pleasure of it. Then he sees that he is powerless to exit self-love.

It follows that here, in this situation—when he sees now how he is immersed in self-love because of our nature—it is regarded as having achieved a certain degree in the work. This means that he has reached the degree of truth, called "recognition of evil." Now he knows that he must begin his work anew, for until now he was walking on the way and deceived himself, thinking that he was above everyone, but now he sees his real state.

Therefore, now he has a place of deficiency to pray to the Creator from the bottom of the heart, since now he sees how remote he is from the work of bestowal, that one cannot come out, but only the Creator can help with it. This is the third degree, which is lower than the two previous degrees.

The fourth degree is the lowest compared to the first three degrees. Sometimes the body comes to him with all its arguments and he listens but does not answer at all. However, he takes its arguments seriously and even sees that it is natural that he cannot perform acts of bestowal. And he remains in self-love as he is used to, without any excitement. He is very composed about it and forgets the place and state he had a moment ago, before the body came to him with its questions, when he thought that he was not like the rest of the people, whose work is built on self-love. Rather, now he feels that this is the way to work, the same as everyone works.

It follows that from all the questions that came to him—which must have been a herald from above in order to give him a chance to rise in his degree, either as the first discernments, which is similar to repentance from love, or as the second discernment, which is as repentance from fear, or as the third discernment, which is to have a deficiency, meaning when he could still pray to the Creator—now he sees that it is impossible that man will be able to help himself by himself.

Now he comes to a state where he believes and sees what our sages said (*Sukkah*, 52), "Rabbi Shimon Ben Lakish said, 'Man's inclination overpowers him each day and seeks to put him to death, as it was said, 'The wicked watches for the righteous and seeks to put him to death.' Were it not for the Creator's help, he would not have overcome it, as it was said, 'God will not leave him in his hand, nor convict him when he is judged.'"

He sees that the body really does seek to put him to death, meaning that it wants to separate him from the life of lives with its arguments. Now he sees that he cannot overcome it by himself, and he waits for the Creator to help him. It follows that the questions that came to him were not in vain. Rather, they gave him room to pray from the bottom of the heart. But in the fourth degree, when he takes everything casually, it is as though the questions came to him in vain, pointlessly.

However, we must know that for a person who has started to walk on the path of bestowal and faith, nothing goes in vain. Rather, after some days or hours, he comes to from his situation after hearing the slandering and sees something new: how a person can fall from a high degree to a degree that is the utter lowliness compared to the state that he was in. And still, he had no sense of it. Rather, he felt that as though nothing has happened, and he took it all very peacefully, agreeing to remain in his current state. He is calm and in a reasonable mood, where previously he thought that if he could not advance in spirituality he would rather die than live. He was always quivering and agitated about how to advance, and always looked at calm people who engage in Torah and *Mitzvot* dryly, without any thought or mind, but simply going by rote.

But now he doesn't feel that he should receive support from anyone, or that he lacks a deficiency. Rather, it is simply natural that person wants to live in peace and not search for faults in himself, but sentence himself to a scale of merit. That is, he has many excuses for everything he thinks is a flaw. But mainly, he wants to live painlessly because he remembers that previously, when he did think about spirituality, he was full of suffering and was always worried. Now, thank God, he has no concerns over spirituality and lives like all other people.

But later, when some awakening comes to him from above, he becomes concerned with spirituality again. At that time he sees something new—man is not his own boss. Rather, he is in a catapult, tossed from above as they choose, and he is in the hands of those above. That is, at one time he is given thoughts that he should throw away all the corporeal matters that pertain to his own benefit. Another time he is tossed down into the corporeal world, meaning he forgets about all the spiritual matters.

It turns out that even the fourth degree is a degree, for he is given a chance to learn from this to see the truth, for by this he can come to cling to the Creator by seeing that he is dependent on the Creator. At that time he will awaken to ask of the Creator to help him out of self-love and achieve love for the Creator.

However, this is a long way. The order is as Baal HaSulam said, that one should say, "If I am not for me, who is for me?" One should say that everything depends on man, since the choice is given entirely to man, and he should not wait until an awakening comes to him from above.

But after the fact he should believe that it is all Private Providence, and man cannot add anything to His work. Rather, he must do as it is desired above, and he has no free choice. This is the best and shortest way, since one spares time and suffering, for one does not suffer due to the prolonging of time.

It follows that we find four discernments when a person begins to walk in the order of work of bestowal and faith:

1) When the body comes to him with its arguments of slander, he accepts them with love. He says, "Now I have a chance to keep the commandment of faith above reason, for otherwise I would be working only within reason." This pertains to repentance from love, meaning that he loves this repentance.

2) When the body comes to him with its arguments of slander, although he overcomes them, he does not like this work, since it is hard work to overcome when he hears slander. This is similar to

repentance from fear, when sins become to him as mistakes, as he would be happier if they did not come to him.

3) When the body comes to him with its slander, he surrenders under its arguments and hasn't the strength to overcome. At that time he feels bad about himself because previously he thought that he was already regarded as being among the servants of the Creator, but now he sees that he has nothing. He regrets it, but he cannot help himself. It follows that the situation he is in pains him.

4) When the body comes to him with its slandering, he crumbles under its load, does everything the body tells him, and takes everything calmly. He promptly forgets that he was ever a servant of the Creator and feels good about himself, as though nothing has happened. Instead, he enjoys his situation because now he has no suffering from not thinking about the work of the Creator, and he wants to continue all his life in this state. Sometimes he doesn't even think about that, meaning he doesn't think at all about life's purpose, but is simply happy as he is.

These four states can be compared to four degrees that our sages said: 1) a righteous who is happy, 2) a righteous who is suffering, 3) a wicked who is suffering, 4) a wicked who is happy.

Although our sages are referring to high degrees, with respect to the relation, we can still compare. We will call the first state, which is similar to repentance from love, "a righteous who is happy." This means that he feels nothing as bad because the sins has become for him as merits.

We will call the second state, which is similar to repentance from fear, "a righteous who is suffering," as *The Zohar* interprets above: "A righteous who is suffering—when the evil is under his authority." That is, he controls it, for he has repented on the slander he had heard from his body. But since the sins have not become merits, it follows that he has sins but they are as mistakes, since the evil is under the authority of the good. It follows that he still has evil, but the good controls it.

The third state is when he surrenders under the evil when he hears slander from the body. He doesn't have the strength to repent on the slander and accepts it. However, he regrets not being able to overcome it. We can call this "a wicked who is suffering." Although he is wicked, meaning he is not repenting, he feels unpleasantness in this situation, which means that he is suffering from not having the strength to overcome.

The fourth state is when he accepts the slander calmly, and doesn't even feel that he has just heard slander. We can call this "a wicked who is happy." That is, although he is wicked, he is happy this way and does not feel any flaw about himself.

Hear Our Voice

Article No. 39, Tav-Shin-Mem-Hey, 1984-85

In the *Slichot* [prayers for pardon], we say, "Hear our voice, the Lord our God, have mercy and pity on us, and accept our prayer mercifully and willingly." In the Monday and Thursday litanies we say, "Have pity on us, O Lord, with Your mercy, and give us not to the hands of the cruel. Why should the nations say, 'Where is their God?' Hear our voice and pardon us, and do not abandon us in the hands of our enemies to obliterate our name. In the end, we have not forgotten Your name; please do not forget us."

We should understand why it ends, "In the end, we have not forgotten Your name; please do not forget us." It implies that this is the reason why we ask that the Creator will help us, because it says, "In the end, we have not forgotten Your name." What reason and cause is there in "In the end, we have not forgotten Your name," for which we say, "please do not forget us"?

To understand the above, we must know how are the nations who are asking heretic questions, since we say, "Why should the nations say, 'Where is their God?'" We also need to understand why we say to the Creator, "Give us not to the hands of the cruel." Who are the cruel? Also, it seems that if we were not placed in the hands of the cruel in exile, it would not be so terrible and we would not need to pray to be delivered form the exile among the nations.

We will explain this according to our way. Since we are born after the *Tzimtzum* [restriction] and the concealment, and only the will to receive for ourselves is revealed in us, it lets us understand that we should work only for our own benefit. By becoming enslaved to self-benefit, we become remote from the Creator. It is known that near and far relate to disparity of form and equivalence of form.

For this reason, when a person is immersed in self-reception, he is separated from the life of lives. Naturally, he cannot feel the flavor of Torah and *Mitzvot* [commandments], for only when he believes that he is keeping the Creator's commandment not for his own benefit can he adhere to the Giver of the Torah. Since the Creator is the source of life, at that time a person feels the taste of life and calls the Torah, "Torah of life," and the verse, "This is your life and the length of your days," comes true.

But during the separation everything is dark for him. Although our sages said, "One should always engage in Torah and *Mitzvot Lo Lishma* [not for Her sake], and from *Lo Lishma* he will come to *Lishma* [for Her sake]," there are many stipulations to this. First he needs to have a need to achieve *Lishma*. A person thinks, "What am I losing by engaging *Lo Lishma*, for which I should always remember the reason why I am learning *Lishma*? It is not in order to receive a corporeal or spiritual reward. Rather, the reason I am learning *Lo Lishma* is to thereby achieve the degree of *Lishma*.

At that time the question, "Why do I need to work for something I don't need?" awakens in him. The body comes to him and says, "What will I gain by your desire to work in order to bestow, called *Lishma*? If I exert in *Lo Lishma*, will I receive something important called *Lishma*?"

In truth, it is to the contrary. If he tells his body, "Work in Torah and *Mitzvot Lo Lishma*, which is the reason by which you will achieve *Lishma*," the body will certainly disrupt him, if this is his purpose, to achieve *Lishma*. It brings many excuses to a person why he cannot do the work of *Lo Lishma*.

Perhaps this is the reason why the body disrupts people who learn *Lo Lishma* so that it will lead them to *Lishma*, and does not let them engage even in *Lo Lishma*, since the body is afraid "lest the man will achieve *Lishma*."

This is not so for the kind of people who do not learn with the intention to achieve *Lishma*, and engage in Torah and *Mitzvot* because the Creator commanded us to keep His Torah and *Mitzvot*, in return for which we will be rewarded in the next world. During the study of Torah they do not aim to exit self-love and be able to keep Torah and *Mitzvot* in order to bestow. It follows that since he is not going against the body, meaning against self-love, the body does not object so much to keeping Torah and *Mitzvot*, since the body's view is that it will keep everything in its own authority, meaning in self-love.

But for those who intend during their engagement in Torah and *Mitzvot* to be rewarded with *Lishma*, it is difficult to observe even *Lo Lishma*, since the body is afraid that it might lose all the self-love and will do everything for the Creator, leaving nothing for the body. It follows that there is a difference even in the *Lo Lishma*, meaning in the intention of the *Lo Lishma* itself. If the intention is to remain in *Lo Lishma* and not to go further, meaning achieve *Lishma*, a person can persist in learning Torah because his body does not pose much resistance.

But if a person aims, while engaging in *Lo Lishma*, to thereby achieve *Lishma*, it contradicts the view of the body. While it is true that he is still engaging *Lo Lishma*, but since the aim is to achieve *Lishma*, the body will resist every single movement and will present obstructions over every little thing.

This means that when those who do not go for the goal of achieving *Lishma* look at the obstructions that people who are walking on the path to achieving *Lishma*, they laugh at them. They say that they don't understand them, that they take every little thing as a tall mountain, and every little thing becomes a huge barrier for them, and they have to muster great strength for every single movement. They do not understand them and tell them: "Take a look for yourselves and see how unsuccessful your way is. We, thank God, study and pray, and the body has no power to deter us from engaging in Torah and *Mitzvot*. But you, with your way, you yourselves say that every little thing you do is as though you have conquered a tall mountain."

We can compare this to what our sages said (*Sukkah*, 52), "In the future (referring to the days of the Messiah), the Creator will take the evil inclination and slaughter it before the righteous and before the wicked. To the righteous, it will seem like a tall mountain. To the wicked, it will seem like a hairsbreadth." Although there it discusses the days of the Messiah, we can take an example from there, meaning explain here that those who intend to achieve *Lishma* are regarded as righteous, since their aim is to be righteous, meaning that their intention will be only for the Creator. To them the evil inclination is regarded as a tall mountain

Those who haven't the goal of achieving *Lishma*, meaning to exit self-love, are considered "wicked" because the evil, called "receiving in order to receive," remains in them. They themselves say that they do not want to exit self-love, and to them the evil inclination seems like a hairsbreadth.

This is similar to the story that is told about Rabbi Bonim: He was asked in the city of Danzig, Germany, why Polish Jews are liars and wear dirty clothes, while German Jews are truthful and wear clean clothes. Rabbi Bonim replied that it is as Rabbi Pinhas Ben Yair said (*Avoda Zarah*, 21), "Rabbi Pinhas Ben Yair said, 'Torah leads to caution, cleanness leads to abstinence, and fear of sin leads to holiness.'"

Therefore, when the Jews of Germany began to adopt cleanness, the evil inclination came to them and told them, "I will not let you engage in cleanness because cleanness leads to other things until you finally arrive in *Kedusha* [holiness]. It follows that you want me to allow you to achieve *Kedusha*. This will not happen!" What could they do? Because they yearned for cleanness, they promised it that if it would stop interfering with their work on cleanness they would go no farther, and it has no reason to fear that they might achieve *Kedusha*, for they are truthful. For this reason, the Jews of Germany are clean, since the evil inclination does not disturb them.

When the evil inclination saw that Polish Jews are engaging in cleanness, it came to them, as well, and wanted to obstruct them because they would achieve *Kedusha*, and it opposes it. They said to it, "We will not go farther." But what did they do? When he left them, they kept going until they reached *Kedusha*. When the evil inclination saw that they are liars, he promptly fought with them over cleanness. Therefore, because Polish Jews are liars, it is hard for them to walk in cleanness.

In the same way, we should understand those who engage *Lo Lishma* and say that our sages promised us that from *Lo Lishma* we come to *Lishma*, and therefore we need not make great efforts to achieve it, but that this will eventually come. Therefore, we have no business with the view that we should always remember that everything we do in Torah and *Mitzvot* is in order to achieve *Lishma* and this is our reward, and this is what we expect.

Rather, we will engage in *Lo Lishma* and in the end it will come, as our sages promised us. This is why the evil inclination does not come to divert them from engaging *Lo Lishma*, since it sees that they have no desire whatsoever to achieve *Lishma*, so it does not bother them at all, as with the story about Rabbi Bonim.

But with those who do yearn to achieve *Lishma*, the evil inclination sees that they engage in *Lo Lishma* because there is no other way but to begin in *Lo Lishma*, as our sages said, "He should not engage *Lo Lishma* unless because from *Lo Lishma* we get to *Lishma*," and they sit and wait, "When will I achieve *Lishma* already?"

When the evil inclination sees that they are exerting to achieve *Lishma* through the remedy of *Lo Lishma*, it promptly comes to them and does all kinds of things to disrupt them, so they do not achieve *Lishma*. It does not let them do even tiny things *Lo Lishma* because of fear, since they are exerting to achieve *Lishma*, as in Rabbi Bonim's reply.

Accordingly, there are two discernments in *Lo Lishma*: 1) His purpose in *Lo Lishma* is to achieve *Lishma*. He always examines whether he has already taken a step in his work toward arriving at *Lishma*. When he sees that he has not moved an inch, he regrets it and pretends that he has not even started with the work of the Creator, since his gauge in Torah and *Mitzvot* is how much he can aim for the Creator. For this reason, when he sees that he cannot even aim the smallest thing for the Creator, he feels as though he hasn't done a thing in the work of the Creator, and regards himself as a useless tool.

At that time he begins to contemplate his purpose. Days are passing and he cannot come out of his state; all he wants is self-love! Worse yet, each day, instead of looking at disruptions in the work as though they are nothing, he sees them as tall mountains; he always sees a great barrier in front of him that he cannot overcome.

Baal HaSulam said about such states that a person advances precisely in these states, called "states of *Achoraim* [posterior]." However, one is not allowed to see it so he will not regard it as *Panim* [anterior], for when a person sees he is advancing, his power of prayer weakens because he sees that the situation is not so bad since in the end he is advancing, though in small steps. It might take a little longer, but he is moving. But when he sees that he is regressing, then when he prays the prayer is from the bottom of the heart, according to the measure of suffering that he feels due to his poor state.

But this you will understand what we say in the litany, "Have pity on us, O Lord, with Your mercy, and give us not to the hands of the cruel." We must know who are the cruel. We should know that when we speak of individual work, then man is the collective. That is, he contains within him the nations of the world, as well. This means that he has lusts and views of the nations of the world, and he is in exile among the nations of the world that exist within him. This is called "the hands of the cruel."

We ask of the Creator, "Give us not to the hands of the cruel." In corporeality, a cruel person is one who gives troubles to people mercilessly, not caring that he is hurting others. Likewise, in the work of the Creator, when a person wants to take upon himself the burden of the kingdom of heaven, the views of the nations of the world in him come and torment him with the slander he hears from them. He must fight them, but they are stronger than him and he surrenders and is compelled to listen to them.

This pains and torments him, as it is written, "And the children of Israel sighed from the work and cried out, and their cry from the work went up to the God, and God heard their groaning." Thus, we see that man's suffering from the evil inclination is the reason why he should have room for prayer. It follows that precisely when he is at war with the evil inclination and thinks that he cannot advance, precisely here he has room for progress.

Baal HaSulam said that a person cannot appreciate the importance of the time when he has serious contact with the Creator. It follows that a person feels that he is in the hands of the cruel, and the nations of the world in him have no mercy on him, and that their cruelty against him is especially when they ask him as it is written, "Why should the nations say, 'Where is their God?'" This is a question of heresy, that they want to obliterate the name of Israel from him, as it is written, "Do not abandon us in the hands of our enemies to obliterate our name."

It follows that the main thing they want is to uproot Israel's faith in the Creator. With these arguments they separate him from the Creator so he cannot connect to the Creator, to adhere to the life of lives and feel the taste of spiritual life. This is why he says that although he hears each day their spirit of heresy, as it is written, "Why should the nations say, 'Where is their God?'" but "we have not forgotten Your name," meaning I still remember the address to turn to.

That is, although only the Creator is left within us, and not what there is in the name, since they cause the name that stays in us to be dry and tasteless, still, "we have not forgotten Your name. This is why we ask, "Please do not forget us," meaning that He will give us the strength to approach Him so we can attain what is contained in the holy name.

Tav-Shin-Mem-Vav

(1985 - 1986)

Moses Went

Article No. 1, Tav-Shin-Mem-Vav, 1985-86

It is written in *The Zohar* (items 1-3): "'Moses went.' Rabbi Hizkiya started, 'Leading to the right of Moses the arm of his glory, dividing the water before them.' Three holy siblings walked among them. Who are they? Moses, Aaron, and Miriam. We have established that Aaron is Israel's right arm, as it is written, 'When the Canaanite, King of Arad ... heard that Israel was coming through the sites.' 'Through the sites' means that Israel were as a man walking without one arm, supporting himself in each place, since 'sites' means 'places.' Then 'he fought against Israel and took some of them captive,' since they were without a right arm. Come and see, Aaron was the right arm of the body, which is *Tifferet*, hence it is written, 'Leading to the right of Moses the arm of his glory.'"

We should understand the allegory that he gives about the verse, "When the Canaanite ... heard." RASHI interpreted that he heard that Aaron had died and the clouds of glory had departed, as a man who is walking without an arm. What does it mean that Aaron was the right arm? We should also understand from the allegory that when one who has no arm walks, he supports himself in every place. We should know that everything we want to do must have a reason that necessitates doing it. According to the importance of the reason, so is the ability to exert in order to obtain one's wish.

For this reason, when a person begins to walk in the work of the Creator and wants to work in faith and bestowal, he wants to know what is the reason that one must walk specifically in this way. Each one understands that if the work was based on reception and knowing, the work would be better and more successful. That is, the body, called "self-love," would not resist this work so strongly, since although the body desires rest and does not want to work at all, if it were on the basis of reception and knowing, it would certainly be easier and more people would engage in Torah and *Mitzvot*.

Baal HaSulam said that the Creator wanted the body to resist so that man will have to have His help. Without help from the Creator, it is impossible to achieve the goal, and this was in order for man to be able to rise to a higher degree each time, as our sages said, "He who comes to purify is aided." The holy *Zohar* asks, "With what is he aided? With a holy soul. When one is born he is given a soul. If he is rewarded with more..." Therefore, man is given work so he can rise in the degrees of holiness.

But in the order of the work, meaning in order for a person to ask for the Creator's help, we need to be careful because when one comes to work, the body tells him, "Why are you so upset? In any case, you cannot overcome your nature, called 'self-love.' You cannot come out of it, and only the Creator can help. So why are you straining yourself, making such great efforts to exit self-love? You're working for nothing! Why do you need this work?"

Baal HaSulam said about this that before each action one wants to perform he must say that the choice is only up to him. At that time he must not say that the Creator will help him. Rather, he must make every effort he can, and he needs the Creator only to complete the work, and he cannot finish the work for the above-mentioned reason.

Our sages said about this (*Avot*, Chapter 5, tractate 21): "He would say, 'It is not for you to finish the work.'" Therefore, it can be said, "Why do I need to work? If I cannot finish it, what good is my work?" This is why the tractate continues, "Nor are you free to idle away from it."

Thus, we see two things here that seem to contradict one another: On the one hand, a person is told to work "as an ox to the burden and as a donkey to the load." This implies that the holy work depends on man, meaning that he can finish it. On the other hand, we say as it is written, "The Lord will finish for me."

The thing is that both are needed. On the one hand, a person must make a choice, meaning to have a desire to work for the Creator. If he could finish his work he would remain in his current state because he would feel that he is complete because he would see that all his actions are for the Creator, so what else is missing? Therefore, there is no longer any need to draw the light of Torah.

However, in order to have a need to progress in the Torah, since the Torah is the names of the Creator, which the Creator desired to reveal to the creatures, and according to the rule, "There is no light without a *Kli* [vessel]," then how can one receive the light of Torah when he hasn't the *Kli*, called "need and deficiency"? For this reason, when one begins to work and sees that he cannot finish the work, he acquires a need and deficiency for the light of Torah.

It is as our sages said, "The light in it reforms him." And then, each time he wants to become purer, he must receive greater help from above. This is why we need both, and there is no contradiction between them, since each has its unique role.

This is similar to what we see in corporality, as every conduct that applies to spirituality extends to corporeality. We see that the order is that when a person is standing on the street carrying a heavy load, and he is asking passersby to help him lift the sack onto his back, everyone tells him they have no time, and "Please ask someone else, since there are many people here who can help you, and you don't really need my help." But if a person is carrying a heavy sack on his back and the sack is dropping off and is about to fall to the ground, and people pass by him and he is asking for their help to put the sack on his back so it does not fall, we see that at that time, when the sack is about to fall off his back, no one will tell him, "I have no time; ask someone else to help you." Rather, the first one next to him will immediately help him.

We should understand the difference between whether the sack is standing on the ground and he is asking for help, in which case everyone has his own excuse not to help him, and whether the sack is on his back and is about to fall, so the first person next to him helps him. We should understand that it is different with someone who is in the middle of the work, who has already begun the work and we can see that he is asking for help so he can continue the work, meaning that the load on his back is about to fall and so we help him.

But if he only wants to begin the work now, we tell him, "No rush. Pretend that the desire to begin the work came a little later; this is not so terrible." For this reason, everyone sees that he does not need immediate help, but can wait until he finds someone with spare time to help him.

The lesson is that when a person waits for the Creator to help him and says, "Now I can work, but before the Creator gives me a desire and craving, I cannot overcome the desires of my body, and I sit and wait for the Creator to help me so I can begin the work of the Creator."

This is similar to a person waiting for any person passing by him to place the heavy sack on his back. Likewise, that man is waiting for the Creator to give him strength and help him, and place the burden of the kingdom of heaven on his back, as it is written, "as an ox to the burden and as a donkey to the load." He wants the Creator to help him with these burden and load and then he will begin the work. At that time he is told, "Wait for an opportunity, and in the meantime stay with the sack of assuming the burden of the kingdom of heaven below on earth."

This is not so with one who has already begun the work, and is not saying that he will wait until the Creator gives him the desire to do the holy work and then he will begin to work. Rather, he does not want to wait because the craving to work and reach the truth pushes him forward though he does not see that he will have the ability to go forward alone, like Nahshon.

However, he sees that he cannot continue this work and is afraid that the burden of the kingdom of heaven, which he is now carrying, is beginning to fall off from him so he begins to call out for help, since he sees that each time, the burden he has taken on himself begins to fall. It is like a person carrying a sack on his back and sees that the sack is beginning to fall. We see that in corporeality, each one he asks for help helps him right away, and no one puts him off for later.

Similarly, in spirituality, one who begins to see that the burden and load are beginning to fall off from him, meaning the work he had previously assumed, to be "as an ox to the burden and as a donkey to the load," and he sees that soon he will be in descent, so he cries out to the Creator and receives help. It is as our sages said, "He who comes to purify is aided," as is written in *The Zohar*.

Conversely, Baal HaSulam said about one who waits for the Creator to help him first and then he will have the strength to work, that it is as it is written (Ecclesiastes, 11), "He who guards the wind will not sow and he who looks at the clouds..." meaning that he stands and waits for the Creator to send a spirit of repentance. This man will never reach the truth.

Now let us return to the matter we asked, "What is the allegory about a person walking without an arm and is supporting himself in every place, and when Aaron dies the arm departs and then the Canaanite can fight against Israel?" We need to know that the right arm is regarded as *Hesed* [mercy], which is the vessel of bestowal. That is, he wants only to do mercy and bestow. By his power, Aaron drew this power to the people of Israel. Because of it no one could fight against the people of Israel, since it is the conduct of the body that it comes to a person and makes him see that if he listens to it, it will give him many pleasures. But if the body hears that his only desire is to bestow, he sees that it hasn't the strength to speak with him.

They received the power of bestowal from Aaron the priest, which is the quality of *Hesed*, and were adhered to him. Therefore, they were under his governance. Hence, when Aaron died, he lost the power of bestowal and the war of self-reception began, for the body could now find a place to argue with him. This is why he gives the allegory of a man walking without an arm, having to support himself in every place he finds where he can find support.

Here the lesson is that since they lacked the power of above reason, called "mind," as well as the power of bestowal, called "heart," the body demanded support for every effort that it made. That is, it asked, "On what basis are you demanding of me to give you the strength to work?" Since he had no *Hesed* so he could say, "I am going above reason," since this is the quality of Aaron, whose is regarded as *Hesed*, called "bestowal" and "above reason."

This is called, "hangs the earth on nothing." Baal HaSulam interpreted that faith above reason means that he has no support, but everything is hanging in midair. It says, "Hangs the earth," where "earth" means the kingdom of heaven. "On nothing" means without any support.

Therefore, when Aaron died they had no one to draw this power so they went within reason and naturally supported themselves in each and every place. That is, wherever they saw that they could receive support so the body would want to work in Torah and *Mitzvot* [commandments] they would accept it. This is called "through the sites," as a person who is walking without an arm. Naturally, the Canaanite came to fight against Israel because within reason they have the dominance to fight. But above reason they cannot argue with this path because he does not need any support.

It follows that the whole exertion begins when a person wants to go above reason and needs to receive that power from above. This comes to them through the quality of Aaron, but now he himself must draw that force, meaning ask of the Creator to help him.

At that time he begins to discern between two things: 1) one who waits for the Creator to help him receive this power, and stands and waits for it, and 2) one who hasn't the patience to wait for the Creator to help him, but rather begins to work and then yells for help from the Creator and says, "For the waters are threatening my life." And because he has already come to a clear understanding that only the Creator can help him he receives the help.

The order of the prayer should not be as lip service. Rather, when he is faced with danger he should not yield before the governance of evil that comes to him with strong arguments and wants to distract him from the work of wanting to take upon himself the burden of the kingdom of heaven. They make every effort to disrupt him with everything they can do.

We see how the poet is giving us a clear picture of the evil that is standing before us. It is written in the *Selichot* (*Selichot* [prayers for pardon] for the fourth day of the Ten Penitentiary Days), "To You, O Lord, I call, O dreadful and terrible. Do not hide Your face in the day of trouble, when cursed ones arise against us ... saying, 'You must not accept God, bowing before Him dividedly, and without sanctifying He who does much pardons, nor fear the Godly dread. When I hear this, my heart trembles; this I will reply to my adversary: 'God forbid that I should forget and leave the portion of the God of my father.'"

It turns out that when one wishes to take upon himself the burden of the kingdom of heaven, and burden means "as an ox to burden and as a donkey to the load," meaning that both the donkey and the ox resist assuming this work, but do it coercively. Why do they resist when they feel that they are working, but when they enjoy the work, meaning when they are eating, although this is also work, they are enjoying during the act so it is not considered "work"?

When a person has no right arm, regarded as desiring mercy, at which time he enjoys the work, the *Sitra Achra* [other side] has no contact with this work so she can fight. But when Aaron dies, namely when he has not been rewarded with Aaron's quality of *Hesed*, the outer ones come to him and tell him all kinds of words of heresy, and then it is work in two ways.

Lend Ear, O Heaven

Article No. 2, Tav-Shin-Mem-Vav, 1985-86

"'Lend ear, O heaven.' Rabbi Yehuda started, 'I opened for my beloved. 'The voice of my beloved knocks.' He says, 'The voice of my beloved knocks' is Moses, who admonished Israel in several arguments, in several quarrels, as it is written, 'These are the words,' 'You have been rebellious,' and 'In Horev you provoked,' as it is written, 'knocks.'" (In the *Sulam* [Ladder commentary], items 1-2) "Although Moses admonished Israel, all his words were with love, as it is written, 'For you are a holy nation to the Lord your God,' and 'The Lord your God has chosen you to be His people,' 'but because the Lord loved you,' as it is written, 'Open to me, my sister, my wife,' affectionately."

We should understand the words of the holy *Zohar*.

1) If he gives so many praises to the people of Israel, as it is written, "For you are a holy nation to the Lord your God," and "The Lord your God has chosen you to be His people," how can we speak of admonition? If they are a holy people, what else is missing in them?

2) What does that teach us for posterity, since they are two opposites in the same carrier? That is, either they are a holy nation, or they are not!

3) There is a rule: "Love covers all transgressions." The writing says (Deuteronomy, 7:7), "The Lord did not desire you nor choose you because you were more numerous than all the nations, for you were the fewest of all peoples ... but because of the Lord's love for you." Therefore, how is it possible to find transgressions in them, since "Love covers all transgressions"?

The thing is that it is known that there is the matter of two writings that deny one another until the third writing comes and decides. "Lines" in spirituality means that the quality of *Hesed* [mercy] is called "right line." *Hesed* means that he only wants to do good to others and wants nothing in return. He longs for the love of the Creator and has no concern for himself. Rather, all his aspirations are only to bestow contentment upon his Maker, and for himself he is content with little. That is, he has no regard for what he has, namely good flavors in Torah, in prayer, or in *Mitzvot* [commandments], but is happy with his lot.

Here, in spirituality, when a person introspects and says that he believes in Private Providence, that everything comes from above, meaning that the Creator has given him a thought and desire to serve the Creator and engage in Torah and *Mitzvot* although he feels no flavor in Torah and *Mitzvot*. Still, he does not mind it and says that he is satisfied with being able to keep the commandment of the Creator. This, alone, is to him as though he has made a fortune. And even though he does not attain the greatness of the Creator, whatever he does have satisfies him and he believes it is a gift from Heaven that he was given the thought and desire.

He sees that others were not given this. Rather, all they aspire for is to attain corporeal things, meaning to be favored by people or delight the body with things that animals use, as well. But he, on the other hand, was given a thought and desire to serve the Creator, "and who am I that He has chosen me?" It is as we say, "Blessed are You, O Lord, who chooses His people, Israel, with love."

It turns out that we bless the Creator for choosing us, meaning that we were given a thought and desire to keep Torah and *Mitzvot*.

Therefore, when he looks at others, who haven't that desire for Torah and *Mitzvot* that he has, he says that He has chosen him over others to serve Him. Although He has given him only a small service, without any intellect and reason, he says that even this service, the least of the least, is more than his own worth because when he looks at himself through the eyes of the greatness of God, he says that he does not deserve even this. Therefore, he is certainly as happy as though he has been rewarded with a service fit for great men.

The right line comes from the upper *Sefirot*. This discernment is called the *Sefira* [singular of *Sefirot*] *Hesed*, pertaining to equivalence of form with the Creator—as He gives, so the lower one wishes to give to the upper ones. This is regarded as equivalence of form, where he does not regard what he has in vessels of reception. Rather, his only measurement of wholeness is his ability to bestow.

Even if he cannot bestow much, he settles for this because he examines his lowliness compared to the Giver, and compared to other people whom he sees as more virtuous than him. Still, he was given from above a thought and desire that they were not given, and he does not say about anything, "My power and the might of my hand."

For this reason, he is always satisfied and has nothing to add to his work. Rather, he thanks and praises the Creator as much as he can, and thanks and praises Him in all kinds of praises. And even when he does not give the praise and gratitude that he thinks he should give to the Creator, he does not regret this because he says about himself, "Who am I to always speak to the King, as is suitable for important people, and not to lowly ones like me?" It follows that he is always in wholeness and has nothing to add.

And if he sometimes forgets about matters of work and his mind is immersed in worldly matters, and after some time he remembers about spirituality and sees that the whole time he was dealing with corporeal matters of this world, he still does not think about the time he was separated. Instead, he is happy that the Creator has summoned him from among all the people and told him, "Where are you?" He promptly begins to thank the Creator for reminding him that he should think about spirituality.

It follows that even in that state he does not think about deficiencies and regrets that he has completely forgotten about work-matters this whole time, but he is happy that at least now he can think about the work of the Creator. It follows that now, too, he is in a state of wholeness and will not come to a state where he is weakened from the work, but will always be in wholeness. This is called "right line," *Hesed*, which is wholeness.

However, this depends on the extent to which a person believes in Private Providence, meaning that the Creator gives everything—the light, as well as the *Kli* [vessel]—meaning both man's desire and deficiency for this, that he is not so adhered to the Creator, and also the feeling in his body of lack of keeping of Torah and *Mitzvot*. The Creator gives everything. The light is certainly something that the Creator must give because the flavor in Torah and *Mitzvot* certainly belongs to the Creator. It is as we say on the night of *Yom Kippur* [Day of Atonement], "For she is like clay in the hands of the potter. When He wishes He gives abundantly; when He wishes He gives sparingly. So are we in Your hands, Keeper of mercy."

It follows that if a person sees that a desire to study awakens in him, even one hour a day, and when he is praying he sees that for a few minutes he knows he is praying and does not forget that he is wrapped in a *Talit* [prayer shawl] and *Tefillin*, and his heart thinks every thought in the world, and then he remembers for a few minutes that he is crowned in the *Talit* and *Tefillin* and that now he is in the middle of a prayer, and he begins to think to whom he is speaking during the prayer. He feels that he is not simply speaking, but is standing before the King, and he believes in "You hear the prayer of every mouth." Although he sees that he has already prayed many times and his prayer was not answered, he still believes above reason that the Creator does hear the prayer, and the reason his prayer has not been granted is that he probably did not pray from the bottom of the heart. Therefore, he takes upon himself to pray more intently "and the Creator will certainly help me and grant my prayer." Then he promptly begins to thank the Creator for reminding him that he is now crowned with *Talit* and *Tefillin*. He feels good since he looks at other people, how they are still asleep, while with me, "the Creator has awakened me in the middle of the prayer," so he is joyful.

If a few more minutes pass and he forgets once more where he is, and thinks about the ox and the donkey, and he is suddenly awakened once again from above, it makes sense that he would complain that he has forgotten about the whole thing—that he is in the synagogue now. However, he does not want to hear about it. Rather, he is happy that he has been reminded. It follows that in this way he only looks at "do good," meaning that he is happy that now he was able to do good and does not notice that until now he was roaming the world of separation.

He can feel all this to the extent that he recognizes his value, that he is not better than other people, and that they even have the spirit of heresy and no affinity to Judaism. He also sees that there are people who do not even pay attention to Judaism, but they live like all other animals, with no concern for any purpose in life. Rather, they think that their whole lives, which they regard as being at a higher level than that of animals, is that they are also concerned with respect, and they understand that sometimes it is better to relinquish lust in order to obtain respect. But as far as Judaism is concerned, even if they were circumcised by their parents, they themselves pay no attention to it because other things interest them more.

When he looks at them, he sees that he does not know why he has been privileged more than them with the Creator's giving him a thought and desire to engage in Torah and *Mitzvot* even if only in action. That is, he sees that he is still far from achieving the degree of *Lishma* [for Her sake], but he says, "In any case, I have been privileged with *Lo Lishma* [not for Her sake], as our sages said, 'From *Lo Lishma* we come to *Lishma*.' Thus, at least I'm on the first stage of *Kedusha* [holiness]." He contemplates how happy he is that the Creator has ushered him into the first degree of *Kedusha*, called *Lo Lishma*, how much he should thank and praise the Creator, especially that if a person is rewarded and is given a thought of engaging in the secrets of Torah, although he does not understand a single word that is written there, it is still a great privilege that now he is adhered to the study of the internality of the Torah.

In other words, he believes that they speak only about Godliness and he has room to delve in his thought, since "everything I'm learning is of the holy names, so I must be very fortunate. Therefore, all I need to do is thank and praise the Creator. That is, the vitality of the whole world comes only from nonsense, while I have been rewarded with entering the first stage of *Kedusha*, called *Lo Lishma*." This is regarded as "right line," meaning wholeness, which requires no correction.

However, it is written, "right, and left, and between them a bride." That is, we also need a left line. We really need to understand this: If he feels that he is in wholeness and can thank and praise the Creator all day and all night, what else does he need? However, he himself knows that it is *Lo Lishma*, and man's purpose is to work for the Creator, and he says that he has not achieved this degree. So how can one rise in degrees if he does not feel deficient?

There is a rule that if a person is asking something from the Creator, it must be from the bottom of the heart. This means that one should feel the deficiency in the heart, and not as lip-service. This is so because when one is asking for luxuries, which you can live without, no one has mercy on that person when he yells and cries for not having something many others do not have. And although he yells and cries to be given it, it is uncommon that there will be people who will pity him. However, when one is yelling and crying for a deficiency that he has, but the rest of the world has that thing and he does not, then when he yells and cries out for people's mercy, then he is heard, and anyone who can help tries to help him.

It is the same here in the work of the Creator. When he tries to find wholeness in the right line, although he knows he has to try to make all his works be for the Creator, he also knows that man must keep what is written, "His delight is in the law of the Lord, and in His law he meditates day and night" (Psalms 1). He does not observe this but he is trying with all his might to feel wholeness in the right line. At that time, although he knows he still has no wholeness, he still cannot ask the Creator to give him strength to be able to keep "And in His law he mediates day and night," and cry out to the Creator to help him achieve *Lishma*, unless as luxuries and not as necessities.

This is so for the above-mentioned reason that when one asks for something and yells and cries for not having it, but other people in his town also do not have it, he cannot say that this is a necessity, but rather a luxury, and one does not cry or beg for luxuries. But here, when he is walking on the right line and sees that other people do not have what he has since only a tiny portion of the world has what he has in spirituality, then how can he say that demands of the Creator to bring him close so he can engage *Lishma*? This is a luxury, and one cannot ask for luxuries from the bottom of the heart, meaning that that deficiency will reach the depth of the heart. He himself is saying that what he has is already a great thing, so how can he ask the Creator to have mercy on him concerning a luxury, to give him the strength to engage *Lishma*, meaning in order to bestow contentment upon his Maker?

It follows that it is impossible for one to ask the Creator to guide him how to walk on the path of truth, since he does not have such a need, for we say about luxuries, meaning about something that others do not have, "trouble shared is trouble halved." Therefore, he has no chance of ever achieving recognition of evil, that the fact that he cannot engage in Torah and *Mitzvot* for the Creator is bad. It follows that he accepts the state of *Lo Lishma*, and although this way is called a "path of falsehood," and not the "true path," he will never feel that he is marching on the path of falsehood, as it is written in the "Introduction of The Book of Zohar" (item 175).

Therefore, one must also walk on the left line. However, one must allocate only a small amount of time for scrutinizing the left line. Most of the time he should be in the right line, since only those who have an inner attraction to achieve *Lishma* are allowed to walk on the left line, too. However, those who feel that they are not among workers, who think that they cannot overcome their desires, they must not walk on the left line. For this reason, even those with an internal attraction to achieve *Lishma*, although they can walk on the left line, they need to be careful not to walk on the left line for more than a short period of time, and only at a set time. And not at any time, but according to the time each one allots himself to scrutinize the left line.

The schedule should be that either one sets one's daily schedule, or a weekly schedule, or a monthly one. It is each according to his feeling, but he should not change the schedule he had decided on in the middle. If he wants to change in the middle because the body comes to him and lets him understand that "it is more like you to have a different schedule than the one you have arranged for yourself," then he must tell his body, "I have my schedule. When I make another schedule, meaning if I have made a schedule for the whole week, when the week is over I will begin to make a new schedule, then you can come to me and tell me to make another schedule than the one I want to make. But I cannot change the schedule in the middle."

However, we should know the meaning of the left line, since there are many discernments in the left line. There is a left line that is complete darkness. This is called "*Malchut* being the quality of judgment and rising in each and every *Sefira* and becoming darkness." That is, no light shines there. There is also a left line called "*Hochma* without *Hassadim*." This is also called "darkness," but the darkness there is only with respect to the light. With respect to the *Kelim*, his *Kelim* have already entered *Kedusha*, meaning that he can aim when he uses the vessels of reception in order to bestow, as well.

It follows that that left line is a great degree. It is called "darkness" due to the plentiful abundance that appears then. As long as he hasn't a clothing of *Hassadim*, he is forbidden to use that light because while using he might fall into receiving in order to receive due to the plentiful abundance that he cannot overcome and receive in order to bestow. This is why we need the left line; this is why the left line is very important.

First we need to know that there is no time or space in spirituality. Therefore, what is the meaning of right and left lines?

The thing is that anything that does not require correction is called "right line," and something that requires correction is called "left line." We find this matter concerning the placing of *Tefillin*. Our sages said (*Minchot* 37), "Rabbi Yosi Hachorem: 'How do we know that we place on the left? He learned it where Rav Natan learned it: Rav Ashi said that it is written, 'from your hand,' with a blunt *Hey*. RASHI interpreted that writing with a blunt *Hey* implies female, left, as he said that she is as powerless as a female."

This means that "left" is regarded as weak and powerless, and that it must be given strength. This is why we see that wherever we want to give an example of something that requires correction we call it "left." This is why after the left line we need the middle line, which corrects the left line. And this is why we call that which needs correction by the name, "left," so as to know that now we need to make corrections.

The corrections that correct the left are called "middle," since the line shows the deficiencies in the right, meaning that the right itself does not show any deficiency until the left line comes. That is, by his engagement in the left line he sees that there are deficiencies in the right. Once he has entered the left he loses the wholeness he had in the right, therefore now he is in a state of deficiency.

However, there are many discernments we should make in the deficiency that the left line shows, meaning what is the reason that there is a deficiency in the left. That is, the left says that there is a deficiency in the right. But sometimes we do not see any deficiency in the left line, and then who is showing that there is a deficiency in the left line, too, once the left has shown that there is a deficiency in the right? Thus, the way of the left must be wholeness. Hence, what is the reason that there is a deficiency in the left, for which he calls it, "left"? There are many discernments about this; it is all according to the issue because in any situation, a person finds a different reason and it is impossible to determine the reason. Rather, it is all on a case-by-case basis.

The left in the beginning of the work is criticism on the right—if it is right to remain in falsehood because we were given Torah and *Mitzvot* because we have the bad, called "self-love," meaning to care for nothing, but rather every means is acceptable in order to obtain the goal of satisfying our will to receive with every possible satisfaction. It is called "bad" because it obstructs us from achieving *Dvekut* [adhesion] with the Creator and exiting self-love, as the animate mind necessitates. Rather, the goal is to be rewarded with *Dvekut* with the Creator, after which he will receive the delight and pleasure that exist in the thought of creation, called "His desire to do good to His creations." With this one can please the Creator because by this the Creator completes His goal from potential to actual—for the creatures to feel the delight and pleasure He has contemplated in their favor.

Since this will to receive, regarded as self-love, is all that obstructs this, it is called "bad." To exit this bad, He has given us Torah and *Mitzvot*, to reach the degree called "servant of the Creator." It is not that he is working for himself, but rather to achieve the degree of *Lishma*.

In the right, he delights with the wholeness of *Lo Lishma*, which means that he is walking on the path of falsehood and wants to stay there. But although he knows he is in the degree of *Lo Lishma*, why is it considered that he wants to stay in *Lo Lishma*?

This follows the rule that one cannot ask the Creator from the bottom of the heart about a deficiency for a luxury, but rather only for a necessity. Since he is already happy that he is in *Lo Lishma*, even after all of his excuses he has—that it is good to be happy even in *Lo Lishma*, he nonetheless can no longer feel a deficiency to need this necessarily. Rather, this will be as luxury for him if we can engage in Torah and *Mitzvot Lishma*. Thus, he must stay in the right line.

Therefore, he should work with attention and criticism on the right line, meaning to see the deficiencies in the right line. Because of it, to the extent that he feels the deficiencies, meaning that the deficiencies he sees mean nothing because man's impression with the deficiencies depends on the extent to which it touches his heart to feel the deficiency as incomplete and his inclination toward the truth and his loathing of lies, so if that deficiency touches the heart, meaning that the situation he is in pains him, then the previous state of right line, when he had wholeness, is inverted in him to suffering. At that time he can pray to the Creator from the bottom of the heart because now the *Lishma* is as important to him as life because through it he clings to the life of lives. But when he was attached to the right line, the *Lishma* was a luxury in his eyes, meaning that he could live without it, too, but one who wants to improve his life and be above others has to try to achieve the degree of *Lishma*.

When one sees that he does not regard *Lishma* as luxuries, meaning to be above others, but that now he feels that he is the worst of them because he sees how far he is from the Creator and from the quality of truth, more than the rest of the people, although he does not see them going on the path of *Lishma*, it does not change anything that he sees no one going on the path of *Lishma* because with matters that concern the heart, one is not impressed by others. Although it is said, "trouble shared is trouble halved," these maxims do not change his situation.

By way of allegory, if a person has a toothache and is crying and yelling, and he is told, "Why are you yelling? Can't you see that there are other people here, at the dentist's clinic, whose teeth are hurting just as yours?" We see that he does not stop crying because of his toothache. The fact that there are other people like him changes nothing for him. If he is really in pain, he cannot look at others so as to find relief for his own pain, if he is really hurting.

Similarly, if a person has really come to feel that he is far from the truth, he will not be comforted by the fact that everyone is taking the path of falsehood. Rather, day and night he longs to come out of that state. At that time a person acquires the need to achieve *Lishma* because he can no longer tolerate the falsehood.

But since that *Kli* [vessel] is not made all at once, meaning that the desire that the person receives from the left line is not made at once, but that desire forms in him gradually until it reaches the complete measure, and before this he still cannot achieve *Lishma*, since there is no light without a *Kli*, it means that he cannot be awarded *Lishma* before he desires it, and that desire grows within him slowly. Penny after penny joins into a great amount, meaning it is filled into a complete desire, and then the *Lishma* can dress in that desire because he already has a complete *Kli*, meaning a complete desire to be rewarded with *Lishma*.

However, we must know that when he is on the left line, meaning when he criticizes himself, he is in separation. This is so because he feels that he is immersed in self-love and does not care about being able to do something for the Creator. In that state he cannot exist because man can live only from the positive and not from the negative.

Therefore, a person must enter the right line once again, meaning keep Torah and *Mitzvot Lo Lishma* and say that there is wholeness in it, as we have explained above. We need to know the fundamental rule that there is a difference between *Ohr Pnimi* [Inner Light] and *Ohr Makif* [Surrounding Light]. *Ohr Pnimi* means that the light shines inside the *Kelim* [vessels]. This means that the light dresses in the *Kli* because there is equivalence between the light and the *Kli*, and the *Kli* can already receive the light in order to bestow. But *Ohr Makif* means illumination from afar. This means that although the *Kli* is still far from the light, since the *Kli* is in order to receive and the light is pure bestowal, yet the light shines from afar, as in, surrounding the *Kelim*.

This is why when we engage in Torah and *Mitzvot Lo Lishma* we still receive illumination in the form of *Ohr Makif*. It follows that through *Lo Lishma* we already have contact with the upper light, although it is illumination from afar. This is why it is called "positive," and a person can receive vitality from this and exist.

By appreciating the *Lo Lishma*, he appreciates the service of the Creator in general, that it is worthwhile to engage in Torah and *Mitzvot* in any manner. Baal HaSulam said that in truth, one cannot appreciate the value of keeping Torah and *Mitzvot* in *Lo Lishma*, for in the end there is nothing to add in actions. Rather, he keeps the commandment of the Creator and this is why this is regarded as the first stage in the work, of which our sages said, "From *Lo Lishma* we come to *Lishma*." For this reason, man should receive vitality and wholeness from the right line, at which time he receives the light of the Creator as Surrounding Light.

Afterwards he must criticize his actions once again, his engagement in the right line, and once again to shift to the right line. By this the two lines grow in him. However, these two lines contradict one another and they are called "two writings that deny one another until the third writing comes and decides between them."

Yet, we should know that the Creator gives the third line, called the "middle line," as our sages said, "There are three partners in man: the Creator, his father, and his mother. His father sows the white; his mother sows the red; and the Creator places a spirit and a soul in him." According to the above, it turns out that two lines belong to the lower one, and the middle line belongs to the Creator. This means that the two lines cause him to be able to pray from the bottom of the heart to the Creator to help him out of self-love and achieve *Dvekut* with the Creator, since when a person prays from the bottom of the heart, his prayer is answered.

However, we should know that there are many aspects to the three lines.

Man Is Rewarded with Righteousness and Peace through the Torah

Article No. 3, Tav-Shin-Mem-Vav, 1985-86

In *The Zohar* (*Lech Lecha*, item 1), Rabbi Aba explains why Abraham was rewarded with the Creator telling him *Lech Lecha* [Go forth] more than all his contemporaries. It writes, "Rabbi Aba started and said, 'Listen to Me, you stubborn-hearted, who are far from righteousness.' 'Listen to Me, you stubborn-hearted' means how hard are the hearts of the wicked. They see the trails and ways of Torah and do not look at them. Their hearts are hard since they do not return to their Master in repentance. This is why they are called, 'Stubborn-hearted who are far from righteousness,' meaning far from the Torah, and hence far from righteousness."

Rabbi Hizkiya said, "They are far from the Creator. And because they are far from the Creator they are called stubborn-hearted." The meaning of the verse is "far from righteousness." Why? It is because they do not wish to approach the Creator, for they are stubborn-hearted. And because of it, they are far from righteousness.

Because they are far from righteousness, they are far from peace, meaning they have no peace, as it is written, "'There is no peace,' said the Lord to the wicked." What is the reason? It is because they are far from righteousness, hence they have no peace.

We should understand why when Rabbi Aba says that being far from righteousness means that they are far from the Torah, and therefore far from righteousness. On the one hand, he says that righteousness is called Torah, and then he says that by moving away from the Torah they move away from righteousness. This implies that the Torah is the reason for righteousness, but we do not see any connection between Torah and righteousness.

We see that the nations of the world have no Torah, as our sages said, "He says His words to Jacob," and still they give *Tzedakah* [righteousness/almsgiving]." Does giving *Tzedakah* require believing in the Creator and keeping the Torah and *Mitzvot* [commandments], and only then can one give *Tzedakah*? Rather, he says that they are far from *Tzedakah* because they are far from the Torah.

He also said that because they are far from the Torah, they are far from *Tzedakah*. This implies that the Torah is the reason by which we can keep *Tzedakah*. That is, the most important thing for us is to achieve *Tzedakah*. How can we achieve such a high degree? Through the Torah.

Thus, we should understand the greatness and importance of *Tzedakah*, which means that the Torah is a lower degree than *Tzedakah* because through the Torah we can achieve *Tzedakah*. We need to understand this.

Also, it is difficult to understand the words of Rabbi Hizkiya in what he adds to the words of Rabbi Aba and says, "Who are the stubborn-hearted? Those who do not want to approach the Creator. And because they do not want to approach the Creator they are far from *Tzedakah*." How can we understand this? Does this mean that through approaching the Creator they will be rewarded with a higher degree, which is *Tzedakah*?

We should also understand why Rabbi Hizkiya says, "Since they are far from *Tzedakah*, they are far from peace." This is even more perplexing because once he has clarified for us the importance of *Tzedakah*, meaning in Rabbi Aba's view, *Tzedakah* is more important than Torah, and in Rabbi Hizkiya's view, *Tzedakah* is greater than approaching the Creator. Now he comes and says that if they do not have the degree of *Tzedakah*, they cannot achieve the degree of peace.

Thus, we should understand what is the degree of peace. It is implied that after all the work he will achieve the degree of peace. That is, the first degree is either Torah or approaching the Creator, the second is *Tzedakah*, and the third is peace. This requires clarification.

We find that *Tzedakah* is called "faith," as it is written about Abraham, "And he believed in the Lord, and He regarded it for him as righteousness." Thus, because faith is regarded as *Tzedakah*, we can already know the importance of *Tzedakah*. It is not as it seems literally. Rather, *Tzedakah* implies faith.

What is faith? It is regarded as *Tzedakah*? We see that one who gives *Tzedakah* [almsgiving] to the poor does not expect the poor to repay him in some way for the almsgiving he has given him. It is especially so with concealed almsgiving; he certainly does not plan to receive anything in return. Therefore, *Tzedakah* means that he is doing something without any reward.

But since the faith we should take upon ourselves must be without anything in return, it means that we must believe in the greatness of the Creator, which holy *Zohar* calls, "For He is great and ruling." He is to have no thought that he is taking upon himself the burden of the kingdom of heaven and by this he will receive from Him some reward. Rather, he is working entirely in order to bestow. This is why faith is called *Tzedakah*, to interpret for us the form that the faith we are taking on ourselves should have.

However, we must pay attention to how we achieve such faith, which is in order to bestow. Our nature is only to receive and not to bestow. Therefore, what can one do in order to achieve bestowal? He is telling us that it is done precisely through the Torah, as our sages said (*Kidushin* 30), "I have created the evil inclination, I have created for it the Torah as a spice."

In the "Introduction to the Study of the Ten Sefirot" (item 11) he says, "However, we find and see in the words of the sages of the Talmud that they have made the path of Torah easier for us more than the sages of the *Mishnah*. This is because they said, 'One should always engage in Torah and *Mitzvot*, even *Lo Lishma*, and from *Lo Lishma* he will come to *Lishma*.' That is, the light in it reforms him. Thus, they have provided us with a new means instead of the penance presented in the above-mentioned *Mishnah*, *Avot*: the 'Light in the Torah.' It bears sufficient power to reform one and bring him to engage in Torah and *Mitzvot Lishma*."

By this we will understand the words of Rabbi Aba, who said that "far from *Tzedakah*" means that they are moving away from the Torah, hence they are far from *Tzedakah*. We asked, "Is the Torah the reason for achieving *Tzedakah*? Is it impossible to give *Tzedakah* without Torah?" The thing is that *Tzedakah* refers to faith. It is impossible to achieve real faith before one has equivalence of form with the Creator, meaning that all of one's actions are only in order to bestow contentment upon the Creator.

He says in the "Introduction of the Book of Zohar" (item 138): "It is a law that the creature cannot receive disclosed evil from the Creator, for it is a flaw in the glory of the Creator for the creature to perceive Him as an evildoer. Hence, when one feels bad, to the same extent, denial of the Creator's guidance lies upon him, and the Operator is concealed from him."

The reason is that before a person is rewarded with vessels of bestowal he is unfit to receive the delight and pleasure from Him. It follows that he feels bad and therefore cannot be awarded real faith before he has corrected the evil in him, called "receiving in order to receive."

It follows that through the Torah, which reforms him, meaning that by receiving vessels of bestowal he will be rewarded with faith, which is called *Tzedakah*, which is "faith because He is great and ruling," and not that the basis of his faith is in order to receive some reward.

Now we will understand what we asked about the words of Rabbi Hizkiya, where he explains the meaning of "stubborn-hearted." He explains that because they move away from the Creator, they move away from *Tzedakah*. We asked, "Can approaching the Creator be a reason that we will have the ability to do *Tzedakah*? What is the connection between them?" It is written in the *Sulam* [commentary on *The Zohar*], "Rabbi Hizkiya does not dispute Rabbi Aba. Rather, he interprets more than him." We asked, "But Rabbi Hizkiya's explanation is even more difficult to understand!"

According to what we explained above, Rabbi Hizkiya explains more what it means that they are called "stubborn-hearted," for which they are far from *Tzedakah*, since regarding what Rabbi Aba says, that they have moved away from the Torah, they think that they simply need to learn Torah and by this they will be rewarded with *Tzedakah*, called "faith." However, Rabbi Aba's intention is that through Torah they will achieve equivalence of form, called "vessels of bestowal," since they cannot achieve real faith before they have vessels of bestowal, as it is written in the *Sulam* ("Introduction of the Book of Zohar").

This is why Rabbi Hizkiya elaborates more and says more simply that "stubborn-hearted" are those who move away from the Creator. That is, they do not want to approach the Creator because they are stubborn-hearted, therefore they are far from *Tzedakah*. This is as we said above, that it is impossible to be rewarded with faith, which is *Tzedakah*, before we are rewarded with nearing the Creator, called equivalence of form, which are vessels of bestowal.

Perhaps that reason why Rabbi Aba does not interpret the same as Rabbi Hizkiya is that Rabbi Aba wants to tell us two things at once, meaning the reason and the advice. The reason why they have no faith is that they have no vessels of bestowal. The advice for this is to engage in Torah, where by the light of Torah they will be awarded equivalence of form, regarded as all their actions being only to bestow. At that time they will be rewarded with *Tzedakah*, which is real faith.

And concerning Rabbi Hizkiya's addition that through *Tzedakah* they will be rewarded with peace, we asked, "If *Tzedakah* is such a great thing, which refers to faith, then what is peace? It implies that peace is even more important!"

We should interpret that peace is the completion of the work. Before one is rewarded with vessels of bestowal, he has no room for faith. Once he has vessels of bestowal and has been rewarded with faith, he obtains the purpose of creation, which is to do good to His creations. This means that then he feels the delight and pleasure that the Creator has created to do good to His creations. At that time one is rewarded with peace.

But before one has been rewarded with *Tzedakah*, which is faith, on the basis of vessels of bestowal, he does not have the *Kelim* to obtain the delight and pleasure, since the good is lacking the correction of not being the bread of shame, for which there was the correction of *Tzimtzum Aleph* [first restriction]. Only when the creatures have that correction, called "vessels of bestowal," there will be a place where the light of the Creator (which is to benefit His creations) can be present.

Prior to this he is in strife with the Creator, as he says in the *Sulam* ("Introduction of the Book of Zohar," item 175): "Peace, too, complained that he was all strife because he cannot engage in *Mitzvot* [commandments] in order to bestow, but with a mixture of self-pleasing." By this he is always in strife with the Creator, since he thinks he is a complete righteous and does not feel his faults at all. That is, he does not feel that his entire engagement in Torah and *Mitzvot* is *Lo Lishma* [not for Her sake], and he is angry at the Creator for not rewarding him as much as a complete righteous should be rewarded.

Thus, we see that before one is rewarded with *Tzedakah*, which is faith in the Creator on the basis of vessels of bestowal, which brings one to approach the Creator, it is impossible to have peace. It follows that the end of the work, when the goal is achieved, is when we achieve the degree of peace. That peace cannot be achieved before we go through the preliminary stages, which are approaching the Creator, then faith, called *Tzedakah*, and finally the goal, which is called "peace."

Concerning Hesed

Article No. 4, Tav-Shin-Mem-Vav, 1985-86

It is written in the holy *Zohar* concerning *Hesed* [mercy] (*Lech Lecha*, item 382): "Why was he not called Abraham thus far? We explained that thus far he was not circumcised, and now he has been circumcised. Once he was circumcised he connected with the *Hey*, which is the *Shechina* [Divinity], and the *Shechina* was in him. This is why now he is called Abraham, with a *Hey*. It is written, 'These are the generations of the heaven and earth when they were created.' We learned that He created them with a *Hey*, and we learned, in Abraham, meaning that *BeHibaraam* [when they were created] has the letters of Be Avraham [in Abraham]. This means that the world was created for Abraham.

"He asks, 'What are they saying?' That is, 'Why are they disputed in interpreting *BeHibaraam*?' He replies, 'It is *Hesed*. When he says that *BeHibaraam* implies Avraham, who is *Hesed*, and the world, which is the *Shechina*, was created for *Hesed*. This is why he says that He created them with a *Hey*, meaning the *Shechina*.

"But one does not dispute the other because everything comes down together. That is, if there is *Hesed* in the world, the *Shechina* is in the world, as well, and vice versa. Hence, the two meanings—*Hesed* and *Shechina*—are one thing, and the world was created for *Hesed* and for the *Shechina*. We should understand why he interprets that *BeHibaraam* means *Be Avraham*, which is *Hesed*, meaning that the world was created for *Hesed*."

We should understand the matter of *Hesed*. Is this not something that concerns only what is between man and man? Did the Creator create the upper worlds—the world of the angels, and the seraphim—only so that each one will deal with mercy with one's friend, so that Reuben will deal with mercy with Shimon? What will the Creator get out of this? Can such a thing be said? Accordingly, we must understand what is *Hesed* [mercy], as he said that the world was created for *Hesed*.

It is known that the purpose of creation is to do good to His creations. Therefore, we should ask, "Why are there two explanations about the verse, 'These are the generations of the heaven ... when they were created,'" one because of the *Shechina* and the other because of Abraham, who is *Hesed*?

We should say that from the verse, "When they were created," they explain only how to achieve the goal, called "to do good to His creations." This means that the creatures must attain the complete delight and pleasure. That is, when they receive delight and pleasure, they should not feel any unpleasantness, called the "bread of shame."

To correct this, there was the *Tzimtzum* [restriction], which is a concealment on the delight and pleasure. It is as the holy ARI says (*The Study of the Ten Sefirot*, Part 1, p 1): "Know, that before the emanations were emanated and the creatures created, an upper simple light filled the whole of reality, and there was no vacant place. ... When it came into His simple will to create the worlds ... to bring to light the perfection of His deeds ... then He restricted Himself."

It follows that the concealment we see on spirituality, meaning, although we should believe that "The whole earth is full of His glory," but if all the creatures in the world felt the glory of the Creator, who would want to engage in lowly things when they see the importance of the glory of spirituality? After all, a person can receive an image of what he had in the past.

If, for example, a person imagines that the most important period he had was when he felt that it was worthwhile to adhere to spirituality, and he looked at himself and the entire world, how time passes aimlessly and pointlessly, and engages only in trivialities. Then, when he is high-spirited, the world seemed to him like little children playing with toys.

Similarly, we sometimes see a little child taking a rope, putting it on another's shoulder and telling him, "You be the horse and I'll pull the reigns." They both enjoy this game. And if we tell the children, "Why are you playing with false things? You are not a wagon-driver and he is not a horse," they will not understand what we are telling them.

When a person depicts the time when he had the most important state in life, he looked at how people engage only in corporeality as a grownup looking at little children playing. It follows that all we need so we can engage in Torah and *Mitzvot* [commandments] is the revelation. That is, to reveal the delight and pleasure hidden in them so we will see them openly. Then, who would not want delight and pleasure? Who would be able to degrade himself and walk into a henhouse and peck in the trash like them, and be happy and joyful about it, when he can enjoy the life of a human? That is, his sustenance would be what delights people and not what delights beasts and animals. All this is said when he feels the difference between the vitality of people and the vitality of beasts, animals, and fowls.

But during the concealment, when he does not see any other life in the world but that the one that he enjoys is the vitality of the whole world, when he looks at other people relinquishing corporeal matters in search for spiritual life, they look at them as foolish, mindless children. Little children are allowed to play with important things, and they throw them away and take meaningless things instead.

While they can enjoy corporeal things, they throw them away and contemplate attaining spiritual possessions. To them, the spiritual matters are meaningless, meaning things that have no value. But it is all because of the concealment on spirituality.

Now we will explain the two interpretations of the word *Hibaraam* [when they were created], where the first means *Hesed*, and the second means *Shechina*. We ask, "Is it worthwhile to create the next world and this world for *Hesed*?" As we explained above, according to the purpose of creation, which is to do good to His creations, the delight and pleasure cannot be revealed before they can receive in order to bestow. Therefore, it is impossible to achieve the goal in full.

This is why we need to explain what is said about *BeHibaraam*, meaning that through them they will fulfill the purpose of creation, and without them it is impossible to achieve the purpose of creation in full. This is why interpreting that Be Avraham [in Abraham] is *Hesed* means that by engaging in the quality of *Hesed* they can achieve the quality of bestowal, after which they will be able to receive the pleasure, and that reception will be regarded as bestowal.

It is as he says in the *Sulam* [commentary on *The Zohar*] ("Introduction of the Book of Zohar," item 175), where he brings the words of our sages: "Upon the creation of the world, when He said to the angels, 'Let us make man in our image,' *Hesed* said, 'Let him be created, for he does mercy.' Truth said, 'Let him not be created, for he is all lies.'"

He interprets there the words of our sages, that *Hesed* said, "Let him be created": "But *Hesed* said, 'Let him be created because he does mercy,' since the *Mitzva* [commandment] to do good that he does is necessarily a clear act of bestowal by which he will gradually become corrected until he can engage in all the *Mitzvot* [commandments] in order to bestow. Thus, he is guaranteed to finally achieve his goal of engaging *Lishma* [for Her sake]. This is why *Hesed* argued that he should be created."

It follows that saying *BeHibaraam* means that *Hibaraam* is needed only as a means but not as a goal, as it is known that the purpose of creation is to do good to His creations. Rather, it is counsels how the creatures can receive the goal, meaning be able to receive the delight and pleasure. Because there must be equivalence of form between the giver and the receiver, and since they are opposite in form, they will never be able to receive the delight and pleasure.

This is why one is saying that the means is *Hesed*, where through the quality of *Hesed* that each does with the other, they will be rewarded with vessels of bestowal and be able to receive the delight and pleasure, and another says that it is *BeHibaraam*, meaning *Hey Beraam* [created them], namely the *Shechina*. This does not mean that he disputes him, but when he says that He created them with a *Hey*, it means that *Malchut*, which is the *Shechina*, is implied here in *BeHibaraam*, meaning a small *Hey*.

The holy ARI interprets (presented in Gatehouse of Intentions, item 43), "This is the meaning of *BeHibaraam*, *BeHey Beraam* [created them with a *Hey*], since all the creatures were five *Partzufim*, both in *Atzilut* and in *BYA*. This is the meaning of the small *Hey* of *Malchut de AK* after she was diminished at the end of her *ZAT*."

He interprets there (in *Ohr Pashut* [commentary below the text]) that the world of *Tikkun* [correction], called *ABYA*, emerged from another *Malchut*, that was mitigated by the quality of *Rachamim* [mercy], called *Tzimtzum Bet* [second restriction], where there was diminution in *Malchut*. This is why *Malchut* is called "small *Hey*."

This means that the *Hey* in *BeHibaraam* is interpreted to refer to the *Shechina* who received correction called "the association of the quality of mercy with judgment." This means that *Malchut*, called "the quality of judgment," is the root of the creatures, namely the will to receive, the *Kli* [vessel] that must receive the purpose of creation—to benefit His creations—and is the vessel of reception for the delight and pleasure that is the substance of the creatures, meaning the desire to receive delight and pleasure from Him. But due to the correction of equivalence of form, there was a rule that this vessel of reception must not be used unless it can aim to bestow. This is called "restriction and judgment."

The world cannot exist without this correction, called "receiving in order to bestow," or there is no disclosure of abundance to the lower ones due to the *Tzimtzum* and judgment that was made for the purpose of correcting the world. However, how is it possible to change the nature of creation, which is reception, into one of bestowal?

Therefore, to be able to correct the vessels of reception to work in order to bestow, there had to be a correction called "association of the quality of mercy with judgment," known as *Tzimtzum Bet*. This means that *Bina*, the quality of mercy, called "bestowal," mingled with *Malchut*, which is reception. Through that merger of mercy with judgment that is done by the remedy of Torah and *Mitzvot* [commandments], we can achieve the abundance although it is against our nature.

This matter is presented in "Preface to the Wisdom of Kabbalah" (item 58): "This is the meaning of our sages' words: 'In the beginning, He contemplated creating the world with the quality of *Din* [judgment]. He saw that the world does not exist and preceded the quality of *Rachamim* [mercy], and associated it with the quality of *Din*.' ...'He saw that the world does not exist' means that in this way, it was impossible for man, who was to be created from this *Behina Dalet*, to assume acts of bestowal. ...Therefore, He preceded the quality of *Rachamim* and associated it with the quality of *Din*. Through this association, *Behina Dalet—Midat ha Din—*was incorporated with sparks of bestowal in the *Kli* of *Bina*."

According to the above-said, it follows that we have the means by which to achieve the purpose of creation to do good to His creations, only thanks to the small *Hey*. This is because the judgment in the *Hey*, which is the quality of judgment, diminished into the quality of mercy. This means that part of the desire to receive diminished and received into it the quality of *Rachamim*, as was said above, that in the roots, the vessels of reception included the quality of bestowal, called *Rachamim*.

By this we will understand why the holy *Zohar* concludes that "one does not dispute the other because everything comes down together. That is, if there is *Hesed* in the world, the *Shechina* is in the world, as well, and vice versa. ...and the world was created for *Hesed* and for the *Shechina*."

This implies that it means that both, meaning the quality of *Hesed* and the *Shechina*, which was corrected with the quality of *Rachamim*, aim for the same thing—that through them the creatures would achieve the purpose of creation, which is to delight His creatures. This is why he says, "If there is no *Hesed* there is no *Shechina*."

That is, without the correction of *Hesed* in the world, where through the quality of *Hesed* they can receive in order to bestow, there would not be the *Shechina*. That is, the correction that was done in *Malchut*, called "association of the quality of mercy with judgment," would not help. However, the quality of *Hesed* does exist in the world, meaning that *Malchut* was corrected with the quality of *Hesed*, which is *Rachamim*, and this helps to achieve the goal.

However, we should understand why *Malchut* is called *Shechina*. Baal HaSulam said that the holy *Zohar* says, "He is *Shochen* [dweller]; she is *Shechina*." This means that where the Creator is revealed it is called *Shechina*. This is called "instilling of the *Shechina*," meaning that there the Creator is revealed.

For this reason one should always pray to be rewarded with the kingdom of heaven, also known as "faith." That is, one should pray that he will be rewarded with faith. But there is a question: If he knows that he lacks faith in the Creator, then to whom is he praying, for only when he believes in the Creator can it be said that he is asking the Creator to give him what he wants?

We can interpret this according to what is written in the "Introduction to the study of the Ten Sefirot" (item 14): "'He whose Torah is his trade.' The measure of his faith is apparent in his practice of Torah because the letters of *Umanuto* [his trade], are the same [in Hebrew] as in *Emunato* [his faith]. It is like a person who trusts his friend and lends him money. He may trust him with a pound, and if he asks for two pounds he will refuse to lend him. He might also trust him with one hundred pounds, but not more.

Also, he might trust him enough to lend him half his property, but not all his property. Finally, he may trust him with all his property without a hint of fear. This last faith is considered 'whole faith,' and the previous forms are considered 'incomplete faith.' Rather it is partial faith, whether more or less."

Thus, we see that there is partial faith. When he has partial faith, it can be said that a person should pray to the Creator to help him since he has only partial faith, so he wants the Creator to help him achieve complete faith. And since it is impossible to be awarded complete faith before one is rewarded with equivalence of form, as said in the previous articles and presented in the "Introduction of the Book of Zohar" (p 138), hence there are those corrections, as written above concerning *BeHibaraam*: 1) through the quality of *Hesed* they will achieve equivalence of form, which is regarded as Abraham; 2) he says that he is *Hey*, meaning the *Shechina*. That is, *Malchut* received into her the quality of *Rachamim* by which they will come into bestowal, and then the purpose of creation to do good to His creations will come true.

Concerning Respecting the Father

Article No. 5, Tav-Shin-Mem-Vav, 1985-86

It is written in the holy *Zohar* (*Vayera*, item 141): "Rabbi Shimon started and said, 'A son honors his father, and a servant his master.' 'A son honors his father' is Isaac with respect to Abraham. He asks, 'When did he honor him? When he tied him at the altar ... and he did not resist doing his father's will.' 'And a servant [honors] his master' is Eliezer with respect to Abraham. When he sent Eliezer to Haran, who did there all that Abraham wished, he honored him, as it is written, 'And the Lord has blessed my master.' And it is written, 'He said: 'I am Abraham's servant,'' to honor Abraham. Indeed, a man who brings silver and gold and gems and camels, and who is respectable and handsome, did not say that he was Abraham's beloved or his kin. Rather, he said, 'I am Abraham's servant,' to raise Abraham's merit and honor in their eyes."

(In item 145) He says, "This is why it is written, 'A son honors his father, and a servant his master.' And you, Israel, My sons, it is a disgrace for you to say that I am your father or that you are My servants. 'If I am a father, where is My honor? And if I am a master, where is the fear of Me?'"

We should understand the words of the holy *Zohar* when it says that "The Lord says, 'And you, Israel, My sons, it is a disgrace for you to say that I am your father.'" This implies that we need to tell someone that the Creator is our father, but we cannot say it because we are ashamed. So we must know to whom we are to say that He is our father. We must also know what is the shame for which we are unable to say it, as it is written, "It is a disgrace for you."

This is generally perplexing. After all, each day we say, "Our father, our King." And during the Eighteen Prayer we say, "Return us, our Father, to Your law," so to whom else are we to say that the Creator is our father and we are ashamed to say it, and for which the Creator is angry and says, "If I am a father, where is My honor?"

We should interpret this: We need to say that "The Lord is our father" relates to the Creator. We always say, "Our Father, Our King," and for this the Creator is angry: how are you not ashamed to say to Me that I am your father while you show Me no respect, as it is said, "If I am a father, where is My honor?" That is, the Creator says it is a disgrace for you to call Me "Our Father," and I see that to you, My honor is in the ground, which is called "*Shechina* [Divinity] in the dust." Thus, how are you not ashamed to call Me "Our Father"?

"And if I am a master, where is the fear of Me?" You say that you are all servants of the Creator, but I do not see that you have fear, meaning the fear of heaven that you should take upon yourselves. A servant is one has no authority of one's own, as our sages said, "He who has bought a slave has bought his Rav." Rather, he is annulled before the master, and all that he receives from the master is only so he can serve the master and not for himself.

But I see that you are taking the opposite route. That is, you want Me to serve you, meaning that I will satisfy your self-love, and all you are coming to ask of Me is how to increase your authority. That is, you are the masters and I am your servant, and you walk around all day with complaints about Me that I owe you and that if you could receive from Me by force you certainly would.

What did the Creator do so they would not receive by force? He did something small: He created darkness in the world, called "concealment," in case the creatures are unwilling to be servants and work for Him, called "receiving in order to bestow contentment upon one's Maker," as our sages said, "cleave on to His attributes." It is known that as long as one is in vessels of reception, the more one receives, the worse one is, meaning farther from the Creator. Therefore, He has made a great correction that when the vessels of reception govern a person he does not see anything of *Kedusha* [holiness] from which he can derive pleasures.

Rather, he sees only those pleasures that he can see, called "pleasures of separation." It is as the holy ARI says, that the *Klipot* [shells/peels] were given a slim illumination for all the corporeal pleasures so they may exist. This light of corporeality is all that we can see as having pleasure. But over spirituality lies a cloud of darkness that covers all the spiritual pleasures. Thus, they do not receive by force when the landlord does not want to give because they see no pleasures. Hence, those whose wish is only self-love flee from any true thing where there is delight and pleasure because darkness covers the earth.

For this reason, a person cannot begin to work *Lishma* [for Her sake] right away, but must begin in *Lo Lishma* [not for Her sake]. In *Lishma*, which is the true way, the body must flee from this work, as every kind goes to its kind. Since man was created with vessels of reception in order to receive, when he sees a thought, word, or action that does not yield anything for his vessels of reception, he promptly flees from them because this is not his kind. His kind is the nature in which he was created—receiving in order to receive, and not to give anything.

In order for a person who begins the work of the Creator not to flee from the work of bestowal because this is not his kind, we must begin with *Lo Lishma*. That is, he keeps the Torah and *Mitzvot* [commandments] that the Creator has commanded us in return for reward from Him for our work. This is so because we could work only for corporeal things, to make money and gain respect, and enjoy rest. We relinquish obtaining money, honor, and other lusts that the body requires of us to do, and which would delight us, and instead keep the Torah and *Mitzvot* that the Creator has commanded us.

We see that when we demand something of the body, that it will relinquish the pleasures it thinks it can enjoy, it asks, "What will you get out of it?" That is, "These new works you want to do, will they give you greater pleasures? If not then why do you need to change your work-place? You are used to working for this landlord but now you want to work for the Creator because He needs your work? Will He pay you a higher salary, meaning more pleasures? Will you enjoy more than in the work you are already used to?"

We should say to it: "Until now we had small gains, meaning imaginary pleasure, but now you will make great profit and your pleasure will be real pleasure because the Creator wishes to give you a spiritual reward. However, without work it will be bread of shame, which is why we were given Torah and *Mitzvot*, and we must believe that He will certainly pay us for relinquishing our needs, from which we could enjoy, in return for a real reward, which is a spiritual reward.

And although we do not know yet what is spirituality, we nonetheless believe it is a great thing compared to which all the corporeal pleasures are as a tiny candle, as explained in the words of the ARI, who says that due to the breaking of the vessels and the sin of the tree of knowledge, sparks fell into the *Klipot* in order to sustain them, so they would not be cancelled as long as they are needed. But the majority of the delight and pleasure is found in the worlds of *Kedusha*. Therefore, it is worthwhile for us to work in Torah and *Mitzvot* by which we will be rewarded with the next world in return for our work in Torah and *Mitzvot*.

However, once a person has begun the work of the Creator and wants to know the real work, he is told, "If I am a master, where is the fear of Me?" That is, the proper way is for the servant to work only for the landlord and not at all for himself. Yet, you are working only in order to be rewarded with the next world; you want reward for your work. The slave works without any reward, and the landlord provides his needs for him only so the servant will be able to work for Him, but the servant has no property that can be said to belong to the servant. Rather, there is only one authority there—the authority of the landlord.

Indeed, all our work in Torah and *Mitzvot* should be in order to achieve equivalence of form, which is *Dvekut* [adhesion] with the Creator. Engaging in Torah and *Mitzvot* is not as we thought before—that the Creator wants us to keep His Torah and *Mitzvot* and He will later pay us for this. Rather, the Torah and *Mitzvot* we were given to keep is because we need it! That is, by keeping Torah and *Mitzvot* we will receive the light of the Torah, and through that light we will then be able to achieve equivalence of form because the light in it reforms him.

Thus, what is the reward we should ask for in return for the body's work? It is that we relinquish the needs of the body for the purpose of keeping Torah and *Mitzvot*. It is impossible to work without reward, since it immediately asks, "Why are you relinquishing the pleasures that you can enjoy? What will you gain?"

The answer is that all our gain is that we are rewarded with serving the Creator. This is very important because it is true, meaning that he will be rewarded with clinging to the King of Kings. But when all the pleasures he has are built on taking every delight and pleasure into serving himself, and receiving pleasure in clothes of reception pertains to animals and not necessarily to humans, the highest of all creatures, so he enjoys the same dresses that animals enjoy. This is unbecoming of him.

Rather, all the dresses where man wants to receive pleasure should be garments of vessels of bestowal. That is, it is impossible to work without pleasure, but he measures his pleasures in how much he can bestow upon the King. That is, if he wishes to know how much work he receives from his work he should not measure how much he enjoys his work, meaning how much pleasure he derives from serving the King. Rather, he should measure by actions, meaning how much he wants the King to enjoy his work. It follows that all of his importance is in that he is serving the King.

It follows that if one wants to test if he is advancing in the work, he should do it in two ways: 1) by looking at the reward he hopes to receive from the Creator. If he is receiving a greater reward each day then the gauge is the vessels of reception. 2) How much he enjoys delighting the Creator, and all his reward is that he is bestowing upon the Creator. For example, if he is serving the greatest man in the country, he enjoys it. But if he is serving the greatest in the generation, he certainly enjoys it more. Therefore, he wants the Creator to be greater and more important in his eyes each day. This is the real measurement.

Confidence

Article No. 6, Tav-Shin-Mem-Vav, 1985-86

It is written in the holy *Zohar* (*Toldot*, item 122-125): "Rabbi Elazar started and said, 'Happy is the man whose strength is in You, happy is the man who strengthens in the Creator and places his trust in Him.' We can interpret confidence as did Hananiah, Misha'el, and Azariah, who trusted and said, 'If it be so, our God...' meaning they trusted the Creator to deliver them from the furnace. But he says that it is not so. Rather, come and see, if He does not deliver them and the Creator does not become one for them, His Name will not be sanctified in the eyes of everyone. But after they knew that they did not speak properly, they restated, 'But even if He does not, let it be known to you, O king.' That is, they said that whether He saves or does not save, you should know that we will not bow unto idols.'

"However, one should not trust and say, 'The Creator will save me' or 'The Creator will do this and that for me.' Rather, one should place one's trust in the Creator to help him, as it should be when he exerts in the *Mitzvot* [commandments] of the Torah and exert to walk in the path of truth. And when one comes to purify, he is aided. In that, he should trust the Creator to help him. He should place his trust in Him and trust none other than Him. It is written about this, 'His strength is in You.'

"'Rails in their hearts' means that one should establish one's heart properly, so no foreign thought may come in it. Rather, his heart will be as that rail that is built to pass through it to every place that is needed, to the right and to the left. 'And his heart shall be sincere,' meaning whether the Creator does good to him or to the contrary, his heart will be ready and corrected never to question the Creator under any circumstances.

"Another thing: 'Happy is the man whose strength is in You.' It is as you say, 'The Lord will give strength to His people,' meaning Torah. 'His strength is in You' means that one should engage in the Torah for the sake of the Creator, meaning the *Shechina* [Divinity], who is called 'Name' because anyone who engages in the Torah and does not exert *Lishma* [for Her sake], it is better for him not to be created. 'Rails in their hearts' is as you say, 'Lift up a song for Him who rides in the prairies, whose name is the Lord,' meaning to extol He who rides in the prairies.

"Also, 'Rails in their hearts' means that one should engage in the Torah with the aim to extol the Creator and make Him respected and important in the world, meaning to aim his heart so his engagement in the Torah will draw abundance of knowledge for him and for the whole world, so the name of the Creator will grow in the world, as it is written, 'And the earth shall be full of the knowledge of the Lord.' Then the words, 'And the Lord shall be king over all the earth' will come true."

According to the above, it is difficult to understand the confidence that the holy *Zohar* interprets for us and says, "However, one should not trust and say, 'The Creator will save me' or 'The Creator will do this and that for me,'" since we see that if someone asks his friend to do him a favor, if that person is his friend and knows that he has a kind heart then he trusts him to do as he asks. But how can it be said that he trusts him even if he does not do as he asks, as it is written, "One should not trust and say, 'The Creator will save me'"?

Another perplexing point is that he says, "He should place his trust in ... none other than Him." It is written about it, "His strength is in You." We need to understand this, since on the one hand he says that he should not say that the Creator will save him, meaning that there should be trust even when He does not save him, like Hananiah. In that case, how can we speak of the doubt, that he should trust none other, which means that another will certainly help and save him?

That is, it is as though there is someone who can save him for certain, and this is why there is a prohibition on trusting someone other than the Creator, although he does not know if He will save him. How can it be said that there is someone who can save him? He brings the example of Hananiah, Misha'el, and Azariah, and there, how can it be said that they should not trust another, as though there is someone in the world who can save them from the furnace? Can this be said?

To understand the words of the holy *Zohar*, we first need to remember the purpose of creation, meaning that there is a goal on the part of the Creator, which the Creator desired from Creation. And also, there is a purpose on the part of the creatures, meaning the purpose that the creatures must achieve, that we can say that they came for their purpose, meaning the reason why they were created.

It is known that from the perspective of the Creator, the goal is that He wishes to delight His creations. This is why He has created the creatures, so as to impart them with delight and pleasure. And since He wants the benefit He gives them to be complete, He has made a correction that before the creatures can receive in order to bestow, they cannot receive any abundance, called "delight and pleasure." This is so because the nature of the branch is to resemble its root. And because the root of the creatures is to bestow upon the creatures, when the creatures engage in reception they feel unpleasantness.

Hence, a correction was made, called *Tzimtzum* [screen] and *Masach* [screen], where only by these can the creatures receive in order to bestow, and then they can enjoy the delight and pleasure that were in the thought of creation. The purpose of the creatures is that they must achieve *Dvekut* [adhesion], called "equivalence of form." That is, as the Creator wishes to delight His creatures, the creatures should also arrive at a state where their only wish is to bestow upon the Creator.

For this reason, those who want to enter the path of truth, to achieve *Dvekut*, must accustom themselves to make every thought, word, and action have the aim to bring contentment to the Creator through the *Mitzvot* that they do and the Torah in which they engage. They must not consider what they can receive from the Creator for wanting to please Him. That is, they must not think, "What will the Creator give me?" meaning that they can extract from the Creator's authority into their own. This would cause them to create two authorities: an authority of the Creator and an authority of the creatures, which is the opposite of *Dvekut*, for *Dvekut* means unification, when two things become one as they unite with one another.

Conversely, two authorities imply separation. This reception when they think of themselves, of receiving something from the Creator into their own authority, makes them more separated than they were thus far.

By this we understand the words of the holy *Zohar* that were said about the verse, "Sin is a disgrace to any people, since 'All the good that they do, they do for themselves.' This brings up the question, "Why is it not enough to say that they are not being rewarded when they engage in acts of mercy—meaning when they bestow, do good—since their intention is not the act of mercy but rather the reward they will receive in return, which is called "for themselves"? That is, they engage in mercy not with the aim to do good to another, but rather aim that the good that they do for another will bring them some reward. It makes no difference whether it is money or honor, as long as they receive reward for their will to receive.

However, we should understand that this means that saying "sin" implies that it would be better if they did not do the mercy.

Can this be said? After all it is no crime to do mercy, so why is it considered a sin?

According to what we explained about people who wish to walk on the path of truth, meaning to be rewarded with *Dvekut* with the Creator, who aspire for equivalence of form, when they are in "sit and do nothing," they do not demand anything for their vessels of reception. Thus, they are not doing anything to drive them away from the Creator.

But when they perform an act of mercy, they ask the Creator to give them some reward into their vessels of reception. Thus, they are asking for something that will separate them from the Creator. This is why the mercy is considered a sin (but this does not refer to Torah and *Mitzvot* because regarding Torah and *Mitzvot*, our sages said, "One should always engage in Torah and *Mitzvot Lo Lishma* [not for Her sake] because from *Lo Lishma* we come to *Lishma* [for Her sake]").

However, according to the rule that it is impossible to do anything without pleasure, how can we work in order to bestow and not receive any reward into our own authority, but rather annul ourselves to Him and cancel our own authority so that only the singular authority remains, namely the authority of the Creator? What are the fuels that will give us the strength to work so we can work in order to bestow?

The fuel that gives strength to work should come from serving the King, and according to the importance of the King, since the Creator has placed a power in nature that we derive great pleasure from serving an important person. Thus, man feels pleasure according to the importance of the King. That is, if one feels that he is serving a great King, to that extent his pleasure grows. Therefore, the more the King is important, the more he enjoys his work.

The pleasure he receives from serving the King is that the greater the King, the more he wants to annul before Him. It follows that all the delight and pleasure he receives does not enter man's authority, but rather he wants to annul before the King to the extent of the

King's greatness and importance. Thus, there is only one authority here, called "singular authority."

But when he wants to receive some reward from the King for his work then he has two authorities separated from one another. It follows that where man should achieve *Dvekut* with the Creator, he achieves separation from the Creator, which is the complete opposite from the goal that the creatures should achieve.

It follows that the reason that gives him strength to work is only that he can bestow upon the King. But before one has reached a state where he feels the greatness of the Creator, he is at war with the body because it does not agree to work without reward, and it cannot work because of the great pleasure of serving the King because it does not feel it, as it lacks the sensation of the greatness of the King. Even more so, it is because it lacks faith, meaning to believe that there is a King in the world.

Our sages said (*Avot*, Chapter 2), "Know what is above you. The eye sees and the ear hears, and all your works are written in the book. When he has faith that there is a supervisor in the world, the calculations of His greatness and importance begin. When he has faith that there is a supervisor in the world, this faith brings him the sensation of importance even when he does not consider the greatness of the Creator. Still, he already has the strength to work in serving the Creator."

However, since he lacks faith and has only partial faith (see "Introduction to the Study of the Ten Sefirot," item 14), when he wants to work in order to bestow, the body promptly comes and yells out loud, "Are you crazy?! You want to work without pay, and you are saying that you want to serve the King, which is itself a great reward. This pertains to those who feel the King, and whom the King examines every movement that they make. They can say that they are working because it is a great privilege to serve the King, but not you!"

This causes the war of the inclination: At times he overcomes the body, and at other times the body overcomes him. He says to the body: "The fact that I don't feel the greatness of the King is your fault because you want to receive everything in your own domain, called 'receiving in order to receive,' but there was a restriction and concealment on this discernment, so it is impossible to see anything of truth. Therefore, let me out of your desire and let's begin to work in order to bestow, and you will certainly see the importance and greatness of the King. Then you yourself will agree with me that it is worthwhile to serve the King and nothing in the world is more important than this."

For this reason, when a person wants to work only in order to bestow and not receive anything, and all his calculations are about bringing contentment to the Creator through his work—that he wants to bring Him contentment—and he does not regard himself at all, how can one know if he is really on that path? Perhaps he is deceiving himself and his intention is only to receive? That is, he is giving in order to receive and not walking on the path of truth, meaning that all he wishes is to be a giver in order to give.

Here one can criticize oneself, meaning one's intention. When he prays to the Creator to help him with the war of the inclination so the inclination will not come to him and wish to control him with its complaints against his work, the Creator will give him a desire only to want to work for Him with all his heart and soul. And certainly, there is no prayer without confidence that the Creator hears the prayer, for if he has no confidence that the Creator will hear his prayer, he will not be able to pray if he is not certain that someone hears his prayer.

This brings up the question: "If he sees that his prayer is not heard, meaning that it is not granted as he understands it should be granted—that he is given what he is asking because the Creator is merciful and gracious, and if He heard He would certainly give what one is asking—then why is his prayer not answered? Doesn't the Creator hear the prayer? Can this be said?"

However, one should believe that the Creator does hear the prayer, as we say in the Eighteen Prayer, "For You hear the prayer of every mouth of Your people, Israel, with mercy." However, we should believe what is written, that "My thoughts are not your thoughts." That is, the Creator knows what is best for man, meaning for his wholeness, and what can obstruct his wholeness.

Therefore, we should say that the Creator always hears and answers according to man's best interest, and this is what He gives us. Thus, one should believe that the states that a person feels are what the Creator wants us to feel because it is in our favor.

It follows that the confidence that we should have in the Creator is that the Creator certainly hears our prayers and answers them, but not according to our understanding, but according to the Creator's understanding of what we should be given. It therefore follows that the confidence is primarily about trusting the Creator that He helps everyone, as it is written, "His mercy is over all His works." However, the confidence should not be that the Creator will help us according to our understanding, but according to the Creator's understanding.

There are people who think that the confidence is according to what a person thinks he needs, that the confidence should be with regard to that, and if he does not believe that the Creator must help him according to man's understanding, it is not regarded as believing and trusting the Creator. Rather, one should have confidence precisely as man wants it.

By this we can understand the words of the holy *Zohar* when we asked about its saying, "However, one should not trust and say, 'The Creator will save me' or 'The Creator will do this and that for me.' Rather, one should place one's trust in the Creator to help him, as it should be." It brings evidence from Hananiah, Misha'el, and Azariah, who said, "Whether He saves or does not save." The holy *Zohar* says there that when one comes to purify he is aided, and in this he will trust the Creator to help him and trust in Him and not place his trust in another besides Him.

It is written about it, "His strength is in You." We asked, "What does it mean that he will 'not place his trust in another'?" Is there anyone else who can help him, for which there is a commandment not to trust another? He speaks of trust in relation to Hananiah, and who could have saved them from the furnace, for which he had to give a prohibition on trusting another?

The thing is that when a person wishes to walk on the path of truth, meaning that all his works will be for the Creator, called "in order to bestow and not for his own benefit," he must believe that the Creator knows what to give him and what not to give. In order for one to avoid deceiving himself and see each time if he is walking on the path of bestowing contentment upon the Creator, he needs to see himself, and whatever his state, he must be pleased.

He should trust that this must be the Creator's will, so I do not mind what state I am in. Rather, I must toil and pray for what I understand, and trust in the Creator that He will help me, for my own benefit. But the Creator knows what is to man's benefit, not man. Here one can criticize one's engagement in Torah and *Mitzvot* [commandments], if one's intention is that he wants to bestow upon the Creator and not for his own benefit, meaning that his aim is not to bestow in order to receive.

For this reason, when one establishes the order of one's work and goes to pray to the Creator, he should trust in the Creator that He will receive his prayer. At that time he should trust in the Creator, meaning that the measure of confidence concerns the Creator's view, and not that he will trust another.

And who is the other? It is man himself. That is, the measure of confidence that the Creator will help him should be as the Creator understands, and not as man understands.

Man is called "other," as our sages said (*Sukkah*, 45b), "We learn that anyone who combines work for the Creator with another thing is uprooted from the world, as it is said, 'Only for the Lord.' This means that it should be only for the Creator, without self-gratification, called 'reception.' This means that even when he aims the *Mitzva* [commandment] for the Creator but wants a little bit for himself, as well, he is uprooted from the world."

What does it mean that he is "uprooted from the world"? Are those who are not rewarded with aiming all their works uprooted from the world? We need to understand to which world they are referring. According to what we learn, they mean the eternal world, called "the world of the Creator." This means that the name of the Creator, who is called The Good Who Does Good, is apparent there. There, His thought is revealed—to do good to His creations.

This is the purpose for which He has created the world, and from that world he is uprooted. That is, he cannot be rewarded with the delight and pleasure being revealed to him because of the correction of the *Tzimtzum* [restriction], which was in order for man to be awarded *Dvekut* [adhesion], called "equivalence of form." For this reason, when one wants to receive a little for oneself, as well, to that extent he moves away from *Dvekut* with the Creator and therefore cannot be awarded the delight and pleasure found in the purpose of creation. Thus, he is uprooted from that world.

It follows from all the above that if one wants to know if he is not deceiving himself and wants to serve the Creator with the intention only to bestow contentment upon the Creator, and the holy *Zohar* says that when he prays to the Creator to help him, he should certainly have confidence that the Creator will help him. Otherwise, if he has no trust, how can he ask? If he does not trust the Creator to help him, he has no room for prayer because one cannot pray and ask a favor of someone unless he knows that that person can do him this favor.

Therefore, he must certainly be sure while he is praying to the Creator that He will certainly help him. And if one sees that the Creator has not helped him as he understands, he doubts the Creator, that He might, God forbid, not hear the prayer. This is why the holy *Zohar* says that he should pray and trust the Creator that He will certainly help him as He understands, since that person wants to engage specifically in matters that are only for the Creator's sake and not for his own sake.

Thus, what difference does it make how he works to bestow upon the Creator? That is, he must believe that if the Creator sees that it will be to man's benefit if he works in whatever state he is in, it does not matter what one thinks will bring the Creator more pleasure, if He helps him according to man's understanding of what brings the Creator more delight.

Rather, he should trust in the Creator to help him according to His understanding. This is what the holy *Zohar* calls, "One should place one's trust in the Creator to help him, as it should be." This means that what the Creator understands, that the person should be only in that state. And concerning the state one is in he should ask the Creator to help him. (That is, in the state he is in, and he understands that this is what he needs, what he understands is what he will ask, but the Creator will do as He sees fit.)

When can it be said that he agrees to the Creator's will and does not insist on saying that he wants the Creator to help him according to his wish? This happens precisely when one asks what one understands, and prays that the Creator will help him as he understands, yet annuls his will before the Creator's will. Then it can be said that he has placed his trust in the Creator to help him as it should be, meaning as the Creator understands and not as man understands.

This is called "Cancel your will before His will," as our sages said (*Avot*, Chapter 2). But if he has no desire to achieve any purpose while he prays to the Creator to help him reach, it clearly cannot be said that he will annul his will before the will of the Creator and say, "I want what I want and what I understand that I need, but You will do to me as You see fit." Then it can be said that he is annulling his will before the Creator's will.

But why does one need to annul his desire? What if he has no desire to annul? It is as though it is not wholeness, since it makes sense that if one agrees with the Creator's will it is certainly better than if he has a different desire than that of the Creator, and he must annul it, as though he has something bad and he must cancel the bad. Would it not be better if he had no bad at all?

The thing is that it is known that for the spiritual *Kli* [vessel] to be fit to receive the abundance of delight and pleasure, it must meet two conditions: 1) to have *Aviut* [thickness], which is the desire to receive delight and pleasure, 2) to have a *Masach* [screen] not to receive according to one's craving and desire for the delight and pleasure, but according to the Creator's delight. This is called "receiving in order to bestow contentment upon his Maker."

However, if he has no vessels of reception, meaning no craving to receive delight and pleasure, he is unfit to receive abundance from above because there is no satisfaction without a need. For this reason, one must try to make for oneself a lack—to crave that the Creator will bring him closer and give him the abundance that the Creator can give, and which he is craving to receive. At the same time, he cancels his desire and trusts the Creator to help him and give him what the Creator understands to be in his favor. Therefore, at that time he has no complaints that the Creator did not help him according to man's understanding.

This is regarded as cancelling his desire and saying, "I do my part," meaning what I understand to be in my favor, "and I understand and believe that the Creator probably knows my situation better, and I agree to go and engage in Torah and *Mitzvot* as though the Creator has helped me as I understand He should answer my prayer. And although I see that He did not give me any answer to my request, I still believe that the Creator has heard my prayer and answered me according to what is good for me. For this reason, I must always pray that the Creator will help me according to my understanding, and the Creator helps me according to what He understands is good for me."

This brings up a question: "Since the Creator helps according to His understanding anyhow, what is man's prayer for?" The Creator does not answer the prayer that a person prays and does as He understands that He should do. Thus, how does man's prayer help? What is His benefit from our prayer for what we understand that we need, while He answers as He understands?

We must know that the prayer we pray is for what we need, and we certainly know what we need and we want the Creator to answer our prayer as we understand it—that if He grants our wishes we will be happy people because He has given us all that we needed, we should know that there is a rule: There is no light without a *Kli*. That is, there cannot be satisfaction without a need.

It follows that even if a person knows what he needs, it is still not considered a deficiency that is destined to be filled, since what man thinks he needs does not mean he has a deficiency. A deficiency means that he is truly deficient of something. A deficiency is not something we do not have. There are many things we do not have, yet they are not regarded as deficiencies that can be satisfied.

For example, if there is a citizen in a certain country, and there are elections for presidency in that country, and someone was elected as president, while the citizen remained an ordinary person, it does not pain him whatsoever that he did not become president. But there is another person in the country, who thought he would become the president. He exerted great efforts among friends and famous people to help him become president, but in the end someone else became president and he was left with only his desire.

There is certainly a difference between those two people, although they have the same absence, namely that they are not presidents. However, there is a huge difference between the one who exerted to become president and was left dissatisfied, and the other one, who despite not becoming president does not suffer from not becoming president. That is, even if they wanted to make him president, he has no *Kelim* [vessels] for it, meaning knowledge of how to handle a presidency.

Rather, the *Kli* for the filling is the desire for something, and a desire means that he is tormented over the thing he wants. And even if he has a desire for something and thinks that this is already regarded as desire, it is still not a real lack making this desire fit for reception of the fulfillment.

The reason is that a deficiency means suffering over what one does not have, and filling means pleasure of obtaining what one wants. It follows that according to his suffering from the negation, so is his delight with the filling.

Now we will come to understand the meaning of the prayer we pray for the Creator to help us as we understand, and believe what is written, "For You hear the prayer of every mouth," and at the same time trust the Creator to hear the prayer of every mouth. However, we should not trust that the Creator should help us according to our understanding, but trust that the Creator will help us according to His understanding.

We asked, "So what is my prayer for, if the Creator will do as He understands?" However, the prayer increases the desire for the filling because the more one prays, the more the deficiency in him grows. That is, he begins to feel a lack for what he prays. When he began to ask for fulfillment of his lack he still did not have the feeling that he really needed what he asked. He simply saw that others were asking some fulfillment and heard from the friends that we should ask the Creator for some fulfillment, so he, too, started praying to the Creator to give him what he wants. However, he did not truly feel that he needed what he asked; it still did not settle in his heart.

Because of the many prayers he prays he begins to examine if he really needs what he is asking, or is it only an accessory, meaning that he is asking for luxuries. That is, he does what must be done as a Jew, but he wants luxuries, meaning to have a better life in spirituality and not be an ordinary person like everyone else who are serving the Creator.

This examination of the prayers he prays makes him realize that he really needs the Creator's help to keep anything in spirituality, since the prayers he prays each time bring him to notice that he is beginning to examine himself, why he is praying. These prayers, which our sages have established for us, do I really need what they said we should pray for, or do I need other things, meaning things that my body understands it needs to ask?

It turns out that as his prayers multiply he begins to acquire a real need until it torments him that he is lacking. This gives him a real desire for the Creator to bring him closer, and this is considered that the Creator is helping him, as it is written in the holy *Zohar*, "Rather, one should place one's trust in the Creator to help him, as it should be," meaning that the confidence should be that the Creator will help him with the prayers as the Creator understands he should be answered.

Now we will explain the rest of the words of the holy *Zohar*: "Another thing: 'Happy is the man whose strength is in You' is as you say, 'The Lord will give strength to His people,' meaning Torah. 'His strength is in You' means that one should engage in the Torah for the sake of the Creator, meaning the *Shechina* [Divinity], who is called 'Name.'"

We should understand what he says there in the *Sulam* [Ladder commentary on *The Zohar*]: "for the sake of the Creator, meaning the *Shechina* [Divinity], who is called 'Name.'" It is known that our whole intention should be to bestow contentment upon the Creator. Thus, what does it mean that he says about what the holy *Zohar* says, that one should engage in the Torah for the sake of the Creator, meaning the *Shechina*, who is called "Name"? This implies that we should aim all the engagement in Torah and *Mitzvot* for the *Shechina*. We need to understand the meaning of "for the *Shechina*." And also, we find in several places in the holy *Zohar* that we must aim the engagement in Torah and *Mitzvot* to "raise the *Shechina* from the dust." Thus, we need to understand the different wording between the Creator and His *Shechina*.

In previous articles we presented what Baal HaSulam explained about the words of the holy *Zohar* where it says, "He is *Shochen* [dweller], and she is *Shechina*." He said that it means that the place where the *Shochen* is revealed is called *Shechina*. Thus, they are not two things but one. That is, we have light and *Kli*. In other words, we attain the Creator only through the *Kelim* [vessels] that attain Him. Therefore, when we speak of the Creator, we speak only of how the Creator is revealed to us through the *Kelim*.

But we do not speak of light without a *Kli* at all. We call the thought of Creation, to do good to His creations, by the name *Ein Sof* [infinity/no end], meaning the benefactor. That is, the benefactor bestows upon the creatures. The *Kli* in which the abundance appears is called *Malchut*, who is called *Shechina*, in whom the delight and pleasure are revealed.

It therefore follows that the Creator wants to bestow delight and pleasure upon the creatures, but the lower ones have no *Kelim* to receive due to the oppositeness of form between the receivers and the giver. Thus, the delight and pleasure are not revealed. At that time there is evil inclination in the world because it portrays spirituality, meaning bestowal, as bad, and only what he can receive in order to receive as good.

For this reason, the lower ones have no place where they can work in order to bestow, since one does not harm oneself. Thus, a person cannot have the motivation to work in order to bestow, hence the upper abundance that is the delight and pleasure cannot be revealed to the lower ones.

It follows that the name of the Creator, the general name, Good Who Does Good, is hidden and concealed from the lower ones. This name is called *Shechina*, which is the name of the Creator with regard to the Good Who Does Good, and this name is in exile. That is, where one begins to work a little bit in order to bestow, one promptly feels exile in this work—that he wants to escape from such states. It is so because as long as one is immersed in self-love he has no idea about the work of bestowal, and when he begins to feel that he is walking on the line of bestowing and not receiving anything, it becomes dark for him and he wants to escape from that state like one who wants to escape from the exile he was given.

This is similar to a man who sinned against the government and was sentenced to exile. He always contemplates how to escape from there. Likewise, when one feels that the receiver will not receive anything from this work, he has no desire to work and wants to escape the campaign altogether. This is why at that time it is considered that the name of the Creator, which is *Shechina*, is regarded as being in exile, meaning that a person tastes exile in this work.

For this reason we pray to the Creator and engage in Torah and *Mitzvot* "to raise the *Shechina* from the dust," meaning that this place of the *Shechina*, which is the name of the Creator, meaning the Good Who Does Good, will appear in vessels of bestowal. But a person feels the taste of dust in this work, and this, too, is the meaning of the *Shechina* in exile, when one tastes in it the taste of exile and wants to escape from this work, meaning from the holy work, where *Kedusha* [holiness] means to bestow contentment upon the Creator.

For this reason we must ask for personal redemption, where each one feels that he has come out of exile. That is, when he works in order to bestow he should feel that he is in the land of Israel, meaning that his desire will crave only *Yashar-El* [straight to the Creator], which is called *Eretz Ysrael* [Land of Israel].

The sign of this is whether one can say wholeheartedly what we say in the blessing for the food: "Let us thank You, the Lord our God, for bequeathing our fathers with a desirable, good, and broad land." That is, besides having to pray for the general redemption, we must also pray for personal redemption.

It follows that in a place, when he was in exile, meaning when he tasted the taste of exile, when the image of bestowal only for the Creator and not for himself would come to him, he felt the taste of exile and dust. And at the time of redemption, when he comes out of exile, he feels in the work of bestowal the taste of a desirable, good, and broad land.

Thus, the land of exile means that we feel that taste of suffering and always reflect on how to escape from that land. Coming out of exile means that he has come to a desirable, good, and broad land. We say about this land: "Let us thank You, the Lord our God." This is called *Eretz Yashar-El* [a land (desire) straight to the Creator], and this is the redemption we should aspire to achieve.

However, a question naturally arises, "Why do we feel the taste of dust in the work of bestowal and want to run from it as one who is in exile?" Although there are many reasons for it, we should add another one: There is a rule that there is no light without a *Kli*, meaning that there is no fulfillment without a lack. Hence, first we must enter the exile and feel the torment in this work because the body, which is called "will to receive," kicks and resists this work because it is against its nature, and through the suffering it feels in exile.

That is, precisely those who engage in work of bestowal and the body resists, but they do not surrender to the body's arguments and suffer the torments of the body, meaning their body's resistance, but they do not escape from the campaign but are always at war with the inclination. At times he prevails, and at other times the body prevails, so he is always in ups and downs and his soul is never at peace.

Then he suffers because he is not like other people, who promptly flee from the work when they see that the body resists the work of bestowal, and do not suffer because they are not in this work of tasting exile when the body resists them because they surrender to the body's governance and speak about it like the spies who slandered the land of Israel.

As we said in the previous articles where we brought the words of the holy *Zohar*, they naturally have no *Kelim* [vessels] in which to receive the redemption, as explained in the essay, "The Giving of the Torah," that the exile is a matter of absence that precedes existence, which is the redemption. Therefore, you find all the letters of *Geula* [redemption] in *Gola* [exile], except for the letter *Aleph*, which points to *Alupho Shel Olam* [Champion of the world/the Creator], as our sages said. This teaches us that the form of absence is but the negation of existence.

For this reason, when we say in the blessing for the food, "Let us thank You," we say, "and for delivering us, the Lord our God, from the land of Egypt, and for redeeming us from the house of slaves." This teaches us that to reach the desirable, good, and broad land, we must first go through a stage of making the *Kelim*, meaning to be in the land of Egypt, and see that we are slaves serving Pharaoh King of Egypt, and the torments of exile bring us a need to pray to the Creator to deliver us from exile, as was said (Exodus, 2:23), "And the children of Israel sighed from the work, and they cried out, and their cry went up to God." It follows that exile is a *Kli*, and redemption is the light and the abundance.

It turns out that the name of the Creator—which he explains there in the *Sulam*—being the *Shechina*, who is called "the name of the Creator," when we asked, "How can it be said that we aim in the Torah and *Mitzvot* for the sake of the *Shechina*, we explained this with what Baal HaSulam said, that the *Shochen* [dweller] and the *Shechina* [Divinity] are one and the same, and the place where the *Shochen* is revealed is called *Shechina*.

We can understand this with an example: If we refer to someone as smart, rich, or generous, are these names different matters, meaning a different body than the person himself? That is, when the wisdom of they call him "wise," or "rich," meaning according to what others see. It follows that his name is only a revelation of the Creator.

The Importance of a Prayer of Many

Article No. 7, Tav-Shin-Mem-Vav, 1985-86

It is written in *The Zohar*, *Vayishlach* [And Jacob Sent], (p 13, Item 45 in the *Sulam* Commentary), "Come and see. Rabbi Shimon said, 'A prayer of many rises before the Creator and the Creator crowns Himself with that prayer because it rises in several manners: One asks for *Hassadim* [grace], another for *Gevurot* [strength], and another for *Rachamim* [mercy]. It consists of several sides—the right side, the left side, and the middle. And because it consists of several sides and manners, it becomes a crown and is placed on the head of the Righteous One who lives forever, meaning *Yesod*, who imparts all the salvations to the *Nukva*, and from her to the entire public. And come and see, Jacob consisted of all three lines; this is why the Creator wanted his prayer, for it was in utter completeness—of all three lines, like a prayer of many. This is why it is written, 'Then Jacob was very much afraid and distressed,' since the Creator made it this way for him, so he would pray because He craved his prayer."

We see in the words of *The Zohar* that it interprets a prayer of many as a single person, saying that Jacob consisted of all three lines. But in all the places where it writes about a prayer of many, it literally means that many pray, as our sages said (*Berachot*, p 8a), "Rabbi Yochanan said in the name of Rabbi Shimon Bar-Yochai, 'Why is it written, 'And I, my prayer is a time of good will unto You, O Lord.'' When is it a time of good will? When many pray."

This means that many pray together, literally. Also, we should understand what *The Zohar* says, that "A crown is placed on the head of the Righteous One who lives forever." What does it mean that it becomes a crown on the head? A crown means the crown of the king, like the crown of the kingship. And what does it mean that the crown on his head is made of the prayer? What makes us understand the importance and greatness of a prayer? Since he wishes to reveal to us the importance of the prayer, he tells us, "Know that the crown for the king is made of the prayer."

It says that it is called *Yesod* and that it gives all the salvations to the *Nukva*, and from her to the entire public. We should understand why the crown is made specifically on *Yesod*, since it is known that we pray to *Ein Sof*, so what does it mean that a prayer of many becomes a crown specifically on *Yesod*? And also, why does it say that *Yesod* imparts to the *Nukva*, and from the *Nukva* to the public?

Baal HaSulam explained the matter of a prayer of many as a person praying for the many; this is called "a prayer of many." This is why a prayer of many is called "a time of good will." When a person prays for himself, he has slander and questions whether his prayer is truly worth acceptance. But when he prays for the public, it becomes irrelevant to scrutinize him and to see if he is worthy of his prayer being answered, since he is not asking for anything for himself, but only for the public.

This is why it was said that a prayer of many is called "a time of good will" and his prayer is answered. And according to what is explained in several places in the *Sulam* Commentary, a prayer of many relates to *Malchut*, who is called "the assembly of Israel" or "the Holy Divinity." She is called "many" because she contains all the souls. And since Divinity is in exile, we ask about the exile of

Divinity, which is sometimes called "Divinity in the dust," since all those names indicate to us the content of the purpose of creation, which was in order to do good to His creations.

It is known that for Him to reveal the perfection of His deeds, there was the first restriction. This means that in a place where there is only a *Kli* called "receiving in order to receive," the upper bounty will be hidden from that place. The abundance comes only to a place where it is possible to aim in order to bestow. And since by nature man is born only to receive, in that place that he sees, his receiver—called "self-love"—cannot receive. Instead, he must do everything for Divinity, meaning for *Malchut*, for only by that will His glory appear in *Malchut*. This is so because only when the Creator can appear to the lower ones will His glory be seen. It was written that the place where the *Shochen* [dweller] appears is called *Shechina* ["dwelling," but also "Divinity"].

This is called, "Let His great name be magnified and sanctified," since the name of the Creator, who is called "The Good Who Does Good," appears in the world. This is so because everyone obtains the purpose of creation called, "To do good to His creations," since now there is a *Kli* that is fit for reception, being the intention to bestow, called *Dvekut* [adhesion] with the Creator.

It turns out that since by nature the creatures are only about reception in order to receive, and since they cannot work in order to bestow without overcoming their nature, they cause *Malchut* to remain in the dust, meaning they cannot see her merit. This means that they cannot see what she can receive from the Creator because everything is hidden due to the restriction.

However, we need some introspection. That is, we should believe what our sages tell us, that all the pleasures in corporeal delights are but a tiny candle compared to the pleasures that exist in spirituality. As it is written in the *Sulam* Commentary ("Introduction of The Book of Zohar," p 173), "This is the meaning of the breaking of the vessels that preceded the creation of the world. Through the breaking of the vessels of *Kedusha* [holiness/sanctity] and their fall into the separated *BYA*, holy sparks fell along with them to the *Klipot* [shells], from which came the pleasures and love of every kind into the domain of the *Klipot*, which pass them on for man's reception and for his delight."

It therefore follows that the majority of pleasures are in *Kedusha*, while we see the contrary, that in corporeality everyone sees things that can be enjoyed. But in the toil in the Torah and *Mitzvot* [commandments], it is impossible to tell a person to engage in Torah and *Mitzvot* without promising him reward for his work. This is because while one engages in keeping the *Mitzvot*, he finds it completely tasteless, but when he is promised a reward and he believes it, he can work in Torah and *Mitzvot* because he will be rewarded.

This is not so when he engages in corporeal things such as eating, drinking, money, honor, etc. A person does not ask, "Why must I deal with these mundane matters?" since where one feels pleasure, he doesn't ask about the purpose of receiving the pleasure. All he can think about while receiving the pleasure is how to enhance the pleasure in quantity and quality. God forbid that one should ever contemplate the matter of reception of pleasure, meaning, "Why do I need to receive pleasure?"

Sometimes, a person receives pleasure from something for which he did not pay a thing. Although it gives him much pleasure, the question still arises in him, "What is the purpose of that pleasure?" For example, a pleasure that costs no money is the pleasure of rest. There is no need to buy this pleasure, for one receives it free of charge. Still, many times a person asks himself, "What will I gain by enjoying this rest?"

But when a person experiences true delight and pleasure, the purpose of this delight never even occurs to him. And if it does happen that he should contemplate the purpose of this pleasure that he's enjoying now, it is a sign that the pleasure he is feeling is not real pleasure, since he can still contemplate its purpose. This is a sign that there is a deficiency in that pleasure, and where there is deficiency, he can contemplate a different purpose than what he is feeling now.

From all the above, it follows that the majority of good taste and pleasure in life are found in Torah and *Mitzvot*, since this is where the upper light is deposited. It is written about it in the *Sulam* Commentary ("Introduction of The Book of Zohar," p 242, "Visions of the Ladder," Item 1), "When one is rewarded with listening to the voice of His word, the 613 *Mitzvot* become *Pekudin*, from the word *Pikadon* [deposit]. This is so because there are 613 *Mitzvot*, and in each *Mitzva* a light of a unique degree is deposited, which corresponds to a unique organ in the 613 organs and tendons of the souls and the body. It follows that while performing the *Mitzva*, one extends to the corresponding organ in his soul and body, the degree of light that belongs to that organ and tendon. This is considered the *Panim* [face/anterior] of the *Mitzvot*."

It follows that by keeping Torah and *Mitzvot*, the purpose of creation—to do good to His creations—becomes revealed. However, he says in the *Sulam* Commentary that this comes specifically after one is rewarded with keeping the Torah and *Mitzvot* in the form of "Listening to the voice of His word." But when he keeps Torah and *Mitzvot* in the form of "That fulfill His word," before they are rewarded with listening, the *Mitzvot* are called *Eitin* [tips/counsels], and they are regarded as *Achor* [back/posterior]. It means that the upper light that belongs to that *Mitzva* is still not shining in them, but they are regarded as counsels by which to come to the light of *Panim*, which belongs to the *Mitzva*.

And all the work and the strengthening that one needs to overcome his desire and thought, which obstruct him from going on the path of truth, apply only when he is in *Achoraim* [back], in the form of "That fulfill His word." This is so because in that state, he still doesn't feel the upper light that is clothed in Torah and *Mitzvot*. Hence, he does everything because he believes it is a great privilege to be rewarded with engaging in Torah and *Mitzvot*, even when he doesn't feel its importance but does everything with faith above reason, for this is man's purpose—to achieve *Dvekut* with the Creator—and he does everything to achieve it. As a result, he observes everything and makes great efforts wherever he can, and his sole intention is to achieve wholeness.

And he sees that after all the efforts and prevailing when he wishes to overcome the obstructers that stand against him, he is still standing on the outside, since *Dvekut* means equivalence of form, and he still did not move an inch from self-love, which is an opposite act from *Dvekut* with the Creator. In that state, he goes to pray to the Creator to enlighten him so he can raise Divinity from the dust. This means that the kingdom of heaven—as she appears to a man when he wants to work only for her, to disclose the glory of heaven in the world—tastes like dust in that state. And he sees that everyone is like him, disrespectful toward the glory of heaven because they cannot appreciate her importance. This is called "a prayer of many," meaning that he prays for the collective.

Two discernments must be made: 1) *Malchut* is called "many" because she contains all the souls. 2) A prayer of many, when he prays for the collective, means that the collective will be rewarded with the importance of Torah and *Mitzvot*, that they will be rewarded with 613 deposits that the upper light shines in each and every *Mitzva*.

It follows that at the end of the day, the two discernments of "many" become one. This means that he prays for the public to be rewarded, for the greatness and importance of *Malchut*—who is called "many"—to be seen, which occurs when everyone is rewarded with vessels of bestowal. At that time, the 613 *Mitzvot* will be revealed, as in "Listening to the voice of His word," at which time the 613 *Mitzvot* are called 613 deposits.

The above-mentioned means that a prayer of many is not rejected when one prays for the collective. The collective is called "the whole of Israel," and the collective is called "the Holy Divinity." And since the collective comprises several discernments, *The Zohar* says that the reason why the prayer of the collective is accepted is that there is wholeness in it. It writes, "And the Creator crowns Himself with that prayer because it rises in several manners, since one asks for *Hassadim*, another for *Gevurot*, and another for *Rachamim*."

We should understand why a prayer must consist of all of them. The rule is that all the discernments that we discern in spirituality are revelations that should be disclosed for the purpose of correcting the lower ones. It follows that the matter of three lines that we say—that perfection means that the three lines are revealed there—means that the Creator wishes to give to the lower one's abundance so they can use them and there will not be any flaw there. This is unlike how it was in the world of Nekudim where there was the breaking of the vessels because there was no correction of lines there, as the holy Ari says.

In other words, when the upper one gives some abundance to the lower one, he wishes that the abundance that the lower one receives will benefit the lower one. But if the *Kli* where the abundance should go is imperfect, all the bounty will go to the external ones. This is the issue with the breaking of the vessels—that the bounty went outside of *Kedusha* [holiness/sanctity]. For this reason, the bounty is not poured out to the lower ones, and it is considered that the prayer was not accepted.

And here comes the matter of correction of lines in the collective. It means that the many, which is *Malchut*, consists of the collective. In other words, there is a correction called "three lines" by which the abundance remains in *Kedusha* and does not go to the external ones. Hence, such a prayer can be accepted, meaning that she can be given abundance.

The Zohar interprets about that, "Because Jacob consisted of three lines," since Jacob is called "the middle line," which includes the right and the left. This is why the Creator wanted his prayer, for it is in utter completeness, comprising all three lines, like the prayer of many. In other words, there are no delays on the part of the Creator in imparting the abundance below, since His desire is to benefit His creations. However, it is as though He waits for the vessels of reception of the lower ones to be fit for reception.

Thus, when there is a proper *Kli* on the part of the lower one—meaning that the prayer is the *Kli* that is fit for reception—it must be on the condition that the abundance will not be lost, meaning that the abundance will not go to the external ones, to the *Klipot*. This is why there is a correction on the *Kli* of *Malchut* that she should transfer the bounty to the lower ones, and this correction is called, "correction of lines."

Now we will explain the rest of the words of *The Zohar*, which we asked about what it said. It writes, "And because it consists of several sides and manners, it becomes a crown and is placed on the head of the Righteous One who lives forever, meaning *Yesod*, who imparts all the salvations to the *Nukva*, and from her to the entire public."

We asked, "But do we not pray to *Ein Sof*?" Thus, what does it mean that the prayer of many becomes a crown specifically over *Yesod*? The thing is that the order of the imparting of the bounty that comes to *Malchut* is called *Yesod*. This means that all of the first nine *Sefirot* give their essence to *Yesod*, and he is called "all."

It follows that we always speak from the perspective of the giver and the receiver of the bounty, who is called *Malchut*. Thus, since the Emanator wishes to bestow and waits for the lower ones to give the proper *Kelim* for reception of the abundance, when the prayers go up—when the prayers are arranged in such a way that is fit for acceptance—they are called "a *Kli* for reception of the abundance." It follows that the *Kli* rose to the giver, and since the general giver is *Yesod*, it is considered that the prayer rose to *Yesod*.

Accordingly, this follows the rule, "The act below awakens the act above." It means that upon the awakening of the lower ones, who wish to draw near to the Creator and be rewarded with *Dvekut* with the Creator, they ask for the Creator's help. It is as our sages said, "He who comes to be purified is aided" (*Zohar*, Noah, p 23, and in the *Sulam* Commentary, Item 63). If a person comes to purify, he is aided with a holy soul and he is purified, sanctified, and he is called "holy."

Thus we see that when a man wishes to improve his actions, he causes a *Zivug* above, by which abundance is poured below. This is called raising MAN, meaning causing a deficiency above. But we should understand how we can say that the lower ones cause a deficiency above. And we should also know the meaning of "deficiency." It is known that a *Kli* is called "a deficiency," meaning that if there is a deficiency, there is room to place the filling there and fill the deficiency.

There are no delays in bestowing on the part of the Emanator, for His wish is to do good. The reason why we see that there is concealment of the light is because the lower ones have no *Kelim* to receive the abundance. Hence, when the lower one awakens to purify himself but lacks the strength, he asks the Creator to help him. Then this deficiency rises, so now the upper one has a *Kli* for giving him abundance, and this is called raising MAN.

It follows that when the prayer, which is a deficiency—what the lower one seeks for his deficiency to be satisfied—rises to the giver, and the giver is called *Yesod*, who bestows upon the assembly of Israel, called *Malchut*—it becomes a crown on His head. This is so because a crown means *Keter* [crown], indicating to the King's crown, meaning the importance of the King. This means that when there is disclosure of His light, everyone recognizes the importance of the Creator.

However, during the concealment of the face, Divinity—the place where the King appears—is called "exile" and "dust." This is so because no taste is discerned in spirituality, but the Torah and *Mitzvot* seem to taste like dust to them. And all this is because the lower ones do not have the *Kelim* to receive the abundance. And because of that, His glory is desecrated among the nations, meaning that before a person is rewarded with the discernment of being Jewish, he is similar to the nations, as it is known that each person is a small world and consists of all seventy nations, as well as of Israel.

But then, during the concealment, when the upper bounty cannot appear to the lower ones because they do not have the proper *Kelim*, whatever illumination they are given will go to the *Klipot*.

The Importance of a Prayer of Many

Because of that, the upper abundance had to be hidden from them. This is called, "The crown has fallen from our head," meaning that the importance of the Creator is desecrated.

But when a person comes to purify, when he wishes for the Creator to bring him closer and give him the vessel of bestowal by which to be rewarded with *Dvekut*, all the upper bounty that will be revealed will be in order to bestow. In other words, he wishes to be given strength from above to have the ability to always be in *Kedusha*, which is *Dvekut*.

Then a crown is made of his prayer, the King's crown, since then the importance of the King is recognized. And this is the meaning of what *The Zohar* says, that the prayer "Becomes a crown and is placed on the head of the Righteous One who lives forever, meaning *Yesod*, who imparts all the salvations to the *Nukva*, and from her to the entire public." This is so because through the prayer, the upper abundance is given to the lower ones, at which time the delight and pleasure are revealed. This is called "a crown," the King's crown, the importance of the King.

Concerning Help that Comes from Above

Article No. 8, Tav-Shin-Mem-Vav, 1985-86

Our sages said (*Sukkah*, 52), "Rabbi Shimon Ben Lakish said, 'Man's inclination overcomes him every day and seeks to to put him to death, as it is said, 'The wicked watches the righteous and seeks to put him to death.' If the Creator did not help him, he would not overcome it, as it is said, 'The Lord will not leave him in his hand or condemn when he is judged.'"

It is written in *The Zohar* (*Vayishlach*, item 10): "Rabbi Hizkiya said, 'Why then is it written, 'And Jacob was left alone'? Where were all the camps of messengers that you say surrounded him and came with him?' Rabbi Yehuda said, 'Since he brought danger upon himself by remaining alone at night and seeing the danger with his eye. Since they came to guard him only from an invisible danger, they parted him.' Then he said, 'I am not worthy of all the mercies and all the truth that You have shown Your servant.' These are the camps of holy messengers that surrounded him and now parted him for he had put himself in evident danger. Rabbi Yitzhak said, 'This is why the holy messengers parted him. They surrounded him and have now parted him because he put himself in evident danger.'"

Accordingly, there is a question: "When did the messengers part from him?" They parted when he put himself in danger. That is, first he put himself in danger, and then the messengers parted from him. It was said about this, "And Jacob was left alone." That is, when they saw, they parted. We should say—"as one comes in and one comes out."

We should understand why the messengers did not come to guard him in the face of evident danger. It is as though we say that they are unable to keep him from real and evident danger. If so, when can they keep him, when it is not evident? And if the danger is not evident, who knows that there is danger here that requires keeping? That is, to whom should it be evident, to the person? Or if the messengers see that there is evident danger, they leave although the person does not know?

To explain this in the work, we first have to know what is the danger there. Afterwards we will explain what is "evident danger." It is known that the work begins from the right line. "Right" means something that does not require correction. That which requires correction is called "left," as our sages said, "We place the *Tefillin* on the left, as it was said, 'And it shall be a token on your hand.'" *Yad-Koh* [your hand]. Our sages said, "The left pushes away and the right pulls closer."

For this reason, when a person is taught to walk in the ways of the work he begins from the right because the right there poses no danger to the spiritual life, since he can always add because the right line is called *Hesed* [mercy]. This means that a person appreciates the Torah and *Mitzvot* [commandments] and says that the Creator has been merciful with him by giving him a thought and desire to observe Torah and *Mitzvot*. And even the simplest intention, meaning that he does not know what thoughts to think during the performance of *Mitzvot* and while engaging in the Torah, but simply knows that he is observing the commandment of the Creator, who commanded us through Moses, this is enough to commit him to observe the Torah and *Mitzvot* according to his ability, and this is enough for him.

Therefore, upon each and every deed he does in Torah or engagement in *Mitzvot* he thanks and praises the Creator for being merciful with him, giving him a thought and desire to observe the Torah and *Mitzvot*. Hence, in each and every *Mitzva* [singular of *Mitzvot*] he thanks and praises the Creator for awarding him with a grip in Torah and *Mitzvot*, regardless of how much. Rather, whatever time he has when the body lets him learn he learns, and as much as he can he exerts to keep the *Mitzvot*. He is happy that he can keep the Creator's will, which was not given to other people like him, meaning that the Creator did not give them the understanding and desire to keep the commandments of the Creator.

One who walks on this line is still not regarded as walking on the right line because we see that when there is only one line and a person does not see another line, it is impossible to say that this is called the "right line." We can say "right" only when there is another line. Then I can say that one is "right" and one is "left."

Therefore, when guiding a person to walk in the path of the Creator, he is told, "Know that the Creator does not want anything from you but only that you will observe the Torah and *Mitzvot* in utter simplicity. This is enough for you. You do not need great intentions like the great righteous. Rather, the Creator requires man to observe Torah and *Mitzvot* according to man's understanding, each according to his quality, meaning with his innate talents. It is impossible to require man to engage in Torah and *Mitzvot* the same as those who are very capable or brave, but each according to the quality with which he was born.

It is as the holy ARI says, "There is not a day that is like another or a moment that is like the next, and there is no man who is like another, and the galbanum [type of incense] will correct what the frankincense [another type of incense] will not correct." That is, each person should correct his self and the quality with which he was born. One is not required to do more than the might of the mind and strength with which he was born.

It follows that one line is when he is told that he does not need to find deficiencies in his work. Rather, if he keeps Torah and *Mitzvot* in utter simplicity it is a great thing since he is observing the King's commandments. Man should calculate and appreciate his work in utter simplicity. That is, if he is praying and saying a verse or a blessing, whether the blessing on the *Mitzvot* or the blessing on pleasure, he should think then to whom he is speaking. Certainly, to the extent that he pictures before whom he stands he will feel differently while saying the blessings and while praying. Even if he does not know the meaning of the words, it is still very important because it does not matter what he says but to whom he is speaking!

Therefore, when observing some *Mitzva*, such as wearing *Tzitzit* [prayer shawl], he looks at the fact that there are some Jews in the world who were not given the opportunity to wear a *Tzitzit*, but he was given the privilege of keeping the commandment of the Creator. He should be very thankful to the Creator for this!

Therefore, to the extent of his simple mind, according to his belief in the greatness of the Creator and that it is a great privilege that he can do what the Creator wants, for these reasons he says the blessing, "Blessed are You, O Lord." That is, he blesses the Creator and thanks Him for rewarding him and giving him what He did not give other people.

Also, when he blesses on pleasures, he also thanks the Creator for rewarding him with believing that the Creator has provided him with the pleasures that people can enjoy. But other people do not have this reward of believing that the Creator has given them all the things with which people can enjoy. And also, a person says during the Eighteen Blesses in the morning, "Blessed are You, O Lord, for not making me a gentile," thanking the Creator for making him Israel.

We therefore see that we must thank the Creator for the smallest things we have in *Kedusha* [holiness/sanctity], and regard it as great. Although we cannot appreciate it, we should still believe it. I heard from Baal HaSulam who once said that as much as we understand the importance of Torah and *Mitzvot Lishma* [for Her sake], in truth, *Lo Lishma* [not for Her sake] is far more important than we appreciate *Lishma*.

This means that we cannot appreciate the contentment that the Creator derives from our desire to do His will. And each act that is done below, in this world, causes awakening above, in the upper world, as it is said in the holy *Zohar*, "An act below awakens an act above." Since man has not yet been rewarded with entering the King's palace and attaining the lights that are renewed by the works of the lower ones, we must believe that this is so.

That is, when a person comes to the synagogue and says there one verse for the Creator, to the Creator, this act is priceless because at that time a person does the deed, and there is nothing more to add in the action. This is a sign that there is wholeness in the act, and it is as important to the Creator as though he has kept it with all the intentions of the complete righteous. In other words, he is told that there are righteous who add only intentions to the actions, but there is nothing more to add to the act itself, as said above. It was said about the act, "Do not add and do not subtract."

However, he is told that the work of intentions is not for him, that it belongs only to a chosen few. Thus, if this is his wholeness, he puts all his energy into keeping what he received by upbringing. By this he knows that all he has to do is maintain the quantity. As for the quality, meaning to improve the intentions, namely the reasons that make him keep Torah and *Mitzvot*, he knows what he was told in his upbringing that in general he will have this world and the next world for his work in observing Torah and *Mitzvot*. This is called "one line" and not the "right line" because there is still no left here, of which we can say that this line is called "right," since there is no "right" without "left."

In this way there is no danger that he might lose the spiritual life of *Kedusha* [holiness/sanctity]. Rather, he is always advancing because his calculations are measured by the action, and each day he adds new actions. Therefore, he is always moving forward because he always sees that each day he adds new actions. For example, when he reaches the age of twenty, he knows that he has seven years of observing Torah and *Mitzvot*. And when he reaches the age of thirty, he has acquired seventeen years of Torah and *Mitzvot*.

It follows that this path is secured and there is no danger here to his spiritual life since he has a basis on which to look and measure his progress. Hence, this path is regarded as a safe path and there is no danger here to his spiritual life. That is, on this way he will not fall from his degree or ever despair because he sees that he is not succeeding in his work. Instead, he will always be at peace. His only regret in the work will be that it pains him that other people around him do not serve the Creator like him. This is his only regret in his work. But in himself he finds that he has much to be happy about, that thank God he has possessions of Torah and *Mitzvot*.

However, when he is told that there is another way, called "left line," which means that on this way a person sees that although he engages in Torah and *Mitzvot* he must still correct himself during the work, and that the correction is not on the action, but that he must correct the intention, meaning with what intention he does what he does, namely the reason that makes him keep Torah and *Mitzvot*, this is already regarded as a dangerous way.

This is so for two reasons: 1) He is told that it is true that it is impossible to work without reward. Rather, any person who does any work, whether great or small, needs fuel that will give him strength to work. If he is told that the reward is that he will bring contentment to the Creator, meaning that "His wish will be only to bestow upon the Creator," the body does not understand this reason as sufficient to give him strength to work, since it is against human nature because the substance of man is the will to receive in order to receive.

For this reason, when he works in one line, meaning that the basis of his work in this world is that he will receive reward in this world and in the next world, the body can understand that for himself, meaning to enjoy and be rewarded it is worthwhile to work.

However, when he is told that he must work with intentions and aim with each action he is doing to bring contentment to his Maker, he is left powerless in the work since then his body demands explanations: "How can I work and relinquish many things that the body can enjoy so the Creator will enjoy?" There is danger in this path that he might lose all of his spiritual life, even what he has acquired while engaging in one line.

2) The second reason for danger is that even if he prevails each time and wants to work in order to bestow, he sees that he cannot overcome in the intention, but always sees the opposite—that when he worked in one line he saw he was advancing. That is, if he spent ten years of work then he had ten years of Torah and *Mitzvot*, and if he has been engaging twenty years in Torah and *Mitzvot*, then he has a possession of twenty years.

But here, on the right line, it is to the contrary. If he has spent three years and cannot aim his work in order to bestow, then he is more shattered and broken since he has been working on the path of bestowal for three years, but he has nothing to show. That is, he has no possession even though he has put in three years of work. It is even more so if he put in five years and so forth. Therefore, the longer he has exerted in the work, the more he sees that he is worse.

But Baal HaSulam said that in truth, on the one hand we can say that a person did advance toward the truth in recognizing the evil. Before he began the work, he thought he would be able to overcome his evil. It is as our sages said (*Sukkah*, 52), "To the wicked, the evil inclination seems like a hairsbreadth, and to the righteous like a high mountain."

But on the other hand a person needs to see the truth as it is, meaning that by this his evil did not move an inch, and this might put him in danger of despairing because he would say that *Lo Lishma* [not for Her sake] is worthless, since the essence of the work is to bring contentment to the Creator, and he sees that he will not be able to overcome. It turns out that by walking on the left line he might, God forbid, be repelled completely from spiritual life, for he has already flawed the *Lo Lishma*. It turns out that he is empty both ways and has no grip on the life of *Kedusha*.

For this reason, people are guided by only one line. If they wake up by themselves and have a drive of their own to start searching for the truth, if they are guided to walk by this way forever or only when in the beginning of the work, they are not shown the left line—that they must correct themselves to do all their works for the Creator.

This is as Maimonides says (end of *Hilchot Teshuva*), "Sages said, 'One should always engage in Torah, even *Lo Lishma*, since from *Lo Lishma* he comes to *Lishma*. Therefore, when teaching children, women, and the uneducated, they are taught to work out of fear and to receive reward. Until they gain knowledge and acquire much wisdom, they are told that secret bit-by-bit and are accustomed to this matter with ease until they attain Him and know Him from love.'"

Therefore, we must walk on the right line, as well as on the left line, means that even if he knows that there is a truth called *Lishma*, still, the way he walked in it when he had only one line, now that line has received a new name and it is called "right line." However, what does it add to us that now we call the one line, "right line"? The explanation is that now there is an intention on the right line. That is, by changing the name, "one line" to "right line," a special intent is attached to this name, which did not exist when it was called "one line." This is why it is forbidden to cancel the left line and walk on the right line, since there is no right without left. Thus, we must say that when he was walking in one line, he did not know if there is another way. But now that there is the left line opposite it, the one line is called "right line."

This means that the wholeness he is receiving now is not because he is walking without deficiencies but because he feels whole and happy with his work as before he went into working in the left line, but for a different reason. Here, in the right line, the wholeness is because he sees that he is a simple person and knows that there is a true path, meaning that you must engage for the sake of the Creator, but he sees that he is far from it. That is, his body does not allow him to annul himself completely before the Creator, that his only direction in life will be to bestow. And yet, he sees that the Creator did give him strength to have some contact with holiness, and others do not have this power. It follows that he thanks and praises the Creator for this. It follows that in such a state he is in wholeness.

However, now that he has begun to work on the left line and understood that the work of bestowal is the main thing, it is difficult for him to be content with less. If he should work, he should work in order to achieve wholeness. But to make efforts to be rewarded with only a touch on the holy work, for this the body has no fuel. This is called, as it is written, "Wherever there is a deficiency in *Kedusha*, there is grip for the *Klipot* [shells/peels]." That is, the *Klipot* make him think, "Should you work so hard for such a small reward, meaning to have such a small grip in *Kedusha*?"

It follows that the *Klipot* have the strength to remove him from the *Kedusha* to a great extent. That is, he is not told that it is not worthwhile to exert for *Kedusha*. "*Kedusha*, meaning serving the King, is certainly a great thing, but you see for yourself that you haven't the strength for it." Therefore, at that time awakens the danger that he will fall from the work completely because now the body has a grip in his work since man himself sees his deficiencies in the work.

But in the work on one line he knew that this was his wholeness because he was instructed from the beginning that *Lishma* belongs to great people who were born with great natural talents and good qualities, and with great powers to overcome their bodies. That is, they control themselves and can carry out what they like, and no one can stop them.

As for you, what's required of you is only according to your ability. That is, do what you can, and by that you have done your duty, since the Torah was not given to the ministering angels but to all the people, each according to his ability.

However, once he begins to walk on the left line he feels that he, too, should achieve *Dvekut* [adhesion] with the Creator and work in order to bestow, and henceforth he will not be able to feel wholeness in the work of the right line because the left will be obstructing him. Here begins the work of faith above reason. That is, he must believe that the work of *Kedusha* is very important work. Therefore, he does not mind if he is rewarded with true wholeness or the wholeness he deserves. That is, he still does not have the great privilege of doing the holy work completely, but to a very small extent. But he regards it as a great fortune, whose value he cannot even measure.

It follows that in this work, when he walks on this line, he appreciates the *Kedusha* so it constantly increases its importance. This is so because he should believe in its greatness above reason, although he still does not actually feel it. He must tell himself: "The reason I must believe above reason in the importance of Torah and *Mitzvot* is that I am still not worthy of feeling its importance and greatness, as it is known that as long as one is still immersed in self-love, he is unfit to feel the delight and pleasure that is clothed in them. But in truth, when I am worthy, I will see it in actual fact."

It therefore follows that the reason he must believe above reason is not because of a deficiency in the light that is clothed in Torah and *Mitzvot*. Rather, the lack is in the *Kli* [vessel] of the lower one, which is still unfit for it. But the Creator knows when I am fit, and will certainly let me feel the taste of Torah and *Mitzvot*." It follows that we should believe above reason not because we cannot feel the good in it, since the light is concealed and we cannot attain it. If that were so then what does it mean, "For they are our lives," which is said about the Torah and *Mitzvot*? Rather, he should believe above reason as long as he has not corrected his vessels of reception. But when he completes his correction, the delight and pleasure will spread in everything holy in which he engages.

Therefore, if he walks on the right line and believes above reason in its importance, to the extent of importance that he attributes to the Torah and *Mitzvot* he can appreciate even the smallest thing, meaning even a touch, meaning even *Lo Lishma* of *Lo Lishma* can also delight him because with this act he is observing the commandment of the Creator.

However, afterwards he must shift to the left line, meaning criticize the work—whether the work he is doing is a way to achieve *Dvekut* with the Creator, as our sages said, "I have created the evil inclination, I have created the Torah as a spice," if he is really going toward this purpose. This is regarded as putting himself in danger. When he is on the left line, his work is mainly to pray, meaning to cry out to the Creator to help him from above, as our sages said, "He who comes to purify is aided."

By this we can interpret the meaning of the angels who surrounded Jacob, as mentioned in the words of the holy *Zohar*, that the angels came to guard him, meaning that it is help that comes from above to assist him so he can continue his way. However, help comes from above when a person has already begun the work and stands midway and cries out for help. But before he has begun the work he is not given assistance.

Therefore, when Jacob has begun the work and has put himself in danger and asked the Creator to help him, the angels were sent to keep him so he could win the war into which he has already entered. But when he has completed the work that he began and received help from the angels, and wanted to begin a new work, called "small cans," and the beginning of the work is in darkness, called "night," this is called "evident danger," since a dark place, called "left line," is dangerous, then he should start alone. Afterward, when he sees that he cannot, he begins to ask the Creator to help, and then he will receive help from above.

Concerning the Hanukkah Candle

Article No. 9, Tav-Shin-Mem-Vav, 1985-86

It is written in *Masechet Shabbat* (23b): "Raba said, 'Clearly, between 'a candle for his house' and a 'Hanukkah candle,' a candle for his house precedes because of domestic peace." RASHI interprets that "candle of his house" refers to Shabbat [Sabbath], and he is poor and cannot afford to buy oil for two candles. As for domestic peace, it is as is said below, "My soul has been devoid of peace." This is the lighting of the candles on Shabbat, when his household regret sitting in the dark.

However, a Hanukkah candle is not for domestic peace because it is forbidden to use its light, as we say after lighting Hanukkah candles, "These candles are holy; we have no permission to use them but only to see them."

We should understand the following: 1) He explains that a Shabbat candle precedes a Hanukkah candle because of domestic peace. This requires explanation. Is this a good enough reason to cancel the *Mitzva* [commandment] of Hanukkah candles, which is so important because of the sanctity in them, to the point where our sages said that it is forbidden to use their light, as we say, "These candles are holy; we have no permission to use them but only to see them"? Do we cancel this *Mitzva* because of domestic peace, which is a corporeal matter? 2) We need to understand the connection between a Shabbat candle and domestic peace, which we learn from the verse, "My soul has been devoid of peace," which is the lighting of candles on Shabbat.

To understand the above we must first explain the three above matters: 1) What is Shabbat? 2) What is domestic peace? 3) What is Hanukkah?

Our sages said that Shabbat is a similitude of the next world (*Berachot*, 57). Also, it is written in the Shabbat Evening Prayer: "You have sanctified the seventh day for Your name, the purpose of the creation of heaven and earth." "Purpose" means that this is the purpose for which Heaven and Earth were created.

Also, it is known that the purpose of creation is to do good to His creations, meaning for the creatures to receive delight and pleasure, and this is called "the purpose of creation." What precedes the purpose is the time of work. This brings up the question, "If the purpose is to do good, why this work?"

The answer is that in order to avoid the bread of shame we were given work, which is called the "correction of creation." This means that through this correction we will be able to receive the delight and pleasure because we will already have equivalence of form with the Creator in the sense that the creatures wish to bestow upon the Creator as the Creator wishes to bestow upon the creatures. It turns out that working in order to bestow eliminates the bread of shame.

According to this, the work that we were given refers to the correction of creation and not to the purpose because the purpose is to enjoy and not to work. Thus, our need for correction does not refer to the pleasure, since the Creator gives it, as it is the purpose. But in order to receive the complete delight and pleasure—and complete means that we can receive the delight without feeling unpleasantness—we were given work because the work is that we have to change the *Kelim* [vessels] we have received by nature, and obtain different *Kelim*, called "vessels of bestowal." When we receive the delight and pleasure in vessels of bestowal, there is no place for unpleasantness upon receiving the abundance.

Two states explain to us the two discernments we described concerning achieving the complete purpose of creation: 1) The order of correction of creation that we work in Torah and *Mitzvot* [commandments] in order to bestow is regarded as using vessels of bestowal. This means that since there are deeds and there are intentions, in that state we use acts of bestowal, regarded as Torah and *Mitzvot*. These acts are regarded as engaging in the form of, "As He is merciful, so you are merciful."

That is, man wants to bestow upon the Creator as the Creator wants to bestow upon the creatures. Therefore, if he acts like the Creator, meaning follows His ways, then the person wants the Creator to pay him for his work for the created beings. However, here there is also the work of the intention, which is to aim that the intention will be similar to the action because sometimes, although the act is giving, the aim is otherwise. That is, the reason he gives is in order to subsequently receive reward. This is called *Lo Lishma* [not for Her sake].

For this reason if a person wants to perform an act of giving there is a lot of work. And the reason that compels him to engage in giving is that he has a reason that causes him to give and not receive, meaning that usually, when we love someone a desire awakens in the heart to give to the loved one, since this expresses our love for that person.

Alternatively, an important person also awakens in our hearts to disclose love for him by giving him a gift. This is called "His mouth and heart are the same," meaning that the act and the intention are the same and his heart does not harbor a different intent from the act of giving because the reason is the intention to bestow. This is called *Lishma* [for Her sake].

It is explained that in the second state, which is the purpose of creation, we can use the vessels of reception. This means that we engage in reception of pleasures but the reason we want to receive pleasure is not to satisfy our wishes, that we crave pleasures and this is why we now want to enjoy. Rather, there is a completely different reason here—the opposite of our action.

We crave to bestow upon the Creator, and for ourselves, we do not want to receive into our will to receive because it would separate us from the Creator. However, what can we give to the Creator so He will enjoy it? What can we say, so to speak, that He needs? There is only one thing we can say: Since He has created creation in order to delight His creatures, we want to receive the delight and pleasure because we want to satisfy His wish, which is to do good.

Now we can explain the question, "What is Hanukkah?" As we explained the first state, it is the work of correction of creation, which is to obtain the vessels of bestowal, with which we can then achieve the purpose of creation. We can call this "spirituality" because we do not want to do anything for ourselves, but only for the Creator, as our sages said, "An offering, meaning a burnt offering, is all for the Creator, completely spiritual."

The miracle of Hanukkah was about spirituality, as we say (in the blessing "On the Miracles"), "When the wicked kingdom of Greece stood over Your people Israel to make them forget Your law and move them from the laws of Your will, You, with your many mercies, stood up for them at the time of their plight."

According to what we explained, "spirituality" means using vessels of bestowal. The domination of the Greeks is expressed in forbidding anything that has to do with vessels of bestowal because there was control over the work of Torah and *Mitzvot* there, as well.

This was on the outside. It is far more so in the thought—they would govern the thought so they would be unable to aim anything for the Creator. Rather, they wanted the people of Israel to be immersed in self-love, by which they will be separated from the Creator. All the thoughts of the *Sitra Achra* [Other Side] are only about removing them from the Creator, and remoteness and separation come only by disparity of form, known as "self-love."

Concerning the Hanukkah Candle

Baal HaSulam said about what our sages asked (*Shabbat*, 21b), "What is Hanukkah?" He explained that the answer is *Hanu* [parked] *Koh* [here/thus far], meaning that they parked here. This means that *Chaf-Hey* [*Koh*/25th] of *Kislev* [the date when Hanukkah begins] was not the end of the war, but only a pause. It is like an army that wants to start a new, major assault, so it lets the soldiers rest and regain their strength so they can continue the war. He said that there are fools who think that they received the order not to go forward into enemy territory but to rest because they have finished the war and there is no need to defeat the enemy anymore.

It turns out that Hanukkah is still not the completion of the goal, but only the correction of creation. It completes the vessels of bestowal, meaning acts of bestowal, and this is why it is forbidden to use the light of Hanukkah, since using is an act of reception, and the miracle was only on acts of giving—that they can do them and aim to bestow, which is called *Lishma*.

The miracle was that they emerged from the domination of the Greeks and could go with faith above reason. But the *Klipa* [shell/peel] of the Greeks was governing Israel so as not to do anything unless he knows why and what purpose this work will bring him, and especially to aim everything above reason.

According to what we explained, it follows that although a Hanukkah candle implies a spiritual miracle, which is that the people of Israel were liberated from the dominion of the Greeks, it was only half a thing. That is, only the vessels of bestowal were corrected by the miracle of Hanukkah, and this is regarded as correction of creation, but still not the purpose of creation.

But Shabbat, which is a similitude of the next world, is regarded as the purpose of heaven and earth, regarded as the "purpose of creation," meaning the completion of the final purpose. That is, a likeness of what will appear at the end of correction illuminates on Shabbat.

Therefore, Shabbat is the time for reception of pleasure, meaning that we are using vessels of reception and only need to aim in order to bestow. This is regarded as all the people in the world having to achieve this degree, as it is written, "For no outcast shall be outcast from Him." Rather, everyone will achieve the goal in full, meaning to receive, but in order to bestow.

Now we will explain what we asked about the connection between Shabbat and domestic peace. It is known that "house" is called *Malchut*, who is the receiver of the upper abundance in vessels of reception in order to bestow. However, *Malchut* has many names, and the name "house" indicates wholeness, as it is written in the *Sulam* (Ladder commentary on *The Zohar*, Noah, p 88, item 249): "You should know that when a person is in full wholeness, he is regarded as dwelling in the house. The word 'house' implies *Nukva de ZA*, who illuminates in *Mochin de GAR*, as it is written, 'A house shall be built with wisdom.' Therefore, those who receive from her are regarded as dwelling in the house. However, when a person needs corrections because he is incomplete, he needs keeping so the outer ones do not grip him and make him sin. Therefore, he must come out of the house because he is forbidden to receive these high *Mochin* for fear that the outer ones will suck from him. He must go out to the path of the Creator, meaning receive the corrections he needs. At that time he is permitted to receive *Mochin* from the *Zivug* of ZA and Leah, for because they are *Ohr Hassadim* that is covered in *Hochma*, there is no suckling from them to the outer ones. These *Mochin* are called 'hostel' because they are intended for travelers. Therefore, although Noah was righteous and wholehearted, he compares him to a traveling guest."

Thus, we see that we should make two discernments in the order of the work: 1) a state called "house," 2) a state called "traveling guest." When a person is still incomplete, he must come out and be in a state of traveling guest, which is the path of the Creator, in order to receive corrections, by which he will achieve wholeness. This is why these people are called "traveling guests," for they are still in the middle of the way and have not achieved the goal they should achieve.

Although they are righteous, like Noah, who was righteous and wholehearted, he was still deficient because he corrected only the vessels of bestowal, called "spiritual vessels." As mentioned above, this is called the "correction of creation," since he can already bestow in order to bestow, which his called *Lishma*.

By this we understand what the *Hanu-Koh* [Hanukkah] candle comes to imply—it is only a pause and not the end of the work. For this reason, it is forbidden to use the light of the Hanukkah candle because the miracle was on spiritual vessels, and vessels of bestowal cannot be used so as to enjoy the light. This is why they are only to be seen.

But a Shabbat candle—where Shabbat is regarded as "the purpose of heaven and earth," which is a similitude of the next world—is called the "purpose of creation," to do good to His creations, that they will receive delight and pleasure. Hence, this light is received in vessels of reception, called "receiving in order to bestow." That is, they are using the vessels of reception.

This is called a "house," as in "A house shall be built with wisdom," where *Malchut* is the root of the souls, called "assembly of Israel," and receives abundance for the souls. When the lower ones are fit for reception of *Ohr Hochma* [Light of Wisdom], it is called *Mochin* [light/pleasure] *de Shabbat*, meaning *Mochin de Hochma*, and *Mochin de Hochma* is the light of the purpose of creation. It follows that Hanukkah candle and Shabbat candle imply two dissimilar discernments.

Now we will explain what we asked about the connection between domestic peace and Shabbat, for which our sages said that it precedes the Hanukkah candle. The *Sefira* [singular of *Sefirot*] *Yesod* is called "domestic peace" because it bestows upon *Malchut*, since *Malchut* is the root of the souls. When *Malchut* is as a dot, meaning that it illuminates only as a tiny dot, the souls do not have the abundance they need. This is called "*Shechina* [Divinity] in exile." At that time the *Klipot* [shells/peels] prevail and wish to control matters of sanctity, and there is a lot of work for the lower ones. This created the division between *Kedusha* [holiness/sanctity] and *Tuma'a* [impurity].

Upon the arrival of *Yesod de Gadlut* [adulthood/greatness], it imparts the upper abundance to *Malchut*, meaning imparts upon her the light of *Hochma*. At that time domestic peace is made, as it is written, "When a man's ways please the Lord, He makes even his enemies be at peace with him." This is why *Yesod* is called "peace," since it makes domestic peace, when the powers of *Klipa* are cancelled, as it is written, "When Shabbat begins, it becomes unique and separates from the *Sitra Achra*, and all are crowned with new souls" (*Kegavna* [a prayer] on Shabbat Eve).

It follows that when the "house," which is *Malchut*, receives the abundance of Shabbat, peace is made, and then all the judgments are removed from her. This is why the Shabbat candle implies the abundance of the end of correction, while the Hanukkah candle indicates the light attained in the middle of the work, which is in order to be able to continue and complete the work. This is why a Shabbat candle is called "domestic peace," after the abundance that comes from *Yesod* to *Malchut*.

Concerning Prayer

Article No. 10, Tav-Shin-Mem-Vav, 1985-86

Our sages said in *Masechet Taanit* (p 2): "To love the Lord your God and to serve Him, this is a prayer. You say, 'This is prayer,' or is it only work?' We should say, 'with all your hearts.' Which is work in the heart? It is prayer."

We should understand why prayer is regarded as work. Is it work to pray to the Creator to grant our wishes and requests? And if our sages said so then they want to imply to us that there is a special meaning to the prayer—that it is work and not simply a prayer. Thus, what is the issue to which our sages imply?

Indeed, it cannot be said that a person prays and asks to be given something if he has no desire for it. Only when a person feels he lacks something does he go and ask for that filling, related to the lack, from the one who can fulfill it, since one asks only from one who has what he needs, and he also knows that he wants to give and to do good to others.

Accordingly, when a person comes to pray and ask the Creator to satisfy his need, his prayer should be clear. That is, he should clearly know what he needs. That is, when he comes to ask from the Creator he should picture himself speaking to the King, and the King can make him the happiest man in the world at once because nothing is missing in the King's house. Thus, first one must carefully examine before the prayer so he knows what he really needs, that if the King fulfills his lack he will not need anything more and will be the most complete man in the world.

According to what we learned—that the purpose of creation is to do good to His creations—it follows that on the part of the Creator there are no hindrances on bestowing delight and pleasure upon the creatures. This means that the reason why the Creator created in the creatures a lack, called "desire to receive," was in order to satisfy the deficiency. As we explained, a lack is called torment and affliction if he cannot satisfy his need.

Therefore, all the lack that was created was with the intention to feel pleasure through it, since the lack is included in the intention to do good. This follows the rule that the craving for something gives the pleasure from satisfying it. It is known that even when we give to a person a meal fit for kings, if he has no desire for the meal he cannot enjoy it.

Therefore, when a person feels a lack and has no satisfaction for it, he comes to ask the Creator to grant him his wishes. In general, a person asks only for delight and pleasure. As we learned, on the part of the Creator, a person does not need to pray that the Creator will give him delight and pleasure because His wish is to do good to His creations. Therefore, no one should be asked for anything if the Giver wishes to give.

It follows that before one goes to ask of the Creator to grant his wishes, he should first examine what he needs. This is what he should ask of the Creator. It seems as though the Creator does not give to a person without a person asking first. This means that because asking is not included in the purpose of creation, which is to do good to His creations, but is something that emerged later, from the creature, for this reason the creature must ask the Creator to give him. But we should not ask that the Creator will want to give delight and pleasure because this is His wish, as said above, that His wish is to give delight and pleasure to the lower ones.

However, we should know that since there was the matter of the *Tzimtzum* [restriction], called "correction of creation," as it is known that it is so that the Creator's gift will not be unpleasantness, called "bread of shame." And since we attribute this correction to the lower one, called *Malchut de Ein Sof*, who is called "the *Kli* [vessel] that received the upper light," and once this receiver received the abundance, a craving for equivalence of form awakened. This is why she did the *Tzimtzum*.

He says in *The Study of the Ten Sefirot* (p 9, "Inner Reflection"): "The upper light does not stop illuminating to the creatures for even a minute, and the whole matter of *Tzimtzum* and *Histalkut* [departure] of light that are mentioned here relate only to the impression and reception of the *Kli*, meaning the middle point. This means that although the upper light does not stop illuminating, the *Kli* still does not receive any of its illumination because it diminished itself."

As said above, not receiving in order to receive does not relate to the purpose of creation. Rather, it is attributed to the correction of creation. It is an act of the lower one who strives for equivalence of form. It follows that the lower ones cannot receive delight and pleasure although the upper one wants to give because they need vessels of bestowal, and this pertains to the receiver and not to the giver, as we said, that the lower one, called *Malchut de Ein Sof*, made the *Tzimtzum*. This is why this *Kli* relates to the lower one, meaning that the lower one will want to receive only if it can aim in order to bestow.

For this reason, when a person comes to pray to the Creator to give him what he needs, we should say that he actually needs something that does not come from the purpose of creation. Rather, what he needs is something that comes from the lower ones. That is, *Malchut*, who is called the "lower one" because she receives abundance from the upper one, made a new *Kli* to receive abundance only in this *Kli* called "vessel of bestowal." Therefore, all he should pray for is that the Creator will give him this *Kli* because this is all he needs.

However, here there is room for scrutiny. If the lower one must make this *Kli* because it pertains to the lower one, as we said above that *Malchut* did it, then why does a person not make this *Kli* by himself, but must ask the Creator to give him this *Kli*? Moreover, we say about this *Kli* that the lower one must make it. We tell him that this is all he needs to ask from the Creator, but if this pertains to man's work then why does he need to ask the Creator?

The matter is clarified more in the words of our sages who said (*Berachot* 33b), "Rabbi Hanina said, 'Everything is in the hands of the Creator except for fear of the Creator, as it was said, 'And now, Israel, what does the Lord your God ask of you but fear?'"

RASHI interprets "Everything is in the hands of the Creator" as follows, "Righteous and wicked do not come by heaven. He has given this to man and has placed before him two ways, and he must choose fear of heaven."

The matter of fear is explained in the *Sulam* [Ladder commentary on *The Zohar*] ("Introduction of the Book of Zohar," item 203): "Indeed, both the first fear and the second fear are not for his own benefit, but only out of fear that he will lessen bringing contentment to his Maker." According to the above, it means that fear is that person must aim everything he does to be in order to bestow contentment upon the Creator.

We asked, if this is so, and bestowal is something that man must do, why did we say that he should ask this from the Creator, since it was said, "Everything is in the hands of the Creator except for fear of the Creator"? We should know that man cannot go against the nature with which he was created. Since the Creator created man with a nature of wanting to receive, as we said that it is impossible to enjoy the pleasures without a desire for the pleasure, and we learned that the essence of creation, regarded as "existence from absence," is the will to receive, hence when one wants to do something in order to bestow it is considered going against nature. This is why we cannot change our nature. Accordingly, if man cannot change nature, why did our sages say, "Everything is in the hands of the Creator except for fear of the Creator?" This implies that man does have the strength to change it.

We can interpret that there are two things here: 1) a desire, regarded as only a potential, that he wants to bestow; 2) that he also has the ability to carry out his thought in actual fact.

Therefore, we should interpret that the demand from man to choose to walk in ways of bestowal, he should know that this is the *Kli* to receive the purpose of creation—to receive the delight and pleasure—and if he hasn't these *Kelim* he will remain in darkness without light. Once he knows this in complete certainty and begins to intend to carry out acts of bestowal, he sees that he cannot go against nature.

Here comes the time of prayer, and not before, since there is no such thing as asking for urgent help—asking for vessels of bestowal, which are *Kelim* in which he can receive life and without which he is regarded as dead, as our sages said, "the wicked in their lives are called 'dead.'" This is because by nature, man asks for help only when he cannot obtain what he wants by himself, since prior to this there is the matter of shame, as our sages said about the verse, "Chrome gorges for the sons of men." "When man needs people, his face changes to be as chrome. What is chrome? There is a bird in the cities near the sea, whose name is Chrome. When the sun shines on it, it turns into several colors" (*Berachot*, p 6).

It is known that the corporeal nature that we were given is such that through it we learn spiritual matters. Therefore, before one knows that he cannot obtain the vessels of bestowal by himself, he does not ask the Creator to give them to him. It follows that he does not have a real desire for the Creator to answer his prayer.

For this reason, one must work to obtain the vessels of bestowal by himself, and after all the work that he has put into it without obtaining it begins the real prayer from the bottom of the heart. At that time he can receive for help from above, as our sages said, "He who comes to purify is aided."

But since this prayer is against nature, since man was created with a desire to receive, which is self-love, how can he pray to the Creator to give him the force of bestowal while all the organs oppose this desire? This is why this work is called "prayer," meaning he must make great efforts to be able to pray to the Creator to give him the force of bestowal and annul man's force of reception.

This is why our sages said, "'And you shall work' is prayer, the work in the heart." By this we will understand why they refer to prayer as "work in the heart." It is because one must work a lot on himself to cancel self-love and assume the work of obtaining vessels of bestowal. It follows that on the desire to have vessels of bestowal he must work with himself to want to pray, to be given the force of bestowal.

A Real Prayer Is over a Real Deficiency

Article No. 11, Tav-Shin-Mem-Vav, 1985-86

The writing says, "These are the names of the sons of Israel who came to Egypt. ...And a new king arose over Egypt, who did not know Joseph. ...And the Egyptians compelled the sons of Israel to labor rigorously ... And it came to pass that the sons of Israel sighed because of the work, and they cried out, and their cry because of the work went up to God ... and God heard their groaning."

We should understand why it is written, "and their cry because of the work went up to God." Did they not have greater torments in Egypt? Here it seems that their cry, meaning their torments, were only from the work. It is also written, "And God heard their groaning," meaning that hearing the prayer was over their groaning, which is only about the work.

We shall interpret this according to our way. It is known that before a person begins to work in order to bestow, but for reasons that are written in the holy *Zohar* ("Introduction of the Book of Zohar," items 190-191), that there are two reasons for engaging in Torah and *Mitzvot* [commandments]: 1) to have the pleasures of this world. If he does not observe the Torah and *Mitzvot* he is afraid that the Creator will punish him. 2) To have the pleasures of the next world. His fear that he may not be given causes him to observe Torah and *Mitzvot*.

When the reason that compels him to observe Torah and *Mitzvot* is his own benefit, the body does not resist so much because to the extent that he believes in reward and punishment he can work and feel that each day he is adding more. And this is the truth, that each day of performing *Mitzvot* and engaging in the Torah joins the day before, and so he adds to his possessions of keeping Torah and *Mitzvot*.

The reason is that his intention is primarily the reward, and he is not thinking about the intention, meaning that his aim will be to bestow. Rather, he believes in reward and punishment, and that he will be rewarded for what he is doing. Therefore, his aim is only to do perform proper actions in every detail. Otherwise, if the actions are improper, it is certain that his work will not be accepted so as to reward him for them. When he sees that the work he is doing is fine, he has nothing more to worry about.

For this reason, his concern is only with the quantity, meaning that he should try to do more good deeds. If he is a wise disciple then he knows he should delve deeper into his learning and be more meticulous in the *Mitzvot* he is performing—to keep them according to the law according to everyone's view. He always tries to be rigorous with judgments that are usually treated more lightly, while he tries to be more rigorous, but he has no other worries.

It follows that such people—whose reason for observing Torah and *Mitzvot* and assuming the burden of the kingdom of heaven is to be rewarded in this world and in the next world—do not need the Creator to have the strength to engage in Torah and *Mitzvot*, since to the extent of their faith in reward and punishment the body allows them to keep, each according to his degree.

This is not so with people who want to do the holy work in order to bestow without any reward, and want to observe Torah and *Mitzvot* because of the greatness of the Creator, and it is a great privilege for them to be allowed to serve the King, as it is written in the above-mentioned holy *Zohar*: "Fear, which is the first, is that one should fear one's Master because He is great and ruling, the essence and the root."

He interprets there, in the *Sulam* [Ladder commentary on *The Zohar*], that there are three manners to fear of the Creator: 1) fear of punishments in this world, 2) fearing punishments of Hell, as well. Those two are not real fear because he is not keeping the fear because of the commandment of the Creator, but for his own sake. It follows that his personal benefit is the root, and fear is the branch and results from his own benefit. But fear that is the essence is that he will fear the Creator because He is great and rules over everything.

It follows that the greatness of the Creator is the reason that compels him to observe Torah and *Mitzvot*. This is regarded as his desire being only to bestow upon the Creator, called "bestowing contentment upon his Maker and not for his own benefit."

Here begins the exile, meaning that he is not permitted to aim his work to be in order not to receive reward, since it is against nature. And although one can force oneself although the body disagrees, just as one can practice abstention although it is against nature, but this pertains to actions. That is, to do things against the body's will he can go above reason, called "against the body's will."

However, he cannot go against his feeling and intellect, meaning to say that he feels otherwise than he does. For example, if a person is cold or hot, he cannot say that his feeling is untrue, and force himself to say that he understands otherwise than what his mind does, or that he feels otherwise than what he is feeling. His only option is to say what he sees.

It follows that when one wants to keep Torah and *Mitzvot* in order to bestow upon the Creator, it is the nature of the body not to move at all unless it sees that it will have some reward. Thus, he has no way to work for the Creator and not for his own benefit.

Here begins the exile, meaning the torments that as much as he works he sees no progress. For example, if he is twenty, he can say that he has acquired possessions of twenty years of engagement in Torah and *Mitzvot*. On the other hand, he can say that he has been keeping Torah and *Mitzvot* for twenty years but has not achieved the ability to do anything in order to bestow, rather everything is built on the basis of self-love.

It follows that all the torments and pains he suffers are because he cannot work for the Creator. He wants to work in order to bestow, but the body is enslaved to the *Klipot* [shells/peels] and does not let him have this aim. At that time he cries out to the Creator to help him because he sees that he is in exile among the *Klipot*, they govern him, and he sees no way that he will be able to emerge from their control.

It follows that at that time his prayer is regarded as a real prayer because he cannot come out from this exile, as it is written, "And He brought Israel out from their midst, for His mercy is forever." Since this is against nature, only the Creator can deliver Israel from this exile. But since it is known that there is no light without a *Kli* [vessel], meaning that there is no filling without a lack, and the lack is the *Kli* that receives the filling, for this reason, before one enters exile, meaning if he does not see that he cannot deliver himself from the exile by himself, it cannot be said that he should be brought out. This is so because although he cries, "Get me out of the state I am in," it is not a real prayer because how does he know that he cannot come out by himself?

Rather, this can be said precisely when he feels the exile, meaning that he will pray from the bottom of the heart. There are two conditions for praying from the bottom of the heart: 1) His work must be against nature. That is, he wants to do everything only to bestow, and wants to exit self-love. At that time it can be said that he has a lack. 2) He begins to exit self-love by himself and exerts in it, but cannot move an inch from his state. At that time he becomes needy of the Creator's help and his prayer is real because he sees that he cannot do anything by himself. Then, when he cries out to the Creator to help him, he knows this from the work, as it is written, "And the sons of Israel sighed because of the work." This means that by working and wanting to achieve the degree of being able to bestow upon the Creator, they saw that they could not emerge from their nature so they prayed from the bottom of the heart.

By this we will understand what we asked about the verse, "and their cry because of the work went up to God." This means that the worst torments, over which was all their crying out, was only over the work, and not over other things. Rather, it means that they were crying out over their situation—that they could not emerge from self-love and work for the Creator. This was their exile, which tormented them—that they saw that they were under their control.

It follows that in the exile in Egypt they obtained *Kelim*, meaning a desire that the Creator will help them emerge from the exile, as we said above that there is no light without a *Kli*, for only when we pray a real prayer, when one sees that he cannot be saved, and only the Creator can help him, this is considered a real prayer.

What Is the Main Deficiency for which One Should Pray?

Article No. 12, Tav-Shin-Mem-Vav, 1985-86

It is known that Creation is called "deficiency." This is why it is called "existence from absence." Man was created full of deficiencies. Therefore, for man to succeed in the work when he is going to satisfy his deficiencies he must first know what is the main deficiency to which he should give preference over all his deficiencies. Since there are spiritual deficiencies and corporeal deficiencies we must first clarify which we defined as "spiritual" and which we defined as "corporeal."

In the essay, "Preface to the Wisdom of Kabbalah" (item 11) it is written, "Now you can understand the real difference between spirituality and corporeality: anything that contains a complete desire to receive, in all its *Behinot* [discernments], which is *Behina Dalet*, is considered 'corporeal.' This is what exists in all the elements of reality before us in this world. Conversely, anything above this great measure of desire to receive is considered 'spirituality.'"

What Is the Main Deficiency for which One Should Pray?

It follows that corporeality means that which relates to satisfying our will to receive. Thus, everything that one does for one's own benefit is called "corporeality," and what he does to benefit the Creator is called "spirituality."

It is therefore clear that we do not need to create the *Kli* [vessel] for corporeality, meaning the desire to satisfy the self-gratification, a *Kli* of wanting to receive in order to receive, since the Creator gave us such *Kelim* [vessels] at the onset of Creation, as it is known that the thought of creation, called "His desire to do good to His creations," created the will to receive existence from absence, that we should want to crave to receive delight and pleasure. Also, the Creator satisfies that *Kli* as He wishes. Thus, we do not need to ask for vessels of reception.

Therefore, the prayer we give for corporeality is only for the filling, meaning that the Creator will satisfy everything we feel we need since the sensation of lack is what makes us suffer. And the suffering we feel are the reason that we do everything we can to satisfy our wishes.

This is not so when we need to pray for spirituality, that the Creator will satisfy our deficiencies, since the lack for spirituality was the reason for the prayer that the Creator will grant our wishes since we are suffering because our deficiency has not been fulfilled, as this deficiency has yet to be born in us, meaning the lack to satisfy the *Kli*, called "vessel of bestowal," which is the difference between spirituality and corporeality. The corporeal *Kli* is called "vessel of reception," and wants to satisfy its self-gratification. A spiritual *Kli* is called "a *Kli* that wants to satisfy the benefit of the Creator," contrary to one's own benefit.

This *Kli* is absent in the nature of creation since by nature, man is born with only a *Kli* for self-gratification. The reason we say to our bodies that we must work to benefit the Creator is that it does not understand what is being said to it, as it cannot grasp not considering its own benefit and thinking all day about benefitting the Creator. It is especially so when it hears that we should relinquish pleasures that pertain to self-love in favor of benefitting the Creator.

This thing is so foreign to the body when it hears that one should work only in order to bestow that it immediately becomes a smart aleck and asks, "I would like to know if you see other people walking in this line for whom you, too, want to do the same? True, I would agree with you, but see for yourself how many people you see whose every thought in life is only to see to the benefit of the Creator and not their own? If we assume that you know that there are people who are walking on this line, how much time and effort did they put into having the ability to do everything only to bestow? And especially, how long should this take, a month, two months, a year, two years?" And it becomes even more of a smart aleck and asks, "Did all those who invest time and effort achieve this degree of being above to aim all their works to bestow?" With these words they can divert a person from the work pertaining to the path of bestowal. It follows from all the above that concerning spirituality, called "bringing contentment to one's Maker," a person has no such deficiency. On the contrary, if he does get a thought that we should do something to bestow upon the Creator without any reward, all the body's thoughts and desires immediately protest and cry out, "Do not be a fool and an exception to go against the majority, who know that the reason that compels one to work is self-benefit."

Only with this force he can engage in Torah and *Mitzvot* [commandments]. Although he knows that he should engage *Lishma* [for Her sake], but there is a general answer to this, that he is keeping what our sages said, "One should always engage in Torah and *Mitzvot Lo Lishma* [not for Her sake] because from *Lo Lishma* he will be rewarded with *Lishma*." However, he should not be concerned with this, meaning to test if he has really come closer to *Lishma*. Rather, he knows that the good is bound to come, meaning that he will certainly achieve *Lishma*, so he does not need to think about the meaning of *Lishma* because he need not scrutinize the details of things he is not supposed to do. Rather, he lives like the majority.

Therefore, there is a big difference between the prayer that one prays for corporality and the prayer one prays for spirituality. For spirituality, one must first pray for the *Kli*, meaning for a deficiency, to feel pain and sorrow at not having this *Kli*, called "desire," meaning to crave to bring contentment to one's Maker.

It therefore follows that he need not pray for satisfying the deficiency, as in corporality when he has a need and asks for the satisfaction of the need, since he still has no *Kli* of spirituality. Hence, when one comes to pray for spirituality he must pray for the *Kli*—that the Creator will give him a *Kli* of wanting to bestow upon the Creator. Afterwards, when he has a *Kli* that pertains to spirituality he will be able to pray for the abundance to enter the spiritual *Kli*.

It follows from the above that the real deficiency for which one must pray to the Creator should be the *Kli*. This follows the rule, "There is no light without a *Kli*." When he prays for a real deficiency that he is lacking comes the granting of the prayer when the Creator gives him a new *Kli*, as it is written, "And I will remove the stony heart from your flesh, and I will give you a heart of flesh."

I heard about this deficiency from Baal HaSulam, who said in the name of his teacher, the ADMOR of Pursov, about the verse, "Command Aaron" (Leviticus, 6:2). "RASHI interprets, "Command' means rushing promptly and for posterity. Rabbi Shimon said, 'the writing should rush primarily where the pockets are empty.'" He interpreted it to mean that "pocket" is a *Kli* in which to put money. Usually, we exert and worry about getting money. And he said, "One should be most concerned where the pockets are empty, meaning where there is no *Kli*."

It is as we explained that in spirituality one need not pray that the Creator will give him abundance and lights. Rather, first he must see that he has a *Kli*, meaning a desire and craving to bestow upon the Creator, since by nature we want only to receive and not to give.

It follows that when one enters the holy work and wants to achieve completion, he must exert with all his might to obtain the desire to want to bring contentment to one's Maker. This is where one should focus all one's prayers—that the Creator will help him and give him this new *Kli*. He must say before Him: "Lord of the world, as You have given me when I first came into this world a *Kli* to only receive for my own sake, I now ask that You will give me a new *Kli*, to have a desire only to bestow contentment upon You."

We might ask, "How can one pray to be given a *Kli* called 'desire to bestow,' when we say that he does not need this *Kli* because he does not feel that he will lack it?" How, then, can one ask for something that one does not need?

Although he sees that he does not have the *Kli* called "desire to bestow," it does not mean that one needs everything that he does not have. It is written about the upper *Sefirot* that the *Sefira* [singular of *Sefirot*] *Bina* desires mercy although we learned that through *Tzimtzum Bet* [second restriction] she departed from *Rosh de AA* [*Arich Anpin*]. Still it is regarded as though she did not depart, for although she has no *Hochma*, it is not considered a deficiency because she does not need it.

We see that something that one does not have is regarded as a lack precisely when he needs it. Moreover, one must feel pain at not having. That is, even when he feels he needs it but is not tormented at not having it, it is still not considered a deficiency. Hence, how can one pray for something for which he has no deficiency?

This is why one must think about the purpose of creation, which we know is to do good to His creations. When one begins to criticize that good, which is among the creatures, meaning their delight in the world from the delight and pleasure that the Creator wants to give to them, yet he cannot find it among the creatures, it makes him realize that there must be a reason that denies the delight and pleasure from the creatures, and for which the upper abundance cannot be revealed, and why the purpose of creation cannot be completed.

When he looks at himself he says that everything he sees—that the creatures did not receive the abundance—must be because they are not observing Torah and *Mitzvot* as one should observe the commandments of the King. It is as our sages said, "The Creator wished to reward Israel, therefore He gave them plentiful Torah and *Mitzvot* [commandments]." This means that through Torah and *Mitzvot* we can be rewarded with the delight and pleasure.

However, the question is, "Why are we not observing the Torah and *Mitzvot* as is appropriate when serving the King?" He says that it is because we lack the sensation of the importance of Torah and *Mitzvot*, and that we lack the importance of the *Mitzva* [commandment] that He has commanded us to keep His Torah and *Mitzvot*.

At that time a person comes to a resolution that only the Creator can correct this. That is, if He reveals to us a little bit of light of Torah and *Mitzvot* so we may feel the pleasure in them, we will certainly be able to serve the King with our hearts and souls, as it should be with those who feel the greatness of the King. Hence, for what should we pray to the Creator? To give some upper abundance. Then everyone will engage in Torah and *Mitzvot* properly, without any negligence.

However, we see what the holy ARI says, that the *Nukva* was improper there, hence there was the breaking. The *Ohr Pnimi* ["Inner Reflection," commentary inside *The Study of the Ten Sefirot*] interprets the words of the ARI that since the upper abundance should come into the *Kli* to receive the abundance in order to bestow, since the light was greater than the *Kli* was ready to receive—meaning that the *Kli* should receive light precisely according to its ability to aim in order to bestow, and it could not aim to bestow with such a great light—the light had to enter *Kelim* [vessels] whose desire is in order to receive.

This is called *Klipa* [shell/peel]. It follows that the *Kelim* broke. Thus, should abundance come into these *Kelim* it will all go to the outer ones, to the *Klipot* [plural of *Klipa*]. This is similar to saying that the *Kli* was broken so we do not place anything in it because it will all spill out.

Therefore, one must not pray to be given abundance from above, since it will all go to the outer ones. Instead, he should pray to the Creator to give him a *Kli*, which is a desire and craving to bestow upon the Creator. When he has that *Kli*, the upper abundance will appear to man and he will feel the delight and pleasure that were in the thought of creation to do good to His creations. Therefore, we should ask the Creator for what we really need, which is a vessel of bestowal, and we need not pray for anything else.

Come unto Pharaoh
– 2

Article No. 13, Tav-Shin-Mem-Vav, 1985-86

The *Zohar* asks, "It is written, 'Come unto Pharaoh,' but it should have said, 'Go unto Pharaoh,' etc. Since the Creator saw that Moses was afraid and other appointed emissaries could not approach him, the Creator said, 'Behold, I am against you, Pharaoh, king of Egypt, the great monster that lies in the midst of his Niles.' The Creator had to wage war against him, and none other, as it is written, 'I am the Lord,' which they explained, 'I and not a messenger.'" Thus far its words (in the beginning of the portion, *Bo* [Come]).

The difference between "come" and "go" is that "come" means that we should walk together, like a person who tells his friend, "Come."

We should understand it because *The Zohar* asks why the Creator needed to go with Moses. It is because Moses alone could not fight him, but the Creator Himself and none other. Thus, why did he need Moses to go with the Creator? After all, it says, "I and not a messenger." Thus, what is the point of the Creator going to Pharaoh, who is called "great monster," with Moses? He could have gone to Pharaoh without Moses.

We should also understand what our sages said (*Kidushin* [Matrimony] 30b), "Rish Lakish said, 'Man's inclination overcomes him every day and seeks to kill him, as it is said, 'The wicked watches the righteous,' and if the Creator did not help him, he would not overcome it, as it is said, 'The Lord will not leave him in his hand.''"

Here, too, arises the question, "If a person cannot prevail by himself and needs the Creator's help, why this doubling?" In other words, either the Creator gives a person the strength to overcome alone, or the Creator will do everything. Why is it that two forces seem to be required here, one of man and subsequently the force of the Creator? It is as though only the two of them can conquer evil, and one force is insufficient.

It is known that man's perfection is that he must reach the purpose of creation to obtain the purpose for which the world was created, which is called "to do good to His creations." In other words, the creatures should come to receive the delight and pleasure that He contemplated to delight them.

Prior to that, creation is still not considered a creation that befits the Creator, since it is known that from the perfect Operator, perfect operations should emerge. This means that everyone should feel the beauty of creation and will be able to praise and glorify creation, that everyone will be able to glorify and thank the Creator for the creation He has created, and that everyone will be able to say, "Blessed is He who said, 'Let there be the world.'" In other words, everyone should bless the Creator for having created a good world filled with pleasures, where everyone is joyful and happy from the contentment they feel from all the pleasures they are experiencing in the world.

However, when a person begins to examine if he is truly satisfied with his life and how much contentment he is really deriving from himself and from his environment, he sees the opposite—everyone is suffering, in torment, and each person suffers differently. But one should say, "Blessed is He who said, 'Let there be the world,'" so he sees that he is only saying it superficially.

However, it is known that the delight and pleasure cannot appear in the world before the world has *Kelim* [vessels] of bestowal, since our vessels of reception are still contaminated by self-reception, which is heavily restricted in its measure and separates us from the Creator (meaning that there was the first restriction on the vessels of reception so the abundance would not shine there, see in the "Introduction of the Book of Zohar," p 138).

Obtaining the vessels of bestowal is where disputes and wars begin, since it is against our nature. And this is why we were given Torah and *Mitzvot*, to achieve the degree of bestowal, as our sages said, "I have created the evil inclination; I have created the spice of Torah" (*Kidushin* 30).

Also, we were given the *Mitzva* [commandment/good deed] of "love thy friend as thyself," and Rabbi Akiva said, "This is the great rule of the Torah" (*Beresheet Rabba, Parasha* 24). In other words, by working in love of friends, a person accustoms himself to exit self-love and achieve love of others.

However, we should understand what we see before us, that there are people who exert in love of friends and still do not come an inch closer to love of the Creator so they can work in Torah and *Mitzvot*, due to the love of the Creator. This means that they say they are in fact advancing a little in love of friends, but they see no progress in love of the Creator. However, we should know that in love of friends, too, there are degrees, meaning we must contemplate the obligation to love of friends.

We can compare it to a two-story building with a ground floor, as well. The King is on the second floor, and one who wishes to come to the King—whose only goal is to converse with the King face-to-face—is told that he must first climb to the first floor, since it is impossible to climb to the second floor without first climbing to the first floor.

Certainly, everyone understands that this is so. However, there is a reason why they must first climb to the first floor—it is called "corrections." In other words, by climbing to the first floor, one can learn how to address the King face-to-face, and will be able to ask the King for his wish.

That person, who hears that he must first climb to the first floor and subsequently to the second floor, understands it very well. But since his only wish is to see the King's face and he cares for nothing else, this makes what he is told—that he must climb to the first floor—a burden and a toil for him.

However, he has no choice, so he climbs to the first floor. He is not interested in seeing what is there, although he heard that the first floor is where one learns how to speak with the King. But he pays no attention to that, for this is not his goal. His goal is the King, not what he can learn on the first floor. His goal is not the study, but to see the King's face. Why should he waste time on trifles, since everything is naught compared to the King? Thus, why should he take interest in what is taught on the first floor?

Hence, when he climbs to the first floor, he has no desire to stay there. Instead, he wishes to quickly climb to the second, to the King Himself, for this is all he wants. However, he is told, "Without knowing the rules that abide on the first floor, you will certainly blemish the King's honor. For this reason, you cannot hope to be able to climb to the second floor before you learn all that there is to learn on the first floor."

Similarly, with love of friends, we heard that it was impossible to be rewarded with love of the Creator before one was rewarded with love of friends, as Rabbi Akiva said, "love thy friend as thyself is the great rule of the Torah." Therefore, while engaging in love of friends, he is not considering love of friends as being valuable, but as redundant.

He keeps it because he has no choice, but he is constantly looking for the time when "I will be rewarded with the love of the Creator, and I'll be able to rid myself of the love of friends. This work is burdensome to me because I can hardly stand my friends, for I see that they all have different traits than mine and I have nothing in common with them. But I have no choice, since I was told that without love of friends I won't be able to achieve love of the Creator. So against my will, I sit with them.

"However, I can ask myself, 'What am I getting from the friends?' Only one thing: I am correcting myself through self-torment by sitting with them and tolerating their talks, which I dislike and which are against my nature. But what can I do? I am told that I must suffer in this world, so I do: I sit and wait for the time when I can run from them and avoid seeing the lowliness that I see in them."

It turns out that he is not taking from the love of friends the remedy called, "love of others," but only because he was told that he has no choice, for otherwise he will not achieve love of the Creator. This is the reason why he engages in love of friends and keeps all the obligations to which the friends commit him. But what he should learn from them is miles away from him.

This means that he is not exiting self-love and he is not reaching love of others. He is observing the love of friends not out of love, but out of fear, since he is not allowed into love of the Creator before he enters the love of friends. As a result, he fears not observing love of friends because he will not be allowed into love of the Creator.

This is similar to the allegory about not being allowed onto the second floor where the King sits, until he climbs to the first floor. The idea is that he will learn the rules of how to keep the King's honor, so it would seem reasonable that he would be happy to go onto the first floor, since now he is learning how to be watchful of the King's honor.

It would benefit him because afterwards, when he enters the King's palace, he will not blemish the King's honor. And therefore, while he is on the first floor, he pays attention to all the rules that apply there and to becoming accustomed to them, since he wants to come into the King, to bestow upon the King, and not at all to be contemptuous of the King's honor.

This relates only to one who wishes to come before the King to give contentment to Him. But one who wishes to come in before the King for self-reception considers what is found on the first floor as redundant. It is of no interest to him. He goes up to the first floor only because he is afraid, since he knows that he will not be allowed to climb to the second floor before he climbs to the first floor. He feels no need to study the laws that are taught there—how to avoid blemishing the King's honor—since the only reason he wants to come before the King is for purposes of self-love.

Therefore, we should know that we were given love of friends to learn how to avoid blemishing the King's honor. In other words, if he has no other desire except to give contentment to the King, he will certainly blemish the King's honor, which is called "Passing on *Kedusha* [holiness/sanctity] to the external ones." For this reason, we mustn't underestimate the importance of the work in love of friends, for by that he will learn how to exit self-love and enter the path of love of others. And when he completes the work of love of friends, he will be able to be rewarded with love of the Creator.

We should know that there is a virtue to love of friends. One cannot deceive himself and say that he loves the friends, if in fact he doesn't love them. Here he can examine whether he truly has love of friends or not. But with love of the Creator, one cannot examine oneself as to whether his intention is the love of the Creator, meaning that he wants to bestow upon the Creator, or his desire is to receive in order to receive.

But we should know that after all the corrections that man is given to do without the Creator's help, he will not be granted any progress in the work of bestowal. And we asked, "Why, then, should one do things in order to later be rewarded with the help of the Creator? After all, the Creator can help even without the work of the lower ones, and man's work on progress in the work will not help in any case."

However, if one does not begin to work, he doesn't know that he cannot triumph over the inclination. But when a person begins to walk in the work of the Creator and does what he can do, then he can offer a true prayer for the Creator to help him.

But why would the Creator want him to offer a true prayer? With a flesh and blood, you can say that he wants him to make a genuine plea because when a person makes a genuine plea of his friend, his friend gives him true gratitude. The flesh and blood, who chase honors, the gratitude that he gives him is as though he is belittling himself before him and he enjoys it.

But as for the Creator, does He need to be given people's respect? Therefore, why would the Creator want a person to make a heartfelt prayer?

The thing is that it is known that there is no light without a *Kli*. It is impossible for one to give something that is very important, and if one has no desire for something, he will slight it and discard it. It will be lost because the need for something matches what he needs; this gives the importance. To the extent of the importance, he keeps the gift from being lost, for otherwise everything will go to the *Klipot*.

This is called "nursing the *Klipot*," meaning that everything goes to the vessels of reception, which take into their authority everything that a person slights in matters of *Kedusha*. From this we know why one should begin the work. But why doesn't the Creator give one the strength to complete the work alone, without His help?

It is known what *The Zohar* interprets concerning what our sages said, "He who comes to be purified is aided." It asks, "With what?" And it says, "With a holy soul," meaning he receives illumination from above, which is called *Neshama* [a soul], called "attaining Godliness," which means that he is included in the thought of creation to do good to His creations.

It follows that by having a *Kli* and a desire for vessels of bestowal, he receives the light, called *Neshama*. Thus, both are required. In other words, a person should begin, and by that he receives a *Kli*. And by being unable to finish, he cries out to the Creator for help, and then he receives the light.

Now we can understand what is written, "Come unto Pharaoh, for I have hardened his heart and the heart of his servants, that I might show these My signs in the midst of them."

A question arises, "Why did the Creator harden Pharaoh's heart?" The text answers, "That I might show these My signs in the midst of them." And the interpretation is, "Why has the Creator hardened man's heart and he cannot win the war against the inclination by himself?"

The answer is, so man will cry out to the Creator, and by that will have the *Kli*. And then the Creator will be able to place the letters of Torah within him, inside the *Kli*. This is the soul that the Creator gives him as help.

This is considered, "The Torah and the Creator are one." "My signs" refers to the letters of the Torah, as in the names of the Creator. This is the "doing good to His creations," which is the thought of creation to do good to His creations. This comes to a person specifically when he has a *Kli*, and this *Kli* comes through the hardening of the heart, for then there is a place where he can cry out to the Creator for help, and He helps him with a holy soul.

Now we can see the matter of "Come unto Pharaoh," meaning both of us, together. In other words, a person should begin and then see that he cannot defeat it, and this is implied in Moses being afraid to approach him. And then the Creator said, "Behold, I am against you, Pharaoh," meaning that then comes the help from the Creator. And with what? With a holy soul, as written in *The Zohar*.

It follows that the hardening of the heart, in the words, "For I have hardened his heart," was to make a place for a prayer. And this prayer is not like one of flesh and blood, who wants respect, to be asked so he will be respected. Rather, the purpose of the prayer is for him to have a *Kli*, a need for the help of the Creator, for there is no light without a *Kli*. And when a person sees that he cannot help himself in any way, then he has a need for the Creator's help.

This is the meaning of what our sages said, "The Creator craves the prayer of the righteous." Here, too, there arises the question,

"But does the Creator need man's surrender, that he will ask of Him?" However, since His wish is to benefit His creations, but there is no light without a *Kli*, He craves the prayer of the righteous, for by that they disclose the *Kelim* [vessels] into which He can impart. It follows that when a person sees that he cannot overcome the evil in him, this is really the time for asking for the help of the Creator.

Now we can understand what the Creator said (Exodus 6), "And I will take you to Me for a people, and I will be to you a God; and you shall know that I am the Lord your God, who brought you out from under the burdens of the Egyptians."

In *Masechet Berachot* (38a), our sages wrote about it as follows, "'Who brought you out from under the burdens of the Egyptians.' The sages ... Thus said the Creator unto Israel: 'When I bring you out, I will do for you something to show you that it is I who brought you out from Egypt, as it is written, 'That I am the Lord your God, who brought you out.'"

This means that it is not enough that the Creator brings the people of Israel out of Egypt, that they were liberated from the torment that they suffered there. When speaking of the work of the Creator, there arises the question, "Was this not enough?" Now they have been liberated from the enslavement of the exile after not being able to serve the Creator due to Pharaoh's rule, and all that they built for themselves, whatever position in the work, was all swallowed in the earth, as our sages said (*Sutah* p 11), "Pithom and Ramses. Rav and Shmuel, one said her name was Pithom. And why was her name Ramses? For his head *Mitroses* [splinters] first." RASHI interprets, "When they built some, it would splinter and fall. They would rebuild, and it would fall. And one said, 'Her name is Ramses, and why was her name Pithom? It is because first is first, it was swallowed by the *Pi Tehom* [mouth of the abysss].'"

We therefore see that there is no dispute between Rav and Shmuel regarding the facts, only regarding the interpretation. The fact was that everything that they built would fall. This means that every time they built for themselves some structure in the work, the

Egyptians came, meaning the alien thoughts of the Egyptians, and ruined all their work. In other words, all the work that they did with all their efforts to overcome and to serve in the work of holiness was swallowed in the ground.

Thus, each day they had to start over, and it seemed to them as though they were never engaged in the work of holiness. Moreover, each time they contemplated moving forward, they saw that not only did they not progress, they even regressed, since new "who" and "what" questions would always surface in their minds.

Accordingly, we should understand this exodus from Egypt as their finally having the ability to serve the Creator without the alien thoughts of the Egyptians. Thus, what does this knowing in the words, "And you shall know," come to tell us? That we must know that it is the Creator who delivered them from the land of Egypt. And there is more we should wonder about, since we began the examination at the enslavement in Egypt, when they were being worked in hard labor, and they were liberated from that, so what else did they miss?

But what is hard labor? Our sages explained the verse, "All their labors which they rigorously imposed on them" (*Sutah* 11b). "Rabbi Shmuel Bar Nahmany said, 'Rabbi Yonatan said, 'They replaced men's work with women's work, and women's work with men's work. And the Egyptians made the children of Israel serve *Ba-Parech* [with rigor].'' Rabbi Elazar says, *Be Peh Rach* [with a soft mouth].'"

We should also understand the matter of hard labor in the work of holiness. We should make two discernments:

1. The act called "the revealed part," which a person can see and where one cannot say that he is erring or deceiving himself, since it cannot be said that there is a mistake about something that is visibly apparent. This is so because with the act of *Mitzvot* and the study of Torah, he sees, and others can also see if he is carrying out actions of Torah and *Mitzvot* or not.

2. The intention. This is called "the hidden part," since others cannot see the intention behind one's acts. And he, too, cannot see the intention in the act, since it is possible to be mistaken about intention and to mislead oneself, for only in apparent things, called "the revealed part," everyone can see the truth. But what one cannot trust himself when it comes to intentions in the heart or thoughts in the mind. It follows that this is hidden from himself and from others.

Now we can interpret the meaning of hard labor, which was said to be "Replacing men's work with women's work." "Men's work" means that he is already a *Gever* [man], that he can *Lehitgaber* [overcome] his evil and engage in Torah and *Mitzvot* in action. Thus, what should he do when he is already called "a man," meaning a man of war, who can fight with his evil in action? Now it is time for him to begin his work in the second discernment, meaning in the concealed, which is the aim. In other words, henceforth, he should try to aim all his actions to be in order to bestow contentment upon the Creator and not for his own benefit.

And what did the Egyptians do when they saw that he was a man who could exit their rule and enter holiness? They swapped their work and gave them women's work. This means that all their work was in women's work, that is, the Egyptians made them think, "Who needs intentions? The actions are what count, and here, in actions, you will succeed, as you can see—you are a man, you can prevail over the evil in you and engage in Torah and *Mitzvot* in every detail and precision, and you must put all your efforts into being more meticulous in Torah and *Mitzvot*.

"However, you should not engage in intentions! This work is not for you, but only for a chosen few. If you begin with the work of bestowing, meaning noticing that you must aim everything to be in order to bestow, you will not have the energy to be so meticulous in the revealed action, where you will not deceive yourself because you see what you are doing. Therefore, there is where you can expand in every detail and precision in your actions.

"But with regard to intentions, you have no real test. Thus, we advise you for your own good, and do not think, God forbid, that we want to divert you from the work of holiness. On the contrary, we want you to rise in the degrees of holiness."

This is called, "Replacing men's work with women's work." Where they should have done work that belongs to men, they explained to the people of Israel that it would be best for them to do women's work, meaning what belongs to women.

"And women's work with men's work" means that those people do not have the power to overcome. Rather, "They are as feeble as a female," meaning that they were weak in keeping Torah and *Mitzvot* and didn't have the strength to keep and observe the *Mitzvot*, even in the revealed form, which is called "only in action." And all the work of overcoming was only on the action, not on the intention.

The Egyptians came to them and made them think, "We don't want to interrupt your holy work. On the contrary, we want you to be true servants of the Creator. In other words, we see that you wish to serve in the work of holiness, so we are advising you that the most important thing is not the action; it is the intention. Therefore, instead of exerting to overcome in action, accustoming yourselves to overcome your body, to study for another hour or to pray for another half hour trying to answer 'Blessed be He,' and 'Blessed be His name,' and 'Amen,' not to mention in the middle of the repetition of the cantor. Who needs it?

"The main aim is for the Creator. That is where you need to focus all your efforts. Why waste your strength on trifling things? Indeed, the Halacha [religious law] says that you must keep all those little things, but this work is not for you; it's work for women. You need to engage in men's work. The fact that you want to engage only in action is unbecoming to you. You should focus primarily on the intent, meaning use every bit of energy you have to aim that everything will be for the Creator. However, don't think for a minute that we are trying, God forbid, to interrupt your work of the Creator. We want the contrary—for you to rise up the ladder of holiness and achieve perfection, meaning that all your actions will be only in order to bestow contentment upon your Maker."

And since they were at the degree called "women" and still did not have the strength to overcome, not even in the part of the action—considered that they are as feeble as females—the Egyptians made them see that the important thing was the aim *Lishma* [for Her name]. By that, the Egyptians made certain that they would not have the strength to continue and overcome in the work of holiness.

It is as Maimonides says when he wrote (*Hilchot Teshuva* [Laws of Repentance], *Parasha* no. 10), "The sages said, 'One should always engage in Torah, even in *Lo Lishma* [not for Her name], since from *Lo Lishma* he will come to *Lishma* [for Her name].' Therefore, when teaching the little ones, the women, and the illiterate in general, they must be taught to work out of fear and to receive reward. When they gain knowledge and acquire much wisdom, they are to be shown that secret bit by bit, and must be accustomed to it with ease, until they attain it, and know Him and serve Him out of love."

The Egyptians advised those who were under the discernment of women not to follow the words of Maimonides. On the contrary, even though they were at the degree of women and little ones, they made them understand that they should immediately begin the work on aiming *Lishma*. By that, the Egyptians made certain that they would remain in their domain, outside of *Kedusha* [holiness/sanctity].

Thus, this is called "hard labor," as Rabbi Shmuel Bar Nahmany interpreted, "*Ba-Parech* [with toil] means BePricha [fragile/crumbling]." And RASHI interpreted, "In crumbling and breaking of the body and the waist." The reason is that when replacing men's work with women's work, and women's work with men's work, it will be as we explained, since men's work was to overcome and advance and aim for the intention *Lishma*, but they weakened them in this work because the Egyptians resisted this work. Hence, besides having to toil in overcoming so they could aim in order to bestow, they had more work in that the

Egyptians made them think that all of this work was redundant, that the work of bestowal did not relate to them, but only to a chosen few.

This is called "twofold work": 1) straining to aim in order to bestow, and 2) fighting them and saying that it is not true, that they will be able to achieve *Lishma*, and not as the Egyptians said, that they should do women's work. And this was the Egyptians' whole intention, to prevent them from approaching the work of bestowal.

Also, they replaced the work of men with that of women, which, as we said, is worthless because it is keeping Torah and *Mitzvot* only in action. This means that their entire war against the inclination is only over the action, and not, as Maimonides says, that women's work should be only about doing things and not teaching them that they must intend *Lishma*.

Therefore, when the Egyptians came and told them that they had to do men's work, meaning aim to bestow, it was hard work for them: 1) Concerning *Lishma*, you are totally incapable of it. 2) Overcoming the body and keeping practical *Mitzvot* was harder for them before the Egyptians' alien thoughts came and made them think that the act of *Mitzvot* without intention was completely worthless and degraded the importance of Torah and *Mitzvot* in *Lo Lishma*. Thus, now, through the Egyptians, the work in the form of women was degraded, and this caused them hard labor, as it was said that it is the breaking of the body and the waist.

It follows from all the above that there are three meanings to the word *Perech* [toil/hard labor], yet there is no contradiction between one interpretation and the other. Rather, all three things were there, and each interpreted according to his own issue:

3. In the first interpretation of Parech, Rabbi Elazar says it is "in *Peh Rach* [soft mouth]."

4. Rabbi Shmuel Bar Nahmany said "In *Pericha*," which means breaking.

5. Rabbi Shmuel Bar Nahmany, "Rabbi Yonatan said, 'They replaced men's work with women's work, and women's work with men's work.'"

However, they all interpret hard labor as *Pericha* [friable], meaning the breaking of the body. And the reason why it was hard work to the point that they called this work, "Labor that breaks the body and the waist," is that they replaced men's work with women's work, and women's work with men's work. This caused them the hard labor.

And yet, why did they listen to the views of the Egyptians? It is because they spoke to Israel with *Peh Rach* [a soft mouth], meaning that the thoughts of the Egyptians came to Israel with a soft mouth. That is, everything they told them to do was not to turn them away from serving the Creator, God forbid. On the contrary, they wished to guide them to walk in the ways of the Creator successfully, so they would not waste time in vain, meaning that they would see no progress in the work of holiness. And since they were spoken to with a soft mouth, it was hard for them to overcome these thoughts.

This implies that when he says that they replaced men's work with that of women, he explains why they listened to the Egyptians. The answer is, because of the *Perech*—that they spoke to Israel with *Peh Rach* [a soft mouth]. Thus, it is for the two above reasons that they came to work in hard labor, as Rabbi Shmuel Bar Nahmany says, *Perech* means work of *Pericha* [breaking], which is work that breaks the body.

Accordingly, we should understand why it is not enough for the people of Israel that the Creator brought them out of Egypt, out of their enslavement so they could engage in Torah and *Mitzvot*, each according to his attainment, and the *Klipa* of Egypt didn't have the strength to resist their work.

Indeed, how great is the miracle and who can appreciate the importance of the matter? When a person considers the amount of suffering and torment that he feels while being in exile under the enslavement of Pharaoh King of Egypt, and to the extent of the darkness of Pithom and Ramses that he assumes in his heart, which they were building. And now, the gates of the *Klipa* of Egypt were opened before them all at once and they came under their own authority. This means that now they were free to engage in Torah and *Mitzvot* as they wished, without any interruptions. What joy and elation it brings to a person when he compares the time of darkness to the time when it illuminates. It is as it is said, "He who separates between darkness and light."

According to the above, we should understand the necessity to know that only the Creator delivers them from the burdens of the Egyptians, as our sages said, "When I bring you out, I will do for you something to show you that it is I who brought you out from Egypt, as it is written, 'That I am the Lord your God, who brought you out from under the burdens of the Egyptians.'"

The thing is that we must always remember the goal that we must reach. And since the purpose of creation is to do good to His creations, our goal is to receive the delight and pleasure that He has contemplated on our behalf. But for the purpose of correction, called *Dvekut* [adhesion], which is about equivalence of form, we have to work to obtain the vessels of bestowal.

Yet, this is only the correction of creation; it is not wholeness. Wholeness means knowing the Creator, knowing and attaining the Torah, which is called "the names of the Creator."

Accordingly, it is not enough that we already have the strength to keep Torah and *Mitzvot* without any interruptions, for this is only a correction, not the complete goal. The complete goal is to obtain the knowledge of the Torah, as in, "The Torah, Israel, and the Creator are one." This is why our sages said, "This is what the Creator said to Israel, 'And you shall know that I am the Lord your God, who brought you out,' I and not a messenger." This means that every single one should come to know the Creator, and this is called "Torah," the names of the Creator.

What Is the Need to Borrow Kelim from the Egyptians?

Article No. 14, Tav-Shin-Mem-Vav, 1985-86

It is written (Exodus 11), "Speak now in the ears of the people that each man will borrow from his neighbor and each woman from her neighbor vessels of silver and vessels of gold. And the Lord gave the people's favor in the eyes of the Egyptians."

Our sages said (*Berachot*, 9b), "The disciples of Rabbi Yanai said, "'Do' means please. The Creator said to Moses, 'Please go and tell them, Israel, to please borrow vessels of silver and vessels of gold from the Egyptians so that that righteous will not say, 'He kept, 'And they enslaved them and afflicted them,' and then, He did not keep 'And they will come out with many possessions.'"

This is perplexing. If the Creator wanted to keep His promise to Abraham, as it is written, "And afterwards they will come out with many possessions," could He not make the people of Israel wealthy without borrowing vessels from the Egyptians? It seems like fraud, for it seems that they initially borrowed by deceit, meaning without intending to return.

We should also understand why the Creator said to Moses to implore Israel to borrow vessels from the Egyptians, as is said above, that "Do" means please [request]. Also, what is this imploring? It seems to mean that the Creator knew that they would object to it, so He asked Moses to speak to Israel. Thus, we should understand the reason for Israel's objection to this.

We should also understand the words, "And the Lord gave the people's favor in the eyes of the Egyptians." How can we understand such a thing, which is completely contradictory? Although anything is possible from the perspective of the Creator, but from the literal perspective this is difficult to grasp, as it is written (Exodus, 1:12), "And the more they afflicted them, the more they multiplied and the more they spread out, and they detested the sons of Israel." Our sages said, "It shows that they were as thorns in their eyes" (*Sutah*, 11).

It follows that from thorns, meaning being unable to stand the people of Israel and seeing them as thorns, they now turned completely around and the Egyptians liked the people of Israel.

In the Creator's promise to Abraham, "And afterwards they will come out with many possessions," we should understand the whole matter that is presented there (Genesis, 15:6), "And He said to him, 'I am the Lord who brought you out of Ur of the Chaldeans to give you this land to inherit it.' And he said, 'Lord God, by what will I know that I will inherit it?' And He said to Abram, ... 'Know for certain that your descendants will be strangers in a land that is not theirs, and they will be enslaved and oppressed four hundred years ... and afterward they will come out with many possessions.'"

Here, too, we should understand the answer that Abraham received to the question, "By what will I know that I will inherit it?" since the Creator's answer was to this question, as it is written, "And He said to Abram, 'Know for certain that your descendants will be strangers in a land that is not theirs, where they will be enslaved and oppressed four hundred years ... and afterward they will come out with many possessions.'" Thus, the question was about guarantees on the inheritance, and the answer to the guarantee was that the people of Israel will be in exile. But is exile a guarantee for inheriting the land?

Baal HaSulam explained the meaning of this question: It is known that there is no light without a *Kli* [vessel]. That is, it is impossible to receive filling if there is no lack. A lack is called a *Kli*, and when Abraham saw what the Creator wanted to give his sons, he said, "I do not see that my sons will have a need for that spiritual inheritance of the land." He said, "If they receive a small illumination they will be content because the smallest degree in spirituality brings more pleasure than all the corporeal pleasures in the world. Accordingly, when they receive some small illumination they might think that there are no greater degrees than what they have attained, and will therefore have no need to ask for anything more."

And because of this, Abraham's question to the Creator was, "By what will I know that they will have the need to inherit the spiritual land?" Thus, he was asking the Creator to tell him how it might happen that they will have light without a *Kli*. Abram understood that the Creator gives the light, but the *Kelim*, meaning a desire for greater lights than they already received, who would make them see that they need to achieve greater ascension than they feel now?

There is a rule in spirituality that anything spiritual that comes to a person makes him feel unsurpassable wholeness, since anything spiritual is a complete feeling, without any deficiency. Otherwise it is not regarded as "spiritual," for only in a corporeal matter can there be pleasure, and still we feel that there is a greater pleasure. This is not so in spirituality.

Thus, Abraham wondered how and through what they would have a need to ask the Creator to give them greater degrees, called "inheritance of the land." He said that the Creator's reply to him, "Know for certain that your descendants will be strangers in a land that is not theirs" means that from here, meaning from the exile in Egypt they will have a need to ask the Creator to give them greater strength each time.

The reason is that when a person begins to advance in the work of the Creator and wants all his actions to be in order to bestow, he sees that he cannot prevail. At that time one asks the Creator to help him, as our sages said, "He who comes to purify is aided," and the holy *Zohar* asks, "How is he aided? With a holy soul."

Indeed, everything that they overcame in the work sank in the earth, as he says about their building of Pithom and Ramesses. That is, each day they had to start their work anew because everything they built went into the abyss and they always saw themselves as though they had never begun to work because they did not remember any word of Torah that concerns work and always reflect on themselves, "Where is our work, the efforts we put into the work? Where did they go?"

It is even more difficult to understand how the *Klipa* [shell/peel] of Pharaoh could swallow all their work to the point that they did not feel that they ever engaged in serving the Creator, that their goal was to achieve wholeness, and they knew what they wanted. Suddenly, they have come to a state where they forgot everything and no *Reshimot* [recollections] remained in them from their work.

All this was deliberate. The Creator has prepared a *Klipa* for this purpose so as to constantly keep them in a state of beginning. It is known that all beginnings are tough, so they will be forced to ask the Creator to help them, as said above, that "He who comes to purify is aided," and as the holy *Zohar* says that each time they receive a "holy soul," which is a force from above, meaning that each time they receive additions to the soul. This accumulates into a great amount, as it is known that "What is given from Heaven is not taken back" (*Hulin* 60).

However, although each illumination received from above departs for the time being, in the end, when he completes the amount of labor that one must do, as in "Everything that is in the might of your hand to do, that do," he receives at once everything he had received one at a time. He thought that it all went to the *Klipot*, but then he receives everything back.

What Is the Need to Borrow Kelim from the Egyptians?

According to the above, it follows that the whole matter of the exile in Egypt was in order to receive *Kelim* [vessels] and a need for the great lights, called "inheritance of the land." This is what Abraham was perplexed about and said that he did not see that his sons would have a need for these great lights. And since there is no light without a *Kli*, it turns out that even if there is a desire to give them, they have no *Kelim* in which to receive.

For this reason they were given the exile in Egypt where through the questions and arguments of the Egyptians they will be continuously emptied from what little *Kedusha* [holiness/sanctity] they had acquired, for they suckled from them. For this reason they will always need to ask the Creator to illuminate their way for them so they can go forward. But they say that they kept going backwards, which is why the ARI wrote that at the time of the exodus from Egypt the people of Israel were in forty-nine gates of impurity until the King of Kings appeared to them and redeemed them.

This seems to contradict reason, since it is known that Moses and Aaron came to Egypt and spoke to the sons of Israel about the Creator wanting to bring them out from Egypt. They performed all the tokens in Egypt, and they saw the ten plagues that the Egyptians suffered, and this must have brought Israel closer to *Kedusha*, and not the opposite—that they kept failing to a deeper gate of *Tuma'a* [impurity], to the point that when it was time to come out of Egypt, meaning when they had to have the best preparation for reception of the light of redemption, we see that when they received the light of redemption they were in forty-nine gates of *Tuma'a*. Is this possible?

As Baal HaSulam explained, the exile in Egypt was in order to obtain the *Kelim* of the Egyptians. But it was only to borrow, and later to return to them. He interpreted that this matter of the Creator saying to Abraham, "Your descendants will be strangers in a land that is not theirs," was a guarantee of the inheritance. This meant that they would have a need to receive the abundance from the Creator, since wanting to come out of the enslavement of the Egyptians can be only through the help of a holy soul. Then they will need the Creator's help each time, and from this they will have a need to draw higher degrees.

Now we will explain the meaning of the exile in Egypt and the lending of the *Kelim* from the Egyptians. We see that when Moses and Aaron came to the sons of Israel, as it is written (Exodus, 4:29), "And Moses and Aaron went and gathered all the elders of the sons of Israel, and Aaron said all the words that the Creator had said to Moses, and performed the tokens before the eyes of the people, and the people believed and heard."

We see from this that as soon as Moses and Aaron came to the sons of Israel they accepted all the words that the Creator had said to Moses with faith above reason. And everything that the Egyptians made them understand with all the questions and doubts about the faith of Israel did not count at all because they went above reason. For this reason, the fact that the whole time they were in exile could not impact them at all now.

That is, once Moses and Aaron came to the sons of Israel with the Creator's desire to take them out of exile, they promptly took it upon themselves not to listen henceforth to the arguments of the Egyptians, who came in the name of Pharaoh, king of Egypt—that it is better for them to remain under their governance, and who tried to make them see that the way of the Egyptians was true and they should not listen to what Moses and Aaron were telling them. "We see that you are yelling, 'Let us go and sacrifice to our God.' This made you think that you should leave Egypt and follow them. And we understand that you want to listen to all that they are telling you with eyes shut. Can this be, while we are making perfect sense? You have nothing to reply to us, yet you insist that you are willing to go all the way according to the words of Moses and Aaron."

From this we see that after Moses and Aaron came with the message of the redemption—that now they were coming out of enslavement, for they were unable to do the holy work, they were happy with this message and did not need any exaggerations of flavors of Torah and *Mitzvot*. Rather, they were happy precisely with this, meaning with being able to simply observe in practice. This gave them complete satisfaction and they delighted in doing their Master's will, as it is written, "Therefore they cry out, 'Let us go and sacrifice to our God'" (Exodus, 5:8).

It follows that now that they are coming out from the exile in Egypt with *Kelim* that do not need anything, but as it is written, "And the people believed and heard," and they have no need to inherit the land that the Creator had promised to Abraham, as it is written, "Know for certain ... and afterwards they will come out with many possessions," meaning that the exile was a guarantee that they would have the need to receive the delight and pleasure, which is the inheritance of the land that the Creator sought to give to his descendants but they still did not have the *Kelim* for this and were content with little.

This is why, "And the Lord said to Moses, 'Speak now in the ears of the people that each man will borrow from his neighbor and each woman from her neighbor vessels of silver and vessels of gold.'" According to what Baal HaSulam interpreted, we should say that it means that they will take the vessels of silver and vessels of gold that the Egyptians have, meaning take their desires and longings, namely all the doubts that they had about the way of the people of Israel.

The Egyptians were always demanding that everything you do must be with reason and understanding, and your engagement in overcoming in order to exit self-love and to do everything in order to bestow is the wrong way because the Creator is good and does good. When He created the world, He certainly did it to benefit His creations, meaning that we, creatures, will enjoy the delight and pleasure. But you are leaving the right path and taking on a path that is completely against the purpose of creation. You are telling us that this is the true way, that you do not need anything for self-love but to do everything in order to bestow contentment upon the Maker.

But whenever the people of Israel heard Egypt's slander about the path of bestowal they would run from them, meaning they ran from these thoughts when they came to confuse the thoughts of the sons of Israel and instill their views in the hearts of the sons of Israel.

For this reason, the Creator knew that they would not want to hear Egypt's questions and doubts of "who" and "what," but they did not have the *Kelim* in which to place the many possessions, since there is no light without a *Kli*. That is, a person cannot be given anything for which he has no desire. Therefore, if He were to ask the sons of Israel, "What do you want Me to give you?" They would say, "We do not want anything from You. On the contrary, our only aspiration is to give to You, and not that You will give to us." Thus, how can they receive the delight and pleasure, called "many possessions," which is considered that He wants to give them *Nefesh*, *Ruach*, *Neshama*, *Haya*, *Yechida*? They have no need for this!

This is why the Creator wanted them to take the Egyptians' *Kelim*, meaning their questions and doubts, and all their desires, which are the *Kelim* of the Egyptians. But they were not to really take those *Kelim*, only borrow them. That is, they would take the Egyptians' *Kelim* only to have a need to satisfy those deficiencies, but not to really keep those *Kelim* because the *Kelim*, meaning these thoughts and desires do not belong to the people of Israel. It is only a temporary borrowing, so as to later return to them.

That is, afterwards, meaning once they received the filling that belongs to these questions, precisely through them it will be possible to bestow upon them the filling. This is similar to receiving the lights that belong to their *Kelim*, which are called "vessels of reception in order to receive." However, they promptly threw away their *Kelim* and used the lights that belong to their *Kelim*, but received everything in order to bestow contentment upon the Maker.

This is similar to what Baal HaSulam interpreted regarding Haman and Mordechai. He said that we see that when Ahasuerus wanted to glorify Mordechai, as it is written (Esther 6:3), "And the king said, 'What honor or dignity has been bestowed on Mordechai for this?' ... and the king said to him, 'What is to be done for the

What Is the Need to Borrow Kelim from the Egyptians?

man whom the king desires to honor?' ... Haman said to the king ... let them bring royal apparel.'"

Accordingly, he asked, "How can such a thing be? If the King wants to honor Mordechai, he asks Haman 'What is to be done for the man whom the king desires to honor?'" He answers that this implies to the order of imparting abundance upon the lower ones. The Creator certainly wants to give honor and greatness to the righteous, which is Mordechai the righteous. But should He ask the righteous, "What do you want Me to give you?" the righteous will say that he does not want to receive anything. On the contrary, all he wants is to bestow upon the King.

This is why he had to ask the Haman in him, who understands that it is good to receive, and then he said, "And do so to Mordechai the Jew," meaning that he will receive the honor and greatness not in the *Kelim* of Haman, which are called "receiving in order to receive," but in receiving in order to bestow.

Similarly, we should explain concerning the borrowing of the *Kelim* from the Egyptians, when the Creator asked Moses to ask Israel to borrow *Kelim* from the Egyptians. We asked, "Why did the Creator have to ask Israel for such a thing? Why would the people of Israel not want to borrow these *Kelim*?" The answer is that when Moses and Aaron came as the Creator's emissaries to bring the people of Israel out from the exile, it is written, "And the people heard and believed," meaning with faith above reason. They did not need anything or had any desire for high degrees. They were content with being able to engage in Torah and *Mitzvot* without any disturbances from the Egyptians.

This is similar to what we said above, that he said that if the king were to ask Mordechai the righteous, "What honor and greatness do you want me give you?" He would reply that he does not want to receive anything from the king, but on the contrary, he wants to give to the king. This is why the king asked Haman what to do with a man whom the king desires to honor. Haman knew what to ask. He said, "Let them bring royal apparel which the king has worn, and the horse on which the king has ridden, and on whose head a royal crown has been placed." This is why the king needed Haman's *Kelim*, meaning what Haman understood that one should receive from the king.

For this reason he had to ask Moses to ask Israel for a favor—that they will borrow the *Kelim* of the Egyptians, meaning temporarily, so they will have desire and craving to satisfy all the lacks that the Egyptians demanded to satisfy. He had to ask because the people of Israel would settle for what they had and would always run from their thoughts and desires, but now they hear the questions and doubts of the Egyptians.

And since He promised Abraham that afterwards they will come out with many possessions, He needed them to take the Egyptians' *Kelim* only as lending and then give them back. That is, they have nothing to do with their wishes, and what they took was only temporarily, to be able to receive the lights, called "inheritance of the land," which the Creator had promised to Abraham.

Now we can understand what we asked about how the matter was turned from one end to the other, since the writing says, "and they detested the sons of Israel," meaning that they were as thorns, and afterwards, "And the Lord gave the people's favor in the eyes of the Egyptians." Wanting to hear their questions gave "favor" because they thought they were going their way. "And the Lord gave the people's favor" by telling them to borrow the *Kelim* from them, since this was what the Egyptians wanted.

A Prayer of Many

Article No. 15, Tav-Shin-Mem-Vav, 1985-86

It is written in *The Zohar* (*Beshalach* (When Pharaoh Let), and in the *Sulam* Commentary, Item 11), "And she said, 'I dwell among my own people.' He asks, 'What does that mean?' He replies, 'When *Din* is present in the world, one should not part from the collective and be alone because when the *Din* is present in the world, those who are noticed and are noted alone are caught first, even if they are righteous. Hence, one should never retire from the people because the mercy of the Creator is always on the whole people together. This is why she said, 'I dwell among my own people,' and I do not wish to part from them.'"

"When *Din* is present in the world" refers to the desire to receive, which is self-love, the nature in which the creatures are born, due to His will to do good to His creations. And because there was a desire for equivalence of form so there would not be the bread of shame, a sentence [*Din*] was passed that it is forbidden to use the vessels of reception, except when one knows that he can aim for the reception to be in order to bestow. Then, one is permitted to use the vessels of reception.

Accordingly, the meaning of "When *Din* is present in the world" is that when the whole world is immersed in self-love, there is darkness in the world because there is no room for the light to draw the creatures down due to the disparity of form between the light and the creatures who receive the light. It is on this disparity of form that the sentence was passed that the upper abundance will not be given to the creatures.

Therefore, when a person awakens and wishes for the Creator to bring him closer, meaning give him vessels of bestowal, which is called "bringing closer," he asks the Creator to help him. However, it is known that the help that comes from the Creator is called "upper abundance," which is called *Neshama*, "a soul." It is as *The Zohar* says, that the aid received from above is in a holy soul.

For this reason, when a person comes to ask the Creator to bring him closer to Him, but he is seen alone, it means that he understands that the Creator must bring him closer personally. Yet, why does he think that the public can remain in its current state and that only he should be treated differently by the Creator?

It is because he understands that he has merits that others do not. And although these are individuals who do not belong to the collective because they understand that they deserve to draw near the Creator more than others and consider themselves righteous, they are caught first. In other words, the *Din*, which is self-reception, is present in them more than in all the others, and they become worse than others in the qualities of self-love.

This is so because he thinks that he deserves more than other people. In other words, it is enough for other people to have what they have, but when he considers himself, he deserves more than the rest of the people. This thought is considered actual reception, meaning 100% self-love. It follows that self-love begins to develop in him more than in others.

It therefore follows that he is constantly working in self-love. And yet, to his own eyes, he seems righteous, since he wishes to work as a giver. He tells himself that his request of the Creator to bring him closer is right because what is he asking? For the Creator to give him strength to keep Torah and *Mitzvot* in order to bestow. And what fault could there be in wishing to serve the King?

With that, we can interpret the words of *The Zohar*. It advises those people with an inner demand, who cannot accept the state they are in because they do not see any progress in the work of God, and believe what is written (Deuteronomy 30:20), "To love the Lord your God, to listen to His voice, and to cleave unto Him; for this is your life, and the length of your days." They see that they lack love and *Dvekut* [adhesion/cleaving], and they do not feel the life in the Torah or know how to find counsel for their souls to come to feel in their organs that which the text tells us.

The advice is to ask for the whole collective. In other words, everything that one feels that he is lacking and asks fulfillment for, he should not say that he is an exception or deserves more than what the collective has. Rather, "I dwell among my own people," meaning I am asking for the entire collective because I wish to come to a state where I will have no care for myself whatsoever, but only for the Creator to have contentment. Therefore, it makes no difference to me if the Creator takes pleasure in me or can receive the pleasure from others.

In other words, he asks the Creator to give us such an understanding, which is called, "entirely for the Creator." It means that he will be certain that he is not deceiving himself that he wants to bestow upon the Creator, that perhaps he is really thinking only of his own self-love, meaning that he will feel the delight and pleasure.

Therefore, he prays for the collective. This means that if there are a few people in the collective who can reach the goal of *Dvekut* with the Creator, and this will bring the Creator more contentment than if he himself were rewarded with nearing the Creator, he excludes himself. Instead, he wishes for the Creator to help them because this will bring more contentment above than from his own work. For this reason, he prays for the collective, that the Creator will help the entire collective and will give them that feeling—that they receive satisfaction from being able to bestow upon the Creator, to bring Him contentment.

And since everything requires an awakening from below, he gives the awakening from below, and others will receive the awakening from above, to whomever the Creator knows will be more beneficial for the Creator.

It follows that if he has the strength to ask for such a prayer, then he will certainly face a true test—if he agrees to such a prayer. However, if he knows that what he is saying is only lip service, what can he do when he sees that the body disagrees with such a prayer to have pure bestowal without a hint of reception?

Here there is only the famous advice—to pray to the Creator and believe above reason that the Creator can help him and the whole collective. And he should not be impressed if he sees that he has already prayed many times but his prayer was not answered. This brings one to despair and the body mocks him and tells him, "Can't you see that you cannot do a thing? And as if you are completely hopeless, you are now asking of the Creator to grant you things that are unacceptable to reasonable people."

At that time, the body argues, "Do tell me, who among the pious and practical people wish for the Creator to give them something that is completely unreasonable? Moreover, you can see for yourself that you were not granted even smaller things than the demand you are making now of the Creator to help you, even though you asked the Creator to help you. And now you say that you want to ask the Creator to grant you something great. It is indeed a very important thing because there aren't many prayers in the world that ask the Creator to give them strength to do things for the collective, that the whole public will be rewarded with delight and pleasure by your labor. This is called 'pure and clean bestowal without a hint of self-love.'

"And you think that your prayer for small things was not granted, but great and important things are certainly priceless." For example, we might say that it is worthwhile to go to a certain person who has such precious paraphernalia that you'd have to search the entire world to find such objects, since they are found only among a chosen few. And a person from the middle-class came, who barely had the usual paraphernalia in his house, and it suddenly occurred to him that he, too, should try to obtain those objects, too, which are found among the chosen few. Certainly, if someone heard about it he would laugh at him.

It is the same for us. When a person is not educated, but is below average, yet wishes to ask the Creator for *Kelim* [vessels] that are found with a chosen few in the world, here the body itself mocks him. It tells him, "You fool, how can you even think of asking the Creator for something that even learned people do not have? How can I give you strength to work on such nonsense?"

And here begins the real work, since man's work in this world is to exit the domain of the evil inclination, which is called "receiving in order to receive." And now he wishes for the Creator to help him walk on the path of pure and clean bestowal without a hint of self-reception.

It follows that this work is truly against the evil, since he does not wish to leave any possessions with it. Rather, now he wants his work henceforth to not be for the will to receive. Rather, he asks the Creator that even what he worked for before, and what was registered in the domain of the will to receive, will all be moved from its authority to the authority of the Creator.

It follows that now he prays for the Creator to give him the strength to repent. That is, the Creator will give him the strength to bring all the deeds that were for the will to receive back to the Creator's domain, both those of the past, and those of the future. It is as Maimonides says (Laws of Repentance, Chapter 2), "Repentance must be for the past, as well."

He writes, "What is repentance? It is for the sinner to leave his sin and remove it from his mind, and resolve in his heart never to do it again, as it is written, 'Let the wicked forsake his way.' And he should also regret the past, as it is said, 'For after I turned back, I repented,' and He who knows all mysteries will testify that he will never return to this sin."

Now we can understand the importance of a prayer of many, as it is written, "I dwell among my own people." *The Zohar* says, "One should never retire from the people because the mercy of the

Creator is always on the whole people together." This means that if one asks the Creator to give him vessels of bestowal, as our sages said, "As He is merciful, you be merciful, too," one should pray for the whole collective. This is because then it is apparent that his aim is for the Creator to give him vessels of pure bestowal, as it was written, "The mercy of the Creator is always on the whole people together." It is known that there is no giving of half a thing from above. This means that when abundance is given from above to below, it is for the whole collective.

For this reason, one must ask for the whole public, since any abundance that comes from above, always comes for the whole people. This is why he says, "The mercy of the Creator is always on the whole people." Thus, there are two meanings to that, since to have pure bestowal, it would have been enough to pray for only one person besides himself. But there is another issue here—a person must ask for a whole thing because it is a rule in spirituality that what comes is always a complete thing, and all the observations are only in the receivers. For this reason, one should ask for the whole collective.

And since the abundance comes to the whole collective, and since there is no light without a *Kli* [vessel], meaning it is impossible to receive fulfillment if there is no vacancy for it where the filling can enter, he is therefore answered for that prayer that he was making for the public. It is as our sages said (Baba Kama, 92), "Anyone who pleads for mercy on his friend is answered first, since he needs the same thing." It means that although the abundance comes to the collective, the collective lacks the *Kelim*.

In other words, the abundance that comes from above is enough for the whole people, but without *Kelim*—deficiencies, so they can fill the cavities—the public does not attain the abundance that comes from above. Rather, he who has deficiencies is answered first.

The Lord Has Chosen Jacob for Himself

Article No. 16, Tav-Shin-Mem-Vav, 1985-86

In *The Zohar*, *Teruma* (item 1), Rabbi Hiya interprets the verse, "The Lord has chosen Jacob for Himself." These are its words: "Rabbi Hiya started, 'For the Lord has chosen Jacob for Himself, Israel for His merit.' How beloved are the sons of Israel by the Creator, Who desires them and wishes to unite with them and bond with them, and He has made them a unique nation in the world, as it is written, 'And what one nation on Earth is like Your people Israel,' and they desired Him and bonded with Him. It is written about it, 'The Lord has chosen Jacob for Himself,' and it is written, 'For the Lord's portion is His people.' And to the rest of the nations He has given ministers and rulers over them while He took Israel for His portion."

We should understand the following about the above words of Rabbi Hiya:

1) He begins to interpret, "For the Lord has chosen Jacob for Himself." This means that the Creator has chosen Jacob because he says that He wanted them and wanted to unite and bond with

them. Afterwards he interprets to the contrary and says, "They desired Him and bonded with Him," as it is written, "For Jacob has chosen the Lord for himself."

2) What does it mean when he says, "and He has made them a unique nation in the world," as it is written, "And what one nation on Earth is like Your people Israel"? After all they are a nation among the seventy nations of the world, so what does "one nation" mean? It seems to imply that He made them one nation.

3) He interprets, "For the Lord's portion is His people," to mean that He has given the rest of the nations ministers and rulers over them, and took Israel to His portion. We should understand what it means that He has given the rest of the nations ministers and rulers, but took the people of Israel to His portion.

It is known that there are two types of guidance: The first is called "private Providence," and the second is called "guidance through reward and punishment." They contradict one another, and Baal HaSulam interpreted that one cannot attain this with the external mind, but only when one has achieved one's wholeness in one's inner degree can one attain this.

The order of man's work is that we were given the work of the Creator with guidance through reward and punishment. This is why one must not say, "I am waiting for the Creator to give me desire and craving to engage in Torah and *Mitzvot*, and when He feels that I am feeling a good feeling I will keep the Torah and *Mitzvot*. It is forbidden to say that since we are as "clay in the hands of the potter," in the hands of the Creator. How does our overcoming help to work against the view of our bodies? We are told that we must not look at our bodies, which demand that we satisfy their wishes. Rather, we must accustom our bodies and convince them to follow the rules of Torah whether they agree or not.

We must believe in reward and punishment—that everything depends on our actions, to the extent that we persuade our bodies to follow the laws of Torah. Our sages said, "The reward is according to the labor (*Avot*, Chapter 5): "Ben He He says, 'The reward is according to the labor.'"

Baal HaSulam said that we must keep the two above types of guidance in the following manner: Before the act, meaning during the preparation, when he is about to keep the Torah and *Mitzvot*, he must believe in Providence of reward and punishment. Then, "Everything that is in the might of your hand to do, that do." That is, everything depends on man's work: To the extent of one's strength to overcome in Torah and *Mitzvot*, so he will be rewarded.

But after the work he should say that he believes in private Providence. It follows that since it is difficult for a person to say after all the efforts he put in, how can he say that it is private Providence? It follows that afterwards he is still working in reward and punishment. That is, if he tries to believe that it was private Providence he will receive reward for this. If he cannot believe in private Providence, it follows that he is punished for not wanting to believe in private Providence.

Therefore, by believing in private Providence and that it is not up to him, but the Creator has chosen to connect with him, he must praise and thank the Creator for choosing him. This applies to each and every discernment. That is, for even the smallest action in spirituality that one is rewarded with doing he should thank the Creator for giving him a thought and desire to do this thing.

One should accustom oneself to this work. When he rises before dawn, whether he woke up by himself or a friend woke him up, he should believe that although he overcame his idleness and got out of bed—with great effort, and he certainly deserves gratitude and a great reward for such great effort—he should still believe that the Creator has given him the desire to overcome all the thoughts he had when he rose out of bed.

It follows that it is the opposite of what one thinks, meaning that the Creator deserves gratitude for giving him the power and desire to overcome all this thoughts and desires. It follows that on the one hand the Creator has chosen him, and this is called "private

Providence." On the other hand, Jacob has chosen the Creator, and this is the meaning of reward and punishment.

Now we will explain what we asked, "What does it mean when he says, 'and He has made them a unique nation in the world'?" After all, there are seventy other nations in the world, and the verse says, "And what one nation on Earth is like Your people Israel"?

It is known that singular and plural in spirituality are interpreted as disparity of form and equivalence of form, as it is written (Exodus, 19:2), "And Israel camped there before the mountain." RASHI interpreted, "As one man with one heart." This is why it is written, "camped," in singular form [in Hebrew]. However, the rest of the pauses are with complaints and disputes, this is why it is written there "camped" in plural form [in Hebrew]. It follows that singular refers to equivalence of form.

With the above said we should interpret that the Creator has made the people of Israel. Although they are many, as in, "As their faces are not similar to one another, their views are not similar to one another" (*Berachot*, 58). Still, He has made them a unique people in the world, which is a great novelty. That is, although they are a nation, meaning plural, they still have the singular form through equivalence of form. As it was at the time of the giving of the Torah, so should be the wholeness of the people of Israel, meaning to become one.

It is presented in the article, "The *Arvut* (Mutual Guarantee)" (item 23): "This is why the text refers to them in singular form, as it is written, 'and there Israel camped before the mountain,' which our sages interpret 'as one man in one heart.' This is because each and every person from the nation completely detached himself from self-love … It turns out that all the individuals in the nation have come together and become one heart and one man, for only then were they qualified to receive the Torah."

We therefore see that the Creator made it so the people of Israel would achieve wholeness by giving them the power to all be of equal form, which is to bring contentment to one's Maker.

We should also explain the third question. We asked about His giving the rest of the nations ministers and rulers, while taking Israel for Himself, for His own portion. We should interpret this in the work in one person, meaning in one body. When a person attributes everything that happens in the world to the Creator, who does and will do all the deeds, he is regarded as a part of the Creator because there is no other authority in the world. At that time he is considered a part of the Creator. When he does not attribute everything that happens in the world to the Creator, but says that they are other forces, which are not *Kedusha* [holiness/sanctity], he is in a state of "nations of the world," meaning having appointees and ministers. However, this is when he is in a state of "the rest of the nations of the world."

The Agenda of the Assembly

Article No. 17, Tav-Shin-Mem-Vav, 1985-86

In *Masechet Berachot* (p 32), our sages wrote, "Rabbi Shamlai said, 'One should always praise the Creator, and then pray.' From where do we have that? From Moses, as it is written, 'And I pleaded.'" Baal HaSulam interpreted that when one wishes to ask for a favor from another, he must know, a) if he has what he asks of him, because if he doesn't, there is no point in asking, and b) that he has a kind heart. This is so because he may have what he asks, but not the kind of heart that would give.

Hence, first one needs to praise the Creator, meaning believe that the Creator has everything that one is asking for, and that the Creator is merciful and grants everyone his wish for the best.

It turns out that when the friends gather in one place, the assembly is certainly for a purpose, since when one allocates part of his time—which he would use for his own needs, relinquishing his engagements, and partaking in an assembly—he wishes to acquire something. Thus, it is important to try that when each of the friends goes home, he should see what he came to the assembly with, and what he has acquired now that he is going home.

Sometimes during the assembly of friends, everyone feels good during the meeting. At that time, it does not occur to them to contemplate with which possession they will go home, meaning what I have in my hand, which I acquired at the assembly of friends and did not have before I came to the society. And then he sees that he has nothing.

This is similar to what is written (Deuteronomy 23:25), "When you come into your friend's vineyard, you may eat grapes until you have satiated your soul, but do not put any in your vessels." We should interpret it that when the friends gather, this is called "Your friend's vineyard," when you sit and eat and drink together, talking about this and that, and the body enjoys during the action. This is similar to, "You may eat grapes until you have satiated your soul."

But when you go home and wish to see what you have in your *Kelim* [vessels], to take some livelihood home, when we leave the gathering and wish to examine what we have in our *Kelim* after all the partying, we see that, "But do not put any in your vessels." In other words, there is nothing in the *Kelim* with which to revive the soul after the assembly.

However, when one exerts, he should make certain that it is not without reward. It is as we say in the prayer, "And came unto Zion," "Lest we touch in vain." Rather, when one goes to an assembly, he should acquire nourishments there so that when he goes home he will be able to see if he has something to put in the *Kelim*. Then he will have the nourishments to feed himself until the next meeting. And until that time, he will have from what has been prepared, meaning from what he has acquired during the assembly of friends.

Therefore, first one must praise the importance of the gathering, and then see what to acquire from that activity. It is as our sages said, "One should always praise the Creator, and then pray." In other words, the beginning of the assembly, meaning the beginning of the discussions, which is the beginning of the assembly, should be about praising the society. Each and every one must try to provide reasons and explanations for their merit and importance. They should speak of nothing but the praise of society.

Finally, its praise should be disclosed by all the friends. Then they should say, "Now we are through with Stage One of the assembly of friends, and Stage Two begins." Then each will state his mind about the actions we can take so that each and every one will be able to acquire the love of friends, what each person can do to acquire love in his heart for each and every one in the society.

And once Stage Two is completed—suggestions regarding what can be done in favor of society—begins Stage Three. This concerns carrying out of the friends' decisions about what should be done.

And regarding the praise of society, in *Matan Torah* (The Giving of the Torah), p 137, he introduces the matter of love of friends, that by bonding with the friends he can obtain the greatness of the Creator. The whole world is immersed in self-love, and he wishes to go by the path of bestowal. But this is against the common view because this is the nature we were born with due to the purpose of creation, which is, as was said, "His will to do good to His creatures."

And all our power to resist it, to act to the contrary—that not only do we not want to receive for ourselves, but we rather want to give, which is considered that all our actions will be only in order to bestow contentment upon our Maker—is because it is within the nature of bestowal that when one gives to an important person he enjoys it. It turns out that without pleasure, one cannot do anything because it is against nature.

However, we can replace the pleasure. This means that instead of receiving pleasure from an act of reception, we will wish to receive pleasure from an act of bestowal. This is called "equivalence of form." We should say that as the Creator enjoys giving to the creatures, we should enjoy giving to the Creator.

Otherwise, meaning if we have no joy or pleasure while we give to the Creator, we are blemishing the equivalence of form. It is as our sages said, "There was no joy before Him as on the day when heaven and earth were created." There was no joy before the Creator since the day the world was created like the joy that He is destined to rejoice with the righteous in the future (*The Zohar*, 1, 115).

Therefore, if we have no joy while we are keeping the commandments of the Creator, then if one aims in order to bestow, it is not considered equivalence of form because one can only be glad where there is pleasure. It turns out that if he has no delight or pleasure in giving to the Creator, it is still not regarded as equivalence of form, that he has room to receive the upper abundance, since he is still lacking the pleasure that the Creator has while giving to the creatures.

It therefore follows that the whole basis upon which we can receive delight and pleasure, and which is permitted for us to enjoy—and is even mandatory—is to enjoy an act of bestowal. Thus, there is one point we should work on—appreciation of spirituality. This is expressed in paying attention to whom I turn, with whom I speak, whose commandments I am keeping, and whose laws I am learning, meaning in seeking advice concerning how to appreciate the Giver of the Torah.

And before one obtains some illumination from above by himself, he should seek out like-minded people who are also seeking to enhance the importance of any contact with the Creator in whatever way. And when many people support it, everyone can receive assistance from his friend.

We should know that "Two is the least plural." This means that if two friends sit together and contemplate how to enhance the importance of the Creator, they already have the strength to receive enhancement of the greatness of the Creator in the form of awakening from below. And for this act, the awakening from above follows, and they begin to have some sensation of the greatness of the Creator.

According to what is written, "In the multitude of people is the King's glory," it follows that the greater the number of the collective, the more effective is the power of the collective. In other words, they produce a stronger atmosphere of greatness and importance of the Creator. At that time, each person's body feels that he regards anything that he wishes to do for holiness—meaning to bestow upon the Creator—as a great fortune, that he has been privileged with being among people who have been rewarded with serving the King. At that time, every little thing he does fills him with joy and pleasure that now he has something with which to serve the King.

To the extent that the society regards the greatness of the Creator with their thoughts during the assembly, each according to his degree originates the importance of the Creator in him. Thus, he can walk all day in the world of gladness and joy, meaning he enjoys every little thing that he does concerning the work of the Creator. This is so because if he remembers that he should contemplate spirituality for even a minute, he immediately says, "I am already grateful and praising and glorifying the Creator," since he believes that now the Creator has called him and wishes to speak with him.

And when a person imagines that the King is calling him and tells him that he wants to play with him, what joy would he experience then, and what high spirits would he have? Certainly, in that uplifted state, he would not think any trifle thoughts. He would only be a little embarrassed at not knowing the King's laws and manners—how to behave when the King speaks to him.

But he considers what he does know how to do for the King as a great fortune, since he nonetheless knows some rules by which to keep the King's commandments, which he learned at school when he was young. And now that he has grown and wishes to serve the King, he will certainly miss the knowledge of the King's laws.

It turns out that his concern is that he does not know what gives the King more pleasure, which act or which intention. And other than that, he lives in a world that is all good. While gathering for the assembly, this is what the society should think, and to speak of the greatness of society, as it is written, "One should always praise the Creator, and then pray."

It is the same with the society. When we wish to demand something of the society, and this is called "praying," we must first establish the merit of the society, and then "pray," meaning demand of the society to give us what we want from it.

Thus, first we need to see what the society has, which possessions they have, which we can receive from them by bonding with them. Perhaps we do not need the possession that the society has, but moreover, we run as far away from it as possible.

Accordingly, when one comes to the assembly of friends, he should always see whether or not the friends have the goal that he craves, that each of them has some grip on that goal. And he thinks that by everyone bonding together for one goal, each will have his own share, as well as the shares of the whole of society. It follows that each member of the society will have the same strength as the whole of society together.

Each one should seriously consider the purpose of the gathering—that it should bring about a sensation, following the assembly of friends, that each one has something in his hand which he can put in his vessels, and that he is not in the form of, "But do not put any in your vessels." Each one should consider that if he does not sit especially attentive during the assembly, not only does he himself lose, but he also corrupts the whole of society.

This is similar to what is written in the Midrash (*Vayikra Rabbah*, Chapter 4): "Two people went inside a boat. One of them began to drill beneath him making a hole in the boat. He told him, 'Why are you drilling?' And he replied, 'Why should you care; I am drilling under me, not under you?' So he replied, 'You fool! Both of us will drown together with the boat!'"

And after they speak of the importance and necessity of the society, there begins the order of correction—how and with what can we reinforce the society to become one bloc, as it is written, "And there Israel camped before the mount" (Exodus 19), and it was explained, "as one man and one heart." The order should be that anyone with a suggestion that can improve the love of friends, it should be discussed, but it must be accepted by all the friends, so there is no issue of coercion here.

Thus far we discussed the connection between man and man, which is to bring us the connection between man and God, as it is written in *Matan Torah* (The Giving of the Torah), p 137. It follows that as they speak of the importance of love of friends, and that its whole importance is that it leads us to the love of the Creator, they should also think that the love of friends should bring us into the importance of the love of the Creator.

Who Causes the Prayer

Article No. 18, Tav-Shin-Mem-Vav, 1985-86

Our sages wrote (*Mesechet Berachot* 32), "One should always praise the Creator and then pray." This shows us that one should believe that when a person comes to a state where he feels his fault in the work of the Creator—when he feels that his faith is not as it should be, that is, able to believe that the Creator is benevolent, and this feeling, when he sees that he cannot thank the Creator and say wholeheartedly, "Blessed is He who said, 'Let there be the world,'" meaning that he so enjoys the world that he thanks the Creator for having created the world so he has what to enjoy—if he doesn't feel the delight and pleasure that can be received, it is hard for him to be thankful for it. And this pains him that he cannot praise the Creator for the world He has created and say wholeheartedly, "Blessed is He who said, 'Let there be the world.'"

And that deficiency pains him, meaning he says that this feeling must have come to him because he is remote from the Creator, meaning immersed in self-love. This causes him to part from the Creator, meaning that he doesn't feel the greatness of the Creator because the Creator is hidden from him.

And therefore, he cannot see the truth, as it is written, "For it is your life and the length of your days." And also, he cannot feel the importance of the Torah, as it is written, "For this is your wisdom and your understanding in the eyes of the nations, who will hear all these statutes and say, 'Surely this great nation is a wise and understanding people.'"

When a person introspects and thinks, "Where is this excitement that the nations are saying about us, 'Surely this ... is a wise and understanding people,' because of the Torah, because we keep what is written, 'Observe and do them; for this is your wisdom and your understanding in the eyes of the nations.' So why don't I feel the importance of Torah and *Mitzvot*?"

In that state of reflection, when he feels how remote he is from any reverence for the work of the Creator, he begins to awaken and think, "Something must be done. I cannot stay in that state of lowliness for the rest of my life." Certainly, this is the time when a person begins to pray to the Creator to bring him closer to Him and to help him from above, as our sages said, "He who comes to be purified is aided."

In other words, He should lift the concealment of the greatness and importance of *Kedusha* [holiness/sanctity] from him, so he can overcome all the ignoble thoughts and desires that come from self-love, and that all his concerns will be only about how he can do something for the *Kedusha*, called "in order to bestow contentment upon his Maker." And certainly, this can only be to the extent that he believes in the greatness and importance of the Creator.

Thus, he asks the Creator to open his eyes so he will see and feel the greatness and importance of the Creator, as it is written (Psalm 88), "Lord, why do You reject my soul? Why do You hide Your face from me?" And then it is a prayer from the bottom of the heart. That is, at that time, a person wants the Creator to heal his heart, as it is written (Psalm 147), "Who heals the brokenhearted and binds up their sadness."

And then one probably thinks that the awakening for the prayer that the Creator will bring him closer to Him came from himself, and he awaits the Creator's salvation, that He will help him by granting his prayer. That is, that He will bring him closer to Him, as he is praying now because now he feels His lack, which he didn't feel before.

Therefore, when a person doesn't receive from the Creator what he thinks the Creator should give him, he becomes angry that the Creator is not granting his prayer. As for other people, he believes that He is not bringing them closer because they have no desire for spirituality. But he is not like other people, who have no affinity to the Creator, so the Creator doesn't need to bring them closer anyway.

But this man, who prayed for the Creator to help him come closer to Him, the Creator Himself can see that he is not like other people. Rather, he is higher than the populace; he understands the world and its purpose, and he contemplates the purpose for which he was created and what he must achieve. But when he looks at other people, he sees their lowliness—that all their thoughts and actions are for their own benefit—and he feels that he understands differently because his mind and qualities are more virtuous and worthy than those of other people.

Moreover, sometimes he sees that he is even more virtuous than the people in his group. He sees that they occasionally think of spirituality, but he—his every thought and all his desires are only about spirituality. He always wants to exit self-love, and all his requests of the Creator are only for Him to deliver him from this lowliness. And he doesn't see that his friends are equally serious, thinking only about spirituality.

For this reason, he is upset with the Creator for not granting his prayer, leaving him in his current state like the rest of the friends, and is not considerate of him, meaning with his prayer, which is truly prayed from the bottom of the heart. Thus, regarding the granting of the prayer, he finds a fault above.

And he asks himself, "But it is written, 'For You hear the prayer of every mouth,' and 'every mouth' means that the whole mouth should ask the prayer, meaning that his whole body demands that the Creator will help him. But as for the rest of the people, their prayers are not answered because it is not with 'every mouth.'"

Baal HaSulam said about it, "It is written, 'And it shall come to pass that before they call, I will answer, and while they are still speaking, I will hear.'" He interpreted that when a person feels his fault and prays for the Creator to help him, it is not because a person feels his fault, and this gives him reason to pray. Rather, the reason is that he is favored by the Creator, and the Creator wishes to bring him near.

At that time, the Creator sends him the sensation of his own fault and calls upon him to join Him. In other words, it is the Creator who brings him near by giving him a desire to turn to the Creator and to speak to the Creator. It follows that he already had the granting of the prayer even before he prayed. That is, the Creator brought him closer by enabling him to speak to the Creator. This is called, "Before they call, I will answer." That is, the Creator brought that person near Him before the thought appeared in the man's mind that he should pray to the Creator.

But why did the Creator choose him and give him the call to come to Him and pray? To this, we have no answer. Instead, we must believe above reason that this is so. This is what we call, "Guidance of Private Providence." One must not say, "I'm waiting for the Creator to give me an awakening from above, and then I will be able to work in the work of holiness." Baal HaSulam said that in regard to the future, a person must believe in reward and punishment, meaning he must say (*Avot*, Chapter 1), "If I am not for me who is for me, and when I am for me, what am I, and if not now, then when?"

Thus, one mustn't wait another moment. Instead, he should say, "If not now, then when?" And he must not wait for a better time, so "Then I will get up and do the work of holiness." Rather, it is as our sages said (*Avot*, Chapter 2), "Do not say, 'I will study when I have time,' lest you will not have time."

But after the fact, said Baal HaSulam, one must believe in private Providence—that it was not the person who called upon the Creator, but the Creator who called upon the person and told him, "I want you to speak to Me." It follows that the reason for the nearing did not come from the individual but from the Creator. For this reason, one mustn't think that the Creator did not hear the prayer. Rather, He brought him near even before he turned to the Creator to bring him near Him.

This is called, "Before they call, I will answer." It follows from the above that if a person has awakened to sense his ignoble state, it did not come from the individual. Rather, the Creator sent him this feeling so he would ask to be brought closer. Therefore, as soon as one has a thought that he is remote from the Creator and wishes to pray to the Creator to bring him closer, he mustn't pray until he first thanks the Creator for having called upon him to bring him closer.

The Creator wants man to pray to Him. And when a person does self-analysis into why he suddenly remembered that there is spirituality and that he should try to obtain something in spirituality, if he immediately says that the Creator sent him this thought, then he can pray.

This is the meaning of what our sages said, "One should always praise the Creator." In other words, as soon as one begins to contemplate his situation concerning spirituality, he should promptly praise and thank the Creator for having given him the thought and desire for spirituality. Afterwards, when he knows that the Creator is calling him, he immediately begins to thank and praise the King for having brought him closer. This is when he can pray for his situation, since he sees that he is lacking Torah and doesn't know any distinction between true and false, and he prays for the Creator to show him the path of truth.

Now we can understand what our sages said (*Midrash Rabbah, Toldot*, 63, Mark 5), "'And the Lord answered him.' Rabbi Levi said,

'There is an allegory about a prince who was striving to take a pound of gold from his father. He was striving from within and he was striving from without, since in Arabic, 'striving' means 'asking.'" He interprets there the gifts of priesthood, that 'taking a pound means that his father, too, wished to give it, and was striving opposite him to hurry his taking.'"

From what we have explained, the reason that a person wants to draw near comes from the Creator. The Creator does not wait for a person to wake up, but awakens the person. Afterwards, one prays that the Creator will bring him closer. We can understand it with the allegory that he gives about the verse, "And ... answered him," which means that Isaac prayed to the Creator.

And he gave an allegory about that, meaning that his father, that is, the Creator, conspires from within, meaning that his father gave him a thought and desire to pray to Him, and afterwards the prince conspires from without. In other words, the people of Israel are princes, and they are standing outside the King's palace and wish to draw near the Creator, meaning enter the King's palace. This means that his father in heaven started first.

Concerning Joy

Article No. 19, Tav-Shin-Mem-Vav, 1985-86

The *Mishnah* says (*Taanit*, 26), "From the beginning of Av we diminish joy. From the beginning of *Adar* we increase joy. If he is deliberating with idol-worshippers, let him judge it on *Adar*." We should understand the meaning of increasing joy and diminishing joy. After all, joy is a result of some reason that caused him joy, and we can only diminish or increase the reasons. Therefore, we should know which reason will bring us joy.

Our sages, who told us to increase joy, referred to joy of *Kedusha* [holiness/sanctity]. Accordingly, we should consider to which reason they told us to refer so it would bring us joy of *Kedusha*. We should also understand what they said, "If he is deliberating with idol-worshippers, let him judge it on *Adar*." After all, we are in the land of Israel, and there are several towns where there is not even one gentile. And even if we find a gentile in town, what should be the deliberation with him?

It seems that judging the idol-worshippers on *Adar* is a perpetual custom and not an incidental matter. That is, if there is a rare incident where Israel is deliberating with a gentile he will go and judge him on the month of *Adar*. Therefore, we need to understand to which idol-worshippers they are referring that they are deliberating with.

We see that there is an order of two manners in our prayers: 1) an order of songs and praises to the Creator, 2) an order of prayers and litanies. We also see that the two are opposite. This is so because naturally, when someone asks one's friend to give him something, the extent of the request depends on the extent of his need for it. If the thing he is asking his friend for is something that touches his heart and necessary, to the extent of the necessity for the matter, he tries to do everything he can to obtain what he is seeking.

Accordingly, when a person prays to the Creator to grant his wish, he should see that his prayer is from the bottom of the heart, meaning to feel his deficiency. To the extent of his feeling, his prayer can be more sincere. Thus, his prayer will not be as lip-service but rather from the bottom of the heart.

To feel his deficiency, he must see the truth, to see that he has a great lack and he is an empty *Kli* [vessel] as far as matters of *Kedusha* are concerned. When he feels that he is the worst person in the world, he can say that his prayer is honest because he feels that his deficiency is the greatest in the world and there is no one who is like him.

Opposite that is the second discernment in the order of our prayer, meaning psalms, songs, and praises. We see that usually the amount of gratitude that one gives to another is measured by the benefit he has received from his friend. For example, when someone helps another obtain something small that he needed, the gratitude is small, as well.

But we see that if someone gives someone a job when jobs are hard to find, he has been jobless for months and is indebted to the grocery store, and the store owner has already told him he must stop selling groceries, he has given up on searching for loans to provide for his necessities, and he suddenly meets a person whom he wanted to ask for a loan, but that person offers him a job with good conditions and tells him, "Why look for loans? I'll give you a job. I heard that you are trustworthy, so although I have many workers, I don't have anyone I can trust. I will pay you well so you can pay your debts quickly, so why should you need a loan from me?"

We can picture the gratitude he would give to this person. He does not need to thank him verbally because his whole body thanks him, as it is written, "All my bones shall say." If we picture a person who was sentenced to life imprisonment, and another person came and liberated him, what gratitude would all his organs give to his savior?

It follows that if one wishes to give high praise to the Creator so it becomes as "All my bones shall say, 'Lord, who is like You, Who delivers the afflicted from him who is too strong for him,'" then one should picture oneself as the happiest person in the world, if he wishes to give great praise to the Creator. Otherwise, if he feels that something is still missing, that he wants the Creator to help him, then the gratitude he gives to the Creator will not be as "All my bones shall say."

Therefore, we see two complete opposites in the order of our prayer, which brings up the question, "What can one do when he sees that they are so remote from one another?" Normally, we see the oppositeness in many things. One example is the order of lights that illuminate in the *Kelim* [vessels]. It is known that there is an inverse relation between *Kelim* and lights. In the *Kelim* the big and fine *Kelim* appear first. That is, *Keter* appears first and the *Sefira* [singular of *Sefirot*] *Malchut* appears last. In the lights it is the opposite: the small ones appear first: first *Malchut*, and finally *Keter*. It is known that when we speak from the perspective of the *Kelim* we say that the order is *KHB ZON*, and when we speak from the perspective of the lights, we say that the order is *NRNHY*.

Another example is that Baal HaSulam said that we see oppositeness in the order of man's work. On the one hand, our sages said (*Avot*, Chapter 4), "Be very, very humble." On the other hand, they said, "And his heart was high in the ways of the Lord." That is, if he really humbles himself before each and every one, he will not be able to overcome those who mock his walking in the path of the Creator, since he humbles himself before everyone. Instead, at that time he should say, "And his heart was high in the ways of the Lord." That is, he should not be impressed by anyone who tells him, "This work that you took upon yourself fits skillful and brave people, who are accustomed to overcoming obstacles and received good upbringing. That is, since they were little they have been accustomed to giving the work of the Creator the prime importance. But you are not like that. You should settle for being an important landlord, meaning see that your children learn Torah and the work of the Creator, and then you will be an important landlord and your daughters will marry disciples of Torah. It is inappropriate for you, middle-aged man, to begin to walk in the path of the work that leads to Torah *Lishma* [for Her sake], and completely not for self-benefit. Get off this path and do not pine for matters beyond your level."

At that time he has no choice but not to be impressed with them and keep the words of our sages, "Let him not be ashamed before the scoffers." It follows that then he must go by the way of pride. But on the other hand, he must keep "Be very, very humble." However, according to the rule, "There are no two opposites in one carrier," how can both be in one person? There are many other examples of two opposites in the work of the Creator, but there can be two opposites in one carrier at two times, meaning one at a time.

The root of the matter is as it is written in the "Introduction to the Book of Zohar" (items 10-11), "How is it possible that the chariot of impurity and *Klipot* [shells/peels] would emerge from His holiness, since it is at the other end of His holiness?"

He says there: "This will to receive, which is the very essence of the souls by creation, is *Tuma'a* [impurity] and *Klipot*. This is so because the disparity of form in them would separate them from Him. And in order to mend that separation, which lies on the *Kli* [vessel] of the souls, He has created all the worlds and separated them into two systems, which are the four worlds ABYA of *Kedusha*, and opposite them the four worlds ABYA of *Tuma'a*. He imprinted the desire to bestow in the system of the ABYA of *Kedusha*, removed the will to receive for themselves from them, and placed it in the system of ABYA of *Tuma'a*."

He also says there: "How will those two things, which are opposite in form from one another, be corrected? For this reason, the reality of this corporeal world was created, meaning a place where there is a body and a soul, and a time of corruption and a time of correction. For the body, which is the will to receive for itself, extends from its root in the Thought of Creation, through the system of the worlds of *Tuma'a*, and remains under the authority of that system for the first thirteen years. This is the time of corruption. Afterwards begins the time of correction, which is after thirteen years. By engaging in Torah and *Mitzvot* [commandments/good deeds], when he engages in order to bestow contentment upon his Maker, he begins to purify the will to receive for himself imprinted in him, and slowly turns it to be in order to bestow."

It turns out that as soon as the creature is created, he consists of two opposites: 1) vessels of reception, 2) vessels of bestowal. There is no greater oppositeness than this. These two opposites come in one carrier, but one at a time, and it seems as though there is a middle line that contains both of them: 1) the will to receive, 2) the will to bestow.

The middle line contains both of them when the will to receive is included in the will to bestow, called "receiving in order to bestow." It follows that the two forces are included in this middle line, meaning reception and bestowal together.

Accordingly, the answer to our question, "How can there be in man's work complete wholeness and deficiency in utter lowliness in the same carrier?" is that this can be in two times. That is, one needs to divide the order of one's work into two ways: 1) One way will be on the path of "right," called "wholeness." This is so because when one begins to turn, one should first turn to the right, called "wholeness," and then to the left. It is so because man can walk specifically on two legs, whereas on one leg you cannot speak of walking.

"Right" means wholeness because when one comes to take upon oneself the work of the Creator, the order is that one should assume the burden of the kingdom of heaven "as an ox to the burden and as a donkey to the load." The "ox" refers to the mind, called "ox," from the verse, "Let the ox know its owner," referring to faith above reason.

A "donkey" refers to the heart, called "donkey," as in, "and a donkey, its master's crib," referring to self-love. Therefore, when saying, "to work in order to bestow contentment upon one's maker," he regards it as a load, and he always wants to throw off his shoulders. He is always searching what he can eat from this work, meaning what pleasure his will to receive might derive.

When he takes upon himself this work he says, "I should see for myself, meaning always check if I am not deceiving myself that I am on the right path, that it is the proper one, meaning keeping Torah and *Mitzvot* because of the commandment of the Creator and not for any other reasons. However, I am keeping the words of our sages, who said, 'One should always engage in Torah and *Mitzvot*, even if *Lo Lishma* [not for Her sake], since from *Lo Lishma* he will come to *Lishma* [for Her sake].' Thus, why should I think whether I am keeping Torah and *Mitzvot* with all the intentions so that everything will be for the Creator?

"However, I have a great privilege that the Creator has given me a thought and desire to keep something in Torah and *Mitzvot*. According to the rule, with something important we do not regard the quantity but the quality. Rather, even if it is a small amount, if the quality is what matters, even something small of high quality is very important. For this reason, since the Creator has commanded us through Moses to keep Torah and *Mitzvot*, I do not care how much I can keep it. Rather, even if I have the worst and foulest intentions, in the act I do observe as much as my body permits.

"And although I am incapable of overcoming the desires of the body, I am still glad that at least I have the strength to keep the commandments of the Creator in some way because I believe that everything comes by Providence. That is, the Creator has given me the desire and strength to observe Torah and *Mitzvot*, and I thank Him for this because I see that not everyone have been given this privilege of observing the *Mitzvot* of the Creator." He should say that he cannot even value the greatness and importance of keeping the Creator's commandment even without any intention.

We can compare it to a child who does not want to eat, who derives no pleasure from eating, so the parents force the child to eat whether he wants to or not. And although the child has no pleasure, in the end, even by coercion, it helps the child, as well, so he can live and grow. However, it would certainly be better if the child wanted to eat by himself, meaning if he enjoyed the food. But even without pleasure and completely by coercion it still benefits the child.

We should say likewise in serving the Creator. Even if we keep Torah and *Mitzvot* by coercion, meaning we force ourselves to keep and our bodies resist anything that is of *Kedusha* [holiness/sanctity], still, the act he performs does its thing, and by this he can come to a state where he has a desire to observe. At that time, all the things he did are not in vain. Rather, everything he did enters *Kedusha*.

We can interpret this with what our sages said about the verse, "He will sacrifice it before the Lord according to his will" (*Arachin*, 21). "Our sages said, 'Will sacrifice it' indicates that he is forced. But it is written, 'according to his will.' How is this so? He is forced until he says, 'I want.'"

This means that the words "before the Lord, according to his will" bewildered our sages. It means that everything he does with regard to bringing himself close to the Creator is not regarded as an act if he does not want to work for the Creator, which is called "according to the Lord's will." Instead, that person is still unable to do things to benefit the Creator, which means that his deeds are worthless, as though he has not done anything because they are still not according to the Creator's will.

However, it is written, "He will sacrifice it." This means that he is forced, meaning even by coercion. That is, when he does not want to work for the Creator it is still called "sacrifice." But this is perplexing, since he does not want to sacrifice the offering to the Creator, so the beginning of the verse contradicts its end.

They said about this: "He is forced until he says, 'I want.'" That is, this follows the rule that our sages said, "One should always engage in Torah and *Mitzvot* even *Lo Lishma*, since from *Lo Lishma* he comes to *Lishma*" (*Pesachim* 50b). This means that by subjugating himself each time, although the body does not agree to work for the Creator because where he does not see self-gratification he cannot do a thing.

Still, he does not notice the body's complaints and says to his body: "Know that even by force, you are doing the Creator's commandments. It will not help you to resist the work. It is said that practical *Mitzvot* have the power to bring one to *Lishma*." This is the meaning of "He is forced," meaning that he forces himself and does not listen to any logic and reason that the body tries to explain to him, but tells it, "In the end he will achieve *Lishma*." This is the meaning of "until he says, 'I want.'" That is, from *Lo Lishma* we come to *Lishma*, which is called "I want."

Therefore, each time he remembers while performing some act of *Kedusha*, great joy immediately awakens in him that he was rewarded with having some contact with matters that the Creator commanded him to do. Although he knows that everything he does is *Lo Lishma*, he is still profoundly happy since our sages have promised us that from *Lo Lishma* we come to *Lishma*.

He is even happier because our sages said, "He who repents from love, sins become for him as merits, and he who repents from fear, sins become for him as mistakes." It follows that when he is

Concerning Joy

rewarded with working *Lishma*, all the *Mitzvot* he had performed *Lo Lishma* will enter *Kedusha* and will be as important as though he had performed them *Lishma*.

Thus, even while he is still working *Lo Lishma*, it is as important to him as though he is working *Lishma*. That is, he thinks that everything he does is certainly more important than sins and are bound to be corrected into being good, and he regards everything he does, even the smallest thing, as a great *Mitzva* [commandment]. It is as our sages said (*Avot*, Chapter 2), "Be careful with a lesser commandment as with a greater one, for you do not know the reward for the commandments."

For this reason, when he calculates the works he is doing, whose *Mitzvot* he is observing, and when he says some words of Torah, he tells himself, "Whose Torah am I learning?" And when he blesses for pleasure, such as before drinking or before eating bread, he thinks, "To whom am I speaking now?"

It turns out that then he is in utter wholeness, and that wholeness begets joy because at that time he is adhered to the Creator, just as he assumes that he is speaking to the Creator, who is good and does good. Naturally, he receives joy from the root, for the root of all creations is the Creator, who is called "the Good Who Does Good."

Our sages said, "Good to him and does good to others." This means that at that time he can believe that the Creator is doing good to him and to everyone. This means that then he can believe above reason that this is really so, even though he concludes with his external intellect that he does not see the good in completeness.

But now, through the calculations he does with his work in Torah and *Mitzvot*, when he is somewhat adhered to some extent to the Creator, he has the power to believe above reason that this is really so. Naturally, "truth will show its way." The result of his thinking that now he is speaking to the Creator is a great awakening of joy, as it is written, "Majesty and splendor before Him, strength and joy are in His place."

We should understand in relation to whom it was said that there is joy in His place. Certainly, all the names we mention are from the perspective of the creatures, meaning according to the perception of the creatures. However, in the Creator Himself, our sages said, "There is no thought or perception in Him at all." Rather, everything is said only from the perspective of the creatures.

Therefore, this means that those who feel that they are standing before Him feel majesty and splendor, as well as those who think that they are standing in His place, since "place" means "equivalence of form."

But there is another meaning, that interest is a mirror, as I heard from Baal HaSulam, that in the place one thinks, there one is. Thus, if a person thinks that he is standing and speaking with the King, then he is in the place where the King is present, and then he feels as it is written, "strength and joy are in His place."

By this we can understand what we asked about what our sages said, "From the beginning of *Adar* we increase joy." We asked, "Why increase joy?" That is, joy is a result of some reason, so what is the reason that could evoke the reason to bring us joy?

According to the above, it pertains to increasing advancement on the right line, called "wholeness." When a person is in a state of wholeness, it is called "equivalence." That is, the whole, which is the man, is now adhered to the Whole, as it is written, "The blessed adhere to the blessed, and the cursed does not adhere to the blessed." Therefore, if one is in a state of criticism, called "left line," he is in a state of "cursed," and then he is separated from the Whole. For this reason at that time he can feel only darkness and not light, for only light brings joy.

However, we should understand why specifically on the month of *Adar* we should increase joy, and why can't we be on the way of the right all year long? We should reply to this that since the miracle of Purim was on the month of *Adar*, when the light of the end of correction illuminated, as it is written in *The Gate of Intentions* (*The Study of the Ten Sefirot*, Part 16, p 1813, item 220),

Concerning Joy

"Therefore, in the future [end of correction], all the holy days will be cancelled but the scroll of Ester [Purim]." The reason is that there has never been such a great miracle, not on any Shabbat or on any good day.

For this reason, the preparation for such a great light should be joy, which is the preparation to greet an esteemed guest, which is the light of the end of correction. Hence, by preparing through increasing joy, we extend the light called "the days of feast and merriment."

This follows the rule that is written in the holy *Zohar*: "The act below awakens the act above." That is, according to the work of the lower ones, the work above awakens. This means that when the lower ones engage in joy, in the same manner they extend light of joy downward, as it is written (Esther, 9:21), "And Mordecai wrote, to oblige them on those days when the Jews rid themselves of their enemies, and it was a month which was turned for them from sorrow into gladness and from mourning into a holiday, that they should make them days of feasting and rejoicing," by which they will extend the light of the end of correction that illuminated then.

We should discern concerning the extension of the joy. We said that the reason for this is that at that time a person thanks the Creator for bringing him closer. It follows that when he gives thanks, he engages in bestowal because he thanks and praises the Creator for giving him a thought and desire to have some contact with spirituality.

But now he does not want the Creator to give him anything. Therefore, he is not asking anything from the Creator, and now his only aim is to give thanks to the Creator. It follows that now he has *Dvekut* [adhesion] with the Creator because he is engaging in bestowal. Thus, by this, joy and wholeness are drawn to him from the *Dvekut* because now he is adhered to the Whole one. This is the meaning of increasing joy by this.

This is not so when he engages in litany, for a prayer that is from the bottom of the heart is full of deficiencies, since to the extent of the sensation of lack so is his prayer deeper. It follows that then he cannot be happy. Thus, the reason for the gladness is when he engages in praise and gratitude and not when he engages in examining deficiencies.

According to the above we can interpret what our sages said, "If he is deliberating with idol-worshippers, let him judge it on *Adar*." This means that there is deliberation with a foreigner as though it is customary that Israel deliberate with foreigners. Does this belong to people who engage in Torah and work, and who do not engage in any work or trade?

In the work, we should interpret that this refers to the idol-worshippers that there are in all of Israel, meaning in one body. Those people who want to walk in the path of the Creator, their bodies resist them. It is as our sages said about the verse, "There shall be no foreign God in you." They said, "What foreign God is there in man's body? It is the evil inclination." This is called "idol-worshippers," since it resists being Israel. This is regarded as deliberating. And then, on the month of *Adar*, when they were rewarded with the miracle and there was joy and merriment to the Jews because they feared the Jews, and it was turned into the opposite—that the Jews governed their enemies—for this reason on this month one can sentence the foreigner within him, and he will certainly succeed on this month, for it is regarded as "turned to the contrary," as it is written, "And the Jews governed their enemies."

We must remember that one deliberates with one's idol-worshippers because each one argues, "It is all mine." Israel argues that the body was created only to be Israel and a servant of the Creator, and not for self-love, while the foreigner within him argues, "It is all mine," too, meaning that the whole body was created with a desire to receive because the body needs to see only to its will to receive. Why should it think about wanting to bestow? It shows several proofs that it is right because this is what everyone does.

That is, it tells him, "Go see what everyone is doing. Is there anyone who is concerned with others while his own needs have not been satisfied? There are very few people, not more than a handful, whose needs have been satisfied completely, so they began to see to others' well-being. However, even then they watch very carefully that their concern for others will, God forbid, not blemish their self-love. But you are saying, 'It is all mine,' meaning to completely avoid thinking about self-love. Instead, you want to use all your energy to serve others, and you excuse your desire to work for the friends, which is called 'love of others,' by telling me that this is not the end, but that you think that by engaging in love of others you will be able to achieve love of the Creator. That is, you want to be completely annulled before the Creator. But then, what shall become of the body, if you want to give your whole body to the Creator, to completely annul before Him? You tell me, how can I agree to this? This is very difficult to grasp. Therefore, I am forced to argue, 'It is all mine,' and not let you move one step forward."

In that state, there is a big war because each one says that he is right. The Israel in him argues that since the Creator created us with the intention that His will is to benefit His creations, He certainly knows what is good for the creatures. That is, He understood that only by doing everything in order to bestow contentment upon the Creator they will have the strength to receive the highest degrees, called "revelation of Godliness," which dresses in the inner mind and inner feeling in the heart. Thus, only in this way they will be able to receive all the delight and pleasure that the Creator wanted to give to the creatures.

This would not be so if they received with vessels of reception. Besides causing separation, there is the matter of being content with less. That is, we must believe what is written in the holy *Zohar*, that there is a faint light that shines in the *Klipot* [shells/peels] to sustain them. That is, all the pleasures in the corporeal world are as faint light compared to the delight and pleasure that is found in *Kedusha* [holiness/sanctity].

In other words, even a small degree of *Kedusha*, such as *Nefesh de Assiya*, contains more pleasure than all the worldly pleasures. If one were to receive the abundance in the desire to receive for one's own benefit, he would settle for this and would not be able to go and attain higher degrees because for self-gratification, this illumination of *Nefesh de Assiya* is satisfactory, and he would have no need to add anything to the pleasures he was enjoying.

However, when one is taught to work in order to bestow contentment upon one's Maker, one cannot say, "I settle for what I have been granted," since everything he receives is to benefit the Creator. Therefore, he cannot say, "I have enough, since I pleased the Creator by receiving a little upper light and it pleases the Creator so I do not want to receive anymore."

It is forbidden to say, "I have enough because I already pleased Him by receiving this small illumination from Him." Instead, one should try to bestow more and more contentment upon the Creator each and every time. And since each joy above is when the purpose of creation, which is to do good to His creations, actually reaches the lower ones—and this is what pleases above—hence, on the month of *Adar*, when the time of the miracle awakens—as it is written, "and it was turned into the opposite, that the Jews governed their enemies"—the time is ripe to awaken the foreigner within him. It is as our sages said (*Berachot* 5), "One should always vex the good inclination over the evil inclination," as it was said, "be angry but do not sin." RASHI interprets "vexing the good inclination" to mean making war with the evil inclination.

Here it means that on the month of *Adar* he can defeat the evil inclination, since then, when there was the miracle from above, it is as our sages said (*Shabbat* 88), "They observed and received." They observed what they already received. RASHI interprets, "What Rabba said, that the generation received it in the days of Ahasuerus, was because of the love of the miracle that was done to them."

But on the month of Av, the time of the ruin of the Temple, when we should mourn it, then the meaning of what our sages said "diminishing joy," is the way in which we engage on the month of *Adar*—in the right, in order to awaken the miracle that appeared on the month of *Adar*. It is as our sages said, "For the love of the miracle they observed and received."

But on the month of Av, when we must mourn the ruin of the Temple, we must work on the left line, meaning criticize our actions, that we must be in the path of *Kedusha*, which is in order to bestow, and how one is remote from bestowal.

When one thinks about this, he is in a state of remoteness from *Kedusha* and is immersed in self-love, where his whole basis for engaging in Torah and *Mitzvot* is in order to satisfy the will to receive with every possible satisfaction.

Therefore, when considering one's lowliness he can awaken the pain of the ruin of *Kedusha* that there is in each and every one. And then the verse, "All who mourn Jerusalem is rewarded with seeing the comfort of Jerusalem" comes true.

Should One Sin and Be Guilty

Article No. 20, Tav-Shin-Mem-Vav, 1985-86

It is written in *The Zohar, Vayikra* (item 251): "We learned that it is written, 'Should one sin and be guilty.'" Why does he first say, "Should one sin," and finally, "and be guilty"? He replies that we learned that "should one sin" means that these are the transgressions with which the creatures have sinned, as it is written, "of all the sins of man." "And be guilty" is as you say, "the guilt is returned to the Lord," where "and be guilty" means "will be corrected." That is, "should he sin" means if he corrects his works and returns what he has robbed. Rabbi Yosi said, "This means that the word, "returns," means he returns by himself, since it is not written "will return," which is imperative, but precisely, "returns," meaning by himself.

We should understand why he says, "Should one sin." Which transgressions are called "sin," where it is written, "of all the sins of man"? We should understand this, since is there a transgression that is not considered a sin? He brings an evidence to this, as it is written, "from all of man's sins." Afterwards he interprets the verse "about theft," which applies specifically between man and man.

Should One Sin and Be Guilty

But what about the *Mitzvot* [commandments] between man and the Creator? We shall explain this in the work. It is known that all the sins come because of the will to receive, which was imprinted in the creatures by the thought of creation "to do good to His creations." After there was a prohibition on receiving in order to receive, which is the correction of the *Tzimtzum* [restriction] that was done in order to avoid the "bread of shame," because of this correction, the worlds of *Klipot* [shells/peels] emerged by cascading.

Then, through the sin of *Adam Harishon* with the tree of knowledge, two systems emerged, as in "God has made one opposite the other." Thus, there is ABYA of *Kedusha* [holiness/sanctity] and opposite it ABYA of *Tuma'a* [impurity].

From here stem all the sins—by wanting to receive only in order to receive. This means that man was created by nature with self-love, meaning that he cares only for his own benefit. Only by the *Segula* [remedy/virtue] of Torah and *Mitzvot* [commandments] can he be corrected to work in order to bestow. Before he receives this correction, called "in order to bestow," he wants to swallow everything into his own domain, meaning to take everything out from the Creator's domain and bring it into man's domain.

Three discernments extend from this in our world: 1) forbidden things and permitted things. 2) We make two discernments in permitted things: mandatory or optional. 3) The intention, meaning we should aim with forbidden things, too, not to do them, so it is for the purpose of bestowing. With permitted things, whether mandatory or optional, the intention should be to bestow and not for self-benefit, but he keeps Torah and *Mitzvot* because of the commandments of the Creator, for he believes in the Creator, that He will enjoy his keeping everything that He has commanded us. This should be his sole intention with everything he does, in positive *Mitzvot* [commandments to do something], negative *Mitzvot* [commandments not to do something], and in optional matters. He tries to aim everything for the Creator while engaging in them.

It follows that if a person receives pleasure into his own authority, his sin is that he takes out from the Creator's domain into his own domain, since everything should enter the Creator's domain, and man is only the Creator's servant and has no authority of his own. Rather, everything should be in his Master's domain, and the servant has no authority of his own.

However, when he receives the pleasures that exist in the world into his own domain it seems as though there are two domains. This is regarded as extracting from the domain of the Creator, whose world is His, and letting into his own domain.

Concerning extracting from his friend's domain into his own, we should discern two manners: 1) His friend does not see that he extracts from his friend and lets it into his own domain. This is called a "thief." That is, if his friend does not see, he has the courage to let his friend's possession into his own domain. But if he sees that his friend might see him taking things and letting them into his own domain then he will not steal.

2) Sometimes he takes his friend's possession even if his friend resists. This is called "robbing." He robs his friend even if his friend sees, but he is not fazed by his yelling that it's a robbery and he does not allow it. He insists, meaning he does not have the power to overcome the passion that he has for his friend's possession, and he is compelled to rob. The reason he is not impressed by the other looking at him taking is that his will to receive is already fully developed.

Baal HaSulam said that the difference between a thief and a robber is that the robber has a bigger will to receive than the thief. Therefore, when a thief knows that the owner will see him in the act, the shame gives him strength to overcome and relinquish the theft. But the will to receive of a robber is so strong that nothing can disrupt him from carrying out his scheme. His desire and passion are so great that he does not consider anything and carries out his plan.

Now we can explain what we asked above about wanting to imply that he says, "Should one sin," meaning which of those sins that are called, "sin," as it is written, "of all the sins of man." We should interpret what he says, "of those sins that are called, 'sin,'" after which he brings evidence from the verse, "of all the sins of man." What does "of all" mean? We should interpret that he is implying to the root from which all the sins come, namely the will to receive, with which all the actions in the world begin, and with which all the works are concluded. That is, we were given this desire to correct so it works in order to bestow. When the general will to receive is corrected in order to bestow, it will be called the "end of correction."

This means that all the corrections we must exert in Torah and *Mitzvot* are only to correct the will to receive so it works in order to bestow, and then we will be rewarded with *Dvekut* [adhesion], and we will be able to attain the purpose of creation—to do good to His creations.

It follows that at the end of correction, when everything is corrected and there is nothing more to correct, everything should enter *Kedusha*. That is, even sins must enter *Kedusha*, or a part of the will to receive will be missing, left outside without correction. We said that the intimation that the verse, "of all the sins of man," means everything that extends from this root. That is, we have to know that all sins extend from the rudimentary will to receive, as we know that this is the root of all the creatures. Therefore, if even one sin remains, since it extends from the root, which is the will to receive, it, too, must be corrected into working in order to bestow, or this deficiency will be apparent in the root, meaning in *Tzimtzum Aleph* [first restriction], which was done on the rudimentary will to receive so we will receive everything that exists in the thought of creation to do good to His creations in the *Kelim* [vessels] that have been corrected into working in order to bestow.

We can understand this through a depiction. Let us assume that His desire to do good to His creations is for one hundred kilograms of pleasure. Naturally, He had to prepare a *Kli* [vessel] with one hundred kilograms of deficiency. Otherwise, there is no place to put the one hundred kilograms of pleasure because there can be filling only in a place of lack. It follows that if we fill the *Kelim* [vessels], meaning deficiencies, and *Kelim* are left outside—meaning some of the *Kelim* that belong to the one hundred kilograms of deficiency are unclean and unfit to be filled with the abundance that belongs to them—the abundance that He wished to give, the one hundred kilograms of abundance, His desire is not fulfilled because some of the *Kelim* belong to the part of the abundance that still did not receive what belongs to them.

It follows that all the *Kelim* that emerged at the time of creation must enter *Kedusha* [holiness/sanctity]. By this we will understand what the holy *Zohar* says, "The angel of death is destined to be a holy angel." This is as said above, that since all the bad comes from the will to receive that the Creator created and then restricted, which is called "correction," all of the one hundred kilograms of will to receive that He has created must be received through the correction called "receiving in order to bestow." These discernments that we cannot correct before the end of correction are called *Klipot* [shells/peels] and *Tuma'a* [impurity], and *Sitra Achra* [other side], but at the end of correction all the *Kelim* must enter *Kedusha* for the above-mentioned reason. Otherwise, there will be a lack in the abundance, since all the *Kelim* must receive the abundance that belongs to their share.

Now we can understand what is written, "of all the sins of man." It pertains to the root of the sins, called "will to receive." This is why it is written, "Should one sin and be guilty." The meaning of the verse, "of all the sins of man," is not sins between man and man specifically, as it is interpreted afterwards about the verse, "and be guilty." It is as you say, "the guilt is returned to the Lord," where "and be guilty" means that he will correct his works and will return the theft he has robbed, which implies specifically between man and man.

However, we should interpret that the root of all the sins is the will to receive in order to receive, which is what a person receives from the Creator, meaning from His domain, and lets everything into his own domain, which is called "theft." That is, he extracts from the domain of the Creator although the Torah screams and says it is forbidden to receive into one's own domain or it is considered having two domains—the Creator's domain, and he takes the pleasures from the Creator's domain into his own. It follows that he is not regarded as a thief but as a robber, for although the Creator sees him taking, his will to receive is so strong that he cannot resist it, which is why he is considered a robber and not a thief.

And what is his correction? He returns the theft that he has robbed, meaning repents and corrects so that all his works enter *Kedusha*. That is, he extends a desire that all his works will be in order to bestow. This is why he interprets "Should one sin and be guilty," that "and be guilty" means correction.

Rabbi Yosi adds and says, "This means that what is written, 'and returns,' means returning by himself, since 'and returns' is not written as imperative, but rather 'returns' is precisely by himself. That is, there is 'repentance from fear,' when sins become for him as mistakes, and this is regarded as such, although he returns the theft." However, this is still not regarded as voluntarily. Rather, since he still has fear, he returns the theft. But this is not regarded as "by himself," meaning of his own volition, so we can say that he is happy with returning the theft. Rather, it is as though he has no choice.

Repentance from fear still does not correct the sin, since with repentance from fear, since become only as mistakes. Hence, there are *Kelim* that are still outside of *Kedusha*, meaning that the upper abundance cannot dress in them. Therefore, His desire, which was to do good to His creations, to bestow upon the lower ones, still has nowhere to clothe. It is as though there is a deficiency in the purpose.

Therefore, we were given a correction called "repentance from love." At that time sins become for him as merits. The *Kelim* that were as "sins," which are desires to receive that belong to the upper abundance from the perspective of the purpose of creation, are unfit to receive the abundance. But when merits are made from these *Kelim*, they are fit for clothing the upper abundance, and then the completion of the goal, which is to benefit His creations, can come true to the extent of the abundance that He wanted to give them. Now all the *Kelim* that belong to the general will to receive that divided into several parts (for it is easier to correct smaller parts) have entered.

This is as the allegory that Baal HaSulam said concerning the correction of the tree of knowledge (*Panim Masbirot* p 56), about a king who wanted to send gold coins overseas to his son, but all his countryfolk were thieves, so he changed the gold coins into pennies and penny by penny join into a great amount, and by this everything will be corrected.

Concerning Above Reason

Article No. 21, Tav-Shin-Mem-Vav, 1985-86

Concerning above reason, we should use this tool both between friends and between an individual and the Creator. However, there is a difference between them. Between an individual and the Creator, this tool must remain forever. In other words, one must never underestimate this tool, called, "faith above reason." But between friends, if he can see his friend's virtue within reason, it is all the better.

And yet, the nature of the body is to the contrary—it always sees his friend's fault and not his virtues. This is why our sages said, "Judge every person favorably." In other words, although within reason you see that your friend is wrong, you should still try to judge him favorably. And this can be above reason. That is, although logically he cannot justify him, above reason he can justify him nonetheless.

However, if he can justify him within reason, this is certainly better. If, for example, he sees that the friends are at a higher degree than his own, he sees within reason how he is in utter lowliness compared to the friends, that all the friends keep the schedule of arriving at the seminary, and take greater interest in all that is happening among the friends, to help anyone in any way they can, and immediately implement every advice for the work from the teachers in actual fact, etc., it certainly affects him and gives him strength to overcome his laziness, both when he needs to wake up before dawn and when he is awakened.

Also, during the lesson, his body is more interested in the lessons, since otherwise he will lag behind his friends. Also, with anything that concerns *Kedusha* [holiness/sanctity], he must take it more seriously because the body cannot tolerate lowliness. Moreover, when his body looks at the friends, it sees within reason that they are all working for the Creator, and then his body, too, lets him work for the Creator.

And the reason why the body helps him shift to in order to bestow is as mentioned—the body is unwilling to tolerate lowliness. Instead, everybody has pride, and he is unwilling to accept a situation where his friend is greater than him. Thus, when he sees that his friends are at a higher level than his own, this causes him to ascend in every way.

This is the meaning of what our sages said, "Counters' envy increases wisdom." In other words, when all the friends look at the society as being at a high level, both in thoughts and in actions, it is natural that each and every one must raise his degree to a higher level than he has by the qualities of his own body.

This means that even if innately he has no craving for great desires or is not intensely attracted to honor, still, through envy, he can acquire additional powers that he doesn't have in his own nature. Instead, the force of the quality of envy in him has procreated new powers within him, which exist in the society. And through them, he has received those new qualities, meaning powers that were not installed in him by his progenitors. Thus, now he has new qualities that society has procreated in him.

It turns out that a person has qualities that his parents bequeathed to their children, and he has qualities that he acquired from the society, which is a new possession. And this comes to him only through bonding with the society and the envy that he feels toward the friends when he sees that they have better qualities than his own. It motivates him to acquire their good qualities, which he doesn't have and of which he is jealous.

Thus, through the society, he gains new qualities that he adopts by seeing that they are at a higher degree than his, and he is envious of them. This is the reason why now he can be greater than when he didn't have a society, since he acquires new powers through the society.

However, this can be said if he truly sees the friends at a higher degree than his own. But at the same time, the evil inclination shows him the lowliness of the society and makes him think, "On the contrary, this society that you wish to bond with is not for you. They are many degrees below your own. Thus, from such a society, not only will you gain nothing, but rather, even the inborn forces that you have, which are small, are larger than those within this society.

"Thus, you should in fact stay away from them. And if you do want to bond with them, at least see that they all obey you, meaning follow your understanding of how the society should behave: how they sit when they gather, how they study, and how they pray. In other words, either they are all serious, and God forbid that they should even smile or ever discuss the friends' worldly matters—if they make a living, or how they make a living, easily or with difficulties, if he has a job where he doesn't suffer, or has a difficult landlord who gives him a hard time, or if his co-workers don't mock him for being orthodox," etc.

All those matters are of no importance and it is a waste thinking about them, for they are only corporeal matters. He, on the other hand, came to partake in an assembly of Israel for a noble purpose, which is to be a true servant of the Creator."

It follows that when he wishes to forget about his corporeality—when in fact, his corporeality deeply concerns him and he lets it go and does not want to remember—the friends come and begin to discuss their friends' corporeality. And he does not care about his friends' corporeality, since now he wants spirituality, "So why are the friends suddenly messing up my mind with mundane stuff which is of no concern to me at all? Is this why I want to forget about my corporeality, to make time to think about the friends' corporeality, can this be?" Thus, "You'd better listen to me and stay away from them," his body tells him, "And you will certainly be more successful. Why mess up your mind with such nonsense?"

Therefore, when the body shows him the inferiority of his friends, what can he answer his body when it comes with arguments of a righteous one? In other words, the body doesn't advise him to turn away from the society because the body is suggesting that he be wicked. On the contrary, the body tells him, "By staying away from the society, you will be righteous and you will think only about your spirituality, and when necessary, of your corporeality, as well."

Therefore, if a person believes that without a society it is impossible to advance and achieve love of the Creator, since this is the springboard for exiting self-love and entering love of the Creator, he has no other choice but to go above reason. He should tell his body, "The fact that you see that they are not really at the degree of craving to attain the love of the Creator as you desire it—meaning, since you are my body, I see in you that you are holier than the rest of the bodies of the friends, since you wish to be a servant of the Creator.

"I see that you are advising me to leave the friends because their bodies already display their inferiority and they haven't the strength to conceal their improper traits, since people normally hide the evil in them from one another so that others will respect them because they have prominent qualities. But here, their evil is so great that they are unable to overcome the evil and hide it so that others will not see them. Thus, from my perspective, they are certainly ignoble.

"However, without a society I will not gain anything, despite all my good qualities. Thus, above reason, I will keep what our sages said (*Avot*, Chapter 4), 'Be very, very humble.' In other words, I must go above reason and believe that they are standing at a higher degree than mine. And then, to the extent of my faith, I will be able to receive encouragement and strength from the society and receive from them what the society can give."

It follows that the only reason he is accepting the love of friends above reason is because of necessity, for lack of other options, but within reason he sees that he is right.

However, it is precisely here, meaning concerning friends, that within reason is more important than the degree of above reason. This is so because in truth, when a person wishes to bring himself closer to *Dvekut* [adhesion] with the Creator, through the work that he wishes to do only in order to bestow, the evil begins to appear in him. And the matter of recognition of evil is not an intellectual matter. Rather, it is a sensation in the heart.

This means that he should feel about himself that he is worse and lower than the whole world. And if he hasn't come to feel it, but thinks that there is someone who is still worse than he, then he probably has not obtained recognition of evil. In other words, the evil is still hidden in his heart and still hasn't been disclosed in him.

This is so because it is possible to see evil only when he has some good. For example, it is impossible to detect any dirt in the house if it is dark. But when you turn on a lamp, you can see that there is dirt there.

Also, if one does not do good deeds, does not engage in Torah and prayer, and wish to draw near the Creator, he has no light to illuminate his heart and to allow him to see the evil in his heart. It turns out that the reason why he is still not seeing that there is more evil in his heart than in all of the friends is that he needs more good. For this reason, he thinks that he is more virtuous than his friends.

It therefore turns out that his seeing that his friends are worse than he comes from his lack of the light that will shine for him, so he will see the evil in himself. Thus, the whole matter of evil that is in man is not in finding the evil, since everyone has this evil, called "will to receive in order to receive," which is self-love. Instead, the difference is entirely in the disclosure of the evil. In other words, not every person sees and feels that self-love is bad and harmful, since a person doesn't see that engagement in satisfying his will to receive, called "self-love," will harm him.

Yet, when he begins to do the holy work on the path of truth, meaning when he wishes to achieve *Dvekut* [adhesion] with the Creator, so all his actions will be for the Creator, by that he receives a little more light that shines for him each time, and then he begins to feel self-love as a bad thing.

It is a gradual process. Each time he sees that this is what obstructs him from achieving *Dvekut* with the Creator, he sees more clearly each time how it—the will to receive—is his real enemy, just as King Solomon referred to the evil inclination as "an enemy." It is written about it, "If your enemy is hungry, feed him bread, for you will heap burning coals on his head."

We therefore see that in truth, a person should feel that he is worse than others because this is indeed the truth. And we should also understand what our sages said, "Counters' envy increases wisdom." This is precisely within reason. But above reason, his friend's merit is not evident enough to say that he is envious of his friend, so it would cause him to work and toil because his friend compels him, due to envy.

Baal HaSulam interpreted a phrase by Rabbi Yohanan, "The Creator saw that righteous were few. He stood and planted them in each and every generation," as it is said, "For the pillars of the Earth are the Lord's, and He has set the world upon them." RASHI interprets, "Spread them through all the generations," to be a basis, sustenance, and a foundation for the existence of the world (*Yoma* 78b). "Few" means that they were growing fewer. Hence, what did

He do? "He stood and planted them in each and every generation." Thus, by planting them in each generation, they would multiply.

We should understand how they would multiply if He planted them in each and every generation. We should understand the difference between all the righteous being in a single generation, and being scattered through all the generations, as is understood from the words of RASHI's commentary, that by spreading them throughout the generations the righteous would increase.

He, Baal HaSulam, said, "By having righteous in each generation, there will be room for people who do not have the innate qualities to achieve *Dvekut* with the Creator. However, by bonding with the righteous that will be in each generation, through adhering to them, they will learn from their actions and will be able to acquire new qualities through the righteous that will be in each generation. This is why He spread the righteous in each generation, so that in this way the righteous will increase."

And as was said, the same can be obtained by adhesion of friends—new qualities by which they will be qualified to achieve *Dvekut* with the Creator. And all this can be said while he sees the merits of the friends. At that time, it is relevant to say that he should learn from their actions. But when he sees that he is better qualified than they are, there is nothing he can receive from the friends.

This is why they said that when the evil inclination comes and shows him the lowliness of the friends, he should go above reason. But certainly, it would be better and more successful if he could see within reason that the friends are at a higher degree than his own. With that we can understand the prayer that Rabbi Elimelech had written for us, "Let our hearts see the virtues of our friends, and not their faults."

However, between an individual and the Creator, it is a whole other matter. In other words, above reason is better. This means that if he takes upon himself faith above reason, his work is in the right direction. This is not so within reason, although a person's intellect grasps differently. In other words, every person knows and understands that if he didn't have to believe, but His Providence were revealed throughout the world, meaning to all the creatures, the whole world would certainly engage in Torah and *Mitzvot*, and there would be no place for secular people. Rather, everyone would be orthodox.

However, His Providence is not revealed to the lower ones. Instead, they must believe. Yet, faith is a difficult thing, since the Creator gave us intellect and reason to see each thing according to our own eyes. We consider everything that concerns human relations according to our best judgment, and there is nothing that will give us distinctions except our minds, as our sages said, "A judge has only what his eyes see" (*Baba Batra* 131). It follows that we conduct all our matters within reason, not above reason.

And for this reason, when a person begins with the work of the Creator and he is told that he must assume faith above reason, he begins to think: "But I see that the Creator gave us reason so as to understand everything according to the intellect, meaning according to the way our minds grasp. Thus, how can I take upon myself something that is against my mind?" It is a very difficult thing for the body to understand that it is in its interest to do the work of holiness in above reason.

Above reason applies to both mind and heart. This is why not every person can enter the work of holiness in the form of bestowal, which is work above reason. Therefore, when teaching the rest of the world the work of the Creator, the order is as Maimonides said, that they begin in *Lo Lishma* [not for Her name] until they gain knowledge and acquire much wisdom, and then they are told that the essence of the work is in order to bestow, which is called, "work for the Creator."

However, we should understand why above reason is better. The contrary seems to make more sense—that if serving the Creator were clothed within reason, more people would come and want to be servants of the Creator. Baal HaSulam said about it that one should not think that when the Creator gives us His work in the form of above reason, it is a low degree. Rather, we should believe that it is a very high degree, for only by that does one have a chance to be able to work in order to bestow. Otherwise, he would have to fall into in order to receive.

Therefore, although more people would be serving if the work had been within reason, they would never be able to achieve *Dvekut* with the Creator, which is the work in order to bestow. Hence, although there would be an increase in quantity, in terms of quality, it would be impossible for man to be able to receive the delight and pleasure that the Creator wishes to give to the creatures, according to His desire—to do good to His creations.

Thus, for the delight and pleasure that the creatures will receive to be flawless, meaning to avoid having the bread of shame, there was the correction of the *Tzimtzum* [restriction]—that the upper abundance would not shine unless it was where there is equivalence of form. This is considered that the creatures receive the abundance in vessels of bestowal. And when there are no vessels of bestowal in the creatures, they must remain in the dark, which is called, "they will die without wisdom."

However, we should know that although there is the light of Torah in *Lo Lishma*, as well, of which our sages said, "One should always engage in Torah and *Mitzvot* in *Lo Lishma* because from *Lo Lishma* we come to *Lishma*, since the light in it reforms him," afterwards, one must reach *Lishma*. In other words, he should come to work above reason in mind and heart.

But between a man and his friend, if he can work in love of friends within reason, meaning if he tries to see the friends as being at a higher level of holiness than himself, this is certainly better. In other words, if he sees within reason that the friends are closer to *Dvekut* with the Creator than he, it is certainly better than if he had to believe above reason.

Thus, in truth, he sees that he is at a higher degree than the friends. Within reason, he always sees the friends as low. However, he believes above reason that he should say—because it is a *Mitzva* [commandment/good deed]—that he should believe that it is not as he sees it. Certainly, if he can see within reason that the friends are at degrees of holiness, it is all the better.

Similarly, we can interpret the verse (Samuel, 16:7), "But the Lord said to Samuel, 'Do not look at his appearance or at the height of his stature, because I have rejected him; for it is not as man sees, for man looks to the eyes, but the Lord looks to the heart.'"

We therefore see that when the Creator sent Samuel to anoint one of the sons of Yishai [Jesse], Samuel understood by what he saw in his eyes that Eliav, son of Yishai, was fit to be the king of Israel instead of King Saul, but the Creator disagreed with his perception. In the end, they brought David, who was herding the cattle, and David was red-headed with fair eyes and good appearance, "And the Lord said, 'Arise, anoint him; for this is he.'"

What does that teach us? There are two things that we see here:

1) From the perspective of Samuel, he understands Eliav's virtues—according to his mind—as being fit to be king over Israel. But the Creator told him, "No, do not follow your own reason," since when concerning the Creator, reason is worthless. Rather, since the Creator wanted to enthrone a king, this is called "between an individual and the Creator," where there is no room for reason, "For My thoughts are not your thoughts, neither are My ways your ways." Rather, what did the Creator tell him? "For it is not as man sees, for man looks to the eyes, and the Lord looks to the heart."

According to the above, we can interpret that "For man looks to the eyes" is good between a person and his friend. In that case, it is good if one can go within reason, that it is in accord with what one sees.

This is not so with, "And the Lord looks to the heart." In other words, concerning matters of the Creator, it is above reason and one must not look according to his own eyes, but above reason. Thus, two discernments must be made here: 1) Between a person and the Creator, above reason is better; 2) between a person and his friend, within reason is better.

This is why the Creator told him, "Do not look at his appearance," since following his eyes is good between a man and his friend. If you can see the friend's merits within reason, it is all the better. But this is not so here, when I want to anoint him as king. This operation belongs to Me. I want him as king. This is called "between a person and the Creator." Here, the proper work is above reason, since precisely in this way it is possible to achieve reception in order to bestow. Otherwise, he will fall into receiving in order to receive, which causes separation and remoteness from *Kedusha* [holiness/sanctity].

However, here arises a question, after one has decided to go above reason and not look at all the questions that the body begins to ask. When he begins to work on the path of bestowal and faith above reason, and overcomes the obstacles—the questions that the body brings him from the world over—and closes his eyes and doesn't wish to look at anything that contradicts the mind and heart, but has decided to go only above reason, after this decision, sometimes he suddenly brings great excuses that the body must agree with.

Thus, he sees that now he is going within reason. But what can he do when now he sees, through the excuses he received from above, that he tells himself, "What can I do now that I have no place where I can work above reason? I see now that everything I do in order to bestow is how it should be."

Thus, he no longer has any questions about serving the Creator, which force him to work above reason. But since the work is primarily above reason, what can he do when he is in such a state?

Baal HaSulam said that when a person is rewarded with some disclosure from above and now he feels that it is worthwhile being a servant of the Creator, it follows that thus far he had work in the form of above reason: the body disagreed with this work and he always had to overcome, and needed the Creator to give him strength above reason. But now he no longer needs the help of the Creator, since now he feels that he has a basis on which to build his structure. In other words, he already has support on which to rely.

Thus, now he is blemishing the faith that he was using before, since now he can already say, "Thank God I am rid of the burden of faith, which was a burden and load to me." But now I already have a basis within reason because now I have received some awakening from above so that the body agrees that it is worthwhile to keep Torah and *Mitzvot*. It turns out that by that he is blemishing the faith.

And Baal HaSulam said that at that time, one must say, "Now I see that the real way is actually to go above reason. And the evidence of that is the fact that now I have been rewarded with some illumination from above, only because I have taken it upon myself to go above reason. This is why I was rewarded with the Creator bringing me a little closer to Him and giving me some awakening from above."

And this illumination that he has now received gives him an answer to all the questions. It turns out that this testifies to the above reason. Thus, what should I do now so I will continue with above reason? There is only to reinforce and to start looking for ways to dress his work in above reason.

It turns out that by that, he did not blemish his faith at all, since he was walking in it before he was rewarded with any illumination from above, since even now he is not receiving the illumination as a foundation on which to build the structure of his work. Rather, he is taking the illumination as a testimony that he is on the right track, that he is in faith above reason. Only in this form of work does the Creator bring a person closer to Him and gives him room to draw nearer to Him, since this nearing will not let him fall into the vessels of reception, which are called "within reason," since the Creator sees that he is trying to go only above reason.

It follows from all the above that concerning above reason, there is a difference between a person-and-the-Creator and a person-and-his-friend. Between a person and his friend, if he can see the friends' merits within reason it is better. But if within reason he sees only the friends' faults, he has no choice but to go above reason and say,

"What I see, hear, and feel is all wrong and untrue. It is impossible that I was mistaken about the friends I have chosen to bond with, meaning that I miscalculated.

"That is, I thought that I would grow richer in spirituality through them, since they had possessions that I did not. Hence, if I were to bond with them, I could rise to a higher degree than I thought. But now I see that in fact, I am discerning otherwise. And I heard that Baal HaSulam said that the only thing that can help a person out of self-love and be rewarded with the love of the Creator is the love of friends. Hence, I have no choice but to bond with those friends, although in my view, I would be better off staying away from them and avoid bonding with them.

"However, I have no choice and I must believe above reason that indeed, all the friends are at a high degree, but I cannot see their virtue with my eyes." This is the reason why he must believe above reason. But when he sees the merit of the friends within reason, he can certainly derive great benefits from the friends. But what can he do? He has no choice.

However, it is a different order between a person and the Creator. In a place where one can go above reason, it is better. Therefore, where one can be assisted from within reason, being rewarded with some illumination from above, then he can say, "Now I see that it is worthwhile being a servant of the Creator because I feel a good taste in the work."

It follows that he took this feeling—that he finds meaning in the work—as a basis and foundation upon which to build his Judaism. And now that he understands with his reason that it is worthwhile to keep Torah and *Mitzvot*, his whole foundation is built on this condition. This means that when he finds meaning in the work, he should obey the voice of the Creator. Thus, if he does not find meaning in the work, he cannot keep the *Mitzvot* of the Creator.

It is known that assuming the kingdom of heaven must be done "With all your heart and with all your soul." In other words, even if He takes one's soul from him, meaning even if he has no livelihood, not even *Nefesh*, he is still committed to being a servant of the Creator and to not present any conditions before the Creator, telling Him, "If you do as I wish, according to what I understand that I need—meaning that I feel a lack in this, and if You satisfy my need—I promise to be a servant of the Creator. But if You do not satisfy all my wishes—those I understand that I need—I cannot take upon myself everything that You command me through Moses."

However, one should assume the burden of the kingdom of heaven without any conditions, meaning even above reason. Moreover, one must say, "Our having to work above reason is not because the Creator cannot give us reason." Rather, we must believe that it is all to our benefit. It turns out that between a person and the Creator we should try to keep it above reason, and if he receives some reason, he should do as mentioned above.

If a Woman Inseminates

Article No. 22, Tav-Shin-Mem-Vav, 1985-86

The holy *Zohar* (*Tazria*, item 9), asks, "We learned that 'A woman who inseminates first, delivers a male child.' Rabbi Aha said, 'We learned that the Creator sentences whether a drop will be male or female, and you say, 'A woman who inseminates first, delivers a male child.' Thus, we do not need the Creator's sentence.' Rabbi Yosi said, 'Of course the Creator discerns between a drop of a male and a drop of a female. And because He has discerned it, He sentences whether it will be a male or a female.'"

He interprets in the *Sulam* [Ladder commentary]: "There are three partners in a man: the Creator, his father, and his mother. His father gives the white in him, his mother—the red in him, and the Creator gives the soul. If the drop is a male, the Creator gives the soul of a male. If it is a female, the Creator gives the soul of a female. This discernment that the Creator discerns in the drop—that it is fit for a soul of a male or a female—is regarded as a sentence of the Creator. If He did not discern it and did not send a soul of a male, the drop would not become a male. Thus, the two statements do not contradict one another. Rabbi Aha said, 'delivers a male child,' but does she deliver because she inseminates? It depends on conception! This verse should have said, 'A woman who conceives delivers a male child.' Rabbi Yosi said, 'A woman, from the day she inseminates and conceives to the day she delivers has no other word in her mouth but whether her child will be a male.'"

We should understand the above matter. What does knowing about a woman inseminating first give us? And also, he tells us that the greatness of the Creator is that He knows how to discern between a drop of a male and a drop of a female. Is this the greatness from which one should be inspired and by which to take upon himself to be a servant of the Creator? We should also understand what Rabbi Aha is asking, "A woman who inseminates and conceives." It should have said "male." Rabbi Yosi explains, "A woman, from the day she inseminates and conceives to the day she delivers has no other word in her mouth but whether her child will be a male." That is, she is concerned about her child being a male. What does knowing what is in the mouth of a woman give us? What will happen if we know this concern of a woman, that she is worried about her child being a male?

To understand all this we will explain what is written in the essay, "Preface to the Wisdom of Kabbalah" (item 57): "The whole purpose of the *Tzimtzum* that unfolded in *Behina Dalet* was to correct it, so there would be no disparity of form in it, as it receives the Upper Light. In other words, to create man's body from that *Behina Dalet*. ...Through his engagement in Torah and *Mitzvot* in order to bestow contentment upon his Maker he will turn the force of reception in *Behina Dalet* into working in order to bestow. By this he equalizes the form of reception to complete bestowal, and then will be the end of correction, since this will bring *Behina Dalet* back to being a vessel of reception for the Upper Light, while being in complete *Dvekut* [adhesion] with the Light without any disparity of form. Yet, this requires one to be included with the higher *Behinot*, above *Behina Dalet*, so as to be able to perform good deeds of bestowal. ...This is because *Behina Dalet*, which should be the root of man's body, was entirely in the form of vacant and empty space, devoid of

Light, as it was of opposite form from the Upper Light. Thus, it is considered separated and dead. If man had been created from her he would not have been able to correct his actions whatsoever, since there would be no sparks of bestowal in him at all."

To correct this was the matter of the association of the quality of mercy with judgment, since the world cannot exist on the quality of judgment, as it is written (item 58), "'He saw that the world does not exist' means that in this way it was impossible for man, who was to be created from this *Behina Dalet*, to acquire acts of bestowal, by which the world will be corrected in the desired amount through him. Through this association, *Behina Dalet*—the quality of judgment—was incorporated with the sparks of bestowal in the *Kli* [vessel] of *Bina*. By this, man's body, which emerged from *Behina Dalet*, was integrated with the quality of bestowal, too, and could perform good deeds in order to bestow contentment upon his Maker until he turns the quality of reception in him to be entirely in order to bestow. Thus, the world will achieve the desired correction from the creation of the world."

He interprets the association of the quality of mercy with judgment in the *Sulam* (*Tazria*, item 95): "You already know that there are two points in *Malchut*: the first is *Malchut de* [of] *Tzimtzum Aleph* [first restriction], which was not mitigated in *Bina*, the quality of mercy, and is therefore unfit to receive any Light, since the force of the *Masach* [screen] and *Tzimtzum* [restriction] is over it. The second point is the point of *Malchut* that was mitigated with the quality of mercy, which is *Bina*. All the lights that *Malchut* receives are from the second point. Hence, the first point is concealed within it, and only the second point is revealed and governs it, and is therefore fit to receive the Upper Lights. For this reason, *Malchut* is called 'the tree of knowledge of good and evil,' since if one is rewarded, it is good, for the first point is concealed and only the second point governs. At that time there is abundance in *Malchut* and the lower one receives from her. If he is not rewarded, for he is a sinner, there is power in the serpent to reveal the first point in *Malchut*, which did not partake in *Bina*, and then she is bad."

Now we can interpret the words of the holy *Zohar* concerning, "If a woman inseminates and delivers a male child." We asked, "What does it teach us if a woman who inseminates first delivers a male child?" According to the words of the holy *Zohar*, there are two forces within us: 1) the quality of judgment, which is regarded as a female, called *Malchut*, 2) the quality of mercy, which is regarded as a male, namely a male force, meaning bestowal, as our sages said, "As He is merciful, so you are merciful."

These two forces govern man, but at times the quality of judgment is concealed and the quality of mercy rules, and at times the quality of mercy is concealed and the quality of judgment rules. We should know that "insemination" is similar to one who sows wheat in the ground. The seeds decay and wheat that is good to eat begins to grow. We also try to fertilize the soil by which the wheat will grow good to eat.

By this we can explain the verse, "If a woman inseminates." If a person wants to begin the work to achieve *Dvekut* [adhesion] with the Creator, and wishes to enjoy "man's food," and not "animal food," his order of work should be that he will sow the "woman" in him, called "will to receive."

That is, he should place his vessels of reception in the ground and try to make self-reception rot in the ground. The more he fertilizes it, meaning tries to understand and feel that self-love is as loathsome to him as manure, and the more he tries to see the lowliness of self-love and wants his self-love to rot, this is called "If a woman inseminates," meaning the female in him, the vessels of reception. He buries this in the ground, meaning he wants his self-love to rot, and then she "delivers a male child," meaning vessels of bestowal. By trying to cancel his vessels of reception, meaning self-love, he is rewarded with vessels of bestowal.

This is similar to burying wheat in the ground so it will rot, and by this he will have wheat fit to be food for man. "Food" means that we enjoy it. That is, before one begins to work on the path of truth he enjoyed only what entered the vessels of self-love. Now he enjoys things that enter the vessels of bestowal, which is called "food for man" and not "food for beast," which are beastly pleasures. This is called "If he is rewarded, the quality of judgment is concealed." That is, the will to receive is concealed and does not rule, and only the will to bestow, called "the quality of mercy," rules.

"Rewarded" means that he wants to be pure, meaning bestowing. "Thick" means desire to receive. Because he wants to achieve the quality of mercy, he is rewarded with the disappearance of the vessels of reception. That is, they do not govern, but the quality of mercy governs, which is called "bestowal" and "male." This is called "delivering a male child," where the child is born through the woman's insemination, meaning by burying the will to receive in the ground, meaning that he wants to receive all his joys in vessels of bestowal.

This is not so if the man inseminates first, if the beginning of his work is the vessels of bestowal, of which he consists from the root of the correction. Through the association of the quality of mercy with judgment, he desires to bury the vessels of bestowal, called "male," and then she "delivers a female." This means that then the quality of judgment is revealed in him and governs, while the quality of mercy, called "male," disappears and he is powerless to do anything with vessels of bestowal.

At that time he eats only animal food, and he is placed only in self-love, like animals. That is, if he sows in the ground the vessels of reception, called "female," then food for man comes out, meaning the power to bestow. But if he buries the forces of bestowal in the ground, then she "delivers a female," and all his food is in vessels of reception, regarded as delivering a female. By this we will understand what Rabbi Yosi replied to Rabbi Aha's question, that the Creator discerns between a drop of a male and a drop of a female, and because He has discerned it, He sentences it to be a male or a female.

We asked, "What does that teach us?" Our sages said, "He who comes to purify is aided," and the holy *Zohar* says, "with a holy soul." It follows that when the woman inseminates first, meaning that the beginning of his work is to sow, meaning bury the woman in him in the ground, namely his will to receive for himself, and all his thoughts are about how to be rid of self-love, and this is what he asks from the Creator, then the Creator discerns whether the drop is of a male, meaning that he wants the Creator to give vessels of bestowal. At that time the Creator gives him the soul of a male. That is, He gives him power from above, called "holy soul," by which he can be a giver, if the Creator sees that his intention in the work of Torah and *Mitzvot* [commandments] is to purify himself because he wants to exist the *Tuma'a* [impurity] of self-love, so the Creator gives him a soul of a male.

If the Creator discerns that the drop is of a female, meaning that the man inseminates first, namely that the beginning of his work is to expand his vessels of reception, that his root, called "the association of the quality of mercy with judgment," but he intends only to receive greater reward through his actions, as it is written in the holy *Zohar*, "they howl as dogs saying 'Give us the wealth of this world, and give us the wealth of the next world,'" it follows that his aim was only to expand the possessions that belong to self-love.

It follows that by sowing, meaning by burying the mingling he has with the quality of mercy, he causes the quality of mercy, which is the force of bestowal, to be concealed. This is called "sowing," when we place and conceal the wheat in the soil, and the wheat becomes hidden in the ground. This implies to us that the force of bestowal has been concealed, and the force of reception is revealed. This is called, "she delivers a female child."

It follows that what Rabbi Yosi said—that the Creator discerns whether a drop is a male or a female—comes to teach us that one should not say, "I have been engaging in Torah and *Mitzvot* for so long, and have been observing everything, slight and serious, but I do not see that the Creator is helping me from above so I can ascend the degrees of holiness." He asks, "Where is the help from above, as our sages said, 'He who comes to purify is aided'?"

Rabbi Yosi comes and says about this that the Creator discerns what is the drop—whether a male, if you want the work of bestowal, or the work of a female, meaning that all your work is to receive reward, called "giving," but in order to receive. Therefore, he cannot say that the Creator does not hear his prayer. Rather, the Creator hears and knows what he is praying, meaning that he does not want to bury his self-love in the ground at all, so how can the Creator give him what he does not want?

It is known that there is no light without a *Kli*. A *Kli* is called a deficiency, and "light" is the filling of the deficiency. If a person has no deficiency to feel that he has no desire to bestow, this is the essence of man's lowliness, for which he is removed from *Kedusha* [holiness/sanctity] and is unable to be rewarded with *Dvekut* [adhesion] with the Creator. This is regarded as not having a *Kli* to receive the filling. This is why Rabbi Yosi says that the Creator discerns which drop it is, meaning what a person wants the Creator to place there, which soul, meaning light that is clothed in vessels of bestowal, namely that He gives him light so as to have the force of bestowal, or the force of reception. For this reason, he must not complain to the Creator because He gives one what one wants.

This is as our sages said, "How is repentance? When He knows the mysteries will testify that he will not turn back to folly." This means that by the Creator giving him a soul of a male, meaning light, so as to have the power to bestow, by this the testimony of the Creator appears, when He "testifies that he will not turn back to folly," since the Creator has given him the soul. By this he is certain that henceforth he will not work for self-love but only in order to bestow.

It is written similarly in the words of the holy *Zohar*, that he who comes to purify is aided. And this is what Rabbi Yosi said, that the Creator certainly discerns whether a drop is of a male or of a female. And because He has discerned it, He sentences whether it is to be a male or a female. This is regarded as "He who knows the mysteries will testify that he will not turn back to folly." However, how can one come to want to bury his self-love, which we call a *Kli*, and the

Creator will give him light within this *Kli*, meaning the soul of a male in a *Kli* that comes by burying the will to receive, called "If a woman inseminates"?

It is very difficult for a person, once he has been created, to keep the quality of judgment revealed and the quality of mercy concealed. The beginning of man's creation is as in, "Man is born a wild ass," and the quality of mercy in him is a black dot, which does not shine. For this reason, he has no need or lack that will engender in him a thought that he needs vessels of bestowal. Rather, his only concern is to satisfy everything that self-love demands. If the Creator helps him to completely satisfy the will to receive, he will feel that he is the happiest man on earth, and what else does he need?

It follows that who can tell him that he needs a lack called "desire to bestow"? He hears a novelty: He is told that he needs a lack. That is, the name *Kli*, called "deficiency," will now be what he lacks, meaning that he needs a lack, and the satisfaction will be receiving the lack. It follows that the names *Kli* and *Ohr* [light] refer only to the deficiency.

To understand this, we should precede with the words of our sages, that a prayer is called "work in the heart." Why is prayer called "work in the heart"? After all, the prayer is only with the mouth. We should interpret that a prayer is called "deficiency," when one wants his request to be granted, meaning to obtain a deficiency in that he has no need to want to bestow, but all he wants is self-love. But how can one demand something for which he has no need, although he hears that he is told, "This is all you need"? But if he does not feel, what should he do in order to feel that he is deficient?

Our sages gave us an advice about this, which is called "prayer," which is the work in the heart. That is, a man says, verbally, that he lacks the desire to bestow, and the heart tells him that all he needs is to satisfy everything that self-love demands and not think of deficiencies, but of fillings. For this reason, he has a lot of work with his heart to want to ask for a deficiency that completely contradicts the will to receive, which is the creature's very essence. At times the heart prevails, and at times the mouth prevails. It follows that then his mouth and heart are not the same because we need to know that in the end it is the heart that governs man, and not the mouth.

This is why it was said that man must work with his heart, to agree to ask for lack, meaning that the Creator will satisfy his lack, namely that here the filling is called "lack." This is the meaning of "The Creator will satisfy his need," meaning that the lack is regarded as filling.

Now we can understand that the only way to obtain a deficiency, that we are lacking the desire to bestow, is by prayer, which is a "medium" between man and the deficiency. That is, one prays for the Creator to give him something for which he has no deficiency, that he will lack it. It follows that the *Kli* that is called "deficiency" is a deficiency with respect to the feeling, meaning that he does not feel its lack, and the prayer is that the Creator will give him the light, which is the filling of his lack. It therefore follows that the filling is a lack. Thus, he has no other choice but to pray to the Creator to give him a deficiency, and this is what connects the *Kli* with the light.

It is as Baal HaSulam said in the name of the ADMOR of Pursov about what Rabbi Shimon said, "The writing should rush primarily where the pockets are empty." A "pocket" means a *Kli* where one puts money. A "pocket" means deficiency, and "money" is the filling of the deficiency. Thus, if a person has no pocket, namely a deficiency, it is even worse than not having the filling because it is regarded as being unconscious. It follows that where one has no sensation of lack that he does not have a *Kli* of desire to bestow, he must hurry himself. With what? With prayer, which is the medium between the *Kli* and the light, between deficiency and deficiency, and the filling, where he already feels that deficiency that he cannot work in order to bestow.

Now we will explain what we asked about Rabbi Yosi's answer to Rabbi Aha's question about why it is written that "If a woman inseminates, she delivers a male child," since the matter depends on conception, and it should have said, "If a woman inseminates and conceives a male child." Rabbi Yosi replied that "from the day when she inseminates and conceives, a woman has no other word in her mouth but whether her child will be a male." We asked, "What does it teach us, what the woman says?"

According to what we explained about the order of the work, we should interpret "If a woman inseminates" to mean the person who buries the self-love in the ground so that a male will grow out of it, meaning that he will be rewarded with a desire to bestow. It follows that as soon as he begins the work of obtaining the desire to bestow, called "If a woman inseminates," the work in this direction begins and he begins to say, "I wish I will deliver a male."

That is, we must go through a process of loathing self-love and feeling the measure of evil found in self-love. It is not enough to decide not to go on the path one is used to marching and wanting to change one's habits. Rather, to him the measure of harm that self-love causes him should be revealed to him, for only by seeing what he is losing can he be certain that he will not regret midway.

This is similar to the sentence concerning a stranger who comes to convert (*Yevamot*, 47a): "Our sages said, 'A stranger who comes to convert is told, 'What did you see that you have come to convert? Don't you know that these days Israel are afflicted, pushed, despised, maddened, and tormented (RASHI interpreted "despised" as in "low" and "coerced," as "dethroned and coerced)?' If he said, 'I know and I am not worthy,' he is accepted at once.' The Great Book of *Mitzvot* wrote, 'The reason is so he will not say afterwards, 'Had I known, I would not have converted'" (*Yoreh De'ah*, item 268)."

Wanting to exit self-love and begin the work of bestowal is similar to leaving all the states in which he lived, dropping everything off, and entering an area where he has never been. For this reason, he must go through conception and months of pregnancy until he has the ability to acquire new qualities, which are foreign to the spirit he has received since birth. Everything he has received from the environment with which he grew up and which reared him with their views and thoughts was entirely on the basis of self-love. He always thought about controlling others, and where he thought he would find a place where he could control he realized it is worth an effort, since it yields pleasure to the will to receive, and the majority supported him. This is regarded as receiving strength for his aspirations from the public, meaning he saw that everyone behaved this way so the body knew that it was worthwhile to exert to acquire power or respect or money. Everything focused on one line, called "desire to satisfy his *Kli*," which is called "self-love."

But now that he has come to convert, meaning exit self-love, where he thought about controlling others, now he is told he must make every effort to control himself and that he is forbidden to control others. And where each day he contemplated how much he has gained that day, which he put into the bag of self-love, now he is told that he should contemplate each day how much profit he has gained that he can put in the bag of love of others.

Accordingly, we should interpret what is said to one who comes to convert. It means that the person who was until now like a gentile, as it is written, "And they mingled with the nations and learned from their works," the holy *Zohar* says, "Every person is a small world in and of itself," namely that each person consists of the seventy nations, which correspond to seven qualities, each of which consists of ten. This is why they are called "seventy nations," and the Israel in him is in exile, under the rule of the nations.

Therefore, when a person comes to take upon himself (the burden of) the kingdom of heaven and exit the exile to which he surrendered and to whom he listened until now—meaning he had to do what they asked and thought that this is how it should be, but the point in the heart has awakened in him and now he has come to work for the Creator—he is tolled, "Until now the nations did not humiliate the Israel in you. This means that your body still did not resist. But now that you want to be 'Israel,' while you have still not emerged from their governance, they despise the 'Israel' in you, since the body will not let you work in order to bestow. Therefore, first you must think if you want to take upon yourself this great work."

But afterwards the nations of the world, too, surrender, meaning the body. However, before he completes his work he must go through months of pregnancy. For this reason, a person is not told the real meaning of annulling self-love. Rather, he must receive this information bit-by-bit, which is called "months of pregnancy." This means that although it is said, "If a woman inseminates and delivers a male child," the truth is as Rabbi Aha says, that it is not as people think that as soon as you inseminate, meaning as soon as you decide to bury your will to receive you "deliver a male child." Rather, the matter depends on pregnancy. This means that although he has agreed to bury his will to receive, he still does not even know the real meaning of annulling self-love.

Rather, knowing the real nature of the will to receive is not something that one can feel at once, since the will to receive must be qualified and prepared so as to have the strength to relinquish real pleasures, which are eternal pleasures, if he has no exercises to accustom himself each time with greater self-love. That is, when a person begins the work of bestowal, he is constantly given from above greater pleasures even in corporeal things, so he accustoms himself to relinquish pleasures and receive them only in order to bestow.

Now we can understand what our sages said, that to the wicked, the evil inclination seems like a hairsbreadth, and to the righteous as a high mountain. We asked, "Is there a difference in reality?" But since a person should be prepared to have the ability to receive the eternal pleasures in order to bestow, he is constantly given more pleasure in everything, as exercises to learn how to use his vessels of reception, called "will to receive," and still be able to receive it in order to bestow. Otherwise he will relinquish this great pleasure.

It follows that he must go through nine months of pregnancy, by which he acquires strength, called "desire to bestow." If he sees that something disrupts the desire to bestow he has the power to repel it, and then he is called "delivers a male child." That is, once he has been through the process of "months of pregnancy," and not in the middle of the work, meaning that as soon as he begins the work he wants to see the power of bestowal that he has attained. Otherwise he is angry and says, "I have already started the work of sowing, so where are the fruits that I should obtain?" Rabbi Yosi explains about it that "A woman, from the day she conceives to the day she delivers has no other word in her mouth but whether her child will be a male." This means that although she has not delivered, she cannot wait and wants to deliver right away.

Concerning Fear and Joy

Article No. 23, Tav-Shin-Mem-Vav, 1985-86

The holy *Zohar* asks (*Aharei*, item 2 in the *Sulam* [Ladder commentary]), "Rabbi Yitzhak started, 'It is written, 'Serve the Lord with fear, and rejoice with trembling.' It is also written, 'Serve the Lord with joy, come before Him with singing.' These verses contradict one another. But we learned, 'Serve the Lord with fear,' since any work by which one wishes to serve one's Master requires fear first, to fear Him. And because of the fear of his Master he will later be rewarded with performing the *Mitzvot* [commandments] of the Torah with joy. This is why it is written, 'What does the Lord your God ask of you but fear,' and by this he will be rewarded with everything.'"

We should understand what fear is. We see that fear and joy are two opposites, and how can fear be a reason for joy, as he says, "Because of the fear of his Master he will later be rewarded with performing the *Mitzvot* of the Torah with joy," since they contradict one another?

We should also understand why the Creator wants to be feared. What does it give Him? It is like a person walking into a henhouse telling them, "If you take upon yourselves to fear me, I will give you food and water. I will give you everything you want in return for fearing me." Can it be said that man has any consideration whether the chickens respect him?

It is much more so with the creatures toward the Creator—what value and importance can we say that the Creator has for the creatures fearing Him? It is so much so that our sages said that a person must do nothing but engage in fear, as it is written, "What does the Lord your God ask of you but fear?" It is also written (Ecclesiastes, 3), "God has made it so that people fear Him," which means that everything that the Creator did, He did so that He will be feared.

To understand the above, we should remember the purpose of creation, meaning the purpose for which the Creator created Creation. It is known that the reason is His desire to do good to His creations. However, in order to bring to light the perfection of His deeds, meaning so there will not be the "bread of shame," He has made a correction called "*Tzimtzum* [restriction] and concealment," where before one has vessels of bestowal it is impossible to see or feel His existence, called "recognition of the Creator."

This means that although we say each day in the prayer, "The whole earth is full of His glory," we still have no feeling of it. Rather, we must believe above reason that this is so. The reason is that although there are no changes in the light, because "there is no absence in spirituality," there are nonetheless changes on the part of the *Kelim* [vessels], and the *Kelim* limit the light. It is so because in the *Kelim* we discern the greatness of the abundance—their impression from the abundance. If one has no *Kelim* that can be a clothing for the light, then no light is apparent in reality, according to the rule: "There is no light without a *Kli* [vessel]." That is, we must know one thing: We can speak of what we attain in our sensations.

Baal HaSulam said an allegory about the *Tzimtzum*: It is like a person covering himself so no one will see him. Can it be said that a person who hides himself so that others will not see him does not see himself because of it? Likewise, the Creator has made the

Tzimtzum and concealment so the lower ones will not see Him while they are immersed in self-love, which is receiving in order to receive, which causes disparity of form and separation between the Giver, who is the Creator, and the receivers, who are the creatures.

And since there is no reception in our root, which is the Creator, when a person does engage in reception he feels unpleasantness, called "bread of shame." This is why there was a correction on the part of the lower ones—that we attribute the *Tzimtzum* to the lower ones. That is, the lower ones need the *Tzimtzum* and concealment since precisely through this correction they will be able to correct the reception into aiming to bestow. But from the perspective of the upper one there are no changes. All the changes are only the qualification of our *Kelim*, as much as they can receive in order to bestow.

Accordingly, since the delight and pleasure do not illuminate in a place of separation, a person is unable to acquire complete faith prior to correcting one's will to receive. It is as he says ("Introduction of the Book of Zohar," item 138), "It is a law that the creature cannot receive disclosed evil from Him, for it is a flaw in His glory for the creature to perceive Him as an evildoer, as it is unbecoming of the complete Operator. Hence, when one feels bad, denial of the Creator's guidance lies upon him to that same extent, and the superior Operator is concealed from him."

From this we see the necessity of the correction of bestowal: Not only is it impossible to receive the delight and pleasure that has been prepared for us, but there is something here that removes us from faith in Him, and this is the worst!

Now we can understand the meaning of fear. We asked, "Does the Creator need us to fear Him?" According to what we explained, fear is as it is written in the *Sulam* [Ladder commentary on *The Zohar*], that man fears that perhaps he will not be able to overcome and receive in order to bestow, as it should be, but will receive in order to receive, which would cause him separation, not necessarily from the delight and pleasure that he will not be able to receive, but he fears that he will not come to deny His faith. It follows that he can actually come to the *Sitra Achra* [other side].

This is the meaning of "God has made it so that people fear Him." Through this fear there will be a twofold great correction: 1) they will have faith in the Creator, 2) they will be able to receive the delight and pleasure that the Creator wants to give them.

It follows that the Creator wants to be feared so that we will have the *Kelim* to receive the delight and pleasure. By this we will have faith in Him, as it is written in the *Sulam* (p 138), "Fear is safekeeping that we will not be removed from His faith."

From this we will understand what is written, "What does the Lord your God ask of you but fear?" It means that He wants to give us abundance, but what detains is the disparity of form, for the light cannot clothe in vessels of reception. Hence, when a person is afraid and vigilant to always keep his intention in order to bestow, the Creator can give him His bestowal in completeness, without any unpleasantness, called "bread of shame."

By this we understand what we asked, "How can fear be reason for joy?" With the above said, it is simple: By having fear, meaning by being careful to always use the vessels of bestowal, the Creator can give him the delight and pleasure because he has vessels of bestowal. And certainly at that time he will have joy from the abundance he has received in order to bestow. It follows that the fear causes the joy, and if he has no fear he is removed from everything.

The Difference between Charity and Gift

Article No. 24, Tav-Shin-Mem-Vav, 1985-86

It is written (Proverbs, 15:27), "He who hates gifts will live." This means that it is forbidden to receive gifts, for it causes the opposite of life. Thus, how do people receive gifts from one another? We should also ask about what the Creator said to Moses, "I have a good gift in My treasure, and its name is Shabbat. I wish to give it to Israel, go and notify them" (*Beitza*, p 16).

We see that it is customary that one can ask another for charity, but we have never seen someone asking another for a gift. For example, we sometimes see that before Passover, when a person must prepare *Matzot* [Passover unleavened bread] and wine and so forth for Passover, he goes to the collector of charity or to some wealthy person and asks him to help him prepare groceries for Passover. He tells him of his dire state and receives what he asks.

However, we have never seen anyone approaching his friend and asking for a gift. For example, now before Passover, his wife is asking him to buy her a diamond ring that is worth at least two hundred dollars. He tells his friend that since he is in financial difficulties

The Difference between Charity and Gift

and cannot buy the ring she wants, he wants his friend to give him the money as a gift to buy his wife the ring for Passover.

We also never heard that in any town there is a collector of gifts, meaning that there will be a collector of charity in town, as well as a collector of gifts. Rather, the usual way is that gifts are given and not requested. That is, when someone loves another, a desire to please him awakens in him, and this is why he gives him a gift. It is impossible to speak of asking for gifts or a special place in town were gifts are given.

However, we should understand the real reason why we do not ask for gifts, and do ask for charity. There is an arrangement in every town to help the needy so they have their sustenance and can exist in the world. Today it is also established in every country that there is an office that tends to those in need.

The reason is very simple: There is a difference between necessity and luxury. Necessity is what one must receive in order to be able to exist. Otherwise, if he did not receive the necessary assistance, he would not be able to exist in the world. Our sages said about this (*Sanhedrin* 37): "Anyone who sustains one soul from Israel, it is as though he has sustained a whole world." This pertains to necessity, without which he will not be able to exist. A person cannot relinquish this and not ask for help, for "All that a man has he will give for his life."

This is why people are not ashamed to ask for charity, since it is more or less a matter of life and death. The other, meaning the giver, also understands that he should give him what is requested. The closer the matter is to life and death, the more openly the receiver demands, and the more the giver takes interest in the receiver's situation. Likewise, the farther it is from life and death, the more coldly the giver relates to the state of the receiver. However, everything follows the track of necessity.

This is not so with luxuries. One who asks for luxuries is ashamed to ask. And the giver, too, does not listen to one who is asking for luxuries. For this reason, we should discern between charity and gift. With charity, the answer to the request of the receiver comes. That is, if the receiver of charity asks then he is given.

It follows that charity comes by an awakening of the lower one because he feels his deficiency. That is, when he sees that he cannot exist in the world without the giver's help, the receiver is not ashamed but goes and despises himself before the giver, since he has no other choice.

But a gift comes entirely from the giver. That is, if the giver awakens to do something, to reveal the love to his loved one, he sends him a gift. It therefore follows that a gift comes by the awakening of the bestowing upper one, but charity comes by an awakening of the receiver.

One who receives the charity should go to the giver and make him see the need for the charity that he is asking of him. To the extent that the receiver can clarify the need that he will come for his aid, and to the extent that he can make him see that it is a complete must, then he receives what he is asking of the giver.

However, the main reason is, as we learn, that when we must use anything that is not in the root we feel unpleasantness about it, as he says (*The Study of the Ten Sefirot*, Part One, *Histaklut Pnimit* [Inner Reflection], item 19), "It is known that the nature of every branch is equal to its root. Therefore, every conduct in the root is desired and loved and coveted by the branch, as well, and any matter that is not in the root, the branch, too, removes itself from them, does not tolerate them, and hates them."

It turns out that there is no reception in our root. Therefore, when one must receive he feels shame, which is unpleasantness, because it does not exist in our root. For this reason, when one needs one's friend's help, if it is necessary, we say that there is no choice because nothing is more important than saving one's life.

However, there are many discernments concerning risk to life. Therefore, anything that is necessary makes us suffer the shame and ask for help. But necessity is not the same for everyone. Each person has a different measure. That is, what one person may consider luxury, another may consider necessity.

Thus, it is difficult to determine the boundary on what is considered luxury and what is considered necessity. Although we can say about something one wants that you can live without, that it is luxury, if one cannot live without it, it is necessity. But this, too, cannot be a one hundred percent accurate gauge.

For example, our sages wrote (*Ketubot*, p 67b), "A man came to Rabbi Nehemiah and told him, 'What do you eat?' He replied, 'Red meat, and antique wine. Do you want to have lentils with me?' He had lentils and died." We see from the story that although everyone agrees that red meat and antique wine are certainly luxuries, to this man they were such a necessity that because of it he died.

We also see there, in the words of our sages, "Our sages taught, 'sufficient for his need, whatever he lacks' (Deuteronomy, 15). 'Sufficient for his need': You command me to sustain him but you do not command me to enrich him. 'Whatever he lacks': even a horse to ride and a servant to run before him. It was said about Old Hillel that once he took for a poor man who grew up wealthy a horse to ride on and a servant to run before him. Once, he could not find a servant to run before him so he ran before him three miles."

We can therefore see that according to the words of our sages about the verse, "whatever he needs," that even a horse to ride on and a servant to run before him fall into the category of necessity, and not luxury, since here we are speaking of a poor man, as the Gemarah writes, that Hillel took a poor man who grew up wealthy. And certainly, what we give to the poor is called "charity," meaning necessity. Even when it is a horse to ride on and a servant to run before him, it is still regarded as necessity. Thus, we cannot put a limit on where "necessity" ends and "luxury" begins.

It therefore follows that the poor man can ask to be given, as charity, what others regard as luxury. This means that we said that the poor man asks for charity does not feel shame because to him the charity is necessary. However, we cannot discern between charity and gift, which is considered luxury. Rather, it depends on the nature of the person.

Each person has his own gauge to determine necessity and luxury—because he can live without it. When a poor man does not have the courage to ask of another, it falls under the definition of a gift, which comes to him only as an awakening of the giver.

However, who can determine if what one asks of one's friend falls under the category of charity or gift? Only the Creator knows one's measure—that thus far it is considered necessity, and henceforth it is considered luxury.

Now we will speak of those terms in matters of work. We need to discern during the prayer, when a person asks the Creator to help him in the work, if he is asking the Creator for charity, meaning necessity, without which he tells the Creator that his life is pointless, meaning that he feels bare and destitute, without Torah and without *Mitzvot* [commandments]. He feels that there is not a spark of truth in him, and all his actions are built on hypocrisy and lies. That is, the whole foundation on which he builds his building of *Kedusha* [holiness/sanctity] is one of self-love.

He feels that each day he is regressing, where he should have progressed. But he sees the opposite, meaning that when he started the work of holiness he felt more importance in Torah and work, and this was why he took upon himself Torah and work—since it was worthwhile to retreat from the vanities of this world and cling to Torah and *Mitzvot*, for it would bring him happiness and meaning to life, and he was very excited.

But now he does not understand where he took those forces. That is, now, if someone told him, "Drop it all, retreat from the vanities of this world, and begin to work the work of holiness," there is no doubt that he would not be able to listen to him in his current state, both intellectually and emotionally.

He should certainly tell himself that then he had faith and confidence, but now he is far from all those. It turns out that the whole time he was engaged in the work it was in order to draw closer to the truth, which is *Dvekut* [adhesion] with the Creator, to which he yearned. But now he has retreated ten degrees, meaning now he lacks the zeal for the Torah and the importance of Torah.

It is even more so with prayer: He has no desire for prayer because the body tells him, "What will you get from praying? You can see for yourself that the more you want to work, the lower you become, so why do I need this work?" Thus, how can one exert where he sees that he cannot move one step forward?

Man enjoys rest and is incapable of relinquishing rest unless he knows that he will have greater pleasure or something more required. At that time he has a reason to relinquish the rest, though not without a reward. Therefore, when he sees that his work did not earn him anything from of what he thought he would earn, he loses the strength to work and remains powerless.

He looks at himself and says that if anyone would come to him and say, "Know that in a little while, some months or years, you will come to a state of despair, meaning that you will have no progress, but to the contrary, that each year you will be lowlier than you feel now, for now you are lowly, therefore you want to begin the true work so as to achieve the true goal for which you were created. Therefore, I am telling you that you are wasting your efforts, since I know many people who thought as you do—that if you only make a small effort you will immediately see results, meaning some progress in the true work."

I would reply to him: "You belong to the spies who slandered the land of Israel. It is just as the holy *Zohar* interprets (*Shlach*, item 63), 'And they returned from touring the land.' 'Returned' means they returned to the evil side, returned from the path of truth. They said, 'What have we got so far? We have yet to see good in the world. We have labored in Torah but the house is empty, and who will be awarded that world and come inside it? It would be better if we did not toil so much.' They told him, and he said, etc., 'We labored and toiled to know the part of that world, as you advised us. And it is also flowing with milk and honey. That upper world is good, as we know from the Torah, but who can be rewarded with it?'"

That is, now he says that after some time of work, if these thoughts had come to him in the beginning of the work, when he took upon himself that he must exit the ordinary situation, called "going by rote," and be a true servant of the Creator, he would tell these thoughts: "You are messengers of the spies. This is why you come to me, to stop me from entering the land of *Kedusha*, called 'holy work.'" He would not listen to them. But now he sees that he himself is feeling the argument of the spies, and now it seems to him that these are not arguments of the spies, but his own arguments, meaning that he feels that everything he feels is true.

As we have said above, the question that awakens is "What is the truth?" Was he at a higher degree in the beginning of the work than he is now after several years of work and labor? If so, what can be said about such a state? All his work was in vain. And not only in vain, since in vain means that he did not gain anything, and he is in the same state as before he entered the work of holiness in order to bestow.

But here it is not so. Rather, he has lost and declined from his previous state. That is, he is lacking the importance and zeal for Torah and *Mitzvot*, the energy and confidence he had. When he looks at himself today, he is in a state of "I could not care less." So it seems as though one should say that he has declined from his previous state, when he began his work.

But in truth, it is not so. There is a rule that there is no light without a *Kli* [vessel]. This means that the Creator does not satisfy the lower one's need if he does not have a real need.

A need does not mean that he does not have something. It is as I wrote in the allegory (Article no. 6, *Tav-Shin-Mem-Vav*), that there were elections in the country to elect a president. There were two candidates for presidency, and several lobbyists, each of whom wanted the president he supported to be elected. In the end one was chosen, and now there was a calculation regarding the deficiency.

The Difference between Charity and Gift

Someone felt that he was not the president, since in the end there is only one president.

We should say that all the people in the country have a lack, for we must say that they are not presidents. However, we should distinguish the amount of pain they feel at not being presidents. We should say that although ordinary citizens are not presidents, they do not feel any deficiency about it.

Those who engaged in making someone a president, but another president was elected, are in pain because of this deficiency that the one they worked for did not become president. However, the one who really suffers is that person who thought that he would be made president, who exerted to win the elections, to make his countryfolk elect him, but in the end his rival was elected. He feels the real suffering. We can say about him that he had the real need to be a president because he has exerted for it, and according to the efforts he has exerted, to that extent he feels the suffering.

It therefore follows that here, in the work of the Creator, in the beginning of his work he had energy and confidence, and great importance for Torah and prayer because at that time he had grace of holiness, and felt that the work of the Creator is important. However, this was still not considered a "deficiency" that the Creator will satisfy, a deficiency is called *Dvekut* [adhesion] with the Creator, since the lack and pain of not having *Dvekut* with the Creator was still not felt in him as he has not exerted for it because he has just begun the work.

But when he does not see results over a long period of time of making efforts, and he does not see a satisfaction of his deficiency, torments and pain begin to form in him because he has made efforts but sees no progress in his work. At that time the thoughts begin to come one-by-one. Sometimes it is with sparks of despair, and sometimes he grows stronger, but then he sees once more that he has fallen from his state, and so on repeatedly. Finally, a real deficiency forms in him, which he has obtained through exertion in ascents and descents. These ascents and descents leave him with pain each time at not having been granted *Dvekut* with the Creator. Finally, when the cup has been filled sufficiently, it is called a *Kli*. Then the filling of it comes from the Creator, since now he has a real *Kli*.

It follows that his seeing that now—after several years of work—he has retreated, this happens deliberately so he will ache at not having *Dvekut* with the Creator. It turns out that each time he must see that he is approaching the making of the *Kli*, called "real deficiency." That is, his gauge of *Katnut* [infancy/smallness] and *Gadlut* [adulthood/greatness] of the deficiency is to the extent of the suffering he feels at not having the filling, which is called here "*Dvekut* with the Creator," where all he wants is only to bring contentment to the Creator. Before the deficiency is completed, it is impossible for the filling to come in full. It is known that what comes from above is always complete. Thus, the deficiency should be full, as well, meaning that he will feel pain and deficiency at not having anything. That is, he should feel that he has no Torah, no work, and no fear of heaven.

Although in practice, he engages in *Mitzvot*, learns Torah, gets up before dawn, and is careful with the slight and serious things, and if other people did what he does they would regard themselves as complete righteous, but he feels that he is completely empty. This is so because he wants to be rewarded with *Dvekut* with the Creator, and for this one must have one thought, meaning that all his works will be in order to bestow, and he sees he is very far from this.

Therefore, he tells himself, "What am I gaining by engaging in Torah and *Mitzvot*? My whole calculation was that through this I will achieve *Dvekut* with the Creator. Yet, I do not see that I have moved one bit closer. On the contrary!" Thus, this person is not asking for luxuries, but only for necessity, to have something with which to revive his soul with some spirituality so he will not be immersed in self-love.

It turns out that he feels that he is completely devoid of spirituality. However, other people do not have this feeling of being

The Difference between Charity and Gift

far from spirituality. Rather, we see that the rest of the people, if they can pray each day in a Minyan [a minimum of ten participants in a prayer] they feel complete. It is even more so with people who come to study their daily page after work—they feel themselves as whole, and have no demand of the Creator to help them have the strength to walk on the path of the Creator. Rather, they pray for the Creator to help them continue their routine. Thus, they are already satisfied with life.

Even more so, those "whose Torah is their work" certainly feel whole and always praise the Creator for giving them the mind and desire not to sit among the idle. Although they pray to the Creator to help them with the matter of *Lishma* [for Her sake], which they had heard existed, they regard it as luxury. They observe the essence of Torah and *Mitzvot*, but do not have this matter of working *Lishma*. It is true that one should engage *Lishma*, but this pertains to a chosen few.

Thus, even when they pray that the Creator will grant them with learning Torah *Lishma*, they regard it as luxury and not as necessity, for thank God they feel that they are among the chosen ones in the nation, that they are in the "light of the vanities of Torah," and for them, "their Torah is their craft."

Thus, it turns out the same, that two people ask the Creator to grant them their requests. We should discern between them not by the prayer, but by the reason for the prayer: one wants it because his soul desires luxuries, so he is asking for a gift. But it is impolite to ask for gifts. Therefore, his request cannot be granted since one does not ask for presents, but it comes only from the giver, meaning that the giver awakens to give the gift to the receiver. For this reason it turns out that the lower one is full of grievances at the Creator for not hearing his prayer, since he is praying for gifts each day but he is not being heard. Therefore, he argues that there is something wrong, God forbid, with the upper one.

But the upper one argues that the lower one is wrong, since he is crying about receiving presents. What he thinks he needs is only a luxury to him. Therefore, if he corrects himself and sees the truth, meaning that he demand necessity, which is charity, then charity is given by the awakening of the lower one, as it is customary for the poor to ask. And the more the request is necessity, the more it is accepted.

This is what is explained above (*Ketubot*, p 67b), that meat and wine may be luxuries for every person, but for the one who came to Rabbi Nehemiah it was necessity. The evidence is that he gave him lentils to eat and he died.

By this we will understand why we see that once a person has made great efforts to achieve *Dvekut* with the Creator, in the end he sees that he has become worse than when he began to do the holy work to correct himself. That is, it is as though the corrections he had made were in vain, useless, but to the contrary.

The answer is that in truth, he went a great deal forward, but we should discern between progress toward the light and progress toward the *Kli*. Human nature is to regard progress toward the light, since light is all that man wants. It follows that things that do not illuminate do not interest him at all, for what will it give him if he has a great deficiency? There is a rule that man wants things that bring him pleasure, so when he wants to know if he has advanced, he examines how much closer he is to the light.

But the truth is that there is no light without a *Kli*. Therefore, first he must advance toward the *Kli*. That is, there is such a thing as advancing in deficiency. In the beginning of his work his deficiency was not revealed to him and he craved the light, although then, too, he had a deficiency—that he did not have light.

But this is similar to what people do: Sometimes a person loses some important object that is worth one hour of his work according to what he earns per day. If, for example, he makes eight dollars a day, he will not work for less than one dollar an hour. Rather, rest will be more important to him. But if he loses an object that is worth one dollar, he will search for it two hours until he finds it. This brings up the question: "Why did he just work an hour to earn half a dollar?"

The answer is that there is a difference between denying profit and losing from the capital. What he possesses and then loses, even if it is a small thing, it is important to him because he had already had it but then lost it. This is not so with something that he did not obtain. A great thing is worth exerting for, but otherwise rest is more important to him.

The same rule applies to us. When he had a desire to achieve *Dvekut* with the Creator, that deficiency is called "prevention of profit." That is, he is deficient that perhaps he will not profit, so he goes to work. But this is still not considered a real deficiency, fit for clothing the upper abundance.

But if he has already invested several years of work it is like losing from the capital. That is, he has lost several years of work without gaining anything. Then this deficiency is regarded as such because this deficiency creates in him torments and pains.

Thus, we see that the great efforts he has made, thinking that soon the Creator will help him and he will be rewarded with *Dvekut* with Him, so he was advancing concerning the desire for *Dvekut* because of the great efforts he has made, so the more he sees that he is exerting, the more he sees the opposite—that the body resists the matter of bestowal altogether.

At that time the understanding that he needs His help forms in him. Then, he is not asking for luxuries, but wants to be a simple Jew who believes in the Creator, that He, the blessed One, His name is the "Good Who Does Good." He wants to praise the Creator and say to Him: "Blessed is He who said, 'Let there be the world,'" just so, without any great attainments in *Torah* and *Mitzvot* with intentions, but very simply to be able to praise the Creator and thank Him for creating him.

Since now he sees that he does not even have the desire for Torah and work he had when he began to work, it is for two reasons, which are one: 1) The reason he began to assume the burden of Torah and *Mitzvot* was built on vessels of reception. Initially, the body longed to receive the delight and pleasure because he felt that he could receive from spirituality more satisfaction in life, meaning that the will to receive would have what to receive, since corporeal pleasures did not give him satisfaction in life. But now that he has begun to work in order to bestow, his body resists it.

The body agrees to labor where it can gain. But now that he has told the body, "Keep Torah and Mitzvot and by that, meaning by keeping Torah and Mitzvot, you will be able not to give the body any pleasure or reward for your work." Because of it, when the body hears that it will have reward for itself, but that its reward will be to have the strength not to give the body any reward for its work, this is the reason why now he has no strength to work as he did before he began to work in order to bestow, when the body expected greater pleasures than what it received from corporeal pleasures. Therefore, for this he had fuel and did not encounter any preventions from the body, since the body expected the desire to receive to gain more pleasures now.

However, we must know that the body has no other language, that it should want to work the holy work. Our sages said about this, "One should always engage in Torah and Mitzvot Lo Lishma [not for Her sake] for by that he will come to Lishma [for Her sake]." It follows that the beginning of his entrance to the work was just fine. That is, we must promise the body that God forbid that we should blemish its will to receive. On the contrary, by keeping Torah and Mitzvot, the will to receive will have real satisfaction in life, and his will to receive will feel that specifically by keeping Torah and Mitzvot he will feel that throughout the world, he is the happiest man in his generation.

But after he has begun the work and begun to know that the main thing is to achieve Dvekut with the Creator, called "doing everything in order to bestow," the body begins to resist this work. However, there is great benefit in this resistance of the body, since by this a person develops a great deficiency, meaning he suffers from being far from Dvekut with the Creator. At that time, the more he regrets, the more he becomes needy of the Creator's help, since then he sees that he cannot exit self-love by himself, but only the Creator

The Difference between Charity and Gift

Himself can help him. This is not a matter of understanding, but a matter of feeling. It is as it is written (Psalms, 127), "If the Lord does not build the house, they who built it labored in it in vain."

It follows that one should believe that all the twists and turns that have brought him to his current state were so he would have the ability to give an honest prayer from the bottom of the heart. However, the evil inclination brings man opposite views, so where one can ask the Creator from the bottom of the heart, meaning when the mind and heart have come to a decision that now only the Creator can help him, because now he can pray a true prayer, the evil inclination comes and brings him to despair, as the spies argue. We can say about this, "The ways of the Lord are straight; the righteous walk in them and the wicked fail in them."

With the above-said we will understand what we asked about the verse, "He who hates gifts will live." It does not mean that he should not receive gifts. However, if he hates the gifts because he wants to work in order to bestow, therefore he hates being a receiver but receives the gifts because the Creator wants it. This is called "receiving in order to bestow," since he would not awaken the Creator to give him luxuries. Rather, he is asking the Creator for necessity. And it makes no difference whether for another it is regarded as luxury, since each one works according to one's own feeling, and does not mind what his friend has. If later the Creator gives him a gift, he receives it in order to bestow.

It follows that if a person asks the Creator to give him vessels of bestowal, it depends on a person's character. That is, we can say that for one it is luxuries and for another it is necessity.

The Measure of Practicing Mitzvot

Article No. 25, Tav-Shin-Mem-Vav, 1985-86

We were given 613 *Mitzvot* [commandments] to perform in practice. Even without the intention, if he merely aims that now he is performing one of the *Mitzvot* that the Creator has commanded us, if we settle for observing the *Mitzva* [singular for commandments] without thinking about any intention, but only straightforward, then he has done his duty.

However, we should keep all the *Mitzvot* according to the conditions in each *Mitzva*. For example, a person may keep the *Mitzva* of *Tzitzit* [tassels—adornment consisting of cords fastened at one end], as it is written, "They shall make for themselves tassels on the corners of their garments." However, there are distinctions concerning the material from which the *Talit* [a prayer shawl that is worn during the morning Jewish services (on each edge of which there is a *Tzitzit*] is made, as well as the length and width of the *Talit*. Also, there are distinctions in the *Tzitzit* itself—the material from which it is made—wool, flax, or other materials—as well as the number of fringes, its length, and so forth.

The conditions in the *Mitzva* of *Tzitzit* should certainly be applied. Otherwise it is regarded as an incomplete practice of the

Mitzva, and is a deficiency in the act. Also, there is adornment in the practice of *Mitzvot*, as our sages said about the verse, "This is my God and I will praise Him," and there are many other precisions to make.

This matter applies to every performance of *Mitzvot*, whether *Mitzvot* from the Torah, from our sages, or *Mitzvot* that we keep because of customs, as our ages said, "Israel's customs are Torah" (*Minchot*, 20b), "and our father's customs are Torah."

The extent of precisions, meaning how meticulous we should be with the *Mitzvot*, was given to us in the *Mitzva* not to eat leaven on Passover. An example of how meticulous we should be: This was given to us on Passover, since leaven implies the evil inclination. For this reason we have many restrictions and precisions. This was given to us as an example of how we should be careful not to come, God forbid, into actually transgressing. Therefore, we were given precisions that will make us stay away from the transgression itself, as well as keep the *Mitzva* itself.

However, the Baal Shem Tov said, "Let him not be too meticulous." That is, one should not dedicate all his senses and time to precisions. Rather, as much as one can, one should keep the *Mitzvot* with all their details and precisions, but without excess. Perhaps this is why we do not apply the same strictness and precisions to all the *Mitzvot* as we do on Passover, for we need our energy for the intentions in the actions, too. Otherwise we will not have much time for intention.

This means that we must also think about the intention, as it is written, "I have created the evil inclination, I have created the Torah as a spice." Thus, we must dedicate time and effort to the intention, too, meaning see to what extent the evil inclination is corrected through the Torah and *Mitzvot*. That is, we must criticize our desire, called "will to receive," to see if we have become more distant from using the will to receive and moving away from it, and how much we have entered the work of bestowal. That is, we must constantly check ourselves so as to know for certain the measure of hatred we have acquired to hating our vessels of reception, and to craving vessels of bestowal.

Therefore, when one engages in some *Mitzva*, he must first know that he is keeping the *Mitzva* in a straightforward manner—that now he is not thinking of anything but the *Mitzva* he is performing, meaning to know that he is observing the commandment of the Creator and believe that the Creator has commanded us through Moses to keep His commandment. By keeping the 613 *Mitzvot* that He has given us, as well as through the *Mitzvot* of our sages, and by keeping the customs of Israel, which are also Torah, everything he does should be with the intention that he wants to delight the Creator. He was given a great privilege from above to be able to speak with the Creator. Therefore, when he blesses, both blesses on pleasures and blesses on *Mitzvot*, he should know and think a little bit to Whom he is giving the blessing, to Whom is he giving thanks.

One should depict that if he were allowed in to see the most important man in town, whom not everyone is permitted to approach, how would he feel when he entered and spoke to him? Or if he were permitted to come to the most important person in the country, what joy he would have. And also, if he imagines that he were allowed in to speak with the most important person in the world, who speaks only to a chosen few, how happy and elated he would be that he was given this great importance, which others are not so fortunate to have? We see that in our world, this gives us satisfaction and contentment in life.

Accordingly, the question is, "Why can't we depict this calculation and depiction of importance we have for a person, if he is respected in corporeality, that we can speak to someone so important, while regarding spirituality, when we speak to the Creator we do not have this feeling of sensing with whom we speak, so as to tell ourselves, 'Look how many people in the world do not have the privilege of speaking to the King of the world'? But to us, the Creator has given a thought and desire to come in and speak with Him."

However, a person must believe in what our sages said, "If the Creator did not help him, he would not overcome it" (*Kidushin*, 30). Thus, we should say that now the Creator has approached us and helped us, so why are we not inspired by the Creator and our hearts are not rejoicing?

However, when one speaks words of Torah and prays to the Creator, or when one blesses, he should imagine that he is speaking to an honorable person, to the King of the world, and wish that it will help him. That is, after all the depictions, it is still not the same as speaking to an honorable person in corporeality and the feeling he has then, where he feels the importance without any work. But in spirituality, he must toil with various depictions until he feels some importance that he is speaking to the Creator.

However, the matter is very simple: In corporeality, he sees that people respect him. Hence, the individual is influenced by the importance that the public has, and takes upon himself to serve him because of the importance he has absorbed from the public in regard to that person.

But with respect to the Creator, a person cannot see the true measure of people's appreciation of the Creator. Rather, everything is built on faith. Where one must believe is where labor begins, for then doubts are born and one must decide whether yes and no.

There is a lot of work in spirituality when a person must appreciate the Creator, and for this to relinquish several things that the body enjoys. He feels as painful when he relinquishes his pleasures, and all in order to win the Creator's approval and be allowed to come in and speak with Him, so He will let him feel with Whom he speaks, meaning that the Creator will be revealed to him and will not be so concealed.

But if he could receive the importance of the Creator from other people, as it is in corporeality, he would have no work. However, there is a special thing about *Kedusha* [holiness/sanctity], called "*Shechina* [Divinity] in exile" or "*Shechina* in the dust." It shows us the unimportance, which is the opposite of importance.

Naturally, we cannot receive importance from the public because we see that the public has no appreciation or regard for spirituality, from which he can receive support to rely on and go with what he was given importance, so he can relinquish the worldly life, called "corporeal life," in order to take upon himself to serve the Creator in order to bestow and not for his own sake.

This is so because he does not see that others appreciate spirituality enough to make it worthwhile to relinquish self-love. This is so because when he begins to look at other learners of Torah and observers of *Mitzvot*, he does not see them with enough importance to cause them to work in order to bestow. Naturally, he does not receive the importance of spirituality as he receives the importance of corporeality from the public.

In corporeality he sees that there is a public that appreciates someone. It does not matter who or what they appreciate, but he is influenced by them. But in spirituality he does not see that anyone, not even individuals, appreciates spirituality. So what can he do to acquire importance that will make it worthwhile for him to work in order to bestow?

It follows that man has a lot of work to exert to do what he can in order to obtain some importance, so he will understand that it is a great privilege that he has been rewarded with serving the Creator and keeping His *Mitzvot* in utter simplicity, meaning without any great intentions. Rather, one should simply feel happiness and vitality in keeping what the Creator has commanded us.

That is, he should think that now he is doing the King's will, and the King enjoys my doing His will. One should believe above reason that the Creator has sent him his thoughts and desires, which caused him to observe the *Mitzvot*, and that it came to him as an awakening from above. That is, now the Creator is calling him: "Come to Me; I want to give you a service in My palace." When one thinks this, the heart is elated and fills with joy, and then he feels high spirited.

It therefore follows that it does not matter what he does. It is all the same, as it is written, "Be careful with a slight *Mitzva* as with a serious one, for you do not know the reward for the *Mitzvot*." It can be said that it does not matter which *Mitzva* of the Creator a person keeps because his only thought is to bring contentment to the Creator.

Therefore, a person can derive great joy from small actions, since the main thing is not the greatness of the *Mitzva*, but the measure and importance of the Giver of the *Mitzva*. That is, it is according to his appreciation of the King.

When a person reflects, he sees that he must satisfy the desire, to have fulfillment. However, there are those who work to satisfy their own desires, meaning what the heart demands. This is called "lust." Conversely, there are those who need to satisfy the will of others, what they require of him, meaning to dress, and live in an apartment, as they require, etc. This falls under the category of honor. And there is also fulfilling the Creator's wish, what He demands, which is keeping of Torah and *Mitzvot*.

However, one should ask oneself: "Is serving the Creator really so important to me that I feel such great importance? So why after all the calculations, I forget everything, enter the corporeal world, stop everything related to *Kedusha*, and take upon myself to fulfill others' desires and not the Creator's, although I said that the Creator's will is so important, more important than to satisfy my own desire?

"When I worry about satisfying my own desire, it falls under the category of lust. When I try to satisfy others' desires it falls under the category of honor. I want to satisfy those two out of self-love. But when I want to do the King's will, that state is very important because at that time I exit self-love, called 'beast,' and enter the category of 'man,' as our sages said, 'You are called 'man,' and the nations of the world are not.'"

Thus, as soon as one comes out of the state of Torah and prayer he says that even the smallest thing he does in *Kedusha* is so important to him that it makes him very happy that he has been rewarded with entering the domain of *Kedusha*, and what fool would want to come out of the state of emotional satisfaction and elation? He feels that he is the happiest man in the world because he had the great privilege of exiting the beastliness that he was in all the time.

All of a sudden he is summoned to come before the King and speak with Him. At that time he looks at himself, how he is always immersed in worldly lusts like all other beasts. But now he sees that he has become a real man. He becomes very critical of his surroundings, how lowly they are, to the point that he can barely stand to be near them and speak to them because he cannot stoop so low as to speak to people devoid of the spirit of *Kedusha*, who are so immersed in self-love that he can barely stand them.

After all this, after some time, even a moment later, after all the criticism he passed on his surroundings, he completely forgets about the spirituality he was in and enters the corporeal world with all the beastly lusts. He does not even remember when he came out, the moment when he came out of the spiritual state into the corporeal state he is in now.

Thus, the question is, "When he was in the spiritual state and was delighted with his situation, was this a lie? Was it only a dream? Or is it to the contrary, that the previous state is his real state, and what he feels now, that he is immersed in beastly lusts, is a dream?"

The truth is that a person must believe that when the Creator appears to him a little bit, he begins to feel the importance of the King and is drawn to Him and annuls as a candle before a torch. If he continues to appreciate the herald he has heard from above, and to the extent that he can regard it, to that extent his aspiration for spirituality grows and he begins to feel that he has emerged from the corporeal world and entered a world that is nothing but good.

But if he forgets to appreciate that call—that he has been called to come speak to the King, and begins to enjoy and instill the joy he has into his vessels of reception, and he is not cautious to thank and praise the Creator for bringing him closer to Him, he is promptly repelled and ejected from the King's palace.

This happens so fast that he has no time to feel that he has been ejected. Only after some time he comes to, and sees that he has

The Measure of Practicing Mitzvot

been thrown out. But when he is ejected from the King's palace he remains unconscious, and therefore cannot feel the moment of ejection.

It is known that in corporality, too, if a person falls from a high floor to the ground, if you ask him how he fell he does not remember anything. All he knows is that now he is in the hospital, but he does not remember anything: who picked him up, who brought him to the hospital, everything is forgotten.

It is the same in spirituality. When he is ejected from the King's palace he does not remember who ejected him, meaning what caused him to fall off his state where he was in utter completeness, full of joy with his situation. He also does not remember when he fell from his high state into the ground, so as to say, "Up to that point I was fine, and at that moment I fell." He cannot remember the moment when he fell from his state. But after some time he opens his eyes and begins to see that now he is in the corporeal world.

This recovery—the consciousness he has regained when he sees that now he is outside the palace—can happen after several hours or even after several days. Suddenly, he sees that he is immersed in worldly lusts, and that once he had a state of ascent.

Now let us return to the matter from which we began, namely the greatness of the quality of practicing *Mitzvot* and words of Torah and prayer in utter simplicity, without any intentions but to learn Torah, since the whole Torah is the names of the Creator, and whether he understands the connection he has—that he is learning—meaning the fact that he is learning with the person.

That is, one should not say, "What does this come to teach us?" Rather, every word he learns is a great thing for his soul. And although he does not understand it, he must believe in the sages, who have instructed us so.

It is likewise in the prayer. He should know and believe that each and every word that our sages have arranged for us was said with the spirit of holiness. For this reason, we must regard each and every word, meaning that he has the privilege that the Creator has given him the thought and desire to observe His commandments, and to thank the Creator for it. He should believe that everything he does in spirituality, while others did not merit this, is because the Creator has chosen him to serve Him.

A person should reflect on how the King is calling him and gives him some understanding to at least keep His commandments so that he will have some contact with the Creator. Likewise, one should depict the importance of the King as much as one can and derive from this joy and elation. This is the path of truth.

That is, we should believe in the importance of the Creator although the body is still not impressed to the extent that he is seemingly serving a flesh and blood King, since there the public revere the King and the individual is influenced by the public. But in spirituality a person cannot see that the public revere the King and the value of annulling before Him is hidden from him. Instead, we must believe that this is so. This is called "right line," meaning without any intentions. Rather, even if he engages with the littlest understanding, he should regard it as though he is doing a great service.

It is as our sages said (*Avot*, Chapter 2, *Mishnah* 1), "Be careful with a slight *Mitzva* as with a serious one, for you do not know the reward for the *Mitzvot*." That is, it does not matter to us what service we do for the King, with which service we bring contentment to the King. Rather, we have one thought: that the Creator will be pleased with what I am doing.

Thus, it does not matter if this work is important or not, since I have no consideration of myself. It can be an unimportant work that not many people want, therefore he wants to do it because it is more needed than important work that many people want.

However, the question is, "Why can't a person feel the light that shines in Torah and *Mitzvot* as soon as he begins the work?" Instead, he must believe that there is a hidden light there, which he cannot see. It would certainly be better if the importance about it were revealed to all, for then everyone could observe the Torah and *Mitzvot*.

Thus, why is there a concealment on Torah and *Mitzvot* to the point that each and every one must labor and toil, and perform all kinds of works in order to be able to say that the whole of the corporeal world is not worthwhile compared to Torah and *Mitzvot*, as our sages said (*Avot*, Chapter 4, 22), "One hour of repentance and good deeds in this world is better than the whole of the life in the next world, and one hour of contentment in the next world is better than all the life of this world."

However, we were given this concealment so as to have room for choice, meaning to have the ability to work in Torah and *Mitzvot* for the Creator, meaning in order to bestow. Otherwise, if the light that is hidden in Torah and *Mitzvot* were revealed, he would work only because of self-love. But then he would not be able to criticize himself and see if his aim is to bestow or for his own sake.

But because we were given the Torah and *Mitzvot* to keep during the concealment, we can keep them in utter simplicity, and say, "If my aim is to bestow, why should I mind what taste I feel?" Therefore, if one wants to be rewarded with anything, he must take upon himself to keep Torah and *Mitzvot* in utter simplicity.

A Near Way and a Far Way

Article No. 26, Tav-Shin-Mem-Vav, 1985-86

In the portion, *Beshalach* [When Pharaoh Sent], we find that the text tells us, "God did not lead them through the land of the Philistines, for it was near; lest the people change their minds when they see war and return to Egypt." This means that a near way is not good. Regarding the second Passover, we see (Numbers, 9:10), "Speak to the sons of Israel, saying, 'Should any man be impure for the soul, or on a far way for you, he should make a Passover for the Lord on the second month.'" This means that if he is on a far way, he cannot do the Passover in its time.

We see that the portion, *Beshalach*, tells us that the near way is not good, as it is written there that He did not lead them for it was near, but that the far way is better. In the portion, *Behaalotcha* [When You Raise (the candles)], it is written that one who is on a far way is put off for a second Passover. This implies that the far way is worse than the near way.

First we must know that the ways to which the Torah relates surely imply a far way and a near way with respect to achieving the completion of the goal. Thus, it is difficult to understand how it can be said that the near way is not good. That is, the reason that the

Torah gives us for this is that they will see war and return to Egypt. But near means close to the Creator. If he is close to the Creator, how can it be said that they will regret and return to Egypt? We understand the opposite—if the people had regretted on a way that is far from the Creator, it could be said, "lest the people change their minds when they see war and return to Egypt."

In the portion, *Re'eh* [See] (Deuteronomy, 14:24), the writing says, "If the distance is so great for you that you cannot carry it, since the place where the Lord your God chooses to set His name is too far from you." Baal HaSulam gave an explanation about this and asked, "What is the reason that the text gives us the reason for 'If the distance is so great for you that you cannot carry it'?" He said that since man must assume the burden of the kingdom of heaven and must be as an "ox to the burden and as a donkey to the load," and man cannot carry it, meaning that it is hard for him to bear the load, which is the meaning of, "cannot carry it," for this reason the road will be far for you.

This is not so if one did take upon oneself the burden of the kingdom of heaven. He would see that everything is near him. That is, a person sees that "the place where the Lord your God chooses to set His name," meaning the place where God has chosen to set His name, is far from him. This is as it is written, "And let them make Me a Temple and I will dwell within them." That place is far from the person, meaning from being able to make in his heart room for instilling the *Shechina* [Divinity]. He is far from understanding such a thing—that one will have the strength to make room for instilling the *Shechina* in his heart. This is so because he will not be able to carry it, meaning he will not want to take upon himself the accepted way, "as an ox to the burden and as a donkey to the load."

It therefore follows that one should exert all of one's energy only on this. That is, one should always seek advice how to take upon himself the above-mentioned burden. One should focus all of one's work, meaning in everything that one does in Torah and *Mitzvot* [commandments], one should desire that these works will bring him the assuming of the burden of the kingdom of heaven not in order to receive reward, and that this is where "the Lord your God has chosen to set His name."

It is known that His name is called *Malchut*, who is called *Shechina*. This is as the holy *Zohar* writes, "He is *Shochen* [dweller]; she is *Shechina* [Divinity/where He dwells]." It is as Baal HaSulam says, that the place where the Creator is revealed is called *Shechina*, and the Creator is called *Shochen*. However, when is He called *Shochen*? When there is someone who attains the *Shochen*. At that time he says that *Shochen* and *Shechina* are not two things, but one. That is, the *Shochen* is called "light without a *Kli* [vessel]," and the *Shechina* is the place where the Creator is revealed. It follows that all that there is in the place where the Creator is revealed is the Creator, and nothing else. However, there is light and *Kli*, meaning there is a *Kli* that attains the light.

It therefore follows that the place where the Creator has chosen to set His name is as we learn, that we need to correct our vessels of reception to be in order to bestow contentment upon the Creator. This is the meaning of equivalence of form. Then, in that place, the name of the Creator appears.

Thus, how can it be said about a near way, "And God did not lead them, for it was near"? After all, a far way means as it is written concerning the second Passover, that one who was on a far way is put off for a second Passover. It is as it is written in the portion, *Re'eh* (Deuteronomy, 14:24): "If the distance is so great for you that you cannot carry it." According to Baal HaSulam's interpretation, remoteness of location stems from being unable to carry it, meaning to tolerate the burden of the kingdom of heaven. Therefore, how can it be that the far way is better than a near way?

In *Masechet Iruvin* (p 53b), he writes there in the name of Rabbi Yehoshua Ben Hananiah, who said, "Once I was walking along the road and saw an infant sitting at a crossroads. I said to him, 'My son, which way leads to the city?' He said to me, 'This one is long and short, and this one is short and long.' I followed the short and long. When I arrived at the city, it was surrounded by gardens and orchards. I went back and told him, 'My son, did you not tell me, this one is short?' He replied, 'My Rav, did I not say "Short and long"?'" This means that there is an issue of near and far, and far and near.

It is written in the portion, *Nitzavim* [Standing] (Deuteronomy, 30:11): "For this commandment which I command you today is not beyond you, nor is it far. For the matter is very near you—in your mouth and in your heart to do it." This means that "near" is a good way, as it is written, "In your mouth and in your heart to do it," and not as in the portion, *Beshalach*.

To understand the above we must interpret this with regard to the beginning of the work. There is a matter of work in practice, and there is a matter of working on the intention. That is, one should work on the intention, too. This means that while observing the *Mitzvot* [commandments], one should have a good intention, meaning with which intention he is performing the *Mitzvot*, namely the reason that causes him to keep the *Mitzvot*.

Since we should aim the actions to be not in order to receive reward, and since man is born with vessels of reception, which is that it is impossible to do anything without receiving reward for one's work, for it is in our nature not to make any movement unless we see that it is worthwhile, that we will have more pleasure by relinquishing rest.

That is, we relinquish the state we are in, in order to receive more pleasure than we have now, before we leave the pleasure and go do something else. Thus, it is certainly important that through performing a new act he will receive more pleasure.

Thus, he must do and keep the Torah and *Mitzvot* not because the Creator wants us to keep them and we want to do His will so He will derive pleasure from our obedience to Him. Rather, since He promises us a great reward for listening to Him, we try to keep what He wants from us, since we are looking at the good reward that He will pay us for our work.

This is similar to people working for an owner at a factory. A usual workday lasts eight hours. By the workers working for him, the owner makes money. Therefore, the owner enjoys having workers who do his will.

Some of the workers approach the owner and tell him that since they see that he is troubled by the fact that he has promised someone to deliver products by a certain date, but they see that according to the pace of the work that the workers are producing in eight hours, he will not be able to meet the terms of the contract and provide all the merchandise on time. Therefore, they agree to work overtime for him. Although they must be home immediately after the eight hour workday, since they have children to tend to, and one of them has a wife who is a little sick, so they try to come home immediately after work, but because they see his distress, they are willing to work overtime for him.

Naturally, when the owner hears of his workers' dedication to him, that they cannot stand his sorrow and therefore agree to work overtime because they know that he is stressed because he must meet the contract that he promised the buyer to provide a certain amount of merchandise by a certain date, but according to the pace of work in eight hours he will be unable to keep his promise.

Therefore, the feeling in their hearts toward the giver of the work does not let them rest without doing something for the owner, so they agree to labor more than they are able. That is, although it is passed the workday hours and they have families with many children, and one of them has a wife who is a little sick and he must do the domestic chores, as well, their conscience does not let them leave the owner in distress.

Therefore, they approach him and tell him, "We have decided to work overtime for you." When the owner hears his workers' devotion, he sees a new thing: Before these workers came to him to show him that they sympathize with his affliction, he thought that all the workers had no emotions or conscience. Rather, they worked for him and not for others only because he pays more than others, so they work for him. But now he sees otherwise—that he was wrong about the workers.

But afterwards they tell him: "However, you must know that for overtime, meaning to work at night, too, we want you to pay us for the overtime twice as much as you pay us for regular hours." Then the owner begins to think again: "Is the reason why they want to work overtime really as they say, that they want to help me in my plight? Or is it the opposite? They see I'm in distress and therefore demand more money for overtime because they know I have no choice? They let me see that I need to give them what they want because they tell me of my dire state, so I will know that they know my situation, and so they want to pressure me to pay them for the overtime the money they are asking."

From this we can take an example of our work in keeping Torah and *Mitzvot*, meaning to discern between action and intention. An action means that he intends to do the act that He has commanded us through Moses to keep Torah and *Mitzvot* in all its details, and that we should aim that the *Mitzva* [commandment] we are doing is in order to do His will, that He wanted us to keep Torah and *Mitzvot*.

It follows that the intention that a person should intend is that we should aim that the actions we do are to keep what He has commanded us. This is regarded as intending for the action to be fine, as He had told us through Moses. It is like the judgment concerning blowing the *Shofar* [special horn blown on special days], that "If he blows the *Shofar* in order to learn, or blows in order to sing, and not for the purpose of *Mitzva*, then he has not done his duty" (as it is written in Way of Life, Rules of *Rosh Hashanah*, item 589).

It therefore follows that when we say that *Mitzvot* require intention, it means that he should aim that the act he is performing will be because he wants to keep the commandment of the Creator. Certainly, the act should be according to the law that our sages determined the measures of Torah and *Mitzvot*—how and in what way it should be in the practice of *Mitzvot*.

For example, the *Sukkah* [the hut of the Tabernacle Festival] has several rules to it in terms of shape. Otherwise, the work is deficient. The same applies to studying Torah, and to the negative

Mitzvot [commandments to avoid certain actions]. There are many rules concerning them. If he does not keep the laws concerning them then there is a deficiency in the work of *Mitzvot*. Even if he does everything according to the law, he should still intend that he is performing the *Mitzva* because the Creator has commanded us to do His will by keeping the *Mitzvot* that He has commanded us through Moses.

All this is regarded only as "the practice of *Mitzvot*," but not the intention. This is so because everything he thinks about doing the act that the Creator has commanded us, and all the labors we labor in Torah and *Mitzvot*, are like all the people in the world, who work and labor to be rewarded, and nothing more.

Also, here we need additional attention because when we say that all the work is in the practice of *Mitzvot*, it means that the labor is in the practice, and it cannot be said here that there is work for the reward. Rather, in order to receive reward for the labor, we do not see that a person will need effort to receive reward, since the only reason we labor and relinquish many things is that we are considering the reward, for only the reward compels us to do hard work without minding the quality of the work or the time of the work, for the reward determines everything.

Thus, we should understand why we are saying that there is work on the intention, meaning work on the reward. After all, how can we speak of work here? However, the thing is that when a person engages in Torah and *Mitzvot* and wants his reward to be that the Creator will give him the thought and desire to work not in order to receive reward, the body does not agree to such a reward, since normally we receive reward for work. That is, the work is in concessions of needs that he enjoys, in return for which he will receive greater pleasures than he is conceding. For example, he relinquishes rest, and sometimes sleep, and so forth, and receives in return greater and more necessary pleasures.

This is not so when he relinquishes pleasures by coercion, when the body disagrees and wants reward in order to agree to relinquish all kinds of pleasures. It follows that the work is acts of bestowal, and the reward will be the intention only to bestow, without any reward of reception. For this intention, meaning for this reward, one must work a lot.

This is more difficult than working in practice, although he does not need two different things at a different time for the intention of the reward. Rather, the same work that he does, and at the same time when he is working, are enough for him, and he does not need other actions, but merely thought and intention. What is the intention? That his thought and desire will be like the act.

That is, as he does the work because the Creator has commanded him to do it, so the intention will be only that he wants to keep the commandments of the Creator only for the Creator, without any reward. The fact that all that is demanded of man while performing the act—when he is doing the Creator's will—is to aim while performing the *Mitzva*, not because he is considering the reward, compels him to work day and night. That is, he keeps what is written, "And you shall contemplate Him day and night" not because he is considering the reward, and this makes him work day and night. Rather, his desire to bring contentment to the Creator is the reason why he exerts in the work.

This is similar to the above-mentioned allegory about the workers who agreed to work overtime for the owner at night, but demanded that he pay them twice as much as they receive during regular hours. We see the difference between working in order to receive reward and working not in order to receive reward. No one can say that the workers are faithful to the owner, and this is why they agree to work for him day and night. Rather, they say the opposite about them, that since the owner needs their work they use him and want him to double their pay.

It is the same with work. Although *Lo Lishma* [not for Her sake] is work, and there is nothing to add in terms of actions, but there is the matter of intention here, meaning what the workers intend by working—whether it is to their benefit or to the benefit of the Creator.

It takes a lot of hard work for the body to agree to work for the Creator, meaning to tell the body what I hope for, what reward I want to receive from the Creator for forcing you to work so hard—so the Creator will give me the reward that you will not be able to obstruct me when I want to do everything in order to bestow.

Naturally, the body yells out loud and does all that it can to avoid losing its control. Therefore, it does not let them do the simplest things because it is afraid that by merit of the act he will achieve *Lishma*, which is entirely for the Creator, and it will have no part that it will be able to receive for self-love.

Because of it, we see that for those who want to keep Torah and *Mitzvot* in order to bestow, every little thing is very difficult because the body is afraid in every action it performs that perhaps through the work he is doing the person will achieve *Lishma*, and all the control of the will to receive over the person will be revoked. This is regarded as having work on the reward, as well. It means that he has work to choose the reward he wants for his work in Torah and *Mitzvot*—whether it is reward that pertains to self-love or reward that is "for the Creator alone," and he does not want to give self-love any part of his work, and always thinks, "When will I be granted with having a desire only to bestow contentment upon the Creator?"

Now we can understand what we asked, "How can there be a bad near way," as it is written, "And God did not lead them, for it was near." We can understand what the infant said to Rabbi Yehoshua Ben Hananiah, that "There is a far and short way, and a short and far one," meaning near but far. This means that although it is near, it is far from the goal.

It is known that Maimonides says that we should not disclose the matter of *Lishma*, as he says (*Hilchot Teshuva* [Rules of Repentance], Chapter 10), "Sages said, 'One should always engage in Torah, even *Lo Lishma*, because from *Lo Lishma* he will come to *Lishma*.' Therefore, when teaching little ones, women, and ordinary people, they are taught only to work out of fear and to receive reward. Until they gain more knowledge and acquire much wisdom, they are told that secret bit-by-bit, and are accustomed to it calmly until they attain Him and serve Him out of love.'"

It implies from the words of Maimonides that there is a near way, meaning that it is near to man's heart, meaning in order to receive reward. It follows that it is called "near" because it is close to man's heart. But there is another interpretation of "near way," which is that a person sees each time that he is coming closer to the goal, and for him the goal is called "reward," and he hopes that when he has a certain amount of Torah and *Mitzvot*, he will promptly receive reward for his work, as it is known that being a hired worker pays only in the end (*Baba Metzia*, 65).

Therefore, he believes that when he finishes his work in this world he will receive his reward in the next world, besides having *Mitzvot* whose reward is in this world, too, as it is written, "These things that a man eats, their fruits are in this world, and the capital awaits him for the next world."

It therefore follows that each day he feels that he has something in his hand, meaning the reward of a day's work, and each day joins a year, and a year to a year. For example, a person who begins to observe *Mitzvot* at age thirteen, which is the time when *Mitzvot* become mandatory, by age twenty he is happy that thank God, he already has seven years of work written to his account. By age thirty he is extremely happy because he already has seventeen years of work written in his book. It follows that each time he works he can be happy that his reward is growing from day to day. This work is called "close to his heart," since he is certain about his advancing reward.

This way is called "near way" because it is agreeable to the heart, since if one sees progress on his way, that way sits well with the heart because he has what to examine. In the work he does, he sees that each day he has a certain amount of work in Torah and *Mitzvot*, and everything is written in his book, as it is written (*Avot*, Chapter 3), "He would say, 'All is in deposit, and a fortress spreads over all of life. The store is open and the shopkeeper sells by deferred payment; the book is open and the hand writes.'" Therefore, he is certain that he has a great asset of reward that he has accumulated by working each day and from year to year. For this reason, this way is called "near way." This is also called "a short way" for the above reason, since he does not need a long time for a person to understand that it is worthwhile to walk on this path because this path is close to his heart. This is why it is a short way.

However, it is a long way to achieve the truth, for the Torah and *Mitzvot* to bring him into having the intention only to bestow. It is very far because this way is the opposite of the path of *Dvekut* [adhesion] with the Creator, which is entirely to bestow. Here he begins to walk on a way that his intention will be only to receive reward. But the purpose one should achieve through his labor in Torah and *Mitzvot* is to bring him to work in order to bestow, as our sages said, "I have created the evil inclination, I have created the Torah as a spice." He needs to see that through Torah and *Mitzvot*, the evil in him, called "receiving in order to receive," will be corrected and he will be able to do everything for the sake of the Creator, and not for his own sake. Concerning his own sake, it is as our sages said about the verse, "If a man dies in a tent," that the Torah exists only in one who puts himself to death over it, and not for his own benefit.

This is called "near and far." It is near to his heart for the two above reason, but far from the truth, as Maimonides says (*Hilchot Teshuva*, Chapter 10), "One who works from love, engages in Torah and *Mitzvot*, and walks in the paths of wisdom not because of anything in the world, and not because of fear of evil, and not in order to inherit abundance, but does the truth because it is the truth."

It follows according to the words of Maimonides that the above near way is far from the truth. Accordingly, we can interpret, "God did not lead them through the land of the Philistines, for it was near; lest the people change their minds when they see war and return to Egypt." The matter of "when they see war" should be interpreted to mean that by engaging *Lo Lishma*, the way is the one that illuminates illumination that one must achieve *Lishma*. And since the beginning of the work is in *Lo Lishma*, they will not want to go to war with the inclination because they will fear losing their degree of engaging in Torah and *Mitzvot*.

This is a far way. The Creator wanted to go with them right away to Mt. Sinai and give them the Torah. This is why He told them right away that they must go by the far way. That is, although this work is far from the heart, it is close to the truth, and by this they will be fit to receive the Torah at the foot of Mt. Sinai.

Therefore, it follows that we can interpret "long and short way" to mean short and near. Thus, the meaning will be "far from the heart," meaning that it requires a long time to make the heart see until it can understand that it is worthwhile to work for the purpose of truth, meaning to keep Torah and *Mitzvot* in truth because the Creator has commanded us to keep the Torah and *Mitzvot*, and we want to keep it so that He will enjoy our doing His will.

It follows that the cause and reason for keeping His commandments is the Creator, and not the person. This means that the importance of the Creator compels him to have a desire and craving to serve Him and bring Him contentment. This is called a "far way," which is because it is far from the heart, but close to the truth, where by being shown the truth, he is closer to touching the truth.

However, "near and far" means "short and long." This will mean "close to the heart," for since the body craves pleasures, and he promises it that through his labor in Torah and *Mitzvot* it will receive reward, it follows that the body is the reason for keeping Torah and *Mitzvot*. That is, if he could receive greater pleasure elsewhere, why would he work where the salary is low? This is why this is called "near and short," for it does not require a lot of time to make the body understand that it should assume the burden of Torah and *Mitzvot*.

It is as he says in the *Sulam* ([Ladder commentary on *The Zohar*] ("Introduction of the Book of Zohar," item 191): "1) Fear of the Creator and keeping His *Mitzvot* so that his sons may live and he will be kept from bodily punishment or a punishment to one's money. This is fear of punishments in this world. 2) When fearing punishments of Hell, as well. Those two are not real fear, for he does not keep the fear because of the commandment of the Creator, but because of his own benefit. It follows that his own benefit is the root, and fear is a derived branch of his own benefit." It follows that this is called "long and short, far and near" because of what is written in the portion, *Beshalach*, "God did not lead them through the land of the Philistines, for it was near."

However, in the portion, *Behaalotcha*, it is written regarding the second Passover, "or one who was on a far way is put off for a second Passover." We asked, "This means that the far way is not good, and this is why he was put off for a second Passover?" We should interpret that when a person walks on the near way, meaning close to his heart, he feels that he is closer to *Kedusha* [holiness/sanctity] than others, who are walking on the far way, since each day he feels that the Torah and *Mitzvot* he is performing are accumulating and increasing.

Thus, he has nothing to correct in himself in order to be close to *Kedusha*, for he can see with his own eyes and does not need to believe above reason that he is ascending on the levels of sanctity. After all, he is keeping the Torah and *Mitzvot* in every detail, so naturally his *Kedusha* is growing every day. He feels that he is a complete righteous, and wonders how he can keep what our sages said, "Be very, very humble."

It follows that such a person, from the state he is in with respect to practice, is hopeless to ever be able to make a sacrifice to the Creator, meaning to come near Him with respect to equivalence of form because he does not feel that he is immersed in self-gratification.

However, if he feels that he is far from the Creator, meaning sees that he is still immersed in self-gratification, and yells to the Creator to let him out from self-benefit and into benefitting the Creator, then he can be corrected, meaning he is put off for a second Passover, and then he makes a sacrifice, meaning that then he comes near to the Creator.

It follows that we should discern two types in the work of the Creator: One type includes those who still belong to *Lo Lishma*. The second type are those who already belong to *Lishma*. They are two types, and one cannot understand the other. This is called "long and short, far and near."

The Creator and Israel Went into Exile

Article No. 27, Tav-Shin-Mem-Vav, 1985-86

It is written in *The Zohar, BeHukotai* [In My Statutes] (item 49), about the verse, "And I, too, will torment you seven times for your sins": "Come and see, the Creator's sublime love for Israel is like a king who had an only son who sinned before the king. One day, he sinned before the king. The king said, 'All those days I have been striking you but you did not receive. Henceforth, see what I will do to you. If I expel you from the land, bears might charge you in the field, or wild wolves or murderers could obliterate you from the world. What should I do? Instead, you and I will go out of the land.' Thus, I, too, as it is written, meaning that you and I will leave the land, meaning go into exile, 'And I will chastise you' to go into exile. And if you say that I will leave you, I, too, am with you."

We should understand the meaning of the exit of the people of Israel from the land abroad, which is called "exile among the nations." What does it mean in the work? That is, what is regarded as "land" and what is regarded as "exit from the land"? Also, what does it mean that when one sins he is punished with exile, to be among the nations of the world? How does it help, and what benefit does it yield in the ways of the work? That is, what is the correction in going out to exile to be under the rule of the nations of the world?

We should also understand how it can be said that the Creator, too, leaves the land with the people of Israel into exile, since "the whole earth is full of His glory," and it is written, "His kingship rules over all." He even sustains the *Klipot* [shells/peels], so how can it be said that He will go out to exile with the people of Israel as though He is not in the land?

To understand the above in the work, we first need to know what is the land of Israel, what is abroad, and why exiting from the land abroad is regarded as exile among the nations. We should also understand that exile is a correction for sins. That is, by suffering the exile, the torments of the exile will make them repent, and then it will be possible to bring them back to the land. But it is written, "And they mingled with the nations and learned their works," so what torments of exile are they feeling, which can be a cause for them to repent and return to the land? That is, what can he know about what is good in the land of Israel so as to crave it, and this land will be a reason that will compel him to repent for the love of the land?

It is known that land is called *Malchut*, and the "holy *Shechina* [Divinity], and "the assembly of Israel," which is the inclusion of all the souls. This means that she must receive the delight and pleasure that was in the thought of creation to do good to His creations, meaning that the souls will receive delight and pleasure.

The order of cascading was from the world of *Ein Sof* [no end/infinity] to the world of *Tzimtzum* [restriction], and then to the line on which the five *Partzufim* [plural of *Partzuf*] of *AK* are clothed, then the five *Partzufim* of *Atzilut*. Afterwards, *Malchut de Atzilut* emanated the three worlds *BYA*, and then *Adam Harishon* was created, and the externality of his body, which is similar to the current material body, was made from *Bina de Malchut de Assiya*, as it is written in *The Study of the Ten Sefirot* (Part 16, p 1912, item 43), "Afterwards he had *NRN* from *BYA* and then *NRN* from *Atzilut*."

It therefore follows that *Eretz* [land/earth] is called *Malchut de* [of] *Atzilut*, and it is written about the world of *Atzilut*, "Evil will not dwell with you," meaning that there is no evil there at all, but only in *BYA* are there scrutinies of good and evil. Rather, there the delight and pleasure that He contemplated giving to the souls are revealed. It is as our sages said about the verse, "'In the beginning God created': there is no beginning but Israel, for everything is for Israel, meaning for the souls of Israel."

After *Adam Harishon* sinned with the tree of knowledge, he was expelled from *Atzilut* and descended to *BYA*. Then he began to repent and correct what he had sinned. By this he reentered the Garden of Eden, meaning *Atzilut*. The correction was that he was expelled from the Garden of Eden, as it is written (Genesis, 3:22), "And the Lord said, 'And now, he might stretch out his hand and take also from the tree of life, and eat, and live forever.' And the Lord God sent him out from the Garden of Eden, to till the ground from which he was taken."

Baal HaSulam explained the fear for which he was expelled from the Garden of Eden, as is written, "He might stretch out his hand and take also from the tree of life, and eat, and live forever." He said that since the man sinned with the tree of knowledge, if a person is punished, meaning suffers from the punishment that he was given, this suffering causes him to repent and correct the flaw that he had caused.

But if he is not punished and does not feel suffering from the sin he had committed, he will certainly not understand that he should repent for it. It is as *The Zohar* writes ("Introduction of the Book of Zohar," item 192), "Rabbi Shimon wept and said, 'Woe if I say, woe if I do not say. If I say, the wicked will know how to serve their master.'"

He interprets in the *Sulam* [commentary on *The Zohar*] as follows, "By this he implies that he could not reveal his words in full in this place so as not to harm the wicked. This is because here he came to disclose how to cling to the tree of life, and never touch the tree of death, and only those who have already corrected the discernment of the tree of knowledge of good and evil are worthy of it. But the wicked, who have yet to correct the sin of the tree of knowledge of good and evil, must not know it, for they must first toil in all the labors until they correct the sin of the tree of knowledge. You will also find this in the verse, 'Lest he reached out his hand and took also from the tree of life and ate, and lived forever' (Genesis, 3). After Adam sinned with the tree of knowledge, he was expelled from the Garden of Eden for fear that he would cling to the tree of life and live forever, and the flaw he had caused in the tree of knowledge would forever remain uncorrected."

It therefore follows that when taking a person out from the land, meaning from the kingdom of heaven he had, since he cannot feel the importance of spirituality that he had prior to being taken out from the kingdom of heaven, and he goes to exile, as it is written, "And they mingled with the nations and learned their works," this is regarded as falling under the enslavement of idol worshippers. That is, all the lusts that exist in the nations of the world govern Israel, who have been exiled. At that time they have no connection to spirituality, except what they are used to keeping out of habit. This they observe, but beyond them it does not occur to them that they have anything to correct.

It follows that we should make two discernments concerning the exile: 1) They are exiled under the governance of the nations. The mind and intellect that they had while in the land, when they were in the kingdom of heaven and thought all day about how to exit self-love and achieve the love of the Creator, when they sinned and went to exile, we can interpret this in the work of the individual, as it is known that the general and the particular are the same. This means that if a person sins while being in the land, meaning if he receives some illumination from above and uses it for his own benefit, meaning says, "Now that I have some flavor in Torah and *Mitzvot* [commandments], I don't need faith above reason." This is called a "sin" because he has blemished the faith above reason.

For this reason, he is expelled from the land and falls under the governance of the lusts of the nations of the world. Once he is in exile, he promptly suffers forgetfulness, and does not remember that he was ever in the land, that he was in a state of "kingdom of heaven" and thought only about how to achieve *Dvekut* [adhesion] with the Creator. He wants to continue this way his whole life, meaning to care only about satisfying the needs that the body demands for its own benefit, and does not care about anything.

After some time, and each one has a different calculation with Him (meaning that when a person is judged above, each one has his own calculation as to how long he should be kept in exile until he receives an awakening from above), and he receives an awakening from above and begins to feel that he is in exile, and begins to remind himself that he has fallen from a high roof to a deep pit.

That is, when he was in the land, he remembers that he looked at the whole world as redundant and always thought, "Why did the Creator create the wicked in the world? What joy or benefit can these wicked bring to the Creator?" Instead, now he looks at himself, that he is in exile, and what can he give to the Creator so as to bring contentment above? He begins to feel the suffering that he has descended from man to beast, meaning sees that now he desires beastly lusts, which he did not have prior to being expelled from the land.

Now he begins to crave the Creator, that He will bring him closer and admit him once again into the land, and out of beastly lusts, and give him pleasures from nourishments fit for man, meaning from acts of bestowal, and not that his nourishment will be from food for beasts. It is as our sages said (Peshachim, 118), "When the Creator told *Adam Harishon*, 'Thorns and thistles it shall grow for you,' his eyes teared. He said, 'Will I and my ass eat from the same crib?' Once He had told him, 'By the sweat of your brow you will eat bread,' his mind was immediately eased."

This sounds as though the Creator gave him the knowledge when He said, "Thorns and thistles it shall grow for you." Before the Creator had told him that, he did not see that his nourishment was only thorns and thistles, which is only animal food. We can interpret that the awakening from above came to him and reminded him what he had had before the sin, what high degrees he had had, and with the exit from the Garden of Eden it is as though he has forgotten everything.

This is regarded as the Creator speaking to him, meaning that he received an awakening from above from the Creator, and then he remembered what he had had. At that time he began to feel the suffering from being expelled from the Garden of Eden, and began to cry about being on the same degree as a beast. That is, his nourishment is only that which pertains to self-love, which is called "food for beast." This is the meaning of "His eyes teared and he said, 'I and my ass from the same crib?'" That is, eating, that which nourishes him, will be similar to that of a beast, where he can elicit joy only out of matters that pertain to self-love.

However, when He told him, "By the sweat of your brow you will eat bread," his mind was immediately eased. RASHI interprets "By the sweat of your brow" to mean after you have had much toil in it. We should interpret the meaning of "toil." According to what we learn, if one has already come to feel that he is at a degree that is similar to a beast, it means that the sensation should also be to the extent that brings to suffering, that he will shed tears over his lowly and poor state, as our sages said, "His eyes teared."

Therefore, the suffering he feels at being similar to a beast gives him the strength to want to make great efforts to exit self-love—which is regarded as a beast—and be rewarded with man's food. That is, that now he can enjoy acts of bestowal.

It therefore follows that we should make two discernments regarding the above exile:

1) He is in exile but does not know he is in exile. Rather, he is happy as he is. Instead, he is searching for quantity, meaning more money, more respect, etc. However, he has already forgotten that he was once at a human degree, called "land," which is the kingdom of heaven. It does not even occur to him that he should change his sustenance. Rather, he does not think that the nourishments he receives in vessels of self-love, called "animal food," need replacing, meaning to have thoughts of giving.

It follows that he does not want to change the source of provision, where he is being fed with only that which comes into vessels of self-love. Rather, he wants to replace the matters that come in vessels of self-love. For example, he would like to change his apartment because he no longer enjoys the one he lives in and wants a different apartment, since a new apartment is something he can enjoy. Also, he changes the furniture because he cannot enjoy the ones he has. By having new furniture his will to receive will have something to enjoy.

2) However, he does not want to change his source of provision, meaning to say that his provision should come from a source that gives only to the vessels of bestowal. This he, God forbid, does not contemplate, as it is known that the receiver cannot understand how can there be provision from giving. The giver is to the contrary. When he sees that he is engaging in reception he is ashamed of himself for doing something he regards as lowly. But in truth, we must change the source of nourishment. There is nourishment that pours into vessels of self-love, and this nourishment comes from the *Klipot* [shells/peels], and there is nourishment that comes into the vessels of bestowal, and this one comes from the worlds of *Kedusha* [holiness/sanctity].

Therefore, according to the two above discernments in exile, the question is, "Who causes one to feel that he is in exile, by which he suffers because he wants to exit the exile, as was said about the exile in Egypt, 'And the children of Israel sighed from the work, and they cried out, and their cry rose up to God from the work'"? We have to say that this awakening came from the Creator, so they would not stay in exile, in a state of oblivion, so the Creator sends the awakening.

It therefore follows that they feel that there is spirituality, but that the spirituality is in a state of lowliness and their heart aches over the fact that the *Shechina* is in exile, and why spirituality has the taste of dust. That is, when they want to work in order to bestow, they cannot appreciate this work as they should feel, that now he is doing the holy work, and not the work of people who are similar to beasts.

But the matter is to the contrary: When he works to man's benefit, he feels good taste in the work. But when he does the work of the Creator, he does not feel any taste. That is, the same act that he does, if he sees that his will to receive has something to receive, that the reward illuminates for him during the work, and this is why he feels good taste, if he replaces the intention during the work and says that he is doing this work not in order to receive reward, he promptly feels his weakness, that he cannot make an effort, and the work begins to slow down right away.

According to the above, it follows that the Creator seemingly comes to him and tells him, "Look at the lowly state you are in. You are just like a beast." Then he begins to suffer that he does not have any feelings of human beings. It pains him and he feels the suffering and pain of being in exile under the rule of the nations of the world. That is, now he feels that he has evil lusts, suitable for the seventy nations.

But before this revelation came to him, so as to feel his lowliness, he lived in a world that was all good, meaning that it did not cause him any deficiency that he was in a state of lowliness. He did not feel that it was lowliness, but rather that he was behaving like everyone else, whose only aspirations are lust, respect, and money. But now that the revelation has come to him from the Creator, that he will see that he is like a beast and not like a man, he suffers, since he would be happy if he could come out of the exile.

But since he is in exile, he sees that he does not see a way out of the exile. It follows that these torments are causing him instability. That is, he does not know what to do. On the one hand, now he sees that he is feeling the truth, meaning the kind of people to whom he belongs, since there are people who belong to beastliness, and there are people who belong to people. And if we want to be more precise, we should discern three kinds: 1) people who have nothing to do with Judaism, 2) people who engage in Torah and *Mitzvot*, but in order to receive reward, 3) people who work not in order to receive reward.

It follows that on the one hand, now he can be very happy that he sees the truth, meaning which type of people he is with, and which degree he should strive to achieve. But at the same time he is feeling pain and suffering at seeing how far he is from *Dvekut* [adhesion] with the Creator. That is, he sees that he cannot do anything for the Creator, and that all that he does is because he wants to receive reward for his actions, but with respect to the desire to bestow, he does not see that he will be able to come out of them by himself.

It follows that he is craving the state when he belonged to the second type, when he had strength to work because the reward illuminated for him, and in his mind he was in a state that is close to the Creator. He would always speak to the Creator and ask Him for reward for his work. He felt complete, and that he did not need a thing because he was certain of the reward, since he was keeping the commandments of the Creator. And the Creator certainly sees that not many people desire to keep His commandments, but he is exerting to keep His commandments, so the Creator will certainly favor him and give him a great reward for it.

Naturally, after such a calculation, a person feels that he is high in the sky among the clouds and looking at the whole world, for undoubtedly, the world exists through their Torah, as our sages said, "The world cannot stand without Torah" (*Midrash Tanchuma, Ki Tavo*). It follows that then he was truly among the happiest people in the world.

But now that he has emerged from the second state, the Creator has illuminated the truth for him, that the work of the Creator is primarily to bestow contentment upon the Creator and not for one's own benefit, and he sees how far he is from the truth, and feels the opposite. That is, where he thought that if instead of *Lo Lishma* [not for Her sake] I had a good feeling, that I am fine with the Creator, meaning that I am trying to obey Him as much as possible, and I am regarded as a "servant of the Creator," and all the reward that the Creator has promised us is surely ready for me, so what else do I need?

It is even more so when I begin to advance in order to bestow. I will promptly be elevated. However, this is not so. Rather, now that he has come to feel the truth, that the main thing is to work to benefit of the Creator, and he should be happy that, thank God, he has gotten on the real track that leads to nearness to the Creator, so he should have been constantly elated and say, "Thank God, I see that the Creator has mercy on me and does not let me labor in vain. Rather, all my labor will now be in order to achieve the goal, called '*Dvekut* with the Creator.'"

However, he feels that his state is the opposite, meaning that he does not have the same joy he had while working in order to receive reward. It is so because he sees that now he has no support from this body, since now he is telling his body, "Know that from this day forth I will not give you any profits in the work, for now I am not working for my own benefit. Rather, I want to work only to benefit the Creator." Then the body does not agree to give strength to work. It follows that now he is in a state of lowliness.

However, before the revelation of the truth has come to him, he was always elated, seeing how each day he was adding in deeds and the reward was guaranteed. But now is the real time when he can give an honest prayer to the Creator to take him out of exile, since before he has received the revelation from above—that he is in exile, controlled by the nations of the world, called "will to receive in order to receive." Thus, he had no deficiency that the Creator could fill, meaning to lead him out of exile. It therefore follows that the Creator has given him the *Kli* [vessel], meaning the deficiency, and then He has given him the light, and both the light and the *Kli* come from above.

By this we can interpret what we asked about what the holy *Zohar* says to Israel when they had sinned, "The Creator said, 'And I will chastise you, to go into exile. And if you say that I will leave you, I, too, am with you.'" We asked, "How could it be that the Creator came out from the land abroad, to exile, since 'the whole earth is full of His glory,' so how can it be said that He is going out?" We also asked, "What the punishment of going to exile adds to us, since everything the Creator does, He does only for man's favor, so what does man gain by going to exile under the rule of the nations of the world?"

According to what we explained above, it follows that saying, "The whole earth is full of His glory," comes to teach us that from the perspective of the Creator there are no changes in the world. Rather, it is as it is written, "You are before the world was created, and You are after the world was created." Thus, all the changes are from the perspective of the qualification of the receivers. That is, to the extent that they can attribute their work only to bestow upon the Creator, to that extent the *Tzimtzum* [restriction] is removed, and the light that is hidden for the lower ones is revealed, and by this the lower ones receive the delight and pleasure.

This is regarded as the people of Israel being in the land, when we feel that the Creator is the land of Israel. That is, since the people of Israel is in the land of Israel, the Creator is named after the action of providing Himself to the creatures so they will recognize and know Him when they are fit for it. If they sin and may blemish, meaning receive upper abundance and pass it on to the *Klipot*, which are self-love, then He must be "taken out" from the land of Israel, meaning that the *Tzimtzum* rises once more and the light departs.

This is regarded as leaving the land, which is the place of the kingdom of heaven, called *Shechina*, and going out to exile under the rule of the nations of the world.

The correction of going out to exile is 1) that first, they will not spoil the abundance. 2) By being in exile, the Creator does not leave them in exile, as we explained above that sometimes a person is in exile but does not know that it is exile, that one must run from that place, meaning from the state where he is and receives nourishment, as that place is called "self-love." Rather, it is to the contrary, he suffers only because he cannot satisfy what the nations of the world require of him, since they control him, meaning he cannot satisfy all the pertaining to self-love.

This is why the holy *Zohar* says, "If I expel you from the land, bears might charge you in the field, or wild wolves or murderers could obliterate you from the world." That is, they will remove you completely from the spiritual world and you will remain only in the corporeal world, called "self-love."

Therefore, in order not to be lost in the exile, the Creator, too, goes out to exile with them. That is, He appears to them in a form of exile. That is, the Creator is called "His name," after the work He does. Since now He gives them exile, meaning that they feel they are in exile, this is regarded as the Creator being out in exile with them. He gives them the sensation of exile so they will not be lost in the exile altogether by not feeling that they have been expelled from the land and that now they are under the rule of the nations of the world.

Now we will understand what we asked, "What is the correction of being expelled from the land?" 1) That they will not spoil what they have attained. This is regarded as knowing his Master and intending to rebel. It means that he knows his Master but cannot be in a state of only to bestow. 2) By being in exile they will feel the need to be only in a state of bestowal, by which they will be rewarded with *Dvekut* with the Creator. Thus, the suffering of exile will reform them. And we should interpret what we asked, "What does it mean that the Creator went out to exile?" that since the Creator is giving them the taste of exile, it is considered that the Creator has come out from the good and pleasant land, giving them, which is to their benefit.

A Congregation Is No Less than Ten

Article No. 28, Tav-Shin-Mem-Vav, 1985-86

It is written in *The Zohar, Nasso* (item 105): "Rabbi Elazar started, 'Why have I come and there is no man?' How beloved are Israel by the Creator, for wherever they are, the Creator is among them. 'And let them make Me a Temple and I will dwell among them.' Every synagogue in the world is called a 'Temple.' 'And I will dwell among them,' since the *Shechina* [Divinity] comes to the synagogue first. Happy is he who is among those first ones in the synagogue, since by them what is completed is completed, meaning the congregation, which is no less than ten. Also, the ten must be in the synagogue at once, and not come one at a time, since all ten are as organs of one body, in which the *Shechina* resides, for the Creator has made man at once, and established all his organs together, as it is written, 'He has made you and established you.'"

We should discern in the above words:

1) Why does he say, "Wherever Israel are, the Creator is among them"? This implies that there is no need for a special place. Afterwards he says, "And let them make Me a Temple and I will dwell among them," meaning specifically in the synagogue.

2) The words, "And let them make Me a Temple and I will dwell among them," imply that first there must be some preparation, meaning "making the Temple," and then "I will dwell," and not just like that.

3) What is the question that he asks, "Why have I come and there is no man?" If you say that the *Shechina* comes to the synagogue first, of course there is still no one there.

4) It is difficult to understand what he says, "The ten must be in the synagogue at once, and not come one at a time." Can it be said that all those who come to the synagogue should wait outside until ten men have gathered, and then they will all enter at once? We have never seen such a thing. So what does it mean that they must not come one at a time?

To understand the above we will explain in the work how to begin the order of the work in a manner of bestowal, called "not in order to receive reward." First, we must remember two things, which are "giver" and "receiver." This extends from His desire to do good to His creations, which is why He has created creatures—to receive the delight and pleasure that He wants to give them. This receiver, namely the *Kli* [vessel] that the Creator created in which to receive the delight and pleasure, is called "desire to receive delight and pleasure." He can enjoy this to the extent of the craving for it. That is, the *Kli* in which we receive pleasure is called "craving."

We attribute these *Kelim* [vessels] to the Creator. That is, the *Kli* that initially received from the Creator is called *Malchut*, or *Behina Dalet* [Fourth Phase (discernment)], which means that it is a craving to receive delight and pleasure. This is called a *Kli* of *Ohr Yashar* [Direct Light]. This is the *Kli* that was used prior to the *Tzimtzum* [restriction], and it is called *Malchut de Ein Sof* [infinity/no end].

Afterwards there was a correction to prevent the bread of shame, since there is a rule in the nature that the Creator has created, that the branch wants to resemble its root. Why is there such a nature? We are forbidden to ask because with respect to the Creator, says the holy *Zohar*, "There is no thought or perception in Him at all." This means that the lower ones cannot attain the thoughts of the Creator.

Everything we say is only in the form of "By Your actions we know You," meaning we speak only through the actions that appear to our eyes, from what we see and can explain, but not before the act that appears before us. For this reason we begin to speak of the first connection between the Creator and the creatures, called "His desire to do good to His creations." Prior to this we cannot speak because we have no attainment in Him. Hence, we only see that in nature, the branch wants to resemble its root.

To correct this, meaning that because the receiver wants equivalence of form with the root, and if it were to receive it would feel unpleasantness, the *Tzimtzum* occurred, called "not wanting to receive in order to receive," but to receive only if he can receive it in order to bestow. This caused us not to be able to receive abundance with the *Kli* called "desire to receive," but rather with a new *Kli*, called "*Ohr Hozer*" [Reflected Light]. It means that the *Ohr Yashar* is regarded as the abundance that the Creator gives to the lower ones, and *Ohr Hozer* is the opposite—that which the lower ones wish to give the Creator.

For this reason, *Ohr Yashar* is called "from above downward," meaning that the upper one, the Giver, namely the Creator, gives to the lower ones. Conversely, the *Ohr Hozer* is called "from below upward," meaning the lower one, who is the receiver, wants to bestow upon the Creator. We attribute this *Kli*, called "in order to bestow," to the lower one because the lower one did it in order to correct itself, since it wants to resemble its root. It is as we learn, that in the world of *Ein Sof*, the *Kli* of *Malchut* received the light in the *Kli* of *Ohr Yashar*, meaning in a *Kli* that came from the upper one. But the *Kli* of *Ohr Hozer* is a *Kli* that the lower one should make.

After the correction to receive only in *Kelim* of *Ohr Hozer* was made, all the worlds and many degrees extended from it. Because this *Kli* extends from the lower one, it cannot be completed at once, but bit by bit, according to the strength of the lower ones. Therefore, since many *Kelim* were made, the lights divide into many degrees. This was not so when what we attribute to the Creator, called "receiving in order to receive," illuminated in the *Kli*. The Creator created this *Kli* at once, in full, so naturally, it was one simple light, without distinction of degrees.

It is as he writes in the book, *Tree of Life* (presented in *The Study of the Ten Sefirot*, p 1): "Know that before the emanations were emanated and the creatures created, the upper, simple light had filled the whole of reality. However, everything was one, simple light, completely equal, and it is called 'the light of *Ein Sof*.'" The reason is that since we attribute this *Kli* to the Creator, it is completed in whole, hence they received one light, without distinction of degrees.

But the *Kli* that we attribute to the lower one cannot be completed at once. Rather, all the work we must exert in is only one—to make a *Kli* called *Ohr Hozer*. This means that the lower one wants to receive delight and pleasure from the Creator only because he wants to bestow upon the Creator, and this is called *Ohr Hozer* [Reflected Light]. When the lower one realizes that he has no desire to receive for himself, but that he wants to delight the Creator, he calculates what he can give to the Creator that the Creator will enjoy.

At that time he sees that he can give only one thing that will delight the Creator. Since the purpose of creation is to do good to His creations, and the Creator wants to give delight and pleasure to the creatures, he says, "I want to receive delight and pleasure because I want to please the Creator." And the more abundance he can receive—meaning that he feels the greatest pleasure from the abundance that he receives—the Creator will certainly enjoy this more.

This is similar to a person who invited over an important person. The man and his household toiled all day and all night so that the important guest would enjoy the food. When the guest ate the meal, which cost him great efforts, and in which he did everything to delight the guest, at the end of the meal he asked the guest, "What do you say about our meal? Did you ever taste a meal like this?"

He replied to him: "To tell you the truth, I don't care what I eat. I never regarded the pleasure I can derive from food, so I wouldn't mind if you prepared a simpler meal, since I hear from you that you put great efforts into it." When the landlord hears this, what pleasure does he have from giving him a big meal?

The lesson is that if a person receives delight and pleasure from the Creator because he wants to delight the Creator by helping Him carry out the purpose of creation—that the Creator wants to delight His creatures—but he says that he derives no joy from the delight and pleasure he receives from the Creator, then what contentment is he bringing to the Creator by saying that he doesn't feel any taste in His delight and pleasure, and that to him it is all the same?

It therefore follows that if one can try to constantly increase what he is receiving from the Creator and appreciate the King's gift, there is a reason for it: He can say to the Creator, "I am receiving great pleasure from You because I know that only with this I can delight You, and this is why I want to receive plentiful pleasures."

However, we must remember that after the sin of the tree of knowledge that *Adam Harishon* sinned, man became as dust, receiving in order to receive. This extends from the worlds ABYA de *Tuma'a* [impurity], as it is written in the "Introduction to the Book of Zohar" (item 25), "It is incumbent upon man to receive strength from above by the merit of Torah and *Mitzvot* [commandments], so he can bestow, and this is called 'Israel,' meaning *Yashar-El* [straight to the Creator]. This means that all his thoughts and desires are only to bring contentment to the Creator. But if he still does not have this desire, it is considered that the person is in exile among the nations of the world, who enslave him to work only for self-love, which is 'receiving in order to receive.' This pertains to the *Klipot* [shells/peels], and not to *Kedusha* [holiness/sanctity], as it is written, 'You will be holy for I am holy.' This means that as the Creator is only about bestowal, your intention will also be only to bestow."

But the opposite of that, meaning when his intention is not to bestow, it is regarded as the opposite of Israel. Rather, it is called "straight to the nations of the world," since they are opposite in form from the Creator, whose desire is only to bestow. But if in this place there is *Yashar-El*—where he is in equivalence of form with the Creator—meaning that there is no other authority there, in that place comes the instilling of the *Shechina*, as it is written, "Wherever I mention My name, I will come to you and bless you." This means that the Creator says, "If I can say that only My name is in this place, and the creature's authority is not in upon it, since the lower one wants only to bestow upon the Creator, then "I will come to you and bless you," meaning that on this place I instill My *Shechina*.

By this we will understand what we asked about the holy *Zohar's* saying that wherever they are, the Creator is among them, which implies that there is no need for a special place. Afterwards it says as it is written, "And let them make Me a Temple and I will dwell among them," meaning precisely in a Temple, and not just anywhere.

We should interpret his saying "wherever they are" to mean wherever "they," meaning *Yashar-El*, are present, where the meaning of *Yashar-El* is straight to the Creator, who are in equivalence of form with the Creator. That is, as the Creator gives mercy, they, too, want only to bestow upon the Creator. And since there is equivalence of form, to that extent the *Tzimtzum* is removed. Hence in this place there is the *Shechina*.

This is called, "And let them make Me a Temple," as it is written, "You will be holy for I the Lord am holy." It follows that "Israel" and "Let them make Me a Temple" are one thing. That is, saying, "And let them make Me a Temple" is preparation and great work to make the place, which is the desire, as Baal HaSulam said, that in spirituality, "place" means desire, meaning a desire of *Kedusha*, which is in order to bestow contentment upon the Creator. This is called "Israel," *Yashar-El*.

Now we will explain the second question, what is the question that he asks, "Why have I come and there is no man?" Certainly, if he says that the *Shechina* comes to the synagogue first, of course there is still no one there, so why does he say, "Why have I come and there is no man"?

However, first we need to understand what "man" means. We should interpret "man" to mean as it is written, "Happy is the man who did not walk in the counsel of the wicked." That is, there is "man" and there is "beast." "Beast" means one who is immersed in self-love and does what beasts do. It follows that the meaning of "Why have I come" means that I have come before you. However, that, too, needs explanation: How can we say that the Creator came to the synagogue first, if "The whole earth is full of His glory?" Thus, what does it mean that the Creator comes to the synagogue before the people who are praying?

We should interpret that it is as Baal HaSulam interpreted the verse, "Before they call, I will answer." It means that when a person goes to pray, it happens because I have given him a thought and desire to come to the synagogue to be a man. In the end, I find him in the synagogue praying for self-love, like a beast. It follows that when he says, "Why have I come," it means "Why have I given him a desire to go to the synagogue, so he will pray for matters of *Kedusha*, which is a Temple, and to be Israel, and in the end "there is no man." Instead, I see that everyone is praying for beastly needs.

Now we will explain what we asked about his saying that there must be ten in the synagogue at once, and not come one at a time. We asked, "Should they all wait outside until ten men have gathered, and then they will all enter together? Have we ever seen such a thing?" He brings evidence from the Creator, "For man, the Creator has made him at once." But we should also understand the evidence itself.

To interpret this we must first understand why we need specifically ten men present in the synagogue, or the *Shechina* will not be able to be there. He gives a reason, that "a congregation is no less than ten." We should also understand this—why specifically ten and not more or less. That is, if there are nine men there, it is not regarded as a congregation, and if there are eleven, it does not add anything, as it is said about testimony: "two as one hundred and one hundred as two" (*Shavuot*, p 42). Rather, it is specifically ten, as our sages said (*Sanhedrin*, 39), "In every ten there is *Shechina*."

It is known that *Malchut* is called "tenth." It is also known that the receiving *Kli* is also called "the *Sefira Malchut*," who is the tenth *Sefira*, receiving the upper abundance. She is called "will to receive," and all the creatures extend only from her. For this reason, a congregation is no less than ten, since all the corporeal branches extend from the upper roots. Therefore, according to the rule, "There is no light that does not have ten *Sefirot*," in corporeality, something is not considered a congregation that can be regarded as important unless there are ten men there, such as the upper degrees.

Now we can understand the meaning of ten, when the Creator asks, "Why have I come and there is no man?" It pertains to "man" and not to "beast," referring to the kingdom of heaven, which is the tenth *Sefira*, meaning we must pray for the exile of the *Shechina*, which the holy *Zohar* calls, "*Shechina* in the dust." Thus, the meaning will be that if the Creator does not find ten there, it means that "I have come first and have given you a desire and awakening to come to the synagogue, to ask for prayer for the exile of the *Shechina*, who is called 'ten,' which is the tenth *Sefira*, and I did not find anyone to pray for the tenth. Instead, I find everyone praying for things that pertain to beasts and not to people."

Similarly, we should interpret what he says, "They must all be at once, and not one at a time." We should interpret that we need the reception of the kingdom of heaven to be at once, and not to say, "Today I want to take upon myself a little bit of the burden of the kingdom of heaven, meaning only when I am at the synagogue. Afterwards, when I go home, I want to enjoy self-love."

That is, he says that he agrees to work in order to bestow some of the time, but not to give all his time only for the glory of heaven. Rather, when one takes upon oneself the burden of the kingdom of heaven he must ask the Creator to make it forever, and not only when he is at the synagogue. We can interpret that having to have ten present at the synagogue at once and not come one at a time means that he should not say, "Now I am assuming a little bit of the kingdom of heaven, and later some more." Rather, each acceptance of the burden of the kingdom of heaven should be at once, meaning at once over his entire life, and not today some and tomorrow some more.

Therefore, if assuming the burden of the kingdom of heaven is over a complete thing, then although he later descends from his degree, since his acceptance was complete, called "ten at once," where "at once" means over his entire life, many pennies join into a great amount, until he is rewarded with faith, which is the permanent kingdom of heaven.

This was not so while assuming the kingdom of heaven was only partial, meaning that he received the kingdom of heaven only for the time being and not permanently. It follows that this is incomplete, so how can he join them into the great amount until he is rewarded with permanent faith? Therefore, when one takes upon oneself the burden of the kingdom of heaven, he should see that it is a complete thing. This is why he says that they should be in the synagogue at once, meaning once and for all. That is, he wants the reception of the kingdom of heaven to be forever.

Lishma and Lo Lishma

Article No. 29, Tav-Shin-Mem-Vav, 1985-86

We find four kinds among observers of Torah and *Mitzvot* [commandments]:

The first kind: Sometimes a person observes Shabbat because his employer forces him. That is, the rule is that if a person has an employee who is desecrating the Shabbat, if he tells the employee, "If you don't stop desecrating the Shabbat I will fire you," the rule is that he has to say that he will observe Shabbat or he will fire him from his job. And where there are no other jobs, he promises the employer to observe Shabbat. It follows that he is observing Shabbat because the employer forces him.

This brings up the question, "Whose Shabbat is he observing? Is it the Shabbat that the Creator has commanded to observe?" Accordingly, is he keeping the *Mitzvot* of the Creator or the *Mitzvot* of the employer, since the employer commanded him to observe Shabbat or he will have no provision? Nevertheless, according to the *Halacha* [Jewish law], he is regarded as "observing Shabbat."

The same rule applies to the rest of the *Mitzvot*. We can put it differently: If a father knows that if he tells his son that he must observe Torah and *Mitzvot* or he will not support him, since the father knows that if he does not support him he will have no provision, and according to the Halacha, the father must see that the son observes Torah and *Mitzvot*, here, too, there is the question, "Whose Torah and *Mitzvot* is he observing? Is it the Creator's, who has commanded us to observe Torah and *Mitzvot*, or is he observing his father's Torah and *Mitzvot*?"

Whatever the case may be, he belongs to people who observe Torah and *Mitzvot*. These are the words of Maimonides (*Hilchot De'ot*, Chapter 6): "He who admonishes his friend first, will not speak harshly to him." What is this about? It is about matters that concern man and man. However, with Godly matters, if he does not secretly repent, he is shamed in public, his sin is made known, he is cursed to his face, and disparaged and cursed until he reforms."

Here, too, there is the question, "Whose *Mitzvot* is he observing, those of the Creator or those of the people who are cursing him?" However, here, too, we see that at the end of the day he is regarded as "observing Torah and *Mitzvot*." That is, when we consider the act he is performing, we find that there is nothing to add to the action. The only question pertains to the intention, meaning to the reason that compels him to observe the Torah and *Mitzvot*. This is the first kind of observing Torah and *Mitzvot*.

The second kind: He observes Torah and *Mitzvot* because of upbringing, since he was born into an orthodox environment, or he was not born into an orthodox environment but later came into one, and it influenced him into observing Torah and *Mitzvot*. The reason for which he observes Torah and *Mitzvot* is that he was told that by this he will have both the life of this world and the life of the next world. Afterwards he began to see that people who are meticulous about Torah and *Mitzvot* are respected and appreciated, and saw how others speak to such people who pray more enthusiastically and dedicate more time to studying Torah. The respect they receive gives him a thrust; it is a fuel for him, and he, too, begins to pray more enthusiastically, and he is more meticulous with each commandment and gesture. By this he has strength to add time in studying Torah.

This is already the second kind of observing Torah and *Mitzvot*, since he wants to observe Torah and *Mitzvot* out of choice, since he understands that by this the Creator will reward him for keeping His commandments. However, he adds another name to the reason that commits him to observe Torah and *Mitzvot*. That is, the respect that he sees that those who observe Torah and *Mitzvot* more diligently than others receive. And besides the respect, those who are meticulous about Torah and *Mitzvot* have other things that the public commit them to work more. It can be money or anything, but there is another reason for which he must observe Torah and *Mitzvot*.

It follows that on the one hand he is higher than the first kind, since here he is observing the Torah and *Mitzvot* of the Creator, since he believes in the Creator. It is unlike the first kind, which does not believe in the Creator and observes Torah and *Mitzvot* out of knowing the punishment—that the employer might fire him—and this is why he has taken upon himself to observe Torah and *Mitzvot*.

However, the second kind was educated into believing in the Creator and observing Torah and *Mitzvot* because the Creator has commanded us to observe Torah and *Mitzvot*. The reward and punishment are not in knowing. Rather, he must believe in reward and punishment, that the Creator is the one who pays the reward, as our sages said (*Avot*, Chapter 2, 21), "You can trust your landlord to pay you for your work, and know that the reward of the righteous is in the future."

Thus, he must believe in reward and punishment. This is not so in the first kind. They do not have to believe in reward and punishment. Rather, the reward and the punishment are revealed. This means that if he does not obey the employer and observes Torah and *Mitzvot* he will certainly be punished, meaning he will be fired and will be jobless.

Also, according to the above-mentioned words of Maimonides that he must be degraded, etc., here, too, he does not need to believe in reward and punishment because he feels the suffering of being chased into taking upon himself to observe Torah and *Mitzvot*. This is something else because he is actually observing the commandment of the employer and not because of the commandment of the Creator, so it is regarded as only the first kind of work of the Creator.

In the second kind he observes the commandments of the Creator but adds another thing, meaning adds another reason to have fuel to observe Torah and *Mitzvot*, such as honor or money, or other things. That is, he has other reasons for which he observes Torah and *Mitzvot*. In the words of our sages (*Sukkah* 45b), this is called "Anyone who joins working for the Creator with another thing is uprooted from the world, as it is said, 'For the Lord alone.'"

We should interpret what it means to combine the Creator with something else. According to our way, we should interpret that if he receives another reason that compels him to observe Torah and *Mitzvot*, it is regarded as being uprooted from the world, since the reason that the cause for observing Torah and *Mitzvot* should be "for the Lord alone," meaning that he observes Torah and *Mitzvot* because it is the Creator's commandment, without an addition of another reason.

It therefore follows that the main flaw with the act is that he blemishes the *Lishma* [for Her sake], since observing *Mitzvot* should be because he works and observes the commandments of the Creator, and because he is working and serving the Creator, and this is why he later comes to ask the Creator to reward him for his work. At that time he is told, "But you also worked for others, so you had others who obliged you to work for them. Go to them so they will pay you the reward for the work you did for them."

This is similar to someone working for Dan [Israeli bus company], and asking for a salary from EGED [another bus company]. They do not want to pay his salary since he did not work for them. Likewise, when a person demands of the Creator to reward him for his work, he is told, "You worked for people, so they will give you honor or money. Go to them and they will pay you." And indeed, they pay him: to the extent of his work, so he is respected.

It turns out that by combining the Creator with another thing—meaning that people, too, commit him to work—he blemishes the *Lishma*. This is why this is regarded as only the second kind, and his work is still not complete, perfect, and clean.

The third kind: He works only for the Creator and not for people. He works humbly and no one knows how much he prays and how much he learns. Therefore, we cannot say that he is working for people, so they will give him something for his work. Rather, he is working only for the Creator, meaning that the only reason that compels him to observe Torah and *Mitzvot* is that he wants to keep the Creator's will.

However, he works for a reward. It is as Maimonides said, "So that no calamities will come to him, and to receive reward in this world," meaning so the Creator will give him health, provision, and contentment from the children, etc., or so He will give him the next world. This is the reason that gives him fuel so he can do the holy work. For this reason, this work is regarded as *Lishma*, since the reason that causes him to observe Torah and *Mitzvot* is only the Creator, meaning that he is working only for the Creator and does not add other things to it.

That is, he has no other reason that causes him to observe Torah and *Mitzvot*. This is regarded as the third kind because he has no desire to work for anyone; only for the Creator. But the reason that obliges him to observe the commandments of the Creator is fear of punishment, or love of the reward.

This is as it is written in the *Sulam* [commentary on *The Zohar*] ("Introduction of the Book of Zohar," item 190): "There is a person who fears the Creator so that his sons will live and not die, or fears a bodily punishment, or a punishment to one's money, hence he always fears Him. It follows that he does not place the fear he fears of the Creator as the root, for his own benefit is the root, and the fear is its result. And there is a person who fears the Creator because he fears the punishment of that world and the punishment of Hell. Those two kinds of fear—fear of punishment in this world and fear of punishment in the next world—are not the essence of fear and its root."

For this reason, since they are not primarily for fear of heaven, we discern this as the third kind. It follows that this work is called *Lishma*, since he worked for the Creator and not for others, too. That is, he did not take anyone else for whom to work, meaning for others, too, so others will respect him. Rather, he comes to the Creator with the complaint: "Since I have been working only for You, and no one knows what I did in observing Torah and *Mitzvot* because I have been working humbly, it is only right that You should reward me for my work."

In this way we should interpret what our sages said, "He who gives a rock to charity so that his sons will live is a complete righteous." The reason is that he is observing the commandments of the Creator. Because the Creator has commanded us to give charity, we give. It turns out that with respect to giving there are no deficiencies here, since he is observing the *Mitzva* [commandment] *Lishma*, meaning for the Creator, and there is no one else obliging him to give charity.

Rather, he is asking for a reward from the Creator, that He will pay for the *Mitzva* that he is observing, and will pay him for the labor he has given only for the Creator and for none other. That is, it is not like the second kind, where he combined another, meaning people from the outside who also caused him to observe and be meticulous with observing Torah and *Mitzvot*.

It is as they said (*Pesachim*, 8a), "And the Tania, he who says, 'This rock is for charity, so that his sons will live, or that I will go to the next world,' he is a complete righteous." RASHI interprets, "He is a complete righteous" in this. They did not say that he is working *Lo Lishma* [not for Her sake], but that he has kept the commandment of his Creator, who commanded to give charity, and even if he intends for his own pleasure, to be rewarded with the next world or that his sons will live.

This means that although he is asking for reward for observing the *Mitzva* [commandment], meaning so that his sons will live, or because he wants the reward of the next world for this *Mitzva*, he is a righteous. The fact that he wants the next world is also regarded as wanting reward, such as so that his sons will live. It is like the above words of the holy *Zohar*, "Whether he wants a reward in this world or in the next world in return for the *Mitzvot*, it is not regarded as the essential fear," since his own benefit is the cause for observing the *Mitzvot*, and not the Creator. Still our sages said here, "He is a complete righteous." It is as RASHI interprets, "Because he is observing the *Mitzvot* of his Creator, who has commanded him to give charity, and also intends for his own pleasure, therefore he is called 'complete righteous.'"

This is as we explained, that because he is working because the Creator has commanded him to observe Torah and *Mitzvot*, and he has no one else who obliges him to observe Torah and *Mitzvot*, this is called *Lishma*, as RASHI interpreted above. It is like the above-mentioned allegory, meaning that he works for Reuven but asks for a salary from Shimon. This is certainly called *Lo Lishma*, for he was working for others at the same time, which is called *Lo Lishma*, and also "the second kind."

(I heard that there are those who try to explain our sages, who said, "One who says, 'this rock is for charity, so that my sons will live,' is a complete righteous." But he conditioning the observing of the *Mitzva*, so they are trying to say that it was written in initials, "he is a *Tzadi-Gimel* [CR]." Afterwards, when they wrote it in explicit words, they turned the *Tzadi-Gimel* into *Tzadik Gamur* [Complete Righteous]. However, they were mistaken in interpreting the initials, since *Tzadi-Gimel* means *Tzedakah Gedolah* [Great Righteousness/Charity], and not *Tzadik Gamur*. However, this is probably not the case, since they cannot explain the other verse, which says, "Or that I will have the next world," since by "next world" he also aims to please himself, the same as "so that my sons will live," as the above words of the holy *Zohar*.)

However, the third kind means that he is working for the Creator, as the Creator has commanded us through Moses to observe Torah and *Mitzvot*, and we are asking for reward from Him, since we worked only for Him, because of the commandment of the Creator, and not for any other reason. This is why it is called *Lishma*. However, this is only the third kind.

The fourth kind observes Torah and *Mitzvot* not in order to receive reward, as our sages said (*Avot*, Chapter 1, 3), "Antiganos, Man of Socho, received from Shimon the Righteous. He would say, 'Be not as servants serving the master in order to receive reward, but be as servants serving the master not in order to receive reward, and let the fear of heaven be upon you.'"

This means that it is specifically not in order to receive reward that is regarded as "for the Creator," as he concludes and says, "and let the fear of heaven be upon you." This means that real fear of heaven is specifically in *Lishma* [for Her sake] without any reward. That is, he does not intend for self-gratification, but his only intention is to bring contentment to the Creator. This is regarded as "clean *Lishma*," without any mixture of self-gratification. This is called the "fourth kind."

However, we know the question, "Is the Creator deficient that He needs the creatures to work only for Him and not at all for themselves, but only for the Creator without a shred of self-gratification? And if they want to enjoy their work, as well, is this work disqualified and not accepted above as a *Mitzva* that is worthy of being received by the King? Why should the Creator mind that man, too, enjoys the work?"

The answer is that it is because there needs to be equivalence of form so there will not be bread of shame. The rule is that the branch wants to resemble its root, and as the Creator is the giver, when a person must receive from someone, he feels it as unpleasant. It follows that the restriction and concealment on our vessels of reception so we do not work in order to receive reward were made in our favor.

Otherwise, it would not be possible to have choice. That is, man would never be able to do and to keep the Torah and *Mitzvot* in order to bestow, since man would not be able to overcome the pleasure that he tasted in Torah and *Mitzvot*, were it not for the restriction and concealment, as it is known that the greater the pleasure, the harder it is to relinquish it.

For this reason, we were given corporeal pleasures where there is only very thin light, which the holy *Zohar* calls "thin light," which fell into the *Klipot* [shells/peels] at the time of the breaking of the vessels. Also, sparks of holiness were added to them after the sin of the tree of knowledge when *Adam Harishon* sinned. These are the pleasures that all created beings pursue. All the wars, murders, thefts, and so forth, that exist in the world are because each one aspires to receive pleasure.

We are meant to overcome these pleasures and receive everything for the Creator. But a person sees how hard it is to exit self-love and relinquish little pleasures. For this reason, were it not for the *Tzimtzum* [restriction], had the real pleasure that exists in Torah and *Mitzvot* were revealed, there is no doubt that they would not be able to relinquish the pleasures and say that he is observing Torah and *Mitzvot* because he wants to bring contentment to the Creator.

However, man cannot agree to observe Torah and *Mitzvot* without any pleasure because of our nature—that we were born with a *Kli* [vessel] called "desire to receive delight and pleasure," so how can we work without any reward?

However, we were given one place on which we can work without any reward. That is, even when we still do not have a taste for Torah and *Mitzvot* due to the *Tzimtzum*, there is one advice, which is to work in greatness of the Creator, how privileged we are to be serving the King.

This, we do have in our nature—that the little one annuls before the great one. We have the strength and motivation to work for the great one, whom the generation regards as the most important and venerable in the world. To the extent of his importance, we enjoy serving him. This pleasure is permitted to receive because enjoying giving is not regarded as bestowing in order to receive, for bestowing in order to receive means that he desires a reward specifically for the service he is giving him.

Conversely, if he works at a factory and knows that the owner enjoys everyone being productive, and anyone who produces more than the usual gives the owner great joy. Therefore, he tries to produce more than other workers do so as to delight the owner. However, afterwards he wants the owner to reward him for trying to please him. This is considered that on the one hand he gives, but on the other hand he wants reward. This is called "bestowing in order to receive reward."

This is not so if a person is serving the king, and says to the king, "I do not want anything in return for the service because I enjoy the service alone, and I do not need to receive any reward, since I feel that anything you give me for the service I am doing for you will blemish my service. All I want is the service. Do not give me any reward, and this is my pleasure, for it is a great honor for me to be rewarded with serving the king."

Of course, he cannot say that he is bestowing in order to receive, since he does not want to receive anything in return. And why does he not want? It is because he derives great pleasure from serving the king. It follows that this is regarded as "bestowing in order to bestow upon an important person," and a person measures the importance of the king according to the extent of his joy of serving the king, since the more the king is important, the more he enjoys, for one who serves the greatest in the city is not as one who serves the greatest in the country, or the greatest in the world.

This is regarded as true bestowal. That is, he enjoys the giving itself, since the main point of bestowing was for the purpose of equivalence of form. That is, as the Creator is the giver, so the creatures want to be givers, and we should certainly say that the Creator enjoys His giving.

It follows that if the creatures bestow upon the Creator and He derives no joy, there is still no equivalence of form here, since the Creator enjoys when He gives to the lower ones. This means that the joy results from the act of bestowal, and if we must receive something in return for the act, then we are blemishing the act and say that there is no wholeness in the act. Rather, to have wholeness we must add something, meaning receive something in return for the act, while the act itself is not so important.

In truth, if we want to do an act of bestowal upon the Creator we must try to enjoy it because the joy of an act of bestowal regards the action, since every single thing that a person wants to do and which is important to him, he gives it a priority to do it first. And the meter by which a person chooses what is most important is that which he enjoys the most.

It therefore follows that if one wants to appreciate the work he is doing for the Creator, he can appreciate it only by receiving great joy. That is, if one can try to derive great joy then he can know that now he is bringing great contentment to the Creator by giving to the Creator when he observes His commandments.

That is, a man desires to bestow contentment upon the Creator but does not know what he can give to the Creator that will delight Him. For this reason, when it is revealed to us that He has given us Torah and *Mitzvot*, and if we observe them He will enjoy, we are certainly happy that now we know what to do for Him. We therefore see that we were given the blessing to do while observing Torah and *Mitzvot*, since we say, "Blessed are You the Lord, Giver of the Torah."

It is written in the *Mitzvot* that we thank Him for giving to us, for example, the *Mitzva* of the *Sukkah* [the hut on Tabernacle Feast]. For example, we are all happy that He instructs us what to do that will delight Him, and we do not need to search for things that will delight the Creator. But the question is, how can we increase our pleasure while performing the *Mitzvot*?

Answer: There is only one way—to try to attain the greatness of the Creator. That is, in all that we do in Torah and *Mitzvot*, we want our reward to be the feeling of the greatness of the Creator, and all our prayers should be to "raise the *Shechina* [Divinity] from the dust," since the Creator is hidden from us due to the *Tzimtzum* that took place and we cannot appreciate His importance and greatness.

Therefore, we pray to the Creator to remove His concealment from us and to raise the glory of Torah. As we say in the Eighteen Prayer of *Rosh Hashanah* [New Year service], "Indeed, give glory to Your people." That is, "Give the glory of the Lord to Your people," so they will feel the glory of the King.

For this reason, one must try to remember the goal while studying Torah, so it will always be before his eyes what he wants to receive from the study, that the study will impart greatness and importance of the Creator. Also, while observing the *Mitzvot*, not to forget the intention that thanks to observing the *Mitzvot*, the Creator will lift the concealment on spirituality from him and he will receive a feeling of the greatness of the Creator.

However, it is hard work observing Torah and *Mitzvot* with the intention to thereby be rewarded with approaching the Creator—to obtain the greatness of the Creator so he can bring Him contentment because of the importance of the Creator, that this will be his reward and he has no desire for any other reward for his work. The body does not agree to work with this intention.

The holy *Zohar* (*Nasso*, items 102-104) says, "Mighty men roam from city to city and are not pardoned. The mixed-multitude ban them among them, and in many places they are given only rations. Thus, there were will be no rise to their fall, not even momentarily. And all the sages and mighty men who fear sin are afflicted, pressed and in grief. They are regarded as dogs, children weighed against fine gold, how they are regarded as clay jars out on every street, etc. These mixed-multitude are rich, peaceful, joyous, without sorrow or affliction whatsoever, robbers and bribers; they are the judges, the heads of the people."

We see in these words of *The Zohar* that it distinguishes between sages and mighty men who fear sin, and judges and the heads of the people, who are regarded as the mixed-multitude. He says that the sages and the mighty men who fear sin are afflicted and stressed, while the judges and the heads of the people are rich, peaceful, and joyous. Why? Because they are the mixed-multitude.

We should understand the meaning of mixed-multitude, that because they are the mixed-multitude they have joy and peace. We see that in the argument that Jacob had with Esau, Esau said to Jacob, I have enough, and Jacob replied, "I have everything." We need to understand the difference between enough and everything.

It is known that the *Sefira Yesod* is called "everything," that it is regarded as *Yesod Tzadik* [righteous], as we say in the prayer, "To You, Lord, is the greatness, the might, the grandeur, eternity, and splendor." It is so because "everything" is *Yesod*, and righteous, called *Yesod*, only gives. The *Sefira Yesod* gives to *Malchut*, as it is known, and as it is written in the holy *Zohar*. This means that the degree of *Yesod* is *Tzadik*, who takes nothing for himself, but all his works are in order to bestow.

Certainly, when a person begins to work on being righteous, meaning not to receive any reward for himself and work only in order to bestow contentment upon his Maker, the body disagrees and gives him obstructions. It does everything it can to interfere with his work. At that time a person is constantly afflicted and has no peace with the situation he is in because he sees that he has not yet come to be a giver upon the Creator. Rather, everything he does is still without the ability to direct it in order to bestow.

He is always afflicted over it because of the sorrow of the *Shechina*, called "*Shechina* in exile." He is in pain that for self-love he has the strength to work, but where he sees that his will to receive will not have anything, he is negligent in the work.

It follows after some time of exerting in the work and wanting to see some closeness to the Creator, he feels each time more of the truth about him: that he is truly remote from *Dvekut* [adhesion] with the Creator. That is, with respect to equivalence of form, as in, "As He is merciful, you, too, are merciful," he is the opposite. Previously he thought that he wanted to bring contentment to the Creator and that there will be some joy in this. He hoped that he would receive for his work the reward of this world, as well as the reward of the next world. But now he sees that he is powerless to work for the Creator, but it is all in order to receive for himself, and not at all to bestow.

What he sees now is that he is worse than when he started the work. When he began to work in the third kind, he had joy and peace because he knew and believed that each day his possessions were accumulating into a great amount, since each day when he does good deeds, the reward of each *Mitzva* is registered to his account. That faith caused him joy and peace because he saw that he was advancing in the work, meaning that his possessions were growing each and every day.

But now that he has moved from the third kind and has begun the work of the fourth kind, which is work not in order to receive reward, he is afflicted and pressed because he is examining himself with vessels of bestowal how much he has already acquired of this *Kli*.

At that time he sees the opposite, that each day as he exerts and wants to achieve closeness to the Creator, meaning to have a desire to bestow, he sees the truth, that each day he is growing more distant. According to what Baal HaSulam said, why does one see that he is growing more distant, since each day he is doing good deeds, and accordingly, the deeds should have brought him closer?

Our sages said, "I have created the evil inclination, I have created the Torah as a spice." Therefore, why does one who begins to work in bestowal see that he is growing worse each day? He says that it is not so, that in truth, he is not regressing each day as he thinks. Rather, each day he is moving forward. The reason he sees that he has become worse is that first one needs to see the falsehood and the evil, and then it is possible to correct them.

But when a person simply wants to block a hole or a crack in a building, and thinks that the hole and the crack are twenty centimeters long, and he works and toils, and finally sees that there are twenty more centimeters to block, it follows that as long as he does not see the real deficiency he is working in vain, meaning he is not correcting anything.

The lesson is that one thinks he has, for example, one kilogram of evil, and wants to fix it. He begins to fix, but then sees that there is another kilogram of evil. It follows that he has not corrected anything. But if he sees the full measure of evil in him, and then fixes it, this is called "complete correction."

This is why Baal HaSulam said that each day when he engages in work in order to bestow he draws closer to the truth, meaning to see the amount of evil in him. In a dark house it is impossible to see that there are dirt and garbage there. But if you bring some light inside then you can see that there are dirt and garbage.

Similarly, when a person begins to engage in Torah and *Mitzvot* in bestowal, the Torah and *Mitzvot* illuminate for him more each time, to see the truth about the measure of evil in him. It therefore follows that each day he is moving forward until he reaches the complete evil within him. Then, when he begins to correct, a complete correction is made, so that afterwards he can put in his *Kelim* [vessels] the delight and pleasure that the Creator contemplated giving to the creatures, as it is written that the purpose of creation is to do good to His creations.

We find this matter in the exodus from Egypt. The holy ARI said that at the time of the exodus from Egypt, Israel were in 49 gates of *Tuma'a* [impurity], until the King of Kings appeared to them and redeemed them. Everyone asks about this: Can it be that the people of Israel, who heard of the mission of the Creator from Moses and Aaron, whom He sent to deliver from the exile in Egypt, as the holy ARI interprets, that the exile in Egypt means that the view of *Kedusha* [holiness/sanctity] was in exile. Moses and Aaron promised the people of Israel that they would come out of exile and enter the *Kedusha*. It is as we say in the *Shema* [Hear] reading, "I am the Lord your God, who brought you out from the land of Egypt to be your God."

Accordingly, it stands to reason that each day they should have risen from degree to degree in *Kedusha*, especially that they saw the ten plagues that occurred in Egypt. Still, the holy ARI says that at the time of the exodus from Egypt the people of Israel were in 49 gates of *Tuma'a*.

However, each day they ascended in the degree of truth and came closer to seeing the measure of evil that they had in the vessels of reception. That is, before Moses and Aaron came to tell them that they must come out of the exile in Egypt, which is the *Klipa* [shell/peel] that suckles from the *Kedusha*, as the holy ARI says, the people of Israel began to move away from them. At that time the *Klipa* of Egypt began to fight them with powerful forces.

That is, the *Klipa* of Egypt let the people of Israel see that it was not worth it to exit self-reception. And concerning the work of bestowal, they let them see that it is difficult and not worth it to work for nothing, that they would not be rewarded with it anyway, since it requires special forces. And the more the people of Israel received strengthening from Moses and Aaron, the more the *Klipa* of Egypt came and weakened them.

It was so much so that each time they overcame the argument of the Egyptians that came into their minds, so they would see that it was not the argument of Egypt, but that the people of Israel would think that these thoughts are their own. This is called "Anyone who is greater than his friend, his desire is greater than him."

It means that to the extent of their strengthening in *Kedusha*, to that extent the *Klipot* strengthened against them. To the extent of the power of the desire to escape, to that extent the other side must show more power so as to keep him in his domain, so he will not escape.

It turns out that in fact, the people of Israel drew closer to *Kedusha* each day, and the evidence of this is that if it is said that they were in 49 gates of *Tuma'a*, it is because that they have already ascended the 49 gates of *Kedusha*, hence there had to be the opposite of *Kedusha*, the 49 gates of *Tuma'a*.

However, before a person completes the work and comes out of the domain of the *Klipot* [shells/peels], he does not see the measure of his entrance into *Kedusha*. All he sees is that each time he is farther away because the opposite of *Kedusha* reveals the evil in him. Before there is light of *Kedusha*, a person cannot see the real form of evil in him. As said above, precisely where there is light we can see the dirt that is in the house.

It follows that one cannot know what he can regard as a good state. That is, it might be that a person feels that he is in a descent, meaning that he sees that he has no desire for Torah and *Mitzvot*. He sees that now he has more passion for self-love than, for example, yesterday. Thus, a person should probably say that yesterday he was in a state where he regarded people who were concerned with corporeal means, with satisfying their will to receive, he stayed away from them and could not see intelligent grownups degrading themselves into being in such a lowly state.

But now he sees that he is one of them and he has no shame in feeling his lowliness. Rather, it is an ordinary thing for him, as though he never thought about spirituality. To understand it better, let us take for example, when a person must get up before dawn. When he is awakened by the alarm clock or by a person, he feels that he must rise to serve the Creator. He begins to feel the importance of the matter, and therefore rises quickly because the sensation of the importance of serving the Creator gives him strength to get up quickly.

Undoubtedly, at that time he is in a state of ascent. That is, it is not corporeality that gives him strength to work, but to him the spirituality, his feeling that now he will have contact with the Creator, in whatever manner, is enough to give him strength to work, and he does not think of anything but the Creator. He feels that now he is regarded as alive, but without spirituality he is regarded as dead. Naturally, he feels that he is in a state of ascent.

In truth, a person cannot determine his state, that he feels he is remote. That is, if he is a person who wishes to walk on the path of bestowal, he must understand that from above he is given a special treatment, that he was lowered from the previous state so he would begin to really contemplate the goal, meaning what is required of man and what man wants the Creator to give him. But when he is in a state of ascent, when he has desire for Torah and *Mitzvot*, he has no need to worry about spirituality. Instead, he sees that he will stay this way his whole life because he is happy this way.

It therefore follows that the descent he has received is for his own good, meaning that he is receiving special treatment, that he was lowered from his state where he thought that he had some wholeness. This is apparent in his agreeing to remain in the current state his whole life.

But now that he sees that he is far from spirituality, he begins to think, "What is really required of me? What should I do? What is the purpose I should achieve?" He sees that he has no power to work, and finds himself in a state of "between heaven and earth." Then, man's only strengthening is that only the Creator can help, but by himself, he is doomed.

It was said about this (Isaiah, 4:31): "Yet those who hope for the Lord will gain new strength," meaning those people who hope for the Creator. This means that they who see that there is no one else in the world who can help them regain strength each time. It follows that this descent is actually an ascent, meaning that this descent that they feel allows them to rise in degree, since "there is no light without a *Kli*."

It follows that when he thought that he was in a state of ascent, he had no desire in which the Creator to place anything, since his *Kli* was full and there was no room to put anything inside. But now that he feels he is in a state of descent, he begins to see his deficiencies and the main reasons that interrupt his achieving *Dvekut* with the Creator. At that time he knows what help to ask of the Creator because he sees the truth, the real obstructer.

According to the above, one cannot say that the Creator has driven him away from the work of the Creator. The proof of this is that he is in a state of descent, meaning that the Creator has thrown him out from the work and does not want him to work for Him. This is not so. On the contrary, because the Creator wants to bring him closer, when he felt that he was in ascent, He could not bring him closer because he had no *Kelim*.

In order to give him *Kelim*, the Creator had to bring him out of his state, and admit him into a state where he feels deficient. Then the Creator can give him help from above, as our sages said, "He who comes to purify is aided. The holy *Zohar* asks, 'With what?' And he replies, 'With a holy soul.'" That is, he is being made to feel that the soul is a part of God above, and then he enters the *Kedusha*. At that time he can go from degree to degree until he completes his soul with respect to what it needs to correct.

It therefore follows that in the first kind, the reason and the cause for observing Torah and *Mitzvot* is people from the outside. In the second kind, the Creator, along with people from the outside, commit him to Torah and *Mitzvot*. In the third kind, only the Creator commits to observing Torah and *Mitzvot*. People on the outside do not commit him, but he himself also causes Torah and *Mitzvot*. In the fourth kind, only the Creator is the cause for observing Torah and *Mitzvot*, and there is no other partner who partakes in committing him to Torah and *Mitzvot*. This is called "for the Lord alone," and this is called "mixed-multitude inside the *Kedusha*."

The Klipa that Precedes the Fruit

Article No. 30, Tav-Shin-Mem-Vav, 1985-86

In the portion, Balak, *The Zohar* writes (item 15), "If you say that so the Creator wished—to give the birthright to Israel, this is improper. Come and see: Esau was a *Klipa* [shell/peel] and *Sitra Achra*. It is known that the *Klipa* precedes the marrow, hence he emerged first. Once the *Klipa* has emerged and was removed, the marrow was found. The first foreskin, which is Esau, is outside. Hence, he emerged first. The covenant, which is the most precious, meaning Jacob, appeared next. Therefore, Esau's early emergence does not regard his birthright, for he is a *Klipa* and foreskin, completely worthless compared to the marrow and the covenant. He only emerged first for the reason that the *Klipa* precedes the fruit."

We should understand why he needs to answer. After all, our sages have already answered this question (introduced by RASHI in the beginning of the portion, *Beresheet* [in the beginning]): "Rabbi Yitzhak said, 'The Torah should have begun from, 'This month is to you...' which is the first *Mitzva* [commandment] that Israel were commanded. What is the reason that it begins with *Beresheet*? It is because 'He has made known to His people the power of His works, to give them the inheritance of nations,' so that should the nations of the world say to Israel, 'You are robbers, for you have conquered the lands of seven nations,' they will tell them, 'The whole earth is the Creator's. He has created it and given it to whom He chooses. At His will he gave it to them, and at His will He took it from them and has given it to us.'"

The same applies with the birthright. First He gave it to Esau, then took it from Esau and gave it to Jacob. We cannot say that birthright is not the same as lands because a land can be sold and given, while birthright is about facts, meaning the one who was born first is called "firstborn," and it cannot be changed. And yet, we see that birthright can also be sold, so we can say that it can be taken from one and given to another. Otherwise, how could Jacob buy his birthright from Esau, as it is written, "and he sold his birthright to Jacob"?

From this we see that birthright is similar to a land, which can be given. Thus, what does this answer that he gives here imply to us, that since a *Klipa* precedes the fruit, being born first does not count as having the birthright?

To understand the matter we must first know what is a *Klipa*, what is marrow, and what is the foreskin, for he calls Esau by the name "foreskin," and what is a covenant, for he calls Jacob by the name "covenant." First we must state the purpose of creation. Afterwards we will be able to explain what is primary and what is not secondary, so as to know the matter of fruit and *Klipa*, which must precede the fruit. What is this necessity, which implies that it cannot be otherwise?

It is known that the purpose of creation is to do good to His creations. For this reason, He has created a creature existence from absence, so that this creature could receive the delight and pleasure that He wants to give them. That creature is called a "will to receive in order to receive." It follows that we can only speak of something that has a desire to receive, or it is not regarded as a creature of which we can speak. A creature is called *Kli* [vessel], and there is no light without a *Kli*. This means that we can speak of light only when it is clothed in a *Kli*.

However, there isn't this *Kli*, called a "desire to receive delight and pleasure," "reception," once the correction called "equivalence of form" has been made, so as not to have the bread of shame. It is known that there is shame when one must receive something, as our sages said about the verse, "Chrome gorges for the sons of men." When a person is compelled to receive from people, his face changes and becomes as chrome. This is why there was the correction called "*Tzimtzum* [restriction] and concealment," to receive pleasure only with the intention to bestow.

It follows that we should discern two things: 1) This most important is the *Kli*, called "desire to receive the delight and pleasure." Without this desire there is nothing to speak of. However, the *Sitra Achra* and the *Klipot* [plural of *Klipa*] extend from this discernment. The order of the cascading of the worlds comes to us as root, meaning that from this point extends open expansion with all the evil. It is as the ARI said, that the *Tzimtzum* is the root of the judgment, meaning that by this there was a *Tzimtzum* not to receive in order to receive, but only in order to bestow. The order was as explained in *The Study of the Ten Sefirot* (Part 1), that initially, the *Tzimtzum* was voluntary, meaning that there still wasn't the prohibition on receiving. Afterwards there was a prohibition on receiving, but there was still no one who wanted to receive in order to receive. That is, there was still no one who wanted to breach the prohibition of the *Tzimtzum*. However, through *Tzimtzum Bet* [second restriction], a new entity was born—someone who wants to receive in order to receive, though there were still no *Klipot*.

The *Klipot* were born after the breaking of the vessels that occurred in the world of *Nekudim*, but there was still no structure of them. Rather, at that time the *Klipot* were called "*Vav* and a dot," and there was still no structure of worlds in them. Only after the sin of *Adam Harishon* with the tree of knowledge, when the *Levushim* [dress/clothing] fell into the *Klipot*, the *Klipot* received the structure of four worlds like the *Kedusha* [holiness/sanctity], and they are called "the four worlds ABYA de [of] *Tuma'a* [impurity]." This is the matter presented in the "Introduction to the Book of Zohar" (item 29): "Know that our work during our seventy years is divided in four:

The First Division is to obtain the excessive will to receive without restraints, in its full, corrupted measure from under the hands of the four impure worlds ABYA. If we do not have that corrupted will to receive, we will not be able to correct it. Thus, the will to receive imprinted in the body at birth is insufficient. Rather, it must also be a vehicle for the impure *Klipot* for no less than thirteen years. This means that the *Klipot* must dominate it and give it of their lights, for their lights increase its will to receive, for the fulfillments with which the *Klipot* provide the will to receive only expand and enhance the demands of the will to receive. If one does not overcome it through Torah and *Mitzvot*, and purifies the will to receive to turn it into bestowal, one's will to receive expands throughout one's life.

The Second Division is from thirteen years onward. At that point, the point in the heart, which is the posterior of the *Nefesh* of *Kedusha* [holiness/sanctity], is given strength. Although it is dressed in his will to receive at birth, it only begins to awaken after thirteen years, and then one begins to enter the system of the worlds of *Kedusha*, to the extent that one engages in Torah and *Mitzvot*. The primary aim of that time is to obtain and intensify the spiritual will to receive. Hence, this degree, which comes past the thirteen years, is deemed holiness. This is considered the holy maid who serves her mistress, which is the holy *Shechina* [Divinity], since the maid brings one to *Lishma* [for Her sake] and he is rewarded with the instilling of the *Shechina*. And the final degree in this division is that he will fall passionately in love with the Creator, as the poet says, "When I remember Him, He does not let me sleep."

Now we can understand what is *Kedusha* and what is *Klipa*. *Kedusha* comes from the words *Kodesh Lehashem* [dedicated to the Creator]. It means that it does not belong to us, meaning that it does not belong to our domain, but that we dedicate it to the Creator. That is, he takes it out from the domain of laypeople and admits it into the domain of *Kedusha*. However, it cannot be said that he admits it into the domain of *Kedusha* if it was not previously in his domain, and then it can be said that he has taken it out from his own domain and admitted it into the domain of *Kedusha*.

Therefore, a person must first be in the domain of the *Klipa* until the age of thirteen years, as it is written in the "Introduction to the Book of Zohar," at which time he feels that he has his own authority because the *Klipa*, called "will to receive in order to receive," is called "disparity of form," which separates him from the Creator. This matter of vessels of reception that one acquires while being under the domain of the *Klipa* until the age of thirteen years lets him feel that he is the landlord, meaning that he can do whatever he wants because he does not feel any authority but his own.

For this reason, when he is told, after thirteen years, that now is the time when you must annul your authority, and say that there is only the authority of the Creator, he begins to think and contemplate, "Why do I need to annul my authority and say that only the Creator is the landlord and I am His servant, and I have no possession, but as our sages said, 'He who buys a servant buys his master.' That is, I need to serve the Creator so as to bring Him contentment."

At that time, man's body, called "will to receive," makes a strong argument: "First I must believe that there is a connection between the Creator and the creatures, and then I must see that it is worthwhile to believe that the Creator is the owner. But for this I must annul my authority and see only that there is contentment to the Creator. What is my gain in this?" However, he understands—once he believes that there is a connection between the Creator and the creatures—meaning that all He wants is to do good to His creations, and all that he needs to see in this state is how the Creator serves him. That is, the Creator is the servant and man is the owner. He is the owner and the Creator must serve man, for man is the master and the Creator is the slave.

The Klipa that Precedes the Fruit

However, when a person is told that he must know that the truth is that the Creator is the landlord and we, creatures, have no say in the world, and whether we accept His kingship over us or we are secular who do not want to assume His kingship, nothing helps us. He does what He wants, and the creatures must obey His orders against their will, as our sages said (*Avot*, Chapter 3, 20), "Man's debt is collected whether willingly or unwillingly."

It follows that even if one does not agree to what he is being told, the fact that he does not want to believe does not change reality—that the Creator is the landlord and does what He wants. However, a person cannot see the truth, and this is why we do not want to believe.

But when a person does not believe it, he cannot take upon himself to be a servant of the Creator, meaning believe that the Creator is the master and we are His servants. Rather, this applies specifically to those with faith.

However, this is not real faith. There is a type of people who believe that the Lord is the Creator and that He has created the world with a purpose called "to do good to His creations." They also believe that the Creator has commanded us through Moses to observe the Torah and *Mitzvot*, that He has given us, but believe all this for profit, meaning that He will pay us for exerting in the work of keeping Torah and *Mitzvot*. They have what to rely on, as our sages said (*Avot*, Chapter 2, 16), "If you learned much Torah, you are given a great reward. You can trust your landlord to pay for your work, and know that the reward of the righteous is in the future [implying the end of correction]."

We therefore see that there is the matter of believing in the Creator and in His law, and keeping every single *Mitzva*, slight or serious. However, it is all measured by profitability, which is in order to receive reward, called *Lo Lishma* [not for Her sake]. However, we must remember what our sages said, "From *Lo Lishma* we come to *Lishma*." Thus, this is already regarded as a degree of *Kedusha*. But when one is told, after thirteen years, that now is the time when you must annul your authority and say that there is no other authority in the world, and you are nothing but a slave serving the master not in order to receive reward, the body resists it. At that time the main work begins, since it is against nature.

Therefore, a person must believe above reason and tell his body: "You must know that you cannot work in bestowing contentment upon the Creator without any reward, since you were born with a nature of wanting to receive, and that nature is necessary, for only this is the whole creation, as it is known that only the will to receive, called 'craving and desire to receive pleasure' is called 'existence from absence.'"

It therefore follows that we are called "creatures" precisely pertaining to the will to receive, which we can call "creation." This desire is found in all the degrees and worlds of *Kedusha*. However, in *Kedusha*, this will to receive is corrected with a correction of intention to bestow. It follows that the basis is the will to receive, and the difference between *Kedusha* and *Tuma'a* and between life and death is only in the intention.

This means that if the reception is in order to bestow, it is called *Kedusha*, since it is equivalence of form. Equivalence of form is called *Dvekut*, as our sages said about the verse, "And to cleave unto Him." They interpreted, "cleave unto His attributes: as He is merciful, so you are merciful," and for this reason he is adhered to the life of lives. It follows that life extends to him from above.

But if he cannot place the intention to bestow on the act, then he is in disparity of form from the Creator, since He is the giver, and the creatures want to receive. For this reason, they are separated from the life of lives, and naturally have only death. This is called *Klipa*, although it comes in the basis of creation. Otherwise, if there is no will to receive there, there is no one to speak of. And yet, if there is no correction of bestowal over it, it is called *Klipa*, *Sitra Achra*, "angel of death," etc.

According to the order of correction, we see that first there must be a desire and craving to receive the pleasures, and then we say that we must know that we must not receive with the intention of self-love. And although there is a great desire to receive the pleasure, I must still overcome the lust and work with myself in such a way that I want to receive the pleasure provided I can aim the reception I will receive now only because the Creator wants me to receive the pleasure, and this is why I am receiving, since I want to please the Creator.

He has already cancelled his own authority, meaning he does not want to receive anything inside the *Kli* called "self-love." But since the Creator wants him to receive, he says, "Now I want to receive delight and pleasure because the Creator wants it, and I want to satisfy the Creator's will." Therefore, now he receives the delight and pleasure.

But in order for man to achieve this degree, regarded as "His only desire is to bestow contentment upon the Creator," here begins the real work, since there are two discernments to make in matters of work: 1) The act. It is difficult for us to relinquish pleasures, regardless of the kind of pleasure. Take, for example, the pleasure of rest. When a person must go to work in order to receive a salary, he goes to work in construction or in a factory, so it is certainly difficult to relinquish the pleasure of rest. But since he will suffer more if he has nothing to eat, he relinquishes rest and takes upon himself labor, since by this he will achieve a greater pleasure.

In what is it great? He gains two things here: not suffering from not having anything to eat, or the suffering of shame when he has nothing to wear. Also, he will have the pleasure of eating and the joy of having nice clothes. This is not so when he relinquishes the pleasure of rest but does not suffer at not having rest, although we can say that when he relinquishes rest he feels suffering of sleep, besides missing the pleasure of sleep. Also, when he works, we can say that in addition to relinquishing the pleasure of rest, he also has the suffering of movement. It is especially so when one is doing physical work—he suffers during the work, as well.

However, this suffering is not like the suffering one feels when he is hungry, or when he must be with people in a place of celebration, such as a Brit [circumcision ceremony] or a wedding, and he has nothing to wear. This makes it easier for him to give up the rest and assume the trouble of labor, since we see what everyone does—giving up rest and going to work. Thus, the suffering from not having must be harder.

The same applies when a person is told, "Give up the rest and start working in Torah and *Mitzvot*." He immediately asks, as in corporeality: "What will be my reward for giving up rest? I want to see the profit." Maimonides says about this (end of *Hilchot Teshuva*): "Your reward will be in this world and in the next world, and you will be saved from affliction and from every misfortune." At that time he can believe what he is told and keep Torah and *Mitzvot* in practice for the Creator. That is, by keeping Torah and *Mitzvot*, he is aiming to what the Creator has commanded us through Moses, and in return we will receive reward for our labor and toil of relinquishing many pleasures that the Torah has forbidden us. In return, we receive reward, just as those who work at a factory or in construction, because we are paid.

The same applies to spirituality. That is, we work for the landlord. It is not that he is the owner of some factory. Rather, we believe that he is the owner of the entire world, and we work for Him. We are told, "Give up the job you have for a small company that pays you very little, and work for the big boss, the owner of the world."

However, this brings up the question: "Why is everyone not working for the owner of the world?" The answer is simple: They do not see an instantaneous reward. Rather, they must believe in the reward—that we will receive when the work is done. For this reason, not everyone can believe in the reward. Hence, since the reward is doubtful and we must believe that in the end we will be paid, not many people want it. Because normally, people work for a guaranteed reward and not for a questionable one, there is a big difference between corporeality and spirituality. However, we must know that the only difference is that here in spirituality, the reward is not instantaneous, but we must believe. This is the only difference.

However, we see that people come and want to keep Torah and *Mitzvot*, although the whole time until they came they were among secular people, and they come and say that they want to repent. When they are asked about the reason that they want to change the way that they were used to, they say that they no longer find meaning in life, meaning in self-love. Because he (a person) does not have anything to receive and put into them (into his desires of self-love), since he has nothing to give them (to the desires of self-love), therefore he wants to keep Torah and *Mitzvot*.

He has heard that one can receive pleasure from Torah and *Mitzvot*, so he will have something with which to delight his will to receive. That is, as long as he sees that he can nourish the will to receive with corporeal pleasures, he has no need to change his way. But if he hears that there is a matter of faith, and that there is a master who leads the world, who did not create the world for no reason, but rather for some purpose, and the goal is called "to do good to His creations," when he hears this, if he is dissatisfied with corporeal pleasures since he cannot find the meaning of life in them, for which it is worthwhile to live and suffer in the world, since each one is suffering according to his degree, so when he hears that there is a place where there is something that illuminates something in life, he can come out of the corporeal pleasures, although we said above that in corporeal pleasures he does not need to believe. But in spirituality, he is in doubt, and must believe that in the end, the glory will come, meaning that in the end he will receive reward. But since he is dissatisfied with corporeal pleasures he can shift to the side of *Kedusha* and observe Torah and *Mitzvot*.

However, when one is immersed in corporeal lusts and finds satisfaction in them, even if temporary, and then he sees that he has no satisfaction, he is already as an infant captured by idol-worshippers, and he is powerless to emerge from their control.

However, even after such people take upon themselves the burden of Torah and *Mitzvot*, sometimes corporeal lusts awaken in them, and then the work is difficult for them. However, we must know that the fact that corporal lusts have awakened in them, meaning that they are beginning to feel flavors in them that they did not taste before, and also all those people who grew up with religious upbringing, who have been keeping Torah and *Mitzvot* since childhood, when they begin to do the work of bestowal there awakens in them greater taste for corporeality than when they first began to engage in work of bestowal. It is as our sages said (*Sanhedrin*, p 75b), "Rabbi Yitzhak said, 'Since the day when the Temple was ruined, the taste of intercourse was taken away, and given to transgressors.'"

We should interpret "Since the day when the Temple was ruined" to mean when the *Kedusha* in man's heart was ruined. "The taste of intercourse was taken away": The term, "intercourse," incorporates all the pleasures. "And was given to transgressors": This is perplexing. Why do transgressors deserve to feel pleasure in corporeal things more than those who are not transgressors? It is as if they deserve the reward of feeling more pleasure than others for committing transgressions.

To understand this we need to see what is customary in the world. If a person can hire a person for a low salary, he will not pay him more. Indeed, every person strives to have workers who will work for them and do everything he asks while paying him less. It is irrelevant to say that he will pay him more than the worker asks. It follows that when speaking of the work of the Creator, when the evil inclination comes to a person and tells him, "Breach the *Mitzvot* of the Torah," the person tells it, "What will you give me?" Then the evil inclination tells him: "In return for obeying me I will give you, for example, two hundred grams of pleasure." So he tells it, "For two hundred grams of pleasure I do not want to breach the Creator's commandments." Then the evil inclination must add another hundred grams until a person can no longer pass up such a delight and must obey the evil inclination.

It follows that to the extent that a person appreciates the sin, to that extent it is difficult for one to breach the *Mitzva*. And since it is difficult to breach the Creator's commandments, and there is a rule that for hard work you must pay well, hence, to the extent that it is difficult for him to commit the transgression, to that extent the evil inclination must give a great reward, meaning a great pleasure in return for the transgression. But when it is not so difficult to breach the Creator's commandment, the evil inclination does not need to give him such a great reward.

It therefore follows that secular people, who do not keep Torah and *Mitzvot* at all, do not feel that they are committing any transgression, as our sages said (*Yoma*, 86b), "If a person commits a transgression and repeats it, it becomes to him as permitted." Thus, the evil inclination does not need to give them a taste for the transgression, since it is not difficult for them to transgress so as to need payment in return for breaching the *Mitzvot*. This is why they do not feel a great taste in the transgression, since he always finds workers who want to work for him, so he does not need to pay them with great pleasures.

This is not so with people who do not wish to commit transgressions, who feel during the act that they are going to commit a transgression and it is difficult for them to do it. Because of it, the evil inclination must let them feel a great flavor in the transgression, or they will not listen to it and keep its orders. Hence, it must pay them with great pleasures.

By this we can interpret the words, "Since the ruin of the Temple." That is, when there is no work of *Kedusha* in man's heart, "the taste has been taken away," meaning the general taste of pleasures, called "intercourse," "and was given to transgressors," meaning that as long as one feels that he is committing a transgression, he feels the flavor. But "If a person commits a transgression and repeats it, it becomes to him as permitted." Then the evil inclination no longer gives him pleasure, since he is working without any reward because he feels no heaviness in committing the transgressions.

Therefore, the orthodox have a big mistake in thinking that the secular enjoy corporeal pleasures. Because they are serving the evil inclination without any reward, since their whole vitality is their objection to religion and they do not have the pleasures that the religious think because the evil inclination does not reward for nothing.

Therefore, do not be surprised if a person sees that when he has begun the work of bestowal he has received more pleasure for corporeal lusts. It is not because he has suffered a descent. On the contrary, because now he does not want to receive in order to receive, but wants only to bestow, when the evil inclination comes to distract him from the work of bestowal it gives him a greater taste for corporeal pleasures so he will listen to it and will not be able to overcome his will to receive.

But before he has begun the work of bestowal, when he engaged in corporeal lusts, he did not have such a great desire for corporeal lusts, since he was engaged in corporeal lusts without much pleasure. But now that he has begun the work of bestowal, if he does not feel a great taste, the evil inclination will not be able to do anything because he will not listen to it. It follows that to the extent that one moves away from self-love he begins to feel greater taste (in corporeal lusts), since otherwise he will not obey it (the evil inclination) at all.

It therefore follows that one need not be alarmed if in the middle of the work he receives a passion for corporeal lusts, even if previously he did not have such lusts. But now, because he needs to constantly correct the vessels of reception, it means that the greater the pleasure, the greater is his desire. When he corrects the desire, meaning overcomes it, each time he sorts out a desire called *Kli*, by taking it out of the *Klipot* and admitting it into *Kedusha*. For this reason, each time he is given a greater lust.

However, each time he should pray to be given strength from above to overcome this *Kli*, called "desire." This is called "correction of the *Kelim* at the root of his soul." These *Kelim* that he must correct, (their correction) begins from the *Kelim*, meaning from a desire to receive corporeality, and finally comes to correcting the *Kelim*, meaning the desires for reception of spiritual things. And he must ask the Creator to give him the force of the *Masach* [screen] over all of them, meaning the assistance from above, as our sages said, "He who comes to purify is aided."

Now we shall come to clarify what we asked, 1) about what the holy *Zohar* explains, that he gave the birthright to Jacob although Esau was born first. It explains that Esau is a *Klipa*, and this is why he came out first and Jacob emerged next. It is so because the order is that the *Klipa* precedes the fruit. We asked, "But there is a simple answer, as RASHI presents in the beginning of the portion, *Beresheet* [In the beginning], as it is written, "'He has made known to His people the power of His works,' so that should the nations say, 'You are robbers,' they will tell them, 'The whole earth is the Creator's. He has created it and gave it to whom He chooses. At His will he gave it to them, and at His will He took it from them and has given it to us.'" Thus, he adds another reason here.

2) Why must the *Klipa* precede the fruit? With the above said, it is simple: since the Creator created the world and Creation is only a *Kli*. It is known that the light is not considered Creation, but rather "existence from existence." Therefore, it cannot be said that He first had to create a correction for Creation, before He has anything to correct. That is, first He created the *Kli*, called "will to receive," and then a correction called "*Tzimtzum* [restriction] and concealment" emerged on that *Kli*. Afterwards there extended to the lower ones the discernment of "the nations of the world," which is the will to receive in order to receive, namely a *Kli* without correction. A *Kli* without correction is called *Klipa*.

Therefore, it cannot be any other way because it is impossible to correct something that has not been born in the world. It follows that by saying, "He created it," it means that He has created the world according to the applied order, meaning that first emerges a deficiency, and then it is possible to correct the deficiency. Hence, according to the rule of root and branch, the receiver in order to receive must emerge first, which is the opposite of the Creator, meaning disparity of form, called "nations of the world," as it is written in the holy *Zohar*, "Among the nations of the world, all the good that they do, they do it for themselves." This is called a "*Klipa* that precedes the fruit," meaning that the *Klipa* is considered that which is unfit for eating because the abundance enters the vessels of reception after the correction of the *Tzimtzum*.

But afterwards comes the correction called "in order to bestow," which is regarded as Jacob. This is called a "fruit" because now there is a correction on the will to receive: to bestow contentment upon the Creator. Now it is possible to eat fruits since there is equivalence of form here between the light and the *Kli*, and then the *Kli* is rewarded with fruits. But concerning the *Sitra Achra*, the holy *Zohar* says, "Another God is sterile and does not bear fruit." This is why it says that Jacob is called "covenant," where making a covenant means that there is equivalence between them. It is as it is written, "For it is a token of an everlasting covenant between Me and the sons of Israel; it is an everlasting token."

It follows that the answer that Rabbi Yitzhak gave, because it is "the power of His works," is the same answer that He has created it according to the order that the *Klipa* precedes the fruit. The branch and root come out, where the *Klipa* must come first, which is receiving in order to receive, and then emerges the correction, which is Israel or Jacob. It follows that when it says, "He took it from them and has given it to us," it is to correct, since such is the order.

Concerning Yenika and Ibur

Article No. 31, Tav-Shin-Mem-Vav, 1985-86

Ibur [conception/impregnation], *Yenika* [nursing], *Mochin* [adulthood/greatness] are three degrees. Once a person has been rewarded with entering *Kedusha* [holiness/sanctity], he begins to attain them. They are called *Nefesh* in *Ibur*, *Ruach* in *Yenika*, and *Neshama* in *Mochin*.

However, even during the preparation for the work, before one has been rewarded with permanent admission into *Kedusha*, these matters still apply. *Ibur* means that a person temporarily *Maavir* [shifts/removes] his selfness and says, "Now I do not want to think of my own benefit whatsoever, and I also do not want to use my intellect, although to me it is the most important thing. That is, since I cannot do something that I do not understand—meaning I can do anything but I must understand the benefit of it—he still says, "Now I can temporarily say that I am taking upon myself at this time that I determine not to use my intellect. Rather, I believe above reason, believe in faith in the sages, believing that there is an overseer who is watching each and every one in the world in Private Providence."

But why should I believe it and I cannot feel that this is so? It makes sense that if I could feel the existence of the Creator I could certainly work for Him and would desire to serve Him. Why then is this concealment? What does the Creator gain by hiding Himself from the creatures? Also, he does not provide any answer to this, but rather answers that with this question, too, he goes above reason and says that if the Creator knew that not making the concealment would be better for the creatures, He would not create concealment.

It turns out that to all the questions that come up in his mind he says that he is going above reason, and that now he is going with eyes shut and only with faith. It is as Baal HaSulam said about the verse (Psalms, 68:32): "Cush shall run to stretch out her hands to God." He said that if one can say, "Cush," meaning that his *Kushiot* [questions] are answers, it means that he does not need answers, but the question itself gives him the answer. That is, he says that now that he has a question he can go above reason. Then, "his hands are to God," meaning that then his hands, namely his vessels of reception—from the words, "Should a hand attain"—then a person is regarded as whole, with God.

Therefore, the beginning of the entrance into the work of the Creator is regarded as *Ibur* [impregnation], when he cancels his self and becomes impregnated in the mother's womb, as it is written, "Hear, my son, your father's instruction, and do not forsake your mother's teaching." This comes from the verse, "For if you call the mother, 'understanding [*Bina*],'" meaning that he cancels self-love, called *Malchut*, whose original essence is called "will to receive in order to receive," and enters the vessels of bestowal, called *Bina*.

One should believe that before he was born, meaning before the soul descended into the body, the soul was adhered to Him, and now he longs to adhere to Him as prior to her descent. This is called *Ibur*, when he completely annuls his self. However, although his heart tells him that only now he agrees to the annulment but later he will regret, we can say about this, "Do not worry about tomorrow."

Also, tomorrow may not be the next day. Rather, tomorrow can be the present or the future. The difference in time can be even an hour later.

It is as our sages said, "Anyone who has what to eat today and says, 'What shall I eat tomorrow?' it is for lack of faith" (*Sutah*, 48). We should interpret that this means that if he has what to eat today, meaning he is willing to take upon himself faith above reason and only thinks, "What will happen later," meaning he already has *Reshimot* [recollections] from states when he thought that he would remain in that state of ascent forever, but then descended once more to a place of lowliness, which is a place of garbage, where garbage means where all the waste is thrown.

That is, during the ascent he thought that the whole matter of self-love is nothing but waste that should be thrown to the garbage. That is, he felt that the will to receive is garbage. But now, during the descent, he himself is descending into the place of garbage so as to receive nourishments from there, like cats poking through trash to find something to eat to sustain themselves. Likewise, during the descent he is like a cat, and not like spoiled people who always select what they should eat and what they shouldn't.

This is the meaning of what we say in the *Hallel* [Praise]: "He raises the poor from the dust, lifts the poor from the trash." Accordingly, it follows that when a person can annul himself a little bit and at that time says, "Now I want to annul myself before the *Kedusha*," meaning not to think about self-love. Rather, now he wants to bring contentment to the Creator, and believes above reason that although he still does not feel anything, he believes above reason, that the Creator hears the prayer of every mouth, and before Him, small and great are equal, and as He can deliver the greatest of the greatest, He can also help the smallest of the small.

This is called *Ibur*, meaning that he passes from his own domain into the domain of the Creator. However, it is temporary. That is, he truly wants to annul himself forever, but cannot believe that there will be annulling forever now since he has already thought many times that it would be so but then descended from his degree and fell to the place of garbage.

However, he does not need to worry about what to eat tomorrow, as was said above, that later he will probably fall from his degree, as this is for lack of faith. Rather, he must believe that the salvation of the Lord is as the blink of an eye. It follows that since he annuls himself for the time being and wants to remain this way forever, it follows that he has the value of *Ibur*.

However, in truth, one must believe that his desire to begin to work the Creator in annulling his self is a call from above, for it is not within man's wisdom. The evidence of this is that during this call, all the questions he had before he was called from above—he had many questions, and each time he wanted to do something in order to bestow the body resisted and could not understand if there is a person in the world who could annul his self before the Creator and not worry at all about his own benefit. He was always under some fear whether he could annul himself to the Creator.

But now he sees that all the thoughts and doubts have been completely burned and he would feel great pleasure if he could annul himself before the Creator. Now he sees that all his reason is worthless, although previously he thought that no one in the world could convince him to annul himself before the Creator, and he would say that this is hard work that not just anyone can come into. But now he sees that there is nothing that interferes with his adhering and annulling before the Creator. Rather, as was said above, since it is an illumination from above, all the obstructers who came and told him the argument of the spies have surrendered to him and vanished from sight.

It is as it is written (Psalms, 103:16), "For the wind has passed over him and he is no more, and his place will no longer know him." It is as it is written, "For the wind has passed over him." When a person receives *Ruach* [spirit/wind] from above, all the obstructers disappear and even his place is not apparent. That is, during the ascent, when he receives spirit from above, at that time he does not understand how can there be a place where the wicked can do something with their arguments.

It follows that during the *Ibur*, when we see that there is a time of abortion, meaning that if the fetus is born before the time of corrections of the *Ibur* has been completed, as some weakness in the impregnation causes an abortion, when the fetus emerges prematurely and cannot exist and dies, it is the same in spirituality. If there is a weakness then a person comes out of the *Ibur* and comes into the air of this world, and all the thoughts that exist in this world fall into his mind, and all the desires of this world cling to him. This is considered that the *Ibur* has died.

In *The Study of the Ten Sefirot*, Part 9 (p 788, item 83), the ARI writes, "There should be doors in a woman, to close them and hold the fetus within so it does not come out until it is completely fashioned. And there should also be in her a force that depicts the form of the fetus."

He explains there in "Inner Light" that there are two forces in the *Ibur*: 1) A depicting force, where the depiction of the fetus is *Katnut* [infancy/smallness], for in order to obtain *Katnut* there is an order, since *Katnut* is preparation for *Gadlut* [adulthood/greatness], and without *Katnut* in the degree there is no *Gadlut*. And as long as he is in *Katnut* he is still incomplete, and wherever there is a deficiency in *Kedusha* there is a grip to the *Sitra Achra*, who might spoil the *Ibur* so it cannot be completed. By this he is aborted, meaning that he is born before the state of *Ibur* has been completed.

It is so because there are twenty-five *Partzufim* [plural of *Partzuf*] in the *Ibur*, meaning NRNHY, and in each of them there is also NRNHY. Therefore, there must be a detaining force, meaning that even in *Katnut* there should be wholeness there. He receives this through his mother, although the fetus in itself has no *Kelim* [vessels] in which to receive *Gadlut* in order to bestow. Still, by annulling before the mother it can receive *Gadlut* from the *Kelim* of its mother. This is regarded as "An embryo is its mother's thigh; it eats what its mother eats."

That is, since it has no choice of its own but rather eats what its mother eats, meaning that what its mother knows is permitted to eat, it eats, as well, it means that he has shifted the choice of what is good and what is bad from himself. Rather, it is all attributed to the mother. This is called "its mother's thigh," meaning that he himself does not merit a name.

There it speaks of upper lights, but the same thing applies during the preparation, when wanting to enter the King's palace—the same orders apply. As there are many discernments there and the *Ibur* is not completed all at once, and it is said that there are nine months of pregnancy until he obtains twenty-five *Partzufim*, in the preparation, too, there are many discernments until he obtains the complete *Ibur* during the preparation. Therefore, there are many ups and downs, and sometimes the *Ibur* becomes corrupted, which is also called "abortion," and we must begin the order of the work anew.

Let us explain the depicting force that exists during the preparation period. The depiction of the *Ibur* is *Katnut*, which means that only in vessels of bestowal, when he engages in Torah and work, he can aim to do everything with the intention to bestow.

That is, the reason why he engages now in Torah and *Mitzvot* is because he believes in the Creator and in His greatness. He takes upon himself that henceforth, all his pleasure will be in that he has a desire to serve the King, and he will regard this as though he has made a fortune, and as though the whole world is looking at him and envies him that he has been privileged with rising to the highest degrees, with which none other has been rewarded. Naturally, he is delighted and does not feel anything bad in the world, but rather that he is living in a world that is all good.

However, all the importance and joy is in that he gives, meaning that he wants to give to the Creator. That is, throughout the day he has one thought: "What should I do that will please the Creator?" That is, on the one hand we say that a person needs to work not in order to receive reward, but only for the Creator. On the other hand, we say that he must enjoy and picture how he can enjoy.

This means that he must depict pictures of greatness and importance of how we appreciate flesh and blood kings or other world leaders, and see how the public appreciates them. Afterwards

Concerning Yenika and Ibur

he should learn from the world how they enjoy serving world leaders and use this for the greatness of the Creator, that when he is serving the Creator he must feel the same pleasure as they enjoy serving world leaders.

Otherwise, if he does not derive great pleasure from engaging in Torah and *Mitzvot*, it is a sign that he does not appreciate the Creator as they appreciate and receive delight and pleasure from serving world leaders.

Therefore, when he speaks to the Creator, he must first depict to whom he is speaking, meaning His greatness and importance. That is, in what manner and what reverence I speak to Him, and He listens and looks at me when I speak to Him.

For example, when a person eats a cake or some fruit, we know we must believe that the Creator has created all these, and now we are enjoying what has been prepared for us to enjoy. We turn to Him for this and thank Him for this, and we say, "We thank and praise You for this pleasure and say, 'Blessed are You, O Lord, creator of the fruit of the tree.'"

At that time a person can monitor what he has just said to the Creator, what reverence he felt while speaking to Him, and what he feels after he has spoken to Him, meaning what impression it has left in him, what elation, since if he truly believes that he spoke to the King, where are the excitement and elation? It is written about it: "If I am a father, where is My honor? If I am a master, where is the fear of Me?"

If we look more closely we can detect two discernments in this act: 1) he enjoys the fruit he is eating. This joy he has from the fruit pertains to the animate will to receive. That is, animals also enjoy eating and drinking. There is no need for man to receive such a pleasure, and this is why this pleasure is called "beastly pleasure."

But the blessing and gratitude he gives to the Creator for it, in this we should make several discernments. In the second discernment in the above action, meaning the joy of thanking the Creator, this pertains specifically to man and is absent in animals. There are many discernments here because in this act, which belongs to man, there are many degrees to discern.

For example, in man we should discern the measure of faith—how much he believes that the Creator has given him all the pleasures to enjoy. Afterwards we should discern—in the speaking that he speaks to the Creator—to what extent he believes that he is speaking to the Creator. Afterwards we should discern to what extent he believes in the greatness and importance of the Creator. In that, it is certain that every person is different. And in a person himself we should discern according to his current state, for because a person is walking, he could be ascending or descending. Thus, in one person we can discern several states, as it is written, "And I will give you moves among these who are standing."

It turns out that in the will to receive pleasure, which by and large pertains to the beast, there is nothing to discern, since it is general pleasure. This is not so with pleasure pertaining to man. There we should already make many discernments. It follows that the foundation of the joy that pertains to man is not attributed to the vessels of reception. Rather, it pertains to bestowal because all his pleasure is built on the Creator. That is, all the fuel from which he has *Kelim* [vessels] for work depends on the greatness of the Creator and not on the measure of man's pleasure. This means that the measure of pleasure depends on the extent to which he assumes the greatness of the Creator.

This is called "pleasure that comes to a person indirectly." He wants to bestow upon the King directly, and to the extent that he depicts the greatness of the King, to that extent he is happier that he is delighting a great king. He receives indirect pleasure from this. It follows that pleasure is permitted only in this manner, for he does not intend for self-pleasure when he is serving the King, but the importance of the King commits him to serve the King.

It turns out that his intention is to delight the King, to make the King happy, so it naturally follows that he enjoys, as well. Such pleasure is permitted because when he receives this pleasure there is no matter of shame here, called "bread of shame," as his pleasure is from giving and not from something he receives directly from the Creator.

When he enjoys something that the Creator gives him it is regarded as pleasure that comes directly from the Giver, as lights. This is called *Ohr Hochma* [Light of Wisdom], which comes to the receiver directly. That is, the receiver enjoys the reception, and this requires a correction called "aiming to bestow." But if his pleasure is because he is giving to the Creator, and he enjoys serving Him, this pleasure is regarded as coming indirectly because his intention is for the King to enjoy and he does not think about enjoying this.

It was said about this: "Serve the Lord with gladness." That is, the joy should come to a person from serving the Creator. However, if he is serving without joy it is for lack of faith in the greatness and importance of the King. Otherwise, there must be joy and elation without any preparation for it, meaning he does not need to see that he will enjoy the work but needs to see that he prepares himself to know Whom he is serving and what is His importance. The joy is the result. Thus, if he has no joy in the work it is a sign that he has no idea about the importance of the Creator, and then he must correct himself in matters of faith.

Thus, he does not need to work on having gladness in serving the Creator. Rather, he must labor to obtain the importance and greatness of the Creator. That is, in everything he does, learns, and engages in *Mitzvot* [commandments], he wants reward for his labor—to be rewarded with the greatness and importance of the Creator. To the extent that he receives the importance of the Creator he will be naturally drawn to annul before Him and will want and crave to serve Him.

Everything we said thus far is regarded as *Ibur* because he must believe that everything comes from the Creator, giving him the thought and desire to annul before Him. At such a time he must find a place for depiction, meaning how he is inspired by this awakening, and criticize, and he will certainly find deficiencies to correct there. But when he sees what is missing there, he cannot be happy because every deficiency causes him suffering, so how can he be happy? On the other hand, it is not good to be so deficient, according to the rule that where there is a deficiency in the *Kedusha* [holiness/sanctity] there is a grip to the *Klipot* [shells/peels], and he might fall from his degree and receive from this weakness in the work.

Therefore, a person must see himself in wholeness, that he has no deficiency. He sees himself as happy with his life and as having where to find pleasure from seeing that there are many people like him who do not enjoy the life that he does, and if they had the pleasure that he has, they would all envy him.

Let us say, for example, that there are prisoners, and no one is allowed to come out of the prison to breathe some air. But one man wins the warden's favor, and no one knows it but he lets him out free one hour a day. He goes home to visit and then returns to the prison. How happy is that man? 1) He is happy because he visits his home. 2) When he looks at the rest of the prisoners, who are not given this freedom, he derives immense delight and pleasure from looking at the others, who are sitting in the prison without seeing any of the light that there is outside.

This means that besides his own pleasure, meaning the pleasure he himself enjoys, he can take pleasure from what is outside of him. He enjoys seeing what he has and what others do not have. It follows that this pleasure comes from outside, meaning from looking outside and seeing how they suffer from not having any leaves, while he enjoys his leaves.

It follows that we should discern two pleasures here: 1) the pleasure he receives from enjoying, 2) the pleasure he receives from having what others do not have, which is called "receiving joy from outside." The lesson is that since we are incarcerated, it is as we say (in the *Kaparot* [atonements] on the eve of *Yom Kippur* [Day of Atonement]), "Dwellers of darkness and the shadow of death, prisoners of poverty and iron, He will deliver them from darkness and the shadow of death."

We have sinned and were placed in prison, where all the prisoners who sinned before the King are placed, where they do not see light their whole life, meaning they were given a life-sentence in prison. They are disconnected from the parents, called "fathers of the world," as our sages said (*Tana de Bei Eliyahu Rabah*, Chapter 25), "When will my deeds reach the deeds of my fathers?"

That is, where there is connection with the fathers, when one knows the good deeds of the fathers, it can be said that he is asking, "When will my deeds reach the deeds of my fathers?" That is, that he, too, will have the ability to do good deeds like the fathers. But because of the sin—as it is said, "For our sins we have been exiled from our land"—we have been placed in prison, completely disconnected from the fathers, meaning we do not know that we had fathers who were adhered to the Creator and we have no idea that it also pertains to us to say of every spiritual matter that we want to do things by which we can adhere to the Creator.

It follows that the people who were sentenced to life imprisonment do not see light their whole lives and accept their situation. They accustom themselves to enjoy only what the warden thinks he should give them for nourishment, and habit causes them to forget what they once had—a life outside the prison, where they enjoyed the life they chose for themselves and did not have to accept the nourishments according to the terms of the prison. However, they have forgotten everything.

The lesson is that one should be happy that the warden loves him and has therefore given him some freedom each day to walk out of jail and enjoy what innocent people enjoy, meaning as though he had never sinned against the King. He walks home and partakes with everyone in his family and the rest of his friends and loved ones, but then he must go back to jail.

This happens every day. That is, when a desire comes to a person to enter the synagogue and pray, and learn a little and feel a little that there is spiritual life, that he finally believes it, meaning that he has faith, it is called "diminutive feeling about all the things in

Kedusha," that he receives illumination from afar. That is, although he is still far from equivalence of form, for because he sinned with self-love, called "disparity of form," he was sentenced to life in prison. Jail is where there is no spiritual life but a place for the wicked who have sinned against the King.

But he was favored by the warden, who gives him a thought and desire to enjoy the life of humans, as in, "You are called 'man,' and the nations of the world are not called 'man,'" since they enjoy man's food, called a "spiritual life," when they are connected to the King of Kings, meaning that they temporarily feel that they are speaking to the King.

When a person pictures that he is favored by the warden, who has given him a temporary leave, although he knows that later he will have a descent and will have to return to prison, even while in prison he can still be happy because he knows from past experience that there are ups and downs. Hence, even when he is returned to prison he knows that sometimes he is favored by the warden who will give him another temporary leave, and in that short while he will be able to see and plead with friends to set him free completely.

This means that even during a descent he sometimes gets thoughts that he is already used to being ejected from the thoughts and desires of sinners who are immersed in self-love. Later, when he receives a call from above, for so he believes, the thoughts and desires he has during the descent, he feels that it is impossible that he will ever be able to come out of self-love, for he sees the body's resistance. Each time the resistance takes on different forms, and each argument is different from the other, but they are all the same in making him see that it is difficult and that there is no such thing in reality that a person can come out of them.

Still, he sees that when an awakening from above comes to him, he forgets all their arguments and they all burn as though they never existed. Now he wants only one thing—to annul before the Creator, and now he feels pleasure specifically in this.

Because of this, when one has some grip in spirituality, even if it is the smallest of the small, he can already feel happy and complete, for two reasons: 1) He has been given a leave. He enjoys being temporarily out of prison, meaning out of Torah and *Mitzvot*. 2) He enjoys seeing that everyone else is in prison. He looks at them with pity and sometimes wants to ask for mercy for them, that the Creator will permit them to come out of prison.

Now we can understand that during the *Ibur*, when his force of depiction is only *Katnut*, when he can barely observe Torah and *Mitzvot* with any intention, he must believe that it is very important that the Creator has given him a place to depart from the rest of the people in the world, who have no connection to Judaism, and whose aspirations are clothed only in beastly pleasures, meaning they settle for that which nourishes and sustains beasts. As for spirituality, they pride themselves in not being stupid like the religious, who say that there is a matter of spiritual life. Instead, they have a strong and clear sense that they are right. They tell themselves, "We are the smartest in the generation in that we don't believe in spirituality, and our life's purpose is only corporeal life."

They know for certain that there is no spirituality in the world, to such an extent that they want to make the religious also know that common sense dictates that there is nothing in the world but corporeal life, just like animals. There are even bigger smart alecks who—because they live like animals—have come to the conclusion that we should not eat animals because the speaking does not have a higher purpose than an animal, so why should we eat them if we are all on the same degree and have the same purpose?

It follows that on the one hand, one should appreciate the thought and desire to do simple things without any understanding or intellect, but completely above reason, and believe that even the small desire to observe Torah and *Mitzvot* was also given to him by the Creator as He favors him. However, he does not know what merit he has over other people whom the Creator has left in the corporeal life while picking him out from among all the people, as in the prison allegory. This matter should bring him joy and wholeness, and because he feels wholeness he can thank the Creator for it. It is as Baal HaSulam said, "To the extent that a person thanks the Creator for having brought him a little closer, to that extent he always receives help from above."

We can interpret that the reason is that if a person understands that he must thank the Creator, it does not mean that the Creator should thank him like flesh and blood. Rather, the question is the measure to which he understands that he must thank Him. At that time he begins to think how much gratitude I should give Him.

There is a rule that to the extent of giving is the extent of the gratitude. For example, if someone helps another person, who did not have a job so as to make a living, and he went and toiled for him and found him a job, naturally, he feels deep gratitude.

But if, for example, a person commits a crime against the government and the judge sentences him to twenty years in prison, and he must leave his family, and he already has sons and daughters that he should marry, and he just started a business, meaning started a company with one hundred workers, but in the meantime he only has fifty workers, and now according to the crime for which he was caught he must be incarcerated for twenty years, he is worried about the outcome of his plans and about his family while he is separated from the world. He says that now he would prefer to die than to live in prison and worry about everything.

And along comes a man who gives him tips by which he is acquitted from all the charges and he is freed. Then the person certainly begins to think what he can give to this man who saved his life. Undoubtedly, now this man has but one concern: "With what can I show this man my heart, that my every bone thanks and praises him." It is as it is written, "All my bones shall say" songs and praises for this man.

It follows that by having to thank him he begins to contemplate the measure of salvation he has given him so as to know what kind of gratitude he should give him. Because of it, when a person thanks the Creator it depends on the extent to which he appreciates the importance of the Creator delivering him from prison for one moment to breathe some more of the air of the world of *Kedusha*.

It therefore follows that a person suffers a descent because he did not appreciate drawing near to the Creator, and not appreciating it caused its loss. It is as our sages said, "Who is a fool? He who loses what he is given." This means that he does not have the intellect to appreciate the measure of nearing Torah and *Mitzvot*, meaning that a person should believe that even the smallest thing in Torah and *Mitzvot* is also very important although he still does not feel its importance.

It follows that faith is in things that man still cannot feel or attain. At that time he must believe in the sages, what our sages told us to believe that it is so, meaning as our sages told us and not as we feel. It is so because our feelings are still not developed in us so as to feel those feelings that extend when knowing we are speaking to the King. This is simple: If one knows that he is speaking to the King, he does not need to prepare himself to feel the importance of the King for it is a natural thing and he does not need to work on it needlessly.

Accordingly, what is the reason that a person is not excited while saying words of gratitude and words of Torah when he believes it is the Torah of the Creator? The reason is that his faith is still not complete faith, meaning that his faith will be as clear knowledge, but rather that his faith is still deficient.

Instead, he must work on believing that he is speaking to an important King, and feeling is something that comes without work, since feeling is only a result of something new that inspires a person. It follows that the main work is the work on faith, to believe that He is a great King.

This is the matter presented in several places in the holy *Zohar*, that one should pray over the exile of the *Shechina* [Divinity], or in other words, the "*Shechina* in exile" or "*Shechina* in the dust." That is, we do not have the importance of the one to whom we pray or speak, or thank for both pleasures and *Mitzvot*. Also, we do not contemplate the value of whose *Mitzvot* we are keeping. All this is called "*Shechina* in exile."

Naturally, we cannot have a feeling for observing Torah and *Mitzvot* because there is a rule that a person is not inspired by something small, to an extent that some excitement will come to him.

It therefore follows that one should serve the Creator with gladness, meaning that in whatever state he is, even if he is in a lowly state and feels completely lifeless while engaging in Torah and *Mitzvot*, he should picture to himself that now he is observing the *Mitzva* [singular of *Mitzvot*] of faith above reason. That is, although the body shows him his lowliness, he can still strengthen himself and say, "My observing Torah and *Mitzvot* without any intention is very important" because in fact, he is observing everything in practice, but lacks the aim. That is, if he also had the right intention, the body would be satisfied and he would feel like a complete human being.

But now the body cannot enjoy Torah and *Mitzvot*, so all that is missing here is the pleasure of the body. But since he wants to work for the Creator, it follows that specifically now, when the body has no pleasure, he can work more in order to bestow. If he believes above reason that this is so, this overcoming is called "awakening from below." Afterwards he must receive sustenance because now he really is adhered to the Creator and wants to serve the Creator with nothing in return.

However, if he cannot go above reason then two officers come to him and put him in prison along with all the sinners against the King. Those two officers are "mind" and "heart." At that time he is sentenced to however long he is sentenced, and then he is given a short leave to examine his behavior. This continues until he is pitied from above and is freed from the prison.

It follows that we need two things: the first is the depicting force, which is *Katnut*, and the second is the detaining force to prevent abortion, meaning not to spoil the *Ibur*. We need the depicting force because there is a rule that there is no light without a *Kli*, meaning no filling without a lack, so if there is no *Katnut*, there will never be *Gadlut*.

However, we need strength to hold on while feeling deficient because deficiency means that it pains him that he is still incomplete. It is known that it is hard to tolerate suffering. If he sees no end to the suffering, he escapes the campaign. It follows that we must give him wholeness so he can hold on and not escape the war of the inclination. However, he must not be given a lie, meaning to deceive himself and say that he is whole, since it is written, "He who speaks falsehood shall not be established before Me."

Therefore, when we say to a person, "You see that everyone is incarcerated," as in the above allegory, "and forget that they even have parents and friends," who are people who engage in Torah and *Mitzvot* and who are friends with their souls. They forget everything and think that all that there is in the world are incarcerated people and a warden who controls them, meaning that they are under the judgment of the evil inclination, and they consider one who goes against their view as insane, meaning that they leave the corporeal life of enjoying the prison and seeks something above reason, meaning to believe that there is greater pleasure than the joys of corporeal life.

But he calculates to himself that he is very privileged that he has been favored by the Creator and that He has delivered him even momentarily from the corporeal life to breathe some air of *Kedusha*. He should be so happy when he considers them and himself. Certainly, this wholeness is considered true wholeness because in corporeality we [see] that a temporary leave, from the above allegory of the prison, gives so much joy to a person when he sees that he has been favored by the warden and all the prisoners have not been privileged with it.

Besides this wholeness being true, a person must make great efforts to appreciate it, since this work lifts the importance of the work by appreciating a small service in spirituality. By this we are later rewarded with enhancing the importance to a point where one can say that he has no way to appreciate the importance of serving the King. This is called *Ibur*.

Ibur means that the awakening comes from the upper one. But during the preparation, which is before one is rewarded admission into the King's palace, where *Ibur* is when he is rewarded with *NRNHY de Nefesh*, there are many ups and down. However, it all enters the *Ibur* since everything comes from the awakening of the upper one.

From the perspective of the preparation, *Yenika* means that he awakens by himself and wants to suckle something from *Kedusha* through authors and books, so he can revive the spirit with spiritual life. For this reason, when he engages in Torah and *Mitzvot* he craves to elicit from them the light of Torah that reforms him, as our sages said, "I have created the evil inclination; I have created the Torah as a spice."

However, in order to elicit the light of Torah we must have faith, as it is written in the "Introduction to the Book of Zohar." The reason is that he believes in the Creator and in His Torah and wants to adhere to Him, but sees that he cannot due to the evil in him, which is the will to receive, and this form causes him to be removed from the Creator. For this reason, his faith is also inconsistent, as it is written in the *Sulam* [commentary on *The Zohar*], that faith cannot be in a person permanently because as long as one does not have fear—which is regarded as constantly fearing that he might not be able to aim to bestow but will crave to receive in order to receive, which is disparity of form—the light of faith cannot be in him permanently.

It therefore follows that there cannot be permanent faith if he has no *Dvekut* [adhesion], called "equivalence of form." But how does one take this force so he can overcome his nature, which is only in oppositeness of form? It was said about this, "One should always engage in Torah and *Mitzvot*, even *Lo Lishma* [not for Her sake], and from *Lo Lishma* he comes to *Lishma* [for Her sake] because the light in it reforms him" (*Pesachim*, 50). It follows that the light in the Torah is what reforms him, but this was said specifically when he wants the light in the Torah in order to reform him, meaning to aim all his actions to bestow upon his Maker.

Then, by reforming him, which means that he has *Dvekut*, then he will be rewarded with permanent faith. But a person who is not concerned with having only partial faith, and learns Torah only where he can derive pleasure that will enter the vessels of reception, and is not concerned with vessels of bestowal, he has no need for the light of Torah to give him the remedy of reforming him. That is, to give him the strength to correct his works so they are only to bestow contentment upon his Maker, which is called *Dvekut*, and by which he will be rewarded with permanent faith.

This is not so if he does not need permanent faith and does not need *Dvekut*, and he expects the light because the light in the Torah comes from the upper one and there is delight and pleasure in this light. It follows that he craves the light not in order to help him turn his vessels of reception into vessels of bestowal. Rather, he wants the light to do the opposite of what it is meant to do.

The purpose of the light is to reform him. "Good" is as it is written, "My heart overflows with a good thing; I say, 'My work is for the King'" (Psalms, 45). That is, "good" means that which awards man with vessels of bestowal. But he wants the light in order to enjoy it, meaning that this light will increase his vessels of reception. This is the exact opposite of what the light should give. He wants to receive from it, and therefore the light will not come to him.

In the "Introduction to the Study of the Ten Sefirot" (item 15), he writes that one should not expect the engagement in Torah and *Mitzvot Lo Lishma* to bring him to *Lishma*, unless he knows in his heart that he has been rewarded with faith in the Creator and His Torah properly, for then the light in it reforms him and he will be rewarded with the day of the Lord, which is all light, since the *Kedusha* of faith purifies man's eyes so they enjoy His light until the light in the Torah reforms him. Likewise, the eyes of the faithless are blinded toward the light of the Creator.

We should interpret what he says, that the light of faith appears to those who have faith. According to what we explained, those who have been rewarded with permanent faith already have abundance.

However, it is as Baal HaSulam said about what is written, "Will bring wisdom to the wise." People ask, "It should have said, 'Will bring wisdom to the fools.'" And he said that since there is no light without a *Kli* [vessel], wisdom cannot be given to the fools, since they have no need. Accordingly, what does "Will give wisdom to the wise" mean? It is for one who has a desire to be wise, who has a *Kli*. He can receive the filling, since there is no filling without a lack.

We should therefore interpret in this way regarding matters of faith, as well. That is, one who has a need for faith because he sees that he has only partial faith, as said above (In the "Introduction," item 14)—and craves to have complete faith—is called "faithful." It means that he has a desire and need for the light of faith. Those people who seek faith, to them the light of Torah appears. This is why it is written that the *Kedusha* of faith purifies man's eyes so they enjoy His light until the light in the Torah reforms him.

It therefore follows that *Ibur* means the awakening from above that a person receives. As the corporeal *Ibur* depends on the parents, here, too, it is upon the calling that comes from above, when one is called upon to repent, and he begins to think other thoughts. Then, all the desires he had prior to the herald he had received from above are burned and do not merit a name.

Conversely, *Yenika* means that he begins to search by himself which *Yenika* [nursing] he will receive from books or authors. He wants to suckle the light of Torah from them in order to have the ability to cling to the Creator and be rewarded with complete faith.

The Reason for Straightening the Legs and Covering the Head During the Prayer

Article No. 32, Tav-Shin-Mem-Vav, 1985-86

It is written in *The Zohar* (*Vaetchanan*, item 10): "Come and see, he who stands during the prayer should straighten his legs and cover his head as one who is standing before the King, and he should cover his eyes so as not to look at the *Shechina* [divinity]." In *The Zohar* (*Vaetchanan*, item 11) he asks, "You say, 'One who is looking at the *Shechina* while he is praying.' But how can he look at the *Shechina*? He replies, 'It is to verify that the *Shechina* is standing in front of him during his prayer. This is why he must not open his eyes.'"

We should understand what the matter of straightening the legs implies, for it seems to be a condition in the prayer, meaning it implies an important issue, so what is it? We should also understand why we must cover the head during the prayer. It cannot be said that it means we must cover the head with the *Talit* [prayer shawl] during the prayer, for this pertains only to the morning prayer. But in the afternoon and evening prayers, which we pray without a *Talit*, how can we speak of covering the head? So what does it imply?

Also, what does it mean to cover the eyes? We cover our eyes when we read the Shema reading, but here he says that during the prayer we should also cover our eyes, so we should know what these words imply. We should also understand the reply of the holy *Zohar* to the question, "How can he look at the *Shechina*?"

He explains that it is to verify that the *Shechina* is standing in front of him during his prayer. But the answer is unclear: What is the connection between closing the eyes and knowing that the *Shechina* is standing in front of him? To understand the above we must return to the whole matter of the work of creation—what it is for and what is the degree that Creation should achieve?

It is known that the purpose of creation was to do good to His creations. To this comes the famous question, "Why then are the delight and pleasure not evident to each and every one of the creatures? Rather, we see the opposite: the whole world is suffering and tormented before they obtain some delight and pleasure. For the most part, when a person introspects, he says what our sages said, "It would have been better not to be born than to be born" (*Iruvin*, 13). In their words, "It would be preferable for man not to be born than to be born."

It is known that the answer is that in order not to have shame, called "bread of shame," we were given a correction called "equivalence of form." This means that every delight and pleasure that one receives should be with the intention to bestow. In order to be able to accustom himself to receive pleasures in order to bestow there had to be a *Tzimtzum* [restriction] and concealment, so we would not see the great pleasures dressed in Torah and *Mitzvot* [commandments] right away.

We can learn the order of the work in order to bestow in corporeal matters, where there are only small pleasures, which the holy *Zohar* calls "thin light," meaning "very faint light." That is, holy sparks fell into the *Klipot* [shells/peels] so they will exist. On that light, which is found in corporeal pleasures, we can learn how to receive them in order to bestow because on smaller pleasures it is easier to accustom ourselves to receive them only in order to bestow. That is, it is easier to say, "If I cannot aim to bestow I give them up and do not want to receive these pleasures because by them I become separated from the Creator."

It is known that He works only to bestow, and the lower one wants specifically to receive. Thus, there is no equivalence of form here. For this reason, meaning, since he wants to adhere to the Creator, the act of reception detaches him from feeling the Creator due to the *Tzimtzum* and concealment that took place so he could accustom himself to be able to do things and direct them to bestow. But if the Providence of the Creator were revealed, the delight and pleasure would be revealed and man would not be able to overcome his vessels of reception.

By this we will understand what our sages said, that during the prayer a man must straighten his legs. *Raglaim* [legs] comes from the word *Meraglim* [spies]. That is, the argument of the spies comes to a person. They saw that it was not worthwhile to commence the work to reach the holy land, which is the land of Israel, for two reasons: 1) What would the will to receive gain if he walked on the path that reaches only the King? That is, he would toil with his work that he is doing for the Creator and the will to receive will not benefit, but lose, and the desire to bestow will gain. But what will the will to receive—which is the heart of the created being—have? 2) Even if we say that it is worthwhile to serve the King, that it brings man great pleasure, not every person is fit for this. This must require special stipulations, which are specifically for people born with great talents and courage, who can overcome all the obstacles found when wanting to approach *Kedusha* [holiness/sanctity].

Rather, it is enough for us to remain on the same level as the whole of Israel. Why should we seek higher degrees than the general public? I don't need to be an exception and I am content with simply keeping Torah and *Mitzvot*, without any intentions. This work will certainly be easier because it is closer to our vessels of reception.

Why should I look at a handful of people saying that the most important is to work for the Creator? Surely, the whole public is working for the Creator, so I will be as one of them. This is called "spies."

It was said that during the prayer he must straighten his legs. This means that he should say that what the spies are showing him, this way—that only a handful of people say that we must walk only in this path—that only this path is the truth, and not the other ways, although they are paths of truth.

This is as our sages said, "One should always engage in Torah and *Mitzvot Lo Lishma* [not for Her sake], and from *Lo Lishma* he will come to *Lishma* [for Her sake]." What our sages said must be true, but this path of trying to walk on the path that leads directly for the Creator is called "the complete truth." This means that he should reply to the spies telling him that what he was doing was wrong, "Now I am going to ask the Creator to help me walk on my way, which I have chosen now, and say that only this is an upright way."

This is the meaning of having to straighten the legs during the prayer. It follows that the prayer that he is going to pray to the Creator is for a deficiency, for if he has no deficiency, he has nothing for which to ask and pray. And what is my deficiency? It is that I see that the spies won't leave me alone, and I don't want to walk in their ways. However, I see that all my thoughts and desires are only for my own benefit, and I see that I cannot do anything for the Creator.

Thus, all I need now, and for which I should ask the Creator, is that He will give me a *Kli* [vessel], called "desire." That is, I am deficient of deficiency, meaning a desire to want to serve the King, and that this will be my every wish and aspiration, and not to worry about things that do not concern serving the Creator.

However, the real reason why a person does not crave to serve the King is not that he does not want to serve the King. Rather,

The Reason for Straightening the Legs and Covering the Head During the Prayer

Baal HaSulam said that the reason is that he does not believe that he is standing before the King. But when he feels that he is standing before the King, his choice becomes annulled and he annuls before the King as a candle before a torch.

It therefore follows that the main thing on which one should work in his labor is to be rewarded with faith, meaning to feel that the Creator exists, as our sages said (*Pirkey Avot*), "The eye sees and the ear hears," since there is concealment over us. But before we exit self-love, we are still under the *Tzimtzum* that was done, so that the place of reception will be dark, without light, which is called "a space vacant of upper light."

For this reason, he asks the Creator to open his eyes so he will feel that he is standing in front of the Creator. He needs this not because he wants to enjoy standing in front of the Creator. Rather, he wants to bestow upon the Creator and cannot do anything because he still does not feel the importance of the Creator. Instead, to him, the *Shechina* is in exile. That is, when it occurs to him to do something for the Creator and not think of his own benefit, the world grows dark on him. It seems to him that now he has passed away from the world and died.

That is, he begins to feel that his entire existence is annulled and he no longer merits a name. For this reason, right at the beginning of his entrance into that state he wants to escape it because at that time he feels the unpleasantness that this situation is causing him, and he cannot continue walking on this path. He understands that if he begins to walk on the path of "Only for the Creator," he should feel life and happiness. But suddenly he sees the opposite.

This brings up the question, "Why is this so?" The answer is that in this state, when he feels this way, he can feel the meaning of "*Shechina* in the dust." That is, he feels that he has fallen so low that he has really stooped to the ground. Afterwards, when he knows what is "*Shechina* in the dust," he can pray to the Creator and do good deeds so the Creator will raise the *Shechina* from the dust.

That is, where he felt that assuming the burden of the kingdom of heaven—meaning to work only for the Creator and not for himself—tastes like dust, he asks the Creator to remove His concealment from him so he will be rewarded with seeing that the *Shechina* is called the "land of the living." That is, precisely by wanting to do everything for the Creator and not for his own benefit, precisely from here one is rewarded with the real life. This is the meaning of the "land of the living," a land from which life springs to all. Conversely, the land of the *Sitra Achra* [other side] is called a "land that consumes its dwellers."

It is known that the matter of reception causes separation from the *Kedusha*. For this reason, "the wicked in their lives are called 'dead.'" Bestowal is called *Dvekut*, as it is written, "And you who cling to the Lord your God are alive every one of you this day." This means that a person wanting the Creator to open his eyes and to be rewarded with faith, meaning to feel His existence, does not mean that he craves the pleasure of feeling that he is standing before the King. Rather, he craves not to be wicked by not wanting to observe the commandment of loving the Creator. And although there cannot be love without pleasure, there is the matter that one wants it directly, and indirectly, something else is drawn.

For example, a person wants to love his children because he wants to enjoy it. Although it cannot be said that he loves the matter and does not feel pleasure about it, for where one feels suffering we cannot speak of love. Only sometimes we say that we are happy about suffering, since by this we might gain something. It is like a person going through surgery in a hospital. He pays the doctor a lot of money, and he does not say that he loves it, but he is happy about it because by this he will gain something important—his life.

Therefore, we cannot say that he wants to love his children and work for them so as to enjoy. Rather, the fact that he wants to love is love that comes naturally and has nothing to do with pleasure. But his love for them gives him joy. It follows that the pleasure derived from love of the children is extended indirectly.

The Reason for Straightening the Legs and Covering the Head During the Prayer

It is the same when a person asks the Creator to bring him closer and give him the light of faith, to feel the existence of the Creator. Naturally, at that time he annuls before the Creator and certainly enjoys. However, this is not what he means. Rather, his intention is that he wants the Creator to bring him closer because he sees that he is wicked and cannot do anything, except for his own benefit. Thus, he truly wants to exit self-love.

It follows that his intention is to exit self-love, and not to receive greater pleasure. That is, since he does not enjoy corporeal pleasures all that much, to give more pleasure to his will to receive, this is his purpose, meaning that he wants his self-love will have more pleasure. Certainly not! On the contrary, he wants to exit self-love altogether.

But the reason that causes him to want to ask the Creator to take him out of self-love and give him the light of faith is only that he is Jewish and must observe Torah and *Mitzvot* because the Creator has commanded us to observe His will. But he sees that he has nothing to do with bestowing upon the Creator. Rather, all his concerns are as those of the gentiles, only self-love. This motivates him to go and ask for something—to be able to be a Jew and not a gentile who belongs to the nations of the world.

However, we should remember that it is impossible to feel the existence of the Creator without feeling pleasure. And yet, this is so when the pleasure comes to him indirectly, meaning when he does not intend it but that it comes to him by itself because it is natural that when we feel that we are standing before the King we feel the importance of the King, and to that extent we are filled with pleasure.

It therefore follows that it cannot be said that he is standing before the King and feels that he wants to annul before the King, and at the same time feel unpleasantness because he wants to annul. Therefore, when a person sees, if he begins to work in order to bestow and feels that by his annulling before the Creator he feels unpleasantness, he should say that this is not the form of the King, but that such a feeling came to him in order to know the meaning of "*Shechina* in exile" or "*Shechina* in the dust."

Then the time is ripe for praying to the Creator to bring him closer, since otherwise he sees that there is no way that he will be able to enter *Kedusha* by himself, since he feels that all the body's organs resist serving the King and annulling his existence, so all his aspirations will be only to serve the King. At that time he is called "deficient," when there is no one in the world who can help him but the Creator Himself.

However, regarding the deficiency, we should make several discernments in order to be fit for fulfillment when praying to the Creator to help him:

1) He has what he needs, but he does not feel its absence. For example, a man has a family of six, and his friends have a family as big as his and live in three rooms, while he lives in an apartment with two rooms. He is content with little and does not feel deficient of another room. Naturally, when he does not feel deficient he does not make efforts to obtain another room. It follows that with such a deficiency we cannot speak of prayer, therefore granting the prayer is irrelevant because "there is no light without a *Kli*, since there is no filling without a lack."

2) He feels its deficiency and begins to try to obtain it. However, after some time of making efforts to satisfy his need he sees that he cannot obtain it so easily and despairs. He begins to tell himself that he does not have to be among the prominent people in the public and can settle for what he has. By man's nature, the laziness helps him justify his lack of effort to a great extent. Hence, now he is restful and carefree because now he does not want anything.

However, since before he despaired he made great efforts to obtain what he wanted, thoughts of the deficiencies, the filling he had hoped to achieve, keep coming to him. And as much as he had exerted to obtain them, it is as though the filling itself is awakening him now to begin the work anew.

The Reason for Straightening the Legs and Covering the Head During the Prayer

At that time a person comes to a state where he asks the Creator to remove all the thoughts that awaken him to feel deficient and work on them. Instead, he prays that no lack will come into his mind. All he wants now, and if he attains this it will be a state he calls, "good," is not to feel any lack.

It therefore follows that the filling he hopes for is not to have a sense of deficiency. This is the entire filling for which he hopes. Now he wants to enjoy the absence of feeling deficiencies, and does not expect the filling of the deficiencies. Rather, the whole satisfaction is in the absence of the feeling of lack. This is what he wants now, that this will be the best state in his life.

This means that should his friend come and ask him, "Do you need anything? I will try to grant you your wish," he will reply to him, "Believe me that now I am in a state where I do not need anything. Now all I want is rest, not to worry about anything. I am embarrassed to tell you since you came to me and you probably came in order to delight me, but to tell you the truth, even you are interrupting my rest by having to try to think what to speak to you about. So I'll tell you the truth, go in peace and do me a favor, tell all our friends not to come visit me if they see that I am not around you, since the only good I feel in my life is rest from all the troubles."

Certainly, when a person prays that the Creator will satisfy such a deficiency he cannot receive satisfaction of such a prayer, which is built on the foundation of despair and idleness. He wants the Creator to help him be lazy, and such a deficiency is not about to be filled because such fillings will not build the world. All the prayers must be for construction, and not the other way around. We must pray for the correction of the world, and idleness will not yield any construction.

3) He feels his deficiency and all the thoughts of idleness and despair cannot satisfy his lack. For this reason he tries to seek advice on how to obtain what he wants. It follows that he is praying to the Creator for the filling of his deficiency because he wants the

construction of the world. He sees that in the state he is in, he is also constructing, but all the buildings he is building are like little children playing and building toy houses then dismantling them, only in order to build once more. It is the building they enjoy.

Likewise, he is looking at the corporeal life. And as the games of the children who are building will not build the world, corporeal pleasures will not be the construction of the world, which must have been created for a purpose and not for little children. So how can he agree to remain among little children?

And although the children laugh at him that he does not want to play with them and do not understand him, thinking that he probably does not have a sense for life and does not know that we can enjoy life, but he is not like everyone else, but seemingly wants to retire from the world and go to the desert to live like the desert animals.

And yet, he cannot give them any answers since he has no common language with them. In any case, he is suffering due to his lack—that he wants to be rewarded with spiritual life. It follows that only in the third discernment of a deficiency can we say that his prayer is called "a prayer," since he demands filling, so he can correct the world, so as to have the ability to receive the purpose of creation, which is to do good to His creations. He believes that all the concealment and restriction that exist in the world is because we haven't the proper tools fit for the abundance of Godliness, which is a vessel of bestowal.

For this reason, he asks the Creator to give him vessels of bestowal. We can obtain this by feeling the greatness and importance of the King. But when the *Shechina* is in exile and when the work tastes like dust, how can we continue this work? This is why a prayer such as this is accepted.

Now we can interpret the words of the holy *Zohar*, when we asked about the intention of saying that we must cover the head and close our eyes as though standing before the King. It is known that the head is called "man's mind." Likewise, the eyes are regarded as the

The Reason for Straightening the Legs and Covering the Head During the Prayer

mind, as it is written, "The eyes of the congregation," which means the elders of the congregation.

Covering and closing mean not looking at what the mind tells him. This means that when a person stands in the prayer, he must believe that he is standing before the King. Although he does not feel the King, he should pray that the Creator will give him the power of faith to feel that he is standing in front of the King. That is, he wants the power of faith that will be just like knowing, meaning that the body will be impressed by the faith that he believes, as though he is seeing the King and is impressed with the King. This is the faith for which he prays.

This is why he says that it is forbidden to open the eyes during the prayer because it is forbidden to look at the *Shechina*. The holy *Zohar* asks, "How can he look at the *Shechina*?" He replies that it is to verify that the *Shechina* is standing in front of him during his prayer, which is why he is forbidden to open his eyes.

We asked, "What is the answer?" The thing is that the faith that a person believes should be exactly as if he is seeing the *Shechina*. Otherwise, if his faith has not reached this level, it is not regarded as real faith. This is the kind of faith for which one should pray, that the faith will work in him as though he is seeing everything with his eyes.

What Are Commandments that a Person Tramples with His Feet

Article No. 33, Tav-Shin-Mem-Vav, 1985-86

It is written in the portion, *Ekev* [Because]: "And it shall come to pass that because you listen ... the Lord your God will keep with you the covenant and the mercy that He has sworn to your fathers." RASHI interprets "And it shall come to pass that because you listen": "If you keep the light *Mitzvot* [commandments] that a person tramples with his feet. You will listen and the Lord will keep, etc., will keep His promise."

We should understand the Creator's stipulation: "If you keep the light *Mitzvot*, I will keep the promises I have given to the fathers. Otherwise I cannot keep them." Surely, the conditions that the Creator wants are not similar to a flesh and blood king, who presents stipulations in favor of the giver. Surely, here they are in favor of the creatures, meaning that otherwise they cannot receive what he has promised. Therefore, we should understand the condition of light *Mitzvot*.

To understand the condition we must first understand the promise that the Creator promised the fathers. Clearly, this does not pertain to corporeality, for the promise was certainly for the Creator to give the people of Israel that they will be rewarded with the purpose of creation, called "doing good to His creations," which is that the souls will obtain the root of their souls, regarded as the five parts of the soul, called *NRNHY*.

In order for the souls to obtain what has been prepared for them to receive, and in order not to feel the bread of shame while receiving the delight and pleasure, we were given the work called "work of bestowal." This means that first, one must accustom himself in this work. In order to have room for choice, meaning to be able to choose the intention with which he observes Torah and *Mitzvot*, there had to be a *Tzimtzum* [restriction] and concealment, for then there is room for choice.

However, if the pleasure were revealed then he would have to observe Torah and *Mitzvot* in order to receive. He would do everything to satisfy his self-love because it cannot be said that he does everything in order to bestow, since when there is disclosure of light, the pleasure is greater than all the corporeal pleasures.

In corporeality we see a rule: The smaller the pleasure—in order to relinquish the pleasure—the less work there is. Also, it cannot be said that the pleasure he receives is with the intention only to bestow if he cannot relinquish it. That is, he must be certain that if he cannot aim to bestow he will be willing to give up the pleasure. Therefore, the smaller the pleasure the easier it is to give it up.

This is why we were given the concealment on the taste of Torah and *Mitzvot* and were given a taste for corporeal pleasures. We must believe in the words of the holy *Zohar* that every delight and pleasure that exists in corporeal things is only a thin light, meaning a very faint light compared to the light of the pleasure that is dressed in

Torah and *Mitzvot*. For this reason, there is a reality where one exercises on corporeal pleasures and afterwards he can come out of the *Tzimtzum* and concealment to some extent, for he can already choose and say that he is receiving this delight and pleasure only because he wants to bestow.

Afterwards, if he passes the trial and receives the small discernment he has attained in the work of the Creator, he is given a bigger degree on which to aim to bestow. Thus he goes from degree to degree until he attains all his NRNHY from the root of his soul. And the NRNHY that a person attains is the 613 ways of the Torah, which are the 613 *Mitzvot* in the Torah and the seven *Mitzvot* of our great sages, which, in *Gematria*, are 620 names that one can attain.

It is written in the book, *A Sage's Fruit: Letters of Baal HaSulam* (Letter no. 17): "It is written in *Tree of Life*, 'The worlds were created only to disclose the names of the Creator.' Thus, you see that since the soul came down to clothe this filthy substance, it could no longer cleave to its root, to its own world, as it was in its root before it came to this world. Rather, it must increase its stature 620 times more than how it previously was in the root. This is the meaning of the entire perfection, the entire NRNHY up to *Yechida*, for which *Yechida* is called *Keter*, implying the number 620."

Now we can see what is the promise that the Creator has promised to the fathers, and how it is possible to attain such wholeness. That question is asked from two sides:

1) The need for this great wholeness. We know that there is no light without a *Kli* [vessel], meaning no filling without a lack. This brings up the question, "How can we have this feeling that we need to obtain the NRNHY?" According to what we explained, all the corporeal pleasures that the whole world is chasing are nothing more than a tiny spark compared to the pleasure in *Kedusha* [sanctity], and when one is rewarded with having even a tiny illumination of *Kedusha* he will feel great satisfaction with it. So who will tell him that he is still deficient to the point that he must obtain the light of

Yechida, or he will feel that he has not yet achieved wholeness? Who will notify this to him?

2) How can one overcome such great pleasures and say that if he cannot aim the reception of these pleasures to the Creator then he gives up the pleasures? From where will he find such strength? After all, we see that even in corporeal pleasures, of which we said that they are but a thin light, sparks that have fallen into the *Klipot*, it is difficult to overcome them and say that we relinquish these pleasures if we cannot aim in order to bestow. And since concerning corporeal pleasures we see that they divide into great pleasures and small ones, it is all the more so in spirituality, where there are many degrees and discernments. So the question is from where will one take such great powers to overcome?

To understand the two above questions, 1) From where will he take the need for greatness, and 2) From where will he take the strength to give up the pleasures so he can be sure that the pleasures he is taking are only in order to bestow contentment upon his Maker, we should precede with the words of our sages (*Kidushin*, 30): "Rabbi Shimon Ben Levi said, 'Man's inclination overcomes him every day and seeks to put him to death,' as it was said, 'The wicked watches the righteous and seeks to put him to death, and if the Creator did not help him, he would not overcome it, as it is said, 'The Lord will not leave him in his hand.'"

We said that there are two questions here:

1) If man has been given the evil inclination, why is he unable to overcome it, but the Creator helps him? After all, choice means that a person can overcome, but here it implies that one has no choice to overcome, but only with the Creator's help. By himself, he cannot overcome it. This brings up the question, "Why did the Creator not give man the strength to overcome it?"

2) If man cannot overcome, why does it say that the Creator helps him? This means that a person must begin to overcome and see that he cannot overcome, and then the Creator helps him. Why does the Creator not help him as soon as the evil inclination comes

to him? What does it add to us that a person begins the work, since he cannot prevail anyway?

Therefore, why does the Creator have to wait until a person begins the work and then the help arrives. What is the benefit from losing time by the Creator waiting for a person to begin the work? Who gains from this loss of time? After all, the Creator should have given the help as soon as the evil inclination comes to a person, before a person begins the work. Why should He wait for a person to start the work and then the Creator will help him?

The thing is, as we said in the previous articles, that the *Tzimtzum* and restriction were in order to correct the world. Otherwise there would not be any possibility for man to be able to even begin the work of overcoming self-love, since by nature, the will to receive controls him, and this is the axis of Creation. What comes afterwards is only a correction, to correct the will to receive.

It turns out that the will to receive is the main thing, and the rest of the things that come later are only to correct it. It follows that the will to receive remains, but corrections are added to it. However, who is the one who undergoes all the corrections? It must be the will to receive.

It is known that even when we say that there is a degree that wants the desire to bestow, it still means that it does not use the will to receive that there is in the degree, but overcomes its desire and engages in the desire to bestow. It follows that the corrections that one should do are only on his vessels of reception, meaning to place on it the intention to bestow. And since the greater the pleasure, the more difficult it is to give it up and say that if he cannot aim to bestow he does not want to receive the pleasure, therefore two things must be corrected here:

1) *Aviut* [thickness], meaning will to receive, so it is not too big, namely that the lower one cannot overcome. For this reason, he must be given smaller lust. Afterwards, when seeing that he can overcome a small pleasure, he is given a greater pleasure. If we see

that he can overcome this pleasure, he is given a greater pleasure, etc., but how do we arrange it?

Therefore, man was given the work in faith above reason, which man slights, from the word "flippant" [in Hebrew]. This means that a person does not respect this work and considers the time he must serve with faith as a state of lowliness. That is, he understands that this work is for women and children, but not for intelligent and acute people.

Conversely, they must understand everything they see happening in the world, so it corresponds with their view and spirit. And when they need to do something but do not see that it is to their benefit, how can they agree to do things that are fit for fools, meaning people who do not scrutinize their thoughts or actions?

For this reason, they always try to avoid such matters. If they sometimes happen to work above reason because they have no choice, since reason is far away from them, they constantly wait for when they can be freed of such states. After all, it is unbecoming of us to live in the air, when the intellect does not understand everything he does as necessary for what he wants to achieve, and he wants to achieve a degree where he is among the prominent ones in the public.

When he looks at the public, how they engage in Torah and *Mitzvot* without any criticism, he says about them that they can observe everything enthusiastically and be meticulous with every detail because they have no sense of criticism. This is why they can be like that, with eyes closed. That is, if they had some brains they would be like me. That is, I observe Torah and *Mitzvot* but I see that this work is unworthy of me. However, I do not have a choice since otherwise I will have no connection with Judaism, and therefore for me everything will be forced and involuntary.

For this reason, as long as I forget that I am going above reason I can do everything like the rest of the people. But when I get the thoughts about the basis on which my Judaism is built, and I have to reply to my body that it is only as in, "The earth hangs on nothing,"

I cannot overcome and say that the foundation of Judaism is based precisely on faith above reason. And specifically now I can keep the commandment of faith, since now I see that I have no basis. But usually, a person falls and lies under the weight of these questions.

Indeed, this is the question of Pharaoh, King of Egypt, who said, "Who is the Lord that I should obey His voice?" For this reason a person says that the path of faith that the Creator has given us to work on, this way will never succeed. And if the Creator had only listened to me He would have let us work on the basis of knowledge, and not on faith. Certainly many people would join in keeping Torah and *Mitzvot*. But in this way, of faith, there are many people who even though they began this work, they escaped from the campaign.

Baal HaSulam said that the Creator chose that we should walk in the path of faith not because man is of inferior degree, so he cannot be guided except by the path of faith. Rather, this is the most successful way. This is why the Creator has chosen this way, so they will take upon themselves the order of their work, by which they will be able to achieve the goal called "doing good to His creations," so the creatures will receive delight and pleasure and will also be in complete *Dvekut*, meaning in equivalence with the Creator. And although the creatures do not understand it, this is the truth.

It therefore follows that although faith is a slight and lowly matter, and we interpreted that slight comes from flippancy, meaning that it is not appreciated, it is still the way by which we can succeed in achieving the goal.

By this we will understand what RASHI interpreted, "If you observe the light *Mitzvot* [commandments] that a person tramples with his feet, You will listen; about this." That is, he referred to faith, which a person tramples with his heels. You will listen about this and then you will have the *Kelim* [vessels/tools] to reach the goal.

This is what RASHI interpreted: "And keep; will keep his promise." This means that the condition He has set is not for the sake of the Creator, as is the way of flesh and blood, who set conditions in favor of the giver. But with the Creator, the condition to observe the light *Mitzvot* aim for man's sake, for precisely by this one can achieve wholeness and be rewarded with what has been prepared for him by the thought of creation.

Now we can explain what we asked:

1) Why does the Creator not help a person when the evil inclination overcomes him, but waits until a person begins the work to overcome, and then helps him, as our sages said, "if the Creator does not help him"? It is akin to a person carrying a heavy load that he does not have the strength to carry, so he asks for help and people come and help him. But when he does not ask for help, no one comes to help him. This can be said between man and man. But why should the Creator wait for a person to begin the work and cry out to the Creator to help him when the Creator knows that he cannot overcome the evil inclination by himself, since the Creator did not give him the strength for it?

2) What is the reason that the Creator did not give him the strength to overcome by himself, but seemingly told him, "I have given you the choice to overcome the evil inclination"? We should say that the Creator did give him the strength to overcome the evil, and at the same time we say that without the Creator's help a person cannot overcome it. It follows that these two matters contradict one another.

We will understand these two questions with the two questions we asked:

1) When a person is rewarded with the smallest degree in spirituality, he feels in it greater pleasure than all the corporeal pleasures, as in the words of the ARI, that all the great pleasures we find in corporeal pleasures—which we see that the whole world is chasing these pleasures and receive through them satisfaction in their lives—all the pleasure in them extends from *Kedusha*, where through the breaking of the vessels and the sin of *Adam HaRishon* with the tree of knowledge, holy sparks fell into the *Klipot* [shells/

peels]. The holy *Zohar* calls this light, "thin light," which descended in order to sustain the *Klipot*. All the corporeal pleasures extend from this, and the smallest degree in spirituality, which is *Kedusha*, where the essence of the light is found, he is certain to derive satisfaction from this and will have no need for *Gadlut* [greatness/adulthood]. Thus, who will tell him that he needs *Gadlut*?

2) From where will he take such great powers that he will be able to receive the great pleasures in order to bestow, or else he will be willing to relinquish them?

It follows that since there is no light without a *Kli*, meaning no filling without a deficiency, for this reason a person must begin the work. When he wants to overcome the evil inclination but cannot, he becomes deficient. When he sees that he cannot overcome he asks the Creator for help. At that time the Creator can give the filling because he already has a *Kli* to receive the filling.

The reason that the Creator did not give him the strength to overcome by himself is that when a person has some filling, he settles for what he has. Then a person has no need to be rewarded with NRNHY of the soul by the Creator helping him, as it is written in the holy *Zohar*, "He who comes to purify is aided. And he asks, 'With what is he aided?' He replies, 'With a holy soul.' When he is rewarded he is given *Nefesh*. When he is rewarded more he is given *Ruach*."

It follows that receiving help from above causes him to need to extend his NRNHY. That is, each time he wants to overcome his evil but cannot, the Creator helps him with a holy soul. But if the person could overcome by himself, from where would he have a need to ask the Creator to give him a higher degree than the one he has?

But now that he is asking the Creator to help him, he is not asking for degrees. Rather, he is simply asking the Creator not to be under the control of the evil. It turns out that the reason why a person wants the Creator to help him have the strength to aim in order to bestow and not be in the domain of the *Sitra Achra* [other side], but that he wants to be in the domain of *Kedusha* [holiness/

sanctity], meaning that his only wish will be to bestow upon the Creator, and this is all he needs, and not any high degrees, but simply to serve the Creator and not himself, this is the force he asks of the Creator. When the Creator helps him, the holy *Zohar* says it with the help of a holy soul. Each help is through a soul that the Creator gives him. Therefore, by this he goes from degree to degree until he attains the completion of the soul, called *NRNHY*.

Now we understand what our sages said, "Man's inclination overcomes him every day." This brings up the question, "Why does he need to overcome the evil inclination every day if he has already received help from the Creator and has defeated it? Why does it need to come to a person once again? And for what purpose does it come each day?"

With the above we understand that since through the help he receives from the Creator, he receives a soul, then each overcoming, when a person wants to overcome and be purer, he thereby receives a soul. This is why these overcomings cause man to be able to attain the *NRNHY* of his soul.

And the second question, "From where will he take strength to overcome?" It is not by his own strength. Rather, this is the help that the Creator gives so he can overcome it. It follows that through one thing there is correction of two things.

Judges and Officers

Article No. 34, Tav-Shin-Mem-Vav, 1985-86

The writing says, "You shall place for yourself judges and officers in all your gates which the Lord your God is giving you." To understand the above according to the rule that the Torah is eternity and applies to all generations, we should interpret the above verse in our generation, too. For this reason, each word requires its own explanation: 1) What are "judges"? 2) What are "officers"? 3) "You shall place for yourself" is singular form. This means that each and every person must place judges and officers. Can it be that each person should do so? 4) "In all your gates." We need to understand how "gates" are related to our time. And also, what does "In all your gates" imply? It means that if there is a gate we should promptly try to place judges and officers there. 5) Especially, what does it imply that he says, "Which the Lord your God is giving you"? What does it imply? Is there anyone else besides the Creator who is giving to the people of Israel?

To understand the above, we first need to mention what we said in the previous articles: 1) The purpose of creation from the perspective of the Creator. 2) The purpose of our work in keeping Torah and *Mitzvot* [commandments], meaning to which degree we should reach by observing Torah and *Mitzvot*.

It is known that the purpose of creation is to do good to His creations, meaning that the creatures will receive from Him the delight and pleasure according to His ability, without any limitations. However, because He wanted His works to be complete, meaning that there will not be the bread of shame, there was a *Tzimtzum* [restriction] and concealment. This means that there is no disclosure of light in *Kelim* [vessels] that work in order to receive. Only once the *Kli* [vessel] called "will to receive" has been corrected to work in order to bestow, then according to his ability to aim to bestow, to that extent the abundance appears. Prior to this they see the opposite of disclosure—feeling only concealment.

It therefore follows that here, meaning after the *Tzimtzum* took place, the work of the lower ones begins. The goal should be that all our thoughts and actions will be with only one intention—to bestow.

However, this brings up the question, "How can there be such a thing?" That is, since man is born a wild ass, from where will he take the strength to be able to come of the nature in which he was created?

For this purpose, we were given work in observing Torah and *Mitzvot*. That is, man should aim while observing Torah and *Mitzvot*, that it will bring him the power to agree to turn all his passions and ambitions to be only about how and with what he might bestow contentment upon his Maker.

Before he began the work of bestowal he thought that this matter of observing Torah and *Mitzvot* will bring him success and blessing so he can delight his body, meaning that by observing Torah and *Mitzvot* the body will have this world and the next world. This was his foundation, on which he built a foundation for himself, for that foundation to be the reason compelling him to observe Torah and *Mitzvot* in all its details, and he had the power to overcome the laziness in his body and prevail in order to obtain the reward.

It is like people who work in corporeality in order to make a living. The body resists working in corporeality, too, since the body would prefer to rest, but the corporeal pay that he sees, which is to his body's benefit, gives him the strength to overcome. Likewise, when the reward for the work is reward for one's body, he has the strength to overcome all the obstacles on his way. Because the reward he hopes for is only for his own needs, the body does not object to it.

That is, although the body enjoys the rest, when it is told, "Give up your rest and you will have pleasure in a way that the pleasure you will receive through the work will be greater than the rest, or that the pleasure you will receive by giving up rest is more necessary than the pleasure you find in rest, since through these pleasures you will be able to exist in the world, otherwise you will be unable to exist." On all these matters the body has the strength to overcome and give up small pleasures in order to obtain greater reward than his work. That is, the reward pays for his concessions, which he demands of his body to make, in order to be happier than he is feeling now, before he has relinquished the pleasures.

But when the body is told, "Work in bestowal," meaning that by observing Torah and *Mitzvot* it will be rewarded with delighting the Creator, namely that a person is told, "Give up your self-love," what will be the reward? That the Creator will enjoy the work of observing Torah and *Mitzvot*. At that time, the body promptly comes and asks the argument of "who" and "what." That is, "What will I gain by the Creator enjoying my work? And how can you work without reward?" This is the "Who" argument," which does not want to work. The body says, "I am willing to work like everyone else, but not on these terms. That is, if I give up my self-love and do everything so the Creator will enjoy, what will be my gain from this work?"

When a person overcomes all the arguments of the body, and thinks that he already has the strength to overcome the body's nature, meaning that now he feels that he can focus his thoughts only in order to bestow, suddenly the body comes to him with new complaints: "It's fine that you want to work for the Creator and not the way everyone else works, in order to receive reward. However, it would be good if, since you have already exerted for a while, you would receive strength from above so you could walk in the way of bestowal. But as you see, you've given much work and didn't move one bit. So you can see for yourself that you cannot walk in this path. You are wasting your energy, working for nothing. Get off this path, escape the campaign."

If a person overcomes all these arguments of the body, the body comes and reveals to him new things, for which a person has no answer. By this it wants to detach him from his work. The body tells him: "It is known that when a person begins to learn some science, he advances each time. If he is talented he advances faster; and if he is less talented he advances slower. And when a person sees that he is not advancing at all in the science, he is told, 'This science is not for you. You need to learn some profession; you are unfit to learn sciences.' We see that this is customary and reasonable."

But here the body argues, "You see according to the efforts you have made in the work of bestowal, that not only did you not move one step ahead, it is to the contrary." That is, before he began the work of bestowal he was not so immersed in self-love. But now that he has made efforts to overcome self-love, he has received a greater desire and feels that now he is more immersed in self-love.

It follows that here, in this work, we see that we are going backwards and not forward. He sees this clearly and actually feels it. That is, previously, before he began to overcome self-love, he thought that this was quite easy to give up self-love in order to be rewarded with spirituality. He always thought, "How can I find a way that I can walk and by which to obtain some spirituality?" However, he never thought that he should worry about emerging from self-love, for this is something not advisable to think about. Rather, all the concerns were about finding the right way that leads to entering the King's palace and meriting the purpose for which man was created.

But now he has come to a state that he had never dreamed of, meaning that self-love would be a stumbling block interfering with reaching the truth. He always thought that he was willing to sacrifice himself in order to reach the truth, but now he sees that he went ten degrees backwards, meaning that he is unwilling to make any concessions on his self-love for the sake of *Kedusha* [holiness/sanctity].

When the body comes to him with such arguments, he "falls under his load." At that time he comes to a state of despair and idleness, and wants to escape the campaign, since now he sees that all the arguments of the body are true arguments.

But the truth is as we said many times. As Baal HaSulam said, there is the matter of advancing toward the truth. That is, before one begins the work of bestowal, he is far from the truth, meaning from feeling the measure of his evil. But later, when he has exerted in overcoming self-love, he advances toward the truth. That is, each time he sees more of how immersed he is in evil, from head to toe.

However, we should understand why we need all this. That is, why is it that before he began the work of bestowal he did not have such a great measure of feeling the evil, but once he has exerted to overcome, the evil has become more clearly sensed in him. Why was everything that should be revealed later not revealed right away, but rather appeared in stages, bit-by-bit?

The thing is that the order of overcoming is gradual. It is as one who practices weightlifting. He begins, say, with lifting 50 kilograms, and gradually adds because through exercises he can keep adding. It is the same in serving the Creator, and this is why we are not given a great taste for self-love in the beginning, since we will probably not be able to overcome. We are giving additional taste of pleasure in self-love according to our work. That is, to the extent that they see that he can overcome, he is given more taste of pleasure in self-love, so he will be able to overcome. By this we will understand what our sages said (*Sukkah*, 52), "One who is greater than his friend, his desire is greater than him."

This brings up the question, "Why is this so?" According to the above-mentioned, it is simple. This is also the order in corporeality: We move from light to heavy. Therefore, before one begins to work in overcoming, he is not given great force of self-love, which he will not be able to overcome because he has not begun the work of overcoming. Therefore, he does not feel a great taste in self-love.

But when he begins to overcome, he is given greater pleasure and importance in self-love so he will have what to overcome. When he overcomes a certain measure of self-love, he is given an even greater measure of importance of self-love. In this way he gradually accustoms himself to overcome pleasures so he can say that everything he is receiving is only in order to bestow.

It follows that self-love becomes to him increasingly difficult to overcome because each time, his will to receive is given more importance so he will have a place to work on overcoming. However, we must understand why we must be given from above more importance and more pleasure to make it difficult to overcome. Concerning this overcoming the corporeality, it would be better if we were not given great importance, but the importance we felt about self-love in the beginning of our work would be enough for us to overcome corporeality and we could promptly begin the spiritual work. But why should I do this work for free, overcoming self-love in corporeal matters? Although each time we have greater overcoming, why do we need to work in self-love, which concerns corporeality?

However, it is a great correction. It is known that the numerous pleasures we feel in corporeal pleasures are only a "thin light" compared to what is found in spiritual pleasures. It therefore follows that even after one has passed the test of overcoming corporeal pleasures, which he can correct only in order to bestow, this test is sufficient only on small pleasures that he can overcome and not receive on condition that he can aim in order to bestow. However, this is not so with great pleasures, and one cannot be given spiritual pleasures which he is bound to take in order to receive.

Therefore, first he must go through the work in corporeal pleasures. There, he is given greater flavors each time then when he began the work. Before he began the work he could taste the taste of pleasure as is ordinarily given to corporeal pleasures. But one who has begun the work of bestowal and wants to be rewarded with spirituality is given more taste in corporeality than the usual. This is so deliberately, so he will become accustomed to greater pleasures than there are in corporeal pleasures. This is a preparation to be immunized in the work of overcoming the great pleasures found in spirituality.

Now we can see that those who want to work the holy work are given additions. That is, they are given additional flavor in self-love. This is not so for people who have no interest in walking in the path of bestowal. It is as our sages said, "Anyone who is greater than his friend, his desire is greater than him." It is so in order to accustom them to the work of overcoming, since for the manifold pleasures found in spiritual pleasures, his usual overcoming of corporeal pleasures will not be enough because the pleasure is in them as a constant, while they are given each time more importance in order to become accustomed to overcoming more each time.

Now we can understand what we asked about the verse where it is written, "You shall place for yourself judges and officers in all your gates." How does placing judges and officers apply to the current time? However, when a person wants to begin the work of the Creator we should make two discernments: 1) Potential. That is, first he makes for himself a plan of what he should, and what he shouldn't do, meaning a scrutiny of good and bad. Doing this in potential is called "judge," who says what must be done. 2) Afterwards we must execute what was in potential. The execution is called "officer."

Since matters of work are not a one-time thing, but rather each day he must exert in the work, hence, the text uses plural form, meaning "judges and officers."

Saying, "You shall place for yourself," in singular form, comes to tell us that this work pertains to each and every individual.

This is why it says, "in all your gates." We should interpret it literally, meaning that a gate is the place of entrance. This means that whenever a person wants to begin the work of the Creator, he must arrange the work in two manners: in potential and in actuality, which are "judges" and "officers."

However, regarding his saying, "In all your gates," we should interpret according to what we see—that there are two kinds of life in our world: 1) corporeal life, 2) spiritual life.

It follows from this that we have two gates: 1) a gate that is similar to a prison gate. This is similar to what is written (in the prayer, "Thank," that we say on the eve of Shabbat in the afternoon prayer): "Dwellers of darkness and the shadow of death; prisoners of poverty and iron." The *Metzudat David* [David's Fortress interpretation] interprets there: "People who sit in a place of darkness are tied by tormenting ties and by chains of iron." 2) A gate that is similar to the King's gate, as it is written, "And Mordechai sat by the King's gate."

At each gate there are guards who are standing guard, but each of the guards acts in the opposite way. That is, the prison guards see that none of the prisoners escape the prison, while the guards at the King's gate see that no one comes through the King's gate.

The thing is that those who are immersed in self-love and have no understanding or feeling of anything more than corporeal pleasures are regarded as being in prison, and the guards do not let them out. By what force do they guard them and not let them out? The moment a guard sees that he wants to exit self-love and begin the work of bestowal he adds to them more pleasure in self-love. By this they tie them with iron chains so they will not want to leave there.

After all the overcoming, when the guards see that the prisoners want to escape self-love and begin to come into the love of the Creator, they promptly give them more flavor and more importance, to the extent that no one ever thought that it was so worthwhile to remain in self-love as they feel now, that self-love is not such a simple matter, as it is written, "Anyone who is greater than his friend, his desire is greater than him." By this the guards have the power to see that no one escapes from the prison.

But the role of the guards who are standing at the King's gate is not to let anyone through the King's gate. What is the power by which they can overcome those who want to come into the King's palace? It is as it is written in the "Introduction to the Study of the Ten Sefirot" (item 133), "It is like a king who wished to select for himself the most loyal of his subjects in the country and bring them in to work inside his palace. What did he do? He issued a decree that anyone who wished, young or old, would come to his palace to engage in the works inside his palace. However, he appointed many of his servants to guard the palace gate, and ordered them to cunningly deflect all those nearing his palace. Naturally, all the people in the country began to run to the king's palace. But the diligent guards cunningly rejected them. Many of them overpowered them and came near the palace gate, but the guards at the gate were the most diligent, and if someone approached the gate, they diverted him and turned him away with great craftiness, until he despaired and returned as he had come. And so they came and went. Only the heroes among them, whose patience endured, defeated the guards and opened the gate. They were instantly awarded seeing the king's face, who appointed each of them to his right place."

It therefore follows that the gates standing at the King's gate deflect with all kinds of arguments that "It is not for you" to enter the King's palace. To each one they make up reasons so these people will understand that it is not worthwhile for them to toil in vain. Especially, through all kinds of arguments, they have the power to deflect them and turn them from the campaign of holy work. This is the meaning of "in all your gates," meaning the prison gate and the King's gate.

Now we will explain the end of the verse where he ends, "which the Lord your God is giving you." We asked, "What does it come to tell us?" It is known that everything comes from the Creator. However, as we explained above, a person who wants to be saved from all those arguments of the guards has only one counsel: faith above reason. This means that everything that the guards say is true. However, the Creator is merciful and gracious, and hears the prayer of every mouth. He gives the power to overcome all the obstacles.

However, there is a rule that one must say, "If I am not for me, who is for me?" That is, a person must not wait for the Creator to help him overcome. Rather, he must overcome by himself and do everything he can do, and only ask that the Creator will help him overcome, meaning help him. If a person tries in any way he can, then he must ask the Creator that his effort will bear fruit. However, a person must not say that the Creator will work for him, but that the Creator will help him in his work to succeed in acquiring the good.

It therefore follows that since man is the worker and the Creator only helps him, a person reflects on why he has been rewarded nearness to the Creator more than others. It is because other people could not exert so much in work above reason and not look at the argument of the body as he constantly prevailed in his work and never looked at his thoughts of despair with which the body wanted to fail him.

It follows that then a person can say, "My strength and the might of my hand have gotten me these riches." In that regard, the verse says that he must know that "the Lord your God is giving you," that it is indeed only God's gift. That is, the fact that you had the strength to place judges and officers in all your gates was but a gift from God.

The Fifteenth of Av

Article No. 35, Tav-Shin-Mem-Vav, 1985-86

It is written in the *Mishnah* (*Taanit*, p 26b): "Rabbi Shimon Ben Gamliel said, 'No days were better for Israel than the fifteenth of Av [11th Hebrew month], and *Yom Kippur* [Day of Atonement], when the daughters of Jerusalem would come out dressed in borrowed white garments, so as not to shame those who do not have. The daughters of Jerusalem would come out and dance in the vineyards. What would they say? 'Young man, lift up your eyes and see what you choose for yourself. Do not cast your eyes on beauty; cast your eyes on family.'" (And on page 31) "Those who did not have wives went there. Our sages taught, 'What would the beauties among them say? 'Turn your eyes to beauty, for a woman is only for beauty.' What would the wellborn among them say? 'Cast your eyes on family, for a woman is only for sons.' In The Eye of Jacob he adds, 'The wealthy among them say, 'Cast your eyes on the wealthy.' What would the unsightly ones among them say? 'Take what you take for the Creator, as long as you crown us with gold coins.'"

We should understand the connection between good days and the daughters of Jerusalem coming out to dance in the vineyards and speaking to young men about matchmaking. What modesty is there here? It implies that the good days that

Israel had caused the daughters of Jerusalem to come out and dance in the vineyards. We should understand the connection between them.

It is known that *Malchut* is called "daughter," as in "Father created the daughter." We make four discernments in *Malchut*. These are called *Hochma*, *Bina*, *ZA*, and *Malchut*, which are called "four *Behinot* [discernments] in the *Aviut* [thickness]."

The first *Behina* [discernment], which is *Hochma*, is called "beauty," for it is known that *Hochma* is called "having beautiful eyes."

The second *Behina* is *Bina*. She is called "mother of the children," and she begot ZON. The quality of *Bina* is that she wants equivalence of form, to be similar to the Giver. For this reason, the merit of *Bina* is that we attribute her to *Keter*, meaning that she wants to resemble *Keter*, who is the Giver.

The third *Behina* is *ZA*. She is called "rich," as it is written, "The rich shall not give more." It is written (*Zohar*, *Ki Tissa*, item 4), "'The rich shall not give more' is the middle pillar, *ZA*, who should not give too much *Yod*. 'The rich shall not give more' is the middle pillar, which, from His essence, leans toward the right, to *Hassadim*, and does not need *Hochma*, hence its title, 'rich.'"

The fourth *Behina*, which is *Malchut*, is called "poor and meager," as it is written, "She has nothing of her own except that which her husband gives her." It is known that *Malchut* is called "faith." It is as was said about Abraham, "And he believed in the Lord and He considered it for him as righteousness." Faith is called *Tzedakah* [righteousness/charity], as one gives charity to the poor without asking anything in return. Such is faith above reason: he does not ask anything in return, but only for the Lord. It follows that it is as though faith is called "meager," like the poor, who do not return anything for the charity that is given to him.

With the above said we can interpret the excerpt about the daughters of Israel coming out. It is known that good days are when there are ascents of the worlds and their disclosure. Therefore, then is the time for disclosure, and then the daughters of Jerusalem come out. Coming out means from concealment to disclosure, and each *Sefira* shows its importance.

It is known that there are four *Behinot* [discernments/phases] of *Ohr Yashar* [Direct Light]. This means that four phases are discerned in *Malchut* herself—in the will to receive, which is *Malchut* with respect to the *Ohr Yashar*, whose quality is to receive in order to receive. Four *Behinot* are discerned there, as it is written ("Preface to the Wisdom of Kabbalah," item 20), "The five discernments of reception in *Behina Dalet* are called by the names of the *Sefirot KHB TM* because prior to the *Tzimtzum* [restriction], while *Behina Dalet* was still the vessel of reception for the ten *Sefirot* included in the Upper Light by way of 'He is One and His Name One,' ... its clothing of the ten *Sefirot* there followed these *Behinot*. Each of the five *Behinot* in her clothed its corresponding *Behina* in the ten *Sefirot* in the Upper Light."

These above-mentioned *Behinot* appear on good days, meaning that each *Behina* reveals its merit. The order is that *Behina Aleph*, called *Hochma*, says, *Bachur* [young unmarried man], meaning one who is worthy of being *Bachur* [also "chosen"] from among the nation. At that time she reveals her merit—that there is beauty in her. That is, *Hochma* is called "the beauty of the eyes," as it is said, "The eyes of the congregation," referring to the sages of the congregation. Therefore, *Hochma* is called "beauties." This is why they said that a woman is only for beauty. Concerning the vessels of reception in general—where the desire to do good to His creations created a *Kli* [vessel] to receive the delight and pleasure—it pertains to light of *Hochma*. This is why a woman is called "vessel of reception only for *Hochma*."

"What would the wellborn among them say?" Being wellborn means that he has a high root. For example, when we say that this man is the grandson of a great man, we mean that his root is a very high root. The *Sefira*, *Bina*, called *Behina Bet*, shows her merit—that she craves equivalence of form, by which we can come to adhere to the root, which is the Emanator and *Keter*. It follows that the *Sefira*

Bina shows that she is attached to the root. This is called "pedigree," meaning that the sons she will bear will have a nature with the same quality as hers, since she has equivalence with the root. This is why it is written, "What would the wellborn among them say? A woman is only for sons."

This means that the vessels of reception, called "woman," must strive to bear sons, meaning that the sons they will bear will be important sons. This is why it was said "Cast your eyes on family," meaning the family pedigree. That is, *Bina* showed her merit—that she is adhered to the root, which is called "equivalence of form," for the root of *Bina* is *Keter*, which is a desire to do good and bestow. Therefore, her merit is that she begets power of bestowal for the sons, who will later bear.

"The wealthy ones among them say, 'Cast your eyes on the wealthy.'" *Behina Gimel*, which is ZA, is called "rich," since one who has *Hassadim* is regarded as rich because he is content with his lot and does not need *Hochma*. He also has illumination of *Hochma*, but he leans toward *Hassadim*. In that respect he is similar to *Bina*, who is the source of *Hassadim*, which extends from the root, *Keter*. She wants to resemble her root, but he has illumination of *Hochma*.

It is written in the holy *Zohar* (Ki Tissa, item 4): "'The rich shall not give more' is the middle pillar, ZA, who should not give too much *Yod*." And it is written, "'The rich shall not give more' is the middle pillar, which, from His essence, leans toward the right, to *Hassadim*, and does not need *Hochma*, hence its title, 'rich.'" It was told not to give too much *Yod*, meaning not to give too much *Yod*, but rather take *Ohr Hassadim* [light of mercy] with illumination of *Hochma*.

This is why it is written, "The wealthy ones among them," meaning *Behina Gimel*, which is the *Behina* of ZA, called light of *Hassadim* in illumination of *Hochma*, for ZA is called "rich." That *Sefira* in *Malchut* shows her merit, as it is written, "Cast your eyes on the wealthy."

"The unsightly ones among them" are the actual *Malchut*, called *Behina Dalet* in *Dalet*, on whom there was the *Tzimtzum* [restriction]. Hence, this *Behina* is called "poor and meager," as it is written in the holy *Zohar*, that *Malchut* is called "poor and meager for she has nothing of her own except that which her husband gives her." It is known that we must assume the kingdom of heaven above reason. This is called "faith," to believe in the Creator although the body comes with many questions, complaints, and demands. At that time we should say, "They have eyes but they do not see, ears, but they do not hear." Instead, we must accept everything above sense and reason. Moreover, this must be as *Tzedakah*, as was said about Abraham, "And he believed in the Lord and He regarded it for him as righteousness."

The reason is that as when you give charity to the poor, you do not ask the poor for anything in return because the poor have nothing to give back except what they are given. So should be the assuming of the burden of the kingdom of heaven—without anything in return, but only for the Creator, as though the Creator has nothing to give back to man in return for his work in assuming the burden of the kingdom of heaven.

Indeed, why should faith be specifically this way? It is because of the known reason that there was a *Tzimtzum* on the vessels of reception so there would be room for work, and by which to achieve equivalence of form, called *Dvekut* [adhesion]. Specifically in these *Kelim* [vessels], called "annulment of vessels of reception," we obtain vessels of bestowal, where one can aim in order to bestow. In these *Kelim* illuminate all the delight and pleasure that the Creator wanted to bestow upon His creations.

However, in the creatures, who were created with vessels of reception, and who are told that they must work above reason, this work is called "unimportant work." It is regarded as unimportant because it is unsuitable for a reasonable person to do things to which the intellect does not agree.

The Fifteenth of Av

It is as Baal HaSulam said about the verse that the Creator said to Moses (Exodus, 4:2): "And the Lord said to him: 'What is that in your hand?' And he said, 'A staff.' And He said, 'Throw it on the ground,' and it became a serpent, and Moses fled from it." He said that Moses' hands are called "faith." It is regarded as "of little importance," since man craves only knowledge. Where he sees that there is no knowledge that he wants to obtain, he cannot attain the matter. He argues that he has already exerted in this work so we can do everything for the Creator but he did not move one bit. Thus, the body tells him, "Give up on this and do not think that you will ever be able to attain it. So get off this path." At that time the Creator tells him, "Throw it on the ground," meaning this is what you should do before the people of Israel. We must know that Pharaoh and Egypt imply the Pharaoh and Egypt that exist in an Israeli heart. "And it became a serpent." That is, as soon as we leave the faith, called "of low importance," we promptly fall into the *Klipot* [shells/peels] for specifically through faith above reason can we be rewarded with all the wholeness.

It follows that the majority of the work is when a person has no intellectual basis on which to build. Also, faith has no basis in his intellect. For this reason, where one does not see that any benefit will arise from this to himself, he promptly loses the energy to work and becomes like a log, without any desire or strength.

But precisely then one can see the truth—whether he has faith above reason, so he can tell his body, which comes to him with arguments that make sense. The body tells him: "Is it not enough for you to see the truth, that it is impossible to go forward your way? Do tell me, how much more proof do you need in order to listen to me, give up, and say, 'Now I have realized that this path of working only for the Creator is not for me. I don't know who it is for, but what I do know is that it is not for me.'"

Although our sages said otherwise (*Sanhedrin*, p 37a), "Therefore, each one must say, 'The world was created for me.' But what can I do if I see that in reality, I cannot keep this reality of saying that I must do everything for the Creator?'" This is why work of faith is regarded as unimportant work.

With the above said we will interpret what the unsightly ones would say, "Take what you take for the Creator, as long as you crown us with gold coins." *Behina Dalet* in *Malchut* is called "poor and meager." As said above, one considers this work unsightly because here he cannot look at the beauty of spirituality, nor at the pedigree in spirituality, or the wealth in spirituality.

Rather, what we do have here are only things that reason and intellect cannot tolerate. It is like an ugly object from which one keeps his distance, as it is written, (*Hulin*, 44), "Stay away from ugliness and its likes." What can they say to a young man who wants to be a chosen one, "Take what you take for the Creator," meaning "We cannot promise you anything of self-benefit. However, if you want to be the chosen ones in the nation, you must take what you take only for the Creator. That is, if you can agree to these conditions, you may take us. Otherwise, there is nothing to speak of."

However, that, too, is not simple. Rather, "We want you to 'crown us in gold coins.'" RASHI interpreted "crown us in gold coins" to mean that after the marriage you will give us jewels and handsome garments. Baal HaSulam said that although a person agrees to take upon himself the bargain for the sake of the Creator, meaning even if she is unsightly, he does not look at anything, but it is like "a bride as she is," she still demands that afterwards he will draw for her the light of Torah. That is, he should try to obtain the flavors of Torah and the flavors of *Mitzvot*, or she will not agree, since "One who does not know the commandment of the upper one, how will he serve him?" This is why they said, "as long as you crown us with gold coins." That is, although in terms of faith it is above reason, afterwards we must extend the light of Torah.

We therefore see two things that are opposite from one another. On the one hand, faith must be above reason, completely unfounded. On the other hand, we must obtain the flavors of Torah and *Mitzvot*.

Similarly, Baal HaSulam said about what we say in the blessing, "Who has created in him, holes upon holes, hollows upon hollows, etc., so that should one of them open or should one of them close, it is impossible to exist and stand before You." He said that closing pertains to faith, which should stay closed. This is the meaning of "Should [one of them] open." Rather, it should stay closed. "Or should [one of them] close" refers to the flavors of Torah and *Mitzvot*. Rather, faith will stay above reason, and the flavors of Torah and *Mitzvot* will be revealed.

What Is Preparation for Selichot

Article No. 36, Tav-Shin-Mem-Vav, 1985-86

It is known that for anything we want, we must prepare the means to obtain it. Accordingly, what must one prepare in order to receive *Selichot* [forgiveness]? In corporeality we see that one does not say to another, "Sorry," unless he has done something that harmed the other person in terms of money, honor, or bodily harm, by causing him some injury. In that case it can be said that one should ask for the other's forgiveness, to forgive the wrong that he has done to him.

There are two things to discern here: 1) If he did not do anything to him, but he is asking him for forgiveness, the other person will look at him as though he is insane. If we saw someone walking on the street saying to everyone, "Sorry, sorry," we would certainly think that he is mad. Forgiveness pertains only to some felony. 2) If another person causes a great loss to another person and apologizes as though he did something small, he will certainly not receive what he has asked for, since he has done a great offense, but he apologizes as though he did something small. It is inconceivable that he will forgive him. Rather, one measures the severity of the damage that he has done to his friend, and to that extent chooses the means that will make his friend forgive him.

We see in corporeal conducts how people behave concerning forgiveness among people, and from the conduct between man and man we should apply the same order between man and God. That is, when one comes to ask the Creator for forgiveness, to forgive his sins, the two above discernments apply, as well: 1) that you do not apologize for anything, but only for hurting another, or you will be perceived as insane, or that you are mocking the other by asking his forgiveness. 2) The request for forgiveness should match the measure of harm to the other.

Therefore, when one comes to ask the Creator to forgive his sin against Him, that he blemished His honor, one must think about his sin against the Creator. This is so because if a person does not feel any sin yet asks for forgiveness, it is as though he is joking. He is yelling and crying and asking the Creator's forgiveness when he does not feel that he has damaged the King's glory whatsoever.

The reason why a person does not feel his sins is as our sages said (*Yoma*, 86), "If a person commits a transgression and repeats it, it becomes to him as permitted." This is the reason why a person does not feel his sins when he comes to ask the Creator for forgiveness.

It follows, according to the second discernment, meaning discerning the measure of the sin, that first one must acknowledge the measure of the flaw that he has flawed in the glory of the King. Otherwise you cannot speak of forgiveness. Thus, one should try as much as possible to be able to ask that He will forgive his sins according to his sins, meaning that they will be of equal weight.

Our sages also said (*Sukkah*, 52), that to the wicked, the sins seem like a hairsbreadth, and to the righteous they seem like a high mountain. The question is, what does this "seem" mean? That is, they said, "Seem to them," but what is the truth?

The thing is that when one does not notice before whom he sins and does not feel the importance and greatness of the Creator, he is faithless. At that time, when he begins to think, "But I'm a Jew, as well," and since now is the month of *Elul*, and it is customary in Israel throughout the generations that since it is a month of mercy, and anyone who is regarded as "Israel" knows that now is the time to ask the Creator for forgiveness for the sins of the house of Israel. Also, we blow the *Shofar* [festive horn] so man's heart will begin to contemplate repentance for sins. At that time one believes that he, too, must have sinned and must ask the Creator for forgiveness.

However, what is the measure of the flaw that he has blemished in the King? A person cannot feel this feeling. Rather, to the extent of one's faith in the greatness of the Creator he can assume the measure of the flaw that he has caused by his sins. Therefore, all those who come to ask for forgiveness without any preparation as to what they are forgiven for are as one who is asking forgiveness of someone although he did terrible things to him, which require true remorse for his actions, yet he is asking forgiveness as though he did something insignificant. Naturally, the request for forgiveness is also without real value as it should be for a real sin.

It follows that before one comes to ask forgiveness he must first reflect on the core of the sin. Afterward he can consider the sins that were caused by the core of the sin. One should know that the core of the sin with which one blemishes, and from which all the sins extend, is that one is not trying to have permanent faith. If he has partial faith, he settles for it.

It is as it is written in the "Introduction to the Study of the Ten Sefirot" (item 14), that if he had permanent faith, that faith would not let him sin. That is, he asks forgiveness from the Creator since he sees that the real reason for all the sins is that he lacks permanent faith. Therefore, he asks the Creator to give him that strength, meaning to have the ability to always have faith steadfast in his heart. Naturally, he will not come and commit sins and blemish the glory of the Creator because he has no feeling of the greatness of the Creator, and because he does not know how to appreciate the glory of heaven, and how not to harm it.

Therefore, he asks forgiveness from the Creator, to help him and give him the strength to take upon himself the burden of the kingdom of heaven above reason, meaning to have the power to overcome and strengthen in faith in the Creator, and to know how to behave between man and God, with some reverence.

This means that when one reflects, he will see that he needs only one thing—to reflect on the difference between Jew and gentile, for which we bless each day, "Blessed are You, O Lord, for not making me a gentile." But one does not pay much attention to what he says, "For not making me a gentile." That is, he does not consider himself: in what way he is Israel and not a gentile. We must know that the main distinction is in the faith—Israel believes in the Creator and a gentile has no faith in the Creator.

Once he knows that difference he must check his measure of faith in the Creator, meaning as it is written in the "Introduction to the Study of Ten Sefirot" (item 14), how much he is willing to make concessions for his faith in the Creator. Then he will be able to see the truth, meaning if he is willing to do things only for the sake of the Creator and not for his own sake, or is he willing to work for the Creator only to a small extent, meaning that, God forbid, he should blemish self-love, or else he will not be able to do anything.

It therefore follows that then is the time when he can see the truth: his true measure of faith in the Creator. From this he can see that all the sins stem only from this reason. By receiving preparation and qualification when he comes to ask the Creator to forgive his sins he can assume the true measure of the flaw, meaning in what way he has blemished the glory of the King and he will know what to ask of the Creator, meaning what sins he has sinned and which he must correct so as not to sin again.

Now we can understand what is written in the portion, *Nitzavim* [Standing] (Deuteronomy, 30:11): "For this commandment, which I command you today, is not beyond you, nor is it far. It is not in heaven, and not beyond the sea, for the matter is very near you—in your mouth and in your heart to do it."

The words, "For this commandment," to which commandment is he referring? We should also understand the meaning of "It is not beyond you." The thing is that the core of the *Mitzva* [commandment] is the *Mitzva* of faith, meaning to believe in the Creator. Afterwards we can keep His *Mitzvot* [plural of *Mitzva*]. All the slanderers and all the obstructions come to the *Mitzva* of faith. The body begins to ask many questions—both questions that the body itself is asking, and questions about faith that the body hears other people.

They come to a person when he wants to take upon himself the burden of the kingdom of heaven "as an ox to the burden and as a donkey to the load," meaning everything above reason. Suddenly, the body becomes smart and begins to investigate and ask "Who" and "What"? Under no circumstances does it let us take upon ourselves the *Mitzva* of faith. The body's questions are so strong that one cannot answer its questions. Then a person becomes bewildered and does not have the strength to overcome its just arguments, according to the reason by which it is asking. The body's questions are a true wonder.

The writing tells us about this: "For this commandment," meaning the commandment of faith, "is not beyond you." That is, you do not need to answer the body's questions, which it asks within reason, since the *Mitzva* of faith is built specifically above the intellect. That is, the external mind, which was given to man, cannot attain it. This is why you do not need to answer its bewildering questions.

Instead, one must believe that all the questions that the body asks do not come in order for you to answer them. It is to the contrary: These questions come to a person so as to give him a place to believe above reason. Otherwise, if the body understood with its intellect that a person wants to work for the Creator, it would be within reason. This would be called "knowing," not "believing," for precisely where one's mind does not grasp, there, if he does something, it is purely on the basis of faith.

It therefore follows that one does not need to be very talented in order to be able to answer the body's questions, since all the answers are "Above reason," called "faith." This is regarded as "It is not in heaven, and not beyond the sea," requiring great tactics. Rather, it is utterly simple, and it is called "It is in your mouth and in your heart to do it," meaning if there is only a desire in the heart then we can overcome.

But the matter of "above reason" requires clarification, since there are many discernments to make there. Baal HaSulam said that above reason means that one should depict for oneself how he would keep Torah and *Mitzvot* if his reason determined that it is worthwhile to engage in Torah and *Mitzvot*. That is, if he felt the taste that is in each and every *Mitzva*.

One must believe that as there are corporeal pleasures, such as pleasures of eating, drinking, and respect, where each thing tastes differently, we must also believe that there is a special taste in each *Mitzva*. Accordingly, if he tasted the change of flavors during his engagement in Torah and *Mitzvot*, what excitement and vitality he would feel during his work? Reason would compel him to create for himself an image in the work that is suitable for a servant of the Creator. He would look at all the things that want to disrupt him from his work as inconsequential, unworthy of his attention.

According to the above-mentioned depiction, which he depicts to himself within reason, he should make the same depiction above reason. That is, although he does not feel that there will be something that reason supports, he still works precisely as if he has strong reason and feeling. When he does this, it is regarded as working above reason.

However, as long as he feels that if he had reason he would be serving the Creator more willingly and more consistently, then he is still working within reason, since there is still a difference between reason and above reason. Precisely when it makes no difference to him, it is regarded as "above reason."